VOLUME 1

# A HISTORY
## OF THE
# REPUBLIC

## THE UNITED STATES TO 1877

The Great Seal of the United States, above, features the bald eagle, a symbol of power. When Congress adopted the Great Seal in 1782, it wanted to emphasize both the importance of the individual states and the unity of the nation as a whole. The eagle wears a shield with 13 vertical stripes — 7 white and 6 red — that stand for the original 13 states. The blue bar above the stripes represents the government of the United States. In one talon, the eagle holds an olive branch, a symbol of peace. In the other, it holds 13 arrows, showing that it is prepared for war. In its mouth, the eagle holds a scroll with the Latin words E PLURIBUS UNUM (Out of Many, One).

On April 30, 1789, in New York City, George Washington took the oath of office as the first President of the United States, as shown in the painting at right. With this oath, the newly independent United States of America took a crucial step toward fulfilling its destiny.

VOLUME 1

# A HISTORY OF THE REPUBLIC

THE UNITED STATES TO 1877

PRENTICE HALL
Englewood Cliffs, New Jersey
Needham, Massachusetts

**James West Davidson/John E. Batchelor**

## James West Davidson

James West Davidson has authored books and papers on a wide range of American history topics including *After the Fact: The Art of Historical Detection* with Mark H. Lytle. With teaching experience at both the college and high school levels, Dr. Davidson consults on curriculum design for American history courses. While completing his Ph.D. at Yale University, he participated in the History Education Project sponsored by the National Endowment for the Humanities and the American Historical Association. Dr. Davidson is an avid canoer. *Great Heart: The History of a Labrador Adventure* is his story of a canoeing trip.

## John E. Batchelor

John E. Batchelor teaches American history to junior high school students in the Guilford County, North Carolina, school system. Mr. Batchelor has also taught language arts and reading. Over the past 15 years, his students have won local, state, and national honors for their creative writing and history projects. Mr. Batchelor has written tests and teacher guide materials, conducted teacher workshops, and evaluated social studies curriculum for local and state boards of education. As a columnist for the Greensboro *News and Record,* Mr. Batchelor has written guest editorials and other articles.

## Second Edition

## Supplementary Materials

Annotated Teacher's Edition
Teacher's Resource Manual

ISBN 0-13-390337-0   10  9  8  7  6  5  4  3

**Cover Design:** Martucci Studio
**Front Matter Design:** Taurins Associates,
  McNally Graphic Design
**End Matter Design:** Taurins Associates,
  McNally Graphic Design
**Maps:** Dick Sanderson and John Sanderson
**Historical Atlas Maps:** General Cartography, Inc.
**Geographic Atlas Maps:** R.R. Donnelley & Sons
  Company
**Charts and Graphs:** Geoffrey Hodgkinson,
  McNally Graphic Design
**Photo Consultant:** Michal Heron
**Photo Researchers:** Susan Marsden Kapsis,
  Barbara Scott

## Credits for Readings and Other Sources

Every effort has been made to trace the copyright holders of the documents used in this book. Should there be any omission in this respect we apologize, and shall be pleased to make the appropriate acknowledgment in any future printings. Acknowledgments appear immediately following each reading.

## Illustration Credits

Frequently cited sources are abbreviated as follows: AMNH, American Museum of Natural History; LC, Library of Congress; MCNY, Museum of the City of New York; MFA, Museum of Fine Arts, Boston; MMA, Metropolitan Museum of Art, New York; NA, National Archives; NG, National Gallery of Art, Washington, D.C.; NMAA, National Museum of American Art; NYHS, courtesy of the New York Historical Society, New York; NYPL, New York Public Library; NYSHA, New York State Historical Association, Cooperstown; SI, Smithsonian Institution; UPI, United Press International; WW, Wide World; Yale, Yale University Art Gallery.

Key to position of illustrations:
*b,* bottom; *l,* left; *r,* right; *t,* top.

**Cover** The Granger Collection; **Page 1** LC;   **5** *t* Arizona State Museum, University of Arizona, silkscreen print by Robert Spray for Margaret Schevill Link, *b* Harry T. Peters Collection, MCNY;   **6** *t* Yale, *b* Mr. and Mrs. John Harney;   **11** National Portrait Gallery, SI;   **12** Independence National Historical Park;   **14** *l to r* SI, Lee Boltin for American Heritage; Memphis Brooks Museum of Art; Texas Memorial Museum; The Rockwell Museum; National Portrait Gallery, SI;   **15** NYHS.

**UNIT 1    Pages 16–17** *l to r* MMA, Gift of H. L. Bach Foundation, 1969; US Naval Academy Museum; British Museum; Bettmann Archive; National Portrait Gallery, London;   **19** NMAA, SI, lent by the US Department of the Interior, National Park Service;   **20** Courtesy of the Library Services Department, AMNH;   **22** US Geological Survey, photo by J.K. Hillers (detail);   **23** *l* © David Muench; *r* © David Muench;   **25** © David Muench;   **29** *l* © David Muench, *r* © David Muench;   **33** Shostal Associates;   **34** Chaco Center, National Park Service;   **35** *t* Shostal Associates, *b* © David Muench;   **37** Dept. of Ethnology, Royal Ontario Museum, Toronto, Canada;   **39** Arizona State Museum, University of Arizona, silkscreen by Robert Spray for Margaret Schevill Link;   **40** British Museum;   **41** Courtesy of the Library Services Department, AMNH;   **43** Peabody Museum, Harvard;   **44** Giraudon/Art Resource, NY;   **49** Bodleian Library Ms. Bodley 264, fol. 218 recto.;   **50** Pierpont Morgan Library;   **52** EPA/Scala;   **54** National Maritime Museum, London;   **55** Museum of Primitive Art, Lee Boltin;   **59** MMA;   **62** NYPL;   **63** Vatican Library;   **66** Arizona Department of Library, Archives and Public Records © David Barr 1982 (detail);   **67** British Museum;   **69** Bettmann Archive;   **73** Bibliothèque Publique, Université de Genève.

*(continued on page 665)*

# Contents

## UNIT 1   The World of the Americas  16

CHAPTER 1  The American Land
            (Prehistory–Present)  18
1  Discovering the Land           19
2  Different Climates             26
Skill Lesson 1: The Parts of a Map  21

CHAPTER 2  The First Americans
            (Prehistory–1600)  32
1  Studying the First Americans    33
2  Peoples of North America       36
3  Great Empires in the Americas   41
Skill Lesson 2: A Painting as a Primary
    Source  43

CHAPTER 3  Europeans Explore
            America (1000–1650)  48
1  The Changing World of Europe   49
2  Search for New Routes to Asia   53
3  Exploring the New World      59
4  Early Claims to North America   65
Skill Lesson 3: Using Latitude and
    Longitude  56

**UNIT 1 REVIEW**                72

## UNIT 2   Settling the New World  74

CHAPTER 4  Planting Colonies
            (1530–1690)  76
1  Spain Builds a Large Empire     77
2  French and Dutch Colonies     83
3  English Settlers in Virginia      88
4  The Pilgrims at Plymouth      93
Skill Lesson 4: Reading a Line Graph  81

CHAPTER 5  English Colonies Take
            Root (1630–1750)  98
1  New England Colonies        99
2  Middle Colonies           105
3  Southern Colonies         109
4  Governing the Colonies     113
Skill Lesson 5: Using a Primary
    Source  116

CHAPTER 6  Life in the Colonies
            (1630–1775)  120
1  The New England Way of Life   121
2  The Breadbasket Colonies    126
3  Two Ways of Life in the South  129
4  A New American Culture      134
5  Growth and Change        138
Skill Lesson 6: Reading a Bar Graph  140

**UNIT 2 REVIEW**              144

# UNIT 3 The Struggle for Independence 146

CHAPTER 7 Crisis in the Colonies
(1745–1775) 148

1 Competing for Empire 149
2 Showdown in North America 151
3 Trouble Over Taxes 156
4 The Split Widens 159
5 The Shot Heard 'Round
the World 163

**Skill Lesson 7: Using a Time Line 167**

CHAPTER 8 The American Revolution
(1775–1783) 172

1 Fighting Begins 173
2 Declaring Independence 177
3 Dark Days of the War 181
4 Other Battlefronts 186
5 Victory at Last 189

**Skill Lesson 8: Comparing Two Points
of View 180**

CHAPTER 9 Creating a Government
(1776–1790) 196

1 The First American Government 197
2 The Constitutional Convention 202
3 We, the People 205
4 Ratifying the Constitution 210

**Skill Lesson 9: Reading a Flow Chart 209**

**UNIT 3 REVIEW** 216

# UNIT 4 Strengthening the New Nation 218

CHAPTER 10 The First Presidents
(1789–1800) 220

1 The New Government at Work 221
2 Staying Neutral 226
3 Political Parties 229
4 Adams Takes a Firm Stand 233

**Skill Lesson 10: Recognizing Fact and
Opinion 232**

CHAPTER 11 Age of Jefferson
(1801–1816) 240

1 Jefferson Takes Office 241
2 The Nation Doubles in Size 244
3 Dangers at Sea 249
4 War Fever 254
5 The War of 1812 256

**Skill Lesson 11: Following Routes on a
Map 247**

CHAPTER 12 The Nation Prospers
(1790–1825) 264

1 The Industrial Revolution 265
2 The Way West 270
3 Changing Times 277
4 America's Neighbors 280

**Skill Lesson 12: Reading a Circle
Graph 274**

**UNIT 4 REVIEW** 286

# UNIT 5   A Growing Nation   288

### CHAPTER 13  Age of Jackson
(1824–1840)   290
1  The People's Choice   291
2  Jackson Takes Office   295
3  Tests of Strength   299
4  Jackson's Successors   304
**Skill Lesson 13:  Reading a Political Cartoon   298**

### CHAPTER 14  Westward Ho!
(1820–1860)   308
1  Oregon Country   309
2  The Lone Star Republic   315
3  Looking Toward the West   319
4  War With Mexico   322
5  From Sea to Shining Sea   325
**Skill Lesson 14:  Using a Diary as a Primary Source   313**

### CHAPTER 15  Two Ways of Life
(1820–1860)   332
1  Industry in the North   333
2  Life in the North   337
3  The Cotton Kingdom   341
4  Life in the South   343
**Skill Lesson 15:  Comparing Two Line Graphs   345**

### CHAPTER 16  The Reforming Spirit
(1820–1860)   350
1  Crusade Against Slavery   351
2  Rights for Women   355
3  Reform Marches On   358
4  Creating an American Culture   361
**Skill Lesson 16:  Using the Card Catalog   364**

**UNIT 5 REVIEW   368**

# UNIT 6   The Nation Divided   370

### CHAPTER 17  The Coming of the War
(1820–1860)   372
1  Differences Over Slavery   373
2  A Great Compromise   375
3  Adding Fuel to the Fire   379
4  A New Political Party   383
5  The Union Is Broken   386
**Skill Lesson 17:  Reading an Election Map   387**

### CHAPTER 18  The Civil War
(1860–1865)   392
1  The Call to Arms   393
2  On the Battle Lines   397
3  Free at Last   401
4  Life in Wartime   403
5  The Tide Turns   408
**Skill Lesson 18:  Using a Table   396**

### CHAPTER 19  The Road to Reunion
(1864–1877)   416
1  Restoring the Union   417
2  The President and Congress Clash   421
3  Changes in the South   425
4  A New Era in National Politics   429
**Skill Lesson 19:  Finding Information in the Library   422**

**UNIT 6 REVIEW   434**

**A Look Ahead**
(1877–Present)   436
1  The American Dream   437
2  Governing a Growing Nation   441
3  A Land of Opportunity   444
4  Becoming a World Power   447

**Reference Section**     **570**

Historical Atlas    572
Geographic Atlas    580
The Fifty States    588
Gazetteer of American History    589
A Chronology of American History    594
Connections With American
   Literature    598

Presidents of the United States    600
Glossary    605
Pronunciation Key    605
The Declaration of Independence    611
Exploring Our Living Constitution    615
The Constitution of the
   United States of America    628
An Overview of Citizenship    650
Index    654

## Focus on Citizenship

Chapter 1   Creating a Map . . . . . . . . . . .31
Chapter 2   Researching a Report . . . . . . .47
Chapter 3   Expressing an Opinion . . . . . . .71
**Unit 1**     Building American Citizenship . .72

Chapter 4   Learning About Citizenship . . . .97
Chapter 5   Learning About Citizenship . . .119
Chapter 6   Evaluating . . . . . . . . . . . . . .143
**Unit 2**     Building American Citizenship .144

Chapter 7   Learning About Citizenship . . .171
Chapter 8   Relating Past to Present . . . . .195
Chapter 9   Learning About Citizenship . . .215
**Unit 3**     Building American Citizenship .216

Chapter 10   Learning About Citizenship . . .239
Chapter 11   Relating Past to Present . . . . .263

Chapter 12   Understanding the Economy . .285
**Unit 4**     Building American Citizenship .286

Chapter 13   Learning About Citizenship . . .307
Chapter 14   Understanding the Economy . .331
Chapter 15   Learning About Citizenship . . .349
Chapter 16   Learning About Citizenship . . .367
**Unit 5**     Building American Citizenship .368

Chapter 17   Learning About Citizenship . . .391
Chapter 18   Learning About Citizenship . . .415
Chapter 19   Learning About Citizenship . . .433
**Unit 6**     Building American Citizenship .434

**An Overview of Citizenship** . . . . . . . . . .650

## Special Features

### Americans Who Dared

John Wesley Powell . . . . . . . . . . . . . . . . . .22
Aztec Soldier . . . . . . . . . . . . . . . . . . . . . .44
Doña Marina . . . . . . . . . . . . . . . . . . . . . .62
Pocahontas . . . . . . . . . . . . . . . . . . . . . . .91
John Winthrop . . . . . . . . . . . . . . . . . . . .101
Paul Cuffe . . . . . . . . . . . . . . . . . . . . . . .139
Pontiac . . . . . . . . . . . . . . . . . . . . . . . . .157
Laura Wolcott . . . . . . . . . . . . . . . . . . . .188
James Forten . . . . . . . . . . . . . . . . . . . . .205
Benjamin Banneker . . . . . . . . . . . . . . . . .237
Dolley Madison . . . . . . . . . . . . . . . . . . . .259
Daniel Boone . . . . . . . . . . . . . . . . . . . . .271
Sequoyah . . . . . . . . . . . . . . . . . . . . . . .301
James Beckwourth . . . . . . . . . . . . . . . . .311
Eli Whitney . . . . . . . . . . . . . . . . . . . . . .343
Frederick Douglass . . . . . . . . . . . . . . . . .353
Mary Boykin Chesnut . . . . . . . . . . . . . . .388
Mary Ann Bickerdyke . . . . . . . . . . . . . . . .407
Parker Robbins . . . . . . . . . . . . . . . . . . .429

### Spirit of America

The Gaspee Incident: Spirit of Justice . . . . .164
Heroes of the Revolution: Spirit of Patriotism .193
Need for a Bill of Rights: Spirit of Religion . .211
Symbols of July 4th: Spirit of Patriotism . . . .269
The People's President: Spirit of Democracy .294
Schools for the South: Spirit of Education. . .420

### Free Enterprise in Action

Eliza Lucas and Indigo . . . . . . . . . . . . . .133
Hunting the Great Whales . . . . . . . . . . . . .336

### Geography in History

The Badlands of South Dakota . . . . . . . . . .25
Shells as Money . . . . . . . . . . . . . . . . . . .37
Estevanico . . . . . . . . . . . . . . . . . . . . . . .65
Witch Hunt in Salem . . . . . . . . . . . . . . . .104
Building the Nation's Capital . . . . . . . . . . .234

## Arts in America

Sor Juana . . . . . . . . . . . . . . . . . . . . . . . . . . . 82
Henry Wadsworth Longfellow . . . . . . . . . . . 363
A Portrait of War . . . . . . . . . . . . . . . . . . . . . 405

## Voices of Freedom

The Star-Spangled Banner . . . . . . . . . . . . . 261
Victory or Death at the Alamo . . . . . . . . . . . 318
The Play of the Century . . . . . . . . . . . . . . . 378

# Skill Lessons

1  The Parts of a Map . . . . . . . . . . . . . . . . .21
2  A Painting as a Primary Source . . . . . . .43
3  Using Latitude and Longitude . . . . . . . .56
4  Reading A Line Graph . . . . . . . . . . . . . .81
5  Using a Primary Source . . . . . . . . . . . .116
6  Reading a Bar Graph . . . . . . . . . . . . . .140
7  Using A Time Line . . . . . . . . . . . . . . . .167
8  Comparing Two Points of View . . . . . .180
9  Reading a Flow Chart . . . . . . . . . . . . .209
10  Recognizing Fact and Opinion . . . . . . .232
11  Following Routes on a Map . . . . . . . . .247
12  Reading a Circle Graph . . . . . . . . . . . .274
13  Reading a Political Cartoon . . . . . . . . .298
14  Using a Diary as a Primary Source . . .313
15  Comparing Two Line Graphs . . . . . . . .345
16  Using the Card Catalog . . . . . . . . . . . .364
17  Reading an Election Map . . . . . . . . . . .387
18  Using a Table . . . . . . . . . . . . . . . . . . . .396
19  Finding Information in the Library . . . . .422

# History Writer's Handbook

Analyzing a Question Before Writing . . . . . . .73
Identifying Parts of a One-Paragraph
    Answer . . . . . . . . . . . . . . . . . . . . . . . . .145
Rewording a Question as a Topic
    Sentence . . . . . . . . . . . . . . . . . . . . . . . .217
Selecting Supporting Information . . . . . . . .287
Arranging Information for Comparison . . . . .369
Arranging Information to Show Cause and
    Effect . . . . . . . . . . . . . . . . . . . . . . . . . . .435

# Maps

Hunters Reach America . . . . . . . . . . . . . . . .21
Physical Regions of the United States . . . . . .24
Climates of the United States . . . . . . . . . . . .28
Native American Cultures . . . . . . . . . . . . . . .38
Great Empires of the Americas . . . . . . . . . . .45
Looking Beyond Europe . . . . . . . . . . . . . . . .51
To India by Sea . . . . . . . . . . . . . . . . . . . . . .57
Columbus Reaches America . . . . . . . . . . . .58
Voyages of Cabral, Balboa, and Magellan . . .61
Spanish Explorers in North America . . . . . . .64
Search for a Northwest Passage . . . . . . . . . .66
Spain and Portugal in the Americas . . . . . . .78
The French Explore North America . . . . . . . .85
New Netherland and New Sweden . . . . . . . .87
The First English Settlements . . . . . . . . . . . .94
The New England Colonies . . . . . . . . . . . . .102
The Middle Colonies . . . . . . . . . . . . . . . . .107
The Southern Colonies . . . . . . . . . . . . . . . .112
Products of the New England Colonies . . . .122
Products of the Middle Colonies . . . . . . . . .127
Products of the Southern Colonies . . . . . . .130
Growth of the Thirteen Colonies . . . . . . . . .136
Major Trade Routes . . . . . . . . . . . . . . . . . .141
North America in 1753 . . . . . . . . . . . . . . . .150
The French and Indian War . . . . . . . . . . . .154
North America in 1763 . . . . . . . . . . . . . . . .156
Lexington and Concord . . . . . . . . . . . . . . .169
The Siege of Boston . . . . . . . . . . . . . . . . .175
The Fight for Independence Begins . . . . . .175
The Revolutionary War, 1776–1777 . . . . . . .182
The War in the West . . . . . . . . . . . . . . . . .186
The War in the South . . . . . . . . . . . . . . . . .191
North America in 1783 . . . . . . . . . . . . . . . .192
Claims to Western Lands . . . . . . . . . . . . . .199
The Northwest Territory . . . . . . . . . . . . . . .201
The Louisiana Purchase . . . . . . . . . . . . . . .247
The Barbary States . . . . . . . . . . . . . . . . . .250
Lands Lost by Indians . . . . . . . . . . . . . . . .255
The War of 1812 . . . . . . . . . . . . . . . . . . . .258
Action in the South . . . . . . . . . . . . . . . . . .258
Early Roads West . . . . . . . . . . . . . . . . . . .272
Major Canals . . . . . . . . . . . . . . . . . . . . . .275
New Nations in Latin America . . . . . . . . . . .282
Election of 1828 . . . . . . . . . . . . . . . . . . . .293
Indian Removal . . . . . . . . . . . . . . . . . . . . .302
Oregon Country . . . . . . . . . . . . . . . . . . . . .310
Independence for Texas . . . . . . . . . . . . . . .317
Trails to the West . . . . . . . . . . . . . . . . . . . .320

War With Mexico . . . . . . . . . . . . . . . . . . . . 324
Growth of the United States to 1853 . . . . . . 326
The California Gold Rush . . . . . . . . . . . . . 328
Products of the North . . . . . . . . . . . . . . . . 334
Products of the South . . . . . . . . . . . . . . . . 342
Growth of Railroads . . . . . . . . . . . . . . . . 369
Slavery in the Territories . . . . . . . . . . . . . 380
Election of 1860 . . . . . . . . . . . . . . . . . . . 387
Choosing Sides . . . . . . . . . . . . . . . . . . . . 394
The Civil War in the East, 1861–1863 . . . . . 399
Union Advances . . . . . . . . . . . . . . . . . . . 411
The Final Battles . . . . . . . . . . . . . . . . . . 412
Election of 1876 . . . . . . . . . . . . . . . . . . . 430

## Historical Atlas

Native American Cultures . . . . . . . . . . . . . 573
North America in 1753 . . . . . . . . . . . . . . . 575
North America in 1783 . . . . . . . . . . . . . . . 577
Growth of the United States to 1853 . . . . . . 579

## Geographic Atlas

The World . . . . . . . . . . . . . . . . . . . . 580–581
The United States . . . . . . . . . . . . . . . 582–583
Physical Features . . . . . . . . . . . . . . . . . . 584
Population Distribution . . . . . . . . . . . . . . 585
Economic Activities . . . . . . . . . . . . . . . . 586
Natural Resources . . . . . . . . . . . . . . . . . 587

# Charts, Graphs, and Time Lines

Time Line, Unit 1 . . . . . . . . . . . . . . . . . . . 16
Time Line, Chapter 1 . . . . . . . . . . . . . . . . . 18
Climates of the United States . . . . . . . . . . . 27
Time Line, Chapter 2 . . . . . . . . . . . . . . . . . 32
Time Line, Chapter 3 . . . . . . . . . . . . . . . . . 48
Time Line, Unit 2 . . . . . . . . . . . . . . . . . . . 74
Time Line, Chapter 4 . . . . . . . . . . . . . . . . . 76
Indian Population of Central America . . . . . . 81
Time Line, Chapter 5 . . . . . . . . . . . . . . . . . 98
Founding of the Colonies . . . . . . . . . . . . . 115
Time Line, Chapter 6 . . . . . . . . . . . . . . . . 120
Trade With England . . . . . . . . . . . . . . . . 140
Population of the Colonies . . . . . . . . . . . . 145
Time Line, Unit 3 . . . . . . . . . . . . . . . . . . 146
Time Line, Chapter 7 . . . . . . . . . . . . . . . . 148
Time Line, Skill Lesson 7 . . . . . . . . . . . . . 167
Time Line, Chapter 8 . . . . . . . . . . . . . . . . 172
Time Line, Chapter 9 . . . . . . . . . . . . . . . . 196
The Federal System . . . . . . . . . . . . . . . . 206
System of Checks and Balances . . . . . . . . 208
How a Bill Becomes a Law . . . . . . . . . . . . 209
Time Line, Unit 4 . . . . . . . . . . . . . . . . . . 218
Time Line, Chapter 10 . . . . . . . . . . . . . . . 220
Money Problems of the New Nation . . . . . . 224
The First Political Parties . . . . . . . . . . . . . 231
Time Line, Chapter 11 . . . . . . . . . . . . . . . 240
American Foreign Trade, 1800–1812 . . . . . 252
Time Line, Chapter 12 . . . . . . . . . . . . . . . 264
A Growing Population in the West . . . . . . . 274
A Growing Population, 1790–1830 . . . . . . . 278
Effect of a Protective Tariff . . . . . . . . . . . 279
Time Line, Unit 4 Review . . . . . . . . . . . . . 287
Time Line, Unit 5 . . . . . . . . . . . . . . . . . . 288
Time Line, Chapter 13 . . . . . . . . . . . . . . . 290
Time Line, Chapter 14 . . . . . . . . . . . . . . . 308

Time Line, Chapter 15 . . . . . . . . . . . . . . . 332
Growth of Railroads . . . . . . . . . . . . . . . . 335
Cotton Production . . . . . . . . . . . . . . . . . 345
Growth of Slavery . . . . . . . . . . . . . . . . . 345
Time Line, Chapter 16 . . . . . . . . . . . . . . . 350
Time Line, Unit 6 . . . . . . . . . . . . . . . . . . 370
Time Line, Chapter 17 . . . . . . . . . . . . . . . 372
Balance of Free and Slave States . . . . . . . 377
Election of 1860 . . . . . . . . . . . . . . . . . . . 387
Time Line, Chapter 18 . . . . . . . . . . . . . . . 392
Resources of the North and South in 1861 . . 396
Time Line, Chapter 19 . . . . . . . . . . . . . . . 416
Election of 1876 . . . . . . . . . . . . . . . . . . . 430
Time Line, 1877–Present . . . . . . . . . . . . . 436
Presidents of the United States,
        1877-Present . . . . . . . . . . . . . . . . . 440

## Historical Atlas

Environment of Early American Cultures . . . 572
Land Claims in North America, 1753 . . . . . . 574
Land Claims in North America, 1783 . . . . . . 576
Growth of the United States, 1790–1853 . . . 578

## Exploring Our Living Constitution

Contents of the Constitution . . . . . . . . . . . 615
Impact of the Constitution on You . . . . . . . 616
Principles of the Constitution . . . . . . . . . . 617
The Right to Vote . . . . . . . . . . . . . . . . . . 618
The Federal System . . . . . . . . . . . . . . . . 620
Separation of Powers . . . . . . . . . . . . . . . 621
Federal Office Holders . . . . . . . . . . . . . . 622
System of Checks and Balances . . . . . . . . 624
Liberties Protected by the First Amendment . 625
Methods of Amending the Constitution . . . . 627

## UNIT 1　The World of the Americas　453

Chapter 1　**The American Land**
(Prehistory—Present)　453

1–1　America the Beautiful
*Katharine Lee Bates*　453

1–2　A European View of North America
*Alexander Mackenzie*　454

1–3　An Indian Prayer for the Sun
*Leslie Spier, ed.*　456

Chapter 2　**The First Americans**
(Prehistory—1600)　456

2–1　An Arapaho Legend
*Ella E. Clark, ed.*　456

2–2　Prayer to the Young Cedar
*Margot Astrov, ed.*　457

2–3　Keeping a Heritage Alive
*Ohiyesa*　458

2–4　Founding the League of the Iroquois
*Elias Johnson*　459

2–5　Farming Methods of the Incas
*Garcilaso de la Vega*　461

Chapter 3　**Europeans Explore
America** (1000–1650)　462

3–1　Leif Ericson Explores Vinland
*A Viking saga*　462

3–2　Marco Polo on the Wealth of Asia
*Marco Polo*　463

3–3　Columbus Lands in America
*Christopher Columbus*　464

3–4　Rescued by Indians
*Alvar Nuñez Cabeca de Vaca*　466

3–5　Cartier and the Indians of Canada
*Jacques Cartier*　467

3–6　Skills Needed in the New World
*Richard Hakluyt*　468

## UNIT 2　Settling the New World　470

Chapter 4　**Planting Colonies**
(1530–1690)　470

4–1　Hardships of the Atlantic Crossing
*Tomas de la Torre*　470

4–2　A Description of Mexico City
*Henry Hawks*　471

4–3　Marquette and Joliet
*Jacques Marquette*　472

4–4　A Virginia Colonist's Despair
*Richard Frethorne*　474

4–5　Pilgrims and Indians Make Peace
*William Bradford*　475

4–6　What to Take to the New World
*Francis Higginson*　476

Chapter 5　**English Colonies Take Root**
(1630–1750)　477

5–1　A Slave's Ballad on an Indian Attack
*Lucy Terry*　477

5–2　Witchcraft in Massachusetts?
*Increase Mather*　478

5–3　Advice for Settlers in New Netherland
*Cornelius Van Tienhoven*　480

5–4　Bacon Rebels
*A member of the Virginia
legislature*　481

5–5　A Colonist's View of the Indians of Virginia
*Robert Beverley*　483

5–6　Contract of an Indentured Apprentice
*An apprentice's contract*　484

Chapter 6　**Life in the Colonies**
(1630–1775)　485

6–1　A Young Girl of Colonial Boston
*Anna Green Winslow*　485

6–2　A Critical View of Philadelphia
*Alexander Hamilton*　486

6–3　A Slave Describes the Middle Passage
*Gustavus Vasa*　487

6–4　Getting an Education in Virginia
*Devereux Jarratt*　488

6–5　Advice on Entering College
*Thomas Shepard*　489

6–6　The Wisdom of Benjamin Franklin
*Benjamin Franklin*　490

6–7　Americans: A New Breed
*Michel-Guillaume Jean
de Crèvecoeur*　492

# UNIT 3　The Struggle for Independence　493

Chapter 7　Crisis in the Colonies
(1745–1775)　493

7–1　Friendship With the Mohawks
*A painting*　493

7–2　Washington Meets With the French
*George Washington*　494

7–3　Wolfe and Montcalm: The Last Battle
*Francis Parkman*　495

7–4　Indians Treat Captives With Kindness
*William Smith*　496

7–5　Paul Revere on the Boston Massacre
*Paul Revere*　497

7–6　Philadelphia's Tea Protest　*Committee
of Tarring and Feathering*　498

Chapter 8　The American Revolution
(1775–1783)　499

8–1　Glory on Bunker Hill　*A poem*　499

8–2　How the Declaration Was Written
*John Adams*　500

8–3　A Loyalist Is Tarred and Feathered
*Ann Hulton*　502

8–4　Lafayette's Impressions of America
*Marquis de Lafayette*　503

8–5　Washington Seeks Help From the Indians
*George Washington*　504

8–6　A Slave's Support for the Patriots
*Phillis Wheatley*　504

8–7　An Eyewitness at Yorktown
*James Thacher*　505

Chapter 9　Creating a Government
(1776–1790)　507

9–1　The Articles of Confederation
*A government document*　507

9–2　No Taxation Without Representation
*Paul Cuffe*　508

9–3　Franklin Asks Support for the Constitution
*Benjamin Franklin*　509

9–4　A Farmer Speaks for the Constitution
*Jonathan Smith*　510

9–5　An Antifederalist Argues His Case
*Anonymous*　511

# UNIT 4　Strengthening the New Nation　512

Chapter 10　The First Presidents
(1789–1800)　512

10–1　The First President Becomes a Legend
*Mason L. Weems*　512

10–2　Washington Advises Neutrality
*George Washington*　513

10–3　Jefferson Opposes the National Bank
*Thomas Jefferson*　514

10–4　Hamilton Supports the Bank
*Alexander Hamilton*　516

10–5　A Song to Unite Americans
*Joseph Hopkinson*　517

Chapter 11　Age of Jefferson
(1801–1816)　518

11–1　The First Republican President
*Thomas Jefferson*　518

11–2　The Shoshones Meet Lewis and Clark
*A Shoshone Indian*　519

11–3　Sympathy for Impressed Americans
*Basil Hall*　520

11–4　Tecumseh Protests Land Sale
*Tecumseh*　521

11–5　Henry Clay Defends War With Britain
*Henry Clay*　522

Chapter 12　The Nation Prospers
(1790–1825)　523

12–1　Pros and Cons of Factory Life
*The Lowell Offering*　523

12–2　Mark Twain on the Lure of Steamboats
*Mark Twain*　525

12–3　A Southerner Objects to the Tariff
*John Randolph*　526

12–4　Monroe Doctrine Declared
*James Monroe*　527

12–5　Americans Sing Praises of Home
*Howard Payne*　528

# UNIT 5  A Growing Nation  529

Chapter 13  Age of Jackson
(1824–1840)  529

13 – 1  The Election of 1824  *Two graphs*  529
13 – 2  A Mother Advises a Future President
*Elizabeth Jackson*  530
13 – 3  Calhoun on the Power of States
*John C. Calhoun*  531
13 – 4  Webster's Defense of National Supremacy
*Daniel Webster*  531
13 – 5  Jackson Warns the Seminoles
*Andrew Jackson*  533
13 – 6  A Campaign Song
*A song from the 1840 election*  534

Chapter 14  Westward Ho!
(1820–1860)  535

14 – 1  Camp Life in the Rockies
*Osborne Russell*  535
14 – 2  A Defense of the Texas Struggle
*William Wharton*  536
14 – 3  Prudencia Higuera's Brass Buttons
*Prudencia Higuera*  537
14 – 4  America's Manifest Destiny
*John L. O'Sullivan*  538
14 – 5  Black Opposition to the Mexican War
*Frederick Douglass*  539

14 – 6  Louise Clappe Strikes Gold
*Louise Clappe*  540

Chapter 15  Two Ways of Life
(1820–1860)  541

15 – 1  At Work on a Clipper  *A sea chantey*  541
15 – 2  Life in a Mill in 1832  *Seth Luther*  542
15 – 3  A Violent Reaction to Foreign-Born Voters
*Louisville Courier*  543
15 – 4  Inventing the Cotton Gin
*Eli Whitney*  544
15 – 5  Memories of a Slave Auction
*Solomon Northrup*  545

Chapter 16  The Reforming Spirit
(1820–1860)  546

16 – 1  A Daring Escape to Freedom
*William Wells Brown*  546
16 – 2  The Case for Slavery  *Thomas Dew
and George McDuffie*  548
16 – 3  A New Approach to Raising Girls
*Elizabeth Cady Stanton*  549
16 – 4  A Country School
*A painting*  550
16 – 5  A Plea for Simplicity
*Henry David Thoreau*  551

# UNIT 6  The Nation Divided  552

Chapter 17  The Coming of the War
(1820–1860)  552

17 – 1  A Question of Slavery in the West
*David Wilmot*  552
17 – 2  How Can the Union Be Saved?
*John C. Calhoun*  553
17 – 3  A Plea to Preserve the Union
*Daniel Webster*  554
17 – 4  The Suffering of Uncle Tom
*Harriet Beecher Stowe*  555
17 – 5  The Dred Scott Decision: A Black View
*Frederick Douglass*  557
17 – 6  Singing the Praises of John Brown
*A song*  557
17 – 7  Mississippi Secedes From the Union
*From the laws of Mississippi*  558

Chapter 18  The Civil War
(1860–1865)  559

18 – 1  The Bonnie Blue Flag
*Harry McCarty*  559
18 – 2  Encouraging Union Soldiers
*Phoebe Cary*  560

18 – 3  Lee Takes Pity on a Union Soldier
*A Union soldier*  561
18 – 4  The Battle of Antietam
*George Washburn Smalley*  562
18 – 5  Issuing the Emancipation Proclamation
*A painting*  563
18 – 6  A Southern Woman Takes Over at Home
*Victoria Clayton*  564
18 – 7  Lee and Grant Meet at Appomattox
*Ulysses S. Grant*  565

Chapter 19  The Road to Reunion
(1864–1877)  566

19 – 1  A Planter Faces the Future
*Susan Dabney Smedes*  566
19 – 2  From the Black Codes
*From the laws of Mississippi*  567
19 – 3  A Former Slave on Reconstruction
*Katie Rowe*  568
19 – 4  Winning and Losing the Right to Vote
*Two drawings*  569

# Getting to Know Your Book

We as authors believe that history begins with a good story. *A History of the Republic: The United States to 1877* is the story of the many different people who settled this land. "Out of Many, One," the motto on the Great Seal of the United States, set a goal for the nation as it grew.

## How the book is organized

The book is organized into 6 units and 19 chapters. The Table of Contents (pages 5–13) lists the titles of units and chapters. It also lists special features, skill lessons, maps, charts, graphs, and time lines in the text. At the back of the book is a selection of readings and other sources and a reference section.

## How each unit is organized

**Unit Opener.** Each unit opens with two pages that give an overview of the unit. Study the opener for Unit 5 below. The unit outline lists the chapters in the unit. The unit time line presents major dates and events. A star after a date shows that a new state entered the Union in that year. The time line also includes a President's band showing who was in office during the years covered in each unit. Pictures with captions illustrate events or developments during this period.

**Unit Review.** Each unit ends with two pages called the Unit Review. It has a summary of each chapter in the unit as well as multiple choice questions to help you review key information. Other questions and activities let you review main ideas and practice skills. A Writer's Handbook offers a lesson on writing a paragraph. Turn to pages 368–369 for the Unit 5 Review.

## How each chapter is organized

**Chapter Opener.** At the beginning of each chapter is a chapter outline that lists the numbered sections of the chapter. A chapter time line shows some of the main events that you'll be reading about. The introduction, called ***About This Chapter,*** gives an overview of the chapter. A picture with caption illustrates an idea from the chapter. Look for these elements in the chapter opener on page 290.

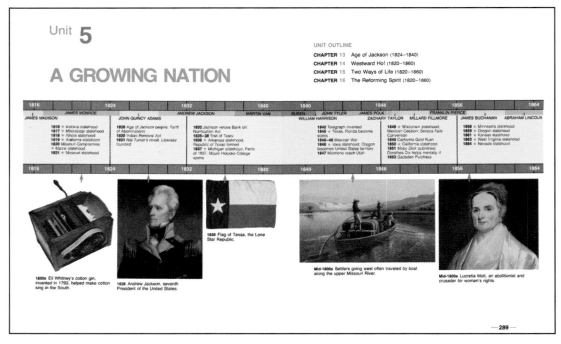

**Individual Lessons.** Each numbered section is a separate lesson. Each lesson begins with **Read to Learn** questions that let you focus on the main ideas of the section and study new vocabulary words. You can find these new words in the Glossary. **Section Review** questions at the end of each section let you locate places on maps, study vocabulary, and review main ideas. Look at these parts of the lesson that starts on page 291.

**Skill Lessons and Special Features.** A skill lesson and two special features appear in every chapter. The skill lessons teach social studies skills such as reading maps and graphs and using time lines. Look at Skill Lesson 13 on page 298. Special features are stories about interesting people and events. Find the list of Special Features in the Table of Contents. Then read one story that interests you right now.

**Maps, Graphs, Charts, and Pictures.** There are more than 100 maps, graphs, and charts in this book and hundreds of pictures. Each tells a story. Captions help show how the visual is related to events in the chapter that you are studying.

**Reading aids.** Reading aids are included to help you read and understand this book. Each new vocabulary word is printed in **dark slanted type.** A definition is given when the word first appears. Important events and ideas are in **dark slanted type,** too. A guide to pronunciation (pro NUN see ay shuhn) helps you read words and names that may be new to you. The Pronunciation Key is on page 605.

**Chapter Review.** Each chapter ends with two pages called the Chapter Review. The Chapter Review has a summary of the chapter as well as different kinds of questions and activities that let you test your understanding of the chapter. It also includes ideas for projects and research reports.

## Readings

A selection of readings and other sources appears on pages 452–569. It contains a variety of readings, including poems, songs, and letters plus colorful paintings, photographs, and cartoons.

This campaign banner shows William Henry Harrison's log cabin symbol. During the campaign, Whigs built log cabins in public places to get people to vote for Harrison.

## Reference Section

The Reference Section can be found on pages 570–667. It includes:

- **Historical Atlas** with maps, graphs, and pictures to illustrate the growth of the United States.
- **Geographic Atlas** with five maps of the United States and one of the world.
- **The Fifty States** with useful information about each state.
- **Gazetteer of American History** with useful information about important places.
- **A Chronology of American History** with major events and developments.
- **Connections With American Literature** with ideas for readings from literature.
- **Presidents of the United States** with a portrait and information about every President.
- **Glossary** with definitions of key terms.
- **The Declaration of Independence** with explanations.
- **Exploring.Our Living Constitution** with a guide for understanding the Constitution.
- **The Constitution of the United States of America** with explanations.
- **An Overview of Citizenship** with a review of the rights of citizens.
- **Index** that tells you where to find a subject in the book.

As you study American history this year, you will use all the different parts of the book. We hope that they will help make history as exciting for you as students as it is for us as historians and teachers.

**James West Davidson**
**John E. Batchelor**

# Unit 1

# THE WORLD OF THE AMERICAS

| Prehistory | | | | | | | 1450 | | | | 1500 |
|---|---|---|---|---|---|---|---|---|---|---|---|

**10,000 YEARS AGO** Last ice age ends
**5,000 YEARS AGO** Farming begins in America
**3,000 YEARS AGO** Mayas drain swamps for farmland

**1001** Vikings reach North America
**1095** Crusades begin
**1300s** Aztecs move into Valley of Mexico
**1400s** Inca empire expands
**1418** Portuguese sailors begin to explore coast of Africa

**1488** Dias rounds Cape of Good Hope
**1492** Columbus reaches America
**1498** Da Gama reaches India

| Prehistory | | | | | | | 1450 | | | | 1500 |
|---|---|---|---|---|---|---|---|---|---|---|---|

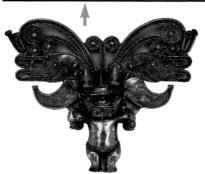

Gold pendant made by Indians in South America.

**1001** Leif Ericson reached Vinland in North America.

**1498** The Portuguese explorer Vasco da Gama.

UNIT OUTLINE

**CHAPTER** 1   The American Land (Prehistory–Present)

**CHAPTER** 2   The First Americans (Prehistory–1600)

**CHAPTER** 3   Europeans Explore America (1000–1650)

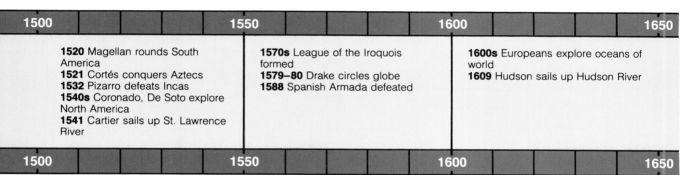

| 1500 | | | | 1550 | | | | 1600 | | | | 1650 |
|---|---|---|---|---|---|---|---|---|---|---|---|---|

**1520** Magellan rounds South America
**1521** Cortés conquers Aztecs
**1532** Pizarro defeats Incas
**1540s** Coronado, De Soto explore North America
**1541** Cartier sails up St. Lawrence River

**1570s** League of the Iroquois formed
**1579–80** Drake circles globe
**1588** Spanish Armada defeated

**1600s** Europeans explore oceans of world
**1609** Hudson sails up Hudson River

| 1500 | | | | 1550 | | | | 1600 | | | | 1650 |
|---|---|---|---|---|---|---|---|---|---|---|---|---|

**1540s** Francisco Coronado searched for gold in the American Southwest.

**Late 1500s** Queen Elizabeth I of England.

# 1

# The American Land (Prehistory—Present)

## Chapter Outline

**1** Discovering the Land
**2** Different Climates
Readings, page 453

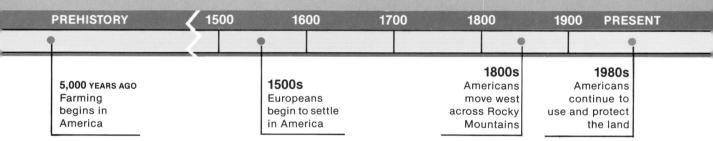

| PREHISTORY | 1500 | 1600 | 1700 | 1800 | 1900 | PRESENT |
|---|---|---|---|---|---|---|

**5,000 YEARS AGO**
Farming begins in America

**1500s**
Europeans begin to settle in America

**1800s**
Americans move west across Rocky Mountains

**1980s**
Americans continue to use and protect the land

## About This Chapter

One hundred thousand years ago, you could have traveled from the northern tip of North America to the southern tip of South America without seeing another person. But you would have seen many kinds of plants and animals in many different landscapes and climates.

As you traveled across the Americas, you would have climbed up and down high mountains and walked into deep valleys. You would have crossed wide rivers and lakes and plodded through windswept deserts. You would have cut your way through steaming jungles and trekked through ice-covered regions.

Many different peoples settled in the Americas. They learned about the land in dif-ferent ways. The first Americans moved across the land, hunting game and gathering food. Later, they discovered ways to make the land produce crops, and they began to farm.

Thousands of years later, Europeans, Africans, and Asians crossed wide oceans to settle in the Americas. They, too, learned to adapt to the many lands and climates of North and South America.

America's history begins with the story of people learning to live in a new land. The physical features, climates, plants, animals, and resources of the land play an important role in this story.

Study the time line above. When did farming begin in America?

In the 1870s, artist Thomas Moran painted the grandeur of the West. This painting shows a canyon carved by the Yellowstone River.

# 1 Discovering the Land

## Read to Learn

★ How did people first reach the Americas?

★ What are the major physical regions of North America?

★ What rivers flow through North America?

★ What do these words mean: geography, glacier, isthmus, mountain, elevation, hill, plain, plateau, tributary?

When the first Americans reached this land thousands of years ago, they spread out in many directions. They developed different ways of life. These differences were due in part to the geography of the Americas. *Geography* includes the physical features, climate, plants, animals, and resources of a region.

Geography influenced the way early Americans lived. Today, geography still affects where and how Americans live. Geography helps to explain history because it shows how people and the land are related.

## The Last Ice Age

According to scientists, the first people to reach America came during the last ice age. The earth has gone through four ice ages. The last ice age occurred between 100,000 and 10,000 years ago. During that time, thick sheets of ice, called *glaciers,* spread out from the arctic regions. Almost one third of the earth was buried under these sheets of ice. In North America, glaciers stretched across Canada and reached as far south as Kentucky.

Glaciers changed the lands they covered. When a glacier moved south, it scooped up soil and huge boulders. When it retreated, or melted, it left behind great heaps of earth and rock. Long Island, New York, was created when a glacier retreated. So were Nantucket and Martha's Vineyard, islands off the coast of Massachusetts. Water from melting glaciers drained into channels, creating large rivers such as the Ohio and the Missouri.

**The land bridge.** Glaciers soaked up water from the oceans like giant sponges. This caused the levels of the oceans to drop. As a result, land appeared that had once been covered by water. Scientists think that during the last ice age a land bridge was exposed between Siberia in Asia and Alaska in North America. Today, this land is under the Bering Sea.

We do not know exactly when people first crossed the land bridge into North America. They may have reached this continent as early as 70,000 years ago. The first Americans were hunters who followed herds of wild animals such as woolly mammoths. Over thousands of years, they moved across North America into South America.

**Temperatures get warmer.** About 10,000 years ago, temperatures rose. Glaciers melted and flooded the land bridge between Siberia and Alaska. The warmer temperatures probably caused the woolly mammoths and mastodons to die out. But the peoples of America adapted to the new conditions. They hunted smaller game, gathered berries and grain, and caught fish.

About 5,000 years ago, some people learned to grow crops such as corn, beans, and squash. These farming people did not have to travel constantly in

Remains of woolly mammoths have been found in the Southwest. Woolly mammoths, or American elephants, grew to be 12 feet high. Armed only with spears and burning torches, early hunters killed these huge animals.

Maps are important tools used by historians and geographers. Maps have many uses. They show physical features such as lakes, rivers, and mountains. They show where people live, how people use the land, and where events took place.

A map shows part of the earth's surface. Almost all maps are flat, but the earth is not. Mapmakers have found ways to put the round earth on flat paper. But all maps, except globes, have some distortion.

To use a map, you need to be able to read its different parts. Most maps in this book have a title, key, scale, and directional arrow. Some also show relief. **Relief** is the difference in height of land that is shown by using special colors. (See the color bands on the map on page 584.)

1. **Look carefully at the map to see what it shows.** The *title* tells you the subject of the map. The *key* explains the meaning of the colors or symbols. (a) What is the title of the map at right? (b) What color shows the land bridge from Asia to North America?

2. **Practice reading distances on the map.** The *scale* helps you read distances on the map in miles or kilometers. On a small-scale map, one inch might equal 500 miles. On a large-scale map, one inch might equal only 5 miles. The map below is a small-scale map. (a) About how far in miles did glaciers stretch from north to south? (b) In kilometers?

3. **Study the map to read directions.** The *directional arrow* shows which way is north, south, east, and west. Generally, north is toward the top of a map, and south is toward the bottom. East is to the right, and west is to the left. (a) In what direction did early hunters travel to reach North America? (b) In what direction or directions did they move after they arrived here?

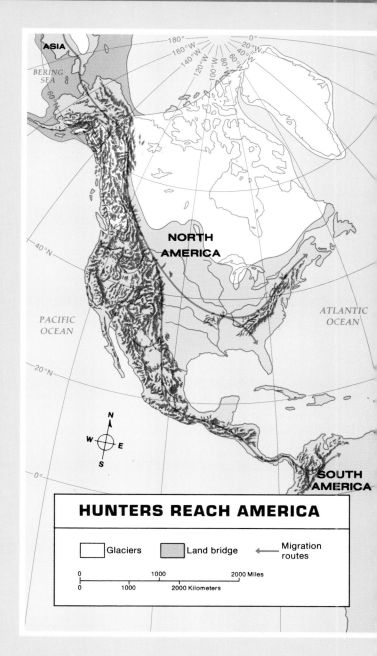

**HUNTERS REACH AMERICA**

☐ Glaciers      ▨ Land bridge      ← Migration routes

0      1000      2000 Miles
0      1000      2000 Kilometers

### John Wesley Powell

In 1879, John Wesley Powell was named to head the United States Geological Survey. His job was to prepare accurate maps of the country. Powell had lost his right arm in the Civil War. Despite this handicap, he braved many dangers to study the land and make maps of the western United States. He also studied the cultures and languages of Native Americans in the West.

search of food. They built the first permanent villages in the Americas.

## Different Landforms

What did the lands settled by the first Americans look like? North and South America are the world's third and fourth largest continents. These two continents plus the islands in the Caribbean Sea are called the *Western Hemisphere.*

As the map on pages 580–581 shows, the Atlantic Ocean washes the eastern shores of North and South America. The Pacific Ocean laps at their western shores. Far to the north lies the ice-choked Arctic Ocean. Far to the south is the Strait of Magellan (muh JEHL uhn), a water passage between the Atlantic and Pacific oceans. Joining the two continents is an *isthmus* (IHS muhs), or narrow strip of land. It is called the *Isthmus of Panama.*

North and South America have many different landscapes. There are high mountains, rolling hills, and long rivers. There are grassy plains, dense forests, and barren deserts. Within these landscapes, there are four basic landforms: mountains, hills, plains, and plateaus (pla TOHZ).

*Mountains* are high, rugged land. They rise to an *elevation,* or height, of at least 5,000 feet (1,500 m) above the surrounding land. Few people can live on the steep, rocky sides of high mountains. Yet, people often settle in valleys between mountains.

*Hills* are also raised parts of the earth's surface. But they are smaller, less steep, and more rounded than mountains. More people live in hilly areas than on mountains because farming is possible.

*Plains* are broad areas of fairly level land. Very few plains are totally flat. Most are gently rolling. Plains are usually not much above sea level. People often settle on plains because it is easy to build farms, roads, and cities on the level land.

*Plateaus* are areas of high, level land. Usually, plateaus rise to at least 2,000 feet (600 m) above sea level. Plateaus can be good for farming if they get enough rain. Some plateaus are surrounded by mountains. Such plateaus are called basins. Basins are often very dry because the mountains cut off rainfall.

## Physical Regions of North America

The mountains, hills, plains, and plateaus of North America form seven major physical regions, as you can see on the map on page 24. These regions offer great contrasts. In some regions, the land is fertile. There, American farmers have been able to plant crops and reap rich harvests. Other regions have natural resources such as coal and oil. These resources have helped make America a strong nation.

**Pacific Coast.** The highest and most rugged part of North America is in the West. Tall mountain ranges stretch from Alaska to Mexico. In the United States, some of the western ranges hug the Pacific. The Cascades and *Sierra Nevada** stand a bit farther inland. The region containing these mountains is called the Pacific Coast. Some important cities of the Pacific Coast are Seattle, Portland, San Francisco, and Los Angeles.

**Intermountain region.** East of the coast ranges is an area known as the Intermountain region. It is a rugged

*Sierra (see EHR uh) is a Spanish word meaning mountain range. Nevada is Spanish for snowy. Spanish explorers were the first Europeans to see these snow-covered mountains.

region of mountain peaks, high plateaus, deep canyons, and deserts. The Grand Canyon, which is more than one mile deep, and the Great Salt Lake are two natural features of this region. Salt Lake City and Phoenix are among the few major cities of the Intermountain region.

**Rocky Mountains.** The third region, the Rocky Mountains, reaches from Alaska through Canada into the United States. Many peaks in the Rockies are over 14,000 feet (4,200 m) high.* The Rockies were a serious barrier to the settlement of the United States. When settlers moved west in the 1800s, crossing the Rockies posed great hardships. In Mexico, the Rocky Mountains are called the Sierra Madre (MAH dray), or mother range.

**Interior Plains.** Between the Rocky Mountains in the west and the Appalachian Mountains in the east is a large lowland area called the Interior Plains.

*The highest peaks in North America are in Alaska. Mt. McKinley, Alaska, rises to 20,320 feet.

America is a land of great natural beauty and varied landscapes. In the photograph at left, waves sweep onto the Pacific coast of the United States. The photograph below shows the Grand Canyon through a limestone arch on the south rim. More than 9 million years ago, the Colorado River began carving this deep canyon in the Southwest.

The western part of the Interior Plains is called the *Great Plains.* The eastern part is called the *Central Plains.*

According to scientists, the Interior Plains were once covered by a great inland sea. Today, some parts are rich in coal and petroleum.* Chicago, St. Louis, and Dallas are in the Interior Plains. The *Badlands* are also found here. See page 25.

---

*The map on page 587 shows where natural resources are located in the United States.

**Appalachian Mountains.** The fifth region, the Appalachian Mountains, runs along the eastern part of North America. The Appalachians are called different names in different places. For example, the Green Mountains, Alleghenies, Blue Ridge, and Great Smokies are all part of the Appalachians.

The Appalachians are lower and less rugged than the Rockies. The highest Appalachian peak is Mt. Mitchell, which is only about 6,000 feet (1,850 m) high. Still, early settlers had a hard time crossing these mountains.

**MAP SKILL** The major physical regions of the United States are shown in different colors on this map. Find the four mountain ranges labeled on the map. Which range is in the eastern part of the United States?

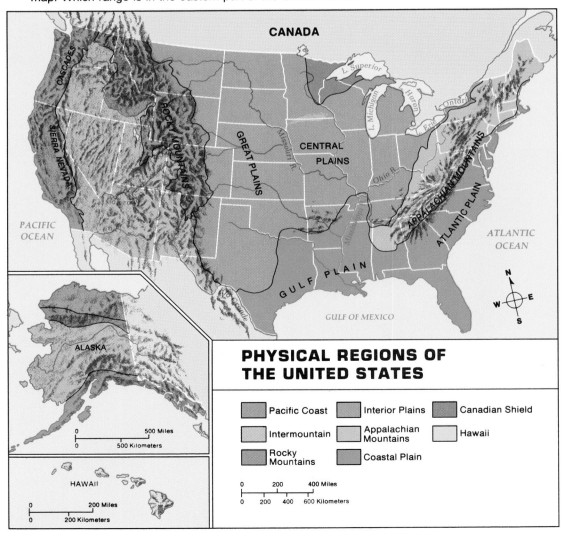

**PHYSICAL REGIONS OF THE UNITED STATES**

Pacific Coast    Interior Plains    Canadian Shield
Intermountain    Appalachian Mountains    Hawaii
Rocky Mountains    Coastal Plain

# Geography in History

## The Badlands of South Dakota

Strange and startling shapes rise up out of the Badlands of South Dakota. The Badlands got their name from the Dakota Indians. They called the area mako sica, or land that was bad, because it had little good water. Later, French and English settlers used words from their own languages to express the same idea.

Wind, weather, and rivers have carved strange shapes in the Badlands and have revealed traces of the ancient history of the Badlands. Rain and wind have exposed the bones of animals that roamed the land millions of years ago. Scientists have found the remains of ancient turtles, camels, and saber-toothed tigers. Today, bear, elk, moose, and deer live there.

People, too, have lived in the Badlands. For hundreds of years, Indians camped in the Badlands during buffalo hunts. In the early 1900s, white settlers built homes there. But lack of water forced many settlers to sell their land. In

1978, the Badlands were made a national park.

★ Why have few people settled in the Badlands?

---

**Canadian Shield.** The sixth region is the Canadian Shield. It is a lowland area. Most of it lies in eastern Canada. The southern part extends into the United States. The region was once an area of high mountains. The mountains were worn away to low hills and plains. The Canadian Shield lacks topsoil for farming. But it is rich in minerals.

**Coastal Plains.** The seventh region is a lowland area called the Coastal Plains. Part of this region, the *Atlantic Plain,* lies between the Atlantic Ocean and the foothills of the Appalachians. It was once under water and is now almost flat. The Atlantic Plain is narrow in the north, where Boston and New York City are located. It broadens in the south to include all of Florida.

Another part of the Coastal Plains is the *Gulf Plain,* which lies along the Gulf of Mexico. The Gulf Plain is rich in petroleum. New Orleans and Houston are major cities of the Gulf Plain.

### Rivers and Lakes

Great river systems crisscross North America. They collect the runoff from rains and melting snows and carry it into the oceans. The longest and most important river system in the United States is made up of the Mississippi and Missouri rivers. This river system flows through the Interior Plains into the Gulf of Mexico. It has many *tributaries,* or branches. They include the Ohio, Tennessee, Arkansas, and Platte rivers.

The Mississippi River carries moisture across the Interior Plains. It also serves as a means of transportation. Today, barges carry freight up and down the river. Today, as in the past, people travel by boat along the river.

The Rio Grande and the St. Lawrence River form parts of the borders between the United States and its neighbors, Mexico and Canada.

Five large lakes, called the *Great Lakes,* also form part of the border between the United States and Canada. The Great Lakes are Superior, Michigan, Huron, Erie, and Ontario. Today, canals connect the Great Lakes, forming an important inland waterway.

The Niagara River connects Lake Erie to Lake Ontario. However, ships cannot use this fast-flowing river because at one point it plunges over broad cliffs, forming the spectacular Niagara Falls. Instead, ships travel through the Welland Canal, which connects these two Great Lakes.

## Landscapes of South America

Like North America, South America has a variety of landscapes. The Andes are a rugged mountain chain. They stretch along the western part of South America. The tallest peaks of the Andes are much higher than those of the Rockies. The Andes plunge almost directly to the Pacific, leaving only a narrow coastal plain. Many people live in the high plateaus and valleys of the Andes.

To the east of the Andes is an interior plain. The plain is drained by three great river systems: the Orinoco, Amazon, and Parana–Paraguay. The Amazon is the world's second longest river. It flows 4,000 miles (6,500 km) from the Andes to the Atlantic.

### SECTION REVIEW

1. **Locate:** Bering Sea, North America, South America, Atlantic Ocean, Pacific Ocean, Sierra Nevada, Rocky Mountains, Great Plains, Appalachian Mountains, Mississippi River.
2. **Define:** geography, glacier, isthmus, mountain, elevation, hill, plain, plateau, tributary.
3. (a) What are the seven physical regions of North America? (b) Describe one feature of each.
4. Where are the Great Lakes?
5. **What Do You Think?** Why do you think the Intermountain region has only a few cities?

# 2 Different Climates

### Read to Learn
★ What are the major climates of the United States?
★ What climates does South America have?
★ What do these words mean: weather, climate, irrigate?

Geographic features such as mountains and rivers have affected the way Americans live. Another feature of geography that has affected Americans is climate. People have had to adapt to different climates in the Americas.

## What Is Climate?

Climate is important to people's lives because it is always there. But just what is climate? How is it different from weather? *Weather* is the condition of the air at any given time and place. *Climate* is the average weather of a place over a period of 20 or 30 years.

Climates have changed over time. During the last ice age, climates grew very cold. The extreme cold affected plants, animals, and people around the world.

Several factors affect climate. One factor is how far north or south of the Equator a region is located. Lands close to the Equator generally have a tropical climate. They usually are hot and wet all year. Lands around the North and South poles have an arctic climate. They are cold all year. Alaska and northern Canada have a subarctic climate with long, cold winters and very short summers. Other lands have both warm and cold seasons.

Another factor that affects climate is altitude, or the height above sea level. In general, highland areas are cooler than lowland areas.

Ocean currents, wind currents, and mountains also influence climate. For example, when winds carrying moisture strike the side of a mountain, the air rises and cools rapidly. As the moisture cools, it falls as rain or snow. Plenty of moisture falls on one side of the mountain. The other side is usually quite dry because the winds have already dumped their moisture.

## Climates of North America

Within North America, climates vary greatly. Many regions have mild temperatures and good rainfall. In such regions, Americans have been able to grow plentiful food crops.

The United States has ten major climates. Look at the map on page 28 and the chart at right. You have read about tropical, arctic, subarctic, and highland climates above. The other six climates are described below.

**Marine.** The strip of land from southern Alaska to northern California is sometimes called the Pacific Northwest. This region has a mild, moist marine climate. The Pacific Northwest has many forests that make it the center of the busy lumber industry.

**Mediterranean.** Most of California has a Mediterranean climate. Winters

## Climates of the United States

| Climate | Weather |
|---|---|
| Tropical | Hot, rainy, steamy |
| Humid subtropical | Humid summers; mild winters |
| Humid continental | Hot summers; cold winters; rainfall varies |
| Steppe | Very hot summers; very cold winters; little rainfall |
| Desert | Hot; very little rainfall |
| Mediterranean | Mild, wet winters; sunny, dry summers |
| Marine | Mild, rainy |
| Subarctic | Very short summers; long, cold winters |
| Arctic | Very cold winters; very short summers |
| Highlands | Seasons and rainfall vary with elevation |

**CHART SKILL** Compare the ten climates on this chart to the climates on the map on page 28. The chart shows the weather found in each climate. Using the map and the chart, find the climate and weather for your state.

are mild and moist. Summers are hot and dry. In many areas, the soil is good, but plants need to be watered in the summer. So farmers and fruit growers *irrigate,* or bring water to, the land.

**Desert.** On the eastern side of the Cascades and Sierra Nevada, the land has a desert climate. This dry region stretches as far east as the Rockies. In the deserts of Nevada, Arizona, and southeastern California, there is almost no rainfall. In many areas, people irrigate the land so that they can grow crops.

**Steppe.** East of the Rockies are the Great Plains. They have a steppe climate with limited rainfall. The short grasses that grow on the Great Plains are excellent for grazing. Huge buffalo herds grazed there for hundreds of years. In the 1800s, settlers, brought cattle to graze on the plains.

**Humid continental.** The Central Plains and the northeastern United States have a humid continental climate. This climate has more rainfall than the steppe. Tall prairie grasses once covered the Central Plains. Today, American farmers raise much of the world's food in this area.

At one time, forests covered much of the northeastern United States. Early European settlers cleared forests to grow crops. But many forests remain, and the lumber industry thrives in some areas.

**MAP SKILL** The United States is a land of many climates. The mild climates of some areas have helped people. In other areas, people have struggled to survive under harsh climate conditions. Locate the state where you live on the map below. What climate or climates are found in your state?

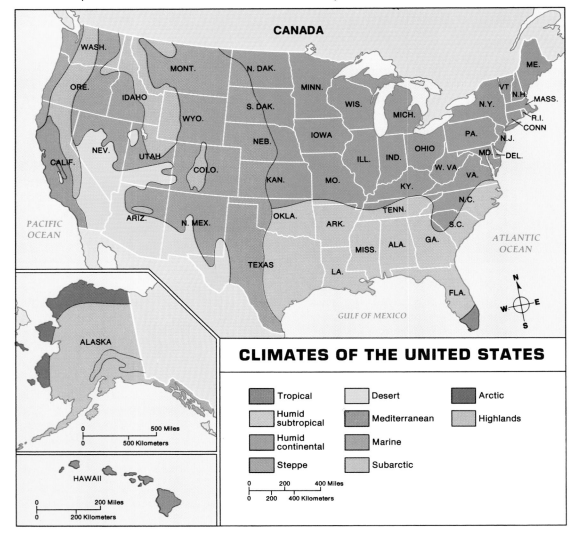

**CLIMATES OF THE UNITED STATES**

- Tropical
- Humid subtropical
- Humid continental
- Steppe
- Desert
- Mediterranean
- Marine
- Subarctic
- Arctic
- Highlands

American climates vary a lot, as these two photographs show. The one at left shows cactus in the desert climate of the Southwest. The one at right shows a cypress forest in the subtropical climate of the Southeast. What differences do you see in the plants of these climates?

**Humid subtropical.** The southeastern part of the country has a humid subtropical climate. Warm temperatures and regular rainfall make this region ideal for growing crops such as cotton, tobacco, and peanuts.

## Climates of South America

South America has many climates. Thick tropical rain forests cover parts of southern Mexico, Central America,* and South America. The huge area drained by the Amazon River is largely rain forest.

The Andes Mountains are a barrier to moist winds. The mountains force the winds to dump rain on the eastern slopes of the Andes. But the western slopes are very dry. In fact, one of the world's driest deserts, the Atacama

*Central America is the part of North America that lies between Mexico and South America.

Desert, stretches along the coast of Peru and northern Chile.

Large parts of Brazil have a savanna climate. These areas have a rainy season when huge amounts of moisture fall. The rainy season is followed by a dry season with no rainfall. Other countries in South America, such as Argentina, Uruguay, and Chile, have climates similar to those in the United States.

### SECTION REVIEW

1. **Define:** weather, climate, irrigate.
2. Name two factors that affect the climate of a region.
3. List the ten major climates of the United States.
4. Describe two climates found in South America.
5. **What Do You Think?** Why do you think climate is important to people's lives?

# Chapter 1 Review

★ **Summary** ★

During the last ice age, hunters moved across the frozen land bridge that connected Asia and North America. They became the first people to settle in the Americas. As these first Americans slowly moved across the two continents, they found many different lands and climates.

Geography is important to the study of American history because it shows how people and the land are related. North America has seven major physical regions and ten climates. For thousands of years, the different lands and climates have affected the way people live.

★ **Reviewing the Facts** ★

**Key Terms.** Match each term in Column 1 with the correct definition in Column 2.

| Column 1 | Column 2 |
|---|---|
| **1.** geography | **a.** narrow strip of land |
| **2.** glacier | **b.** branch of a river |
| **3.** isthmus | **c.** broad area of gently rolling land |
| **4.** mountain | **d.** physical features of a region |
| **5.** hill | **e.** high, rugged land |
| **6.** plain | **f.** average weather over time |
| **7.** plateau | **g.** thick sheet of ice |
| **8.** tributary | **h.** condition of the air at a certain time and place |
| **9.** weather | **i.** raised, rounded part of the earth's surface |
| **10.** climate | **j.** high, level land |

**Key People, Events, and Ideas.** Identify each of the following.

1. Western Hemisphere
2. Isthmus of Panama
3. Sierra Nevada
4. Great Plains
5. Central Plains
6. Great Lakes
7. Atlantic Plain
8. Gulf Plain
9. Badlands
10. John Wesley Powell

★ **Chapter Checkup** ★

1. How did glaciers affect North America during the last ice age?
2. (a) How do scientists think the first Americans reached North America? (b) How did the lives of the first Americans change about 10,000 years ago?
3. Describe the major geographical features of South America.
4. (a) Name four major rivers of North America. (b) Why is the Mississippi River important?
5. Explain two ways that mountains influence climate.
6. Why do farmers in Nevada, Arizona, and southeastern California have to irrigate the land?

## ★ Thinking About History ★

1. **Relating past to present.** (a) How did the first Americans adapt to climate changes after the last ice age? (b) How do Americans today adapt to living in different climates?

2. **Analyzing information.** (a) List two differences between the Great Plains and the Central Plains. (b) How does climate influence these differences?

3. **Understanding geography.** Review pages 26–29. (a) Which American climates are probably the easiest to live in? (b) Which climates are probably the hardest to live in? Why?

4. **Expressing an opinion.** Do you think that geography has as much influence on people today as it did in the past? Explain your answer.

## ★ Using Your Skills ★

1. **Map reading.** Review the map-reading steps in Skill Lesson 1 (page 21). Then study the map on page 24. (a) What is the title of the map? (b) What region is directly east of the Pacific Coast? (c) What region is directly west of the Atlantic Plain? (d) What is the approximate distance in miles east to west across the United States?

2. **Outlining.** Outlining is a way of presenting lots of information in an organized way. An outline helps you summarize and review facts. To outline a chapter, list its main topics and subtopics. Then give facts about each subtopic. To outline Chapter 1, write the first main topic—the numbered title on page 19. (See the sample below.) Below that, write the first subtopic—the subsection on page

19. Under each subtopic, write at least two facts. Complete the outline for Chapter 1.

I. Discovering the Land (main topic)
   A. The Last Ice Age (subtopic)
      1. formed land bridge between Siberia and Alaska
      2. people crossed land bridge to North America
   B. Different Landforms
      1.
      2.

3. **Comparing.** When you compare two or more things, you need to look for ways they are similar and ways they are different. Compare the Rocky Mountains and the Appalachians. (a) How are they similar? (b) How are they different?

## ★ More to Do ★

1. **Creating a travelogue.** As a group project, create a travelogue, describing the route taken by the first people who reached North America.

2. **Identifying place names.** Using a map of the United States, find place names that describe their geography—for example, Rocky Mountains.

3. **Creating a map.** On a blank map of the United States, draw in and label the rivers mentioned on pages 25 and 26.

Include the Great Lakes and the bodies of water around the United States. Use the map on pages 582–583 to find this information.

4. **Exploring local history.** Prepare a report on the land and climate of the area where you live. Describe the rivers, weather, plants, and animals of the area. Then list three ways that climate affects people in your area.

CHAPTER

# 2

# The First
# Americans (Prehistory—1600)

## Chapter Outline

**1** Studying the First Americans
**2** Peoples of North America
**3** Great Empires in the Americas
Readings, page 456

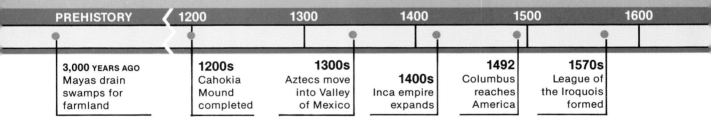

| PREHISTORY | 1200 | 1300 | 1400 | 1500 | 1600 |
|---|---|---|---|---|---|

**3,000 YEARS AGO**
Mayas drain swamps for farmland

**1200s**
Cahokia Mound completed

**1300s**
Aztecs move into Valley of Mexico

**1400s**
Inca empire expands

**1492**
Columbus reaches America

**1570s**
League of the Iroquois formed

## About This Chapter

People have lived in the Americas for thousands of years. The first people to reach the Americas probably arrived about 70,000 years ago. Little is known about them. How did they live? Why did some stay in North America and others move thousands of miles into South America? Today, historians and scientists are trying to answer these and other questions about Native Americans, as the first Americans are called.

Recently, the cameras on a space satellite took pictures over the jungles of Guatemala in Central America. When the pictures were developed, scientists were puzzled by a series of straight lines that cut through the swampy jungle like a giant checkerboard. Two scientists went to Guatemala to learn about the lines. They paddled dugout canoes up streams and deep into the jungle. They found ditches crossing the jungle in the same checkerboard pattern that the satellite photos had shown.

The scientists realized that Native Americans dug these ditches. The people were the Mayas, who lived in the swampy jungle over 3,000 years ago. The Mayas dug the ditches to drain swamps and make fields for growing crops. Later, the Mayas built an empire in Central America. Discoveries such as this one have added greatly to our knowledge of the first Americans.

Study the time line above. Did the Mayas start farming before or after the Aztecs moved into Mexico?

In the 1500s, the Incas built the city of Machu Picchu (MA choo PEEK choo) high up in the Andes Mountains of Peru.

# 1 Studying the First Americans

## Read to Learn

★ How do archaeologists learn about early people?

★ How did some people adapt to life in the desert?

★ What do these words mean: archaeologist, culture, adobe, pueblo, drought?

Like early people in other parts of the world, the first Americans left no written records. How, then, can we learn about the first Americans?

## The Work of Archaeologists

People who did not write left behind other evidence of their lives. For example, when they roasted animals over fires, they left charred bones at their campsites. Some left clay cooking pots as well as weapons and tools made of bone and stone. Scientists who study the evidence left by early people are called *archaeologists* (ahr kee AHL uh jihsts). By studying the evidence, archaeologists have learned much about early people.

Archaeologists are interested in the *culture,* or the way of life, of early people. Culture includes the customs, ideas, and skills of a given people. It also includes their houses, clothes, and government.

The work of archaeologists is hard because much evidence about early people has been destroyed. Their first

Archaeologists have learned a lot about early Indian cultures. Here, an archaeologist measures the size of an ancient roasting pit before she makes a drawing of it.

task is to find evidence that has survived. Sometimes, archaeologists find evidence in unexpected places. A flood might wash away a river bank and uncover ancient bones. Or a bulldozer clearing land might dig up a buried campsite. When such finds occur, archaeologists learn as much as they can before the evidence is removed.

Archaeologists have to work carefully and keep detailed records of everything they find. They often use small picks and soft brushes to uncover an object without damaging it. Once they have dug out an object, they try to analyze, or explain, what it is. By looking closely at an object, archaeologists can learn a great deal about the people who made or used it. A sharp, finely shaped arrowhead suggests that the people were skilled at making weapons. Bits of pottery at a campsite suggest that the people knew how to shape clay into cookware.

## The Mound Builders

Archaeologists have studied the evidence left behind by Native Americans. In recent years, they have learned much about groups of people called the *Mound Builders.* These people built thousands of mounds from eastern Oklahoma to the Atlantic Ocean. The mounds varied in size and shape. See the picture of the Great Serpent Mound at right.

The Mound Builders lived at various times from about 2,800 years ago until the 1700s. Among them were the Adenas, Hopewells, and Mississippians. Between about 900 and 1250, the Mississippians built the great Cahokia Mound in Illinois. It covers 116 acres and is so large it looks like a hill. Dozens of smaller mounds are clustered nearby.

The mounds served different purposes. Some were burial mounds. They were built over the graves of important people. Others were platform mounds. They were shaped like pyramids with flattened tops.

By studying these mounds, archaeologists have begun to learn about the lives of the Mound Builders. To build such large mounds, hundreds of people had to work together. So the Mound Builders must have had strong rulers who could organize large groups of workers. The mounds also show that religion and concern for the dead were important to the people.

## Peoples of the Desert

Many peoples left their mark on the American Southwest. Among them were the *Hohokams* (HOH hoh kahmz) and *Anasazis* (ah NUH sah zeez). Each had their own customs, but they were alike in some ways.

Both peoples made excellent pottery and built their houses out of stone and sun-dried clay bricks, called *adobe.* Both were farmers who raised corn,

The Great Serpent Mound in Ohio was built more than 1,000 years ago. The serpent twists across the land for more than 1,200 feet (365 m). It is about 20 feet wide and 4 feet high. This mound may have been used for religious ceremonies.

beans, and squash. And both developed ways to irrigate the land. The Hohokams irrigated their crops by digging canals from the Salt and Gila rivers in Arizona. The Anasazis built dikes and dams to bring water from streams to their fields.

Some Anasazi villages still stand. They are known as *pueblos* (PWEHB lohz), the Spanish word for villages. In Pueblo Bonito, New Mexico, the houses are several stories high and have as many as 800 rooms. The rooms are tiny, but the Anasazis spent much of their time in the bright, warm plaza outside. The houses have no stairways or hallways. To reach rooms on the upper floors, people used ladders.

The Anasazis are known as Cliff Dwellers because some of them built their homes on cliff walls. They may have done this for protection from warlike neighbors. In the morning, men and women climbed to the top of the cliffs to take care of their crops. They climbed back down to their homes by using toeholds cut into the cliffs.

In the late 1200s, a *drought* (drowt), or long dry spell, hit these lands. The drought forced the people to leave their homes. The Anasazis never recovered from the disaster.

Cliff dwellings such as this one can be seen in the Mesa Verde National Park in Colorado. These cliff homes were built between 1100 and 1300. Archaeologists have found fine pottery, woven fabrics, and decorated walls inside.

1. **Define:** archaeologist, culture, adobe, pueblo, drought.
2. What kinds of evidence have early Native Americans left behind?
3. Why did the Mound Builders build huge earth mounds?
4. **What Do You Think?** Why do you think people today are interested in learning about the first Americans?

# 2 Peoples of North America

### Read to Learn

★ What Native American cultures developed in North America?

★ How did different people adapt to their environment?

★ What do these words mean: igloo, potlatch, hogan, long house?

In 1492, when Christopher Columbus reached the Americas, he thought he had reached the East Indies. So he called the people he met Indians. This term is still used to refer to Native Americans. *Native Americans* are descended from the people who reached America thousands of years ago.

Millions of Native Americans lived in North America before 1492. They spoke hundreds of different languages and developed many cultures.* As the map on page 38 shows, Indians lived in all parts of North America.

## Far North

The Far North is a land of bitterly cold winters and icy seas. The *Eskimos* were one of the peoples who adapted to this harsh land. They survived by making use of everything the land, sea, and sky had to offer. In the winter, they built *igloos,* or houses made of snow and ice. Lamps filled with seal oil kept the igloos warm even in the most bitter cold. In the summer, they made dwell-

---

*Some beliefs and customs described in this chapter are still practiced by Native Americans today.

ings out of animal skins. Eskimo women made warm clothing out of furs and sewed seal skins into waterproof boots.

In winter, several families traveled together in a hunting band. The Eskimos hunted wolves, foxes, and polar bears. When the seas were not frozen, they used kayaks (KĪ aks), or small skin boats, to hunt seals and walruses. Food was often scarce. Therefore, the Eskimos shared what they caught.

In their religion, the Eskimos showed concern for the animals they depended on for survival. The Eskimos believed that each animal had a spirit. So when an Eskimo hunter trapped a female fox, for example, he offered bone needles to the fox's spirit. This offering, he believed, ensured good hunting in the future.

## The West

Indians in the West adapted to many different climates. Among the cultures of the West are the Northwest Coast and Intermountain.

**Northwest Coast.** Unlike the Eskimos, the peoples of the Northwest Coast did not face bitter winters or a scarce food supply. Instead, they enjoyed pleasant weather year round. Magnificent forests and nearby oceans and rivers were rich storehouses of deer, moose, bear, and salmon.

The people made good use of the forests. Men built houses and different

# Geography in History

In plentiful supply along the Pacific Coast, shellfish were a source of food for the peoples of the Northwest Coast. But one kind of shellfish—dentalia—served another purpose. Their tooth-shaped shells were used as money!

Dentalia usually lived in deep waters offshore, so they were hard to reach. Because dentalia were a difficult catch, the Native Americans prized the shells.

The Nootka of Vancouver Island were the main producers of dentalia shells. Off the island, dentalia lived in shallower waters. Using a long broomlike device, the Nootka were able to reach the dentalia, trap them in the wood splints of the broom, and then lift them out of the water.

Once on shore, the Nootka boiled out the flesh of the dentalia. Then they dried

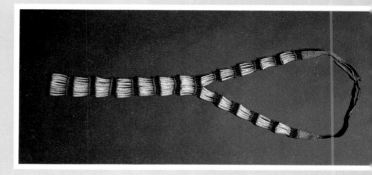

the shells and polished them with sand. As the final step, they grouped the shells by size and strung them together. The longer the string of shells, the greater was the value.

★ Why did Native Americans of the Northwest Coast value dentalia shells as money?

kinds of canoes out of wood. Some canoes were used for visiting. Others were for fishing or for war. The largest canoes were almost 70 feet (20 m) long and could carry up to 60 people. Women wove the soft inner bark of cedar trees into clothes and blankets.

In the 1800s, many groups of people lived in villages with their houses facing the sea. Each house was home to several families. In front of their house, people put up totem poles. A totem pole was a tall wooden post carved with animals or other figures.

Within each village, people were ranked according to how much they owned. A family held a *potlatch,* or ceremonial dinner, to show off its wealth. Sometimes, a family spent years preparing for a potlatch. Many guests were invited, and everyone received gifts. The more gifts a family gave to its guests, the greater fame the family

In the 1800s, Native Americans on the Northwest Coast carved totem poles showing animals such as beavers, bears, and eagles. A totem pole told visitors of the great deeds of a family.

NATIVE AMERICAN CULTURES

| | |
|---|---|
| 0 | 500 |  1000 Miles |
| 0 | 500 | 1000 Kilometers |

MAP SKILL By 1400, about 10 million Native Americans lived in North America north of Mexico. Native Americans spoke at least 500 different languages and had their own cultures. Scholars have divided North America into the culture regions shown here. Name two groups that lived in the Southwest.

won. At one potlatch, the gifts included 8 canoes, 54 elk skins, 2,000 silver bracelets, 7,000 brass bracelets, and 33,000 blankets.

**Intermountain.** In the dry Intermountain region, life was difficult. Without water, few plants or animals were able to live in the region. Native Americans like the Ute and Shoshone had a hard time finding food. They moved around in small groups. Often, a single family spent much of its time looking for food.

## Southwest

In the Southwest, people like the Anasazis learned to farm in a dry, desert climate. Later groups like the *Pueblos* adopted many Anasazi customs. They built adobe houses and grew squash, beans, and corn.

The Pueblos believed that many spirits watched over the land. The spirits caused rain to fall and crops to grow. To keep the spirits happy so that they would give rain and good harvests, each Pueblo village set up a secret society. Members performed ceremonies and dances to please the spirits.

The Pueblos traced family lines through the woman's family. This custom gave women special importance. When a man married, he went to live with his wife's family. The wife owned most of the family property.

Another group in the Southwest were the *Navajos* (NAV uh hohz). At one time, they were hunters and food gatherers. But they learned to farm from the Pueblos. The Navajos lived in **hogans,** or houses built of mud plaster and supported by wooden poles.

The Navajos believed in two kinds of beings: Earth Surface People and Holy People. Earth Surface People included the Navajos and other humans. Holy People included gods. Like the Pueblos, the Navajos believed that they had to please the Holy People. They held special ceremonies to ensure good health and good harvests.

## Great Plains

The peoples of the Great Plains were hunters and farmers. Many lived in villages on hills above rivers. They built their houses with great care. They dug pits for the foundations and used sod from the pits for the roofs. To make walls, they covered poles with grass. Each house had a hole in the roof to let out smoke from the cooking fire.

In the winter, the men hunted animals near the village. In the summer, they went on long trips in search of buffalo herds. Huge herds of buffalo stretched for miles across the plains.

In the spring when the snows melted, the river below the village often overflowed its banks for a few days. When the ground was soft and easy to work, the women used animal bones to break up the soil. They then planted corn, beans, and sunflowers.

Each village was ruled by a council made up of the best hunters. The chief was a council member respected by the others because he spoke well and judged wisely. Sometimes, a village had several chiefs. Each chief served on a different occasion, such as hunting, farming, or going to war.

## Southeast

The Southeast had fertile land with more than 100 kinds of trees and plenty of rain. More Native Americans lived here than in any other area north of Mexico. Among the peoples of the Southeast were the *Natchez* (NACH ihz), who lived in Mississippi and Louisiana. The Natchez were descendants of the Mound Builders. They were farmers and hunters. Dividing the year into 13 months, they named each month after a food gathered or hunted during that time. The names of months included Deer, Strawberries, Little Corn, Mulberries, Turkey, Bison, and Bear.

Men and women shared the work of growing crops. During planting and

The Navajos drew sand paintings to use in healing the sick and in religious ceremonies. This Navajo sand painting shows Father Sky and Mother Earth, two of the most important Holy People.

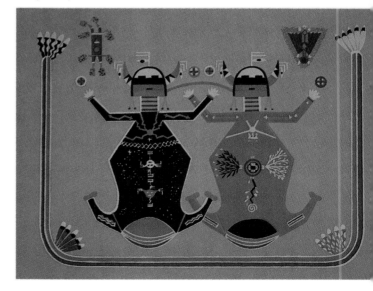

harvesting time, everyone in the village worked together. They moved from one field to the next. Men were also hunters. To hunt deer, they disguised themselves. Wearing a deerskin and antlers, a Natchez hunter could move quite close to a deer before shooting it with his bow and arrow.

The Natchez worshipped the sun as the source of all life. They kept a fire going day and night in a temple to the sun. The Natchez believed in an afterlife. The faithful would enjoy peace and plenty of food after they died. The unfaithful, however, would be forced to live in a swamp swarming with mosquitoes.

The Natchez were divided into social classes. At the top was the Great Sun, or chief. Below the Great Sun were other members of the chief's family, called Suns. Next came the Nobles and then the Honored People. The lowest class was the Stinkards.

Natchez laws required that the male children of a Sun, Noble, or Honored Person marry one class below them. As a result, the male descendants of a Great Sun eventually became Stinkards. The female children could hold on to their higher social class if their marriages were arranged carefully.

## Eastern Woodlands

Many different groups of people lived in the Eastern Woodlands. In the forests and open lands, they hunted game such as deer, bear, and moose. They raised crops of squash, pumpkins, and corn—including popcorn.

The most powerful people in the Eastern Woodlands were the *Iroquois* (IHR uh kwoi), who lived in what is now New York State. The Iroquois lived in *long houses*. A typical long house was about 18 feet (5 m) wide and 60 feet (18 m) long. A hallway ran the length of the long house. On either side of the hallway were small rooms. Each room was a family's home. Families who lived across from each other shared a fire in the hallway.

Women played an important part in Iroquois life. Like a Pueblo man, an Iroquois man moved in with his wife's family when he married. Women owned all the property in the long house. They were in charge of planting and harvesting.

Iroquois women also had political power. The Iroquois were divided into five nations: the Mohawk, Seneca (SEHN ih kuh), Onondaga (ahn uhn DAH guh), Oneida (oh NĪ duh), and Cayuga (kay YOO gah). Each nation had its own

Many Indians of the Southeast lived along the coast and were skilled at fishing. Although fish was their main source of food, they also farmed. Notice the fire built on a pile of sand in the bottom of the boat. It kept the Indians warm while they fished.

This scene shows Indians of the Eastern Woodlands. Indians of this region hunted and farmed. The Indian near the center is grinding corn in a hollow log.

ruling council. Women chose the men who served as council members.

A major problem facing the councils was the constant fighting among the Iroquois nations. Sometime about 1570, the five nations formed a union, called the *League of the Iroquois*. A council of 50 leaders met at least once a year to settle disputes. Again, the women chose the leaders. At meetings, the leaders discussed problems and voted on ways to solve them. Each nation had one vote. The council could not act unless all five nations agreed.

**SECTION REVIEW**

1. **Define:** igloo, potlatch, hogan, long house.
2. List the seven major culture regions of North American Indians.
3. How did the Eskimos adapt to the arctic climate?
4. Why did the Pueblos believe the gods had to be pleased?
5. What power did Iroquois women have?
6. **What Do You Think?** Do you think the place where a group of people lived affected their way of life? Explain.

# 3 Great Empires in the Americas

**Read to Learn**

★ Where was the Maya empire?
★ How did the Aztecs build their capital city?
★ How did the Incas organize their large empire?
★ What does this word mean: pictograph?

Native Americans in Mexico and in Central and South America built large empires. Among them were the empires of the Mayas, Aztecs, and Incas. In each, the people learned to grow great amounts of food. The plentiful food supported a large population.

## Mayas

The Maya empire stretched across large parts of Central America and Mexico. (See the map on page 45.) About 3,000 years ago, the Mayas began clearing the tropical rain forests of this region. The rain forests were difficult and dangerous places in which to live. They were hot and humid and were inhabited by wild animals. Fierce stinging ants, poisonous snakes, and mosquitoes brought disease and death to the people. The Mayas dug canals to drain the swampy land. They learned to grow beans, corn, and squash.

Most Mayas were farmers. They lived in houses with mud walls and thatch roofs. A family raised a few turkeys or deer to be killed for feasts. Maya farmers kept beehives for honey. The honey could be gathered easily because bees in the region did not sting.

**Maya cities.** From time to time, farmers who lived in small villages visited one of the great Maya cities, such as Tikal. In the city marketplace, farmers found woven baskets, blankets, bright feathers for headdresses, jade jewelry, pottery, and tools made of flint. What impressed visitors most, however, were the towering stone temples in the heart of the city. The main temple was shaped like a pyramid and rose up to ten stories high. Smaller temple pyramids stood nearby, each with steep steps leading to the top.

A city had tens of thousands of people. The people were divided into social classes. Priests were the highest class. Next came the nobles. Below them were the peasants, or farmers. At the bottom were the prisoners of war, who were slaves.

**Important advances.** Religion was central to Maya life. Every day, priests performed ceremonies in the temples to please the gods. Religion also led the Mayas to make important advances. Because time and the seasons were sacred, priests studied the movements of the sun and stars. With this information, they developed an accurate calendar.

The Mayas invented a method of writing. They drew *pictographs,* or pictures to represent objects. They carved these pictographs on stone tablets or painted them on paper made from tree bark.

## Aztecs

In the 1300s, the Aztecs moved into the Valley of Mexico. The valley sits between two mountain ranges. The mountains kept rivers from draining into the sea. So the valley was very swampy.

**The wonders of Tenochtitlan.** The Aztecs built their capital city, *Tenochtitlan* (tay noch tee TLAHN), on an island in the middle of a swampy lake. They built canals to drain the lake. Aztec farmers learned to grow crops on the swampland. Using wooden stakes, they attached mats to the floor of the swamp. They then put layers of mud on the mats and planted their gardens. Farmers grew as many as seven crops a year on these floating gardens.

Tenochtitlan was the largest city in the Americas. By 1500, over 100,000 people lived there. People paddled canoes on the canals to bring food and other goods to the city. Three raised roads led into the city. They had drawbridges that could be lifted if an enemy attacked. Within the city, thousands of stone and mortar houses lined the streets. In the center, a great stone pyramid temple rose into the air. Scattered around the city were other temples.

The wealthiest and most powerful Aztec was the emperor. Below him were priests and nobles. Ordinary people included farmers and merchants.

When the emperor walked anywhere in the city, the nobles followed him. They threw cloth in his path so

Historians use primary sources to learn about the past. A ***primary source*** is firsthand information about people or events of the past.

Paintings are one kind of primary source. They show how the people of a certain time and place saw themselves. Often, they give useful evidence about aspects of daily life such as food, clothes, games, and homes.

The picture below was painted on the walls of a Maya temple. Use the following steps to learn how to use a painting as a primary source.

1. **Identify the subject of the painting.** Study the painting carefully. (a) List three things the people are doing. (b) What kinds of plants and animals are shown? (c) What title would you give to this painting? (d) Explain why you chose this title.

2. **Decide what the painting tells about the life of the people.** Study the painting and review what you have read about the life of the Mayas. (a) Where was the painting found? (b) Describe the houses of the people. (c) From this painting, what conclusions can you draw about the daily life of the Mayas?

3. **Decide if the painting is a reliable source.** A painting does not always tell the full story. An artist may have painted it for a special reason or may have left out some details. You need to decide whether it is a reliable source of information. (a) Do you think that the artist showed everything exactly as it was? Explain. (b) Does this painting give you a complete idea of the daily life of the Mayas? Explain.

## Aztec Soldier

To keep their empire strong, the Aztecs needed many soldiers. Aztec soldiers filled the streets of Tenochtitlan, wearing colorful cloaks and headdresses. They often carried bouquets of flowers. In battle, soldiers carried shields and swords and wore quilted jackets as protection against arrows. Their swords were edged with sharp black glass.

that his feet would never touch the ground.

**Religion.** The Aztecs worshipped many gods. Their chief one was the sun god. Every day, they believed, the sun god fought its way across the heavens. They compared the sun's battles to their own wars.

Religion greatly affected daily life. Over 5,000 priests lived in Tenochtitlan. They directed religious ceremonies. Like the Maya priests, they studied the stars and planets and made accurate calendars.

The Aztecs believed that their gods required human sacrifices. When powerful Aztec armies conquered neighboring peoples, they took many prisoners and demanded heavy taxes. The Aztecs used prisoners of war as sacrifices. By the early 1500s, the sacrifice of so many prisoners and the burden of heavy taxes left the conquered peoples ready to revolt against Aztec rule.

## Incas

The Incas built the largest empire in the Americas. In the 1400s, it stretched along the Pacific coast of South America for about 2,500 miles (4,000 km). The Inca capital was the city of Cuzco (KYOOS koh), located in the Andes Mountains of Peru. Find Cuzco on the map at right.

**A well-organized empire.** The Incas had a powerful, well-organized government. The Sapa Inca, or supreme ruler, lived in Cuzco. He had the power of life and death over his subjects. Priests and nobles helped the Sapa Inca rule.

The Incas built an excellent system of roads so that the army could move quickly to put down revolts. Inca engineers built log and stone bridges across rushing streams. In the steep mountain passes, they hung bridges made of ropes over deep gorges.

The Incas also set up a system for sending messages quickly across the empire. Every village had runners ready to carry news. A runner from Cuzco, for example, would carry a message to a village. From there, another runner would speed the news on its way.

**Other achievements.** In addition to building roads and bridges, Inca engineers made temples and forts out of huge stone blocks. Each block weighed hundreds of pounds. Workers moved the blocks up steep mountains without

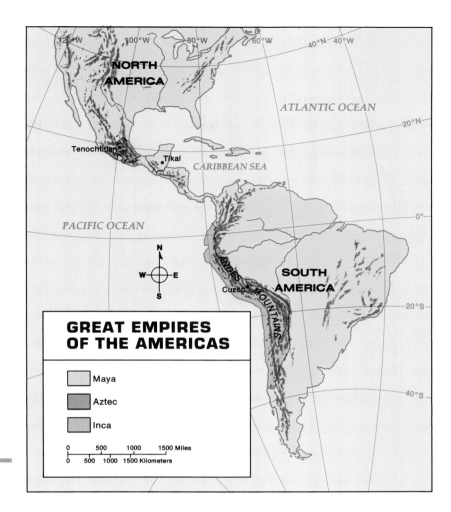

GREAT EMPIRES
OF THE AMERICAS

Maya

Aztec

Inca

| 0 | 500 | 1000 | 1500 Miles |
| 0 | 500 | 1000 | 1500 Kilometers |

MAP SKILL The Mayas, Aztecs, and Incas built empires in the Americas, as this map shows. Which of these three empires was the largest?

the help of animals or wheeled carts.* Each block was cut to fit in place exactly without cement. When earthquakes hit, the blocks slid apart gently but then slipped back together.

Inca farmers built terraces that looked like wide steps on the steep slopes. The terraces kept the rains from washing the soil and crops down the slopes of the Andes. The Incas made advances in medicine. They used quinine to treat malaria. They discovered medicines that lessened pain and performed successful brain surgery.

In the 1520s, a civil war broke out in the Inca empire. The fighting weakened the Incas just when they were about to face a serious new threat—the arrival of explorers from Europe.

### SECTION REVIEW

1. **Locate:** Central America, Mexico, Tikal, Tenochtitlan, Andes Mountains, Peru, Cuzco.

2. **Define:** pictograph.

3. What advances did the Mayas make?

4. Why did the Aztecs build floating gardens?

5. **What Do You Think?** Why do you think the Incas were able to control their huge empire?

---

*Horses once lived in the Americas, but they died out long before the first Americans arrived. Native Americans did not see horses until they were brought to the Americas by Europeans. Native Americans did put wheels on some toy carts but did not use wheels on full-sized carts.

# Chapter 2 Review

## ★ Summary ★

Archaeologists study the evidence left behind by early people. By doing this, they have learned a lot about the lives of the first Americans.

Many different groups of Native Americans lived in North America. The peoples of each culture region adapted to the local climate and resources. Native Americans developed different ways of farming their lands, building their houses, and organizing their lives. In Mexico and in Central and South America, Native Americans built large empires, including the Maya, Aztec, and Inca empires.

## ★ Reviewing the Facts ★

**Key Terms.** Match each term in Column 1 with the correct definition in Column 2.

| Column 1 | Column 2 |
|---|---|
| 1. archaeologist | a. way of life of a people |
| 2. culture | b. Spanish word for village |
| 3. pueblo | c. scientist who studies evidence of early people |
| 4. drought | d. picture that represents an object |
| 5. pictograph | e. long dry spell |

**Key People, Events, and Ideas.** Identify each of the following.

1. Mound Builders
2. Anasazi
3. Native American
4. Eskimo
5. Pueblo
6. Navajo
7. Natchez
8. Iroquois
9. League of the Iroquois
10. Tenochtitlan

## ★ Chapter Checkup ★

1. (a) Describe how archaeologists work to uncover the past. (b) What have archaeologists learned about the culture of the Mound Builders?

2. (a) Why are the Anasazis known as Cliff Dwellers? (b) Why did the Anasazis leave their homes in the late 1200s?

3. (a) List three Indian cultures of North America. (b) Describe how people in each of these cultures got their food.

4. Describe the kinds of work women did in different Indian groups.

5. How did each of the following peoples change the land on which they lived: (a) Mayas; (b) Aztecs; (c) Incas?

6. (a) Why did the Mayas develop an accurate calendar? (b) How did the Mayas record information?

7. (a) Describe three achievements of the Aztecs. (b) Why were many people unhappy with Aztec rule?

8. (a) How did the Incas send messages across their empire? (b) Why was the Inca empire weakened in the 1520s?

## ★ Thinking About History ★

1. **Relating past to present.** How does the work of archaeologists help us learn more about the past?

2. **Understanding other cultures.** Reread "Shells as Money" on page 37. (a) Why could the Nootka harvest the shells? (b) What does this story tell you about the economy of the Northwest Coast?

3. **Understanding geography.** How did geography affect the ways of life of different Native American groups. Give at least three examples.

4. **Applying information.** What evidence shows that the Aztecs had an advanced empire?

## ★ Using Your Skills ★

1. **Map reading.** Review the map-reading steps in Skill Lesson 1 (page 21). Then study the map on page 38. (a) What is the title of the map? (b) List three Native American groups that lived on the Great Plains. (c) Name one group that lived east of the Apaches. (d) Did the Chippewas live north or south of the Natchez?

2. **Making a generalization.** A *generalization* is a true statement based on facts. Before making a generalization, you need to gather facts. Review what you read about the way the peoples of the Northwest Coast lived. (a) List three facts about their way of life. (b) Make a generalization about their life based on the facts you listed.

3. **Comparing.** Compare the Mayas and the Incas. (a) How were they similar? (b) How were they different? (c) Why do you think these differences existed?

4. **Using a photograph as a primary source.** A photograph, as well as a painting, can be used as a primary source. Review Skill Lesson 2 (page 43). Study the photograph on page 33. (a) What does it show? (b) Why do you think the Incas built terraces on the side of the mountain?

## ★ More to Do ★

1. **Working with archaeologists.** As a group project, make a model of a campsite where early Native Americans lived. Then imagine that some archaeologists discover the site. How would the archaeologists describe and analyze what they find?

2. **Eyewitness reporting.** Imagine that you are a newspaper reporter visiting Tenochtitlan in 1450. Write an article describing life in the Aztec capital. Use information in this chapter as well as in encyclopedias and books.

3. **Researching a report.** Write a report on the everyday life of one of the Native American peoples you read about in this chapter. Include information about their homes, eating habits, customs, and government.

4. **Exploring local history.** List the names of parks, lakes, or streets in your local area that suggest a Native American influence. Then give a report about Native American peoples who lived or still live in your area.

# 3

# Europeans Explore America (1000–1650)

## Chapter Outline

1 The Changing World of Europe
2 Search for New Routes to Asia
3 Exploring the New World
4 Early Claims to North America
Readings, page 462

| 1000 | 1100 | 1200 | 1300 | 1400 | 1500 | 1600 |
|------|------|------|------|------|------|------|

**1001**
Leif Ericson reaches Vinland

**1095**
Crusaders leave for Holy Land

**1271**
Marco Polo sets out for China

**1324**
Mansa Musa travels to Egypt

**1492**
Columbus reaches America

**1539–1542**
De Soto explores North America

## About This Chapter

In 1271, 17-year-old Marco Polo traveled east from Venice with his father and uncle. After a long and dangerous journey, the travelers finally reached Peking, China. Marco Polo spent 24 years in China. There, he became an official of the Chinese ruler, Kublai Khan.

When Marco Polo returned to Venice, he wrote a book about his travels. In it, he described the riches of China. He compared the splendid cities of China to the small cities of Europe. "I tell you truly," Polo wrote, "that more boats loaded with more . . . things and of greater value go and come" on one of China's rivers than on all the rivers of Europe. Most people who read Polo's book refused to believe his stories. They called him the Prince of Liars. A few, however, were curious to know more about lands such as China.

At the time of Marco Polo's journey to China, Europe was changing. Eager to increase trade, merchants and rulers looked beyond Europe for new markets. In the 1400s and 1500s, European nations sent brave sailors out to explore every corner of the globe. During this age of exploration, Europeans came in contact with peoples of many different lands. And they soon claimed some of these lands as their own.

Study the time line above. Name two events that happened after Polo's visit to China.

When Marco Polo left Venice for China, his travels helped open new worlds to Europeans.

# 1 The Changing World of Europe

## Read to Learn

★ What was life like in Europe during the Middle Ages?

★ Why did Europeans go on the Crusades?

★ What changes took place during the Renaissance?

★ What do these words mean: feudalism, manor, serf?

Until the late 1400s, Europeans knew nothing about the lands or peoples of the Americas. In fact, for hundreds of years most people in Europe lived and died without leaving their villages. Gradually, however, conditions changed. A new age dawned in which Europeans expanded their horizons and set off to explore new worlds.

## Vikings Reach America

The first Europeans to reach North America were the Vikings. The *Vikings* were fierce, seagoing people from Scandinavia. They braved the stormy seas of the north to trade with and raid neighboring lands. Vikings settled Iceland. And from there, they explored farther west. See the map on page 51.

One Viking explorer was the red-haired, red-bearded Eric the Red. Eric explored a land west of Iceland, which he named Greenland. Actually, Greenland was a harsh land, much icier than Iceland. But Eric chose this pleasant-sounding name in order to attract farmers to settle there.

In 1001, Eric's son, Leif, decided to explore even farther to the west. He

The Vikings were great sailors. In small boats such as the ones shown here, they sailed the Atlantic as far as North America. Viking sailors used only the stars to steer their course at sea.

sailed into the sun until he reached a land where wheat and grapes grew wild. Large salmon swam up river. Leif Ericson named the place **Vinland,** or Wineland, because of the grapes. Vinland was in North America, but no one is sure where.*

For several years, Vikings sailed to Vinland. They brought sheep and cattle to their settlements. About 1013, the Vikings left Vinland. No one is sure why.

The Viking voyages to America remained unknown in the rest of Europe. What was happening in Eu-

*Archaeologists think Vinland was on the northernmost tip of Newfoundland. There, they have found the remains of Viking houses, tools, and weapons.

rope in the years after 1000? Why did no one hear about the Viking discovery? To answer these questions, you need to understand what life was like for most Europeans at the time.

## Europe in the Middle Ages

The Viking voyages took place during the **Middle Ages,** the period from about 500 to 1350. During the early Middle Ages, Europe was divided into many small kingdoms. Life was hard, and most people worried only about surviving. Trade and travel was limited. Except for the Vikings, few people dared to sail far out into the oceans.

During the Middle Ages, kings divided up their lands among powerful nobles, called lords. Lords owed loyalty to their king. But they often acted on their own. The system of rule by lords who owe loyalty to their king is called **feudalism** (FYOOD'l ihz'm).

War was a way of life for many lords. They fought with each other for power and land. Thousands of peasants died in the constant fighting. Many starved when their crops and homes were destroyed.

Each lord had one or more manors. A **manor** included a village or several villages and the surrounding lands. Almost everyone lived on a manor. Most people were **serfs.** Serfs were peasants who had to stay on the manor where they were born.

A manor was self-sufficient. Serfs produced everything they needed. They planted and harvested crops. They raised sheep for wool, which was spun into cloth. And they made their own tools. From time to time, a peddler visited the manor, bringing goods and news from distant lands. In general, however, people knew little about life outside the manor.

## Wider Horizons

By 1050, changes were taking place that made Europeans look beyond the narrow world of the manor. Peasants learned better ways of farming and grew more food. Warfare declined, and trade increased. Towns grew up along the trade routes. Unlike lords or peasants on manors, townspeople were very interested in trade and travel.

**The Crusades.** About this time, too, Christians set out on the Crusades. The *Crusades* were a series of wars aimed at conquering the Holy Land. The Holy Land referred to the places in the Middle East connected with the life of Jesus. For hundreds of years, the Holy Land was ruled by Arab Muslims. They allowed Christians to visit the Holy Land in peace. In the late 1000s, however, the Seljuk Turks conquered the Holy Land. Unlike the Arabs, the Seljuk Turks often attacked and killed Christian visitors to the Holy Land.

In the Middle Ages, all Christians in Western Europe belonged to the Catholic Church led by the Pope. They were not divided into many different churches as they are today. In 1095, the Pope called for a crusade to take the Holy Land from the Seljuk Turks. Thousands of Christians responded to the Pope's call. They sewed crosses to their clothes as badges of faith and set out for the Holy Land.

For 200 years, waves of Christian crusaders marched to the east. Many Christians and Muslims were slaughtered in the fighting.

**Results of the Crusades.** In the end, the Crusades failed to free the Holy Land from Muslim control. But they did help change Europe in several ways. First, shipbuilders of northern Italy and sailors learned a lot from

**MAP SKILL** In the late 1200s, Marco Polo traveled from Italy to China. He brought back stories of the riches of Asia. Later Europeans were eager to trade with Asia. They especially wanted spices from the East Indies. Where are the East Indies?

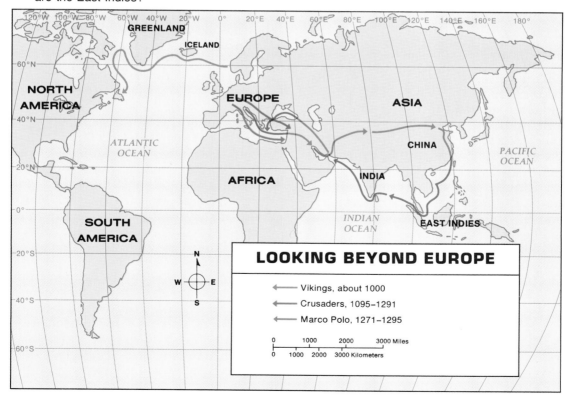

LOOKING BEYOND EUROPE

← Vikings, about 1000
← Crusaders, 1095–1291
← Marco Polo, 1271–1295

0    1000    2000    3000 Miles
0  1000  2000  3000 Kilometers

In 1099, crusaders captured Jerusalem after fierce fighting. Christian knights killed all the defenders and massacred non-Christian families in the city. In this picture, knights fight their way into the city.

building and sailing the ships that took crusaders across the Mediterranean to the Holy Land.

Second, merchants increased their trade with the Middle East. Italian merchants controlled most of this trade. They bought the silks, spices, and cotton cloth that Arab traders brought to the Middle East from far-off Asia.

Third, crusaders returned home with tastes for foods of the Middle East such as rice, oranges, and dates. They introduced other Europeans to the use of spices such as ginger, cinnamon, and pepper. In the days before refrigerators, food spoiled easily. Spices helped cover up the bad flavor of spoiled meat and added variety to meals.

Finally, increased trade and travel made Europeans aware of more of the world. When Marco Polo of Venice traveled overland to China in the 1270s, he found an empire that was far more advanced than any in Europe.

## The Renaissance

In the Middle Ages, books were written by hand, and few people could read. But with the invention of the printing press about 1450, books could be copied more easily than before. As a

result, news and information spread more quickly.

The idea of a printing press grew slowly over hundreds of years. Building on earlier inventions, Johann Gutenberg (GOOT n berg) of Germany took the final step. He invented small pieces of metal engraved with letters of the alphabet. Because these pieces of type could be used and reused to form different words and sentences, they were called moveable type. In 1455, Gutenberg printed the Bible by using moveable type. The age of printing had begun.

The invention of the printing press helped spread the learning of the Renaissance (REHN uh sahns). *Renaissance* is a French word meaning rebirth. During the Renaissance, the period from about 1350 to 1600, Europeans made great advances. They uncovered much of the knowledge collected by the Greeks and Romans in ancient times.

Renaissance scholars were curious about the world. They read ancient Greek and Roman works and learned much from Arab and Jewish scholars. They then made new, practical discoveries of their own. Eagerly, they explored the world of ideas and the physical world around them.

## Rise of Strong Nations

During the Renaissance, strong rulers gained control over feudal lords. They built the foundations of the nations we know today. In England and France, rulers increased their power when many feudal lords slaughtered each other in a long series of wars.

In Spain and Portugal, nation building was a long, slow process. During the Middle Ages, Arab Muslims conquered these lands. Christian knights fought for hundreds of years to drive out the Muslims. By 1249, Portugal had captured the last Muslim stronghold.

In Spain, knights slowly pushed the Muslims south. But the land remained divided among several rulers until the late 1400s. In 1469, Ferdinand, king of Aragon, and Isabella, queen of Castile, were married. Their marriage united much of Spain. The two rulers then joined forces against the Muslims.

European rulers were eager to increase their power through trade. Huge profits could be made trading silks from China and spices from the East Indies.* However, Arab and Italian merchants controlled the rich silk and spice trade because they controlled the trade routes across the Mediterranean. Other Europeans saw that they had only one choice—find another route to Asia.

---

*At the time, Europeans called the East Indies the Spice Islands, or simply the Indies.

### SECTION REVIEW

1. **Locate:** Iceland, Greenland, Europe, Asia, China, East Indies.
2. **Define:** feudalism, manor, serf.
3. What lands did the Vikings explore?
4. Why was life difficult in the Middle Ages?
5. **What Do You Think?** Why do you think the Crusades have been called a "successful failure"?

# 2 Search for New Routes to Asia

### Read to Learn

- ★ What new ways of sailing were developed?
- ★ How did the Portuguese reach India?
- ★ What did Columbus find on his voyages?
- ★ What do these words mean: navigation, caravel, magnetic compass, astrolabe, colony?

Portugal and Spain led the way in the search for a sea route to Asia. Both countries had similar goals. They wanted to find gold and increase trade. Each country, however, chose a different path. Portugal believed it could reach the East Indies by sailing south around the tip of Africa and then east to India. Spain hoped to reach the East Indies by sailing west across the Atlantic Ocean.

### Portugal Leads the Way

Like other nations, Portugal was eager to expand its trade. But because its coast faced the Atlantic, it was cut off from the profitable Mediterranean trading routes. So in the early 1400s, the Portuguese began to explore the Atlantic coast of Africa.

**Prince Henry.** Prince Henry of Portugal knew the problems that faced sailors. He was determined to do what he could to improve *navigation,* or the practice of plotting a course at sea. Because of his efforts, he later became known as Prince Henry the Navigator.

In 1418, Prince Henry set up an informal school for sailors at Sagres (SAH grehz). From there, he sent ships to explore the coast of West Africa.

Sea voyages were difficult and dangerous. Captains knew how to sail with the wind but could not sail well against it. To solve this problem, the Portuguese designed better ships, called caravels (KAR uh vehls). A *caravel* had a rudder for steering and triangular sails. The rudder and triangular sails helped a caravel sail against the wind.

Another problem was getting lost at sea. Captains could steer only by the sun. Also, there were no good maps of the coast of Africa. To reduce the risk of getting lost at sea, Prince Henry invited mapmakers and astronomers to Sagres. They drew up new maps and charts based on information from sea captains.

**New instruments.** Two new instruments also helped sailors. One was the ***magnetic compass,*** a Chinese invention brought to Europe by the Arabs. The magnetic compass showed which

direction was north. With a compass, a captain could steer a straight course. The other instrument was the astrolabe (AS truh layb). The ***astrolabe*** was used to measure the positions of stars. With it, a sailor could figure out his latitude at sea.

By 1460, the year Prince Henry died, the Portuguese had explored a long stretch of the African coast. They brought back gold, ivory—and slaves. Before long, other nations joined Portugal in the African slave trade.

## Gold Kingdoms of Africa

In the 1400s, Europeans knew little about Africa or the many peoples who lived on that large continent. A Spanish map showed an African ruler in the middle of the Sahara Desert. The caption read: "This Negro lord is called Musa Mali. So abundant is the gold in his country that he is the richest and most noble king in all the land."

In fact, Musa Mali's real name was Mansa Musa. He ruled Mali, a kingdom in West Africa. The kingdom of Mali flourished from about 1200 to 1400. In 1324, Mansa Musa traveled from Mali across North Africa to Egypt and the Middle East. He so dazzled the Egyptians with his great wealth that news of his visit reached Europe. Mali's wealth came from trade in gold and salt.

Mali was one of several kingdoms that rose in West Africa. (See the map on page 57.) After Mansa Musa's death, Mali declined. In the late 1400s, Songhai (SAWNG hī) became the most powerful kingdom in West Africa. Timbuktu, located on the Niger River, was a thriving center of trade and learning. The University of Sankore in Timbuktu produced many fine scholars.

## Around Africa to India

To Europeans like Prince Henry, Africa meant gold. In fact, they named part of West Africa the ***Gold Coast.*** The

New instruments and accurate maps helped sailors in the 1400s. This picture shows a geographer at work.

African artists created fine works of art. This bronze sculpture of a woman was made in the African city-state of Benin. The Portuguese traded with Benin in the late 1400s.

Portuguese built forts on the Gold Coast to protect their trade in gold, ivory, and slaves. Before long, they looked beyond Africa to India. They believed that by sailing around Africa, they would reach India and win a share of the silk and spice trade.

In 1488, Bartholomeu Dias (DEE uhsh) sailed around the southern tip of Africa. Dias called the tip the Cape of Storms because of its rough seas. He wanted to sail on to India, but his frightened crew forced him to return home. When King John of Portugal

heard abo[u]t
that Portug[...]
route to India.
of Storms the C[...]

In 1497, Kin[g ...]
ships under the co[...]
Gama. His orders w[...]
coveries and go in sea[...]
May 1498, after sailing [...]
and across the Indian Oc[...]
reached India. (See the m[...]
57.)

The Portuguese had achie[v]ed their goal. From India, they sailed on to the East Indies, the source of spices. And within a few years, they built a rich trading empire in Asia.

## Spain Joins the Search

Like Portugal, Spain wanted a share of the spice trade. But Spain was busy fighting to expel the Arabs. In 1492, the last Arab stronghold fell to the armies of King Ferdinand and Queen Isabella. That same year, Isabella sent a daring sea captain on a voyage of discovery.

**Christopher Columbus.** The sea captain was an Italian named Christopher Columbus. Columbus grew up in Genoa, a busy seaport. As a young man, he sailed on several voyages in the Mediterranean. Later, on a voyage to England, his ship was attacked and sunk off the coast of Portugal. Columbus was wounded but was able to float to shore on an oar.

In Portugal, Columbus heard about the discoveries being made along the coast of Africa. He began studying Portuguese maps and charts. Slowly, he developed his own ideas about how to reach the Indies.

**A plan for sailing west.** Like all educated people of his day, Columbus knew the earth was round. He was convinced that he could reach Asia by sailing west. With favorable winds, he believed, a sailing ship could reach Asia within two months.

To locate places exactly, mapmakers draw lines around the globe. Some lines run east and west. Other lines run north and south. Lines that run east and west are called **lines of latitude.** Each line is numbered in degrees (°). The line of latitude that runs east and west around the center of the earth is called the **Equator.** See the map at right.

Lines that run north and south are called **lines of longitude.** The line of longitude that runs north and south through Greenwich (GREHN ihch), England, is called the **Prime Meridian** (muh RIHD ee uhn).

1. **Locate lines of latitude.** Lines of latitude measure distances north or south of the Equator. The Equator is at 0° latitude. North of the Equator, lines of latitude are numbered from 1° to 90°N, where the North Pole is located. South of the Equator, they are numbered from 1° to 90°S, where the South Pole is located. (a) Which label on the map at right is closest to 20°N? (b) Is Lisbon closest to 20°S? 20°N? 40°N?

2. **Locate lines of longitude.** Lines of longitude measure distances east or west of the Prime Meridian. The Prime Meridian is at 0° longitude. Lines of longitude are numbered from 1° to 180° east or west longitude. (a) What continent or continents does 20°E cross? (b) At what longitude is Cape Bojador?

3. **Locate places using latitude and longitude.** To locate places, you need to combine latitude and longitude. For example, Sagres is located at about 38° north latitude and 8° west longitude (38°N/8°W). (a) What is the latitude and longitude of the Cape of Good Hope? (b) At what latitude and longitude did Vasco da Gama reach India? (c) Which explorer sailed past 20°S/20°W?

Columbus asked the king of Portugal for money and ships for the voyage. The king consulted his experts. They disagreed with Columbus about the length of the voyage, claiming that it would take at least four months. Besides, the Portuguese preferred to explore the route around Africa. So the king turned down his request.

Columbus moved to Spain and set his plan before Queen Isabella. She seemed interested, but it took six years of pleading before she finally agreed to provide ships for the voyage.

**A voyage of discovery.** On August 3, 1492, Columbus set sail. His crew included 90 sailors aboard 3 tiny ships. Columbus commanded the largest ship, the *Santa María*. The other ships were the *Niña* and *Pinta*.

At first, the ships had fair winds. They stopped for repairs in the Canary Islands off the coast of Africa. On September 6, Columbus set his course due west. For a month, the crew saw no land. They grew restless because in those days sailors were never out of sight of land for more than three weeks. Columbus held firm against threats of mutiny.

On October 7, sailors saw flocks of birds flying southwest. Columbus changed course to follow the birds. A few days later, crew members spotted branches floating in the water. A storm blew up, but on the night of October 11,

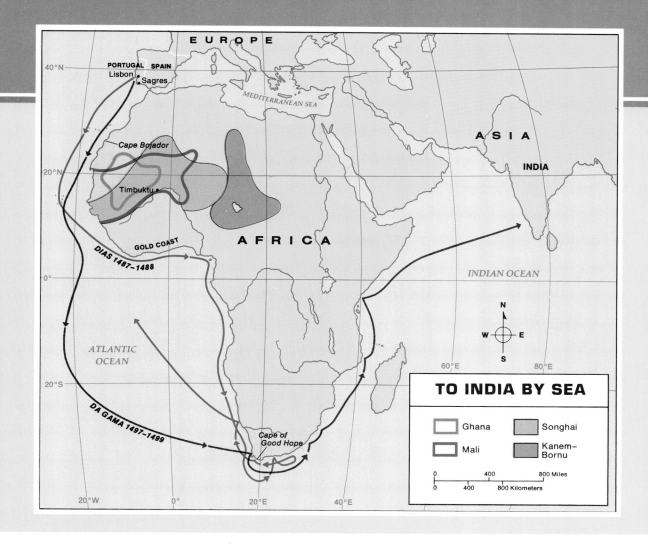

**TO INDIA BY SEA**

Ghana
Mali
Songhai
Kanem–Bornu

0        400        800 Miles
0    400    800 Kilometers

the moon shone brightly. At 2:00 A.M. on October 12, Rodrigo Triana, the lookout on the *Pinta*, spotted cliffs in the moonlight. "Tierra! Tierra!" he shouted. "Land! Land!"

## The New Land

Columbus felt sure he had reached the East Indies. So when the local people paddled their canoes out to his ships, he called them Indians. But the new land left Columbus puzzled. The islanders called themselves Arawaks and wore few clothes. Where were the silks, palaces, and cities of China?

When the local people brought Columbus gold ornaments, he concluded that China must be close. Columbus spent three months exploring nearby islands. He visited Hispaniola* and Cuba. Today, these and other islands in the Caribbean Sea are called the West Indies.

**Later voyages.** In January 1493, Columbus sailed for home. He received riches and honor from Queen Isabella, who named him Admiral of the Ocean Sea and Viceroy of the Indies. The Spanish ruler agreed to finance another voyage.

Columbus made three more voyages to the West Indies. On his second

---

*Today, Haiti and the Dominican Republic are located on the island of Hispaniola.

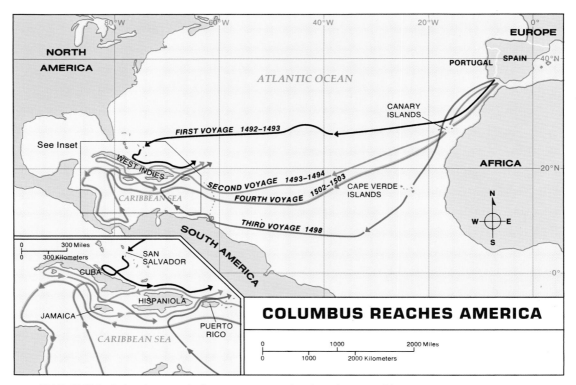

COLUMBUS REACHES AMERICA

MAP SKILL Columbus made four voyages to the Americas, as this map shows. The weather on the first voyage was so fair that sailors worried that their good luck was too good. On which voyage did Columbus reach Puerto Rico? On which voyage did he sail farthest to the south?

trip, he discovered other islands, including Puerto Rico. He set up the first Spanish colony in the New World at Hispaniola. A *colony* is a group of people settled in a distant land who are ruled by the government of their native land.

Columbus had little success on his later voyages. He quarreled with the colonists and was called back to Spain in disgrace. When he died in 1506, he still believed that the land he had discovered was part of Asia.

**Trouble in the conquered lands.** The colonists soon grew discontent because they did not find enough gold to make them rich. They forced the Indians to work for them. When the Indians revolted, colonists killed or enslaved them.

The Indians resisted the Spanish in different ways. The Tainos of Puerto Rico grew angry with Spanish treatment. At first, they did not rebel because they believed that the Spanish were gods who could not be killed.

One old chief decided to test whether the Spanish were gods or mortals. A Spanish colonist ordered some Tainos to carry him across a river. Halfway across, the Tainos let the colonist fall into the water and kept him under for a few hours. For several days, they watched—praying forgiveness from their gods all the while—to see if he would come back to life. When he did not, they spread the news that the Spanish were not gods. A rebellion broke out against the Spanish in which thousands of Tainos were killed.

Christopher Columbus was showered with honors when he returned to Spain after his first voyage. Later, he lost the respect of Queen Isabella because he did not bring back riches from the Indies.

**Naming the New World.** Many explorers followed the route charted by Columbus. They soon realized that the new land was not Asia as Columbus had claimed. In 1499, an Italian merchant named Amerigo Vespucci (vehs PYOOT chee) sailed along the northern coast of South America. When he returned home, he wrote a letter describing "a New World . . . more densely peopled and full of animals than our Europe or Asia or Africa."

In 1507, a German mapmaker read this letter. On a map, he then labeled the new land America, after Amerigo. In this way, America was named after Amerigo Vespucci, not after Christopher Columbus.

### SECTION REVIEW

1. **Locate:** Portugal, Spain, Sagres, Mali, Songhai, Timbuktu, Cape of Good Hope, Indian Ocean, India, West Indies, Hispaniola, Puerto Rico.
2. **Define:** navigation, caravel, magnetic compass, astrolabe, colony.
3. How did Prince Henry encourage exploration?
4. Why were Egyptians and Europeans so impressed with Mansa Musa?
5. **What Do You Think?** Why do you think Columbus risked great danger to sail across the Atlantic Ocean?

# 3 Exploring the New World

**Read to Learn**
★ How did Spain and Portugal divide up the world?
★ What areas did Balboa and Magellan explore?
★ How did Spain win an empire in the New World?
★ What does this word mean: conquistador?

After 1492, many explorers crossed the Atlantic. They risked great dangers in their search for a way to the rich empires of Asia. The explorers did not reach China or India. But they did discover that the New World had its own rich empires. In the 1500s, Spain won an empire in the Americas that made it the richest nation in Europe.

## Dividing Up the World

When the news of Columbus' first voyage reached King John of Portugal, he refused to recognize Spanish claims to the new lands. He said that Columbus had simply found a few islands in the Atlantic Ocean that already belonged to Portugal. To prevent war between Spain and Portugal, the Pope offered to settle the dispute. In 1494, he had them sign the Treaty of Tordesillas. The treaty drew a *Line of Demarcation* (dee mahr KAY shuhn) that divided up the world. (See the map on page 61.)

The treaty gave Spain the right to colonize and trade with the lands west of the line. Spain, therefore, claimed North and South America. The treaty gave Portugal the right to colonize and trade with the lands east of the line. Portugal, therefore, controlled trade with China and the East Indies. The treaty, of course, ignored the interests or wishes of the peoples living in these lands.

Almost by chance, Portugal gained a foothold in South America. In 1500, Pedro Álvares Cabral (kuh BRAHL) set sail for India around Africa. Strong winds blew his ship far off course, and he landed on the coast of Brazil. Cabral realized that this part of South America was east of the Line of Demarcation. So he claimed the land for Portugal.

## Balboa Sees the Pacific

In the early 1500s, Spanish sailors explored the coasts of North and South America, looking for a western route to Asia. Once they realized that these large continents blocked the way, they searched for a route across or around the Americas.

In 1513, Vasco Núñez de Balboa (bal BOH uh) decided to find such a route. Balboa heard from the people of Panama that a large body of water lay to the west. So he set out with 190 men to cross the Isthmus of Panama.

The isthmus was only 45 miles (72 km) wide, but it was covered by a thick, steaming jungle. The explorers hacked a trail through the jungle and waded across swamps filled with mosquitoes. Finally, Balboa climbed a mountain and looked out on a huge ocean. The next day, sword in hand, he waded into the water and claimed the ocean for Spain. He called it the South Sea because he thought it was south of Asia. In fact, he was looking out on the Pacific Ocean.

## A Voyage Around the World

When Balboa saw the Pacific, he thought that the East Indies were nearby. He had no idea how wide the ocean was. Before long, however, Ferdinand Magellan (muh JEHL uhn) discovered the true size of the Pacific.

Magellan was a Portuguese sea captain who made several voyages around Africa to India and the East Indies. He believed that he could find a shorter route to Asia by sailing around South America.

**Departure.** In August 1519, an eager and hopeful Magellan sailed out of Seville harbor in Spain. He was in command of 5 ships and 268 men. When the fleet reached Brazil, problems arose. One ship was destroyed in a storm. The other ships tried to sail around Cape Horn, the tip of South America. But fierce storms drove them back.

For five long months, Magellan waited for better weather. The frightened officers tried to force him to return home. But he boldly crushed the mutiny, leaving the ringleaders to die on the bleak South American coast. Finally, Magellan discovered a passage around Cape Horn. The passage is now called the Strait of Magellan. In November 1520, Magellan led his three remaining ships into the large ocean Balboa had seen earlier. Magellan called it the Pacific Ocean because it was so peaceful compared to the stormy Atlantic.

**Crossing the Pacific.** The Pacific posed new problems because it was so huge. "We remained 3 months and 20 days," wrote one sailor, "without taking on any food or refreshment. We ate only old biscuit reduced to powder and full of grubs . . . and we drank water that was yellow and stinking." Sailors caught rats to eat. When there were no more rats, they ate sawdust and leather so tough that they had to soak it for days before it was soft enough to chew.

Magellan finally reached the Philippine Islands. (Find Magellan's route on the map below.) There, he was killed in a battle with the local people. Magellan's crew sailed on. In 1522, one ship and 18 sailors reached Spain. These survivors were the first Europeans to circle the globe. Magellan's voyage proved that ships could reach Asia by sailing west.

## Spain Wins an Empire

In 1519, the year Magellan set out from Spain, Hernando Cortés (kawr TEHZ), a Spanish adventurer, landed on the coast of Mexico. Cortés had heard

**MAP SKILL** In the 1400s and 1500s, European sailors explored the oceans of the world. They wanted to find an easy sea route to Asia. Follow the route Magellan pioneered on his voyage of discovery. At what latitude did he cross the Line of Demarcation?

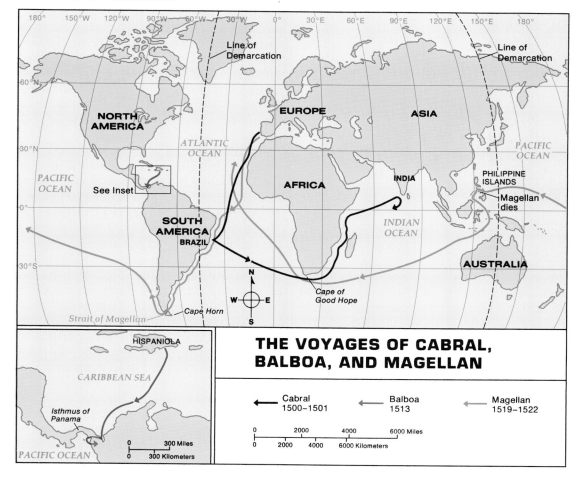

THE VOYAGES OF CABRAL, BALBOA, AND MAGELLAN

Cabral 1500–1501
Balboa 1513
Magellan 1519–1522

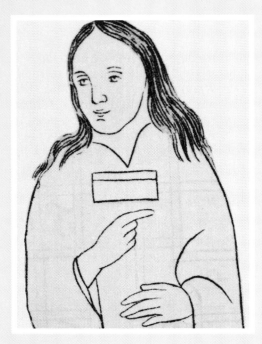

### Doña Marina

A Native American woman known to the Spanish as Doña Marina helped Cortés in his victory over the Aztecs. Although she was of royal birth, Doña Marina was given as a slave to Cortés. She learned Spanish quickly and became an interpreter for Cortés. When Doña Marina heard of a plot by Montezuma to kill the Spanish, she told Cortés, saving him from death.

set up outposts in the Americas. In exchange, the conquistadors agreed to give Spain one fifth of any gold or treasure they captured.

**Cortés takes Tenochtitlan.** Soon after Cortés reached shore, messengers carried word of his landing to Montezuma (mahn tuh ᴢʏoo muh), the Aztec emperor. They reported that fair-skinned strangers had come from the east. The strangers, they said, had come across the sea. The fair-skinned men wore metal armor and had powerful weapons that made loud noises and shattered trees into splinters. (The weapons were cannons.) The messengers also reported that the Spanish had "deer that carry them on their backs wherever they wish to go." (The "deer" were horses, which the Aztecs had never seen before.)

Montezuma hesitated, not knowing what to do. The Aztecs believed that they were descended from a white-skinned god, Quetzalcoatl (keht sahl koh ᴀʜ tuhl). The god was expected to return to their land from the east. What if Cortés and his fair-skinned men were messengers of the Aztec god?

When the newcomers neared Tenochtitlan, Montezuma decided to welcome them as his guests. For more than six months, Cortés negotiated with Montezuma. But he actually held the Aztec leader almost as a prisoner in his own capital. Still, Montezuma refused to call out his army.

Finally, other Aztec leaders forced Cortés out of the city. Cortés turned for help to the people the Aztecs had conquered. Because these people hated Aztec rule, they joined Cortés. In 1521, they captured Tenochtitlan and destroyed most of the city. Within a few years, the mighty Aztec empire had fallen.

**Pizarro defeats the Incas.** Rumors of other rich empires attracted more conquistadors to the Americas. Fran-

about the mighty Aztec empire. Now he wanted to conquer it. His army included 400 soldiers and 16 horses.

Cortés was a *conquistador* (kohn ᴋᴇᴇs tah dohr), or conqueror. The conquistadors were bold warriors, successors to the knights who had driven the Muslims out of Spain. One knight summed up the motives of the conquistadors. "We came here to serve God and the king and also to get rich." Spanish rulers gave conquistadors the right to cisco Pizarro (pee ZAHR oh) heard about the Inca empire when he marched with Balboa across Panama. After several unsuccessful attempts, Pizarro reached Cuzco, the Inca capital, in 1532.

Pizarro found the Incas divided by civil war. He launched a surprise attack and killed the Inca ruler, Atahualpa (ah tah WAHL pah). By 1535, Pizarro had taken control of much of the Inca empire.

**Reasons for success.** Why were Cortés and Pizarro able to conquer two powerful empires with only a handful of soldiers? First, the Spanish had better weapons. They used guns and cannons against the Indians' bows, arrows, and spears. Second, the Aztecs and Incas had never seen horses and were frightened by the mounted Spanish knights. Third, Native Americans like the Aztecs and Incas at first thought the Spanish were gods.

Finally, diseases such as chicken pox, measles, and influenza helped the Spanish. The Aztecs and Incas had no resistance to these European diseases. They caught the diseases from the Spanish and died by the thousands. Many Aztec warriors caught smallpox and dropped dead in battle. The Spanish claimed that the hand of God was striking the Aztecs down.

Aztec and Inca treasures made the conquistadors rich. Spain grew rich, too, especially after gold and silver mines were discovered in Mexico and Peru.

## Spain Looks North

While Cortés and Pizarro were winning riches in Central and South America, other conquistadors explored North America. One was Juan Ponce de León (PAWN say day lay AWN). Ponce de León explored an island Columbus had visited. When Ponce de León saw a beautiful bay in the north, he called it Puerto Rico, or rich port. Later, he put down

A Spanish priest copied this picture from an Aztec painting. It shows how the Aztecs saw the Spanish. The Aztecs were awed by Spanish horsemen. Some thought that a man on horseback was a new kind of animal—half man, half beast.

the Taino rebellion on Puerto Rico and became the island's first governor.

In 1513, Ponce de León explored Florida, hoping to find the Fountain of Youth. This magical fountain, he had heard, would make anyone who bathed in it young forever. He found no fountain or rich kingdoms. But he did take many Indian slaves from Florida to Puerto Rico to replace those who had died or been killed by the Spanish.

Two other conquistadors, Francisco Coronado (koh roh NAH doh) and Hernando De Soto, heard stories of the Seven Cities of Gold. The streets of these cities were said to be paved with gold. Coronado's search led him into New Mexico. In 1540, after great hardships, he found villages of the Zuñis, but no

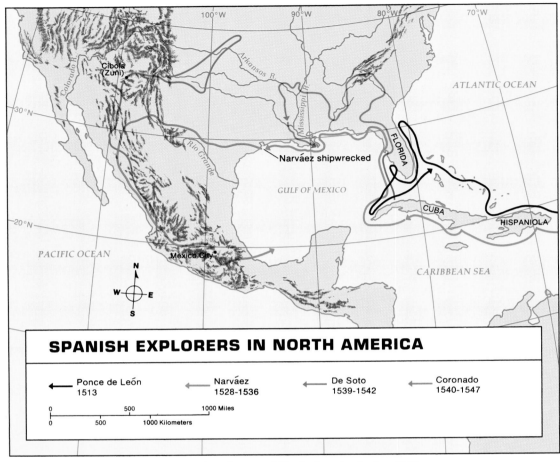

**SPANISH EXPLORERS IN NORTH AMERICA**

| ← Ponce de León | ← Narváez | ← De Soto | ← Coronado |
|---|---|---|---|
| 1513 | 1528-1536 | 1539-1542 | 1540-1547 |

0     500     1000 Miles

0     500     1000 Kilometers

**MAP SKILL** Conquistadors explored parts of North America in the 1500s. They did not find the Seven Cities of Gold as they hoped. But they mapped routes that Spanish missionaries and settlers followed. Which explorer was the first to visit Florida?

gold. From 1539 to 1542, De Soto explored the southeast of the present-day United States. But he died without finding gold. Follow the routes taken by Ponce de León, Coronado, and De Soto on the map above.

At first, the conquistadors were welcomed by the local Indians they met. But when the Spanish started to kill, rob, and enslave the Indians, the Indians fought back. This fierce Indian resistance forced Spain to back off from North America. Instead, Spain concentrated on its empire in the south. Before long, other nations began to claim lands in North America.

**SECTION REVIEW**

1. **Locate:** Line of Demarcation, Brazil, Isthmus of Panama, Cape Horn, Pacific Ocean, Philippine Islands, Puerto Rico, Florida.

2. **Define:** conquistador.

3. What nations signed the Treaty of Tordesillas?

4. Why did conquistadors go to the Americas?

5. How did disease help the Spanish defeat the Aztecs?

6. **What Do You Think?** How do you think Magellan's voyage affected the way Europeans saw the world?

Among the conquistadors was an African called Estevanico (ehs tay vahn EE koh). He was brought as a slave from Morocco to the New World. In 1528, he sailed to Florida with 300 Spanish soldiers and their servants. Under their leader, Pánfilo de Narváez (nahr VAH ehs), the group hoped to find the Seven Cities of Gold.

Disaster struck early. Almost everyone, including Narváez, was killed in battle with Indians, died of disease, or drowned crossing the Gulf of Mexico. Only Estevanico and three other men survived. For eight years, they wandered through Texas, Arizona, and New Mexico, hunting for the cities of gold.

Estevanico learned Native American languages, so he was able to lead the others in their search. Several times, the four men were taken as slaves by Native Americans. Estevanico helped his companions to escape or win freedom.

The four survivors finally reached Spanish settlements in western Mexico.

In 1539, Estevanico again set out to hunt for the cities of gold. He reached the edges of a Zuñi pueblo that shimmered like gold in the sun. But he was killed in battle before he learned whether the city was full of riches.

★ Find the areas Estevanico explored on the map on page 64.

# 4 Early Claims to North America

## Read to Learn

★ What explorers searched for a northwest passage?

★ How did the Protestant Reformation affect Europeans?

★ Why were Spain and England rivals?

★ What do these words mean: northwest passage?

When other European nations saw the rich empire Spain was winning in the New World, they, too, wanted a share. Soon, England, France, and the Netherlands outfitted their own voyages of discovery.

## Search for a Northwest Passage

To the nations of Europe, spices from Asia were still more valuable than land in the New World. But what was the quickest route to Asia? Magellan's passage around South America was too long and dangerous. So English, French, and Dutch explorers looked for a *northwest passage,* or a waterway through or around North America.

**John Cabot.** In 1497, five years after Columbus' first voyage, King Henry VII of England sent John Cabot on a voyage of discovery. Cabot was sure he could find a shorter route across the Atlantic by sailing farther north. He left Bristol, England, on May 2, 1497. On June 24, he reached land, probably an island off Nova Scotia. Like Columbus, he thought that he had reached Asia. He claimed the land for England. On a second voyage, Cabot explored the eastern coast of North America, still thinking he was exploring Asia.

**French explorers.** In 1524, France sent an Italian sailor, Giovanni da Verrazano (vehr rah TSAH noh), on a voyage of discovery. Verrazano searched the coast of North America for a northwest passage. He probably sailed into New York harbor, where a bridge named after him stands today.

France outfitted several more voyages. In the 1530s, Jacques Cartier (kahr tee YAY) sailed past Newfoundland and found the broad opening where the St. Lawrence River flows into the Atlantic. (See the map below.) The opening looked to him like a passage that might lead to China.

Cartier sailed up the St. Lawrence and met a group of Iroquois. They told him about the kingdom of Saguenay (sag uh NAY). The Saguenay, they said,

MAP SKILL The search for a northwest passage sent explorers from many nations across the Atlantic. Find the route Hudson took in 1610. What nation sent Hudson on that voyage? What body of water did he explore in 1610?

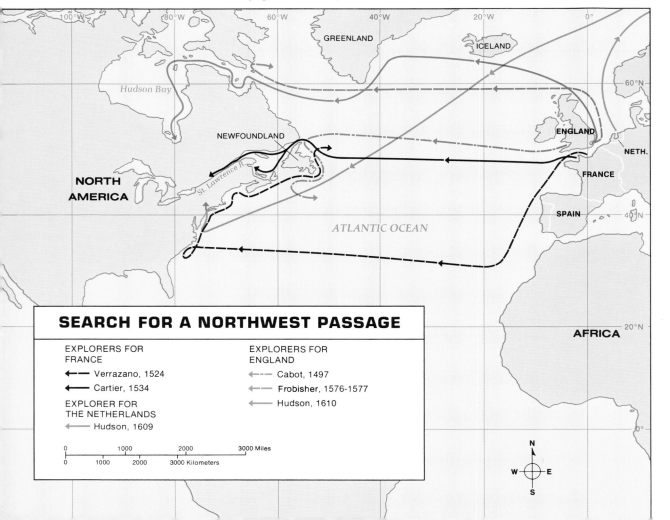

**SEARCH FOR A NORTHWEST PASSAGE**

EXPLORERS FOR FRANCE
←— Verrazano, 1524
←— Cartier, 1534

EXPLORER FOR THE NETHERLANDS
←— Hudson, 1609

EXPLORERS FOR ENGLAND
←--- Cabot, 1497
←— — Frobisher, 1576-1577
←— Hudson, 1610

0    1000    2000    3000 Miles
0  1000  2000  3000 Kilometers

Native Americans sometimes tried to stop European explorers from invading their lands. Here, Martin Frobisher and his sailors battle with Eskimos.

had rich gold and silver mines. Some of the people, they added, hopped around on one leg or flew like bats.

Cartier believed these fabulous stories. In 1541, he left home again to hunt for the Saguenay. As he sailed up the St. Lawrence River, he kept getting reports that the Saguenay were just a bit farther away. In the end, Cartier returned to France without finding the Saguenay or a northwest passage. He did, however, claim many lands for France. Also, he helped build the first French settlements in Canada.

**Frobisher and Hudson.** Two English explorers, Martin Frobisher and Henry Hudson, also searched for a northwest passage. Between 1576 and 1578, Frobisher made three voyages to North America. Although he failed in his main purpose, Frobisher explored parts of northern Canada. Before returning home on one trip, he filled his ship with tons of sparkling ore that he thought was gold ore. The ore proved to be iron pyrite, or fool's gold, which had no value.

Henry Hudson made two trips to North America for England, exploring regions in the far north. Then, in 1609, he agreed to explore for the Dutch. In a small ship, the *Half Moon,* Hudson discovered a wide bay. He hoped that it was a northwest passage. But it turned out to be the river that now bears his name. Hudson sailed up the river about 150 miles (240 km) to where Albany, New York, stands today.

On Hudson's fourth voyage, he sailed again for England. He explored

Hudson Bay, which was named after him. On the way home, Hudson's crew rebelled. They put Hudson, his son, and seven loyal sailors into a small boat and set it adrift. The small boat and its crew were never seen again.

Explorers kept looking for a northwest passage in the 1700s and 1800s. A route to the Pacific Ocean across the top of North America does exist. But it is blocked with ice for most of the year. The first successful trip through this passage was finally made in 1906.

## Rivalries Among European Nations

During the 1500s and 1600s, European nations fought many wars over religion. Until the 1500s, the Catholic Church was the only church in Western Europe. But in 1517, a German monk named Martin Luther called for reforms in the Catholic Church. His call split the Church.

Luther's followers became known as Protestants because of their protests against the Catholic Church. The movement to reform the Church was called the *Protestant Reformation.* In the 1500s, many different Protestant churches were formed. Believers took their faith so seriously that Catholics and Protestants tortured and killed each other in many wars. These religious wars became mixed up with political wars—wars fought for power and territory. When European nations expanded overseas, their wars were carried to these new lands, too.

**Spain and England.** In the late 1500s, Spain was the most powerful Catholic nation in Europe. The Spanish king, Philip II, wanted to force Protestants to return to the Catholic Church. He faced fierce opposition, however.

England was the strongest Protestant nation. But it was not nearly as powerful as Spain. The queen of England, Elizabeth I, was head of the Church of England. She feared the power of Catholic Spain and was determined to prevent Philip from conquering England.

**English Sea Dogs.** Elizabeth knew England was no match for Spain. Yet she allowed daring English sailors to attack Spanish treasure fleets and to raid Spanish colonies in the New World. These adventurers were known in England as Sea Dogs—though the Spanish called them pirates!

Like the conquistadors, the English Sea Dogs wanted to win fame and fortune for themselves. But they also fought for their country against Spain. One Sea Dog, Sir Humphrey Gilbert, joined the search for a northwest passage. Gilbert planned to set up a colony in North America to use as a base for his search and for raids on Spanish treasure ships. He wrote a book for Queen Elizabeth called *How Her Majesty May Annoy the King of Spain.*

**Sir Francis Drake.** Perhaps the boldest Sea Dog was Sir Francis Drake. In 1577, Drake took Magellan's route around Cape Horn. He attacked Spanish settlements in Peru. At one port, Drake's crew grabbed up treasure while Drake forced helpless Spanish officials to dine with him on board his ship, the *Golden Hind.* During the meal, crew members played violins. Drake explored farther up the Pacific coast before sailing west across the Pacific Ocean.

In 1580, Drake returned to England after circling the globe. He received a hero's welcome, especially since the *Golden Hind* was filled with Spanish gold. Queen Elizabeth visited Drake on board his ship. There, she knighted him—Sir Francis Drake—as a reward for his services. King Philip of Spain was furious when he heard this. He demanded that Elizabeth return the stolen Spanish treasure. When Elizabeth refused, Philip prepared for war.

Queen Elizabeth I knighted Drake on board the *Golden Hind*. Drake won his greatest prize when he captured the Spanish ship *Glory of the South Sea*. It carried many chests of gold, silver, and jewels.

**The Spanish Armada.** In 1588, Spain sent a huge fleet, called the *Spanish Armada*, against England. The English were greatly outnumbered, but their ships were faster than the heavy Spanish galleons. During the battle, a violent storm blew up, scattering the Spanish Armada.

The defeat of the Spanish Armada did not mean the end of Spanish power. Spain continued to profit from its colonies in the New World. However, in the years after 1588, England, France, and other nations began setting up their own colonies in the Americas.

**SECTION REVIEW**

1. **Locate:** Newfoundland, St. Lawrence River, Hudson Bay.
2. **Define:** northwest passage.
3. What dangers did explorers face in looking for a northwest passage?
4. Why were Martin Luther's followers called Protestants?
5. (a) How did the English Sea Dogs anger Spain? (b) Why did Queen Elizabeth knight Drake?
6. **What Do You Think?** Why do you think finding a northwest passage was so important?

# Chapter 3 Review

## ★ Summary ★

About the year 1000, the Vikings reached North America. But news of their voyages did not spread to other parts of Europe during the Middle Ages. In the Renaissance, however, European nations began to look overseas. Portugal led the way in looking for a sea route to India.

Christopher Columbus reached the West Indies in 1492. He claimed the land for Spain. In the 1500s, the conquistadors helped Spain win a huge empire in the Americas.

Sailors from many nations explored the oceans of the world in the 1500s and 1600s. Magellan found a route around South America to the Pacific. Other explorers hunted for a northwest passage to the Pacific and Asia.

## ★ Reviewing the Facts ★

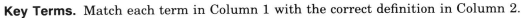

**Key Terms.** Match each term in Column 1 with the correct definition in Column 2.

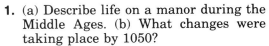

### Column 1
1. feudalism
2. caravel
3. astrolabe
4. colony
5. conquistador

### Column 2
a. instrument used to measure the positions of stars
b. system of rule by lords who owe loyalty to their king
c. group of people settled in a distant land who are ruled by the government of their native land
d. conqueror
e. ship with a rudder and triangular sails

**Key People, Events, and Ideas.** Identify each of the following.

1. Leif Ericson
2. Crusades
3. Renaissance
4. Prince Henry
5. Vasco da Gama
6. Queen Isabella
7. Ferdinand Magellan
8. Hernando Cortés
9. Francisco Pizarro
10. Francisco Coronado
11. Jacques Cartier
12. Henry Hudson
13. Protestant Reformation
14. Queen Elizabeth I
15. Sir Francis Drake

## ★ Chapter Checkup ★

1. (a) Describe life on a manor during the Middle Ages. (b) What changes were taking place by 1050?
2. (a) Why did the Pope call for a crusade? (b) List three results of the Crusades.
3. What improvements were made in sailing in the 1400s?
4. (a) Why did the king of Portugal refuse to help Columbus? (b) What ruler supported Columbus? (c) Why did Columbus' crew rebel during his first voyage?
5. (a) What body of water did Balboa find? (b) Why did he call it the South Sea?
6. Why did Montezuma hesitate to fight the Spanish?
7. Give three reasons why the Spanish were able to conquer the Aztecs and Incas.
8. (a) List three sailors who explored the coasts of North America. (b) What did Cartier hope to find on his voyage up the St. Lawrence?

1. **Relating past to present.** (a) What two nations divided up the world in 1494? (b) What two nations today are competing for influence around the world? (c) Compare these situations.

2. **Analyzing a quotation.** Columbus told his crew: "It is useless to complain, since I have come to find the [East] Indies and so will continue until I find them." How might these words have affected the crew?

3. **Expressing an opinion.** Review the story of Doña Marina on page 62. Do you think Doña Marina was a traitor to her people or a hero? Explain your opinion.

4. **Applying information.** (a) What motives led Portugal and Spain to explore the oceans of the world? (b) How did these motives affect their treatment of the peoples they met?

★ **Using Your Skills** ★

1. **Map reading.** Review the map-reading steps in Skill Lesson 3 (page 56). Then study the map on page 66. (a) At about what latitude did Cabot cross the Atlantic? (b) Who explored farthest south in North America? (c) What is the latitude and longitude of the southernmost point this explorer reached?

2. **Placing events in time.** The time lines at the beginning of each chapter show when important events took place. Study the time line on page 48. (a) When did Leif Ericson reach Vinland? (b) In what year did Marco Polo leave for China? (c) Which of these events took place first?

3. **Ranking.** Review the explorers mentioned in this chapter. Then choose five explorers and rank them according to whose voyages you think had the most important results. Explain your ranking.

4. **Using a painting as a primary source.** Review the steps for using a painting as a primary source in Skill Lesson 2 (page 43). Then study the painting on page 63. (a) What is the subject of the painting? (b) How does the artist show the Spanish? (c) What do you think the artist thought of the Spanish? Explain your answer.

5. **Making a review chart.** Make a large chart with four headings across the top: Explorer, Date(s) of Voyage(s), For What Country, Results of Voyage(s). Fill in the chart for all explorers mentioned in this chapter. Use other books, if necessary, to complete the chart.

★ **More to Do** ★

1. **Preparing a newspaper advertisement.** Prepare a newspaper advertisement that Magellan could have used to get sailors to join his voyage of discovery.

2. **Writing a dialogue.** Write a dialogue that might have taken place between Montezuma and Cortés when they first met.

3. **Drawing a cartoon.** Draw a cartoon showing what Native Americans might have thought of the first Europeans they saw.

4. **Exploring local history.** Find out if Europeans explored your local area. Then prepare a map showing the route they took during their exploration.

# Unit 1 Review

**Chapter 1** The first Americans probably crossed a land bridge from Asia to North America about 70,000 years ago. They found many different physical regions and climates in the Americas. People who settled the land learned to adapt to the geography of each region.

**Chapter 2** Archaeologists have studied the cultures of the first Americans. Native American groups settled in different parts of North America. Each people had its own culture. The Mayas, Aztecs, and Incas built empires in the Americas.

**Chapter 3** During the Renaissance, Europeans explored the oceans of the world. Sailors like Columbus and Magellan charted new routes across the oceans. Other explorers claimed large parts of the Americas for Portugal, Spain, France, and England.

★ **Unit Checkup** ★

Choose the word or phrase that best completes each of the following statements.

1. During the last ice age, much of North America was covered by
   (a) glaciers.
   (b) plateaus.
   (c) tributaries.

2. The climate of the Southeast is
   (a) desert.
   (b) steppe.
   (c) humid subtropical.

3. Archaeologists study
   (a) weather and climate.
   (b) natural resources.
   (c) evidence of early people.

4. The Navajos lived in the
   (a) Pacific Northwest.
   (b) Eastern Woodlands.
   (c) Southwest.

5. The Aztecs built their capital city at
   (a) Tikal.
   (b) Cuzco.
   (c) Tenochtitlan.

★ **Building American Citizenship** ★

1. Over the years, Americans have benefited from the rich resources of the land. Today, many private citizens as well as the United States government are concerned about protecting the American land. How are people trying to protect the land and its resources?

2. Millions of Native Americans lived in North and South America before 1492. As you learned, they developed many different cultures. Today, Native Americans are proud of their traditions and cultures.

Choose one Native American group you read about in this unit. Find out more about the group's history and culture. Then describe how the traditions of the group have survived.

3. During the Renaissance, explorers sailed into unmapped waters. Today, American space explorers are making voyages into new regions. What qualities did Renaissance explorers have that space explorers of today have?

The picture at right was drawn by an Aztec artist in the 1500s. It shows the effects of smallpox on the Aztecs. Study the picture. Then answer the following questions.

1. How does the artist show the effects of smallpox?

2. What do you think the picture in the top part of the drawing represents?

3. Why do you think the artist made the drawing?

4. What does the drawing tell you about the Aztecs?

5. What title would you give this Aztec drawing?

## History Writer's Handbook

### Analyzing a Question Before Writing

Before writing an answer to a question, study the question. Look for the key word and other clues in the question that will help you prepare a good answer.

The *key word* in a question tells you what to do with the topic. Often the key word is an instruction word. Some common instruction words and their meanings are listed below.

Explain: tell how or why
Compare: give similarities and differences
Describe: give details or features
Summarize: tell important ideas in as few words as possible

Sometimes the key word is a question word. Some common question words and their meanings are listed below.

Why: give reasons
How: tell in what way or by what means
What: give specific examples

Other clues in a question are words or phrases that limit the topic. A clue might tell you to limit the topic to a certain person, event, geographic area, or time period. Or it might tell you the number of examples or ideas you need to include.

**Practice** Analyze the following question: *How did the geography of the Far North affect the way of life of Eskimos?*

1. What is the key word in the question?

2. What does the key word tell you to do?

3. What clue tells you to limit the topic to a geographic area?

4. What does the clue *of Eskimos* tell you?

# Unit 2
# SETTLING THE NEW WORLD

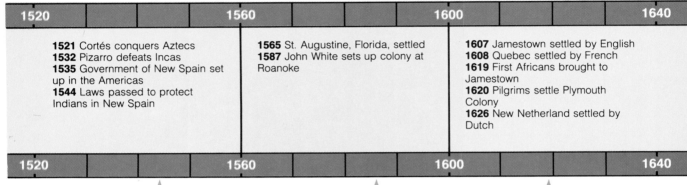

| 1520 | 1560 | 1600 | 1640 |
|---|---|---|---|

**1521** Cortés conquers Aztecs
**1532** Pizarro defeats Incas
**1535** Government of New Spain set up in the Americas
**1544** Laws passed to protect Indians in New Spain

**1565** St. Augustine, Florida, settled
**1587** John White sets up colony at Roanoke

**1607** Jamestown settled by English
**1608** Quebec settled by French
**1619** First Africans brought to Jamestown
**1620** Pilgrims settle Plymouth Colony
**1626** New Netherland settled by Dutch

| 1520 | 1560 | 1600 | 1640 |
|---|---|---|---|

**Mid-1500s** The Spanish made coins from the gold of the New World.

**Late 1580s** The English artist John White painted this Algonquin village.

**1619** The first House of Burgesses was set up in Virginia.

UNIT OUTLINE

CHAPTER 4 Planting Colonies (1530–1690)

**CHAPTER 5** English Colonies Take Root (1630–1750)

**CHAPTER 6** Life in the Colonies (1630–1775)

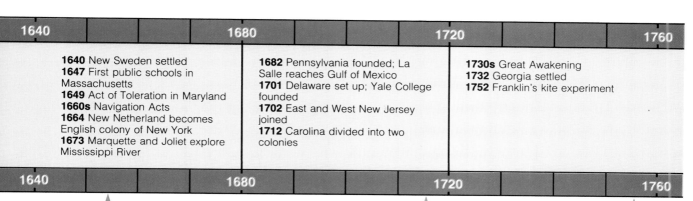

| 1640 | 1680 | 1720 | 1760 |
|---|---|---|---|

**1640** New Sweden settled
**1647** First public schools in Massachusetts
**1649** Act of Toleration in Maryland
**1660s** Navigation Acts
**1664** New Netherland becomes English colony of New York
**1673** Marquette and Joliet explore Mississippi River

**1682** Pennsylvania founded; La Salle reaches Gulf of Mexico
**1701** Delaware set up; Yale College founded
**1702** East and West New Jersey joined
**1712** Carolina divided into two colonies

**1730s** Great Awakening
**1732** Georgia settled
**1752** Franklin's kite experiment

| 1640 | 1680 | 1720 | 1760 |
|---|---|---|---|

**1600s and 1700s** French fur traders explored much of North America.

**1700s** Prudence Punderson embroiders at home.

**1700s** Colonists developed their own industries, such as glassmaking and forging iron.

# 4

# Planting Colonies (1530–1690)

**Chapter Outline**

1 Spain Builds a Large Empire
2 French and Dutch Colonies
3 English Settlers in Virginia
4 The Pilgrims at Plymouth
Readings, page 470

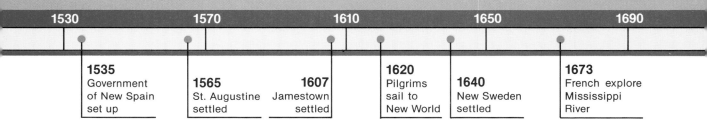

| 1530 | 1570 | 1610 | 1650 | 1690 |
| --- | --- | --- | --- | --- |

**1535**
Government
of New Spain
set up

**1565**
St. Augustine
settled

**1607**
Jamestown
settled

**1620**
Pilgrims
sail to
New World

**1640**
New Sweden
settled

**1673**
French explore
Mississippi
River

## About This Chapter

In 1584, Richard Hakluyt wrote a pamphlet urging Queen Elizabeth I of England to plant colonies in America. He argued that "if England possesses these places in America, Her Majesty will have good harbors, plenty of excellent trees for masts, good timber to build ships . . . all things needed for a royal navy, and all for no price."

Further, he argued that the English would be able to trade with Native Americans, exchanging "cheap English goods for things of great value that are not thought to be worth much by the natives of America." This trade, he said, would make England very rich. The Queen was not convinced by Hakluyt's arguments. But England's rival, Spain, was already setting up colonies in America.

In the 1500s and 1600s, Spain, France, the Netherlands, and Sweden planted colonies in the New World. Despite a slow start, England, too, set up its own colonies.

Early colonists faced terrible hardships. The long journey across the Atlantic used up their food supplies and left many weak and ill. In the New World, settlers had to build homes, grow food, and make everything they needed. Despite the hardships, most early colonies survived with the help of friendly Native Americans.

The New World colonies differed from each other. These differences were due in part to geography and to the varied cultures from which settlers came.

Study the time line above. When was Jamestown settled?

Pilgrims were among the earliest English settlers in North America. Almost 250 years later, George Boughton painted *Pilgrims Going to Church*.

# 1 Spain Builds a Large Empire

### Read to Learn

★ How did Spain govern its colonies?
★ What social classes existed in New Spain?
★ What was Spanish culture like in the New World?
★ What do these words mean: viceroy, pueblo, presidio, mission, peninsular, creole, mestizo, encomienda, plantation?

Between 1492 and 1535, conquistadors won a large empire for Spain. During that time, Spain encouraged them with words but gave them little money for their voyages to the New World. Once Spain began to profit from the riches of the Americas, it paid close attention to its colonies there.

### Governing an Empire

In 1535, the Spanish king, Charles V, set up a system of government in the Americas that lasted for nearly 300 years. He divided his empire into New Spain and Peru. (See the map on page 78.) New Spain included Spanish colonies in the West Indies, Central America, and North America. Peru included all Spanish lands in South America.

The king put a viceroy in charge of each region. A *viceroy* is an official who rules an area in the name of a king or queen. Colonists had little say in their government. The viceroy and other officials chosen by the king enforced a series of laws called the Laws of the Indies.

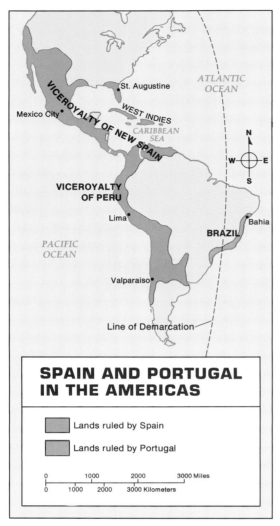

MAP SKILL Both Spain and Portugal built empires in the New World, as this map shows. The Spanish empire included the viceroyalties of New Spain and Peru. Name two settlements in New Spain.

The *Laws of the Indies* allowed Spain to keep strict control over its colonies. The laws said how the colonies should be ruled. They told farmers what to plant and how to raise cattle. They said how and where towns should be built. For example, a town had to be built on high ground with good farmland, woods, and a plentiful water supply nearby.

Under the laws, three kinds of settlements were organized: pueblos, pre-sidios (pray SIH dee ohs), and missions. *Pueblos* were towns that were centers for farming and trade. At the center of the town was the plaza, a large open space. Here, townspeople and farmers gathered on important occasions. At one end of the plaza stood the church, usually the largest building in town. Shops and private homes lined both sides of the plaza.

*Presidios* were forts that housed soldiers. A presidio formed a rectangle and was surrounded by high mud brick walls. Inside the walls were shops, stables for horses, and storehouses for food. Most soldiers lived in large barracks. Farmers settled outside the walls of the presidios and were glad to have military help nearby.

*Missions* were religious settlements run by Catholic priests and friars. Like other Europeans who settled in the New World, the Spanish had no use for Indian religious beliefs. They believed it was their duty to convert the Indians to Christianity.

Priests set up missions throughout New Spain. They forced Indians to live in the missions and learn about Christianity. Each mission supported itself through the work of Indians. With a presidio nearby, priests had soldiers to back up their demands for Indian labor and to put down revolts. By setting up presidios and missions, the Laws of the Indies allowed Spain to rule the conquered Indians.

## Social Classes

Under the Laws of the Indies, people were divided into social classes. At the top were the *peninsulares* (puh nihn suh LAHR ays). They were born in Spain and were sent by the Spanish government to rule the colonies. Only peninsulares could hold the highest jobs in government and the Catholic Church. Although peninsulares were wealthy landowners, most lived in the cities.

**Creoles.** Below the peninsulares were the *creoles* (KREE ohls). They were descended from Spanish settlers who were born in the Americas. Many creoles were wealthy and well educated. But they could not hold the jobs that were kept for the peninsulares. This policy made the creoles resent the peninsulares.

Many creoles owned large farms. There, they grew crops that were in demand in Europe, including bananas, rice, melons, and wheat. Creoles also raised crops that were new to Europeans but that Native Americans had grown for years. These included corn, beans, tomatoes, potatoes, squash, and tobacco. Many creoles took up ranching. They raised horses, sheep, cattle, and pigs on large ranches that stretched for many miles.

**Mestizos and Native Americans.** Below the creoles were the *mestizos* (mehs TEE zohs). These people were of mixed Spanish and Indian background. Mestizos worked on farms and ranches owned by creoles. In the cities, they worked as carpenters, shoemakers, tailors, and bakers. In the 1600s and 1700s, the mestizo population grew rapidly.

The lowest class in the colonies were the Native Americans. Under the strict social system set up by the Spanish, Indians were kept in poverty for hundreds of years.

## Tragedy for Native Americans

Most Spanish settlers hoped to become rich in the New World. To do so, they needed workers to make their ranches, mines, and farmlands profitable. The Spanish government helped settlers by giving them *encomiendas* (ehn koh mee EHN dahs), or the right to demand taxes or labor from Native Americans living on the land.

In the West Indies, the Spanish learned that the best profits could be made by setting up *plantations,* or large estates farmed by many workers. Indians were forced to work on the plantations. They grew sugar cane and tobacco, which plantation owners sent to Spain. Sugar cane was especially valuable because it could be made into sugar, molasses, and rum.

When the Spanish found gold and silver in Peru and Mexico, they forced Native Americans to work the mines. Spanish soldiers marched Indians hundreds of miles from their homes. In the mines, Indians were forced to dig deep, narrow underground tunnels. They worked 12 hours a day, hacking out the rich ore.

**Death from disease.** Thousands of Native Americans died from overwork, mine accidents, and horrible conditions in the mines. European diseases killed millions more. As you have read, Native Americans had no resistance to European diseases. Smallpox, measles, and typhoid wiped out entire towns. (See the graph on page 81.)

Often, there were too few people left in a village to bury those who had died. One Aztec wrote that in village after village, people "could not walk. They only lay in their resting places and beds. They could not move. They could not stir."

**Bartolomé de Las Casas.** Spanish missionaries were concerned about the cruel treatment and high death rate among the Indians. One priest, Bartolomé de Las Casas (day lahs KAH sahs), worked hard to improve conditions for them.

As a young man, Las Casas visited Cuba, Puerto Rico, and other Spanish colonies. Everywhere, he saw Indians dying of hunger, disease, and mistreatment. Horrified, Las Casas returned to Spain and asked the king for laws to protect the Indians.

Spain looked on the Indians as loyal subjects. So in 1544, it passed laws to protect them. The laws said that Native Americans could not be made slaves and allowed them to own cattle and

Spain forced Native Americans to work long hours in gold and silver mines. This painting, done around 1584, shows a silver mine and processing plant in Potosí, Peru. For a time, Potosí was the largest city in the New World because of its rich silver mine.

grow crops. The new laws helped a little but did not end the disease or the mistreatment.

## Slaves From Africa

Las Casas made another suggestion to help the Indians. He advised the Spanish to replace Indians with slaves from Africa. Africans, he said, did not suffer from European diseases as Indians did. Also, many Africans were farmers in their own lands. So they already had useful farming skills.

Spanish colonists agreed with Las Casas. They needed workers for their plantations. Bringing in African slaves seemed like a good way to replace the Indians who were dying off in such large numbers. Europeans had been taking slaves in Africa since the 1460s. Soon, ships were bringing thousands of African men, women, and children to be sold as slaves in the New World.

Before he died, Las Casas regretted his suggestion. He saw that African slaves suffered as much as the Indians. By that time, however, the plantation system had taken hold. In the years ahead, the African slave trade grew. Like the Spanish, other European colonists set up plantations in the New World and brought in African slaves to make them profitable.

## Spanish Culture in the New World

By the mid-1500s, the Spanish had firmly planted their culture in the Americas. They brought with them their language, laws, religion, and learning.

Native Americans also influenced the culture of New Spain. They introduced colonists to new foods, including corn, tomatoes, chocolate, and potatoes. The Spanish wore Indian clothing such as the poncho, a coatlike blanket with a

Historians use graphs to show trends, or developments over time. Graphs are a way of showing *statistics,* or facts in number form. The most commonly used kind of graph is a *line graph.* Other kinds are circle and bar graphs.

A line graph has a grid that is made up of horizontal and vertical lines. A *horizontal axis* runs across the bottom of the grid. A *vertical axis* runs up and down one side of the grid. Information is put on the grid with dots. The dots are then connected to make a *curve.* The curve shows changes taking place over a period of time.

The curve on a line graph shows a trend. If the curve goes up, the graph is showing an upward trend. If the curve goes down, the graph is showing a downward trend. On some line graphs, you might see both upward and downward trends.

Use the steps below to read the line graph at right.

1. **Identify the type of information shown on the line graph.** Most graphs have a title, date, and source. The title tells you what the subject is. The date tells you what time period is covered. The source tells you where the information was found. (a) What is the title of the graph? (b) What time period does the graph cover? (c) What is the source of the graph?

2. **Study the labels on the graph.** Both the horizontal axis and the vertical axis have labels. (a) What do the numbers on the horizontal axis show? (b) What do the numbers on the vertical axis show?

3. **Practice reading the line graph.** The dates on the horizontal axis are spaced evenly. The numbers on the vertical axis are also spaced evenly apart and usually begin at zero. A line graph may show numbers in thou-

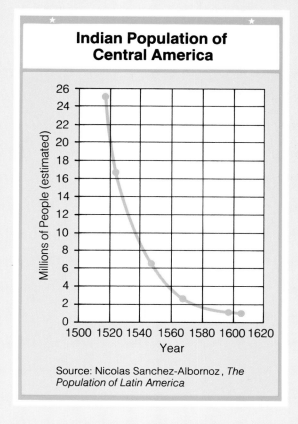

**Indian Population of Central America**

Source: Nicolas Sanchez-Albornoz, *The Population of Latin America*

sands or millions. (a) About how many Native Americans lived in Central America in 1520? (b) About how many lived there in 1540? in 1600? (c) During which period did the population fall the most?

4. **Draw conclusions from the information shown on the graph.** Use the line graph and your reading in this chapter to answer the following questions. (a) In your own words, describe what happened to the population of Native Americans living in Central America between 1520 and 1600. (b) Why did the Indian population in Central America decline so rapidly? (c) What effect do you think the death of so many people might have had on those who survived?

The most famous poet of New Spain was Juana Inés de la Cruz. Born in 1651, she was a brilliant child who could read by age 3. When she was 14, she begged to be allowed to study at the University of Mexico like the men. But she was refused.

Juana Inés became lady-in-waiting to the wife of the viceroy. After a short time, however, she decided to become a nun so that she could go on with her studies in the peace of the convent. As Sor Juana, or Sister Juana, she read widely and learned several languages. She wrote many poems and plays and published essays on science, music, and mathematics.

Sor Juana became well known for her brilliant mind. Educated men and women pleaded for the right to talk to her at the convent. However, some people envied her success. They criticized her for seeking knowledge instead of doing good works. In 1693, Sor Juana sold her library

and went out to care for the sick. A great plague swept Mexico a few years later. While helping victims of the plague, she herself became ill and died.

★ How did Sor Juana contribute to the arts in America?

hole in the middle for the head. Indian words such as canoe, tobacco, and hurricane came into Spanish and English. The word hurricane, for example, came from the Tainos of Puerto Rico. To the Tainos, Juracan was a god who acted like a devil.

The Spanish built their cities on the foundations of Aztec and Inca cities. Mexico City, capital of New Spain, rose on the site of Tenochtitlan. Like the Aztec city, the new Spanish capital had paved and lighted streets, a police department, and a public water system.

Spanish settlers built libraries, theaters, and fine churches. Indian artists decorated Christian churches with paintings of their harvests and other traditions. Printing presses turned out the first European books published in the New World.* By 1551, Spanish colonists had opened universities in the West Indies, Mexico, Ecuador, and Peru. People like Sor Juana (see the picture above) were contributing to the arts in America.

Missionaries and explorers spread Spanish culture across the New World. They trekked as far north as Oregon and as far south as the tip of South America. In fact, Spanish colonies in the Americas became the basis for the

---

*Indians produced books before the Spanish arrived. But most of these were burned by Spanish soldiers and priests.

independent nations of Latin America today.

The Spanish also built settlements in the American Southwest. Spanish settlers were used to its dry climate because it was similar to the climate of Spain. They brought the first horses, cattle, pigs, goats, and chickens to the Southwest. And they planted many kinds of fruit and nut trees.

In 1565, the Spanish built a presidio at St. Augustine, Florida. St. Augustine is the oldest European settlement in the United States.

Place names in the United States show the widespread influence of Spanish culture. States such as Nevada, Colorado, and Montana have Spanish names. Cities in the Southwest such as Los Angeles, El Paso, Santa Fe, San Carlos, and San Antonio were first settled by Spanish missionaries.

## SECTION REVIEW

1. **Locate:** New Spain, Peru, Mexico City, Cuba, Puerto Rico, St. Augustine.
2. **Define:** viceroy, pueblo, presidio, mission, peninsular, creole, mestizo, encomienda, plantation.
3. What were the Laws of the Indies?
4. How did Bartolomé de Las Casas try to help Native Americans?
5. **What Do You Think?** How do you think slavery affected the economy of Spanish colonies?

# 2 French and Dutch Colonies

### Read to Learn

★ What regions did the French explore?
★ Who set up New Netherland?
★ How did Europeans treat the Indians in North America?
★ What do these words mean: coureur de bois?

Spain's rich gold and silver mines in Mexico and Peru made it the envy of other European nations. France, England, Sweden, and the Netherlands sent their own explorers to hunt for treasures in the New World. Although they found no treasure, they all planted colonies in North America.

## The First French Settlements

In the early 1500s, French fishermen discovered rich fishing grounds off the coast of Newfoundland. Each summer, fishermen sailed across the Atlantic and caught tons of cod. They dried the fish on shore before sailing back to France with their catch.

The fishermen did not settle in Newfoundland. But they did trade with Native Americans. They exchanged knives, kettles, and cloth for furs, especially beaver skins. These furs sold for high prices in Europe.

**Samuel de Champlain.** In the early 1600s, France took steps to encourage the fur trade. In 1603, it sent Samuel de Champlain (sham PLAYN) to North America. He brought settlers to the coast of Maine. The climate was so harsh that the settlers soon left. A year later, Champlain set up a colony at Port Royal, Nova Scotia.

In 1608, Champlain followed Cartier's route up the St. Lawrence. He built a trading post under a rocky cliff above the river. The settlement was called Quebec (kwee BEHK). It quickly grew into the center of a thriving fur trade.

**Fur trappers and traders.** Most French colonists were trappers and traders. Because they lived in the woods, they became known as *coureurs* *de bois* (koo RUHR duh BWAH), or runners of the woods.

Coureurs de bois learned how to trap and survive in the woods from Native Americans. Many married Indian women. Indians showed the French how to build and use canoes. In the fall, Indians and trappers paddled up the St. Lawrence to winter trapping grounds. The trip was difficult because they had to carry canoes around rapids.

Indians taught trappers how to make snowshoes. Wearing snowshoes, they climbed through deep snow to find their traps. Trappers slept in wigwams, or Indian houses made of poles and birchbark.

When the snows melted, trappers loaded furs into their canoes for the trip down the St. Lawrence. At the French settlements, they traded the furs for blankets, kettles, and other goods they would use the next winter.

## A Route to the West

The St. Lawrence River was very important to the French in North America. The Appalachian Mountains blocked most routes inland from the Atlantic. However, the St. Lawrence led deep into the heart of America. Led by Indian guides, French trappers and traders explored the St. Lawrence to the Great Lakes.

French Catholic missionaries often traveled with the fur traders. The missionaries were determined to make Native Americans accept Christianity. They set up missions, drew maps, and wrote about the newly explored lands. In 1673, Father Jacques Marquette (mahr KEHT), a priest, and Louis Joliet (JOH lee eht), a fur trader, set out in canoes across Lake Michigan. With the help of Indian guides, they explored south and west until they reached the Mississippi River. They were excited by this discovery, hoping at last to have found a passage to Asia.

After paddling over 700 miles (1,100 km), Marquette and Joliet realized that the Mississippi emptied into the Gulf of Mexico, not into the Pacific. Disappointed, they returned north before they reached the Gulf. Their journey was important, however, because it opened the way for other explorers.

In 1682, Robert La Salle (lah SAHL) explored the Mississippi down to the Gulf of Mexico. La Salle boldly claimed the entire Mississippi Valley for France. He named the region *Louisiana* for the French king, Louis XIV.

To keep Spain and England out of Louisiana, the French built forts along the Mississippi. In the north, Antoine Cadillac built Fort Detroit near Lake Erie. In the south, the French built New Orleans at the mouth of the Mississippi. New Orleans soon grew into a busy trading center.

## New France

The French colony of *New France* grew slowly. Aside from trappers and traders, few French settled there. In the 1660s, however, Louis XIV decided to encourage farmers to go to New France.

**An attempt at farming.** The king put a new governor in charge of the colony. In 1665, the governor set sail for New France with 1,000 farmers. To encourage family life, the governor brought many young women to New France. Some were noble. Others came from middle class or peasant families. Most women were single, but they soon found husbands among the settlers. Peasant women were the most popular because they were used to the hard work of farming.

Despite efforts to encourage farming, trappers still outnumbered farmers. People made more money trapping than farming. Also, only nobles owned the land. Because farmers could not own their own land, they either had to work for the nobles directly or else pay them rent.

Like Spain, France ruled its colony strictly. It gave settlers little freedom. Farmers lived under the close watch of French officials. Coureurs de bois, however, enjoyed more freedom because they lived far from French settlements.

**French influence.** As they hunted for fur, the French explored large parts of North America. Following Indian trails, they mapped routes from the Gulf of Mexico to northern Canada. In

---

**MAP SKILL** French explorers trekked across large parts of North America on foot and by canoe. Find the route taken by Marquette and Joliet. About how many miles did they travel along the Mississippi River?

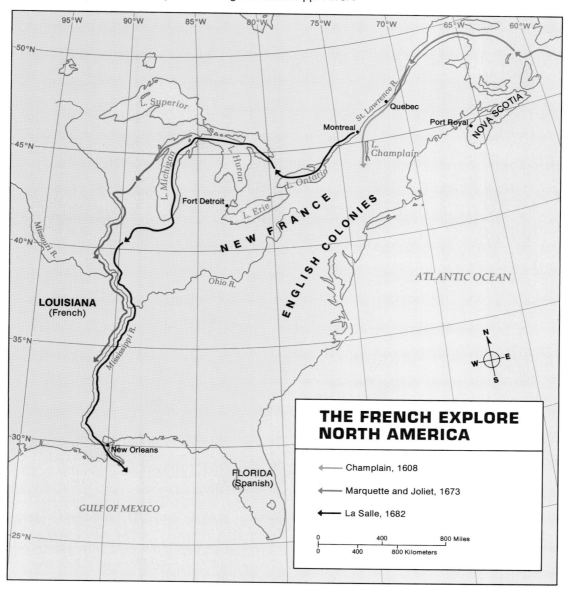

THE FRENCH EXPLORE NORTH AMERICA

⟵ Champlain, 1608

⟵ Marquette and Joliet, 1673

⟵ La Salle, 1682

Father Jacques Marquette and Louis Joliet traveled from Lake Michigan into the Fox River and upstream to Portage, Wisconsin. There, they portaged, or carried, their canoes overland to the Wisconsin River and then paddled downriver to the Mississippi.

1743, French explorers saw the Rocky Mountains for the first time.

The French built towns and trading posts across their large colony. French influence is seen today in place names such as Vermont—green mountain, Terre Haute—high land, and Baton Rouge—red stick.

## New Netherland

In the 1600s, the Dutch set up the colony of *New Netherland* in North America. As you read, the English explorer Henry Hudson made one voyage for the Dutch. In 1609, he found the mouth of a river, today called the Hudson River. The Dutch paid little attention to Hudson's discovery at first. Then in 1626, Peter Minuit (MIHN yoo wiht) led a group of Dutch settlers to North America. In a famous deal, he bought Manhattan Island at the mouth of the Hudson from local Indians.

Minuit called his settlement New Amsterdam. From a tiny group of 30 houses, it grew into a busy port where ships docked from all over the world. The Dutch built trading posts along the Hudson River. The most important one was Fort Orange. Today, Fort Orange is called Albany.

**Fur trading.** The Dutch entered the fur trade. They became fierce rivals of the French and their Indian allies, the Algonquins (al GAHN kwihnz). The Dutch made friends with the Iroquois, longtime rivals of the Algonquins. They gave guns to the Iroquois to fight the Algonquins. With Iroquois help, the Dutch brought furs down the Hudson to New Amsterdam. The French and Algonquins fought back, however. For many years, fighting raged among Europeans and their Indian allies.

**New Sweden is taken over.** About 1640, Swedish settlers arrived in North America. They set up the colony of *New Sweden* along the Delaware River. Swedes built a town where Wilmington stands today. Some Dutch settlers helped their Swedish neighbors, but most Dutch resented the nearby Swedish colony. Fighting broke out between the colonists. In 1655, the Dutch took over New Sweden.

**Dutch influence.** As you will read, England conquered New Netherland in 1664 and made it an English colony. Still, many Dutch customs survived. The Dutch introduced Saint Nicholas to the New World. Every year on the saint's birthday, children put out their shoes to be filled with presents. Later, "Saint Nick" became Santa Claus, and the custom of giving gifts was moved to Christmas Eve.

Many Dutch words entered the English language. A Dutch master was a "boss." The people of New Amsterdam sailed in "yachts." Dutch children munched on "cookies" and "crullers" and listened to ghost stories about "spooks."

## Newcomers and Native Americans

In North America, as in New Spain, European diseases killed thousands of Native Americans. Indians told one Dutch explorer that their people were "melted down" by disease. "Before the smallpox broke out among them," the explorer said, "they were ten times as numerous as they now are."

Rivalry between French and Dutch fur traders also affected the Indians. Each group encouraged its Indian allies to attack the other. Besides, the scramble for fur led to overtrapping. By 1640, beavers had almost been wiped out in the Iroquois lands of upstate New York.

The arrival of European settlers affected Native Americans in other

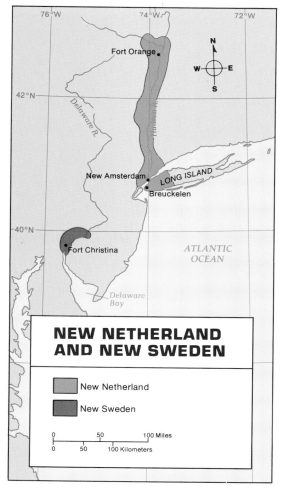

**MAP SKILL** The Netherlands and Sweden both claimed lands in North America. The Dutch settlement at Breuckelen was later called Brooklyn. What is the latitude and longitude of Breuckelen?

### NEW NETHERLAND AND NEW SWEDEN

- New Netherland
- New Sweden

When the Dutch settled the southern tip of Manhattan Island, they called their settlement New Amsterdam. This picture shows New Amsterdam about 1655. Notice the windmill, which produced energy to grind corn.

ways. Missionaries tried to convert Indians to Christianity. Indians gave up hunting with bows and arrows in favor of muskets and gunpowder bought from Europeans. Alcohol sold by European traders had a terrible effect on Indian life.

The French, Dutch, and English influenced fewer Indians than the Spanish because there were fewer Indians where they settled. However, they all seized Indian lands. And settlers from all three nations enslaved Indians and sold them to plantations in the West Indies.

## SECTION REVIEW

1. **Locate:** Nova Scotia, St. Lawrence River, Quebec, Great Lakes, Gulf of Mexico, New France, Hudson River, New Amsterdam, New Netherland, Fort Orange, New Sweden.

2. **Define:** coureur de bois.

3. How did most French colonists make a living?

4. Why did the Dutch become allies of the Iroquois?

5. **What Do You Think?** Why do you think Indians came to see European settlers as invaders?

# 3 English Settlers in Virginia

**Read to Learn**

★ Why is Roanoke known as the "lost colony"?

★ What problems did the Jamestown Colony face?

★ How did life improve for the colonists by the 1620s?

★ What do these words mean: charter, joint stock company, capital, burgess, representative government, stockade?

In the early 1500s, England had little interest in setting up colonies in North America. English explorers searched for a northwest passage and raided Spanish treasure ships. By the late 1500s, however, a few people began to dream of planting colonies.

## The Lost Colony of Roanoke

In 1585, Sir Walter Raleigh raised enough money to send seven English ships to America. The ships reached Roanoke (ROH uh nohk) Island off the coast of North Carolina, but the colonists did not stay in America. In 1587, John White, an artist who had sailed on the first voyage, returned to Roanoke to try again to build a colony. Among the settlers with him were his daughter, Ellinor Dare, and her husband. In Roanoke, Ellinor Dare gave birth to the first English child born in North America, Virginia Dare.

When supplies ran low, White returned to England. But 117 settlers, including his daughter and granddaughter, stayed behind. Before he left, White told the settlers to leave a message carved on a tree if they moved to another place. If they were attacked, they were to carve a cross.

Because of war between England and Spain, White was unable to return to Roanoke until 1590. As White rowed to shore, a sailor played English songs on a trumpet to let the settlers know they were coming. No one answered.

On shore, White found books and rusty armor scattered about the fort the colonists had built. He thought that Indians had dug these up after the colonists left. Then he saw carved on a tree the letters C R O A T O A N—but no cross. On his earlier voyage, White had visited Croatoan Island. The Indians there had been friendly. Bad weather kept White from sailing to the island to look for his family and the settlers. He returned to England without ever finding them.

To this day, no one knows what happened to the "lost colony" of Roanoke. Did they join the Croatoans? Did they starve? Or were they killed by other Indians whose chief had been murdered by the English? The failure of Roanoke and the cost of setting up a colony discouraged other settlements for a time. In the 1600s, however, the English found new ways to raise money to set up colonies in the New World.

## The Jamestown Colony

In 1606, the *Virginia Company* of London received a charter from King James I. A *charter* is a legal document giving certain rights to a person or

In 1590, John White painted this map of Roanoke Island, located off the coast of North Carolina. On earlier trips, White painted scenes of Indian life as well as plants and animals of the New World.

company. The charter gave the company the right to colonize the land between the Potomac River and North Carolina. The land was called Virginia. The charter gave colonists the same rights as people in England.

**Financing the colony.** The Virginia Company was a *joint stock company,* a private trading company that sold shares to investors. For years, merchants had used joint stock companies to finance trading voyages. In a joint stock company, a group of merchants pooled their funds to form a company. Each merchant got shares of stock for the money he put in.

When the company raised enough *capital,* or money for investment, it outfitted ships for a trading voyage. If ships returned safely, the cargoes were sold. Each investor then received a share of the profits.

The Virginia Company financed, or paid for, the first successful English colony. Investors in the company hoped that colonists would find gold mines like those in New Spain.

**Early problems.** The Virginia Company sent its first group of colonists across the Atlantic in 1607. The colonists sailed their three small ships into Chesapeake Bay and up a river they called the James. After landing in a wooded area, they began to build homes. They called their settlement *Jamestown,* after King James I. From the start, they ran into problems. The land was swampy. Mosquitoes were everywhere, and the drinking water was bad. Before long, many colonists died from diseases.

Governing the colony was also a problem. The London merchants were supposed to make laws for the colony. Because the merchants were far away, they chose a council of 13 men to rule the colony. But members of the council quarreled with each other. As a result, little was done to make the colony strong. Colonists spent their days hunting for gold instead of planting crops.

**Captain John Smith.** The Jamestown Colony almost failed that first year. It was saved from disaster by Captain John Smith. Smith, the son of a farmer, had already lived through many adventures in Europe before sailing to America. He grew disgusted with the Jamestown colonists. "No talk, no hope, nor work," he complained. People only wanted to "dig gold, wash gold, refine gold, load gold." But no one found gold, and the colony was running out of food.

Smith then took matters into his own hands. He visited nearby Indian villages to trade for food. Powhatan, a powerful chief who was angry with the English, took Smith prisoner and ordered him put to death. According to Smith, Powhatan's 10-year-old daughter, Pocahontas (poh kuh HAHN tuhs), begged her father to spare him. Powhatan agreed and even sold corn to Smith to feed the hungry colonists at Jamestown.

Because of his success with the Indians, the council put Smith in charge of the colony. Smith told people that they would only get food if they worked. Life in the colony improved when colonists began planting crops. But in 1609, Smith was injured in an accident. After he returned to England, the colony again fell on hard times.

## The Starving Time

The Virginia Company sent more settlers to Jamestown, but most died from disease and starvation. Of 900 settlers who arrived between 1606 and 1609, only 150 survived. During the winter of 1609–1610, these survivors faced "the starving time." They ran out of food and were forced to live on "dogs, cats, snakes, toadstools, horsehides, and what not." By spring, only 60 were still alive.

When it learned of the tragedy, the Virginia Company put a military governor in charge of the colony. The governor had power to make any laws he felt were needed.

Colonists complained that military rule was too strict. One settler was executed for killing a chicken without permission. Another, who stole a few cups of oatmeal, was chained to a tree until he starved to death. Despite military rule, Jamestown remained in trouble. Investors in the Virginia Company feared that they would never make a profit.

## Profits From Tobacco

Several events helped the colony survive and even prosper. First, colonists began to grow tobacco. Europeans learned about tobacco and pipe smoking from Native Americans. One colonist, John Rolfe, learned from the Indians that the Virginia soil was excellent for growing tobacco. Rolfe developed a blend of tobaccos that became popular in Europe.

At first, tobacco helped the young colony prosper, especially when the demand for tobacco grew in Europe. Settlers cleared new land outside Jamestown. For the first time, ships of the Virginia Company returned to England filled with profitable cargoes. But later on, planters produced too much tobacco, and prices fell.

Growing tobacco was hard work. Settlers tried to make Indians work the tobacco plantations. When Indians ran off into the forests, planters looked for other workers. In 1619, a Dutch ship arrived in Jamestown with 20 Africans on board. At least 3 of the Africans were women. The Dutch had seized these men and women in Africa to sell as servants or slaves.

The first Africans in Virginia may have worked as servants and earned their freedom. However, by the late 1600s, Virginia planters had come to depend on a cruel system of slave labor to produce their crops. The system lasted for over 200 years.

*Ætatis suæ 21. Aº 1616.*

AMERICANS WHO DARED

### Pocahontas

Pocahontas was the daughter of Powhatan, an Indian leader in Virginia. Pocahontas was her nickname, meaning "playful one." Her real name was Matoaka. Captain John Smith said that she not only saved his life but also saved the Jamestown Colony from "death and famine." In 1614, Pocahontas married John Rolfe, a planter. Soon after, she visited England. An artist painted this portrait of her dressed like an upper class English woman. Sadly, Pocahontas died in England just before she was to sail home.

## Representative Government

The second event that helped Virginia was a new form of government. In 1619, the Virginia Company sent a governor to the colony with orders to consult settlers on important matters. Settlers who owned land were allowed to elect *burgesses,* or representatives. The burgesses met in an assembly called the *House of Burgesses.* Together with the governor, they made laws for the colony.

The House of Burgesses brought representative government to the English colonies. A *representative government* is one in which voters elect representatives to make laws for them. Although only wealthy men who were landowners could vote, the idea grew up that settlers had a say in how they were governed.

The idea of representative government was deeply rooted in English history. In 1215, English nobles forced King John to sign the *Magna Carta,* or Great Charter. This document gave nobles certain rights. It said that the king could not raise new taxes without first consulting the Great Council made up of nobles and church leaders. Most important, it showed that the king had to obey the law.

Gradually, the rights won by nobles were given to other English people. The Great Council grew into Parliament, a representative assembly. By the 1600s, Parliament was divided into the House of Lords, made up of nobles, and the House of Commons. Members of the House of Commons were elected to office. Only a few wealthy men had the right to vote. Still, English people firmly believed that the ruler must consult Parliament on money matters and obey the law.

## Women in Virginia

The third event that helped the colony was the arrival of women. Most early settlers in Jamestown were men. The first English women in Jamestown were Anne Forest, who came with her husband, and Anne Burras, her young maid. They were on board a supply ship that arrived in 1608. A small number of women lived in the colony during "the starving time."

In 1619, the Virginia Company decided to send 100 women to Virginia to "make the men more settled." The women quickly found husbands among the settlers. The Virginia Company profited from the marriages because it charged each man who found a wife 150 pounds of tobacco.

Life in Virginia was hard. Women had to make everything from scratch—food, clothing, even medicines. Still, after women arrived, settlers took hope that the colony would survive.

## Friend or Enemy

The Indians who lived around Jamestown were farmers. At first, they did not see the English as a threat. In fact, they often felt sorry for the half-starved white settlers who did not know how to grow corn or trap animals.

The English, on the other hand, were suspicious of the Indians. They called the Indians heathens, or non-Christians. They looked down on Indian customs, which were so different from their own. Because they feared attacks by the Indians, settlers built their homes close together. They surrounded their homes with a *stockade,* a high fence made of wooden posts.

As more colonists arrived, they needed land. Because growing tobacco wore out the soil quickly, colonists kept clearing new land. More and more settlements sprang up in Virginia. The Indians soon began to see the colonists as invaders who were taking over their land and giving it out to white settlers from across the Atlantic. They tried without success to negotiate with white officials.

In 1622, Indians attacked and killed about 350 settlers in Virginia. The English, in turn, killed or enslaved the Indians. In the 1600s, the English made many treaties with the Indians in which they agreed to respect Indian land. But in the end, the English

Jamestown settlers welcomed the arrival of supply ships such as this one. Without supplies from England, settlers would have suffered even worse hardships than they did. The two women at left may have been Anne Forest and Anne Burras, who reached Jamestown in 1608.

ignored these treaties. So the fighting continued. More and more Indians were either killed or pushed inland.

SECTION REVIEW

1. **Locate:** Roanoke, Chesapeake Bay, Jamestown.
2. **Define:** charter, joint stock company, capital, burgess, representative government, stockade.

3. (a) List three problems the Jamestown colonists faced. (b) What product helped Jamestown prosper?
4. How was representative government set up in Virginia?
5. How did Native Americans help the Jamestown colonists?
6. **What Do You Think?** How do you think the arrival of women helped the Jamestown Colony survive?

# 4 The Pilgrims at Plymouth

**Read to Learn**
★ Who were the Pilgrims?
★ What did the Mayflower Compact say?
★ How did the Pilgrims survive their first winter?

In 1620, a year after the House of Burgesses was set up in Virginia, another band of settlers sailed to America. They were known as Separatists because they wanted to set up their own church separate from the Church of England. Later, the Separatists were called *Pilgrims*.

## Search for Religious Freedom

The Pilgrims were looking for a place where they could live and worship in their own way. Queen Elizabeth and her successor, King James I, disliked any group that refused to follow

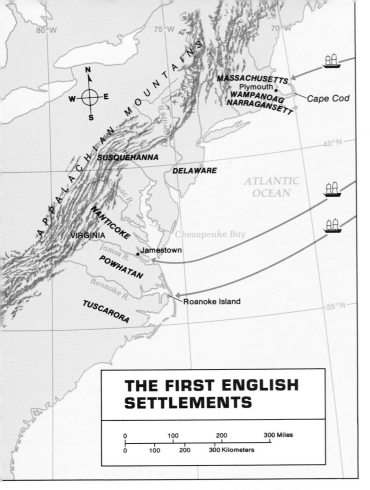

## THE FIRST ENGLISH SETTLEMENTS

```
0        100        200        300 Miles
0    100    200    300 Kilometers
```

**MAP SKILL** In the early 1600s, English settlers planted colonies in Roanoke, Jamestown, and Plymouth. The colony at Roanoke ended in failure. Which of these three colonies was farthest north? What Indians lived near the Jamestown colonists?

the official religion, the Church of England. King James vowed to "harry them [the Pilgrims] out of the land." As a result, the Pilgrims were persecuted, or attacked, for their beliefs.

**From England to Leyden.** In the early 1600s, the Pilgrims left England for Leyden, a city in the Netherlands. The Dutch allowed the newcomers to worship freely. But the Pilgrims did not feel at home in Leyden. They were farmers and did not like city life. They worried, too, because their children were growing up speaking Dutch, not English.

The Pilgrims and some other English people got a charter to set up a colony in Virginia. In September 1620, 101 men, women, and children set sail for Virginia. On the voyage, a storm blew their small, leaky ship, the *Mayflower,* off course. They landed far north of Virginia, at a spot near Cape Cod.

**The Mayflower Compact.** The Pilgrims explored the coast and decided to stay where they were instead of sailing south to Virginia. But their charter did not apply to a colony outside Virginia. So before they went ashore, they drew up an agreement on how they would govern their colony.

Forty-one Pilgrims signed the *Mayflower Compact.* In it, they agreed to consult each other about laws for the colony and promised to work together to make the colony succeed.

The Mayflower Compact began:

> We, whose names are underwritten . . . Having undertaken for the Glory of God, and Advancement of the Christian Faith . . . a Voyage to plant the first colony in the northern parts of Virginia . . . do enact, constitute, and frame, such just and equal Laws . . . as shall be thought most meet [fitting] and convenient for the general Good of the Colony.

Later, when the colony grew too large for everyone to consult together, the settlers chose representatives to an assembly. The assembly made laws for the colony.

## Hard Times—and Success

The Pilgrims called their settlement *Plymouth* because they had sailed from Plymouth, England. When they landed in December, it was too late to plant crops. So they had to live off wild game and whatever food they had left from the voyage.

The Pilgrims spent their first winter in sod houses quickly thrown together. William Bradford, an early governor of Plymouth, wrote that some Pilgrims lived in caves "half a pit and half a tent of earth supported by branches . . . nasty, dank and cold."

In July 1620, the Pilgrims left Holland on the first stage of their voyage to the New World. This painting shows them at prayer as their ship sets sail. Religious faith made the Pilgrims confident of success. "Their condition was not ordinary," wrote one. "Their ends were good and honorable; their calling lawful and urgent, and therefore they might expect the blessing of God."

Bradford described the hardships of that winter. The Pilgrims "had no friends to welcome them, nor inns to entertain or refresh their weatherbeaten bodies," he wrote. "If they looked behind them, there was the mighty ocean which they had passed. . . .What could now sustain them, but the Spirit of God and His grace?"

The Pilgrims had a strong religious faith. They believed that it was the will of God for them to stay in Plymouth. By the spring, almost half the settlers had died of disease or starvation. The survivors refused to give up. They cleared land and planted crops.

Samoset, a Pemaquid Indian from Maine, helped the Pilgrims. He had learned some English a few years before from explorers sailing along the coast. Samoset and other Indians taught the Pilgrims to plant corn and trap animals for furs.

Samoset brought Squanto, a Wampanoag who spoke English, to the Pilgrims. Squanto gave the Pilgrims good advice on planting crops. He showed them how to catch eels from nearby rivers. By treading water, he stirred up eels from the river bottom and then snatched them up with his hands.

In the fall, the Pilgrims had a good harvest. The colony was saved! Because they believed that God gave them this harvest, they set aside a day for giving thanks to God. In the years ahead, the Pilgrims celebrated the end of the harvest with a day of thanksgiving. Americans today celebrate *Thanksgiving* as a national holiday.

## SECTION REVIEW

1. **Locate:** Cape Cod, Plymouth.
2. (a) Why did the Pilgrims leave England for Leyden? (b) Why did they leave Leyden for the New World?
3. Why did the Pilgrims write the Mayflower Compact?
4. **What Do You Think?** Do you think the Pilgrims could have survived without the help of the Indians? Explain.

# Chapter 4 Review

★ **Summary** ★

Spain was the first European nation to build an empire in the Americas. In the 1500s, Spain set up a government that kept its colonies under firm control. A rich culture based on Spanish and Indian traditions grew up in New Spain.

French, Dutch, and Swedish settlers also planted colonies in North America. French settlers were mostly trappers and traders. The Dutch settled along the Hudson River and competed with the French and Indians for control of the rich fur trade.

The first permanent English colony was set up at Jamestown, Virginia. After a desperate struggle to survive, the colony began to prosper. To the north, the Pilgrims built the Plymouth Colony. They, too, suffered through hard times but were helped by friendly Indians.

★ **Reviewing the Facts** ★

**Key Terms.** Match each term in Column 1 with the correct definition in Column 2.

**Column 1**
1. viceroy
2. mestizo
3. coureur de bois
4. charter
5. capital

**Column 2**
a. money for reinvestment
b. runner of the forest
c. document giving certain rights to a person or company
d. person of mixed Indian and Spanish background
e. royal official who rules a colony in the name of a king or queen

**Key People, Events, and Ideas.** Identify each of the following.

1. Bartolomé de Las Casas
2. Samuel de Champlain
3. Jacques Marquette
4. Louis Joliet
5. Robert La Salle
6. Peter Minuit
7. Virginia Company
8. John Smith
9. Pocahontas
10. John Rolfe
11. House of Burgesses
12. Magna Carta
13. Pilgrims
14. Mayflower Compact
15. Squanto

★ **Chapter Checkup** ★

1. Why did the Spanish build missions?
2. (a) List the four social classes in New Spain. (b) How did each earn a living?
3. Describe three things the coureurs de bois learned from the Indians.
4. Why did settlers in New France prefer trapping to farming?
5. In what part of North America did the Dutch settle?
6. How did the English finance the Jamestown Colony?
7. (a) Why did the Indians feel sorry for the first Jamestown settlers? (b) How did their view change?
8. Why did the Pilgrims decide to stay in Plymouth despite the hard times they suffered?

## ★ Thinking About History ★

1. **Relating past to present.** Describe one custom or idea that Americans have inherited from each of the following: (a) Spanish; (b) French; (c) Dutch; (d) English; (e) Indians.

2. **Defending a position.** Bartolomé de Las Casas did more harm than good when he tried to help Native Americans. Defend or criticize this statement.

3. **Learning about citizenship.** Review the descriptions of the governments of New Spain and Virginia. (a) In which colony did people have more say over their government? (b) Why?

4. **Comparing.** Compare the early years of settlers in Jamestown and Plymouth. (a) How were their experiences similar? (b) How were they different?

5. **Analyzing a quotation.** Review the quotation from the Mayflower Compact on page 94. (a) Why did the Pilgrims undertake their voyage? (b) What kinds of laws did they plan to make for the Plymouth Colony?

## ★ Using Your Skills ★

1. **Map reading.** Study the map on page 78. (a) What lands did Spain rule? (b) What lands did Portugal rule? (c) Which country ruled lands east of the Line of Demarcation?

2. **Map reading.** Study the map on page 85. (a) Which explorer or explorers traveled along the Mississippi River? (b) Which French explorer or explorers sailed up the St. Lawrence River first? (c) Using this map and your reading in this chapter, why do you think French explorers traveled where they did?

3. **Making a generalization.** Review the description of relations between Native Americans and Europeans on pages 79, 84, and 87. (a) Make a generalization about the way Europeans behaved toward Native Americans. (b) List three facts to support your generalization.

4. **Outlining.** Review the outlining steps you learned on page 31. Then outline the section "French and Dutch Colonies" on pages 83–88.

## ★ More to Do ★

1. **Creating a map.** On a blank map of North and South America, use different colors to show what lands each of the following countries claimed around 1650: Spain, Portugal, France, the Netherlands, Sweden, and England. Label the main cities or towns in each colony.

2. **Writing a diary.** Write several diary entries of a woman who sailed to Jamestown in 1619. Include her trip across the Atlantic and her first years in Jamestown.

3. **Interviewing.** Imagine that you are a reporter who is interviewing either Squanto or Samoset. Do background research to find out where he came from and what he thought of the Pilgrims. Write up your interview or give it as an oral report.

4. **Exploring local history.** Find out about any monuments in your local area that honor European explorers. Prepare a brochure encouraging people to visit these monuments.

# English Colonies Take Root (1630–1750)

## Chapter Outline

**1** New England Colonies
**2** Middle Colonies
**3** Southern Colonies
**4** Governing the Colonies
Readings, page 477

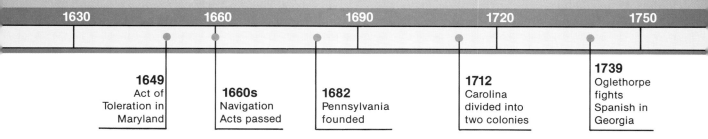

| 1630 | 1660 | 1690 | 1720 | 1750 |
|------|------|------|------|------|

**1649**
Act of
Toleration in
Maryland

**1660s**
Navigation
Acts passed

**1682**
Pennsylvania
founded

**1712**
Carolina
divided into
two colonies

**1739**
Oglethorpe
fights
Spanish in
Georgia

## About This Chapter

Young William Penn spurred his horse toward London. Even though it was night, he rode fast because he carried an important message for King Charles II. At dawn, Penn reached the king's palace. He insisted on delivering his message to the sleepy king. The message came from Penn's father, Sir William, an admiral in the royal navy.

Penn's meeting with the king lasted only a short time. But years later it helped Penn to have served as a messenger to the king. While a student at Oxford University, Penn joined the Quakers, a religious group that the Church of England hated. Penn was jailed for his beliefs even though he was wellborn and the son of an admiral. To avoid further trouble, Penn decided to move to America.

The king owed Penn's father a lot of money. Instead of asking for the money, Penn asked for a royal charter granting him lands to start a colony in America. The king agreed. As Penn said, "The government at home was glad to be rid of us [the Quakers] at so cheap a rate." In 1682, Penn sailed for America, determined to make his colony a place where Quakers could live in peace.

In this chapter, you will read about the colonies England planted along the Atlantic coast of North America. Slowly, the scattered villages and towns grew into 13 English colonies. Each colony had its own story.

Study the time line above. Was Pennsylvania founded before or after Maryland's Act of Toleration?

The English planted 13 colonies in North America. This painting shows Baltimore, Maryland, which grew into a busy harbor in the 1700s.

# 1 New England Colonies

## Read to Learn

★ Why did the Puritans leave England?
★ How were Massachusetts, Connecticut, and Rhode Island founded?
★ Why did fighting break out between settlers and Indians?
★ What do these words mean: emigrate, democratic government, toleration?

During the 1600s, the English set up 13 colonies along the eastern coast of North America. Although each colony was different, they were grouped together by location. From north to south, they were the New England Colonies, Middle Colonies, and Southern Colonies. The first New England Colony was Plymouth, settled by the Pilgrims in 1620. Within a few years, other settlers braved the dangerous trip across the Atlantic to build homes in America.

## Reasons for Leaving Home

Settlers had many reasons for leaving England. Some, like those who went to Jamestown, wanted to get rich by finding gold. Others hoped to improve their lives by owning land. In England, the oldest son usually inherited his father's land. Younger sons had little hope of having land. The colonies offered such people large amounts of land. They gave little thought to the Indians already living there.

For many settlers, religious reasons were as strong as economic ones. As you have read, the Pilgrims left England because they could not worship as they pleased. Other religious groups soon followed.

**Evil and declining times.** Among these groups were the Puritans. *Puritans* were Protestants who wanted the Church of England to become purer by getting rid of Catholic practices. They opposed organ music and the special clothes worn by priests. Unlike the Pilgrims, the Puritans did not want to separate from the Church of England. But they did want reforms made.

Puritans were a powerful group in England. Many were well-educated and successful merchants or landowners. Because they held seats in Parliament, they could make their views known.

King James I disliked Puritans as much as he did Pilgrims, and he made their lives difficult. After he died in 1625, his son, Charles I, moved even more firmly against the Puritans. When Puritans and their supporters in Parliament fought back, Charles dismissed Parliament. He said that he would rule without it. He threatened Puritans with harsh punishments if they did not obey bishops of the Church of England. Puritan leaders decided that England had fallen on "evil and declining times." So they made plans to *emigrate,* or leave their country and settle elsewhere.

**The Great Migration.** The Puritans got a charter from the king to form the Massachusetts Bay Company. The charter gave land in New England to the company. During the winter of 1629, the Puritans prepared to leave home.

The next year, over 1,000 men, women, and children sailed in 17 ships for the *Massachusetts Bay Colony.* Some joined a small group of Puritans who had already settled in Salem. Many went to Boston, which soon grew into the largest town in the colony. Villages sprang up as people flocked to the new colony. Between 1629 and 1640, more than 20,000 settlers arrived in Massachusetts Bay. The movement became known as the *Great Migration.*

## The Massachusetts Bay Colony

Puritans held strong beliefs about how people should live and govern themselves. They felt they had a mis-

In the 1600s, economic conditions in England forced many farm workers off the land. Homeless farmers poured into the cities. When they could not find jobs, some became beggars. English officials urged poor families like this one to go to the New World.

sion to build a new society in the Massachusetts Bay Colony. The new society was to be based on the laws of God. If they obeyed God's laws, Puritans believed, God would protect them. John Winthrop, a leading Puritan, told the settlers "that we shall be as a city upon a hill. The eyes of all people are upon us."

Winthrop, a well-to-do lawyer, helped organize the new colony. He and other officials of the Massachusetts Bay Company had to decide who could take part in the government of the new colony. Under the company charter, only stockholders had the right to govern. At first, Winthrop and a few others tried to follow this rule. But most settlers were not stockholders.

Before long, Winthrop realized that the colony would run more smoothly if more settlers could take part. As a result, all men who were church members were allowed to vote for a governor and for representatives to an assembly called the *General Court*. In fact, only a limited number of men could vote. Still, the idea of representative government was planted in the Massachusetts Bay Colony.

Winthrop was a practical man who listened to others. He was elected governor of Massachusetts Bay many times. Under his leadership, the colony grew and prospered.

## The Path to Connecticut

As the elected governor, Winthrop believed that he had the right to rule the colony as he thought best. Some Puritans disagreed. Thomas Hooker, a minister, argued that an official like Winthrop might mean well but still govern badly. Hooker wanted laws to limit the governor's power.

Rivalry grew up between Winthrop and Hooker. In 1636, Hooker and about 100 supporters decided to leave the Massachusetts Bay Colony. A handful of Puritans had already moved into the fertile Connecticut River valley. Hook-

**AMERICANS WHO DARED**

### John Winthrop

John Winthrop, first governor of the Massachusetts Bay Colony, was reelected many times between 1630 and 1649. He led 1,000 people to Boston in the first wave of the Great Migration. Winthrop firmly believed that people should act according to Christian principles. As a devout Puritan, he commanded the respect of other colonists.

er and his friends took the same path. They drove their cattle, goats, and pigs along Indian trails that cut through thick forests. At last, they reached the Connecticut River valley. There, they built the town of Hartford. Other colonists soon followed Hooker into Connecticut. They set up many new towns along the river.

In 1639, the settlers wrote rules called the *Fundamental Orders of Connecticut*. The Fundamental Orders set

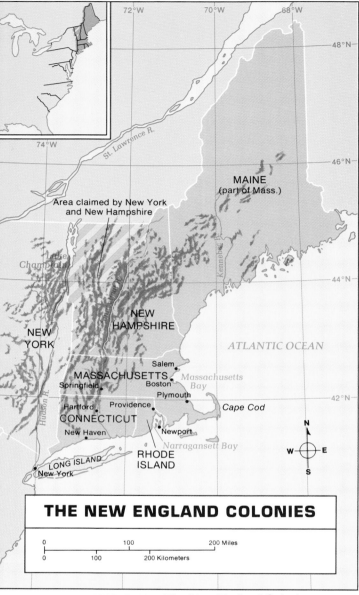

# THE NEW ENGLAND COLONIES

| 0 | 100 | 200 Miles |
| 0 | 100 | 200 Kilometers |

MAP SKILL The New England Colonies were among the first colonies the English set up in America. Name the four New England Colonies. At what latitude is Plymouth?

up a government similar to that of Massachusetts. But the power of the governor was limited. Hooker believed that the people should set limits on the power of the government. Its power, he said, came only from "the free consent

of the people." These two ideas are central to a democratic government. A *democratic government* is one in which the people hold power and exercise it by choosing representatives in free elections.

Connecticut became a separate colony in 1662. That year, the towns along the Connecticut River were joined, and the king gave the colony a royal charter. (See the map at left.)

## Escape to Rhode Island

In the 1630s, other differences grew up among the Puritans in Massachusetts. A young Salem minister, Roger Williams, challenged the governor's authority. Williams was a gentle, friendly man. But his ideas greatly worried Puritan leaders.

**Dangerous ideas.** Williams said that the king of England did not have the right to give land in North America to Puritans or anyone else. The land, he said, belonged to the Indians. English settlers should buy their land from the Indians. Puritan leaders were horrified by Williams' ideas. They saw him as a dangerous troublemaker.

Williams had other ideas that were troubling to Puritan leaders. He said that the business of church and state should be completely separate from each other. He also believed in toleration. *Toleration* means willingness to let others practice their own beliefs. In Massachusetts, Puritans refused to let people with different religious beliefs worship freely. Williams even wanted to allow men who were not church members to vote.

**Flight in winter.** In 1635, leaders of the Massachusetts Bay Colony ordered Williams to return to England. Before Williams could leave, Governor Winthrop took pity on him. He secretly advised Williams to flee. Williams took this advice, escaping in the winter through frozen forests to Narragansett Bay. He stayed with Indians and in the spring bought land from them for a settlement.

In 1644, Williams went to England to get a charter for his colony. At first, the colony was called the Providence Plantations. Later, Providence and other towns became the colony of *Rhode Island*.

**Religious freedom.** In Rhode Island, Williams put his beliefs into practice. He made sure that the church was separate from the state and allowed settlers to worship as they pleased. This drew Catholic and Jewish settlers to Rhode Island. Williams also allowed all white men to vote, even if they were not church members.

## Anne Hutchinson on Trial

Among those who fled to Rhode Island was Anne Hutchinson. Hutchinson and her husband, William, arrived in Boston in 1634. She worked as a midwife, helping to deliver babies. She was herself the mother of 14 children.

Hutchinson was an intelligent and devout churchgoer. Often, she met with friends at her home after church to discuss the minister's sermon. These meetings worried Puritan officials. They believed that only clergymen were qualified to explain God's law. When Hutchinson claimed that many ministers were teaching incorrect beliefs, she was put on trial.

At her trial, Hutchinson answered the questions put to her by Governor Winthrop and other Puritan officials. Winthrop found that she had "a nimble wit and active spirit." Time after time, she showed up the weakness in his arguments. And he could not prove that she had broken any Puritan laws or religious teachings. Finally, after two days of questioning, Hutchinson made a mistake. She said that God had spoken directly to her. To Puritans, this was a terrible error. They believed that God spoke only through the Bible, not to individuals.

In 1638, the General Court sent Hutchinson away from the colony. With her family and supporters, she went to Rhode Island. Later, she moved to the Dutch colony of New Netherland, where she and most of her family were killed by Indians.

## Conflict Over the Land

Massachusetts was the largest colony in New England. It controlled trading and fishing villages along the coast

Anne Hutchinson, shown here, courageously faced her accusers. During her trial, she claimed that she had received "an immediate revelation" from God. Because this claim violated Puritan beliefs, Hutchinson was sent out of the colony along with her husband and 14 children.

Tensions ran high in Salem Village, Massachusetts, in 1692. In the eastern part of the village, commerce was booming. Merchants living there enjoyed economic success and growing political power. But farmers in the western part of the village resented the merchants. They faced hard times and had lost political influence. Historians think that this east-west conflict fueled a terrible panic known as the Salem witch hunt.

The panic broke out when two girls began to suffer strange fits. When coaxed to explain their behavior, the girls accused neighbors of casting spells on them. People were quick to believe that the Devil was at work. Soon, accusations of witchcraft spread like wildfire through all of Salem. Before officials ended the witch hunt 10 months later, at least 200 people were named as witches. Of those put on trial, 20 were hanged.

What role did east-west conflict play in the witch hunt? A map study of Salem Village showed a striking split. Most of the accused witches lived in the eastern part. Most of the accusers lived in the western part. Historians have concluded that the witch hunt was in part a subconscious reaction to east-west conflict. Farmers lashed out against merchants and others in the eastern part by accusing them of witchcraft.

★ What caused east-west conflict in Salem Village?

north of Boston. In 1680, the king of England made these settlements into a separate colony called *New Hampshire.* However, in 1691, Massachusetts absorbed the towns and villages of the smaller Plymouth Colony.

As settlers streamed into the colonies, they took over Indian lands. They argued that Indians had no right to the land because they were not farming it. In fact, most Indians were farmers, even though they did not farm all the land. They also depended on the land for hunting to add meat to their diet.

**Pequot War.** When settlers ignored Indian land claims, fighting broke out. In the 1630s, the English accused the Pequots (PEE kwahts) of killing two traders in the Connecticut Valley. Colonists decided to punish the Pequots. They attacked a Pequot town when most of the men were away and killed hundreds of unarmed men, women, and children.

In the war that followed, most of the Pequots were killed, and the English took over the rich lands of the Connecticut Valley.

**King Philip's War.** In 1675, a Wampanoag leader, Metacom, took a stand against the English who were moving onto Indian lands near Plymouth. Metacom was called King Philip by the English.

In *King Philip's War,* which lasted for 15 months, both sides committed terrible acts. In the end, Metacom was captured and killed. His family and about 1,000 other Indians were sold into slavery in the West Indies. Many Indians were forced to leave their homes and starved to death. As in Connecticut, colonists soon expanded into Indian lands.

This pattern of expansion and war between colonists and Indians was repeated throughout the colonies. And it continued even after the colonies won independence.

═══ SECTION REVIEW ═══

1. **Locate:** Massachusetts, Connecticut, Rhode Island, New Hampshire.
2. **Define:** emigrate, democratic government, toleration.
3. How did Puritans disagree with the Church of England?
4. List one way each of the following differed with the Puritan leaders of Massachusetts Bay: (a) Thomas Hooker; (b) Roger Williams; (c) Anne Hutchinson.
5. **What Do You Think?** Do you think settlers and Indians could have avoided war? Explain.

# 2 Middle Colonies

**Read to Learn**

★ How did England gain New York?
★ What ideas did William Penn have for his colony?
★ What do these words mean: patroon, proprietary colony, royal colony?

South of New England were the Middle Colonies. The Middle Colonies were unlike the other English colonies, which were settled mostly by English people. Many different people settled in the Middle Colonies. Among them were the Dutch and Swedes who lived along the Hudson and Delaware rivers.

## New Netherland Becomes New York

The Dutch colony of New Netherland attracted settlers from many parts of the world. One visitor told of hearing 16 different languages spoken along the busy docks of New Amsterdam.

**Patroons rule the land.** To encourage farming in New Netherland, the Dutch granted huge parcels of land to a few rich families. A single land grant stretched many miles along the Hudson. One grant was the size of Rhode Island. Owners of these manors, or estates, were called *patroons.* In return for land, each patroon agreed to bring over 50 farm families from Europe.

Patroons ruled the lives of settlers on their land. They decided how much land each family would farm and how much rent each must pay. They held their own courts and gave out punishments for any crime committed on their land. Because few farmers wanted to live under the harsh rule of the patroons, the population of New Netherland remained small.

**Peter Stuyvesant.** The Dutch West India Company ran the colony. To improve profits, it gave the governor almost absolute power. One governor, Peter Stuyvesant, was a hard-nosed man who had lost a leg fighting in the West Indies. He believed that New Netherland needed strong rule to survive. So he punished lawbreakers with heavy fines or whippings.

Stuyvesant drove the colony into debt by carrying on many costly wars against the Indians. To pay expenses, he taxed most goods that people bought. When colonists demanded a voice in the government, Stuyvesant told them his authority came "from God and the West India Company, not from the pleasure of a few ignorant subjects."

**The English move in.** In the 1660s, rivalry between England and the Netherlands led to war in Europe. King Charles II of England saw that New Netherland stood between New England and English settlements in Virginia. So in 1664, he sent English warships to New Amsterdam.

Even when the English aimed guns at the city, Stuyvesant swore not to give up. But he had few weapons and little gunpowder. Also, he was so unpopular and had spent so much money fighting Indians that Dutch colonists refused to help him. In the end, he had to surrender without firing a shot.

When King Charles gave New Netherland to his brother, the Duke of York, the colony was renamed *New York* in his honor. For a time, the Duke of York ruled the colony much as the Dutch had. But New Yorkers, especially Puritans who moved to New York from New England, demanded the right to choose an assembly to make laws for the colony. In 1683, the Duke of York finally allowed New York to have its own assembly.

## New Jersey

In 1664, New York stretched as far south as the Delaware River. The Duke of York decided to give part of the colony to two friends, Lord Berkeley and Sir George Carteret. These men set up a proprietary (pruh PRĪ uh tehr ee) colony, called *New Jersey.*

In a *proprietary colony,* the king gave land to one or more people, called proprietors. In return, proprietors gave the king a yearly payment and accepted his authority. Proprietors then divided up the land and rented it to oth-

Peter Stuyvesant was known for his temper and stubbornness. He let no one question his judgment. When one settler criticized him, Stuyvesant replied, "I will make him a foot shorter and send the pieces to Holland."

ers. They made laws for the colony but had to respect the rights people had under English law.

New Jersey occupied the fertile land between the Hudson and Delaware rivers. Like New York, New Jersey was settled by people from many nations. Puritans, French Protestants, Scots, Irish, Swedes, Dutch, and Finns mingled in New Jersey. For a time, the colony was divided into two parts: East Jersey and West Jersey. In 1702, East and West Jersey were joined, and New Jersey became a *royal colony* under the king's control. The colony had a charter that protected religious freedom and an assembly that voted on local matters.

## William Penn's Holy Experiment

Religious freedom was on the mind of William Penn when he founded a colony in 1682. Penn belonged to the Religious Society of Friends, a group organized by George Fox. The group was known as the *Quakers.*

**Religious freedom.** Like the Pilgrims and Puritans, the Quakers were Protestant reformers. But their reforms went further than those of other Protestants. Quakers believed that men and women were equal in God's sight. They saw no need for ministers or priests and refused to pay taxes to the Church of England. They had no use for church ceremonies and felt that it was wrong to wear fancy clothes. Quakers also believed that wars were wrong, and they refused to serve in the army.

In both England and New England, Quakers were arrested, fined, and even executed for their beliefs. As you read at the beginning of this chapter, Penn was jailed for his beliefs. So Penn wanted his colony to protect the religious freedom of Quakers as well as other groups.

Penn named his colony Sylvania, meaning woodlands. But the king changed the name to *Pennsylvania,* or

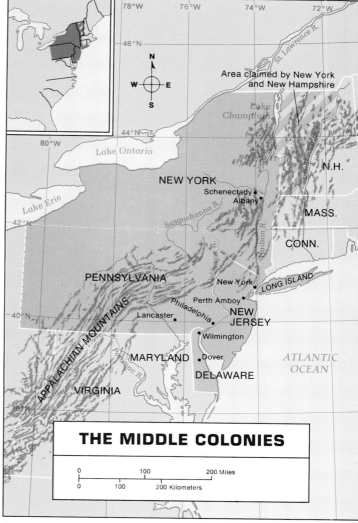

MAP SKILL What are the four Middle Colonies shown on this map? Why do you think these colonies were called the Middle Colonies?

Penn's woodlands, to honor William Penn's father, a well-known admiral.

**The Frame of Government.** Penn wrote the *Frame of Government* to explain how the colony would be run. A governor appointed by Penn and a council of advisers made laws for the colony. A representative assembly accepted or rejected these laws. Later, the assembly won the right to make laws itself. Any white man who owned land or paid taxes had the right to vote.

Penn thought of his colony as a "holy experiment." It was meant to be a model of religious freedom, peace, and Christian living. The Frame of Government allowed freedom of worship for anyone who believed in God. Protestants, Catholics, and Jews went to Pennsylvania to escape persecution.* Penn's beliefs also led him to oppose slavery and act fairly toward Native Americans.

Like Roger Williams in Rhode Island, Penn believed that the land belonged to the Indians. He said that settlers should pay for the land. Native Americans respected Penn for this policy. As a result, the colony enjoyed many years of peace with its Indian neighbors.

Penn advertised for settlers by sending pamphlets all over Europe. Many settlers came from England, Wales, Scotland, and Ireland. Pamphlets were translated into German, French, and Dutch. A large number of German-speaking Protestants moved

*Later, English officials forced Penn to turn away Catholic and Jewish settlers.

to Pennsylvania. They were called the Deutsch (doich), or Germans. Later, the Pennsylvania Deutsch became known as the Pennsylvania Dutch.

**City of brotherly love.** Penn looked up the Delaware River for a spot to build his capital that was "high, dry, and healthy." He had grown up in London, a dirty city with houses crowded close together. Under such conditions, fires were a constant danger. Penn wanted his capital to be "a green country town, which will never be burnt and always be wholesome."

Penn called his capital Philadelphia, a Greek word meaning brotherly love. He drew up a plan for the city. Houses had to leave "ground on each side for gardens or orchards or fields." In the 1700s, Philadelphia grew into the largest, most prosperous city in the English colonies.

**The Lower Counties become Delaware.** Pennsylvania had no outlet on the coast. So Penn asked the Duke of York to give up some land on the lower Delaware River. The duke agreed, giving Penn an area known as the Lower Counties. Settlers in the Lower Coun-

William Penn treated the Delaware Indians with respect. Friendly relations between settlers and Indians helped Pennsylvania prosper. In this painting, Penn and other Quakers present gifts to the Indians as part of a treaty agreement.

ties did not like this change. They did not want to send representatives all the way to Philadelphia to meet in the assembly. So in 1701, Penn gave them their own assembly. The new colony was called *Delaware*. (See the map on page 107.)

(See the map on page 107.)

(See the map on page 112.)

## SECTION REVIEW

1. **Locate:** Middle Colonies, New York, Hudson River, New Jersey, Delaware River, Pennsylvania, Philadelphia, Delaware.

2. **Define:** patroon, proprietary colony, royal colony.

3. (a) Why did few Dutch settle in New Netherland? (b) Why were the English able to seize the Dutch colony so easily?

4. How was each of these colonies formed: (a) New Jersey; (b) Delaware?

5. **What Do You Think?** In what ways do you think William Penn's "holy experiment" was successful?

# 3 Southern Colonies

### Read to Learn

★ Why did Lord Baltimore want to set up a colony?

★ How was North Carolina different from South Carolina?

★ What plans did General Oglethorpe have for Georgia?

Virginia was the first Southern Colony. In the 1600s and 1700s, English settlers established four other Southern Colonies: Maryland, North Carolina, South Carolina, and Georgia. (See the map on page 112.)

## A Safe Place for Catholics

In the 1600s, English Catholics had to worship in secret, facing jail or death if they were caught. A Catholic noble, Sir George Calvert, decided to start a colony in America where Catholics could worship in peace.

**Lord Baltimore.** Calvert's title was Lord Baltimore. He escaped persecution because he was a friend of King Charles I. In 1632, Charles gave him 10 million acres of land north of Virginia. Lord Baltimore named his colony *Maryland* in honor of Queen Henrietta Maria, wife of Charles I. Lord Baltimore died before his colony got under way. But his son, the second Lord Baltimore, sent settlers to Maryland in 1634.

The settlers found much to please them. Chesapeake Bay was full of fish, oysters, and crabs. They could grow tobacco and other crops on the fertile land. When they saw a brightly colored bird, they named it the Baltimore-Bird "because the Colors of Lord Baltimore's Coat of Arms are black and yellow."

**The early years.** Lord Baltimore never visited Maryland, but he made careful plans for the colony. He appointed a governor and council of advisers and set up an elected assembly. He offered land to any man who brought settlers to the colony. A man received 100 acres for bringing over a healthy male servant and 50 acres for each woman or child.

Among those who settled in the colony were a few women like Margaret Brent. Because she brought her own servants, Brent was given land. She started a plantation and managed it so well that she won the respect of other planters, including the governor.

In 1647, when the governor was dying, he asked Brent to take charge of his estate. She did. She also helped prevent a rebellion in Maryland. The

Although Lord Baltimore, shown here, never visited Maryland, he influenced the life of the colony. He strongly supported the Act of Toleration, which gave freedom of worship to people in his colony.

Maryland assembly praised her efforts, saying that "the colony's safety at that time [was better] in her hands than in any man's." But when Brent asked for a place in the Maryland assembly, her request was refused because she was a woman.

Although many Catholics settled in Maryland, Protestants also came to the colony. To avoid problems over religion, Lord Baltimore asked the Maryland assembly to approve an *Act of Toleration* in 1649. The act gave religious freedom to all Christians. However, it did not protect the rights of Jews.

## Rebellion in Virginia

In Virginia, waves of settlers joined the survivors of the early years. Wealthy tobacco planters controlled the best land near the coast. Newcomers could only get land by taking over Indian lands in the interior. When clashes occurred between Indians and settlers, officials in London gave set-

tlers permission "to root out [the Indians] from any longer being a people."

In the 1640s, Indian and white leaders agreed to divide the land. Both peoples enjoyed peace for about 30 years. But as more settlers arrived and took land, fighting broke out again.

In 1676, Nathaniel Bacon, a 29-year-old planter, organized men and women on the frontier. They wanted the governor to do more to protect them from the Indians. When the governor refused, Bacon and his followers raided Indian villages. They then marched on Jamestown, burning the capital. *Bacon's Rebellion* lasted only a short time. When Bacon died soon after, the revolt fell apart. But it showed that frontier settlers were determined to stay and push even deeper into Indian lands.

## The Carolinas

In 1663, King Charles II granted eight nobles a huge tract of land that stretched from Virginia to Spanish Florida. The nobles set up a colony called Carolina, the Latin name for Charles. They had grand plans for Carolina. People who bought land would be given noble titles such as Lord High Chamberlain. The new nobles would have serfs and slaves to work for them. These grand plans did not work out. Instead, settlers set up a government like that of Virginia and Maryland with a governor and elected assembly.

People settled in two different areas of the Carolinas. The areas were far apart and had little contact with each other. In the north, tobacco farmers trickled in from Virginia. They tended to have small farms.

In the south, the first settlers built Charles Town, later called Charleston, where the Ashley and Cooper rivers meet. They tried to raise grapes, oranges, and lemons. But these crops did not do well. So they grew rice, which soon became a major crop.

Planters in the south had large estates worked by slaves.* By the early 1700s, thousands of slaves had been brought to the southern part of Carolina. The northern part had fewer slaves. In 1712, Carolina was divided into two colonies: *North Carolina* and *South Carolina*.

## The Last Colony

In 1732, King George II gave the southern part of South Carolina to

*In the 1600s, the slave system brought to the West Indies by Spain spread to the English colonies. English, Dutch, and French merchants competed for control of the slave trade.

General James Oglethorpe (OH guhl thawrp). The general was a respected soldier and an energetic reformer. Oglethorpe named his colony *Georgia* in honor of the king. Georgia was the last of the 13 English colonies set up in America.

Oglethorpe was concerned about people imprisoned in England for debt. Under English law, debtors could be jailed until they paid what they owed. Conditions in prison were awful. When debtors came out of prison, they often had no money and nowhere to live. Oglethorpe wanted to help debtors and other poor people by paying their passage to Georgia. He believed that in

In 1734, James Oglethorpe returned to England to get support for his colony in Georgia. He brought along a group of Indians, shown at right, who had sold land to him. In England, Oglethorpe got new rules forbidding slavery and rum in the colony. However, the rules were unpopular in the colony and were later dropped.

Georgia the freed debtors could make a new start in a new home.

**A slow start.** In 1733, Oglethorpe and 120 settlers sailed from England to Georgia. They built the town of Savannah above the river of the same name.

Oglethorpe set out strict rules for these first settlers. He limited farms to 500 acres and outlawed slavery. He did not allow the sale of rum in the colony. Under these rules, the colony grew slowly. Some settlers moved to other colonies, where they could own large plantations and slaves. When Oglethorpe eased the rules and allowed slavery, Georgia grew more quickly.

King George II supported Oglethorpe's plan for Georgia, mainly because he wanted a strong English colony on the border of Spanish Florida. Spain was still a rival of England in America. And both countries claimed the land between South Carolina and Florida.

**War with Spain.** General Oglethorpe put his military experience to work. In 1739, Parliament declared war on Spain. Oglethorpe led English forces against the Spanish in Florida. Spain responded by invading Georgia. With the help of the Creek Indians, Oglethorpe and his army forced the Spanish to retreat.

During this time, Mary Musgrove greatly helped Oglethorpe. Musgrove was the daughter of a Creek mother and an English father. She married a planter, John Musgrove, and together they ran a successful plantation.

Because Mary Musgrove spoke both English and Creek, she helped to keep up the friendship between the Creeks and settlers in Georgia. Also, she informed Oglethorpe of Spanish movements on the border between Georgia and Florida.

MAP SKILL The Southern Colonies stretched from Maryland to Georgia. Name three ports in the Southern Colonies. Who ruled the land south of Georgia?

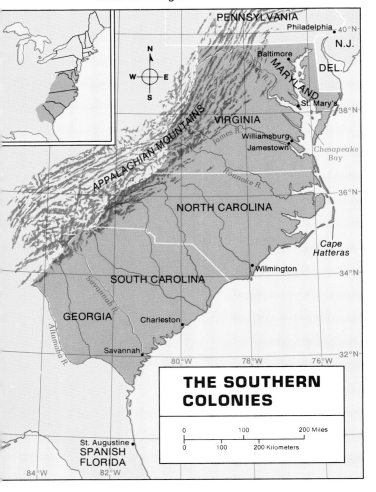

**THE SOUTHERN COLONIES**

| | | |
| --- | --- | --- |
| 0 | 100 | 200 Miles |
| 0 | 100 | 200 Kilometers |

## SECTION REVIEW

1. **Locate:** Maryland, Chesapeake Bay, Virginia, Charleston, North Carolina, South Carolina, Georgia, Savannah, Spanish Florida.

2. (a) Why was Maryland founded? (b) What was the purpose of Maryland's Act of Toleration?

3. Why did Nathaniel Bacon and other frontier settlers rebel in Virginia?

4. Name one difference between North Carolina and South Carolina.

5. **What Do You Think?** Why do you think England wanted a military man like General Oglethorpe to lead Georgia?

# 4 Governing the Colonies

★ Why did England pass the Navigation Acts?
★ What were colonial governments like?
★ What do these words mean: mercantilism, import, export, enumerated article, legislature, indentured servant?

At first, English officials paid little attention to the small, struggling settlements in North America. In time, however, all the colonies except Pennsylvania and Maryland came under royal control. For the most part, England left the colonies to themselves. But it did take a strong interest in trade with the colonies.

## Trade Between England and the Colonies

Like other European countries, England believed that colonies existed for the benefit of the parent country. This belief was part of the economic theory of *mercantilism* (MER kuhn tihl ihz'm). According to this theory, a nation became strong by building up its gold supplies and expanding its trade.

Trade occurs when goods are exchanged. *Imports* are goods brought into a country. *Exports* are goods sent to markets outside a country. Because exports help a country earn money, mercantilists thought that a country should export more than it imports.

**The Navigation Acts.** In the 1660s, Parliament passed a series of laws that governed trade between England and its colonies. These laws were known as the *Navigation Acts.* The purpose of the Navigation Acts was to strengthen England and make it richer.

One law said that only ships built in England or the colonies could carry goods to and from the colonies. Also, it said that most of the sailors on the ships had to be from England or the colonies. This law was designed to keep trade in English hands and train sailors who could serve in the navy in wartime.

Another law required any ship carrying European goods to America to stop first in England. The English collected taxes on the goods before they were sent to the colonies. This law allowed England to profit from trade between its colonies and other nations. Other laws listed certain goods from the colonies that could be sold only in England. These goods included tobacco, cotton, and sugar and were known as the *enumerated articles.* In this way, the laws protected the supply of raw materials that English merchants and workers made into finished goods.

**Benefits and drawbacks.** The Navigation Acts were good for England. In general, they were good for the colonists, too.

The law that limited trade to English or colonial ships encouraged colonists to build their own ships. New England became a center for shipbuilding, and shipbuilders in the colonies made good profits. The colonies benefited from the strong English navy that protected trade. Also, colonial merchants did not need to compete with foreign merchants because they were sure of a market for their goods in England.

Still, many colonists resented the Navigation Acts. They felt that England was treating them like children by telling them what they could or could not do. Also, European goods cost more because they had to be shipped to England first. There, they were taxed before being sent to the colonies.

In the end, many colonists ignored the Navigation Acts or found ways to

Trade between England and the colonies grew in the 1600s and 1700s. Because of the Navigation Acts, ports such as Bristol, England, shown here, bustled with activity.

get around them. Smuggling goods in and out of the colonies became a way of life for some New Englanders. For a time, English officials did little to stop the smuggling. When illegal trade increased, however, England looked for ways to enforce the Navigation Acts.

## The Dominion of New England

In the 1680s, England tried to enforce the Navigation Acts, especially in Massachusetts where smuggling was widespread. In 1686, King James II combined all the colonies from Massachusetts to New Jersey into the *Dominion of New England.* He dismissed their assemblies and appointed Sir Edmund Andros to rule the colonies. Andros did not like Puritans. He

soon made himself very unpopular in New England.

Events in England helped the colonists. In 1688, King James was overthrown in the Glorious Revolution. The new king and queen, William and Mary, ended the Dominion of New England and restored elected assemblies in the colonies.

The revolution in England had another effect. In 1689, William and Mary signed the *English Bill of Rights.* It protected the rights of individuals and gave anyone accused of a crime the right to trial by jury. It outlawed cruel punishments. Also, it said that a ruler could not raise taxes or an army without the approval of Parliament. As English men and women, colonists were protected by this bill.

## Governors and Assemblies

By the late 1600s, each colony had developed its own form of government. Still, the basic setup of each was the same. A governor was sent from England to direct the affairs of the colony. He enforced the laws and appointed a council of advisers to help him rule.

**Elected assemblies.** Each colony had a legislature. A *legislature* is a group of people who have the power to make laws. In most colonies, the legislature had an upper house and a lower house. The upper house was made up of the governor's council. The lower house was an elected assembly. It approved laws and protected the rights of citizens. Just as important, it had the right to approve any taxes the governor wanted.

Sometimes, a governor and assembly disagreed. But an assembly controlled the money. So it could refuse to

**CHART SKILL** The 13 colonies were founded over a period of 125 years. What were the main reasons why the colonies were founded?

## Founding of the Colonies

| Colony/Date Founded | Leader | Reasons Founded |
| --- | --- | --- |
| **New England Colonies** | | |
| Massachusetts<br>  Plymouth/1620<br>  Massachusetts Bay/1630 | William Bradford<br>John Winthrop | Religious freedom<br>Religious freedom |
| New Hampshire/1622 | Ferdinando Gorges<br>John Mason | Profit from trade and fishing |
| Connecticut<br>  Hartford/1636<br>  New Haven/1639 | Thomas Hooker | Expand trade; religious and political freedom |
| Rhode Island/1636 | Roger Williams | Religious freedom |
| **Middle Colonies** | | |
| New York/1624 | Peter Minuit | Expand trade |
| Delaware/1638 | Swedish settlers | Expand trade |
| New Jersey/1664 | John Berkeley<br>George Carteret | Profit from land sales; religious and political freedom |
| Pennsylvania/1682 | William Penn | Profit from land sales; religious and political freedom |
| **Southern Colonies** | | |
| Virginia/1607 | John Smith | Trade and farming |
| Maryland/1632 | Lord Baltimore | Profit from land sales; religious and political freedom |
| The Carolinas/1663<br>  North Carolina/1712<br>  South Carolina/1712 | Group of eight proprietors | Trade and farming; religious freedom |
| Georgia/1732 | James Oglethorpe | Profit; home for debtors; buffer against Spanish Florida |

Among the many kinds of primary sources are photographs and written records. Written records are primary sources if they are firsthand information from people who were involved in an event. Letters, diaries, contracts, laws, and treaties are all primary sources.

The excerpt below is adapted from Gottlieb Mittelberger's *Journey to Pennsylvania.* The book was published after a trip in 1750. Follow these steps to practice using a primary source.

1. **Identify the source by asking who, what, when, and where.** (a) Who wrote the source? (b) What is it about? (c) About when was it written? (d) Where does it take place?
2. **Recognize the author's point of view.** Many eyewitnesses have a particular reason for writing about an event. And they want to share their views with their readers. When you read a primary source, you need to recognize the author's point of view. (a) What is Mittelberger's opinion about the journey to Pennsylvania? (b) What words or phrases show you that he feels strongly about the journey?
3. **Decide whether the source is reliable.** (a) Do you think that Mittelberger gives an accurate view of the journey? Why? (b) Do you think that there is anything left out of his account? (c) Would you say that this is a reliable source for learning about crossing the Atlantic in the mid-1700s? Explain.

 **Journey to Pennsylvania**

When the ships have weighed anchor, the real misery begins. Unless they have good wind, ships must often sail 8, 9, 10 or 12 weeks before they reach Philadelphia. Even with the best wind, the voyage lasts 7 weeks. . . . During the voyage people suffer terrible misery, stench, many kinds of seasickness, fever, dysentery, boils, scurvy, cancer, and the like, all of which come from old, sharply-salted food and meat and from very bad, foul water so that many die miserably.

Add to this misery, the lack of food, hunger, thirst, frost, heat, dampness, and fear. The misery reaches a peak when a gale rages for two or three nights and days so that every one believes that the ship will go to the bottom with all human beings on board.

When ships land at Philadelphia after the long voyage, only those who have paid for their passage are allowed to leave. Those who cannot pay must stay on board until they are bought and released from the ships by their buyers. . . . The sale of human beings in the market on board ship goes like this. English, Dutch, and Germans come on board to choose among the healthy passengers and bargain with them how long they will serve for their passage money. Adults bind themselves to serve anywhere from 3 to 6 years. Young people must serve until they are 21 years old.

Many parents must sell and trade away their children like so many head of cattle. It often happens that whole families are sold to different buyers.

Work and labor in this new and wild land are very hard. Work mostly consists of cutting wood, felling oak trees, and clearing large tracts of forest.

pay the governor's salary until he met its demands.

**On voting day.** Each colony had its own rules about who could vote. In all colonies, only white Christian men over age 21 could vote. In some, only Protestants or members of a particular church could vote. All voters had to own property. Colonial leaders believed that only property owners knew what was best for the colony. A newcomer had to live in the colony for a certain time before he could vote. There were fewer rules for local elections. Often, any law-abiding white man could vote for local officials.

On election day, voters and their families met in towns and villages. Excitement filled the air as people exchanged news and gossip. Candidates greeted voters and offered to buy them drinks. Finally, the sheriff called the voters together. One by one, he read out their names. When called, a voter announced his choice in front of everyone. The candidate often thanked the voter for his support. One observer recorded this election day scene:

| | |
|---|---|
| Sheriff: | "Mr. Blair, who do you vote for?" |
| Blair: | "John Marshall." |
| Marshall: | "Your vote is appreciated, Mr. Blair." |
| Sheriff: | "Who do you vote for, Mr. Buchanan?" |
| Buchanan: | "For Mr. John Clopton." |
| Clopton: | "Mr. Buchanan, I shall treasure that vote in my memory. It will be regarded as a feather in my cap forever." |

## Limited Rights for Many

The right to vote was limited to a few white men. Nonwhites such as blacks and Indians had few rights. Also, women and white servants had limited rights.

**Women.** Like women in Europe at that time, women in the colonies had few legal rights. A woman's father or husband was supposed to protect her. Women were expected to marry at an early age. A married woman could not start a business of her own or sign a contract unless her husband approved of the arrangement.

In most colonies, unmarried women and widows had more rights. They could make contracts and sue in court. In Maryland and the Carolinas, women settlers who were heads of families were offered land on the same terms as men. Margaret Brent, you remember, won respect for managing her plantation so well.

**Indentured servants.** Many men and women who were eager to go to America could not pay for the voyage. So they became indentured servants. An *indentured servant* signed a contract, agreeing to work for a certain length of time for whoever paid his or her way to the colony. The time was usually between four and seven years. At the end of that time, an indentured servant received a set of clothes, tools, 50 acres of land, and freedom. More men than women were indentured servants. Because there were so few women in the New World, women often shortened their terms of service by marrying.

Thousands of men, women, and children came to America as indentured servants. After completing their service, they supported themselves as farmers, merchants, and craftworkers. Some became successful and rose to positions of respect in the colonies.

### SECTION REVIEW

1. **Define:** mercantilism, import, export, enumerated article, legislature, indentured servant.
2. Describe three laws included in the Navigation Acts.
3. How did the English Bill of Rights limit the power of the ruler?
4. How was the legislature organized in most colonies?
5. **What Do You Think?** Why do you think there were fewer rules for voting in local elections than in assembly elections?

# Chapter 5 Review

### ★ Summary ★

Between 1607 and 1732, the English set up 13 colonies along the Atlantic coast of North America. People had many reasons for settling in the colonies.

Puritans, Quakers, and Catholics emigrated to find religious freedom. Others left for economic reasons. People like William Penn and James Oglethorpe founded colonies, hoping to make them models of peaceful living and hard work.

In general, England left the colonies alone. In the 1600s and 1700s, each colony had its own government and laws about voting. However, England regulated the trade of the colonies. The Navigation Acts strengthened England's economy. At the same time, the colonies also benefited from these acts. By the mid-1700s, the English colonies were firmly rooted in America.

### ★ Reviewing the Facts ★

**Key Terms.** Match each term in Column 1 with the correct definition in Column 2.

**Column 1**

1. emigrate
2. toleration
3. patroon
4. proprietary colony
5. indentured servant

**Column 2**

a. someone under contract to work for a certain length of time in exchange for passage to the colonies
b. owner of a manor in New Netherland
c. leave one country to settle in another
d. willingness to let others have their own beliefs
e. land granted by the king to one or more people

**Key People, Events, and Ideas.** Identify each of the following.

1. Great Migration
2. John Winthrop
3. Thomas Hooker
4. Roger Williams
5. Anne Hutchinson
6. Metacom
7. Peter Stuyvesant
8. William Penn
9. Quakers
10. George Calvert
11. Act of Toleration
12. Margaret Brent
13. James Oglethorpe
14. Mary Musgrove
15. Navigation Acts

### ★ Chapter Checkup ★

1. Why did Puritans declare that England had fallen on "evil and declining times"?
2. Why was Roger Williams seen as a dangerous troublemaker?
3. (a) How were the Middle Colonies different from the other English colonies? (b) Name five groups that settled in the Middle Colonies.
4. (a) What beliefs did the Quakers teach? (b) How did William Penn get settlers for his colony?
5. Why did Lord Baltimore want to start a colony in America?
6. (a) What rules did James Oglethorpe set up for his colony? (b) Why did he change these rules?
7. (a) How did the Navigation Acts help England? (b) How did they help the colonies? (c) Why did the colonies resent them?
8. Describe how a person became an indentured servant.

## ★ Thinking About History ★

1. **Relating past to present.** (a) Why do you think Puritan leaders saw Roger Williams as a threat to the Massachusetts Bay Colony? (b) Do you think he would be considered a dangerous person today? Explain.

2. **Analyzing a quotation.** James Oglethorpe believed that once debtors reached Georgia, they could work "in a land of liberty and plenty, where . . . they are unfortunate indeed if they can't forget their sorrows." What do you think he meant by this?

3. **Learning about citizenship.** (a) Which colony or colonies were started by people seeking religious freedom? (b) How did each of these colonies treat other religious groups? (c) Do you think religious toleration was widely accepted in the 1600s and 1700s? Explain.

4. **Evaluating.** As colonies grew, relations between settlers and Indians worsened. War often broke out between the two groups. (a) Why did Indians like Metacom take a stand against the English? (b) How did the views of Roger Williams and William Penn differ from the views of other colonists?

## ★ Using Your Skills ★

1. **Map reading.** Study the map on page 107. (a) Which of the Middle Colonies was farthest north? (b) Which of the Middle Colonies was farthest south? (c) Why do you think the 13 colonies were all on the coast?

2. **Placing events in time.** Review the time line on page 98. (a) What event appears first on the time line? (b) What event appears last? (c) During what period were the Navigation Acts passed?

3. **Comparing.** Compare the way Rhode Island and Pennsylvania were founded.

(a) Who founded each colony? (b) What ideas did each founder have? (c) How were their ideas similar? (d) How were their ideas different?

4. **Chart reading.** A chart shows a lot of information in a clear and simple way. Review the chart on page 115 about the founding of the colonies. (a) Which colony was founded first? (b) During what time period were the Southern Colonies founded? (c) How many colonies were founded by individuals?

## ★ More to Do ★

1. **Writing a play.** As a group project, write a brief play about the trial of Anne Hutchinson and act it out.

2. **Preparing a pamphlet.** Prepare a pamphlet William Penn might have used to attract settlers to his colony.

3. **Exploring local history.** Interview someone who has recently immigrated to your community from another country. Write a report comparing their rea-

sons for leaving their home with the reasons of Europeans in the 1600s and 1700s.

4. **Organizing a debate.** Organize a debate on this statement: "Governments in the early colonies were undemocratic." One group should find information to support the statement. The other group should find information to disprove it.

# CHAPTER
# 6
# Life in
# the Colonies (1630–1775)

**Chapter Outline**

1 The New England Way of Life
2 The Breadbasket Colonies
3 Two Ways of Life in the South
4 A New American Culture
5 Growth and Change
Readings, page 485

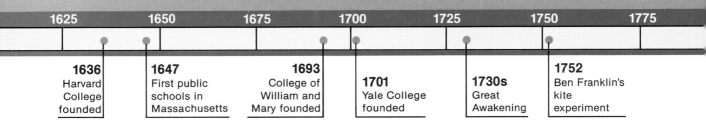

| 1625 | 1650 | 1675 | 1700 | 1725 | 1750 | 1775 |

**1636**
Harvard College founded

**1647**
First public schools in Massachusetts

**1693**
College of William and Mary founded

**1701**
Yale College founded

**1730s**
Great Awakening

**1752**
Ben Franklin's kite experiment

## About This Chapter

In the 1600s and 1700s, thousands of settlers flocked to the English colonies. They found a world very different from their old ones. From New England to the South, settlers experimented with new crops, new building materials, and new ideas. In the end, each region developed its own way of life.

In the 1600s, life was very hard for the newcomers. People in the different colonies knew little about one another. By the 1700s, however, the colonies were well established. Improved trade and travel allowed colonists to learn more about each other.

Even after conditions improved, people worked hard at many tasks. At an early age, children took on important jobs. In 1775, a Connecticut girl wrote this description of her day's work.

> Fixed gown . . . mended Mother's Riding-hood, spun short thread, fixed two gowns for Welsh's girls . . . spun linen, worked on cheesebasket, [combed] flax with Hannah, we did 51 lbs. apiece. Pleated and ironed, read a sermon of Dodridge's, spooled a piece, milked the cows, spun linen, did 50 knots, made a broom of guinea wheat straw, spun thread to whiten, set a red dye, [visited with] two scholars from Mrs. Taylor's, I carded two pounds of whole wool [and then] spun harness twine and scoured the pewter.

Study the time line above. Name three colleges founded in the colonies.

Plantations in the South were often built along rivers. Planters loaded goods on ships bound for England, the West Indies, and Europe.

# 1 The New England Way of Life

### Read to Learn

★ How did geography affect colonists in New England?
★ Why was the meetinghouse the center of town life?
★ What tasks did women perform?
★ What do these words mean: subsistence farmer, surplus, stocks?

The New England Colonies were settled mostly by Puritans and their offspring. Puritan attitudes and beliefs influenced the way of life in these colonies. But geography also affected life in New England.

### The Land and Climate

When the Pilgrims arrived off Cape Cod, William Bradford described the new land as a "country, full of woods and thickets," that had a "wild and savage" look. Settlers soon discovered that New England was, indeed, a land of forests. They organized chopping bees to clear away trees and haul off large boulders that dotted the land.

The rocky soil was not very fertile, and farming methods were crude. As a result, the land wore out. So every few years, farmers needed to clear new land. Most settlers were *subsistence farmers.* That is, they had small plots of land on which they grew enough food for their own needs. When they did produce *surpluses,* or extra food, they traded it for such goods as tools and kettles.

The climate of New England was quite harsh. During the short growing season, families worked from dawn to dusk in the fields. During the long cold winters, deep snows sometimes cut towns off from each other.

Yet sometimes, snow helped farmers. Once farmers began producing more goods, they often waited until the winter to take these goods to the nearest port. When the roads were covered with snow, they loaded butter, maple sugar, and other products onto sleds drawn by oxen. Because the sleds slipped smoothly over the packed snow, the trips were quicker than at other times of the year.

## Using the Land's Resources

New Englanders made good use of their limited resources. The large forests provided lots of timber. Fish and furs were plentiful, and the jagged coastline offered many good harbors.

**Shipbuilding.** Settlers in New England used the forests to supply timber to a busy shipbuilding industry. Lumber was brought from New Hampshire to shipbuilders in Boston. Portsmouth, New Hampshire, and Newburyport, Massachusetts, later became major shipbuilding ports.

The tallest trees were made into masts. Other products used in shipbuilding such as pitch and tar also came from the forests. England encouraged shipbuilding in the colonies. It needed ships for its navy, and its own forests had been cut down years before.

**Fishing and whaling.** Although most New Englanders were farmers, many fished the coastal waters. Fishing people hauled in huge catches. When Captain John Smith visited New England, he caught 60,000 cod in just one month. One New Englander reported, "I myself . . . have seen such multitudes of sea bass that it seemed to me that one might go over their backs without getting one's feet wet." Catches included oysters over a foot long and lobsters over five feet.

Fishing was hard work. When the fish were running, fishermen did not stop to eat or sleep. A cook held food in front of the fishermen so that they could eat while they worked. After fishing boats returned to shore, fish were dried in the sun and sent to other colonies or to England.

MAP SKILL Farming, shipbuilding, and fishing were among the economic activities of New England colonists. Study the map and the key. Name one city where ships were built.

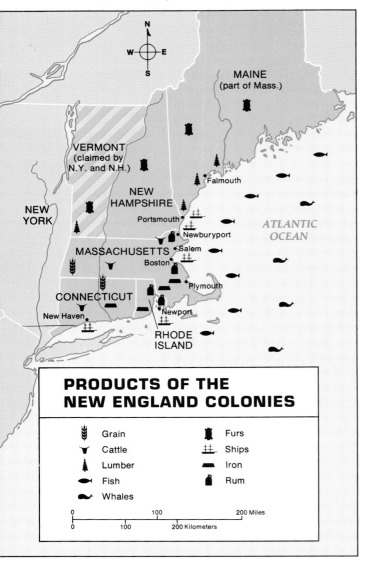

## PRODUCTS OF THE NEW ENGLAND COLONIES

- Grain
- Cattle
- Lumber
- Fish
- Whales
- Furs
- Ships
- Iron
- Rum

0 100 200 Miles
0 100 200 Kilometers

In the 1600s, New Englanders began to hunt whales. Whales supplied settlers with products such as ivory and oil for lamps. Whaling grew into a big business in the 1700s and 1800s.

## New England Towns

New England was a land of towns and villages. Farm families lived in towns and went each day to their fields outside the towns. Puritans thought people should live in towns so that they could worship and take care of local matters as a community.

What did a New England town look like? At the center of most towns was the common, an open field where cattle grazed. Nearby was the meetinghouse. The meetinghouse was the center of town life. As one New Englander observed, it was "built by our own vote, framed by our own hammers and saws, and by our own hands set in the most convenient place for all." The meetinghouse served two purposes. It was the church where Puritans met to worship. It was also used for town meetings.

On the common outside the meetinghouse, many towns set up stocks. *Stocks* were wooden frames with holes for the arms and legs. They were used to punish people found guilty of crimes such as drunkenness and swearing. People could be sentenced to spend a few hours or a few days in the stocks. Passers-by laughed at prisoners and threw rotten eggs or stones at them.

Wooden houses with steep roofs lined both sides of the narrow streets of a town. Often, the second floor of a house was built out over the street. This overhang gave the second-floor rooms more space and protected the first-floor walls from rain.

**Church services.** Religion was at the center of Puritan life. The church enforced rules about behavior, clothing, and education. Attendance at church was required. Services were very different from those of today. Sun-

Puritans used stocks such as those shown here to punish people who broke their strict moral code. Sometimes, people were sentenced to stand with their head and arms in stocks. The public shame and discomfort in the stocks made people think twice about breaking the law.

day services lasted all day. In the morning, the meetinghouse bell rang to call everyone to worship. At midday, people had an hour for lunch and then returned for the afternoon service.

In church, Puritans sat on hard wooden benches. The wealthy sat apart in boxlike enclosures with high walls. During the 1600s, women were seated on one side of the house and men on the other. Children had their own separate section. It was hard for them to keep quiet during the long services. One Connecticut boy was scolded for his "rude and idle behavior in the meetinghouse such as laughing and smiling . . . or pulling the hair of his neighbor."

**Town meetings.** Church services were solemn times, but town meetings could be noisy. Citizens met to discuss questions that affected the town—what roads to build, what fences to repair, how much to pay the schoolmaster. Townspeople argued and then voted on these issues.

Town meetings gave New Englanders a chance to speak out on issues. Unlike the Spanish or French colonists in the Americas, the English colonists had a say in government. This early experience encouraged the growth of democratic ideas in the New England Colonies.

## At Home With the Family

During the long, cold New England winters, life at home centered around the huge kitchen fireplace. The fire-place covered an entire wall of the kitchen. Despite the size of the fire-place, the room was cold because winds blew down the chimney. One New Englander described how the ink in his pen froze even as he sat writing right inside his fireplace.

If the kitchen was chilly, bedrooms were even colder. Thick drapes hung from four posts at each corner of a bed. The drapes helped keep out the cold. Before going to sleep, people put a met-al warming pan filled with hot coals in their beds to heat the sheets.

In the 1600s, New Englanders sat on narrow benches at long tables to eat their meals. Instead of plates, they used trenchers. A trencher was a block of wood hollowed out for food. Two people shared a trencher. In the 1700s, people began to use pewter or china plates.

At meals, children were supposed to eat quickly and remain silent. In some homes, children had to eat standing by

In colonial times, the fireplace was the center of family life. It was used for both cooking and heating the home. In this picture, children inside the fireplace are sitting on the warming bench. Why do you think the warming bench was a popular spot?

Women worked hard raising their families, keeping the house, and doing chores on the farm. This picture shows women on a typical washday. At left, one woman boils water. The others beat and rinse clothes in the stream.

the table or behind their parents, who handed them food! One book of table manners advised children: "Look not earnestly at any other person that is eating." And it warned them not to throw bones under the table.

## A Busy Life for Women

In New England and in other colonies, women worked at many tasks from sunrise to sunset. Although a woman had few legal rights, she worked as an equal partner with her husband to provide for her family. Women helped clear the land. They planted and harvested crops. They ground corn, skinned and cleaned animals, and dried fruits and vegetables such as peppers, pumpkins, and apples. Many women kept geese, and they plucked goose feathers for pillows and mattresses.

In the fall, women made candles for the long winter evenings ahead. First, they melted animal fat in a huge pot. Then, they dipped candlewicks into the fat, letting it cool on the wick. On a good day, a woman could make about 200 candles.

Women spent a lot of time making clothes for the family. They began with wool from sheep and flax from a plant. Wool had to be dyed, greased, and combed before it was spun into thread. Women then wove the thread into cloth or knitted it into socks or mittens. Flax had to be cut, beaten, combed, and sorted before it was spun into linen thread.

Women worked at many jobs outside the home. They were blacksmiths, tinmakers, and weavers as well as innkeepers, merchants, and barbers. They also worked as nurses, midwives, and doctors.

### SECTION REVIEW

1. **Define:** subsistence farmer, surplus, stocks.
2. Why did New England farmers have a hard time producing good harvests?
3. List three ways that colonists made a living in New England.
4. What was the purpose of town meetings?
5. **What Do You Think?** Do you think women in the New England Colonies had harder lives than women of today? Explain your answer.

# 2 The Breadbasket Colonies

### Read to Learn

★ How did geography affect people in the Middle Colonies?

★ How did Swedish, Dutch, and German settlers influence the Middle Colonies?

★ What do these words mean: cash crop, tenant farmer, backcountry?

New Englanders visiting the Middle Colonies saw much that was familiar. But they also found differences. Farms were larger and more spread out. Towns were not the center of life. Unlike New Englanders, who came mostly from England, settlers in the Middle Colonies came from many European countries.

## The Land and Climate

The land and climate of the Middle Colonies were different from those of New England. In the fertile lands of the Hudson and Delaware river valleys, farmers prospered. Winters were less harsh. Summers were warmer, and the growing season lasted longer.

**Cash crops.** Unlike the subsistence farmers of New England, farmers in the Middle Colonies produced surpluses of wheat, barley, and rye. These became *cash crops,* or crops that are sold for money on the world market. The Middle Colonies became known as the *Breadbasket Colonies* because they exported so much wheat and other grain.

Farmers also raised cattle and pigs. Every year, they sent tons of beef, pork, and butter to the ports of New York and Philadelphia. From there, the food was shipped to New England and the South or to the West Indies, England, and other parts of Europe.

**Manufacturing and crafts.** The Middle Colonies produced many kinds of manufactured goods. A visitor to Pennsylvania mentioned that he saw workshops turn out "most kinds of hardware, clocks, watches, locks, guns, flints, glass, stoneware, nails, paper." Pennsylvania became a center of manufacturing and crafts, in part because William Penn had encouraged many German settlers with valuable skills to set up shop there.

Colonists in the Delaware River valley made household and farm tools because they had large supplies of iron ore. They built furnaces to heat the iron ore and turn it into pig iron. At forges, or smaller furnaces, ironworkers puri-

Iron products made at forges were important to daily life in the colonies. Pat Lyon, owner of this forge, was a very successful businessman.

fied the pig iron and made nails, farm tools, and parts for guns.

**Manor life in New York.** In New Jersey, Pennsylvania, and Delaware, farmers earned a legal right to land by clearing, planting, and living on it. In New York, however, a different system existed.

As you read, Dutch patroons owned huge manors along the Hudson River. *Tenant farmers* worked the land and paid rent to the landowner. The manor system did not change when the English took over New Netherland, even though many tenant farmers were unhappy with it. They felt that rents were too high. They resented having to use their own oxen to clear or plow the landowner's fields. At harvest time, they had to leave their own crops in the field while they harvested the landowner's crops.

Several times, angry tenant farmers rioted and attacked manor houses. Many tenant farmers simply left New York. They moved to Pennsylvania or New Jersey, where they could work their own land. Others went north to farm the land in the area that later became Vermont.

## Comfortable Homes

The different peoples who settled the Middle Colonies had their own styles of building. Some colonists built log cabins, which were introduced to America by the Swedes. Sweden was a land of forests. Swedes had built log cabins there long before Swedish settlers came to America.

Dutch houses were common in the towns and cities of New York. The Dutch used brick for building their homes. Their houses had steep roofs topped by weather vanes. Front doors were split across the middle. The top half was opened to let in air and light. The bottom half was closed to keep out geese and pigs. In front, the Dutch built

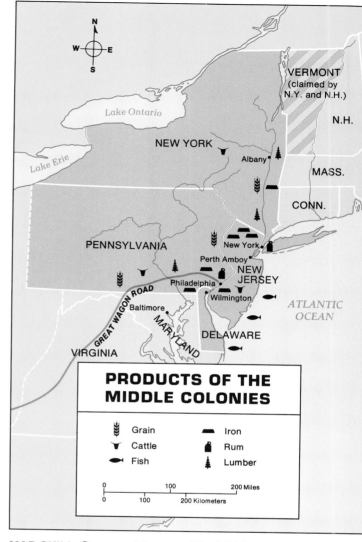

MAP SKILL Compare this map of the Middle Colonies to the map of the New England Colonies on page 122. What similarities do you find in the products of the two regions? What differences do you find?

a wooden porch, which they called a stoop.

German settlers developed a new kind of woodburning stove. It heated a home better than a fireplace, which let blasts of cold air leak down the chimney. Other colonists copied the German stove.

Visitors to the Middle Colonies remarked on the comfortable life of

This painting shows a flax-scutching bee in the Middle Colonies. Flax is a plant with fibers that are spun into linen thread. A bee was a party where many people worked together at a task. The man at far left is breaking the tough stalks of the flax plant. Other men and women pound the stalks to get at the fibers. At bees such as this one, colonists exchanged news with friends and neighbors.

many farm families. A New Englander who stayed with a Quaker family in Philadelphia reported that the people dressed simply, according to Quaker custom. But he marveled at the supper he was served, which included "ducks, hams, chickens, beef, pig, tarts, creams, custards, [and] jellies."

## Moving West

In the 1700s, thousands of Scotch-Irish and German settlers arrived in the Middle Colonies. They set out from Philadelphia and other cities for frontier lands farther west. As settlers pushed the Indians out, they built new towns such as Haverford, Lancaster, and York. When they ran up against the Appalachian Mountains, many turned south and settled in western Maryland and Virginia. This area along the Appalachians was called the *backcountry*.

**The Great Wagon Road.** The route to the backcountry was known as the *Great Wagon Road*. Like most roads, it was rough and rutted with deep mudholes.

Settlers built large wagons, called *Conestoga* (kahn uh STOH guh) wagons, to carry goods along the road. A Conestoga wagon had large wheels that kept goods from getting wet as the wagon bumped through mudholes. The floor curved up at both ends so that goods would not fall out as the wagon went up or down steep hills. A cloth cover stretched over hoops of wood kept out rain and snow.

**Life in the backcountry.** The first settlers in the backcountry took over lands already cleared by Indians. Later settlers had to clear thick forests themselves before they could farm the land. To do this, they used a method they had learned from the Indians. They girdled trees, or cut the bark around tree trunks with axes. Sometimes, they burned around the roots. Both methods killed the trees. Farmers then planted seeds between the dead trees. After a year or two, they cleared away the dead trees.

People used the forests for many of their needs. They built log cabins and made wooden shutters. Indians showed them how to use knots from pine trees to make candles to light their homes. Settlers gathered wild honey from hollow logs and hunted animals for food. Sharpshooters brought home deer, bear, and wild turkey.

---

**SECTION REVIEW**

1. **Locate:** Hudson River, Delaware River, Philadelphia, Appalachian Mountains, Great Wagon Road.
2. **Define:** cash crop, tenant farmer, backcountry.
3. Why were the Middle Colonies known as the Breadbasket Colonies?
4. Why were tenant farmers in New York unhappy with life on the manors?
5. **What Do You Think?** Why do you think settlers pushed into the backcountry rather than stay in the east?

---

# 3 Two Ways of Life in the South

**Read to Learn**

- ★ How did geography affect settlers in the Southern Colonies?
- ★ Why did planters turn to slave labor?
- ★ How was plantation life different from life in the backcountry?
- ★ What do these words mean: tidewater, slave code, racism?

Settlers in the Southern Colonies developed a way of life different from that of other English colonies. The difference was due in part to climate and geography.

## The Land and Climate

In the South, the climate was warmer than elsewhere along the coast of North America. As you have read, Jamestown settlers learned that the climate and soil of Virginia were well suited to growing tobacco. At first, small farmers grew tobacco along with food crops. But tobacco soon wore out the soil. As a result, plantations often replaced small tobacco farms. Plantation owners could rotate crops and leave part of their land idle each year. This way, the soil did not wear out so quickly.

Settlers in other Southern Colonies followed the example of Virginia. By the 1700s, Virginia, Maryland, and parts of North Carolina had become major tobacco-growing areas. South Carolina and Georgia produced rice and indigo. In busy Charleston harbor, ships loaded cargoes of tobacco, rice, and indigo for markets overseas.

Geography affected where southerners built their plantations. They settled along the coast and fertile river valleys because these low-lying areas were good for growing rice. Rivers gave inland planters an easy way to ship their harvests. At harvest time, crops were brought to the river bank and loaded onto ships bound for England or the West Indies.

Along the coastal plain, ocean tides swept up river for quite a distance. As a result, the coastal plain was known as the *tidewater.* The tidewater was a region of plantations. Farther inland, the land was hilly and covered with thick forests. As in the Middle Colonies, this inland area was called the backcountry. Two ways of life grew up in the South, one in the tidewater and the other in the backcountry.

## Growth of Slavery

Tidewater planters needed many workers to make their land profitable. At first, they tried to make Indians work the land. Or they brought indentured servants from England. By the late 1600s, however, planters were buying large numbers of African slaves. Although people in other colonies owned some slaves, most slaves lived in the South.

**Reasons.** Why did southern planters turn to African slave labor? The English saw how slave labor earned profits for the Spanish colonists. Planters believed that Africans were used to warm climates. Then, too, it was hard for blacks to escape because their skin color made it easy to find them. Unlike the Indians, Africans did not know the forests of North America.

Planters preferred slaves to indentured servants because buying a slave was a one-time expense. Indentured servants could leave after they completed their years of service. But planters owned and controlled their slaves as well as their slaves' children forever. Colonists passed *slave codes,* or laws that controlled the behavior of slaves and denied them basic rights. Slaves were seen as property, not as human beings.

Most English colonists accepted slavery. They did not question the justice of owning slaves because of racism. *Racism* is the belief that one race is superior to another. White Europeans believed that black Africans were inferior to them. They claimed to be helping their slaves by teaching them Christian beliefs. A few colonists, however, protested that slavery was unjust.

**MAP SKILL** Study this map of the Southern Colonies. What are the major products of the tidewater, or coastal areas? What are the major products of the backcountry?

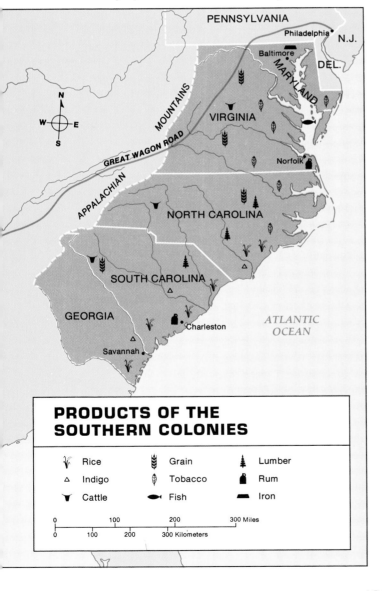

## PRODUCTS OF THE SOUTHERN COLONIES

| | | |
|---|---|---|
| Rice | Grain | Lumber |
| Indigo | Tobacco | Rum |
| Cattle | Fish | Iron |

— 130 —

Quakers spoke out against slavery, and some New Englanders criticized merchants who grew rich from the slave trade.

**The Middle Passage.** During the 1700s, the slave trade grew into a major business. Portuguese, Spanish, Dutch, English, and French ships brought about 100,000 Africans to the Americas each year.

White slave traders built forts on the African coast. They offered guns and other goods to African rulers who brought slaves to the coast. Slaves were forced on board ships and packed into small spaces below decks with hardly enough room to sit up. Often, they were chained together two by two. Once or twice a day, they were taken up on deck to eat and exercise.

Some Africans fought for their freedom during the trip. Others refused to eat. But sailors pried open their mouths and forced them to swallow food. Still others leaped overboard. They chose to die rather than to live as slaves. Many died of diseases that spread quickly in the hot, filthy air below deck.

The horrible trip from Africa to the Americas was called the *Middle Passage.* When slave ships reached American ports, captains sold their human cargo in the marketplace. Planters inspected the slaves to find healthy, strong workers. On the plantation, slaves had to adjust to a strange language and culture—and to a life without freedom.

Slaves helped the Southern Colonies grow. They cleared the land, worked the crops, and tended the livestock. They showed white colonists how to grow rice. Still as slaves, some became fur trappers, sailors, and soldiers. But many did not accept their lot. Sometimes, they tried to escape, attacked their owners, or damaged crops in protest.

This painting was done by an Englishman who served as an officer on a slave ship. Captains crammed their human cargo into the holds below deck. Many slaves died of diseases that spread quickly in the overcrowded and filthy holds.

## Life on a Plantation

Many plantations were almost self-sufficient. People on the plantation produced most of the food and other goods they needed. On a typical plantation, the largest building was the Great House, where the planter and his family lived. Houses were made of wood or brick. The inside walls were plastered with lime ground from oyster shells.

Wealthy planters copied the styles of English manor houses. A planter's house had a parlor for visitors, a dining room, a library or music room, bedrooms for family members, and guest bedrooms. Some houses also had large ballrooms for dancing. The kitchen was often a separate building so that the Great House remained "cool and sweet." As one planter explained, "The Smell of hot Victuals [food]" was "offensive in hot Weather."

Planters made all decisions about the land. They decided which fields to plant, what crops to grow, and when to harvest the crops and take them to market. They also directed the lives of slaves. A planter might own from 20 to 100 slaves. Most slaves worked in the fields. However, some were skilled workers. Black carpenters, barrelmakers, blacksmiths, and brickmakers produced goods the plantation needed. Other slaves worked in the Great House as cooks, cleaners, or servants.

In the Great House on a plantation, Southerners lived in simple elegance. Here, family members enjoy music and dancing. At an early age, children of wealthy planters learned to play musical instruments and practiced graceful dancing steps.

Eliza Lucas was 17 years old when her parents moved to South Carolina from the West Indies. Her father, an army colonel, soon had to leave his family to serve overseas. Because her mother was ill, Eliza Lucas took over the family plantation. The Lucases grew rice in low-lying fields. But Colonel Lucas also owned land where rice could not be grown. He and his daughter wanted to put that land to good use.

Colonel Lucas sent home seeds and plants from all over the world, including ginger, cotton, figs, and indigo. Indigo is a plant whose leaves produce a blue dye. Indigo was grown in the West Indies and sold well in England, where it was used to dye cloth.

Eliza Lucas successfully raised a few indigo plants. So her father sent an overseer, or manager, from the West Indies to help her raise a full crop. But the overseer made a dye of poor quality from the indigo. The young woman found out that the overseer was spoiling the dye on purpose. He was afraid that if she succeeded in growing indigo, West Indian planters would lose business.

Colonel Lucas then sent a black slave skilled at growing indigo to help his daughter. The man showed slaves on the plantation how to raise a good crop. Eliza Lucas then gave indigo seeds to her neighbors. Indigo succeeded beyond her wildest dreams. By 1754, South Carolina was shipping many tons of indigo to England every year. By then, Eliza Lucas had married Charles Pinckney. For the next 40 years, she continued to raise indigo and other crops.

★ How do you think growing indigo helped the economy of the South?

Women kept the household running smoothly. They were in charge of the house slaves and made sure daily tasks were done. These tasks included weeding the vegetable garden, milking the cows, and collecting eggs. Women ran the plantation if their husbands were away or died.

## The Backcountry South

In the backcountry of the South, settlers developed a different way of life from tidewater planters. Many backcountry people came from Pennsylvania along the Great Wagon Road. (See the map on page 127.) They settled in western Maryland, Virginia, and the Carolinas. Many went on to the Shenandoah Valley, where they found rich lands for farming.

In the backcountry, people built log cabins and raised cattle and pigs. Once a year, they rounded up their animals and drove them to markets in Baltimore, Petersburg, or Charleston.

The backcountry was more democratic than the tidewater. There were few very rich families on the frontier. Settlers treated each other as equals. As one visitor noted, "Every man . . . calls his wife, brother, neighbor, or acquaintance by their proper name of Sally, John, James, or Michael." By contrast, tidewater people used terms such as "My dear sir," "Madam," or "Mister." Also, backcountry people wore simple clothes suited to frontier life, not the silks and velvets worn by tidewater families.

Backcountry settlers often quarreled with their governments in the east. These frontier settlers did not elect as many representatives to colonial assemblies as tidewater planters did. So when the government passed laws that were unpopular in the backcountry, settlers there sometimes rebelled to defend their rights.

=== SECTION REVIEW ===

1. **Define:** tidewater, slave code, racism.
2. What cash crops did the South grow?
3. Why did planters prefer slaves to indentured servants?
4. (a) What kinds of decisions did planters make? (b) What kinds of jobs did women do on plantations?
5. **What Do You Think?** Why do you think settlers in the backcountry resented tidewater planters?

# 4 A New American Culture

### Read to Learn

★ How did children in the colonies get an education?

★ What were the social classes in the colonies?

★ Why did Benjamin Franklin become famous?

★ What do these words mean: public school, apprentice, gentry, almanac?

By the mid-1700s, the English colonies had developed a culture different from that of England. Settlers from many lands contributed to the new American culture.

## Education in the Colonies

From the start, colonists worried about how to teach their children what they needed to know in the New World. New England led the way in education. Many Puritans were well educated. They believed that all people should learn to read so that they could study the Bible. As a result, the Massachusetts assembly passed a law ordering all parents to teach their children "to read and understand the principles of religion."

**The first public schools.** In 1647, Massachusetts required all towns with 50 families to hire a school teacher for their children. A town with 100 families had to set up a grammar school for boys to prepare them for college. The law set up the first *public schools,* or schools supported by taxes. Public schools were important because they allowed children from both poor and rich families to get an education.

The first New England schools had only one room for students of all ages. Because there were few coins in the colonies, parents paid the schoolteacher with furs, fruit, green vegetables, and corn.

**Other schools and colleges.** In the Middle Colonies, churches and individual families set up private schools. These schools charged fees. So only children of well-to-do families could afford to attend. In the Southern Colonies, people lived too far apart to bring children together in a school. Planters hired tutors, or private teachers, for their children. Sometimes, a school was set up in an old tobacco shed in the fields. Children rode on horseback or rowed up a river to school.

In 1636, Massachusetts set up the first college to train Puritan ministers. Two years later, John Harvard, a minister, left his library to the college, which then took his name. Puritans in Connecticut set up Yale College in 1701. In Virginia, the College of William and Mary was organized in 1693 to train ministers of the Church of England. Before long, colleges also began training lawyers, doctors, and teachers.

| | |
|---|---|
| A | In *Adam*'s Fall / We finned all. |
| B | Thy Life to mend / This Book attend. |
| C | The Cat doth play / And after flay. |
| D | A Dog will bite / A Thief at Night. |
| E | The Eagle's Flight / Is out of Sight. |
| F | The idle Fool / Is whipt at School. |

A New England schoolbook, or primer, not only taught students to read but also gave moral lessons. From a book such as this one, children learned the alphabet, reading, and spelling. In school, they also studied arithmetic, history, and geography.

**Learning on the job.** Many children had no formal schooling. They learned the skills they needed on the job. In farm families, children learned from their parents and older brothers and sisters.

Children also served as apprentices (uh PREHN tihs ehz). An *apprentice* worked for a master craftsman to learn a trade or craft. For example, when a boy reached age 12 or 13, his parents might apprentice him to a master glassmaker. The young apprentice lived in the glassmaker's home for six or seven years. The glassmaker gave him food and clothing and treated him like one of the family. He was also supposed to teach the boy to read and write and give him religious training.

In return, the apprentice worked without pay in the glassmaker's shop and learned the skills he needed to become a master glassmaker. He was then ready to start his own shop as a glassmaker. Boys were apprenticed to many trades. They became papermakers, printers, clockmakers, or leather tanners.

**Education for girls.** Girls, too, became apprentices, although they had a smaller choice of trades. A girl's parents might send her to become a cook, a needleworker, or a housemaid. However, women learned other trades from their fathers, brothers, or husbands. They worked as shoemakers, silversmiths, and butchers. Quite a few women became printers. A woman often took over her husband's business after his death.

Most schools accepted only boys. In New England, however, girls attended dame schools, or private schools run by women in their own homes. Girls learned many skills at home by helping their mothers to dry meat and vegetables, spin wool, weave, and embroider. Often, parents taught their daughters to read and write.

## Bigwigs and the Meaner Sort

Colonists enjoyed more social equality than people in England. But social classes did exist in the colonies. At the top stood the *gentry*. They included wealthy planters, merchants, ministers, successful lawyers, and royal officials. Below the gentry was the middle class. It included farmers who worked their own land, skilled craftworkers, and some tradespeople. The lowest class, often called the "meaner sort," included hired farmhands, indentured servants, and slaves.

People dressed according to their social class. The gentry showed off their wealth by wearing silks with lace ruffles. People of the "meaner sort" could be fined for dressing like the gentry. Instead of silks, they wore simple clothes made of homespun linen or wool.

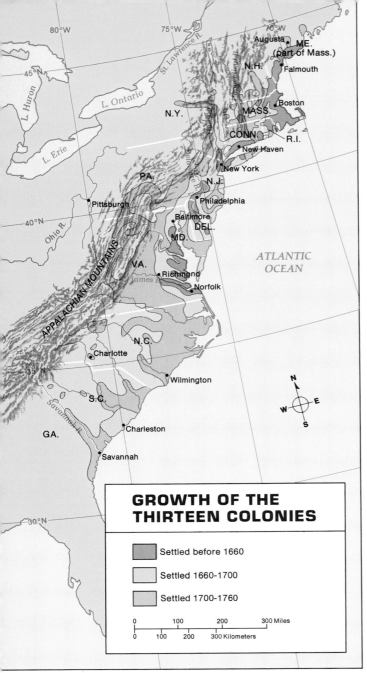

MAP SKILL The 13 colonies grew and expanded in the 1600s and 1700s. In which direction did settlers move as the colonies grew? What barriers to settlement did they have to overcome?

The gentry and middle class copied the popular styles of London. In the 1600s, long curly wigs were in fashion. Wealthy colonists who wore these fancy wigs became known as "bigwigs." By the mid-1700s, men wore smaller wigs tied at the back with a ribbon.

## Benjamin Franklin: An American Genius

People in the colonies could climb the social ladder more easily than in England. One such person was Benjamin Franklin, the son of a poor Boston soap and candle maker. Franklin was born in 1706 and died in 1790. In his long life, he rose from poverty to become famous throughout the world.

**Successful printer.** Franklin was one of 17 children. He left school at age 10 to work for his father. Later, he was apprenticed to his brother James, a printer. Although Franklin had only two years of formal schooling, he never stopped learning. He used his spare time to read and study literature, mathematics, and foreign languages.

At age 17, Franklin ran away from Boston and made his way to Philadelphia. He set up a printing shop that he turned into a thriving business. He published pamphlets, newspapers, and *almanacs,* or books containing calendars and other useful information. Franklin's best-known book was *Poor Richard's Almanac.* Many of its sayings are still quoted today: "Early to bed and early to rise makes a man healthy, wealthy, and wise" and "The sleeping fox catches no poultry."

**Scientist and inventor.** From an early age, Franklin was curious about how things worked. And he was full of ideas for improving things. In 1740, he invented the Franklin stove. It burned less wood and heated homes better than other stoves. He invented the bifocal lens, which let people wear one pair of glasses for both distance and closeup work.

Franklin experimented with electricity. In 1752, he proved that lightning was a form of electricity. To do this, he flew a kite during a thunderstorm. When lightning struck the kite, electricity flowed down a wire attached to the kite. Franklin then invented the lightning rod to protect buildings against damage from lightning.

Benjamin Franklin is shown here conducting his famous experiment with lightning. Franklin became known throughout America and Europe for his work. In 1754, a French scientist wrote him: "We are all waiting with the greatest eagerness to hear from you." Today, scientists say that Franklin was lucky he was not electrocuted when he flew the kite in a storm.

**Energetic leader.** Franklin had ideas about improving city life. He convinced Philadelphia to pave its streets with cobblestones, organize a police force, and set up a fire company. Eager to promote education, he organized the first lending library in America and an academy that later became the University of Pennsylvania.

Franklin had a rich career as a public leader and diplomat, as you will read later on. His practical inventions helped people, and his fame worldwide gave colonists reason to be proud of their home-grown genius.

## The Great Awakening

In the 1730s and 1740s, a religious movement, known as the *Great Awakening,* swept through the colonies. In New England, the Puritan preacher Jonathan Edwards called on listeners to examine their lives and give up their unholy ways. In a famous sermon, "Sinners in the Hands of an Angry God," Edwards described the fiery torments of hell that awaited evildoers.

Between 1738 and 1770, an English minister, George Whitefield (HWIHT feeld), drew huge crowds to outdoor meetings from Massachusetts to Georgia. Whitefield was a powerful speaker.

His voice rang with feeling as he called on sinners to reform. "It was wonderful to see the change soon made in the manner of our inhabitants," reported Benjamin Franklin after hearing Whitefield preach.

The Great Awakening aroused bitter debate. Some people strongly supported it. They listened to traveling preachers and formed many new churches. Other people opposed the movement. They supported established churches.

The movement brought other changes. The growth of new churches forced people to be more tolerant. The clergy lost influence in part because the Great Awakening emphasized a person's own experience in religion.

### SECTION REVIEW

1. **Define:** public school, apprentice, gentry, almanac.
2. Why did Puritans want their children to get an education?
3. What classes existed in the colonies?
4. Describe two ways Benjamin Franklin influenced the colonies.
5. **What Do You Think?** Why do you think the Great Awakening had such an important effect on colonists?

# 5 Growth and Change

**Read to Learn**

★ What was travel like in the colonies?
★ How did trade affect the colonies?
★ What was life like in cities of the colonies?
★ What do these words mean: triangular trade?

In the 1600s, the English colonies had little contact with each other. As the colonies grew, however, people learned more about their neighbors. By the mid-1700s, people from different colonies discovered that they had many interests in common.

## Improvements in Travel

In the 1600s and early 1700s, travel was slow and dangerous. There were few roads. Travelers followed Indian trails through the forests. Even when trails were widened into roads, they were dusty in summer and muddy in winter. Often, there were no bridges across streams and rivers. Early visitors to Boston had to cross the Charles River on a small ferry. Their carriages were taken apart to fit onto the ferry, and their horses swam along behind the boat.

Because travel was so difficult, colonists stayed close to home. Settlers seldom heard from friends or relatives in other colonies. A postal service grew up, but it was slow. In 1717, it took one month for a letter to get from Boston to Williamsburg, a town in Virginia—and two months in winter.

**Franklin's milestones.** In the mid-1700s, colonists tried to improve travel and communication. Ben Franklin had milestones placed along the road between Boston and Philadelphia so that people would know how far they had traveled. He invented a machine that recorded distances as it was wheeled along behind his wagon. At each mile,

he left a large stone on the ground. Roadworkers then put the stone firmly in place.

Along with better roads came better mail service. In 1753, Franklin was appointed postmaster general for the colonies. He set up relay stations along the mail roads. At the relays, mail carriers changed tired horses for fresh ones. As a result, mail moved more quickly.

**The spread of ideas.** As travel and mail service improved, colonists learned more about their neighbors. Taverns sprang up along main roads and in towns and cities. Travelers stopped in taverns to exchange news and gossip with local people.

News and ideas were also spread through pamphlets, newspapers, and books turned out by printing presses in the colonies. The first printing press was set up at Harvard College in 1639. Early presses printed religious books along with histories and travelers' stories. In the 1700s, presses printed pamphlets and newspapers.

Colonial newspapers were short, often only four pages long. They carried news about the other colonies and about England and Europe. This news was often several months old by the time it reached other colonies.

## Trade Expands

The colonies developed a greater sense of unity through trade. As trade expanded, the colonies grew prosperous and strong. Ships of every kind bustled up and down the Atlantic coast. They carried fish, lumber, and other products from New England to the Middle Colonies and the South. The Middle Colonies shipped grain and flour to New England and the South. The Southern Colonies exported rice, indigo, and tobacco to colonies in the north.

**Yankee traders.** Merchants from New England dominated colonial trade. They were known as *Yankees,* a nickname that implied sharp, clever, hard-working people. Yankee traders won a reputation for always getting a good buy and profiting from any deal.

A Yankee ship, wrote one observer, arrived in Puerto Rico loaded with horses and other goods. The crew quickly unloaded the horses. Then, Yankee traders turned their ship "into retail shops, where they dealt out their onions, potatoes, salt fish, and apples, an article which brought a very high price."

**The triangular trade.** Colonial merchants developed many trade routes. One series of routes was known as the *triangular trade* because the three routes formed a triangle. (See the map on page 141.) On the first leg of the journey, New England ships carried fish, lumber, and other goods to the West Indies. There, they picked up sugar and molasses. Molasses was a dark brown syrup made from sugar cane. New Englanders used molasses to make rum. Much of the rum was sold in New England, but some was used to trade.

On the second leg, merchants carried rum, guns, gunpowder, cloth, and tools from New England to West Africa. They used these goods to buy slaves. On the final leg, traders carried slaves to the West Indies. With the profits from selling the slaves, Yankee traders bought more molasses.

Many New England merchants grew wealthy from the triangular trade. In doing so, they often disobeyed the Navigation Acts. Traders were supposed to buy sugar and molasses only from English colonies in the West Indies. But the demand for molasses was so high that New Englanders bought from the Dutch, French, and Spanish West Indies. Although En-

**AMERICANS WHO DARED**

### Paul Cuffe

The 42-ton whaling ship sailed proudly into port. Its captain-owner, Paul Cuffe, and the all-black crew welcomed the sight of home. Cuffe, the son of a free black man and Native American woman, grew up in Massachusetts. At age 16, he went to sea on a whaling ship. After years of struggle, he owned a small fleet of trading ships and made a fortune. Even while he succeeded in business, Cuffe worked hard to win freedom and equality for blacks.

gland opposed this illegal trade, bribes could make customs officials look the other way.

## Growing Cities

Port cities grew as trade expanded. Sailors hurried along docks and piers that were piled high with cargoes. On nearby streets, merchants and craftworkers showed off their goods. Boston, the busiest port in the colonies, had more than 40 wharves.

New York City prospered from trade, too. Its streets were even lighted at night. As daylight faded, a night

As you learned in Skill Lesson 4 (page 81), graphs show statistics in picture form. A bar graph is useful because it shows changes in one or more sets of numbers over time.

The bar graph at right shows the growth of trade between England and the 13 colonies during the period from 1700 to 1750.

There are two kinds of bar graphs. In a vertical bar graph, the bars go up and down. In a horizontal bar graph, the bars go from side to side. Some bar graphs have two or more bars in different colors so that you can make comparisons.

Study the bar graph at right. Then use the following steps to read the bar graph.

1. **Identify the subject of the bar graph.** Like a line graph, a bar graph has a title as well as a horizontal axis and a vertical axis. Each axis is labeled with numbers or dates. Often, a label says that the numbers are in thousands. In this case, you add three zeros to the numbers shown. If the numbers are in millions, you add six zeros. (a) What is the title of the graph? (b) What do the numbers on the vertical axis show? (c) What dates are shown on the horizontal axis? (d) What is the source of the information shown on this graph?

2. **Practice reading the facts on the bar graph.** Notice that the intervals, or spaces, between the numbers and dates are always equal. Also, the numbers on the vertical axis always start with zero. (a) What are the intervals between the dates on the graph? (b) What was the value of trade with England in 1700? (c) What was its value in 1740? (d) In what year was trade worth most? (e) In what year was it worth least?

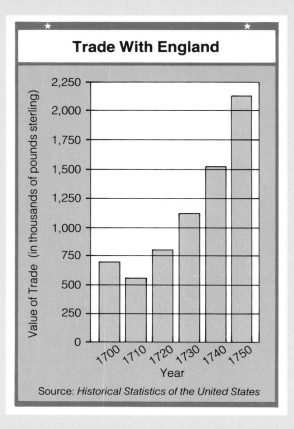

**Trade With England**

Value of Trade (in thousands of pounds sterling)

Year

Source: *Historical Statistics of the United States*

3. **Make a generalization based on the facts on the bar graph.** Study the graph to find facts to support a generalization. (a) Between what years did trade increase the most? (b) Between what years did it decrease? (c) Make a generalization about trade with England between 1710 and 1750.

4. **Interpret the information.** Use the bar graph, the map on page 141, and your reading in the chapter to interpret the information about trade. (a) Why do you think trade was important to England? (b) Why do you think it was important to the colonies? (c) What goods were traded between England and the colonies?

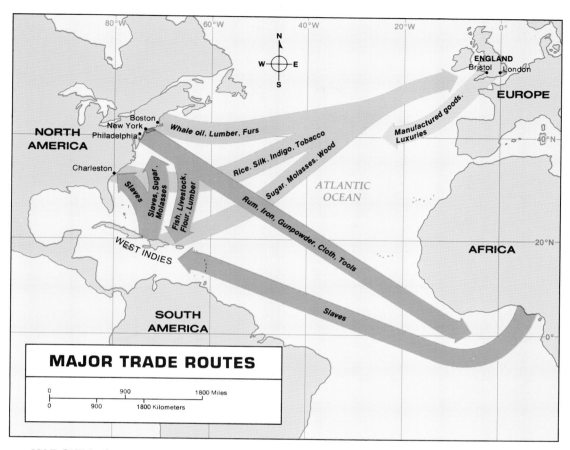

## MAJOR TRADE ROUTES

Map labels: ENGLAND, Bristol, London, EUROPE, NORTH AMERICA, Boston, New York, Philadelphia, Charleston, Whale oil, Lumber, Furs, Rice, Silk, Indigo, Tobacco, Manufactured goods, Luxuries, Sugar, Molasses, Wood, Rum, Iron, Gunpowder, Cloth, Tools, ATLANTIC OCEAN, Slaves, Sugar, Molasses, Fish, Livestock, Flour, Lumber, Slaves, WEST INDIES, AFRICA, SOUTH AMERICA, Slaves

Scale: 0   900   1800 Miles
0   900   1800 Kilometers

**MAP SKILL** Colonists traded with the West Indies, Africa, and Europe in a series of triangular trade routes. Find a three-sided trade route. What goods were traded at each place along the route?

watchman called out: "Lanthorn, and a whole candell-light. Hang out your lights." During the night, he checked the lights, calling out the time and weather. "Two o'clock and fair winds!" Or "Five o'clock and cloudy skies!"

The fastest growing city was Philadelphia. By 1760, its population was the largest in North America. Thanks to Ben Franklin, it boasted the only hospital in North America. It had three libraries and three newspapers—one in German.

In the South, the largest cities were Baltimore and Charleston. Charleston was known as the most elegant colonial city. Wealthy rice planters and their families lived in beautiful mansions and dressed in the latest fashions from London and Paris.

Most Americans lived on farms. Yet cities were important centers. There, people met in great numbers and exchanged news and ideas that would shape events in the years ahead.

### SECTION REVIEW

1. **Define:** triangular trade.
2. Why was travel difficult in the colonies?
3. Name two ways people learned about what was going on in other colonies.
4. Why was molasses important in the triangular trade?
5. **What Do You Think?** How do you think the growth of trade was related to the growth of cities?

# Chapter 6 Review

 **Summary**

Colonists developed different ways of life. This was due in part to the land and climate of the different regions. In New England, for example, the land was poor for farming. The Puritan religion also helped shape the New England way of life.

The fertile land of the Middle Colonies allowed settlers to produce surpluses of wheat and grain. As a result, the Middle Colonies exported foods to other colonies.

To meet the need for workers in the South, planters imported thousands of slaves.

Children in the colonies were educated in different ways. Some learned to read and write in public schools. Others were taught by tutors. Many children learned trades as apprentices. As roads and mail service improved, colonists in different regions learned more about each other. In the 1700s, trade helped the colonies prosper.

 **Reviewing the Facts**

**Key Terms.** Match each term in Column 1 with the correct definition in Column 2.

| Column 1 | Column 2 |
|---|---|
| 1. subsistence farmer | a. belief that one race is superior to another |
| 2. cash crop | b. someone who learns a trade from a master craftsworker |
| 3. tenant farmer | c. goods sold for money on the world market |
| 4. racism | d. someone who grows just enough food to live on |
| 5. apprentice | e. someone who works and pays rent for land owned by another |

**Key People, Events, and Ideas.** Identify each of the following.

1. Breadbasket Colonies
2. Great Wagon Road
3. Middle Passage
4. John Harvard
5. Benjamin Franklin
6. *Poor Richard's Almanac*
7. Great Awakening
8. Jonathan Edwards
9. George Whitefield
10. Yankee

 **Chapter Checkup**

1. How did New England colonists make use of the forests?
2. (a) Describe a typical New England town. (b) Why did Puritans want to live in towns?
3. (a) What manufactured goods did the Middle Colonies produce? (b) Why did Pennsylvania become a center of manufacturing?
4. Why was the Conestoga wagon useful?
5. Give three examples of how plantations were self-sufficient.
6. Why were public schools important?
7. Explain three ways girls got an education in the colonies.
8. (a) How was travel made easier in the 1700s? (b) How did improved travel affect the colonies?
9. What products did each of the following regions export to other parts of the world: (a) New England; (b) Middle Colonies; (c) South.
10. Describe two cities in two different colonies.

## ★ Thinking About History ★

1. **Relating past to present.** Review the description of New England homes and family life on pages 123–125. (a) How was life similar to that of today? (b) How was it different?

2. **Applying information.** Why do you think New Englanders came to dominate trade in the colonies?

3. **Evaluating.** Do you think racism was a major or minor factor in the growth of slavery? Explain your answer.

4. **Comparing.** (a) Compare the ways of life of tidewater planters and people living in the backcountry. (b) What do you think were the most important differences between the two groups?

5. **Analyzing a quotation.** A popular saying Ben Franklin included in *Poor Richard's Almanac* went: "An ounce of prevention is worth a pound of cure." Give an example to show what this means.

## ★ Using Your Skills ★

1. **Map reading.** Study the map on page 136. (a) What does this map show? (b) What areas were settled before 1660? (c) What areas were settled between 1660 and 1700? (d) Why do you think settlers moved inland?

2. **Map reading.** Study the map on page 141. (a) What products did New Englanders export to the West Indies? (b) What products did colonists import from Europe? (c) How were slaves part of the triangular trade?

3. **Making a review chart.** Make a large chart with three columns and three rows. Title the columns New England Colonies, Middle Colonies, and Southern Colonies. Title the rows Land, Climate, and Products. Fill in the chart, using the maps on pages 122, 127, and 130 and your reading in this chapter. (a) How was the land in New England different from that in the Middle Colonies? (b) What crops were produced only in the South? (c) How do you think the land and climate affected the crops and products of the three regions?

4. **Using a painting as a primary source.** Study the painting on page 121. (a) Which building do you think was the Great House? Why? (b) Which building or buildings were the slaves' houses? Why? (c) How do the hill and the houses on it show the different classes in the South?

## ★ More to Do ★

1. **Preparing an oral history.** In groups of two, prepare an oral history in which one student interviews the other about what it was like to be captured as a slave in Africa and sent to the New World.

2. **Researching a report.** Research and write a report on one of the following aspects of daily life in the colonies: (a) food; (b) clothing; (c) games.

3. **Exploring local history.** Prepare a skit about the experiences of early settlers in your community.

4. **Making a model.** Create a model of a New England town or a southern plantation in about 1750.

5. **Eyewitness reporting.** As an eyewitness, describe Benjamin Franklin's experiment with flying his kite during a thunderstorm.

# Unit 2 Review

**Chapter 4** In the 1500s, Spain built a large empire in the Americas. France, too, explored and claimed lands in North America. Although the first English colony at Roanoke failed, Jamestown was settled in 1606. To the north, Pilgrims planted the Plymouth Colony in 1620.

**Chapter 5** In the 1600s and 1700s, the English set up 13 colonies in North America. Many colonists came to America for religious or economic reasons. Each colony had its own government with a royal governor and an elected assembly. However, many people, including women and slaves, did not have the right to vote.

**Chapter 6** The New England, Middle, and Southern colonies differed from each other, in part because of geography. Although each colony had its own way of life, trade and travel helped colonists learn about one another.

★ **Unit Checkup** ★

Choose the word or phrase that best completes each of the following statements.

1. Most settlers in New France were
   (a) farmers.
   (b) fur traders.
   (c) plantation owners.

2. Many of the early English colonies were financed by
   (a) joint stock companies.
   (b) cash crops.
   (c) subsistence farmers.

3. England regulated trade with the colonies in the
   (a) Frame of Government.
   (b) Fundamental Orders of Connecticut.
   (c) Navigation Acts.

4. The Breadbasket Colonies were the
   (a) New England Colonies.
   (b) Middle Colonies.
   (c) Southern Colonies.

5. A successful American printer, scientist, and inventor was
   (a) Benjamin Franklin.
   (b) Jonathan Edwards.
   (c) Mary Musgrove.

★ **Building American Citizenship** ★

1. Many people settled in the 13 colonies to find religious freedom. (a) How did some colonies protect religious freedom? (b) Is religious freedom still a concern of Americans today? Explain your answer.

2. Colonial governments based the right to vote on age, property, religion, race, and sex. What is the right to vote based on today?

3. Town meetings gave New Englanders a chance to speak out on issues. How can Americans today make sure their voices are heard?

4. Racism allowed white settlers to justify slavery in America. (a) How did racism affect relations between settlers and Indians? (b) Why do you think American leaders today speak out against racism?

# ★ Critical Thinking Skills ★

The line graph at right shows the growth of population in the 13 colonies between 1650 and 1750. Study the graph. Then answer the following questions. (Note that the numbers on the vertical axis are in thousands. So you have to add three zeros to them to get the correct population.)

1. How many people lived in the colonies in 1650?

2. What was the population of the colonies in 1700?

3. When did the population reach one million?

4. (a) Did more people settle in the colonies between 1650 and 1700 or between 1700 and 1750? (b) Why do you think more came in that time period?

5. Why do you think the colonies were anxious to get more settlers?

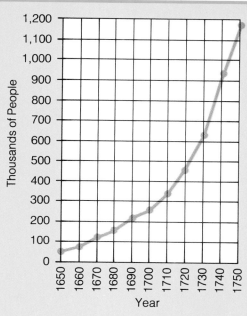

**Population of the Colonies**

Source: *Historical Statistics of the United States*

---

## History Writer's Handbook

**Identifying Parts of a One-Paragraph Answer**

Study the following question. *What ideas of Roger Williams did the Puritans see as dangerous?* To answer the question, you might write a paragraph, or a group of sentences that develop the main idea of the answer.

Begin the one-paragraph answer with a ***topic sentence*** that states the main idea of the answer. For example: *The Puritans saw three ideas of Roger Williams as dangerous.*

Next, write ***detail sentences*** that give information to support the main idea. For example: *Williams wanted to pay the Indians for their land. He argued for separation of church and state. He also supported freedom of worship.*

**Practice** Study the following question. *How did John Smith save the Jamestown Colony?* Now study the following one-paragraph answer.

*John Smith used strong means to save the Jamestown Colony. He bought corn from the Indians to feed the starving colonists. Then he told the people they would only get food if they worked.*

Identify the topic sentence and the detail sentences in the answer.

# Unit 3
# THE STRUGGLE FOR INDEPENDENCE

| 1740 | | | | 1750 | | | | 1760 | | | | 1770 |

**1740s** English settlers and traders move into Ohio River valley

**1754** French and Indian War begins; Albany Plan of Union
**1759** English take Quebec

**1763** Treaty of Paris ends French and Indian War; Pontiac's War
**1765** Stamp Act
**1766** Stamp Act repealed
**1767** Townshend Acts

| 1740 | | | | 1750 | | | | 1760 | | | | 1770 |

**1700s** England and France battled for control of North America.

JOIN, or DIE.

**1760s** Benjamin Franklin's cartoon, "Join, or Die," came to have more meaning when the colonists protested British efforts to tax them.

UNIT OUTLINE

**CHAPTER** 7   Crisis in the Colonies (1745–1775)

**CHAPTER** 8   The American Revolution (1775–1783)

**CHAPTER** 9   Creating a Government (1776–1790)

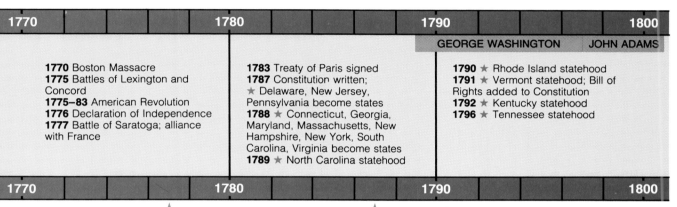

| 1770 | 1780 | 1790 | 1800 |
| --- | --- | --- | --- |

GEORGE WASHINGTON        JOHN ADAMS

**1770** Boston Massacre
**1775** Battles of Lexington and Concord
**1775–83** American Revolution
**1776** Declaration of Independence
**1777** Battle of Saratoga; alliance with France

**1783** Treaty of Paris signed
**1787** Constitution written;
★ Delaware, New Jersey, Pennsylvania become states
**1788** ★ Connecticut, Georgia, Maryland, Massachusetts, New Hampshire, New York, South Carolina, Virginia become states
**1789** ★ North Carolina statehood

**1790** ★ Rhode Island statehood
**1791** ★ Vermont statehood; Bill of Rights added to Constitution
**1792** ★ Kentucky statehood
**1796** ★ Tennessee statehood

| 1770 | 1780 | 1790 | 1800 |
| --- | --- | --- | --- |

**1777** George Washington at the Battle of Princeton.

**1787** The Constitution of the United States.

# 7
# Crisis in
# the Colonies (1745–1775)

## Chapter Outline

**1** Competing for Empire
**2** Showdown in North America
**3** Trouble Over Taxes
**4** The Split Widens
**5** The Shot Heard 'Round the World
Readings, page 493

| 1745 | 1750 | 1755 | 1760 | 1765 | 1770 | 1775 |
|------|------|------|------|------|------|------|

**1740s**
English move
into Ohio
Valley

**1754**
French and
Indian War
begins

**1759**
British take
Quebec

**1765**
Stamp Act
passed

**1770**
Boston
Massacre

**1775**
Fighting at
Lexington
and Concord

## About This Chapter

In the 1760s, colonists faced a deep crisis over this question: Did England have the right to tax them? In August 1765, Thomas Hutchinson, the lieutenant governor of Massachusetts, found himself in the middle of the storm. A few months earlier, Parliament had passed the Stamp Act, which taxed certain goods. Many colonists in Boston were furious about the tax. In fact, some colonists were angry enough to take violent action.

On August 26, Hutchinson and his family were having supper when a messenger burst in. "The mob is coming!" he cried. Hutchinson knew that the mob was after him because he was a royal official. He told his children to go to a neighbor's house, and he prepared to face the mob. But his oldest daughter "protested that she would not quit the house unless I did," recalled Hutchinson. "I could not stand against this and withdrew with her to a neighboring house."

Within minutes, the mob "fell upon my house with the rage of devils." When the mob realized that Hutchinson had fled, they rushed off to find him. Hutchinson hid all night. At dawn, he returned to find his home destroyed.

The violence shocked many colonists. But it was only the beginning. Anger over the Stamp Act grew. So, too, did the quarrel between England and its American colonies. By 1775, the quarrel had reached a point where it could be decided only by war.

Study the time line above. Name two events that happened in the years after the Stamp Act was passed.

Disputes between colonists and England led to a crisis. Here, angry New Yorkers destroy a statue of King George III.

# 1 Competing for Empire

### Read to Learn
★ What nations claimed land in North America?
★ Where did France build forts?
★ Why did Indian nations take sides in the struggle between England and France?

During the 1700s, Spain, France, and England competed for empire around the world. In North America, the 13 English colonies were caught up in these rivalries.

## Rivals for North America

By the late 1600s, England had two rivals in North America: Spain and France. Spanish settlers had expanded slowly into North America. Missionaries led the way into California, New Mexico, and Arizona. Because these settlements were far away from its colonies on the Atlantic coast, England did not see them as a threat.

However, Spain and England often clashed in the West Indies and along the border between Georgia and Spanish Florida. As you learned, Georgia was set up to stop Spain from expanding north from Florida. For years, Spain and England eyed each other with distrust across this border.

**The key to a large empire.** England's other rival was France. France claimed all the land along the Mississippi River. Find New France on the map on page 150. To back their

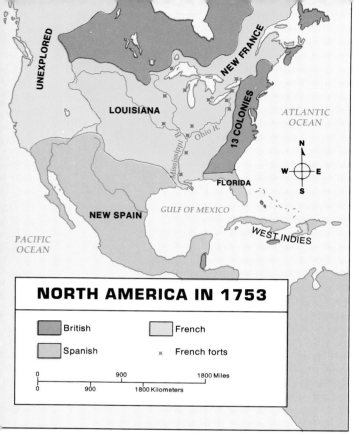

## NORTH AMERICA IN 1753

| | | | |
|---|---|---|---|
| ■ British | | □ French | |
| ■ Spanish | | ✕ French forts | |

0      900      1800 Miles
0      900      1800 Kilometers

MAP SKILL France and Spain claimed land to the north and south of the 13 English colonies in North America. Who claimed land along the Mississippi River?

claim, the French built forts from the Great Lakes to New Orleans. These forts gave France the key to a large empire and blocked the English colonies from expanding to the west.

To the north, France controlled Canada with a string of forts along the St. Lawrence River. These forts were meant to keep an enemy from sailing up the river into New France. Also, the forts protected the rich fishing grounds off Newfoundland and the fur trade around the Great Lakes.

**By right of arms.** English settlers lived in the area between the Atlantic Ocean and the Appalachian Mountains. By the 1740s, however, English traders were moving west from New York and Pennsylvania into the Ohio River valley.

At first, the French tried to scare off the English. In 1749, French soldiers moved down the Allegheny and Ohio rivers. Wherever a stream joined these two rivers, the French put up a sign warning that the land belonged to France "by right of arms."

English traders ignored these warnings. So the governor of New France, the Marquis Duquesne (mahr KEE doo KAYN), had forts built in the Ohio River valley to keep the English out of the French empire.

## Native Americans Take Sides

The lands that Spain, France, and England claimed in North America were not empty. Native Americans hunted and grew crops on these lands. They did not want to give up the land to European settlers. In the 1700s, some Native Americans decided that the only way to protect their way of life was to take sides in the struggle between England and France.

Indians controlled fur trade in the heart of North America. So both France and England looked for allies among the Indians. The French expected the Indians to side with them. Most French in North America were trappers and traders, not farmers. Trappers did not destroy hunting grounds by clearing forests for farms. Also, many French trappers married Indian women and adopted Indian ways.

On the other hand, English settlers were mostly farm families. They cleared land, often ignoring Indian rights. Because the English believed that their culture was superior, they looked down on Indian ways. As English settlers expanded onto Indian lands, Indians fought back.

In the end, both France and England found allies. France's strongest allies were the Algonquins and Hurons. The English looked for help to the powerful Iroquois nations, old enemies of the Algonquins.

An English trader and official, William Johnson, won the respect of the Mohawks, one of the Iroquois nations.

The English invited friendly Iroquois leaders to visit London. A Dutch artist, John Verelst, painted this portrait of the Iroquois leader Ho Nee Yeath Taw No Row. The English called him John Wolf Clan.

Johnson was one of the few English men to marry an Indian woman. His wife, Molly Brant, was the daughter of a Mohawk chief. Johnson urged his Iroquois friends to become allies of the English.

The English also won the help of Indians in the Ohio Valley by charging lower prices for trade goods than the French. Many Indians began buying from English traders. The loss of Indian trade angered the French, who were determined to defend their claims in the Ohio River valley.

## SECTION REVIEW

1. **Locate:** Florida, Mississippi River, Gulf of Mexico, New Orleans, Canada, St. Lawrence River, Ohio River.
2. How did France protect its claim to land in North America?
3. Why did some Indians in the Ohio River valley prefer to trade with the English?
4. **What Do You Think?** How do you think the actions of both England and France increased tensions in North America?

# 2 Showdown in North America

### Read to Learn

★ What role did George Washington play in the French and Indian War?
★ Why did the colonies reject the Albany Plan of Union?
★ What lands did Britain gain by the Treaty of Paris?
★ What does this word mean: population?

Three times between 1689 and 1748, France and Great Britain* went to war. Battles raged in both Europe and North America. English colonists named the wars after the ruling king or queen. There was King William's War, Queen Anne's War, and King George's War. Each war ended with an uneasy peace. In 1754, fighting broke out again in a long conflict, called the *French and Indian War.*

### Drama at Fort Necessity

Scuffles between France and Britain in the Ohio River valley triggered the opening shots of the French and Indian War. Some wealthy Virginians claimed land in the upper Ohio River valley. To protect their claims, they urged the governor of Virginia to build a fort where the Monongahela

---

*In 1707, England and Scotland were joined into the United Kingdom of Great Britain. After that date, the terms Great Britain and British were used to describe the country and its people. However, the terms England and English were still used in the 1700s.

and Allegheny rivers meet. (See the map on page 154.) The governor sent a young officer, George Washington, to carry out this task.

Washington was only 22 years old at the time, but he was an able and brave soldier. Washington grew up on a plantation in Virginia. At age 15, he began work as a surveyor. He later explored frontier lands in western Virginia. In 1753, Washington carried a message to the French in Ohio warning them to pull back their forces. On this dangerous mission, young Washington narrowly escaped death.

In 1754, Washington again headed west from Virginia. This time, he led 150 soldiers to carry out the governor's order to build the new fort. On the way, Washington heard that the French had already built Fort Duquesne where the two rivers meet. But he continued on.

When Washington learned that a French scouting party was camped in the woods ahead, he made a quiet march at night and surprised them. In a brief battle, Washington's troops scattered the French.

Defeat soon followed success. The Virginians, expecting the French to counterattack, hastily put up a stockade. They called it Fort Necessity. A strong force of French troops and Indians surrounded the fort. Trapped and outnumbered, the Virginians surrendered. Later, Washington was released

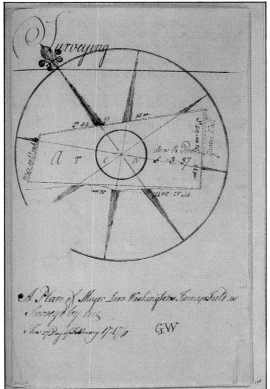

By age 17, George Washington, at left, was the official surveyor for Culpeper County, Virginia. He drew the plan, shown below, of his brother Lawrence Washington's turnip field.

and rode back to Virginia. The clash at Fort Necessity was the first battle of the French and Indian War.

## A Plan of Union

While Washington was defending Fort Necessity, delegates from seven of the English colonies were meeting in Albany, New York. They came together for two main reasons. They wanted the Iroquois to help them against the French. And they wanted to plan a united defense against the French.

The Iroquois leaders who came to the meeting had not decided whether to help the British. They thought that the French were stronger and had more forts than the British. The Iroquois left without agreeing to help, but later they did fight with the British.

The delegates in Albany knew that the colonies needed to work together against the French. Benjamin Franklin proposed the Albany *Plan of Union.* The plan called for a Grand Council with representatives from each colony. The Grand Council would make laws, raise taxes, and set up the defense of the colonies. The delegates approved the Plan of Union. But the colonial assemblies rejected it because they did not want to give up any of their own powers.

## The Balance of Power

The French and Indian War, which began in 1754, lasted until 1763. The war went badly for the British at first. The French had several advantages. For example, New France had a single government that could make decisions more quickly than the 13 separate English colonies. Also, the French had many Indian allies to help in the fight against the British.

But Britain had some advantages. It, too, had Indian allies. In the 13 colonies, the *population,* or number of people, was 20 times greater than that of New France. The English colonies were easier to defend than New France. And the British navy ruled the seas.

**English setbacks.** In 1755, General Edward Braddock led British and colonial troops to attack Fort Duquesne. General Braddock knew how to fight a war in Europe, but he had never fought in the wilderness of North America. A stubborn man, Braddock was called "Bulldog" behind his back.

The British moved slowly because they had to clear a road through thick forests for their cannons and other heavy gear. Washington, who went with Braddock, was upset at the slow pace. Indian scouts warned Braddock that he was heading for disaster. But he ignored their warning.

When the British neared Fort Duquesne, the French and their Indian allies launched a surprise attack. French and Indian sharpshooters hid in the forest and picked off British soldiers, who wore bright red uniforms. Braddock had five horses shot out from under him before he fell, fatally wounded. Washington was luckier. As he later reported, he "escaped without a wound, although I had four bullets through my coat."

Almost half the British were killed or wounded. Washington and other survivors returned to Virginia with news of Braddock's defeat. Washington then took command of a small force. During the rest of the war, he tried to guard the long Virginia frontier against Indian attacks.

For the next two years, the French and their Indian allies won a string of victories. The French captured Fort Oswego on Lake Ontario and took Fort William Henry on Lake George. (See the map on page 154.)

**A confident leader.** In 1757, a new prime minister, William Pitt, took over the British government. Pitt was a bold leader. "I believe that I can save this nation and that no one else can," he claimed with confidence. Pitt decided to try to win the war in North America first.* He sent Britain's best generals to the colonies. Then, he encouraged the colonists to support the war by promising to pay high prices for all goods they supplied to the troops.

Under Pitt's leadership, the tide of battle turned. In 1758, Lord Jeffrey Amherst captured the French fort at Louisbourg. That year, too, the Iroquois persuaded the Delawares to stop

---

*By 1756, the French and Indian War had spread from North America to Europe. There, it became known as the Seven Years War. The British and French also fought in India, where the British suffered defeats at first.

fighting the British. Without the Delawares, the French could not hold Fort Duquesne. When the British took the fort, they renamed it *Fort Pitt,* after the British prime minister. It later became the city of Pittsburgh.

## On the Plains of Abraham

The British kept up the offensive. With the help of their Indian allies, they took Fort Niagara. In 1759, Pitt sent General James Wolfe to attack Quebec, capital of New France. If Britain captured Quebec, France could no longer supply its forts farther up the

**MAP SKILL** During the French and Indian War, Britain and France battled for control of North America. Find Louisbourg, Quebec, and Fort Duquesne on the map. Why do you think Britain wanted to capture these places?

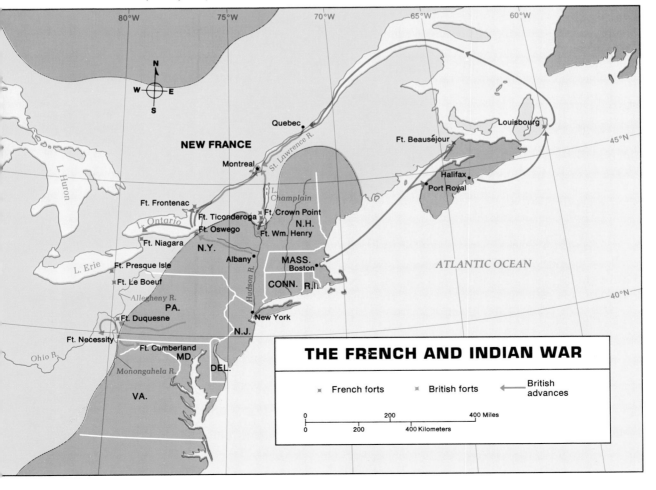

THE FRENCH AND INDIAN WAR

This painting by Sigmund Samuel shows British troops climbing up to the Plains of Abraham. When General Wolfe first saw the cliffs, he said, "I don't think we can by any possible means get up here; however, we must use our best endeavour." They succeeded and surprised the French in Quebec.

St. Lawrence River. Thus, the war would be won. But Quebec was well defended. It sat atop a steep cliff above the St. Lawrence. An able French general, the Marquis de Montcalm, was prepared to fight off a British attack.

Wolfe devised a daring plan to take Quebec. He knew that Montcalm had only a few soldiers guarding the cliff because the French thought that it was too steep to climb. Late one night, Wolfe secretly moved his troops in small boats to the foot of the cliff. British soldiers swarmed ashore and scrambled up the steep cliff onto the *Plains of Abraham* outside the city.

When the sun rose, Montcalm woke to hear that 4,000 British troops were waiting to go into battle. He quickly marched his own troops out to meet them. In the fierce battle that followed, both Wolfe and Montcalm were killed. But Wolfe lived long enough to see the British win.

## British Gains

When news of the British victory reached the 13 colonies, church bells rang out in celebration. The fall of Quebec sealed the fate of New France. In 1760, the British took Montreal, and the war in North America ended. Fighting dragged on in Europe until Britain and France signed the *Treaty of Paris* in 1763.

By this treaty, Britain gained Canada and all French lands east of the

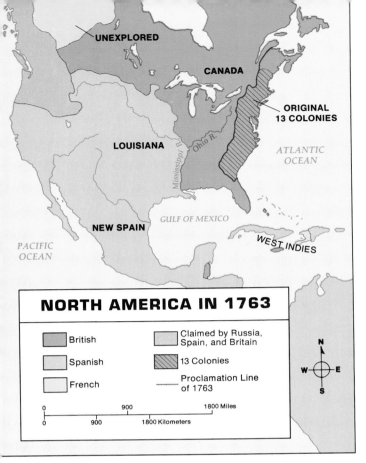

## NORTH AMERICA IN 1763

**Legend:**
- British
- Spanish
- French
- Claimed by Russia, Spain, and Britain
- 13 Colonies
- Proclamation Line of 1763

0    900    1800 Miles
0    900    1800 Kilometers

Map labels: UNEXPLORED, CANADA, ORIGINAL 13 COLONIES, LOUISIANA, ATLANTIC OCEAN, NEW SPAIN, GULF OF MEXICO, WEST INDIES, PACIFIC OCEAN, Mississippi R., Ohio R.

**MAP SKILL** Compare this map to the map on page 150. How was North America in 1763 different from what it had been in 1753?

Mississippi River. (This area is shown on the map at left.) In the New World, France kept only a few sugar-growing islands in the West Indies. Spain, which had entered the war on the French side in 1762, had to give Florida to Britain. However, Spain kept its lands west of the Mississippi, as well as its empire in Central and South America.

After years of fighting, peace returned to North America. Yet within a few years, a new struggle broke out. This time, the struggle pitted Britain against its own colonies.

### SECTION REVIEW

1. **Locate:** Fort Duquesne, Fort Oswego, Louisbourg, Quebec, Montreal.
2. **Define:** population.
3. (a) What was the Albany Plan of Union? (b) Why was it rejected?
4. How did the British victory at Quebec affect the outcome of the war?
5. **What Do You Think?** Why do you think the British were able to win so much of North America by 1763?

# 3 Trouble Over Taxes

### Read to Learn
★ Why did Pontiac fight the British?
★ How did Britain try to get money to repay its debts?
★ Why did colonists object to the Stamp Act?
★ What do these words mean: boycott, repeal?

Britain was pleased with its victory. So, too, were the colonists. They were free of the French threat and could go back to their everyday lives. Their soldiers had fought well, and they had developed good officers like George Washington.

But with victory came problems. How would Britain govern the lands it won from France? How would Britain treat French settlers and their Indian allies? Even more urgent, how would Britain repay the money it had borrowed to win the French and Indian War?

### Fighting on the Frontier

Even before the war between Britain and France ended, trouble flared up in the Ohio Valley. English colonists crossed the Appalachians to settle in the former French lands. Yet

Native American nations already lived there. They included the Senecas, Delawares, Shawnees, Ottawas, Miamis, and Hurons.

The British sent Lord Jeffrey Amherst to the frontier to keep order. In the past, French traders treated Native Americans with respect, holding feasts and giving presents. Amherst refused to do this. He raised the prices on goods traded to the Indians because the British no longer had to compete with the French. Also, he allowed English settlers to build forts on land given to the Indians by treaties.

**Pontiac's War.** Amherst's actions angered Native Americans. They found a leader in Pontiac, an Ottawa chief. One English trader described Pontiac as "a shrewd, sensible Indian of few words, [who] commands more respect amongst these nations than any Indian I ever saw." (See the picture at right.)

War broke out when Pontiac attacked British troops at Fort Detroit. He then called on other Indian nations to join the fight. A number of Indian nations responded to his call. In a few months, they overran most British forts on the frontier. British and colonial troops fought back and regained much they had lost.

In October 1763, Pontiac learned that the Treaty of Paris had been signed. The treaty ended the Indians' hope of receiving French aid. One by one, the Indian nations stopped fighting and returned home. "All my young men have buried their hatchets," said Pontiac. By December, the British again controlled the frontier.

**Proclamation of 1763.** Pontiac's War convinced the British that they must stop settlers from moving onto Indian lands. So the British issued the *Proclamation of 1763*. It drew a line along the Appalachian Mountains and forbade colonists to settle west of that line. Settlers already living west of the line had to leave.

**AMERICANS WHO DARED**

### Pontiac

Pontiac was a strong, proud man and the leader of the Ottawas. He was determined to hold the Ohio Valley against the British. Pontiac believed that Indians could save their land only by returning to their old ways. He carried this message to his followers. A skillful organizer, Pontiac brought many Indian nations together to fight the British.

The proclamation was meant to protect Native Americans and fur traders in the western lands. Britain sent 10,000 troops to America to enforce it. The troops were supposed to patrol the frontier. However, most stayed in cities on the Atlantic coast.

The proclamation angered colonists because it stopped them from moving west. Also, colonists had to help pay for the British troops. Many settlers simply ignored the proclamation and moved west anyway.

## An Urgent Need for Money

Britain faced another problem after the French and Indian War. It was deeply in debt. The British prime minister, George Grenville, decided that the colonists must help pay the debt since they gained the most from the war.

**Sugar Act.** In 1764, Prime Minister Grenville asked Parliament to approve the Sugar Act, which put a new tax on molasses. Molasses, you will remember, was a valuable item in the triangular trade. (See page 141.)

The *Sugar Act* of 1764 replaced an earlier tax on molasses. The earlier tax was so high that any merchant who paid it would have been driven out of business. So most merchants simply avoided the tax by smuggling molasses into the colonies. Often, they bribed tax collectors to look the other way. The Sugar Act of 1764 lowered the tax. But Grenville demanded that the smuggling and bribes be stopped. And he wanted the tax paid.

**Stamp Act.** In 1765, Grenville persuaded Parliament to pass the *Stamp Act*. It put a tax on legal documents such as wills or marriage papers, as well as on newspapers, almanacs, playing cards, and even dice. The Stamp Act required that all legal documents and dozens of other items carry a stamp to show that the tax had been paid. Stamp taxes were used in Britain and other countries to raise money. But Britain had never required its colonies to pay such a tax.

## No Taxation Without Representation

To the surprise of the British, the colonists responded violently to the Stamp Act. Riots broke out in New York City, Newport, and Charleston. In Boston, angry mobs destroyed the homes of royal officials. Agents who were supposed to collect the unpopular stamp tax were run out of town.

The British prime minister, George Grenville, thought the Stamp Act was a fair tax. To his surprise, the colonists claimed it was completely unfair. The stamp, above, was used on wills and insurance policies to show that a five-shilling tax had been paid.

John Adams, a Massachusetts lawyer, noted that the rage of the people was felt in every colony. "Our presses have groaned, our pulpits have thundered, our legislatures have resolved, our towns have voted, the crown officers everywhere trembled."

Why were the colonists so angry at the taxes? After all, Britain had spent a lot of money to protect them during the recent war. And British citizens were paying much higher taxes than the American colonists.

Colonists objected to the taxes because they believed in the principle of no taxation without representation. This principle had its roots in English traditions going back to the Magna Carta. (Review page 92.) Colonists claimed that only they or their representatives had the right to pass taxes. They argued that they did not elect any representatives to Parliament. So Parliament had no right to tax them. The colonists were willing to pay taxes—if the taxes were passed by their own colonial legislatures.

## The Stamp Act Congress

Colonists began to organize against the Stamp Act. In October 1765, nine colonies sent delegates to the *Stamp Act Congress,* which met in New York City. The congress sent petitions, or letters, to King George III and Parliament. In these petitions, the delegates declared that the Stamp and Sugar acts were unjust because Parliament had no right to tax the colonies.

Parliament was in no mood to listen to the petitions of the Stamp Act Congress. But colonists took another action that was more effective. They joined together to boycott British goods. To *boycott* means to refuse to buy certain goods or services. The boycott of British goods took its toll. Trade fell off by 14 percent. British merchants suffered. So, too, did British workers who made goods for the colonies.

Finally, in 1766, Parliament *repealed,* or canceled, the Stamp Act. At the same time, however, it passed the Declaratory Act. In this act, Parliament said that it had the right to make laws and raise taxes in "all cases whatsoever."

When colonists heard that the Stamp Act had been repealed, they were overjoyed. They paid little attention to the Declaratory Act. But the dispute over taxes was not settled. Before long, colonists would face other crises when Parliament again tried to tax them.

## SECTION REVIEW

1. **Locate:** Appalachian Mountains, New York, Charleston, Boston.
2. **Define:** boycott, repeal.
3. What was the goal of the Proclamation of 1763?
4. Why did colonists object to the Stamp Act?
5. **What Do You Think?** Do you think the Stamp Act was unjust? Explain.

# 4 The Split Widens

## Read to Learn

★ How did the colonists respond to the Townshend Acts?
★ What leaders emerged in the colonies?
★ What happened during the Boston Massacre?
★ What do these words mean: writ of assistance, nonimportation agreement, committee of correspondence?

The repeal of the Stamp Act left Britain with its war debt still unpaid. So Parliament passed new taxes, which colonists again protested. As tensions built, violence broke out again.

## The Townshend Acts

In May 1767, Parliament debated the issue of taxing the colonists. During the debate, George Grenville, now a member of Parliament, challenged Charles Townshend, who was in charge of the British treasury.

"You are cowards, you are afraid of the Americans, you dare not tax America!" shouted Grenville.

"Fear? Cowards?" snapped Townshend, "I dare tax America!"

"Dare you tax America?" cried Grenville. "I wish I could see it!"

"I will, I will!" replied Townshend.

The next month, Parliament passed the **Townshend Acts**, which taxed goods such as glass, paper, silk, lead, and tea. Although the taxes were fairly low, Americans still claimed that Parliament did not have the right to tax them.

The Townshend Acts set up new ways to collect the taxes. Customs officers were sent to American ports with orders to stop smugglers. They were allowed to use writs of assistance in their work. A *writ of assistance* was a legal document. It let a customs officer inspect a ship's cargo without giving any reason for the search. Sometimes, customs officers used these writs to keep ships from leaving port until merchants paid them bribes.

Colonists protested the writs of assistance. They said that the writs violated their rights as British citizens. Under British law, an official could not search someone's property without giving a good reason for suspecting that person.

## A Tough Response

The colonists' answer to the Townshend Acts was loud and clear. From New Hampshire to Georgia, merchants and planters signed **nonimportation agreements**. In these agreements, they promised to stop importing goods taxed by the Townshend Acts. They hoped that British merchants who were hurt by the loss of business would force Parliament to repeal the new taxes.

Colonists carried their fight to the newspapers. They wrote letters warning fellow citizens of the danger of letting Parliament tax them. Newspapers in one colony printed letters sent to newspapers in other colonies.

Many angry colonists joined the **Sons of Liberty**. This group was formed during the Stamp Act protests. Members met to talk about ways to protest British policies and protect colonial liberties. The Sons of Liberty agreed to stop using any goods that were taxed and to stop drinking British tea.

Women formed the **Daughters of Liberty**. They pledged to wear dresses of homespun cloth rather than of cloth imported from England. In Rowley, Massachusetts, "thirty-three respectable ladies of the town met at sunrise with their [spinning] wheels to spend the day at the house of the Reverend Jedediah Jewell." At sunset, the women appeared "neatly dressed . . . in homespun."

In cities such as Boston and Charleston, Sons and Daughters of Liberty hung lanterns in large trees,

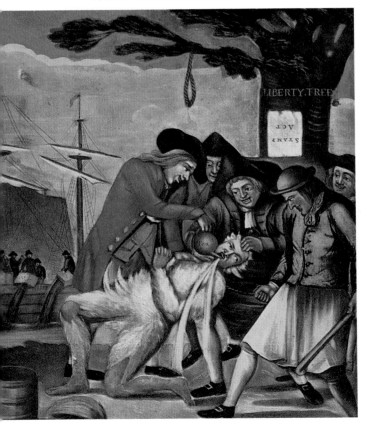

Some colonists tarred and feathered tax collectors to protest British taxes. This drawing by a British artist shows colonists pouring tea down the throat of a tax collector who has been tarred and feathered.

which then became known as Liberty Trees. From these trees, they hung cloth or straw statues dressed like British officials. The statues served as warnings to the officials not to try to collect the unpopular taxes. Sons and Daughters of Liberty visited merchants to persuade them to sign the nonimportation agreements.

## Colonists Find Leaders

During the quarrel with Britain, leaders emerged in all the colonies. In Massachusetts, Samuel Adams of Boston took the lead against Britain. Sam Adams seemed an unlikely leader. He was a failure in business and a poor public speaker. But he loved politics. He was always present at Boston town meetings and Sons of Liberty rallies.

Sam Adams "eats little, sleeps little, thinks much," reported one colonist. "He is most decisive . . . in the pursuit of his objects." Adams worked day and night against Britain. He published a lot of pamphlets and wrote many letters to the newspapers. His fiery arguments made colonists aware of the dangers of British rule.

Another Massachusetts leader was John Adams. John Adams, a lawyer, was more cautious than his second cousin, Sam. His knowledge of British law earned him the respect of many colonists.

In Virginia, George Washington was a member of the House of Burgesses when it protested the Townshend Acts. Another Virginian, Patrick Henry, was well known for speeches that moved listeners to both tears and anger. In a speech against the Stamp Act, Henry attacked Britain so furiously that some people called out, "Treason!" Henry replied, "If this be treason, make the most of it!" Henry's words moved a young listener, Thomas Jefferson. At the time, Jefferson was a 22-year-old law student. Later, he joined the ranks of American leaders.

Among the colonial leaders, Patrick Henry won fame for his spellbinding speeches. Here, he addresses fellow Virginians in the House of Burgesses.

Women like Mercy Otis Warren also took leading roles. Warren wrote plays that made fun of royal officials. The plays were published in newspapers and widely read. Warren's home in Plymouth, Massachusetts, was a meeting place for colonists opposed to British policies.

## Trouble in the Cities

New York and Boston were centers of protest. In 1766, the New York assembly refused to obey the Quartering Act. The *Quartering Act* said that colonists had to pay for the housing of British soldiers. New Yorkers argued that the Quartering Act was just another way of taxing them without their consent. When news of New York's action reached Britain, royal officials angrily dismissed the assembly.

In Boston, too, tempers were rising. The governor dismissed the Massachusetts assembly in 1768 because it asked to have the Townshend Acts repealed. Soon after, two regiments of British soldiers arrived in Boston to protect customs officers from outraged citizens.

To many people, the soldiers' tents set up on the Boston Common were daily reminders that Britain was trying to bully them into paying unjust taxes. When the soldiers walked along the streets of Boston, they risked insults, snowballs, or beatings. The time was ripe for disaster.

## The Boston Massacre

On the night of March 5, 1770, a crowd gathered outside the Boston customs house. Colonists shouted insults at the "lobsterbacks," their name for the redcoated soldiers who guarded the building. Then, they began throwing snowballs, oyster shells, and sticks at the soldiers.

The soldiers stood their ground. Suddenly, a shot rang out—no one knows whether from the soldiers or the crowd. The soldiers fired into the crowd. When the smoke from the musket volley cleared, five people lay dead or dying. Among them was Crispus

Paul Revere, a Boston silversmith, engraved and printed this scene of the Boston Massacre. The picture circulated widely in the colonies. It helped stir up anger against Britain. Revere shows Captain Thomas Preston, at right, ordering his troops to fire on the colonists.

Attucks, a black sailor who was active in the Sons of Liberty.

Sam Adams quickly wrote to the other colonies about the shooting, which he called the *Boston Massacre*. Paul Revere, a Boston silversmith, made an engraving of it. The engraving vividly showed the dead and wounded colonists. As news of the Boston Massacre spread, colonists' outrage grew.

The soldiers were put on trial for the shooting. John Adams agreed to defend them, saying that they deserved a fair trial. He wanted to show the world that Americans believed in justice, even if the British government did not. At the trial, Adams argued that the crowd had provoked the soldiers. His arguments convinced the jury, and the soldiers received light sentences.

## Parliament Backs Down

On the day of the Boston Massacre, Parliament was meeting in London. The nonimportation agreements had crippled trade with the colonies. Under pressure from British merchants, Parliament repealed most of the Townshend taxes. But it left in place the tax on tea. The colonists, it said, must accept the fact that Parliament had the right to tax them.

Americans were delighted with the repeal. So they paid little attention to the tax on tea. They ended their boycott of British goods, and for a few years, calm returned to the colonies. But memories of the disputes left Americans uneasy.

During this period of calm, Sam Adams set up the first *committees of correspondence* to keep colonists informed of British actions. The committees wrote letters and pamphlets to spread the alarm whenever Britain tried to enforce unpopular acts of Parliament. In this way, the committees helped unite the colonists against Britain.

━━ **SECTION REVIEW** ━━━━━━━━

1. **Define:** writ of assistance, nonimportation agreement, committee of correspondence.
2. (a) Why did some colonists join the Sons and Daughters of Liberty? (b) What actions did these groups take?
3. How did Samuel Adams work for the colonists' cause?
4. Why did New Yorkers protest against the Quartering Act?
5. **What Do You Think?** Why do you think Sam Adams called the shooting at the customs house the Boston Massacre?

# 5 The Shot Heard 'Round the World

### Read to Learn
★ Why did Americans protest the Tea Act?
★ How did Britain respond to the Boston Tea Party?
★ Why did General Gage send troops to Concord?
★ What do these words mean: militia, minuteman?

Between 1765 and 1770, Parliament twice passed and then repealed taxes. In 1773, a new conflict over taxes exploded. This time, colonists began to think the unthinkable. Perhaps the time had come to throw off British rule and declare their independence.

## Trouble Over Tea

The new trouble began over tea. Colonists enjoyed drinking tea. Most of it came from the British East India

# Spirit of America

## The *Gaspee* Incident: Spirit of Justice

In the early 1770s, the *Gaspee,* a British ship, patrolled the waters off Providence, Rhode Island, to prevent smuggling. Its commander, William Dudingston, often angered colonists when he stopped small fishing boats at gunpoint.

On June 9, 1772, the *Gaspee* ran aground while chasing a local ship. On hearing this news, a group of Providence merchants rowed out to the stranded ship. Swiftly, they swarmed on board the *Gaspee.* They sent Dudingston and his crew ashore and then set fire to the *Gaspee.*

News of the *Gaspee* affair ignited a storm in London. The king ordered a secret commission to look into the affair. However, colonists learned about the commission. When commission members arrived in Rhode Island, they ran into a wall of silence. They offered a reward for information leading to the arrest and conviction of the guilty parties. But there were no arrests.

In the end, the commission members returned to England empty-handed. Still, colonists saw their coming to the colonies as yet another British attack on American liberties. Committees of correspondence sprang up throughout the colonies to discuss the fears aroused by the *Gaspee* affair.

★ How did the *Gaspee* affair increase tension in the colonies?

Company. The company sold its tea to American tea merchants. In turn, these tea merchants sold the tea to the colonists.

In the 1770s, the British East India Company was in financial trouble. Over 15 million pounds of its tea sat unsold in British warehouses. In 1773, Parliament tried to help the troubled company by passing the *Tea Act.* The act removed some taxes paid by the British East India Company. It also let the company sell tea directly to colonists instead of to American tea merchants. These steps were meant to lower the price of tea so that Americans would buy more of it.

To the surprise of Parliament, colonists protested the Tea Act. American tea merchants were angry because they were cut out of the tea trade. If Parliament ruined tea merchants today, they warned, it might turn on other businesses tomorrow. Even tea drinkers, who would have paid less for tea, scorned the Tea Act. They believed that it was a trick to make them agree to Parliament's right to tax the colonies.

Once again, Americans responded with a boycott. "Do not suffer yourself to sip the accursed, dutied *STUFF*," said one newspaper. "For if you do, the devil will immediately enter into you, and you will instantly become a traitor to your country." Daughters of Liberty brewed homemade "liberty tea" from raspberry leaves. At some ports, colonists refused to let ships unload their cargoes of tea.

## The Boston Tea Party

When three ships loaded with tea reached Boston, Massachusetts, Governor Thomas Hutchinson insisted that the ships unload their cargo. But Sam Adams and other Sons of Liberty had their own plans. On the night of December 16, they met in Old South Church. They sent a message to the governor, demanding that the ships leave the harbor. The messenger returned with the governor's reply. The ships must stay and unload their cargo. Adams stood up and declared, "This meeting can do nothing further to save the country."

His words were a signal. One by one, people left the meeting. A little while later, a crowd of about 50 people dressed as Indians swarmed down to the harbor and boarded the tea ships. "We then were ordered by our commander to open the ship's hatches," recalled one colonist, "and take out all the chests of tea and throw them overboard . . . first cutting and splitting the chests with our tomahawks."

News of the Boston Tea Party, shown here, spread quickly. Other seaports held "tea parties" of their own. Some colonists celebrated the event, but others feared that it would lead to more trouble with Britain.

In three hours, the job was done. The contents of 342 chests of tea floated in Boston harbor. The next day, the cautious John Adams wrote about the event in his diary:

> The people should never rise without doing something to be remembered, something notable and striking. This destruction of the tea is so bold, so daring, so firm . . . it must have such important and lasting consequences that I can't help considering it a turning point in history.

## Britain Responds

Colonists had mixed reactions to the *Boston Tea Party.* Some cheered this firm protest of British rule. Others worried that such action would encourage lawlessness in the colonies. But even those who condemned the Boston Tea Party were shocked at Britain's response to it.

**The Intolerable Acts.** Parliament and King George III felt that the people of Boston needed to be punished. In 1774, Parliament passed a series of laws directed against Massachusetts. First, it shut down the port of Boston. No ship could enter or leave the harbor—not even a small boat. The harbor would remain closed until the colonists paid for the tea and showed that they were sorry for what they had done.

Second, Parliament said that town meetings could be held only once a year unless the governor gave permission for other meetings. In the past, colonists had called town meetings whenever they wished.

Third, Parliament allowed customs officers and other officials who might be charged with major crimes to be tried in England instead of in Massachusetts. Colonists protested. They said that a dishonest official could break the law in America and avoid punishment "by being tried, where no evidence can pursue him."

Fourth, Parliament passed a new Quartering Act. No longer would redcoats camp in tents on the Boston Commons. Instead, commanders could force citizens to house troops in their homes. The colonists called these laws the *Intolerable Acts* because they were so harsh.

**Quebec Act.** About the same time, Parliament also passed the **Quebec Act.** It set up a government for Canada and protected the rights of French Catholics. The Quebec Act included the land between the Ohio and Missouri rivers as part of Canada. The act pleased French Canadians. But it angered the American colonists, in part because the new government in Canada did not include an elected assembly. American colonists were especially upset that western lands, which they claimed, were made part of Canada.

**Colonists react.** The committees of correspondence spread the news of the Intolerable Acts and wrote angrily about the Quebec Act. People from other colonies sent aid to Boston, where the people faced hunger while their port was closed. Carts rolled into Boston with rice from South Carolina, corn from Virginia, flour from Pennsylvania, and sheep from Connecticut.

In the Virginia assembly, young Thomas Jefferson suggested that a day be set aside to mark the shame of the Intolerable Acts. The royal governor of Virginia did not like the idea and dismissed the assembly. But the colonies went ahead with the idea anyway. On June 1, 1774, church bells rang slowly. Merchants closed their shops. Many colonists prayed and fasted all day.

## The First Continental Congress

As sympathy for Massachusetts grew, leaders from the colonies decided to meet. They wanted to unite against the Intolerable Acts. In September 1774, delegates from 12 colonies gathered in Philadelphia at the *First Continental Congress.* Only Georgia did not send delegates.

Historians study events that happened in the past. They often look at these events in **chronological order,** or the order in which they occurred. In this way, they can judge whether or not events are related.

A **time line** is one way to show the relationship between events over time. A time line also shows the dates when events happened.

A time line appears at the beginning of each unit and at the beginning of each chapter in this book. These time lines are called horizontal time lines because they set out dates and events on a line from left to right.

Study the time line below. Then use these steps to read the time line.

1. **Identify the time period covered in the time line.** (a) What is the earliest date shown on the time line below? (b) What is the latest date? (c) What is the period covered by this time line?

2. **Decide how the time line is divided.** Time lines are always divided into equal parts or time periods. Some time lines are divided into 10-year periods. A 10-year period is called a **decade.**

Some time lines are divided into 100-year periods. A 100-year period is called a **century.** The period from 1700 to 1799, for example, is called the 18th century. We live in the 20th century, or the period from 1900 to 1999. (a) List the dates on the top of the time line below. (b) How many years are there between each date? (c) What events occurred during the decade of the 1760s? (d) What century is shown on this time line?

3. **Study the time line to discover how events are related.** Use your reading in this chapter and the time line to answer these questions. (a) When did the Boston Tea Party take place? (b) Was the Tea Act passed before or after the Boston Tea Party? (c) Was there a relationship between these two events? Explain your answer.

4. **Draw conclusions.** Compare the time line below to the one on page 148. Then use your reading in this chapter and the two time lines to draw conclusions about events taking place during this period. (a) What time period is shown on page 148? (b) Which time line shows the longer period of time? (c) What events took place between 1745 and 1763? (d) How do you think these events affected what happened after 1763?

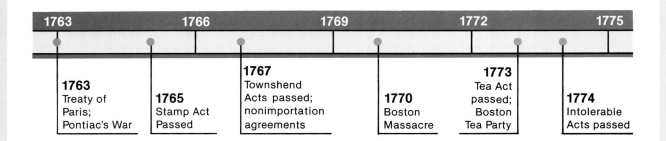

| 1763 | 1766 | 1769 | 1772 | 1775 |
|---|---|---|---|---|

**1763**
Treaty of
Paris;
Pontiac's War

**1765**
Stamp Act
Passed

**1767**
Townshend
Acts passed;
nonimportation
agreements

**1770**
Boston
Massacre

**1773**
Tea Act
passed;
Boston
Tea Party

**1774**
Intolerable
Acts passed

Delegates had different views about what the Continental Congress should do. Some wanted to patch up the quarrel with Britain by getting Parliament to guarantee their rights. Others argued that the Intolerable Acts proved that Britain would destroy their rights whenever it chose. They urged colonists to stand together firmly against Britain.

After much debate, the delegates passed a resolution backing Massachusetts in its struggle against the Intolerable Acts. They agreed to boycott all British goods and stop exporting American goods to Britain until the acts were repealed. They urged each colony to set up and train its own militia (muh LIHSH uh). A *militia* is an army of citizens who serve as soldiers during an emergency.

Before leaving Philadelphia in October 1774, the delegates agreed to meet again the next May. By May 1775, however, events would set the colonists on a new course.

## The British Are Coming!

In Massachusetts, colonists were already preparing to resist Britain. Volunteers, known as *minutemen,* trained regularly. Minutemen kept their muskets at hand, ready to fight at a minute's notice. In towns near Boston, they collected weapons and gunpowder.

Meanwhile, Britain built up its forces. More redcoats landed at Boston, bringing the total number of troops to 4,000. Early in 1775, General Thomas Gage, who commanded the British troops, sent scouts to the towns near Boston. They reported that minutemen had a large store of arms in Concord, a village 18 miles (29 km) from Boston. On April 18, Gage sent about 700 troops to seize the arms by surprise. The troops left Boston quietly at night. But eagle eyes saw them leave. Sons of

Liberty hung two lamps from the Old North Church in Boston. The lamps were a signal to other watchers.

**Paul Revere's ride.** Across the Charles River, Paul Revere and other Sons of Liberty saw the signal. They mounted their horses and rode toward Concord. As Revere passed through each sleepy village, he shouted: "The British are coming! The British are coming!"

In the early morning of April 19, the redcoats reached the common at Lexington, a town near Concord. There, 70 armed minutemen waited under the command of Captain John Parker. The British ordered the minutemen to go home. They refused. A shot broke through the chill air. Later reports disagree over who fired it. (See the two reports on page 217.) In the brief struggle that followed, eight colonists were killed, and one British soldier was wounded.

The British went on to Concord but found no arms or supplies. When they turned back to Boston, they met 300 more minutemen on a bridge outside Concord. Fighting broke out again. This time, the British were forced to retreat. As they withdrew through the woods and fields, colonial sharpshooters took deadly aim at them. Before they reached Boston, the British lost 73 men. Another 200 were wounded or missing.

**Fading hopes for peace.** News of the battles at Lexington and Concord traveled fast. Many colonists saw their hopes of reaching an agreement with Britain fade. Only war would decide the future of the 13 colonies.

More than 60 years after the battles, a monument was set up in Concord. A well-known New England poet, Ralph Waldo Emerson, wrote a poem to be sung at the opening ceremony. In the "Concord Hymn," he created a vivid picture of the clash at Concord. It begins:

**MAP SKILL** In the picture at right, British redcoats fire on minutemen at Lexington. The fighting at Lexington and Concord lasted only a few minutes, but the return to Boston was costly for the British. They faced angry colonists as they retreated. What towns did the British pass through on their way to Concord?

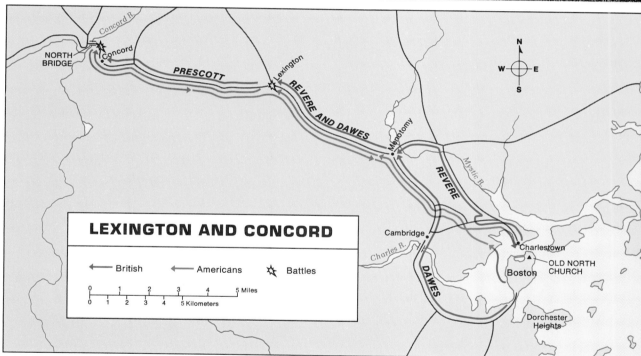

## LEXINGTON AND CONCORD

← British    ← Americans    ☆ Battles

0  1  2  3  4  5 Miles
0  1  2  3  4  5 Kilometers

By the rude bridge that arched the
    flood,
Their flag to April's breeze unfurled,
Here once the embattled farmers stood,
And fired the shot heard round the
    world.

The "embattled farmers" faced long years of war. But at the war's end, the 13 colonies would stand firm as a new, independent nation.

---

## SECTION REVIEW

1. **Locate:** Boston, Lexington, Concord.
2. **Define:** militia, minuteman.
3. What was the goal of the Tea Act?
4. Describe three of the Intolerable Acts.
5. **What Do You Think?** Why do you think delegates to the first Continental Congress were divided over how to respond to the Intolerable Acts?

# Chapter 7 Review

 **Summary**

In the mid-1700s, competition between France and England resulted in the struggle known as the French and Indian War. By 1763, Britain had won control of the French empire in North America.

The war left Britain deeply in debt. So Parliament decided to tax the colonies to help repay this debt. Colonists protested against the taxes passed by Parliament.

To protest the Tea Act, a group of colonists dumped tea into Boston harbor. Britain responded by passing the Intolerable Acts. In September 1774, leaders from 12 colonies met at the First Continental Congress. They planned to meet again in 1775. But by then, minutemen and British troops had clashed at the battles of Lexington and Concord.

 **Reviewing the Facts**

**Key Terms.** Match each term in Column 1 with the correct definition in Column 2.

| Column 1 | Column 2 |
|---|---|
| **1.** boycott | **a.** document letting officials make a search |
| **2.** repeal | **b.** group that informed colonists of British actions |
| **3.** writ of assistance | **c.** army of citizen soldiers |
| **4.** committee of correspondence | **d.** cancel |
| **5.** militia | **e.** refusal to buy or use certain goods or services |

**Key People, Events, and Ideas.** Identify each of the following.

1. Plan of Union
2. Pontiac
3. Proclamation of 1763
4. Stamp Act
5. Stamp Act Congress
6. Townshend Acts
7. Quartering Act
8. Samuel Adams
9. Patrick Henry
10. Mercy Otis Warren
11. Boston Massacre
12. Tea Act
13. Quebec Act
14. First Continental Congress
15. Paul Revere

 **Chapter Checkup**

1. (a) Which Indian nations sided with France in the 1700s? (b) Who helped Britain? (c) Why did Native Americans take sides in the struggle between Britain and France?

2. (a) Why did George Washington lead troops into the Ohio Valley in 1754? (b) What happened at Fort Necessity?

3. Describe the role each of the following played in the French and Indian War: (a) Edward Braddock; (b) William Pitt; (c) James Wolfe.

4. Why did Pontiac fight the British?

5. (a) List three ways Parliament tried to tax the colonies. (b) Describe how colonists responded to each.

6. Why did the colonists protest taxes passed by Parliament?

7. (a) What was the Boston Tea Party? (b) What different reactions did colonists have to it?

8. (a) Why did General Gage send troops to Concord? (b) What happened to them when they reached Lexington?

## ★ Thinking About History ★

1. **Drawing a conclusion.** (a) How did Britain try to prevent clashes between Native Americans and settlers on the frontier? (b) Do you think this policy was likely to succeed? Explain.

2. **Learning about citizenship.** Parliament claimed that it represented all British subjects and had the right to tax the colonies. Colonists replied that only their own representatives had that right. With which side do you agree? Explain.

3. **Relating past to present.** Compare the ways colonists protested unpopular acts of Parliament to the ways people protest unpopular laws today. (a) How are they similar? (b) How are they different?

4. **Analyzing a quotation.** In early April 1775, a British scout near Boston talked to an old man cleaning his musket. "I asked him what he was going to kill. He said there was a flock of redcoats at Boston, which he expected would be here soon; he meant to try and hit some of them, as he expected they would be very good marks." (a) What did the old man mean by "a flock of redcoats"? (b) Was his prediction true? Explain.

5. **Understanding the economy.** Describe two economic reasons why colonists protested British policies.

## ★ Using Your Skills ★

1. **Map reading.** Study the map on page 150. (a) How many countries claimed land in North America? (b) Which country held land around the Great Lakes? (c) What country had control of Florida in 1753?

2. **Map reading.** Study the map on page 169. (a) In what direction did Paul Revere ride when he left Boston? (b) About how far is Lexington from Concord? (c) In what direction did the British travel when they retreated from Concord?

3. **Placing events in time.** Study the time line on page 167 and review your reading in this chapter. (a) Were the Intolerable Acts passed before or after the Boston Tea Party? (b) What was the link between these two events?

4. **Making a generalization.** (a) List three facts about events leading up to the Boston Massacre. (b) Make a generalization based on these facts about the Boston Massacre.

## ★ More to Do ★

1. **Writing a diary.** Write several entries for a diary George Washington might have kept on his way to the Ohio Valley in 1754.

2. **Exploring local history.** Use the maps on pages 150 and 156 and a blank map to show whether your local area was part of the territory claimed by Britain, France, or Spain in 1753. In 1763.

3. **Drawing a cartoon.** Draw a cartoon showing a British view of the Sons or Daughters of Liberty.

4. **Giving a speech.** Give a speech that Patrick Henry might have made in the Virginia assembly after hearing about the battles of Lexington and Concord.

CHAPTER

# 8

# The American Revolution (1775–1783)

## Chapter Outline

1 Fighting Begins
2 Declaring Independence
3 Dark Days of the War
4 Other Battlefronts
5 Victory at Last

Readings, page 499

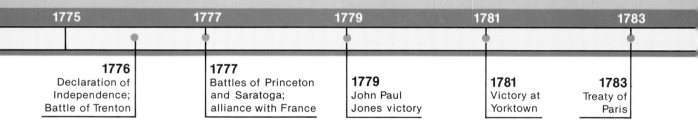

| 1775 | 1777 | 1779 | 1781 | 1783 |

**1776**
Declaration of
Independence;
Battle of Trenton

**1777**
Battles of Princeton
and Saratoga;
alliance with France

**1779**
John Paul
Jones victory

**1781**
Victory at
Yorktown

**1783**
Treaty of
Paris

## About This Chapter

Early in 1775, debate raged across the colonies. A few outspoken leaders called on the colonies to declare their independence from Britain. But most leaders were more cautious. They hoped to get Britain to change its conduct toward the colonies. Still, the issue was discussed everywhere.

In March 1775, Patrick Henry made a passionate speech to his fellow Virginians. "There is no longer any room for hope," he cried. "We have done everything that could be done to avert [prevent] the storm which is now coming on." Henry declared that the colonists must fight to protect their rights. Britain, he said, was not to be trusted. Its army and navy were being sent to America with one purpose—to enslave the colonists.

To those people who argued that the colonies were too weak to fight Britain, Henry replied: "But when shall we be stronger. Will it be the next week or the next year? Will it be when we are totally disarmed? . . . Shall we gather strength by irresolution [lack of decision] and inaction?" Henry's voice rose as he uttered these last words: "I know not what course others may take. But as for me, give me liberty, or give me death!"

Henry's words echoed through the colonies in the days ahead. Between 1775 and 1783, thousands of colonists took up the challenge—to fight for liberty.

Study the time line above. How do you think Patrick Henry's speech might have influenced events in 1776?

John Trumbull painted this picture, *The Battle of Bunker Hill*. In the battle, colonists showed they would fight for their liberties.

# 1 Fighting Begins

**Read to Learn**

★ What did the Second Continental Congress do?

★ How did the colonists defend Bunker Hill?

★ Why did the British leave Boston?

★ What does this word mean: blockade?

Lexington and Concord were the first battles of the American Revolution. In April 1775, no one knew how long the fighting would last. King George III believed that he could soon restore order in the colonies. Meantime, colonists wondered what chance they had of defeating a well-armed, powerful nation like Britain.

## Victory at Ticonderoga

In 1775, each colony had its own small militia. But the colonies had no army to face the British. Even so, less than a month after Lexington and Concord, a daring band of colonists made a surprise attack on Fort Ticonderoga (tī kahn duh ROH guh). The fort stood at the southern end of Lake Champlain and protected the water route to Canada. (See the map on page 175.)

Leading the attack was Ethan Allen, a blacksmith famous for his strength and fierce temper. Allen knew that the fort had many cannons the Americans needed. Allen's followers came from the nearby Green Mountains of Vermont.

Early on May 10, Allen and his *Green Mountain Boys* slipped through the morning mists at Fort Ticonderoga. Quickly, they overpowered the one guard on duty at the gate and entered the fort. Allen went straight to the rooms where the officers slept. In a loud voice, he called out to the British commander, "Come out, you old rat!"

The commander pulled on his uniform and demanded to know on whose authority Allen acted. "In the name of the Great Jehovah [God] and the Continental Congress!" replied Allen. The commander had no choice but to surrender the fort with its supply of gunpowder and about 100 cannons.

## The Second Continental Congress

On the day that Ethan Allen took Ticonderoga, the Second Continental Congress met in Philadelphia. This time, all 13 colonies sent delegates. The situation was very different from what it had been in September 1774. Now, the colonists were actually fighting the British.

Still, the delegates were divided over what to do. A few, like Sam Adams and John Adams, secretly wanted the colonies to declare their independence. But most delegates hoped to avoid a break with Britain. After much debate, the Continental Congress voted to try to patch up the quarrel with Britain. Delegates sent King George III the *Olive Branch Petition.* In it, they declared their loyalty to him. But they asked him to repeal the Intolerable Acts and end the fighting.

At the same time, the Congress took a bold step. It set up the Continental Army and named George Washington as its commander in chief.

## The Balance of Forces

Without wasting time, Washington left Philadelphia for Boston. Riding north, the new American commander knew that he faced a long, hard struggle. The British army was disciplined and experienced. Washington's army was untrained and had little gunpowder and few cannons. Britain was a powerful nation with a strong navy. Its ships could move soldiers quickly up and down the coast. The Americans had no navy to match the British fleet.

Despite these advantages, Britain faced some serious problems. Its soldiers were fighting 3,000 miles (4,800 km) from home. It took months for news to reach Britain or for supplies and fresh troops to reach America. Also, British soldiers often risked attack by colonists once they marched out of the cities into the countryside.

Still, the Americans had certain strengths. They had every reason to fight because they were defending their own homes, farms, and shops. Reuben Stebbins of Williamstown, Massachusetts, was typical of many soldiers. When he heard the British were near his home, he rode off to battle. "We'll see who's goin' t' own this farm!" he cried.

Even though few Americans were trained as soldiers, many owned rifles and were good shots. Also, the Americans were fortunate to have George Washington, who proved to be an excellent leader.

## Battle of Bunker Hill

Even before Washington reached Boston, American forces fought a fierce battle there. Minutemen kept close watch on the British troops under General Gage. They wanted to keep the British from leaving the city.

**Digging in.** At sunset on June 16, 1775, Colonel William Prescott led 1,200 American troops to take up position on Bunker Hill in Charlestown. (See the map on page 175.) From this position, they could fire on British ships in Boston Harbor. Prescott soon saw that nearby Breed's Hill was a bet-

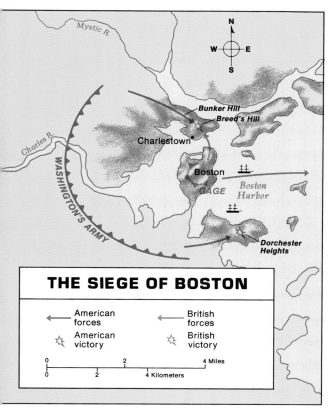

## THE SIEGE OF BOSTON

| | |
|---|---|
| ← American forces | ← British forces |
| ☆ American victory | ☆ British victory |

0      2      4 Miles
0      2    4 Kilometers

## THE FIGHT FOR INDEPENDENCE BEGINS

| | |
|---|---|
| ← American forces | ← British forces |
| ☆ American victories | ☆ British victories |

0      50      100     150 Miles
0   50   100   150 Kilometers

**MAP SKILL** Early in the American Revolution, several battles took place in and around Boston, as the map above shows. After fierce fighting, colonists were forced to leave Bunker Hill and Breed's Hill. Later, they took Dorchester Heights. In 1775 and 1776, fighting took place elsewhere in New England and Canada, as the map at right shows. Name two American victories early in the Revolution.

ter position. So he put his men to work digging trenches there. "Dig, men, dig," he urged. "Dig for your lives." Prescott knew that the trenches must be finished before dawn. Otherwise, the British could easily force them off the hill.

At dawn, the British general, William Howe, spotted the Americans. He ferried about 2,400 redcoats across the harbor to Charlestown. There, the British had to cross rough fields broken by fences to climb Breed's Hill. Each soldier carried a heavy pack that weighed about 125 pounds. It was hot, exhausting work, and the soldiers moved slowly.

The Americans waited in their trenches, watching the British struggle up the hill. Because the colonists had only a small amount of gunpowder, the American commanders warned, "Don't shoot until you see the whites of their eyes!"

**A hot fire.** As the enemy advanced, "we gave them such a hot fire that they were obliged to retire nearly 150 yards before they could rally," recalled Colonel Prescott. Twice, the British advanced up the hill. Twice, they had to retreat from American musket fire. "The oldest officers say they never saw a sharper action," reported Francis Rawdon, a young redcoat.

On the third try, the British pushed over the top. By then, the Americans had run out of gunpowder. Although the British took both Bunker and Breed's hills, it was a costly victory. Over 1,000 redcoats lay dead or wounded. The Americans lost 400.

The ***Battle of Bunker Hill*** was the first major battle of the war. It showed that the American army would not collapse at the first sound of battle. On the other hand, it showed that the British would not be easy to defeat.

## The British Leave Boston

Washington reached Boston a few weeks after the Battle of Bunker Hill. All through the summer and fall, he struggled to make an army out of soldiers from different colonies. "Connecticut wants no Massachusetts men in her corps," he wrote. And "Massachusetts thinks there is no necessity for a Rhode Islander to be introduced into her." Slowly, Washington won the respect of the troops. The army learned to obey orders and work together.

By January 1776, the Continental Army surrounded the British in Boston. The cannons captured at Fort Ticonderoga were dragged on sleds

After the Green Mountain Boys took Fort Ticonderoga, they dragged cannons they had captured across the snow-covered Green Mountains to Boston. There, the cannons were used to fortify Dorchester Heights, which overlooked the city. What problems do you think the Green Mountain Boys faced in bringing the cannons to Boston?

across mountains and forests to Boston. Washington put the cannons on Dorchester Heights, a hill overlooking Boston and its harbor. The British realized that the Americans were dug in too well to be forced out. So in March 1776, General Howe ordered his troops to leave Boston for Halifax, Canada.

Although the British left New England, Washington knew that the war was far from over. King George III ordered a blockade of all colonial ports. A **blockade** is the shutting off of a port by ships to keep people or supplies from moving in or out. Also, the king hired Hessian troops from Germany to help British soldiers fight the colonists.

## Invasion of Canada

While Washington was training one army outside Boston, two other American armies were moving north into Canada. (See the map on page 175). One, led by Richard Montgomery, left from Fort Ticonderoga. The other, led by Benedict Arnold, moved north through Maine. Americans expected French Canadians to help them force the British out of Canada.

Montgomery seized Montreal in November 1775. Then he moved down the St. Lawrence toward the city of Quebec. Arnold had a terrible journey through the Maine woods in winter. His troops were forced to boil candles, bark, and shoe leather for food. Finally, they, too, reached Quebec. But the Americans were disappointed because French Canadians did not come to their aid.

On December 31, 1775, the Americans attacked Quebec during a driving snowstorm. The attack was turned back. Montgomery was killed, and Arnold was wounded. The Americans stayed outside Quebec until May 1776, when the British landed new forces in Canada. Weakened by disease and hunger, the Americans withdrew, leaving Canada to the British.

### SECTION REVIEW

1. **Locate:** Lake Champlain, Fort Ticonderoga, Boston, Bunker Hill, Breed's Hill, Boston Harbor, Montreal, Quebec.
2. **Define:** blockade.
3. Why was Ethan Allen able to take Fort Ticonderoga so easily?
4. How did colonists try to patch up the quarrel with Britain in 1775?
5. **What Do You Think?** How do you think the Battle of Bunker Hill affected the American cause?

# 2 Declaring Independence

### Read to Learn

★ What did Paine argue for in *Common Sense?*
★ What are the main parts of the Declaration of Independence?
★ Who were the Loyalists?
★ What does this word mean: traitor?

Late in 1775, the Continental Congress learned that the king had rejected the Olive Branch Petition and set up the blockade. To many Americans, these actions showed that the colonists could no longer hope to settle their differences with Britain. Still, many colonists did not want to take the final step and declare their independence.

## The Voice of *Common Sense*

Although many colonists thought that the king had ignored their rights, they were still loyal to Britain. Then, in

January 1776, Thomas Paine wrote a pamphlet called *Common Sense*. Paine had only recently moved to Philadelphia from England. But he believed that the colonists should declare independence.

The pamphlet created a great stir in the colonies. In it, Paine answered the colonists' worries about breaking with Britain. He argued that it was foolish "to be always running three or four thousand miles with a tale or petition, waiting four or five months for an answer, which when obtained requires five or six more to explain it in."

Paine asked anyone "to show a single advantage this continent can reap, by being connected with Britain." Besides, he said, America was already at war with Britain. And "since nothing but blows will do . . . let us come to a final separation!"

Between January and July 1776, 500,000 copies of *Common Sense* were sold in the colonies. George Washington wrote that "*Common Sense* is working a powerful change in the minds of men." The pamphlet even changed Washington's habits. Until 1776, he followed the custom of drinking a toast to the king at official dinners. After reading Paine's pamphlet, he dropped this custom.

## Congress Acts

Paine's pamphlet had an effect on the Continental Congress, too. More and more delegates came to believe that the colonies must declare independence. In June 1776, Richard Henry Lee from Virginia offered a resolution saying that "these United Colonies are, and of right ought to be, free and independent States." It was a tense moment. Delegates knew that there would be no turning back once they declared independence. If Britain won the war, they would be hanged as traitors. A *traitor* is a person who betrays his or her country.

In the end, the delegates appointed a committee to draw up a declaration of independence. The committee included John Adams, Benjamin Franklin, Thomas Jefferson, Robert Livingston, and Roger Sherman. Their job was to explain to the world why the colonies were taking such a drastic step. The committee asked Jefferson to prepare the document.

Jefferson was one of the youngest delegates in the Congress. Tall, slender, and quiet, he spoke little in the Congress. But among his friends, he liked to sprawl in a chair with his long legs stretched out and talk for hours. In late June, Jefferson completed the declaration, and it was read to the Congress. The delegates made a few changes.*

On July 2, the Continental Congress voted that the 13 colonies were "free and independent States." Two days later, on July 4, 1776, the delegates accepted the *Declaration of Independence*. Since then, Americans have celebrated July 4th as Independence Day.

## The Declaration of Independence

The Declaration of Independence has three main parts. (An introduction and the text of the Declaration is printed on pages 611–614.) The first part explains the basic rights on which the nation is founded. "We hold these truths to be self-evident," wrote Jefferson, "that all men are created equal, that they are endowed by their Creator with certain unalienable rights, that among these are life, liberty, and the pursuit of happiness."

How do people protect these basic rights? By forming governments, the Declaration said. Governments could exist only if they had the "consent of

---

*One change involved slavery. The delegates dropped a statement that condemned King George for continuing slavery in the colonies.

The signing of the Declaration of Independence was a solemn occasion. But John Adams felt that future Americans would celebrate the event "with pomp and parade, with shows, games, sports, guns, bells, bonfires, and illuminations from one end of this continent to the other."

the governed." If a government took away its citizens' rights, then it was the people's right and "their duty, to throw off such government, and provide new guards for their future security."

The second part of the Declaration lists the wrongs committed by Britain. In the long list, Jefferson showed how the king had abused his power. It backed up the colonists' argument that they had a right to revolt.

The last section declares that the colonies had become "the United States of America." All ties with Britain were cut. As a free and independent nation, the United States could now make alliances and trade with other countries.

John Hancock, the president of the Continental Congress, was the first to sign the Declaration. He signed his name in large, bold handwriting. Other delegates added their names.

## Patriots and Loyalists

John Dunlap of Philadelphia published the Declaration of Independence late on July 4, 1776. Later, Mary Katherine Goddard, a Baltimore printer, produced the first copies of the Declaration that included the names of all the signers. When copies of the Declaration reached towns and villages, people had to decide whether to support the new nation or remain loyal to Britain.

The nation was divided. On one side were *Patriots,* people who supported independence. On the other were *Loyalists,* people who stayed loyal to the king. Many families were split. Ben Franklin, for example, was a Patriot. His son, the royal governor of New Jersey, remained loyal to George III. Loyalists included royal officials as well as many merchants and farmers.

As you learned in Skill Lesson 5 (page 116), people usually have a reason for writing about events or developments in which they are involved. As a result, a primary source, or firsthand account, reflects the author's point of view. Two people writing about the same subject can have different points of view.

The letters below are written by Abigail and John Adams. During the Revolution, John Adams was away from home for long periods. His wife, Abigail Adams, wrote to him often. She kept him informed about their children and their farm, which she kept going. When the Continental Congress was preparing the Declaration of Independence, she wrote her husband the first letter reprinted below. The second letter is John Adams' reply to his wife.

Read the letters. Then compare the two points of view.

1. **Study the contents of each source.** (a) What does Abigail Adams want her husband to do? (b) What is John Adams' response to her request? (c) Who does John Adams mean when he says "another tribe, more numerous and powerful than all the rest"?

2. **Compare the points of view.** (a) What does Abigail Adams think men are like? (b) Does John Adams agree with his wife's view of men? Explain.

3. **Evaluate the usefulness of these sources.** (a) What do these letters tell you about American society in 1776? (b) Do you think these letters are a reliable source of information? Explain.

 **Abigail Adams wrote:**

I long to hear that you have declared independence. And by the way, in the new code of laws that I suppose you will make, I wish you would remember the ladies and be more generous and favorable to them than your ancestors. Do not put such unlimited power in the hands of husbands. Remember, all men would be tyrants if they could. If particular care and attention is not paid to the ladies, we are determined to stir up a rebellion and will not regard ourselves as bound by any laws in which we have had no voice or representation.

 **John Adams replied:**

As to your extraordinary code of laws, I can't help laughing. We have been told that our struggle has loosened the bonds of government everywhere, that children and apprentices were disobedient, that schools and colleges had grown turbulent, that Indians slighted their guardians and Negroes grow insolent to their masters. But your letter was the first hint that another tribe, more numerous and powerful than all the rest, had grown discontented.

Depend upon it, we know better than to repeal our masculine systems. Although they are in full force, you know they are little more than theory . . . in practice, you know, we are the subjects. We have only the title of masters, and rather than give this up, which would subject us completely to the power of the petticoat, I hope General Washington and all our brave heroes would fight.

During the war, many thousands of Loyalists supported the British. There were more Loyalists in the Middle States and the South than in New England. But life was difficult for Loyalists everywhere. Patriots tarred and feathered people who spoke in favor of Britain. Many Loyalists fled to England or Canada. Those who fled lost their homes, stores, and farms.

======= SECTION REVIEW =======

1. **Define:** traitor.
2. Give two reasons Paine thought the colonies should become independent.
3. What are the basic rights set out in the Declaration of Independence?
4. **What Do You Think?** Why do you think many colonists remained loyal to Britain?

# 3 Dark Days of the War

### Read to Learn

★ What major battles were fought in the Middle States?
★ Why was the Battle of Saratoga a turning point in the Revolution?
★ How did foreigners help the Americans during the Revolution?
★ What does this word mean: cavalry?

Most of the early battles of the American Revolution were fought in New England. After General Howe left Boston in March 1776, however, the heavy fighting moved to the Middle States. For the next two years, Americans battled the British in New York, New Jersey, and Pennsylvania. During this time, Americans faced the darkest days of the war.

## Battle for New York

When General Howe left Boston, he by no means gave up fighting. He reorganized his forces in Halifax and then sailed for New York City. Washington expected Howe's move. He marched from Boston to New York to defend the city. But he faced a grim situation. Howe had 34,000 troops, 10,000 sailors, 30 warships, and 400 smaller boats to ferry his troops ashore. Washington had only 20,000 troops. Most of them had little training and no experience in battle. And he had no navy.

Washington divided his troops because he did not know where Howe would land. He sent some to Long Island. In August 1776, Howe made a surprise attack on these troops. In the *Battle of Long Island,* more than 1,400 Americans were killed, wounded, or captured. The rest retreated across the East River to Manhattan.

Washington realized that he could not defend New York against Howe. So he retreated north. All through the fall, he fought running battles with Howe's army. In November, Washington crossed the Hudson River into New Jersey. The British followed, chasing the Americans across the Delaware River into Pennsylvania. (See the map on page 182.)

During the battle for New York, Washington needed information about Howe's forces. Nathan Hale, a young Connecticut officer, offered to go behind British lines. Hale got the information but was captured by the British. He was tried and condemned to death.

"He behaved with great composure," wrote a British soldier, "saying he thought it the duty of every good officer to obey any orders given him by his Commander in Chief." Later, it was reported that Hale's last words were "I only regret that I have but one life to lose for my country."

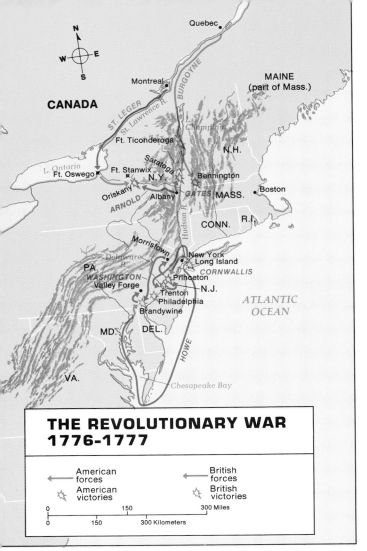

## THE REVOLUTIONARY WAR 1776-1777

← American forces
☆ American victories

← British forces
☆ British victories

0 — 150 — 300 Miles
0 — 150 — 300 Kilometers

**MAP SKILL** In 1776 and 1777, American and British forces fought many battles, as this map shows. In October 1777, Americans won an important victory at the Battle of Saratoga. Describe the route taken by General Burgoyne's army to reach Saratoga.

## A Much-Needed Victory

By December 1776, Washington was very discouraged. "I am wearied to death," he admitted. "I think the game is pretty near up." The Continental Congress fled from Philadelphia, fearing a British attack. Washington's troops were discouraged, too. They were cold and hungry. Every day, soldiers left the army to return home.

Tom Paine, author of *Common Sense,* wrote a new pamphet, called *The Crisis*. In it, he wrote:

> These are the times that try men's souls. The summer soldier and the sunshine patriot will, in this crisis, shrink from the service of their country; but he that stands *now*, deserves the love and thanks of men and women.

**Attack on Trenton.** Washington had Paine's words read aloud to his troops. The Americans needed more than words, however. So Washington decided on a bold move. He planned a surprise attack on Trenton.

On Christmas night, Washington secretly led his troops across the icy Delaware River. Soldiers huddled in the boats as the spray from the river froze on their faces. Once across the river, the troops marched through the swirling snow. General Washington rode up and down the lines. "Soldiers, keep by your officers," he urged.

Early on December 26, the Americans surprised the Hessian troops guarding Trenton and took most of them prisoner. After the ***Battle of Trenton,*** one American wrote in his diary: "Hessian population of Trenton at 8 A.M.—1,408 men and 39 officers; Hessian population at 9 A.M.—0." Most were then prisoners of the Americans.

**Victory at Princeton.** After the Battle of Trenton, the British sent General Charles Cornwallis to recapture the city. In the evening of January 2, Cornwallis saw the lights of Washington's campfires. "At last we have run down the old fox and we will bag him in the morning," he said.

But Washington fooled Cornwallis. Washington left his fires burning and marched behind British lines to attack Princeton. There, he won another victory. From Princeton, Washington moved on to Morristown, where the army spent the winter. The victories at Trenton and Princeton gave the army new hope and confidence.

## A British Plan of Attack

Early in 1777, General John Burgoyne (buhr GOIN) convinced King George to try a new plan of attack. Burgoyne told the king that if the British could cut off New England from the other colonies, the war would soon be over.

Burgoyne's plan called for three British armies to march on Albany from different directions. New England would be cut off when the three armies met in Albany. Britain then would control all the land from Canada to New York. The king and his advisers approved the plan. However, they ordered General Howe to take Philadelphia before he marched to Albany.

**Brandywine and Germantown.** Burgoyne's plan might have worked if General Howe had taken Philadelphia quickly. But he did not. In July 1777, he sailed from New York to the Chesapeake Bay. (See the map on page 182.) As he marched toward Philadelphia, Washington tried to stop him. At the *Battle of Brandywine,* the Americans were defeated.

Howe entered Philadelphia in late September. Washington again attacked the redcoats, this time at Germantown, just outside Philadelphia. But the Americans again met defeat. Washington retreated to Valley Forge, where he set up winter quarters.

Meanwhile, two other British armies under Barry St. Leger (lay ZHAIR) and Burgoyne moved south from Canada on their way to Albany. St. Leger tried to take Fort Stanwix. He had to retreat when Benedict Arnold arrived with a strong American army. General Burgoyne retook Fort Ticonderoga without firing a shot. But his army moved slowly because they had to drag many baggage carts through the woods.

**Turning point at Saratoga.** Burgoyne sent soldiers into Vermont to find food and horses. Patriots attacked and defeated these troops at the *Battle of Bennington.*

Burgoyne's troubles grew. The Green Mountain Boys hurried into New York to help the American army led by General Horatio Gates. At the

In October 1777, Washington attacked the British army, shown here at Germantown. The day was not as clear as this later painting shows. Fog covered the battlefield. The fog caused confusion and kept the Americans from winning a victory.

village of Saratoga, Gates surrounded the British. Twice, Burgoyne tried to break through the American lines. Both times, he was driven back by General Benedict Arnold. Realizing he was trapped, General Burgoyne surrendered his entire army to the Americans on October 17, 1777.

## Alliance With France

The American victory at the **Battle of Saratoga** was a turning point in the war. It ended the British threat to New England and encouraged Americans at a time when Washington's army in Pennsylvania was suffering defeats. More important, it convinced France to sign a treaty with the United States.

In 1776, the Continental Congress had sent Benjamin Franklin to Paris to get help from the French king, Louis XVI. The Americans were in desperate need of weapons and other supplies. They also wanted France to declare war on Britain. France had a strong navy that could be used against the British.

Franklin knew that many French people favored the American cause. France and Britain were longtime rivals. And the French were still unhappy about their defeat by the British in the French and Indian War. Still, Franklin had a hard time. Louis XVI secretly sent some weapons and supplies. Yet the French king did not want to help the Americans openly until he saw that they were likely to win.

The Battle of Saratoga convinced him to help the struggling young nation. In February 1778, France became the first nation to sign a treaty with the United States. In it, Louis XVI recognized the new nation and agreed to give it military aid.

## The Winter at Valley Forge

French aid came too late to help Washington and his army at Valley Forge. During the long, cold winter of 1777–1778, they suffered terrible hard-

ships, while the British in Philadelphia were warm, comfortable, and well fed.

The Americans had little food or clothing. As the winter wore on, soldiers suffered from frostbite and disease. A Rhode Island officer wrote home to beg the governor to send food and clothes. His troops were so ragged looking, he wrote, that others called them "the naked regiment." Some soldiers stood on guard wrapped only in blankets. Many had no shoes and wrapped bits of cloth around their feet.

When news of the army's suffering spread, Americans sent food and clothing to Valley Forge. Women were especially active. They gathered medicine, food, clothing, and ammunition for the army. They raised money to buy other supplies and collected lead objects to be melted into bullets. (See the picture of Laura Wolcott on page 188.)

## Help From Overseas

Help also came from overseas. In 1777, the Marquis de Lafayette (lah fih YET), a French noble, brought many professional soldiers to America. He fought at Brandywine and spent the winter at Valley Forge. The young Frenchman became a trusted friend of General Washington.

Two Polish officers helped the Americans. They were Thaddeus Kosciusko (kahs ee USH koh) and Casimir Pulaski (poo LAHS kee). Kosciusko, an engineer, helped build forts and other defenses. Pulaski trained *cavalry,* or troops on horseback.

Help came from New Spain, too. Bernardo de Galvez* was governor of the Spanish lands of Louisiana during the Revolution. He supplied cattle from Spanish herds in Texas to the Americans. Also, he attacked the British in Florida.

Friedrich von Steuben (STOO buhn) from Prussia improved discipline in the

---

*The city of Galveston, Texas, is named after Bernardo de Galvez.

The harsh winter at Valley Forge was a severe test of Washington's leadership. He kept the army together despite great hardships. Washington had to plead with local merchants and farmers for food supplies. And he wrote daily to Congress to send supplies and new recruits.

American army. Steuben once served in the Prussian army, the best-trained army in Europe. A lively person, Steuben kept everybody in good spirits. He showed the Americans how to use bayonets. Most soldiers had not fought with bayonets. So they used them to roast meat over the fire.

Although Steuben spoke little English, he soon taught Washington's troops how to march. He ordered each soldier to put his left hand on the shoulder of the man in front of him. Then, Steuben called out in his German accent: "Fooorrvarrd march! Von, Two, Tree, Four!"

By the spring of 1778, the army at Valley Forge was more hopeful. "The army grows stronger every day," wrote one New Jersey soldier. "The troops are instructed in a new and so happy a method of marching that they will soon be able to advance with the utmost regularity, even without music and on the roughest grounds." While soldiers drilled, Washington and his staff planned new campaigns against the British.

### SECTION REVIEW

1. **Locate:** New York, Philadelphia, Trenton, Delaware River, Princeton, Albany, Brandywine, Saratoga, Valley Forge.

2. **Define:** cavalry.

3. (a) Name three battles fought in the Middle States. (b) What was the result of each?

4. Why did Americans want an alliance with France?

5. **What Do You Think?** Why do you think foreigners like Lafayette and Steuben helped the Americans?

# 4 Other Battlefronts

## Read to Learn

★ Why did some Indians help the British?
★ How did John Paul Jones become a hero?
★ What role did black Americans and women play in the Revolution?
★ What does this word mean: neutral?

The Revolution was fought on many fronts. While the Continental Army battled in the east, other Patriots fought in the west and at sea.

## War in the West

During the war, Americans continued to move west. In Kentucky, they named one new settlement Lexington, after the first battle of the Revolution. Another settlement was called Louisville, after America's ally, King Louis XVI of France. But as settlers moved west, they often clashed with Native Americans whose lands they were invading.

**Native Americans.** When the Revolution began, many Native Americans wanted to stay *neutral,* or not fight for either side. Yet some Indians did fight. Indian nations such as the Algonquins and Iroquois were divided over which side to help. In Massachusetts, Algonquins helped the Patriots. But west of the Appalachians, some Algonquins helped the British because Patriots were seizing their lands.

In Tennessee, most Cherokees wanted to stay neutral or favored the Patriots. Nancy Ward, a Cherokee leader, warned Patriot settlers of a raid planned by a small group of Cherokees. Settlers responded to the warning by attacking all the Cherokees. This betrayal of trust forced the Cherokees to join the British.

MAP SKILL American and British forces fought for control of lands west of the Appalachian Mountains. Find the route George Rogers Clark took from Fort Pitt to Vincennes. In which direction or directions did he march to reach Vincennes?

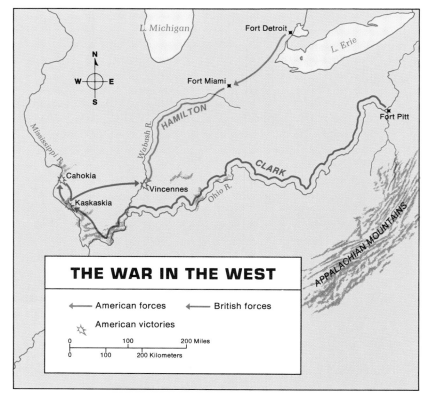

**THE WAR IN THE WEST**

← American forces   ← British forces

☆ American victories

0   100   200 Miles
0   100   200 Kilometers

In this picture of a famous naval battle, the *Bonhomme Richard,* commanded by John Paul Jones, fires on the *Serapis.* After winning the battle, Jones climbed on board the captured *Serapis* and watched his own damaged ship sink.

The British found other Indian allies and supplied them with weapons. The Indians who joined the British did so to protect their homes against white settlers.

**Clark's victories.** In 1778, George Rogers Clark led Virginia frontiersmen against the British in the Ohio River valley. With the help of Miami Indians, Clark captured the British forts at Kaskaskia and Cahokia. (See the map on page 186.)

Clark wanted to take Vincennes, but British forces there far outnumbered the Virginians. So he planned a surprise attack. During the winter, he marched 150 miles (240 km) through heavy rains, swamps, and icy rivers. When Clark's small band of men reached the fort, they spread out through the woods to appear greater in number than they really were. The trick worked. The British commander thought that it was useless to fight so many Americans. In February 1779, he surrendered Vincennes to Clark.

## War at Sea

With its strong navy, Britain was able to blockade and patrol the Atlantic coast. Although the American navy remained small, American ships attacked and captured British ships at sea. One daring American captain, John Paul Jones, even raided the English coast.

In September 1779, Jones fought the most famous sea battle of the war. The battle took place in the North Sea off the coast of Britain. Jones was in command of the *Bonhomme Richard*—named after Franklin's *Poor Richard's Almanac*—when he saw 39 merchant ships guarded by a British warship, the *Serapis.* He attacked the *Serapis* even though it was larger than his ship.

During the battle, British cannon balls ripped through the *Bonhomme Richard,* setting it on fire. The British commander called on Jones to surrender. "I have not yet begun to fight!" replied Jones. He brought his ship in close to the enemy. Americans jumped aboard the *Serapis* and defeated the British in hand-to-hand fighting. The victory made Jones a popular hero.

## Black Americans in the War

By 1775, many blacks had gained their freedom through loyal service.

## AMERICANS WHO DARED

### Laura Wolcott

Laura Wolcott lived in Litchfield, Connecticut, where her family were Patriots. At age 15, she made her own contribution to the cause. In July 1776, New Yorkers tore down a statue of King George III. Pieces of lead from the statue were sent to Litchfield. Women made them into cartridges for Washington's army. Wolcott made at least 4,250 cartridges.

Slavery was declining in the North,* where a number of free blacks lived. Black Patriots hoped that the Revolution would lead to equality. The Declaration of Independence stated that "all men are created equal." Black Americans expected the new nation to live up to this goal and end slavery.

Some white Americans supported the idea of freedom for slaves. James

*In the 1760s, two surveyors, Charles Mason and Jeremiah Dixon, marked the official border between Pennsylvania and Maryland at 39°43′N. The border, known as the Mason–Dixon Line, came to be seen as the dividing line between the North and South.

Otis of Massachusetts wrote that "the colonists are by the law of nature free born, as indeed all men are, white or black." By 1783, Vermont, Massachusetts, and New Hampshire had outlawed slavery. During the war, other states debated the issue.

When the Revolution began, the British tried to win the support of blacks. In 1775, the governor of Virginia stated that all slaves who served the king would be given their freedom. This offer encouraged thousands of slaves to join the British.

Meantime, many free blacks and slaves supported the Revolution. At least seven blacks were among the minutemen who fought at Lexington and Concord. Other black Patriots marched into battle at Ticonderoga and Bunker Hill.

For a time, the Continental Congress refused to let slaves or free blacks serve officially in the army. However, the British success in recruiting slaves made the Congress change its mind. By 1778, both free blacks and slaves were allowed to serve in the Continental Army. They formed all-black fighting regiments and served in white regiments as drummers, fifers, spies, and guides.

## Women in the Revolution

Women supported the Patriot cause in many ways. They worked on the home front, making guns and other weapons. One woman, known as "Handy Betsy the Blacksmith," was famous for supplying cannons and guns to the army.

Women raised money to supply the army with food, clothing, and medicine. They also took over work usually done by men. They farmed the land alone and grew the food so badly needed by the Continental Army.

Women made shoes and wove cloth for blankets and uniforms. Betsy Ross of Philadelphia was one of many women who sewed flags for Washing-

As a child, Phillis Wheatley was brought from Africa to America and sold as a slave. Later, she managed to teach herself Greek and Latin and wrote fine poetry. In one well-known poem, she praised the leadership of General Washington.

ton's forces. Long after the war, the story grew up that Washington asked Ross to make the first American flag of stars and stripes. But the story cannot be proved.

Many women joined their soldier-husbands at the front. There, they washed clothes, cooked, and cared for the wounded. Martha Washington joined her husband as often as possible. She and other women helped raise the army's spirits.

A few women took part in battle. During the Battle of Monmouth in 1778, Mary Ludwig Hays carried water to her husband and other soldiers. The soldiers called her "Moll of the Pitcher" or Molly Pitcher. When her husband was wounded, she took his place, loading and firing a cannon. Deborah Sampson of Massachusetts dressed as a man and fought in several battles. Later, she wrote about her life in the army.

=== **SECTION REVIEW** ===

1. **Locate:** Ohio River, Kaskaskia, Cahokia, Vincennes.
2. **Define:** neutral.
3. Which side did Native Americans take in the Revolution?
4. Why did black Americans support the Revolution?
5. **What Do You Think?** Why do you think women were as important as men in the war effort?

# 5 Victory at Last

### Read to Learn

★ What battles were fought in the South?
★ How were the British trapped at Yorktown?
★ What were the terms of the Treaty of Paris?
★ What does this word mean: ratify?

In 1778, the war entered a new stage. The fighting, which had begun in New England and shifted to the Middle States, now moved into the South.

### Battlefields in the South

Fighting began in the South in the early days of the Revolution. In February 1776, North Carolina Patriots defeated a Loyalist army at the *Battle of Moore's Creek Bridge.* This victory has sometimes been called the Lexington and Concord of the South.

After the French entered the war, the British decided to put their main effort in the South. They counted on the support of Loyalists there. For a time, the British met with success. In December 1779, British troops seized Savannah, Georgia. They later took Charleston, South Carolina. The Americans suffered one blow after another at the hands of the British. "I have almost ceased to hope," wrote Washington after hearing of these American losses.

**Tale of a traitor.** In the summer of 1780, Washington got more bad news. He learned that Benedict Arnold, one of his most talented generals, had gone over to the British side. Arnold had fought bravely in many battles. One soldier recalled that Arnold always led—never followed—his men into battle. "It was 'Come on, boys!' not 'Go on, boys!' He didn't care for nothin'. He'd ride right in."

In 1780, Arnold was in command of the American fort at West Point. Because he felt that he had not received credit for his successes, Arnold offered to turn West Point over to the British. The plot almost succeeded. American soldiers caught the messenger carrying Arnold's offer. West Point was saved. Arnold himself escaped and joined the British.*

**The tide turns.** In the fall of 1780, the Americans began to stem the tide of British victories in the South. Patriots organized hit-and-run attacks on the redcoats. Francis Marion of South Carolina led a small band of men who slept by day and traveled by night. Marion was known as the *Swamp Fox.* He

---

*In America, the name Benedict Arnold came to mean a traitor.

Francis Marion's hit-and-run attacks earned him the nickname Swamp Fox. Banastre Tarleton, a British colonel, claimed that "the devil himself could not catch Marion." Here, Marion and his men cross the Pee Dee River in South Carolina.

appeared suddenly out of the swamps, attacked the British, and then retreated into the swamps. His attacks kept the British off balance.

Two American generals, Daniel Morgan and Nathanael Greene, helped the Patriots to victory in the South. Morgan, a Virginian, commanded a company at the Battle of Saratoga in New York. In January 1781, he defeated a Loyalist and British army at the **Battle of Cowpens** in South Carolina.

Joining Morgan, General Greene used the same hit-and-run tactics as Francis Marion. He won few outright victories, but he did wear down the British. The American successes made the British general, Charles Cornwallis, decide to leave the Carolinas. In April 1781, Cornwallis took his army north into Virginia.

### Victory at Yorktown

At first, Cornwallis was successful in Virginia. Secretly, he sent Loyalist troops to attack Charlottesville, where the Virginia legislature was meeting. Loyalist soldiers almost captured the lawmakers, including Virginia's governor, Thomas Jefferson.

American troops under Lafayette fought back by making raids on the British. Lafayette did not have enough troops to fight a real battle. Still, the American raids forced Cornwallis to pull his troops back to Yorktown, on a peninsula between the James and York rivers. Cornwallis felt safe at Yorktown because he counted on the British navy to supply his troops. But a French fleet under Admiral de Grasse drove the British ships out of the Chesapeake Bay. French troops under the Comte de Rochambeau (roh shahm BOH) had just landed from France. They joined General Washington in New York. Together, they marched into Virginia, boxing in the British army.

Cornwallis held out for three weeks before he surrendered his entire army

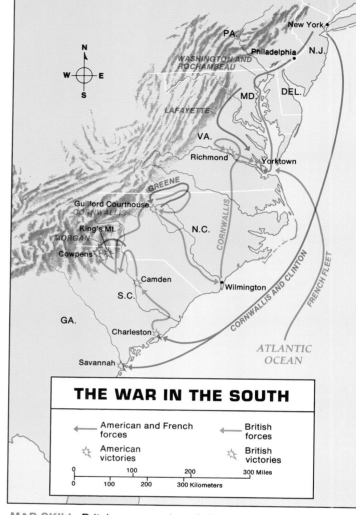

**THE WAR IN THE SOUTH**

American and French forces

British forces

American victories

British victories

0 100 200 300 Miles
0 100 200 300 Kilometers

MAP SKILL Britain won a string of victories in the south in 1779 and 1780. Slowly, Americans turned the tide. In October 1781, French and American forces trapped Cornwallis at Yorktown, forcing him to surrender. How do you think the French fleet helped the American victory at Yorktown?

on October 17, 1781. Two days later, the defeated British soldiers turned over their muskets to the Americans. During the ceremony, the British army band played the song "The World Turned Upside Down."

### A Time for Peace

News of the American victory at Yorktown stunned the British. "It is all over," cried the British prime minister, Lord North. The defeat of Cornwallis convinced the British to negotiate for

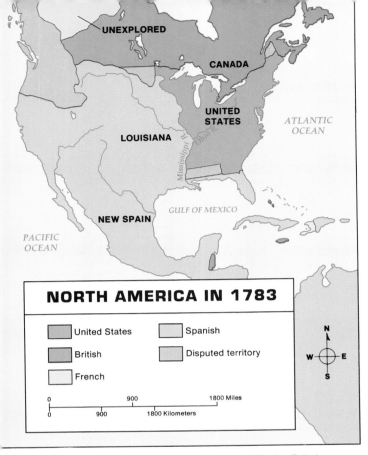

NORTH AMERICA IN 1783

Legend:
- United States
- British
- French
- Spanish
- Disputed territory

UNEXPLORED

CANADA

UNITED STATES

LOUISIANA

NEW SPAIN

ATLANTIC OCEAN

GULF OF MEXICO

PACIFIC OCEAN

0    900    1800 Miles
0    900    1800 Kilometers

**MAP SKILL** By the Treaty of Paris, Britain recognized the United States as an independent nation. What nations held land on the borders of the United States?

peace. Peace did not come at once, however.

Peace talks began in Paris in 1782. Congress sent Benjamin Franklin and John Adams, along with John Jay of New York and Henry Laurens of Virginia, to work out a peace treaty. Because the British wanted to end the war, the Americans got most of what they wanted.

**The Treaty of Paris.** Britain agreed to recognize the United States as a free and independent nation. It recognized the borders of the new nation. The United States extended from the Atlantic Ocean to the Mississippi River. The southern border stopped at Florida, which now belonged to Spain again.

For their part, the Americans agreed to ask state legislatures to pay Loyalists for the property they lost in the war. In the end, however, most state legislatures ignored Loyalist claims. On April 19, 1783, Congress *ratified,* or approved, the Treaty of Paris. This date was exactly eight years after the first shots were fired at Lexington and Concord.

Cooperation between General Washington and the Marquis de Lafayette helped win the war. This painting shows the two men at the Battle of Yorktown in 1781. Reuben Law Reed painted this picture many years after the war from the description of an eyewitness.

Thousands of men and women fought for the American cause. Some joined the Continental Army. Others helped from behind the lines. Among the heroes of the Revolution are the four people shown on these stamps.

In 1777, young Sybil Ludington made a midnight ride like that of Paul Revere. She warned Patriot soldiers of a British attack on Danbury, Connecticut.

Salem Poor, a black soldier, fought at Lexington and Concord and at the Battle of Bunker Hill. After Bunker Hill, Colonel Prescott and other officers asked the Continental Congress to reward Poor as a "brave and gallant soldier."

Haym Salomon, a Jew, left Poland because of religious persecution. In America, he joined the Sons of Liberty and was arrested by the British. Later, he made a fortune in business. When the Continental Congress was desperate for money, Salomon spent his own fortune to help the American cause.

At age 16, Peter Francisco fought at the Battle of Brandywine. In the next four years, he fought in many other battles and was wounded four times. In one battle, he is credited with carrying a 1,000-pound cannon to keep it from falling into British hands.

★ How did the deeds of men and women like these four help the American cause?

**Washington retires.** The war was a long and difficult struggle. Patriots fought against better-armed and better-trained soldiers. French money, arms, and soldiers helped the Americans win major battles. The strength and courage of leaders like Washington were also important to the American victory. In 1781, when Washington marched from New York to Yorktown, men, women, and children turned out along the road to see the commander in chief. People quietly touched his horse or his cloak as he passed.

When peace came, Washington bid farewell to his soldiers and retired to his home in Mount Vernon, Virginia. The new nation still faced difficult tests, however. Americans would once again call on Washington to lead the nation.

#### SECTION REVIEW

1. **Locate:** Savannah, Charleston, Cowpens, Yorktown.
2. **Define:** ratify.
3. How did each of the following help the Patriots: (a) Francis Marion; (b) Daniel Morgan; (c) Nathanael Greene?
4. How did the French help the Americans at Yorktown?
5. **What Do You Think?** Why do you think people touched George Washington's cloak as he rode by on his way to Yorktown?

# Chapter 8 Review

## ★ Summary ★

When the Second Continental Congress met in 1775, members had to decide whether the colonies should declare independence. Thomas Paine's pamphlet, *Common Sense,* helped convince them to draw up the Declaration of Independence. The Declaration explained why the colonies were breaking away from England.

The revolution was fought on many fronts—in New England, the Middle States, and the South. George Washington led Patriot armies through difficult times. The American victory at Saratoga was a turning point because it brought France into the war on the American side. In October 1781, Washington defeated Cornwallis at the Battle of Yorktown, the last major battle of the war. In the Treaty of Paris, Britain agreed to recognize the United States as an independent nation.

## ★ Reviewing the Facts ★

**Key Terms.** Match each term in Column 1 with the correct definition in Column 2.

| Column 1 | Column 2 |
|---|---|
| 1. blockade | a. troops on horseback |
| 2. traitor | b. approve |
| 3. cavalry | c. not fight for either side in a war |
| 4. neutral | d. someone who betrays his or her country |
| 5. ratify | e. shutting off of a port to keep supplies from moving in or out |

**Key People, Events, and Ideas.** Identify each of the following.

1. Ethan Allen
2. Olive Branch Petition
3. Thomas Paine
4. Thomas Jefferson
5. John Hancock
6. Patriot
7. Loyalist
8. Nathan Hale
9. John Burgoyne
10. Marquis de Lafayette
11. John Paul Jones
12. Molly Pitcher
13. Phillis Wheatley
14. Benedict Arnold
15. Admiral de Grasse

## ★ Chapter Checkup ★

1. (a) What advantages did the British have during the Revolution? (b) What advantages did the Americans have?
2. How did the Patriot stand at Bunker Hill help the Americans?
3. (a) What are the three main parts of the Declaration of Independence? (b) What does each part say?
4. Why are the years from 1776 to 1778 often called the dark days of the war?
5. How did France help the United States?
6. How did each of the following people help the Patriot cause: (a) Nancy Ward; (b) George Rogers Clark; (c) Deborah Sampson?
7. (a) Who was the Swamp Fox? (b) How did he help the Americans?
8. What were the terms of the Treaty of Paris?

## ★ Thinking About History ★

1. **Taking a stand.** Loyalists believed that the colonists were betraying their country by declaring independence. Do you agree? Explain.

2. **Relating past to present.** Reread the Declaration of Independence on pages 611–614. In 1776, colonists said that a government must respect certain basic rights of its citizens. Today, these rights are called human rights. (a) According to the Declaration, how did Britain violate, or fail to protect, these rights? (b) Do any countries today violate the human rights of their citizens? Explain.

3. **Analyzing a quotation.** When Cornwallis moved his army to Yorktown, Lafayette saw a chance to trap the British. "Why haven't we a fleet here?" he cried. "If the French army could fall from the clouds into Virginia and be supported by a squadron [of ships] we should do some very good things." (a) What did Lafayette mean by "some very good things"? (b) Did his wish come true? Explain.

4. **Understanding geography.** How do you think geography played a role in each of the following battles: (a) Battle of Bunker Hill; (b) Battle of Trenton?

## ★ Using Your Skills ★

1. **Map reading.** Study the map at right on page 175. (a) What British general's route is shown on this map? (b) In what direction did Benedict Arnold march to reach Quebec? (c) About how far did Montgomery have to travel from Fort Ticonderoga to Quebec?

2. **Constructing a time line.** Make a time line for the American Revolution. To construct a time line, draw a horizontal line on a blank sheet of paper. Label the left end 1775 and the right end 1783. Divide the line into eight equal parts, each representing one year. Complete the time line by writing the names of major battles or other events next to the year in which they happened. (a) What is the first event of the Revolution? (b) What is the last event? (c) During what period were most of the major battles fought?

3. **Outlining.** Review the outlining skill you learned on page 31. Then prepare an outline of the first two sections of this chapter on pages 173–181. Using your outline, write a summary of what happened during the early years of the American Revolution.

## ★ More to Do ★

1. **Drawing a cartoon.** Draw a cartoon about the American victory at Fort Ticonderoga in 1775.

2. **Making a poster.** Make a poster to recruit soldiers for Washington's army.

3. **Organizing a debate.** As a group project, prepare a debate among delegates to the Continental Congress on the following question: "Should the colonies declare their independence from Britain?"

4. **Interviewing.** In small groups, prepare skits in which you interview survivors of the winter at Valley Forge.

5. **Exploring local history.** Write a pamphlet describing how your local area honors events and heroes of the American Revolution.

CHAPTER

# 9

# Creating a
# Government (1776–1790)

## Chapter Outline

1 The First American Government
2 The Constitutional Convention
3 We, the People
4 Ratifying the Constitution
Readings, page 507

| 1776 | 1778 | 1780 | 1782 | 1784 | 1786 | 1788 | 1790 |
|------|------|------|------|------|------|------|------|

**1777**
Articles of
Confederation
written

**1781**
Articles of
Confederation
ratified

**1783**
Treaty of
Paris

**1787**
Northwest
Ordinance

**1788**
Constitution
ratified

## About This Chapter

During the American Revolution, the nation set up its first government under the Articles of Confederation. By 1787, however, many Americans were dissatisfied with the Articles. In May 1787, delegates met in Philadelphia to write a new constitution for the United States.

James Madison was one of the men who attended the Constitutional Convention. He decided to keep "an exact account of what might pass in the Convention." The notes, he felt, would be an important record for future generations.

"I chose a seat in front of the presiding member, with the other members on my right and left hand," reported Madison. In this central place, he could hear all that was said.

He carefully noted "what was read from the chair or spoken by the members." At the end of each day, he wrote up his notes.

Madison claimed his notes were complete. "I was not absent a single day," he wrote, "nor more than a fraction of an hour in any day so that I could not have lost a single speech, unless a very short one."

Thanks to Madison's hard work, we have a full record of the debates that went on at the Constitutional Convention. From his notes, we can see how the Constitution was shaped. The Constitution, written in 1787, still forms the basis of our government.

Study the time line above. Was the Constitution ratified before or after the Treaty of Paris?

With the sun rising behind his chair, George Washington watches as delegates sign the Constitution of the United States.

# 1 The First American Government

**Read to Learn**
* Why did the states want written constitutions?
* What problems did the United States face under the Articles of Confederation?
* What do these words mean: constitution, execute, bill of rights, economic depression?

In 1776, the Declaration of Independence created a new nation made up of 13 independent states. The states faced a long, uphill battle against Britain. The struggle was made even harder because the states had little experience in working together. In the past, Britain made decisions for the colonies as a whole. Now, the new states had to set up not only their own governments but also a national government.

## State Governments

In forming its government, each state wrote a constitution. A *constitution* is a document that sets out the laws and principles of a government. Some states, such as Connecticut and Rhode Island, revised the charters they had before the Revolution. Others, such as Massachusetts, wrote new constitutions, which voters approved.

Americans wanted written constitutions for two reasons. First, a written constitution would clearly spell out the rights of all citizens. Second, it would limit the power of government.

The new state governments were similar to colonial governments. All the states had a legislature elected by voters. Most legislatures had an upper house, called a senate, and a lower house. Every state except Pennsylvania had a governor, who *executed,* or carried out, the laws.

Virginia included a bill of rights in its new constitution. A *bill of rights* lists freedoms the government has to protect. In Virginia, the bill of rights protected freedom of speech, freedom of religion, and freedom of the press. Citizens also had the right to a trial by jury. Other states followed Virginia's lead and included bills of rights in their constitutions.

The new state constitutions expanded the number of citizens who had the right to vote. To vote, a citizen had to be male and over age 21. He had to own a certain amount of property or pay a certain amount of taxes. For a time, women in New Jersey could vote. (See the picture below.) In a few states,

Even after the Revolution, American women had limited political and legal rights. For a time, New Jersey let women vote, as this picture shows. But this right was taken away in 1807.

free black men could vote. But slaves could not vote in any state.

## The Articles of Confederation

While the states were forming their governments, the Continental Congress wrote a constitution for the nation as a whole. Writing a constitution that all the states would approve was a difficult job. In 1776, few Americans thought of themselves as citizens of one nation. Instead, they felt loyal to their own states.

**A weak national government.** The new states were unwilling to give too much power to a national government. They were already fighting Britain. And they did not want to replace one harsh ruler with another. After much debate, the first American constitution, called the *Articles of Confederation,* was completed in 1777. Under the Articles, the 13 states agreed to send delegates to Congress. Each state had one vote in Congress. The Articles gave Congress the power to declare war, appoint military officers, and coin money. Congress was also responsible for foreign affairs.

The Articles of Confederation limited the powers of Congress by giving the states final authority. Although Congress could pass laws, at least 9 of the 13 states had to approve a law before it went into effect. Congress could not regulate trade between states or even between states and foreign countries. Congress could not pass any laws regarding taxes. To get money, Congress had to ask each state for it. No state could be forced to pay.

The Articles created a loose alliance among the 13 states. The national government was weak, in part because it had no president to carry out laws passed by Congress. This weak national government might have worked if the states had been able to get along with each other. But many disputes arose, and there was no way of settling them because the Articles did not set up a system of courts.

**Conflict over western lands.** The first dispute arose even before the Articles went into effect. Every state had to approve the Articles. But Maryland refused. It wanted the land between the Appalachian Mountains and the Mississippi River turned over to Congress.

Virginia and several other large states claimed these western lands. (See the map at right.) As a small state, Maryland worried that the large states would become too powerful unless they gave up their land claims.

At first, Virginia and the other states refused to give up their claims. But Thomas Jefferson and other leading Virginians saw the need for a national government. So they convinced the Virginia legislature to give up its claims. Other large states followed Virginia's lead. Finally, in 1781, Maryland ratified the Articles of Confederation, and the first American government went into effect.

## Many Troubles

The new government faced many troubles. Massachusetts, New Hampshire, and New York all claimed Vermont, but they had no way of settling their dispute. Foreign countries took advantage of the new government's weakness. For example, Britain refused to withdraw its troops from the Ohio Valley as it had agreed to do under the peace treaty. Spain, too, challenged the new nation. It closed the port of New Orleans to American farmers. The port was important to them because they used it to ship goods to the east.

The most difficult problem for the new government was raising money. Congress did not have the power to pass tax laws, and the states did not contribute enough money to meet the government's expenses.

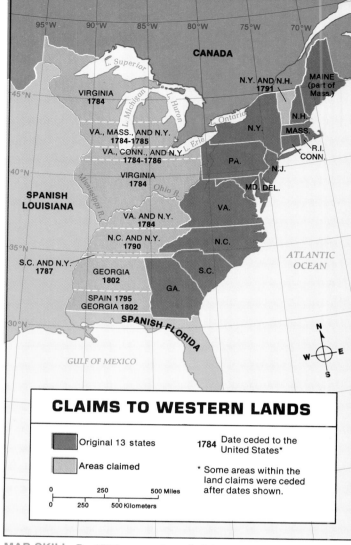

**CLAIMS TO WESTERN LANDS**

Original 13 states

Areas claimed

1784 Date ceded to the United States*

* Some areas within the land claims were ceded after dates shown.

0   250   500 Miles
0   250   500 Kilometers

MAP SKILL  By 1783, a number of states claimed lands west of the Appalachians. Which states claimed the most land? Which states had no land claims in the West?

During the Revolution, the Continental Congress tried to raise money simply by printing paper money. Paper money is valuable only if it is backed by reserves such as gold or silver or by confidence in the government. The Continental dollars Congress printed had no gold or silver backing. Also, few people believed that the government could pay its debts. So Continental dollars soon became worthless.

When Continental dollars became worthless, states printed their own paper money. This caused a great deal

Despite the problems the new nation faced, Americans felt great patriotic pride. This pride was seen in the symbols of the nation. Miss Liberty, who is shown here carrying a flag, stood as a symbol of freedom.

of confusion. How much was a North Carolina dollar worth? Was a Virginia dollar just as valuable? Most states refused to accept money from other states. As a result, trade between states became difficult.

Congress tried to pass a law taxing imported goods. But every state had to approve the tax before it could go into effect. When only 12 states approved it, the tax was defeated.

## Organizing the Northwest Territory

Despite its troubles, Congress did pass two important laws. Both concerned the Northwest Territory,* lands

---

*Americans used the word territory to mean an area that was not yet organized into a state.

lying north of the Ohio River and east of the Mississippi. (See the map on page 201.) Many settlers lived in this region. Every year, more headed west to clear land for farms.

To set up a system for settling the Northwest Territory, Congress passed the *Land Ordinance of 1785.* The ordinance called for the land to be surveyed and divided into townships. Each township would have 36 sections. A section was one square mile and contained 640 acres. (See the diagram on page 201.) Congress planned to sell sections to settlers for $640 each. One section in every township was set aside to support public schools.

Two years later, in 1787, Congress passed the *Northwest Ordinance.* This ordinance set up a government for the Northwest Territory and outlawed slavery there. It allowed the region to be divided into separate territories. Once a territory had a population of 60,000 free citizens, it could ask Congress to be admitted as a new state. The new state would then be "on an equal footing with the original states in all respects whatsoever."

The Northwest Ordinance was important because it set up a way for new states to be admitted to the United States. It guaranteed that new states would be treated just the same as the original 13 states. Eventually, the Northwest Territory was carved into five states: Ohio, Indiana, Illinois, Michigan, and Wisconsin.

## Shays' Rebellion

While Congress dealt successfully with the Northwest Territory, it failed to solve other problems. Among the most serious were the problems of farmers.

During the Revolution, the demand for farm products was high. Farmers borrowed money for land, seed, animals, and tools. But after the war, the nation suffered an economic depres-

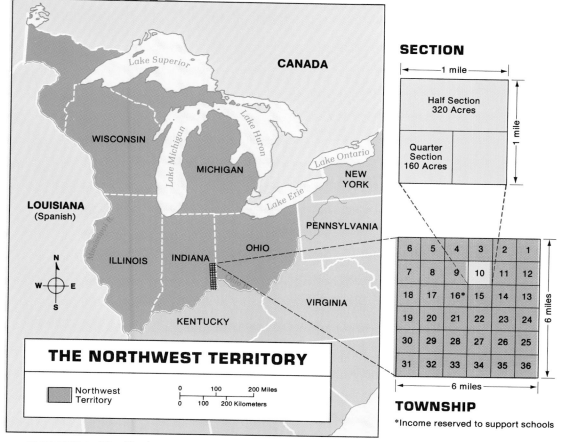

## SECTION

1 mile

Half Section
320 Acres

Quarter
Section
160 Acres

1 mile

| 6 | 5 | 4 | 3 | 2 | 1 |
|---|---|---|---|---|---|
| 7 | 8 | 9 | 10 | 11 | 12 |
| 18 | 17 | 16* | 15 | 14 | 13 |
| 19 | 20 | 21 | 22 | 23 | 24 |
| 30 | 29 | 28 | 27 | 26 | 25 |
| 31 | 32 | 33 | 34 | 35 | 36 |

6 miles

6 miles

## TOWNSHIP

*Income reserved to support schools

### THE NORTHWEST TERRITORY

Northwest Territory

0   100   200 Miles
0   100   200 Kilometers

**MAP SKILL** The Northwest Territory included lands between the Ohio and Mississippi rivers. In the 1780s, Congress set up a system for settling the area. How is each township within the Northwest Territory divided up?

sion. An *economic depression* is a period when business activity slows, prices and wages fall, and unemployment rises. When prices for farm goods fell, farmers could not repay their loans.

Farmers in western Massachusetts were hard hit by falling farm prices. To make matters worse, Massachusetts raised taxes. The courts threatened to seize the farms of people who did not pay their loans and taxes.

Captain Daniel Shays was a Massachusetts farmer who had fought in the Revolution. In 1786, Shays gathered a force of about 1,000 angry farmers. They attacked courthouses and tried to take a warehouse full of rifles and gunpowder. Massachusetts quickly raised an army and ended the rebellion.

*Shays' Rebellion* worried many Americans. It was a sign that the Arti-cles of Confederation were not working. Leaders of several states called for a convention to discuss ways of reforming the Articles. They decided to meet in Philadelphia in May 1787. When they met, however, they took more drastic action.

### SECTION REVIEW

1. **Locate:** Maryland, Virginia, Northwest Territory.
2. **Define:** constitution, execute, bill of rights, economic depression.
3. Why did states want to limit the power of the national government?
4. Describe three problems the nation had faced under the Articles of Confederation.
5. **What Do You Think?** Why do you think Americans in the 1770s and 1780s thought state governments were more important than the national government?

# 2 The Constitutional Convention

### Read to Learn

★ Who were the leaders of the Constitutional Convention?

★ What compromises were worked out at the Convention?

★ What do these words mean: legislative, executive, judicial, compromise?

The delegates who went to Philadelphia in May 1787 had their work cut out for them. Soon after the meeting began, they decided to do more than revise the Articles of Confederation. They chose to write a new constitution for the United States. Between May and September, they forged a document that has been the basis of American government ever since.

## The Convention Opens

The *Constitutional Convention* met in Philadelphia. Every state was supposed to send delegates, but Rhode Island refused. Thus, only 12 of the 13 states were represented.* The meeting took place in the Pennsylvania State House, the same place where the Declaration of Independence had been signed 11 years before.

**Who was there?** The 55 delegates included many leaders from the Revolution. Benjamin Franklin, at age 81, was the senior statesman. George Washington traveled north from his home in Mount Vernon, Virginia. Washington was so well respected by the delegates in Philadelphia that he was at once elected president of the Constitutional Convention.

Quite a few delegates were young men in their 20s and 30s. Among them was Alexander Hamilton of New York.

---

*New Hampshire was reluctant to send delegates. It did not do so until the Convention was half over.

During the Revolution, Hamilton served for a time as Washington's private secretary. Hamilton did not like the Articles of Confederation, which he said were "fit neither for war nor peace." The nation, he wrote, "is sick and wants powerful remedies." The powerful remedy he prescribed was a strong national government.

Another member of the Constitutional Convention was James Madison of Virginia. At first glance, Madison did not impress people. He was short and thin and spoke so softly that he was often asked to speak up. But Madison had much worth saying. He had served in Congress and in the Virginia legislature. A hard worker, he was always eager to learn. Before going to Philadelphia, he collected the latest books on government and politics. Madison arrived in Philadelphia a week early so that he would have time to read and organize his thoughts.

**Need for secrecy.** When the meeting began, the delegates decided to keep their talks secret. They wanted to be free to speak their minds without seeing their words printed in newspapers. "My wish," wrote Washington, "is that the Convention may . . . probe the defects of the Constitution to the bottom, and provide radical cures." He and other delegates wanted to explore every issue and solution, without pressure from outside.

To ensure secrecy, guards stood at the door, admitting only the delegates. The windows were kept closed to keep passers-by from overhearing the debates. But the closed windows made the room terribly hot. As it was, the summer of 1787 was the hottest in many years. New Englanders in their woolen suits suffered terribly. Southerners were more used to the heat and wore lighter clothes.

In 1787, delegates to the Constitutional Convention met in the Pennsylvania State House, renamed Independence Hall. Both the Declaration of Independence and the Constitution were signed here.

## Heated Debate

On May 25, George Washington took his place as president of the Convention. He sat in a high-backed chair at the front of the room. The other delegates sat at tables covered by green cloth. Everyone agreed on the need for action. By May 30, the delegates had voted to write a new constitution instead of revising the Articles of Confederation.

**Virginia Plan.** Early on, Edmund Randolph and James Madison, both of Virginia, presented a plan for the new government. It became known as the *Virginia Plan.* In the end, much of the Virginia Plan was included in the new constitution.

The Virginia Plan called for a strong national government with three branches: legislative, executive, and judicial (jyoo DIHSH uhl). In general, the *legislative branch* of a government passes the laws. The *executive branch* carries out the laws. And the *judicial branch,* or system of courts, decides if laws are carried out fairly.

The Virginia Plan also called for a two-house legislature with a lower house and an upper house. Seats in both houses would be divided up according to the population of each state. States with large populations would elect more representatives than states with small populations. This differed from the Articles of Confederation. Under the Articles, each state had one vote in Congress, no matter what its population.

Small states at once protested this plan. They were afraid that large states would outvote them. Supporters of the Virginia Plan said that it was only fair for a state with more people to have more representatives.

**New Jersey Plan.** The debate over the Virginia Plan almost caused the Convention to fall apart. In June 1787, William Paterson of New Jersey presented a plan that had the support of the small states. The *New Jersey Plan* also called for three branches of government. But it called for a legislature with only one house. Each state would have one vote, no matter what its population was.

## The Great Compromise

The delegates argued to a standstill. The heat caused tempers to rise. Finally, Roger Sherman of Connecticut worked out a compromise between the large and small states. A *compromise* is a settlement in which each side gives up some of its demands in order to reach an agreement.

Sherman's compromise called for a legislature with a lower and an upper house. Members of the lower house, known as the *House of Representatives,* would be chosen by all men who could vote. Seats would be divided up according to the population of each state. The large states liked this part of the compromise because it was similar to the Virginia Plan.

Members of the upper house, called the *Senate,* would be chosen by state legislatures. Each state would have two senators. Small states supported this part of the compromise. Together, the two houses would be the Congress of the United States.

On July 16, delegates narrowly accepted Sherman's plan, which became known as the *Great Compromise.* Each side gave up some demands in favor of the nation as a whole. If the delegates had not agreed to the Great Compromise, the Convention might have broken up without solving the problems facing the United States.

## Compromises Over Slavery

After accepting the Great Compromise, the delegates faced a new question. Would slaves be counted as part of the population? The answer to this question was important because it affected the number of representatives a state would have in the House of Representatives.

The slavery question led to bitter arguments between the North and South. Southerners wanted to include slaves in the population count even though they would not let slaves vote. Northerners protested. They realized that if slaves were counted, southern states would have more representatives than northern states. Northerners argued that since slaves could not vote, they should not be counted.

The debate raged on until the delegates worked out a new compromise. They agreed that three fifths of the slaves in any state would be counted. In other words, if a state had 5,000 slaves, 3,000 of them would be included in the state's population count. This agreement was known as the *Three Fifths Compromise.*

Northerners and Southerners disagreed over another issue related to slavery. By 1787, some northern states had banned the slave trade within their borders. They wanted the new Congress to ban the slave trade in the entire nation. Southerners warned that their economy would be ruined if Congress outlawed the slave trade.

In the end, the two sides compromised. Northerners agreed to let the slave trade continue for at least 20 years. After that, Congress could regulate it if it wished.

## The Final Weeks

Throughout the summer, the delegates made many more decisions about the new constitution. How many years should the President, head of the executive branch, serve? How should the courts be organized? Would members of Congress be paid?

Finally, on September 17, the Constitution was ready. Delegates from each state came forward to sign the document. Washington and the other members of the Constitutional Convention had done a remarkable thing. In a few months, they had set up the framework for a lasting government. Their next job was to win approval for the Constitution.

### SECTION REVIEW

1. **Define:** legislative, executive, judicial, compromise.
2. Why did delegates decide to keep their talks secret?
3. Why did delegates from small states object to the Virginia Plan?
4. What was the Great Compromise?
5. **What Do You Think?** Do you think the Three Fifths Compromise was a reasonable solution? Explain.

AMERICANS WHO DARED

### James Forten

James Forten of Philadelphia was a free black. During the Revolution, he served as a powder boy on an American ship—even though he was only 15 years old. After the war, he became a sailmaker and invented a device for handling sails. He bought his own sail shop and earned a large fortune. Forten devoted his life to ending slavery and urging equal rights for free blacks. He refused to sell sails and rigging to slave ships and used his wealth in the cause of ending slavery.

# 3 We, the People

### Read to Learn

★ How does the Constitution divide powers between the federal government and the states?
★ How does separation of powers work?
★ What do these words mean: republic, federalism, separation of powers, electoral college, checks and balances, bill, veto, override, impeach?

In September 1787, after months of debate and many compromises, the framers of the Constitution returned to their home states. The people of the United States now had their first look at the Constitution. (The complete text of the Constitution is printed on pages 628–649.) The Constitution created a republic. A *republic* is a nation in which the voters elect representatives to govern them.

"We, the people of the United States," the document begins, "do ordain and establish this Constitution for the United States of America." By starting this way, the Constitution makes clear that the power of the government comes from the American people.

## Federalism: A Framework of Government

All over the land, people read the Constitution. They were curious to see how it differed from the Articles of Confederation. A major issue they were interested in was what powers the national government would have and what powers the states would have.

Under the Articles of Confederation, the states had more power than the Congress. But this system had caused problems. Under the new Constitution, the states delegated, or gave up, some powers to the national government. At the same time, the states reserved, or kept, power in other areas. This sharing of power between the states and the national government is called *federalism*. The system of federalism is shown in the diagram below.

Federalism has given Americans a flexible system of government. The people have power because they elect both national and state officials. The federal, or national, government has the power to act for the nation as a whole. And the states have power over important local matters.

**Powers of the federal government.** The Constitution spells out the powers of the federal government. For example, only the federal government has the power to coin money. So states could no longer issue money as they had under the Articles of Confederation. The federal government has the power to regulate trade between states and with other countries. Also, the federal government has the power to declare war.

CHART SKILL Under the federal system, states and the national government divide up power. Name two powers shared by both national and state governments. Who has the power to set up schools?

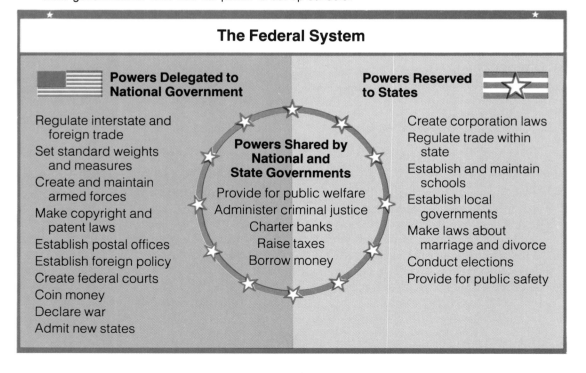

## The Federal System

**Powers Delegated to National Government**

Regulate interstate and foreign trade
Set standard weights and measures
Create and maintain armed forces
Make copyright and patent laws
Establish postal offices
Establish foreign policy
Create federal courts
Coin money
Declare war
Admit new states

**Powers Shared by National and State Governments**

Provide for public welfare
Administer criminal justice
Charter banks
Raise taxes
Borrow money

**Powers Reserved to States**

Create corporation laws
Regulate trade within state
Establish and maintain schools
Establish local governments
Make laws about marriage and divorce
Conduct elections
Provide for public safety

**Powers of the states.** Under the Constitution, states have the power to regulate trade within their borders. They can decide who votes in state elections. They have power over schools and local governments. Also, the Constitution says that powers not given to the federal government belong to the states. This point pleased people in small states who were afraid that the federal government might become too powerful.

**Shared powers.** The Constitution states that some powers are to be shared by federal and state governments. Both governments have the power to build roads. Today, for example, federal roads are called U.S. 169 or Interstate 40. State roads are labeled Connecticut 47 or Arizona 85.

The framers of the Constitution had to decide how the states and the federal government would settle any future disagreement. To do this, they made the Constitution "the supreme law of the land." This means that in any dispute, the Constitution is the final authority.

## Separation of Powers

The Constitution set up a strong federal government. To keep the government from becoming too powerful, the framers of the Constitution created three branches of government. Then, through a system of separation of powers, they made sure that no one branch could become too powerful. *Separation of powers* means that each branch of government has its own powers. The powers are clearly described in the Constitution. (Look at the diagram on page 208.)

**Congress.** Congress is the legislative branch of government. It is made up of the House of Representatives and the Senate. Members of the House are elected for two-year terms. Senators are elected for six-year terms.

Under the Constitution, voters in each state elect members of the House of Representatives. Delegates at the Constitutional Convention wanted the House to represent the interests of ordinary people. At first, the Constitution said that senators were to be chosen by state legislatures. In 1913, this was changed. Today, senators are elected in the same way as House members.

Article I of the Constitution sets out the powers of Congress. Among them, Congress has the power to collect taxes. It can "regulate commerce with foreign nations, and among the several states." In foreign affairs, it has the right to declare war and "raise and support armies."

**The President.** Article II of the Constitution sets up the executive branch of government. It is headed by the President. The executive branch also includes the Vice President and any advisers appointed by the President. The President and Vice President serve four-year terms.

The President is responsible for carrying out all laws passed by Congress. The President is also commander in chief of the armed forces and is responsible for foreign relations.

**The courts.** Article III calls for a Supreme Court. The article allowed Congress to set up other federal courts under the Supreme Court. The Supreme Court and other federal courts hear cases that involve the Constitution or any laws passed by Congress. They also hear cases arising between two or more states.

## Electoral College

The framers of the Constitution debated whether to let voters elect the President directly. But this idea worried them. In the late 1700s, news traveled slowly. The framers argued that New Englanders would probably know little about a candidate for President

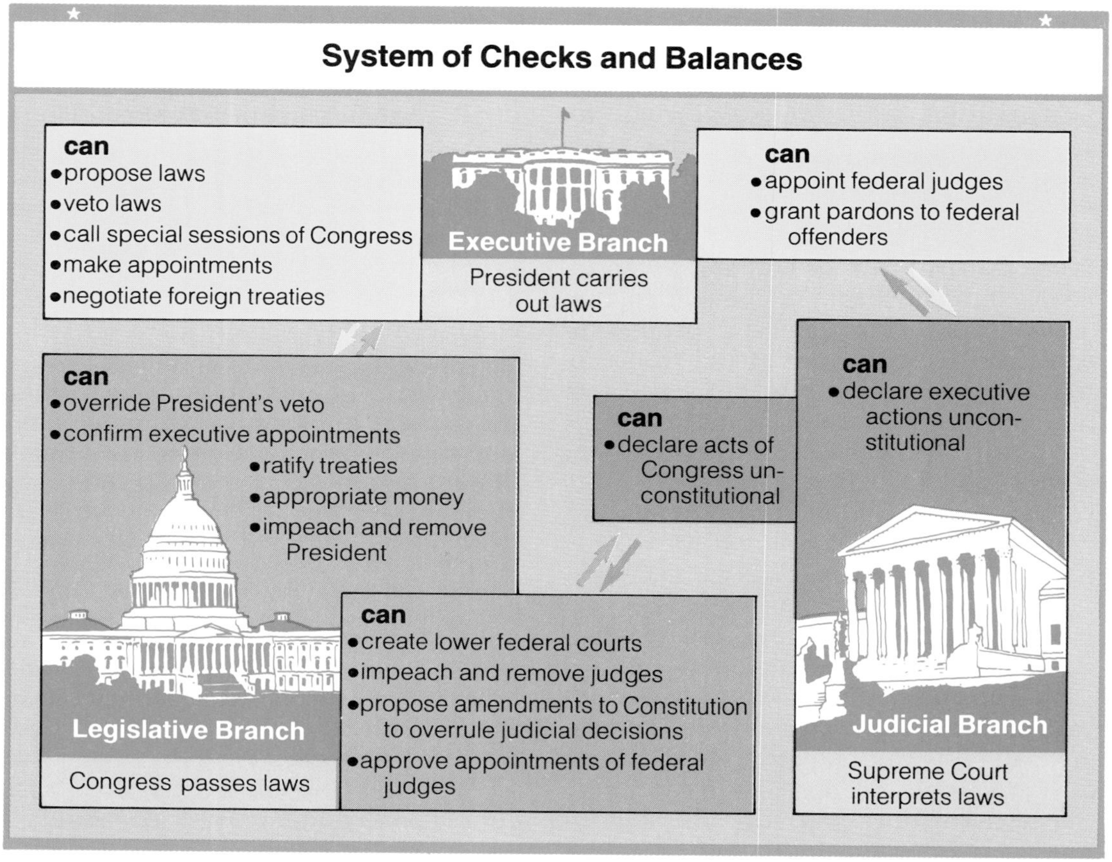

## System of Checks and Balances

**Executive Branch**
President carries out laws

**can**
- propose laws
- veto laws
- call special sessions of Congress
- make appointments
- negotiate foreign treaties

**can**
- appoint federal judges
- grant pardons to federal offenders

**Legislative Branch**
Congress passes laws

**can**
- override President's veto
- confirm executive appointments
  - ratify treaties
  - appropriate money
  - impeach and remove President

**can**
- create lower federal courts
- impeach and remove judges
- propose amendments to Constitution to overrule judicial decisions
- approve appointments of federal judges

**can**
- declare acts of Congress unconstitutional

**Judicial Branch**
Supreme Court interprets laws

**can**
- declare executive actions unconstitutional

CHART SKILL The Constitution sets up a system of checks and balances among the three branches of government. Name one way Congress checks the President. What power does the Supreme Court have to check Congress?

from the South. And a candidate from Pennsylvania would be unknown to voters in Massachusetts or Georgia. So how could voters choose the best candidate for the job?

To solve this problem, the Constitution set up a system for electors from each state to choose the President. State legislatures would decide how to choose their electors. Every four years, the electors met as a group, called the *electoral college.* The electoral college voted for the President and Vice President of the United States.

The framers of the Constitution expected that electors would be well-informed citizens who were familiar with the national government. They believed that such men would choose a

President wisely. The electoral college still meets today, but its function has changed somewhat from the original system.

## Checks and Balances

The Constitution set up a system of *checks and balances.* Under this system, each branch of the federal government has some way to check, or control, the other two branches. The system of checks and balances is another way in which the Constitution limits the power of government.

To do its work, Congress passes *bills,* or proposed laws. A bill then goes to the President to be signed into law. (Study the flow chart at right.) The

A **flow chart** is used to give a lot of information in a simple and easy-to-understand way. A flow chart shows developments in a step-by-step manner. For example, under the Constitution of the United States, Congress has the power to pass bills, which the President signs into law. Over the years, a complicated process has developed whereby a bill actually becomes a law.

Study the flow chart to see the steps through which a bill has to pass before it can become a law.

1. **Identify the parts of the flow chart.** (a) What is the title of the flow chart? (b) What does each of the four columns show? (c) What do the black arrows show? (d) What color shows House action? Senate action?

2. **Practice reading the flow chart.** (a) Where is a bill usually introduced? (b) What happens to a bill after it has been introduced? (c) What happens after the House and Senate have both passed their own forms of a bill? (d) What is the last step a bill goes through before it becomes a law?

3. **Evaluate the information shown on the flow chart.** Every year, about 10,000 bills are introduced in Congress. Only about 1,000 ever make it through the many steps to become laws. (a) Why do you think House and Senate committees hold hearings on bills that have been introduced? (b) Using the flow chart, why do you think only a few bills actually become laws?

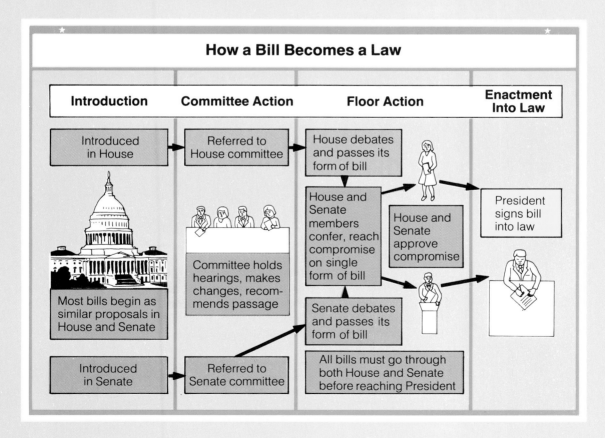

**How a Bill Becomes a Law**

| Introduction | Committee Action | Floor Action | Enactment Into Law |
|---|---|---|---|

Introduced in House

Referred to House committee

House debates and passes its form of bill

House and Senate members confer, reach compromise on single form of bill

House and Senate approve compromise

President signs bill into law

Committee holds hearings, makes changes, recommends passage

Most bills begin as similar proposals in House and Senate

Senate debates and passes its form of bill

Introduced in Senate

Referred to Senate committee

All bills must go through both House and Senate before reaching President

President can check the power of Congress by *vetoing,* or rejecting, a bill. On the other hand, Congress can check the President by *overriding,* or overruling, the President's veto. To override a veto, two thirds of both houses of Congress must vote for the bill again.

Congress has other checks on the President. The President appoints officials such as judges and ambassadors. But the Senate must approve these appointments. The President has the power to negotiate treaties with other nations. But two thirds of the Senate have to approve a treaty before it can become law.

Congress also has the power to remove the President from office if it finds the President guilty of a serious crime. The Constitution describes how this can be done. First, the House of Representatives must *impeach,* or bring charges, against the President. A trial is then held in the Senate. If two thirds of the senators vote for conviction, the President must leave office.

Congress and the President have checks on the power of the courts. The President appoints judges, who must be approved by the Senate. If judges misbehave, Congress may remove them from office.

The Constitution offers a remarkable balance among the three branches of the federal government and between state governments and the federal government. This balance has helped it work for nearly 200 years, longer than any other written constitution in the world. The Constitution has survived, too, because it is a living document. As you will read in this and later chapters, it can be changed to meet new conditions in the United States.

═══SECTION REVIEW═══

1. **Define:** republic, federalism, separation of powers, electoral college, checks and balances, bill, veto, override, impeach.

2. (a) List three powers delegated to the national government. (b) List three powers reserved to the states.

3. (a) List the three branches of the federal government. (b) Name one power given to each.

4. Why was the electoral college set up?

5. **What Do You Think?** How do you think the system of checks and balances limits the power of government?

# 4 Ratifying the Constitution

### Read to Learn
★ What did Federalists and Antifederalists say about the Constitution?
★ How can the Constitution be amended?
★ What rights do the first ten amendments protect?
★ What do these words mean: amend, due process?

In 1787, Americans were divided in their views of the Constitution. Many supported it. But many others were shocked by it. So ratifying the Constitution was a bitter struggle.

### The Debate Goes On

The framers of the Constitution set up a process for the states to decide on the new government. At least 9 of the 13 states had to approve the Constitution before it could go into effect. In 1787 and 1788, voters in each state elected delegates to special state conventions. Then, the delegates met to decide whether or not to ratify the new Constitution.

**The two sides.** In every state, debates went on over the Constitution. Supporters called themselves *Federal-*

For Americans in 1776, the Revolution was not just a struggle for freedom from British control. It was a struggle for freedom in general. For many, the idea of freedom included the right to worship as they pleased.

The original Constitution contained no protection of religious freedom. Americans were worried. Under the newly formed government, how free would they be to worship, or not to worship, as they pleased?

After George Washington became President in 1789, several religious groups wrote to him. Baptists, Quakers, Jews, Presbyterians, Catholics, and others all expressed hopes that he would safeguard their religious freedom.

In his responses, Washington hailed the importance of religion to the new nation. Religion, he said, promoted good deeds, honesty, hard work, and thrift. He promised that the new government would support religious freedom. In one letter, he wrote, "Every man . . . ought to be protected in worshipping the Deity according to the dictates of his own conscience."

Religious freedom became law in 1791. In that year, the Bill of Rights was added to the Constitution. The First Amendment guaranteed religious freedom by stating, "Congress shall make no law respecting an establishment of religion, or prohibiting the free exercise thereof."

★ Why did religious groups write to President Washington?

---

*ists.* They called people who opposed the Constitution *Antifederalists.*

Federalists favored a strong national government. The best-known Federalists were James Madison, Alexander Hamilton, and John Jay. They wrote a series of letters, called *The Federalist Papers,* defending the Constitution. They signed their letters with the names of ancient Roman heroes such as Publius or Cato. People generally knew who the letter writers really were, but it was the custom of the time to use pen names.

Antifederalists opposed the Constitution for many reasons. They felt that it made the national government too strong and left the states too weak. They thought that the Constitution gave the President too much power. Most people expected George Washington to be elected President. Antifederalists admired him. But they warned that in the future a less desirable person might be elected. So they did not want the office to be too powerful.

**Call for a bill of rights.** The main argument of the Antifederalists was that the Constitution had no bill of rights. Americans had just fought a revolution to protect their freedoms. They wanted to include a bill of rights in the Constitution that spelled out these basic freedoms.

Federalists answered that the Constitution protected citizens very well without a bill of rights. Anyway, they argued, it would be impossible to list all the natural rights of people. Antifederalists replied that if rights were not clearly written down, it would be easy to ignore them. Several state conventions refused to approve the Constitution until they were promised that a bill of rights would be added.

**Approval at last.** On December 7, 1787, Delaware became the first state to ratify the Constitution. In June 1788, New Hampshire became the ninth state to approve it. The Constitution could go into effect.

Still, the future of the United States remained in doubt. It was important that all states support the Constitution. But New York and Virginia, two of the largest, had not yet ratified the Constitution. In both states, Federalists and Antifederalists were closely matched. In Virginia, Patrick Henry argued strongly against the Constitution. "There will be no checks, no real balances in this government," he cried. Henry was popular in Virginia. But in the end, Washington, Madison, and other Federalists turned the tide in favor of the Constitution. In late June, Virginia ratified the Constitution.

In New York, the struggle went on for another month. Finally, in July 1788, the state convention voted in favor of the Constitution. North Carolina ratified it in November. Rhode Island, the last state to ratify the Constitution, did so in May 1790.

## We Have Become a Nation

When Americans heard that the Constitution was approved, they held great celebrations. The city of Philadelphia set its celebration for July 4, 1788. As the sun rose that day, church bells rang. In the harbor, the ship *Rising Sun* boomed a salute from its cannons. A huge parade snaked along Market Street, led by soldiers who had served in the Revolution. Horses wore bright ribbons, and bands played popular songs.

As usual, watchmen announced the hour and the weather. But on this day, they added, "10 o'clock, and a glorious star-light morning." They meant that ten stars (or states) had ratified the Constitution. Thousands watched as six horses pulled a blue carriage shaped like an eagle. Thirteen stars and stripes were painted on the front, and the Constitution was raised proudly above it.

Americans celebrated their independence and their new Constitution with parades and picnics. Here, patriotic Americans raise a Liberty Pole as their families watch.

That night, even the skies seemed to celebrate. The northern lights, vivid bands of color, lit up the sky above the city. Benjamin Rush, a Philadelphia doctor and strong supporter of the Constitution, wrote to a friend: "Tis done. We have become a nation."

The nation held its first election under the Constitution in January 1789. The first President was, of course, George Washington. John Adams was elected Vice President. The first Congress was made up of 59 representatives and 26 senators. It met in New York City, the nation's first capital.

## Amending the Constitution

The first Congress turned its attention quickly to the need for including a bill of rights in the Constitution. The framers had provided a way to *amend,* or change, the Constitution. They wanted to make the Constitution flexible enough to change as the times changed. But they did not want changes made lightly. So they made the process fairly difficult.

The first step is to propose an amendment. This can be done in two ways. Two thirds of both houses of Congress can vote to propose an amendment. Or two thirds of the states, meeting in special conventions, can propose an amendment. The next step is to ratify the amendment. Three fourths of the states must vote for the amendment before it can become part of the Constitution.

In the 200 years since the Constitution was adopted, only 26 amendments have been made. Ten of these amendments were added in the first years of the Constitution.

## The Bill of Rights

In 1789, the first Congress passed a series of amendments. By December 1791, three fourths of the states had ratified ten amendments. These ten amendments became part of the Constitution and are known as the *Bill of Rights.*

The Bill of Rights protects certain basic rights. James Madison, who wrote the amendments, said that the Bill of Rights does not *give* Americans these rights. People already have these rights. They are natural rights, he said, that belong to all human beings. The Bill of Rights simply prevents the government from taking away these rights.

The First Amendment guarantees the basic rights of freedom of religion, freedom of speech, freedom of the press, and freedom of assembly, or the right to meet in groups. The next three amendments came out of the colonists' struggle with Britain. For example, the Third Amendment prevents Congress from forcing citizens to keep troops in their homes. Before the Revolution, you will remember, Britain tried to make colonists house soldiers.

Amendments 5 through 8 protect citizens who are accused of crimes and are brought to trial. Every citizen has the right to due process of law. *Due process* means that the government must follow the same fair rules in all cases brought to trial. These rules include the right to trial by jury, the right to be defended by a lawyer, and the right to a speedy trial. The last two amendments limit the powers of the federal government to those that are granted in the Constitution.

=== SECTION REVIEW ===

1. **Define:** amend, due process.
2. Why did Antifederalists oppose the Constitution?
3. How can an amendment be made to the Constitution?
4. List three rights protected in the Bill of Rights.
5. **What Do You Think?** What do you think Dr. Rush meant when he said, "We have become a nation"?

# Chapter 9 Review

## ★ Summary ★

After independence, each state organized its own government. The first national government was set up under the Articles of Confederation. Under the Articles, however, states had final say over most issues. This left the national government too weak to work effectively.

In 1787, delegates from 12 states met at the Constitutional Convention in Philadelphia. They drew up a new constitution, which has been the basis for the government of the United States ever since. The Constitution set up a system of sharing powers between state governments and the federal government. Within the federal government, separation of powers and a system of checks and balances limit the powers of each branch of government. Soon after the Constitution was ratified in 1789, the Bill of Rights was added.

## ★ Reviewing the Facts ★

**Key Terms.** Match each term in Column 1 with the correct definition in Column 2.

| Column 1 | Column 2 |
| --- | --- |
| 1. constitution | a. settlement in which each side gives up something |
| 2. compromise | b. document that sets out the basic laws of a government |
| 3. republic | c. bring charges against someone |
| 4. federalism | d. sharing of power between the national and state governments |
| 5. impeach | e. nation where voters choose representatives to govern them |

**Key People, Events, and Ideas.** Identify each of the following.

1. Articles of Confederation
2. Northwest Ordinance
3. Shays' Rebellion
4. Alexander Hamilton
5. James Madison
6. Constitutional Convention
7. Virginia Plan
8. New Jersey Plan
9. House of Representatives
10. Senate
11. Great Compromise
12. Three Fifths Compromise
13. Federalist
14. Antifederalist
15. Bill of Rights

## ★ Chapter Checkup ★

1. Describe three problems under the Articles of Confederation.
2. Describe one cause and one result of Shays' Rebellion.
3. Compare the Virginia Plan to the New Jersey Plan.
4. What two issues divided northern and southern states during the Constitutional Convention?
5. Why did the framers of the Constitution set up each of the following: (a) separation of powers; (b) checks and balances?
6. How was the Constitution ratified?
7. (a) Why did Antifederalists want a bill of rights in the Constitution? (b) How did Federalists respond to this demand?
8. How does the Bill of Rights protect citizens who are accused of crimes?

## ★ Thinking About History ★

1. **Understanding the economy.** (a) What money troubles did the national government face under the Articles of Confederation? (b) Why did the government print paper money? (c) Why did Continental dollars become worthless?

2. **Relating past to present.** (a) On what issues did the Constitutional Convention have to compromise? (b) Why do you think these compromises were necessary? (c) Describe one local or national issue today on which you think compromise is necessary.

3. **Analyzing information.** Explain how the system of federalism set up by the Constitution solved some of the problems the government faced under the Articles of Confederation.

4. **Learning about citizenship.** How does the Constitution set up a balance between the powers of the states and the powers of the national government?

## ★ Using Your Skills ★

1. **Map reading.** Study the map on page 199. (a) What state or states claimed land around the Great Lakes? (b) Who owned the land west of the Mississippi River? (c) What state or states claimed land directly south of Lake Superior?

2. **Using a diagram.** Study the diagram on page 201. (a) How large is a township? (b) How many sections are there in a township? (c) How large is a section? (d) Can a section be subdivided? Explain.

3. **Making a review chart.** Information that is organized in a chart can be easily reviewed and compared. Make a chart with two columns and three rows. Title the columns Articles of Confederation and Constitution. Title the rows Legislative Branch, Executive Branch, and Judicial Branch. Complete the chart with information from the chapter. (a) What were the major differences between the Articles of Confederation and the Constitution? (b) Were there any similarities? Explain.

4. **Ranking.** Review the Bill of Rights on pages 640–642. Then choose five rights and rank them according to which you think is most important. Explain your ranking.

## ★ More to Do ★

1. **Exploring local history.** Research and write a report describing the adoption of your state's first constitution.

2. **Researching.** Find out more about one of the delegates at the Constitutional Convention. Describe his background and how he came to be a delegate.

3. **Creating headlines.** Create a series of headlines announcing the completion of work on the Constitution.

4. **Organizing a debate.** As a group project, organize a debate between Federalists and Antifederalists. Set up the debate at a state convention called to ratify the Constitution.

5. **Preparing a report.** Write a report about some aspect of American life after the Revolution. You might describe songs, dress styles, schools, or churches.

# Unit 3 Review

## ★ Unit Summary ★

**Chapter 7** During the French and Indian War, Britain drove the French out of North America. After the war, Britain tried to raise money to pay off its debts by taxing the 13 colonies. Colonists protested the new taxes. They claimed that Parliament did not have the right to tax them. The crisis over taxes slowly led to war.

**Chapter 8** In July 1776, a year after the American Revolution began, colonists declared their independence from Britain. George Washington led the Americans in their struggle for independence. Americans suffered many setbacks at first. Finally, with French help, they defeated the British. By the Treaty of Paris, Britain recognized the American nation.

**Chapter 9** The Articles of Confederation set up the first American government. In 1787, however, Americans decided to replace the Articles with a new constitution. Under the new government, states and the national government shared power. Each of the three branches of the federal government had checks on the power of the other.

## ★ Unit Checkup ★

Choose the word or phrase that best completes each of the following statements.

1. Colonists protested against the Sugar and Stamp acts by declaring a
   (a) blockade.
   (b) compromise.
   (c) boycott.

2. Britain responded to the Boston Tea Party by passing the
   (a) Tea Act.
   (b) Intolerable Acts.
   (c) Stamp Act.

3. Colonists who supported Britain during the American Revolution were called
   (a) Loyalists.
   (b) Patriots.
   (c) Federalists.

4. France agreed to help the Americans after the Battle of
   (a) Saratoga.
   (b) Bunker Hill.
   (c) Yorktown.

5. During the Constitutional Convention, the Three Fifths Compromise had to do with
   (a) slaves.
   (b) money.
   (c) land claims.

## ★ Building American Citizenship ★

1. Colonists protested British efforts to tax them because they did not elect representatives to Parliament. (a) Who decides on taxes in this country today? (b) How can people influence what taxes are passed?

2. In 1776, Americans believed that they should explain to the world why they were breaking away from Britain. They did so in the Declaration of Independence. How do people today make known their disagreements with the government?

3. The Constitution set up a federal system. (a) Describe decisions your state government makes that affect your life. (b) Describe decisions the United States government makes that affect your life.

Read the two reports on the Battle of Lexington. Then answer the questions below.

1. On what issue or issues do the two reports differ?
2. Is William Sutherland writing from the British or colonists' point of view?
3. How can you tell which side the Reverend Jonas Clark favors?
4. Can you tell if one of these reports is more reliable than the other? Explain.

 **William Sutherland reported:**

We still went on farther when three shots more were fired, which we did not return. . . . When we came up to the main body, several of our officers called out, "Throw down your arms and you shall come to no harm," or words to that effect. They refused to do this. I heard Major Pitcairn call out, "Soldiers, don't fire. Keep your ranks. Form and surround them." Instantly, some of the villains, who got over the hedge, fired at us, which our men for the first time returned.

 **Rev. Jonas Clark reported:**

Three officers advanced on horseback to the front of the body. One of them cried out, "Villains, rebels, disperse!"—or words to this effect. One of them said, "Lay down your arms . . . why don't you lay down your arms!" About this time, the second of these officers fired a pistol toward the militia as they were dispersing. Another pointed toward our men and with a loud voice said to the troops, "Fire!" which was instantly followed by a discharge of arms.

 **History Writer's Handbook**

### Rewording a Question as a Topic Sentence

The topic sentence in a one-paragraph answer states the main idea of the answer. You can often write a topic sentence by rewording the question.

Look at the following question. *Why was the American victory at Saratoga a turning point in the American Revolution?* By rewording the question, you might write the following topic sentence. *The American victory at Saratoga was a turning point in the American Revolution for three reasons.*

Note that the topic sentence includes the clues in the question. The phrase *for three reasons* covers what the key word *Why* in the question is telling you to do (give reasons). The phrases *at Saratoga* and *in the American Revolution* repeat the clues that limit the topic.

You may reword the question as a topic sentence without covering the key word. For example: *The American victory at Saratoga was a turning point in the American Revolution.* But keep the key word in mind when you later select information for detail sentences.

**Practice** Reword each of the following questions as a topic sentence for a one-paragraph answer.

1. Describe the three parts of the Declaration of Independence.
2. Compare the legislative branches of the Virginia Plan and the New Jersey Plan.

# Unit 4

# STRENGTHENING THE NEW NATION

| 1780 | | | | 1790 | | | | 1800 | | | | 1810 |
|---|---|---|---|---|---|---|---|---|---|---|---|---|

GEORGE WASHINGTON      JOHN ADAMS      THOMAS JEFFERSON

**1787** Northwest Ordinance; Constitution written; ★ Delaware, New Jersey, Pennsylvania become states
**1788** ★ Connecticut, Georgia, Maryland, Massachusetts, New Hampshire, New York, South Carolina, Virginia become states
**1789** ★ North Carolina statehood

**1790s** Lancaster Turnpike built
**1790** ★ Rhode Island statehood
**1791** ★ Vermont statehood; Bank of the United States set up; Bill of Rights
**1792** ★ Kentucky statehood
**1793** Cotton gin invented
**1795** Treaty of Greenville
**1796** ★ Tennessee statehood

**1800s** Whitney develops interchangeable parts
**1803** ★ Ohio statehood; Louisiana Purchase
**1804–06** Lewis and Clark explore Louisiana Purchase
**1807** Embargo Act; *Clermont* launched

| 1780 | | | | 1790 | | | | 1800 | | | | 1810 |
|---|---|---|---|---|---|---|---|---|---|---|---|---|

**Late 1700s** Columbia was an early symbol of the United States.

**1790s** *Daniel Boone Escorting a Band of Pioneers Into the Western Country* by George Caleb Bingham.

**Early 1800s** Thomas Jefferson designed this portable writing desk.

UNIT OUTLINE

**CHAPTER** 10    The First Presidents (1789–1800)

**CHAPTER** 11    Age of Jefferson (1801–1816)

**CHAPTER** 12    The Nation Prospers (1790–1825)

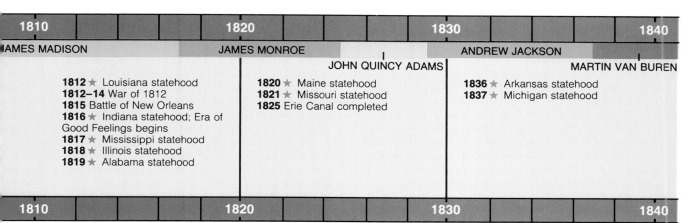

| 1810 | | | | 1820 | | | | 1830 | | | | 1840 |
|---|---|---|---|---|---|---|---|---|---|---|---|---|

JAMES MADISON          JAMES MONROE          ANDREW JACKSON

JOHN QUINCY ADAMS                    MARTIN VAN BUREN

**1812** ★ Louisiana statehood
**1812–14** War of 1812
**1815** Battle of New Orleans
**1816** ★ Indiana statehood; Era of Good Feelings begins
**1817** ★ Mississippi statehood
**1818** ★ Illinois statehood
**1819** ★ Alabama statehood

**1820** ★ Maine statehood
**1821** ★ Missouri statehood
**1825** Erie Canal completed

**1836** ★ Arkansas statehood
**1837** ★ Michigan statehood

| 1810 | | | | 1820 | | | | 1830 | | | | 1840 |
|---|---|---|---|---|---|---|---|---|---|---|---|---|

**1813** During the Battle of Lake Erie, Oliver Perry's ship was crippled by British gunfire. The American commander rowed through heavy fire to another ship.

**1800s** Philadelphia was one of the largest cities in the nation. Here, a Philadelphia man sells oysters outside the Chestnut Street Theater.

CHAPTER

# 10

# The First Presidents (1789–1800)

## Chapter Outline

**1** The New Government at Work
**2** Staying Neutral
**3** Political Parties
**4** Adams Takes a Firm Stand
Readings, page 512

| 1788 | 1790 | 1792 | 1794 | 1796 | 1798 | 1800 |

**1789**
George Washington becomes President

**1792**
Kentucky becomes state

**1794**
Whiskey Rebellion

**1795**
Jay Treaty; Treaty of Greenville

**1798**
XYZ Affair; Alien and Sedition acts

**1800**
Jefferson elected President

## About This Chapter

Early on April 30, 1789, crowds gathered in the streets of New York. They were there to see George Washington take the oath of office as President of the United States. Around noon, Washington arrived at Federal Hall.

Vice President John Adams stepped forward to greet him. Adams had a speech ready, but he was so nervous that he forgot every word of it. Finally, he said, "Sir, the Senate and House of Representatives are ready to attend you to take the oath required by the Constitution." Then, he led Washington out onto a balcony where the crowds could watch the ceremony.

After taking the oath, Washington went inside to make a speech. He looked "grave, almost to sadness," recalled one senator. His voice broke with emotion, said another. "This great man was agitated and embarrassed more than ever he was by the leveled cannon or pointed musket."

Why was President Washington so grave and serious on the day he took office? In 1789, Washington did not know that the nation would grow and prosper. He was the first President of a new nation that many people, especially the British, thought would fail. Washington proved them wrong when he led the nation firmly and set it on the path to greatness.

Study the time line above. In what century did Washington take office?

—220—

In 1789, George Washington rode from Virginia to New York to take office. Here, he passes through Trenton, New Jersey.

# 1 The New Government at Work

**Read to Learn**

★ Who was in Washington's cabinet?
★ How did Hamilton plan to strengthen the nation's economy?
★ What do these words mean: precedent, cabinet, bond, national debt, speculator, tariff?

In April 1789, the newly elected President and members of Congress set about the task of governing the United States.

## Washington in Office

When George Washington took office, he had few guidelines to follow. The Constitution set up a framework of government but did not say just how the government would work. Every action or decision the first President made set a precedent (PREHS uh duhnt). A *precedent* is an act or decision that sets an example for others to follow.

**A dignified leader.** Washington was determined to set an example as a formal, dignified President. When he rode, he mounted a white horse with a leopard-skin saddlecloth. When he drove, he used a carriage pulled by six cream-colored horses. People recognized the President's carriage and greeted him with respect.

Washington was a strong leader. When problems developed, he stepped in to resolve them. But he was careful

President Washington and First Lady Martha Washington, standing on the dais at left, often held formal receptions. Washington received visitors on Tuesday afternoons from 3 P.M. to 5 P.M. Anyone who was properly dressed could come. The First Lady also held teas every Friday evening.

to stay out of day-to-day political battles. As a result, people came to see him as a man who could lead the nation with dignity.

At the end of Washington's first term, the President wanted to retire to Mount Vernon. However, his friends persuaded him to run for reelection. He won easily. When his second term ended in 1796, Washington refused to run for a third term. In doing this, he set a precedent that other Presidents followed until 1940.

**Choosing a cabinet.** The Constitution said very little about how the executive branch of government should be organized. But it was clear that the President needed people to help him carry out his duties. When the first Congress met in 1789, it quickly set up five departments to help the President. They were the State Department, the Treasury Department, the War Depart-

ment, and the offices of the Attorney General and Postmaster General.

Washington chose talented men to head the five departments. This group of officials became known as the *cabinet*. Washington's cabinet included Thomas Jefferson as Secretary of State, Alexander Hamilton as Secretary of the Treasury, Henry Knox as Secretary of War, Edmund Randolph as Attorney General, and Samuel Osgood as Postmaster General.

**Organizing the federal courts.** The Constitution called for a Supreme Court. But it gave Congress the job of organizing the federal court system. In 1789, Congress passed the *Judiciary Act.* The act said that the Supreme Court should have a Chief Justice and five Associate Justices.* It also set up a

---

*Today, the Supreme Court has been expanded to include eight Associate Justices.

system of district courts and circuit courts. Decisions made in these lower courts could be appealed to the Supreme Court.

Washington chose John Jay as the first Chief Justice of the Supreme Court. The justices wore black and scarlet robes like judges in England. But Jefferson convinced them not to wear white wigs like English judges.

## Restoring Confidence

As Secretary of the Treasury, Alexander Hamilton wanted to put the nation's finances on a firm footing. Yet he faced grave problems. During the Revolution, the national government and individual states borrowed a lot of money from foreign countries and from ordinary citizens. Governments borrow money by issuing bonds. A *bond* is a certificate that promises to pay the holder a certain sum of money plus interest on a certain date. For example, if a person pays $100 for a government bond, the government agrees to repay that money with interest in five or ten years. The money a government owes is called the *national debt.*

By 1789, most southern states had paid off their debts from the Revolution. But other states and the federal government had not. When Alexander Hamilton became Secretary of the Treasury, he wanted to make sure that these debts were paid. After all, he said, who would lend money to the United States in the future if the country did not pay its old debts?

**Hamilton's plan.** Hamilton was an energetic young man who wanted to make a name for himself. He suggested a two-step plan for paying off both the national debt and state debts.

First, he wanted to buy up the government's old bonds and issue new bonds. When the nation's finances improved, the government would be able to pay off the new bonds. Second, Hamilton wanted the national government to pay off debts owed by states.

Alexander Hamilton was only 32 years old when he became Secretary of the Treasury. He strongly supported the Bank of the United States, above. The Bank was located on Third Street in Philadelphia, then the nation's largest city.

**Opposition to the plan.** In Congress, James Madison led the opposition to Hamilton's plan. During the Revolution, soldiers and other people were paid for their services with government bonds. Many of these people needed cash. So they sold their bonds to speculators. A *speculator* is someone who is willing to invest in a risky venture on the chance of making a large profit.

Speculators usually paid bondholders only 10 or 15 cents for a bond worth one dollar. If the government repaid the bonds at their full value, speculators stood to make large profits. Madison argued that speculators should not be paid full value for the bonds. After bitter debate, Hamilton managed to convince Congress to accept his plan and repay the national debt in full.

Many southern states opposed Hamilton's idea of repaying the debts owed by the states because they had already paid their debts. Once again, Madison led the fight against Hamilton. When Hamilton saw that Madison had enough votes in Congress to defeat him, he offered the southern states a compromise.

**The compromise.** Hamilton knew that many Southerners wanted to move the nation's capital from New York City to Virginia. Hamilton offered to get his New England friends to vote for a capital in the South if Southerners would support his plan for repaying state debts.

Southerners, including Madison, finally agreed. In July 1790, Congress passed a bill taking over state debts and making plans for the new capital city. Congress decided that the capital should not be part of any state. Instead, it set aside a piece of land on the Potomac River, which it called the District of Columbia. Congress expected the new capital city, called the Federal City, to be ready by 1800. (See page 234.) Meanwhile, it made Philadelphia the nation's capital.

## Meeting Government Expenses

Another part of Hamilton's program to strengthen the nation's economy was to create a national bank. In 1791, Congress passed a bill setting up the *Bank of the United States.* The government deposited the taxes it collected into the Bank. In turn, the Bank issued paper money and paid government bills. By making loans to citizens, the Bank encouraged the growth of new businesses.

The new government had many expenses. It had to pay its employees, build the new Federal City, and keep up the army and navy. As Secretary of the Treasury, Hamilton had to find ways to raise money for the government. The Constitution, you remember, gave Congress the right to pass tax

CHART SKILL As Secretary of the Treasury, Hamilton had to set up a way for the government to meet its expenses. What was the government's income in 1789? How much did it owe?

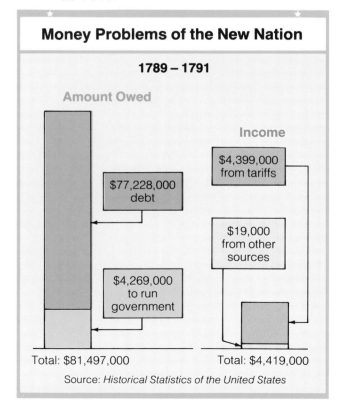

## Money Problems of the New Nation

### 1789 – 1791

Amount Owed

$77,228,000 debt

Income

$4,399,000 from tariffs

$19,000 from other sources

$4,269,000 to run government

Total: $81,497,000

Total: $4,419,000

Source: *Historical Statistics of the United States*

To put down the Whiskey Rebellion, President Washington called out the state militias. Nearly 15,000 troops responded. Here, Washington reviews some of the troops at Fort Cumberland, Maryland.

laws. So Hamilton asked Congress to pass several tax laws. See the chart on page 224.

One law was a *tariff,* or tax, on all foreign goods brought into the country. Hamilton hoped that a tariff would help American manufacturers by making imported goods more expensive than American goods. The tariff was meant to encourage people to buy American goods.

The tariff was more popular in the North than in the South. Industries were growing in the North, and the tariff protected northern manufacturers from foreign competition. Southerners were mostly farmers. They bought more foreign goods than Northerners. They resented the tariff because it made these goods more expensive.

Congress also passed a bill that taxed all liquor made and sold in the United States. Hamilton wanted this tax to raise money for the Treasury. Instead, it led to a rebellion.

## The Whiskey Rebellion

Many farmers in the backcountry raised corn. Corn was too bulky to haul to markets in the East. But whiskey could be carried easily in barrels. So farmers made corn into whiskey and sold the whiskey to earn money. When backcountry farmers heard about the

tax on whiskey, they compared it to the unfair taxes the British Parliament had passed in the 1760s. They refused to pay it.

When officials in western Pennsylvania tried to collect the unpopular tax in 1794, farmers rebelled. Soon, thousands of farmers were marching through Pittsburgh. Supporters of the *Whiskey Rebellion* set up Liberty Trees and sang revolutionary songs.

Washington acted quickly. He called up the militia and took charge of the troops himself. When the farmers heard that 15,000 troops were marching against them, they surrendered peacefully. Hamilton wanted the leaders executed. Washington disagreed and pardoned them. He felt that the government had showed its strength. Now that the crisis was over, he wisely decided to show mercy.

### SECTION REVIEW

1. **Define:** precedent, cabinet, bond, national debt, speculator, tariff.
2. Why did Washington need a cabinet?
3. What did Hamilton want to do about debts owed since the Revolution?
4. Describe two ways Congress tried to raise money.
5. **What Do You Think?** Why do you think Washington chose to stay out of day-to-day political battles?

# 2 Staying Neutral

## Read to Learn

★ How did the French Revolution affect the United States?

★ What was the purpose of the Neutrality Proclamation?

★ Why did war break out on the western frontier?

★ What advice did Washington give in his Farewell Address?

In its early years, the new nation faced many challenges both at home and abroad. Spain, Britain, and Native American nations ruled the lands that bordered the United States. President Washington had to decide how the United States would deal with these other powers.

## The French Revolution

Events in Europe posed unexpected problems for the United States. Late in 1789, ships arriving at American ports brought surprising news from France. On July 14, 1789, a mob in Paris had attacked the Bastille (bah STEEL), a huge prison. Only a few prisoners were held there. But the attack on the Bastille marked the beginning of the *French Revolution*.

The French people had many reasons for rebelling against their king and the nobles who ruled their country. They wanted a constitution and rights similar to those that Americans had just won in their Revolution.

The storming of the Bastille, shown here, marked the beginning of the French Revolution. Lafayette sent Washington the key to the Bastille to show the close ties between the French and American revolutions. Differing reactions to the French Revolution caused divisions in Washington's cabinet.

At first, most Americans supported the French Revolution. They knew what it meant to fight for liberty. Besides, France was America's first ally. And people like the Marquis de Lafayette were working for the cause of liberty in France. Lafayette, you remember, had helped Americans in their fight for independence.

Like most revolutions, the French Revolution soon took a violent course. The French king, Louis XVI, and his family were imprisoned and then executed. In America, opinion was divided. People like Hamilton were horrified at the Reign of Terror that swept France and killed thousands of people. Thomas Jefferson condemned the terror but thought that the violence was necessary for the French to win their freedom. John Adams disagreed. He claimed that the French had no more chance of creating a free government "than a snowball can exist in the streets of Philadelphia under a burning sun."

## Washington Avoids War

The French Revolution worried rulers and nobles all over Europe. They were afraid that revolutionary ideas would spread to their own lands. To prevent this, Britain, Austria, Prussia, the Netherlands, and Spain joined in a war against France. The fighting continued on and off from 1792 to 1815.

The war in Europe affected the United States. In 1778, the United States and France had signed a treaty of friendship. Under the treaty, France could use American ports. Now that France was at war with Britain, it wanted to use American ports to supply its ships and attack British ships.

Washington's cabinet was divided over what course to follow. Alexander Hamilton argued that America's treaty with France was signed with King Louis XVI. Since the king was dead, he went on, the treaty was no longer in force. However, Thomas Jefferson favored the French cause. He was suspicious of Hamilton, who wanted friendly relations with Britain, America's old enemy.

**The Neutrality Proclamation.** Washington wanted to keep the nation from being dragged into a European war. So in April 1793, he issued the *Neutrality Proclamation*. It stated that the United States would not support either side in the war. Also, it forbade Americans from taking any warlike action against either Britain or France.

Despite the Neutrality Proclamation, problems arose. American merchants wanted to trade with both Britain and France. But each of these countries wanted to stop Americans from trading with its enemy.

**Jay's Treaty.** In 1793, the British began attacking American ships that traded with the French colonies in the West Indies. Well-armed British warships chased and captured American merchant ships. On the small French island of St. Eustacia, the British took 130 American ships. When Americans learned of Britain's high-handed action, many wanted to declare war. Washington knew that the United States was in no position to fight a war. So he sent Chief Justice John Jay to Britain for talks.

After much hard bargaining, Jay worked out a treaty in 1794. The British agreed to pay damages for the ships taken in the West Indies. But they refused to make any promises about future attacks. Jay also wanted the British to give up the forts they still held in the Ohio Valley. Britain agreed to do this only after the Americans paid the debts owed to British merchants since the Revolution.

The Senate was unhappy with *Jay's Treaty*. But at Washington's request, it ratified the treaty in 1795. Although the treaty was unpopular, Washington was satisfied that he had avoided war with Britain.

In rural areas, people got together for many occasions. Quilting parties such as this one were popular. They often doubled as engagement parties. The quilt made at the party was presented as a gift to the engaged couple.

## War on the Frontier

During the 1790s, thousands of settlers moved into the Northwest Territory. The large number of white settlers in the Northwest Territory created serious problems. The United States had signed treaties with the Indian nations who lived there. Most settlers ignored the treaties and took land wherever they pleased.

**Indians fight back.** Native Americans resented the people who were invading their lands. As a result, clashes occurred between settlers and Indians. Indians attacked white families who lived far from a fort. White settlers took revenge on Indians, even on those who had not taken part in the attacks. The violence spread.

In 1791, the Miami Indians in Ohio joined with other Indian nations to drive settlers off their land. The Miamis were led by a skillful fighter, Little Turtle. The British in the Ohio Valley encouraged the Indians by supplying them with rifles and gunpowder. When Washington heard the news, he sent General Arthur St. Clair with 3,000 soldiers to fight the Indians. Little Turtle defeated St. Clair's forces.

**Battle of Fallen Timbers.** Washington replaced St. Clair with General Anthony Wayne. Wayne drilled his troops well. In 1794, he marched into Miami territory. A Shawnee leader, Blue Jacket, had taken over from Little Turtle. He gathered his forces at a place called Fallen Timbers. It got this name because a violent windstorm had blown down many trees and created a tangle of logs. The Indians thought that Wayne would have trouble fighting on this ground. But Wayne's troops pushed through the underbrush and defeated the Indians.

The next year, 12 Indian nations signed the *Treaty of Greenville* with the United States. They had to give up about 25,000 square miles (65,000 square km) of land. In return, they received $20,000 and a promise of more payments if they kept the peace.

## Washington's Farewell Address

During his years as President, Washington kept a measure of peace in the new nation. Before he left office in 1796, he wrote some words of advice for his fellow citizens. Washington's *Farewell Address* was printed in newspapers across the country.

In the address, he warned the country against becoming involved in European affairs: " 'Tis our true policy to steer clear of permanent alliances with any portion of the foreign world."

To Washington, the United States was a young nation struggling to get on its feet. It should concentrate on the business of governing at home. However, Washington did support trade with other nations because trade helped the American economy.

Washington's Farewell Address became a guiding principle of American foreign policy. Future Presidents tried to follow his advice though with mixed results.

After Fallen Timbers, Indian leaders had to sign the Treaty of Greenville. Find Anthony Wayne's signature on the treaty above. English names were written next to the symbols marked by each Indian leader.

### SECTION REVIEW

1. (a) What did most Americans think of the French Revolution when it began? (b) How did their views change?
2. What did the Neutrality Proclamation say?
3. Why did Washington send Chief Justice Jay to Britain?
4. Describe one result of the Battle of Fallen Timbers.
5. **What Do You Think?** Why do you think Washington advised Americans to "steer clear of permanent alliances"?

# 3 Political Parties

### Read to Learn
★ Why did political parties form in the United States?
★ What ideas did each party support?
★ How did newspapers influence politics?
★ Who was elected the second President of the United States?

In 1789, there were no political parties in the United States as there are today. In fact, President Washington and other leaders of the new nation mistrusted political parties. Yet before Washington left office in 1796, two parties had developed.

## Against All Warnings

During the 1700s, most Americans distrusted political parties. In his Farewell Address, Washington warned that parties caused "jealousies and false alarms." Jefferson echoed this warning. He said, "If I could not go to heaven but with a party, I would not go at all."

Americans had good reason to distrust political parties. They had seen how parties worked in Britain. Parties, called factions in Britain, were made up of a few people who schemed to win favors from the government. They were more interested in personal profit than in the public good. American leaders wanted to keep factions from forming. But disagreements between two of Washington's chief advisers spurred the growth of political parties.

The two parties that developed in the 1790s were led by Secretary of the Treasury Alexander Hamilton and Secretary of State Thomas Jefferson. Hamilton and Jefferson were different in many ways. Hamilton was a short, slender man. He spoke forcefully, dressed elegantly, and sparkled with energy. He was much in demand at formal parties.

Jefferson was tall and a bit gawky. Although he was a Virginia aristocrat, he dressed and spoke informally. "He spoke almost without ceasing," recalled one senator. "Yet he scattered information wherever he went" and sparkled with brilliant ideas.

## Two Views on Government

Hamilton and Jefferson had very different views about what was good for the country. Hamilton wanted the federal government to be stronger than state governments. Jefferson believed that state governments should be stronger.

Hamilton supported the Bank of the United States. Jefferson opposed it because he felt that it gave too much power to wealthy investors who would help run it. Also, Jefferson interpreted the Constitution strictly. He argued that nowhere did the Constitution give the federal government the power to create a national bank.

Hamilton interpreted the Constitution more loosely. He pointed out that the Constitution gave Congress the power to make all laws "necessary and proper" to carry out its duties. He reasoned that since Congress had the right to collect taxes and the Bank was necessary to collect taxes, then Congress had the right to create the Bank.

Hamilton wanted the government to encourage economic growth. His programs favored the growth of trade, manufacturing, and cities. He favored business leaders and mistrusted the common people. Jefferson believed that the common people, especially farmers, were the backbone of the nation. He thought that crowded cities and manufacturing might corrupt American life.

Finally, Hamilton favored Britain, an important trading partner of the United States. Jefferson favored France, America's first ally and a nation whose people were struggling for liberty and freedom.

## Parties Take Shape

At first, Jefferson and Hamilton disagreed only in private. But when Congress began passing Hamilton's program, Jefferson and his friend, James Madison, decided to organize support for their views. They moved quietly and cautiously at first.

In 1791, they went to New York State, telling people that they were going to study its wildlife. In fact, Jefferson was interested in nature and traveled as far north as Lake George. But he and Madison also met with such important New York politicians as Governor George Clinton and Aaron

Burr, a strong critic of Hamilton. Jefferson asked Clinton and Burr to help defeat Hamilton's program by getting New Yorkers to vote for Jefferson's supporters at the next election.

**Republicans and Federalists.** Before long, leaders in other states began organizing to support either Jefferson or Hamilton. Jefferson's supporters called themselves *Democratic Republicans.* Often, the name was shortened to Republicans.* Hamilton and his supporters were known as *Federalists* because they favored a strong federal government. Federalists had the support of merchants and shipowners in the Northeast and some planters in the South. Small farmers, craftworkers, and some wealthier landowners supported the Republicans.

**Newspapers wave the banner.** Newspapers influenced the growth of political parties. Newspaper publishers took sides on the issues. The most influential newspaper, the *Gazette of the United States,* was published in Philadelphia, which was still the nation's capital in the 1790s. John Fenno, publisher of the *Gazette,* strongly supported Hamilton's programs. Jefferson's friend Philip Freneau started a rival paper, called the *National Gazette.* It published articles supporting the Republicans. (See Skill Lesson 10 on page 232.)

Between 1790 and 1800, the number of American newspapers more than doubled—from about 100 to over 230. These newspapers played an essential role in the new nation. They kept people informed and helped shape public opinion.

---

*Jefferson's Republican party was not the same as today's Republican Party. In fact, Jefferson's Republican Party later grew into today's Democratic Party.

---

CHART SKILL By the 1790s, two political parties had formed. Describe two differences between the parties on economic issues.

## The First Political Parties

| Federalists | Republicans |
|---|---|
| 1. Led by A. Hamilton | 1. Led by T. Jefferson |
| 2. Wealthy and well-educated should lead nation | 2. People should have political power |
| 3. Strong central government | 3. Strong state governments |
| 4. Emphasis on manufacturing, shipping, and trade | 4. Emphasis on agriculture |
| 5. Loose interpretation of Constitution | 5. Strict interpretation of Constitution |
| 6. Pro-British | 6. Pro-French |
| 7. Favored national bank | 7. Opposed national bank |
| 8. Favored protective tariff | 8. Opposed protective tariff |

## Choosing the Second President

When Washington retired in 1796, political parties played an important part in choosing his successor. The election of 1796 was the first in which political parties played a role. Each party put forward its own candidates. The Republicans chose Jefferson as their candidate for President and Aaron Burr for Vice President. The Federalists chose John Adams for President and Thomas Pinckney for Vice President.

The election of 1796 had an unusual result. According to the Constitution, each elector cast two votes. He could cast them for any two candidates. The person receiving the most votes would become President. The person with the next highest total would become Vice President.

Many primary sources, such as letters, diaries, and speeches, express the opinions of the people who wrote them. Therefore, when historians study primary sources, they have to recognize fact and opinion. A *fact* is something that actually happened. It is known to be true because it can be proved or observed. An *opinion* is a judgment that reflects a person's beliefs or feelings. It is not necessarily true.

Often, writers present a series of facts to back up an opinion. For example, in the Declaration of Independence, Jefferson listed facts to support the opinion that George III had tried to establish "an absolute tyranny over these states."

In the letter below, Alexander Hamilton writes about political differences between himself and the party led by Madison and Jefferson.

1. **Determine which statements are facts.** Remember that facts can be checked and thereby can be proved. Use your reading in this chapter to help answer these questions. (a) Choose two statements of fact in Hamilton's letter. (b) How might you prove that each statement is a fact?

2. **Determine which statements are opinions.** Writers often show that they are giving an opinion by saying "in my view" or "I think" or "I believe." (a) Choose two statements in which Hamilton gives his opinion. (b) How can you tell each is an opinion?

3. **Determine how a writer mixes fact and opinion.** Reread the last sentence of the letter. (a) What did Hamilton mean by a "womanish attachment to France and a womanish resentment against Great Britain"? (b) Is it true that Jefferson supported France and opposed Britain? (c) What country did Hamilton want the United States to support? (d) Why do you think Hamilton mixed fact and opinion in the statement?

---

 **Alexander Hamilton wrote:**

It was not until the last session of Congress that I became completely convinced that Mr. Madison and Mr. Jefferson are at the head of a faction that is hostile toward me. They are motivated by views that, in my judgment, will undermine the principles of good government and are dangerous to the peace and happiness of the country.

Freneau, the present publisher of the *National Gazette,* was a known Antifederalist. It is certain that he was brought to Philadelphia by Mr. Jefferson to be the publisher of a newspaper. At the same time as he was starting his paper, he was also a clerk in the Department of State.

His paper is devoted to opposing me and the measures that I have supported. And the paper has a general unfriendly attitude toward the government of the United States.

On almost all questions, great and small, which have come up since the first session of Congress, Mr. Jefferson and Mr. Madison have been found among those who want to limit federal power. In respect to foreign policy, the views of these gentlemen are, in my judgment, equally unsound and dangerous. They have a womanish attachment to France and a womanish resentment against Great Britain.

Abigail and John Adams are shown here soon after they married. During the Revolution, they were often apart. Abigail Adams' letters to her husband give a fascinating look at these two brilliant people and the early years of the new nation.

When the ballots of the electoral college were counted, John Adams had 71 votes. So Adams, a Federalist, became President. Thomas Jefferson had 68 votes. So Jefferson, a Republican, became Vice President. In 1804, the system was changed by the Twelfth Amendment. It required electors to vote separately for the President and Vice President. Meanwhile, Adams took office in March 1797 as the second President of the United States.

# 4 Adams Takes a Firm Stand

**Read to Learn**
★ Why did many Americans want war with France?
★ Why did Adams become unpopular with his own Federalist Party?
★ What were the Alien and Sedition acts?
★ What do these words mean: alien, sedition, unconstitutional, nullify?

Like Washington, John Adams faced many problems when he took office. But Washington had been very popular and was respected as "the father of his country." When George Washington died in 1799, Henry Lee of Virginia wrote that he was "first in war, first in peace, first in the hearts of

Soon after taking office, President Washington chose the exact location on the Potomac River for the Federal City, as the capital was then called. Although the area was wilderness, it offered advantages. It was within reach of states in the North and West as well as in the South. And it was safe from attack.

Hoping to turn the wilderness into a beautiful city, President Washington

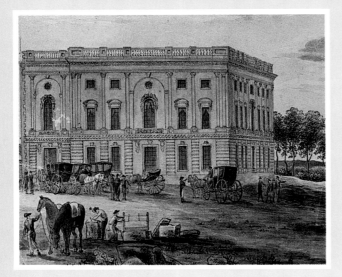

hired the French architect Pierre Charles l'Enfant to draw up plans. L'Enfant designed a capital he said would be "magnificent enough to grace a grand nation."

Besides a design, building a new capital called for money and labor. But business people and workers did not see the wilderness as pleasant or profitable. They chose to stay in Philadelphia and other older cities. So work on the city went slowly.

In 1800, President Adams and the government moved from Philadelphia to the Federal City. Instead of a magnificent city, members of Congress found a village of muddy wagon tracks, unfinished buildings, and swampy fields. One member called the capital "wilderness city." Another described it as "a mud hole."

Renamed Washington, D.C., the capital was slowly finished. Like the nation itself, it grew out of the wilderness and became a source of pride to Americans. Its broad avenues and stately buildings were a dream come true.

★ Why did it take a long time to build the nation's capital?

his countrymen." Adams did not enjoy the same high level of fame and respect.

### The XYZ Affair

Foreign affairs occupied much of President Adams' attention. When the United States ratified Jay's Treaty with Britain in 1795, France had responded with anger. French warships seized some American ships in the West Indies. When the United States sent an ambassador to Paris to discuss the problem of neutral rights, the French refused to see him.

Adams was determined to work out a solution. In 1797, he sent three new ambassadors to Paris. This time, the Americans were received. But the French foreign minister, Maurice de Talleyrand, said that there would be delays before talks could begin.

**A secret offer.** Talleyrand was a shrewd man but not very honest. He sent three secret agents to offer the Americans a deal. The agents were blunt. "You must pay money," they told the Americans. "You must pay a great deal of money." Talleyrand wanted $250,000 for himself and a loan to

France of $10 million. "Not a sixpence!" replied one of the Americans angrily.

The Americans reported the incident to President Adams, referring to the agents as X, Y, and Z. When Adams made the *XYZ Affair* public in 1798, most Americans were outraged. People repeated the slogan "Millions for defense, but not one cent for tribute!" They were willing to spend money to defend America, but they would not pay bribes to another nation.

**Spending for defense.** The XYZ Affair ignited war fever in the United States. But President Adams resisted the pressure to declare war on France. Like Washington, he wanted to keep the country out of European affairs. Still, he could not ignore French attacks on American ships. So he moved to strengthen the American navy. At the same time, Congress created the Department of the Navy.

Up and down the coast, shipyards fitted out small boats with guns and cannons. They built nearly a dozen frigates. Frigates were large, fast sailing ships that carried as many as 44 guns. The best-known frigate, the U.S.S. *Constitution,* was launched in 1797 (before the XYZ Affair).* Later, it was nicknamed "Old Ironsides" because its wooden hull was so strong that it seemed to be made of iron.

Talleyrand was so impressed by the new American navy that he stopped attacking American ships. He also assured Adams that if American ambassadors came to France, they would be treated with respect.

## A Split in the Federalist Party

Many Federalists, led by Alexander Hamilton, wanted to ignore Talleyrand's offer to negotiate. They thought that the United States would benefit

*After 100 years of service, the U.S.S. *Constitution* was retired from active service in 1897. It can be visited today in the Boston Navy Yard.

from a war with France. War, they said, would force the United States to build a strong army as well as a navy. These Federalists also hoped that war with France would weaken support for Jefferson and the Republicans, who were sympathetic to the French.

President Adams was a Federalist, but he disagreed with Hamilton's wish for war. The growing disagreement between Adams and Hamilton led to a split in the Federalist Party. Hamilton and his supporters were called *High Federalists.*

Adams delayed building up an American army. Instead, he sent new ambassadors to France. Although

In the late 1790s, fears of war led the new nation to strengthen its navy. This print shows the building of the frigate *Philadelphia*.

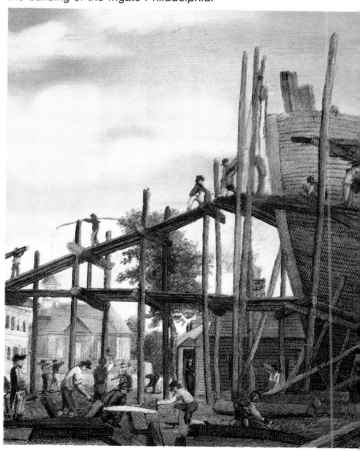

Hamilton no longer held office, he attacked Adams, calling him "unfit for a President." Hamilton urged Federalists in the Senate to block approval of the ambassadors to France. In turn, Adams threatened to resign and let Vice President Jefferson take office. At the thought of a Republican President, Hamilton backed down.

When the American ambassadors reached France, they found a young army officer, Napoleon Bonaparte, in power. Napoleon was interested in expanding French power in Europe. He did not want to be bothered fighting the United States. So he signed an agreement known as the *Convention of 1800.* In it, France agreed to stop seizing American ships.

Adams kept the nation out of war. But peace cost him the support of many Federalists and split his party.

### The Alien and Sedition Acts

In 1798, while talks were still going on with France, the High Federalists in Congress passed several strict laws. The laws were known as the Alien and Sedition acts. They were meant to protect the United States in case of war.

The *Alien Act* allowed the President to expel any *alien,* or foreigner, who was thought to be dangerous to the country. Another law made it harder for immigrants to become citizens. Before 1798, a white male immigrant could become a citizen after living in the United States for 5 years. Under the new law, immigrants had to live in America for 14 years before they could become citizens.

The High Federalists passed this act because many recent immigrants supported Jefferson and the Republicans. The act would keep these immigrants from voting for years.

Republicans hated these laws. They were even more outraged by the *Sedition Act. Sedition* (sih DISH uhn) means the stirring up of rebellion against a government. The Sedition Act said that citizens could be fined and jailed if they criticized public officials.

Republicans argued that the Sedition Act violated the Constitution. The First Amendment, they said, protected an American's freedom of speech. One Republican warned that the act would make it a crime to "laugh at the cut of a congressman's coat" or "give dinner to a Frenchman." Republican fears were confirmed when several Republican newspaper editors and even a congressman were fined and jailed for their opinions.

### The Kentucky and Virginia Resolutions

Vice President Jefferson believed that the Alien and Sedition acts were *unconstitutional,* that is, not permitted by the Constitution. Jefferson could not turn to the courts for help because the Federalists controlled them. Instead, he called on the states to act. He argued that a state had the right to *nullify,* or cancel, a law passed by the federal government.

Urged on by Jefferson, the Kentucky and Virginia legislatures passed a series of resolutions in 1798 and 1799. The *Kentucky and Virginia resolutions* said that each state "has an equal right to judge for itself" whether a law is constitutional. If a state decides that a law is unconstitutional, Jefferson said, it has the power to nullify the law.

The Kentucky and Virginia resolutions raised important questions. Did states have the power to decide if laws were constitutional? Did states have the power to nullify laws passed by Congress? These questions were left unanswered at the time because other states did not support the movement to nullify the Alien and Sedition acts. In the end, the Alien and Sedition acts were changed or dropped. However, the question of a state's right to nullify laws would come up again.

## Election of 1800

By 1800, the fear of war with France had died down. As it did, Federalist power declined. The Republicans hoped to sweep the Federalists out of office. In the election of 1800, they pointed out that Federalists had raised taxes to prepare for war with France. Also, they made an issue of the unpopular Alien and Sedition acts.

Jefferson ran as the Republican candidate for President. Aaron Burr ran for Vice President. Adams was again the Federalist candidate with Charles Pinckney for Vice President.

**A tie vote.** Republicans won a large victory in Congress. In the race for President, Republicans beat the Federalists. But when the electoral college voted, Jefferson and Burr each received 73 votes. The tie vote raised this question: Who would be President—Jefferson or Burr?

According to the Constitution, in the case of a tie vote, the House of Representatives decides the election. The House voted 35 times. Each time, the vote remained a tie. Even though the people clearly meant Jefferson to be President, Burr would not step aside. At last, the House made Jefferson President. Burr became Vice President.

Congress took steps to prevent another confusing election. It passed the Twelfth Amendment, which was ratified in 1804. The amendment required electors to vote separately for President and Vice President.

**Federalist power fades.** With the election of a Republican President, the Federalist era came to an end. After 1800, Federalists won fewer seats in Congress. In 1804, the Federalist leader, Alexander Hamilton, was killed in a duel with Aaron Burr.

The Federalist Party lost power largely because it distrusted the ordinary citizen. Although the party declined slowly after 1800, it left its mark. Federalists helped the nation

## AMERICANS WHO DARED

### Benjamin Banneker

Benjamin Banneker, the son of a freed slave, became a respected astronomer and mathematician. He was largely self-taught. From studying books, he made a clock—without ever seeing one. In 1790, he was chosen as a surveyor for the Federal City. But he gained more fame from his almanacs, which were full of useful scientific information.

during its early years. And a Federalist President, John Adams, kept the nation out of war.

### SECTION REVIEW

1. **Define:** alien, sedition, unconstitutional, nullify.
2. How did Talleyrand insult the United States?
3. How did Adams and Hamilton differ on the question of war with France?
4. (a) Why did the Federalists support the Alien and Sedition acts? (b) Why did the Republicans oppose them?
5. **What Do You Think?** How do you think the Kentucky and Virginia resolutions fit in with Jefferson's ideas on government?

# Chapter 10 Review

## ★ Summary ★

In 1789, George Washington took office as the first President of the United States. Although he faced many problems during his two terms, he led the nation on a course of peaceful growth. Washington chose able men to serve in his cabinet. As Secretary of the Treasury, Hamilton tried to strengthen the nation's finances.

Foreign affairs occupied the attention of both Washington and Adams, the second President of the United States. Both Presidents kept the United States out of war. But Adams did this at the cost of splitting his party.

In 1800, Thomas Jefferson was elected as the third President of the United States. By this time, political parties were playing a major role in American politics.

## ★ Reviewing the Facts ★

**Key Terms.** Match each term in Column 1 with the correct definition in Column 2.

| Column 1 | Column 2 |
|---|---|
| **1.** cabinet | **a.** tax |
| **2.** tariff | **b.** foreigner |
| **3.** alien | **c.** cancel |
| **4.** sedition | **d.** stirring up of rebellion against a government |
| **5.** nullify | **e.** group of officials who head up executive departments |

**Key People, Events, and Ideas.** Identify each of the following.

1. Judiciary Act
2. Bank of the United States
3. Whiskey Rebellion
4. Neutrality Proclamation
5. Jay's Treaty
6. Treaty of Greenville
7. Farewell Address
8. Alexander Hamilton
9. Thomas Jefferson
10. XYZ Affair
11. John Adams
12. Convention of 1800
13. Alien Act
14. Sedition Act
15. Kentucky and Virginia resolutions

## ★ Chapter Checkup ★

1. (a) Describe Hamilton's plan for paying off state and national debts. (b) Who objected to his plan? (c) Why did they object?
2. What was the cause of the Whiskey Rebellion?
3. Why did Washington issue the Neutrality Proclamation?
4. Describe one cause and one result of war on the frontier in the 1790s.
5. (a) How did political parties develop? (b) Who supported the Federalists? (c) Who supported the Republicans?
6. Describe two results of the XYZ Affair.
7. How did differences between Adams and Hamilton affect the Federalist Party?
8. What important issue was raised by the Kentucky and Virginia resolutions?

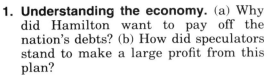

## ★ Thinking About History ★

1. **Understanding the economy.** (a) Why did Hamilton want to pay off the nation's debts? (b) How did speculators stand to make a large profit from this plan?

2. **Relating past to present.** (a) What advice did Washington give in his Farewell Address? (b) Do you think Americans today would still agree with his advice? Explain.

3. **Expressing an opinion.** Do you think the Alien and Sedition acts were necessary to protect the nation? Why?

4. **Learning about citizenship.** (a) What problems did the first Presidents of the United States face? (b) Give two examples of how strong leadership helped the new nation.

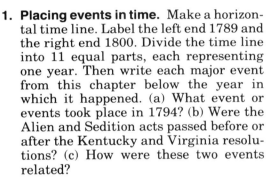

## ★ Using Your Skills ★

1. **Placing events in time.** Make a horizontal time line. Label the left end 1789 and the right end 1800. Divide the time line into 11 equal parts, each representing one year. Then write each major event from this chapter below the year in which it happened. (a) What event or events took place in 1794? (b) Were the Alien and Sedition acts passed before or after the Kentucky and Virginia resolutions? (c) How were these two events related?

2. **Skimming a chapter.** Skimming is a useful reading skill. When you skim a chapter, you read the chapter quickly to get a general idea of what it is about. To skim a chapter in this book, look first at the Chapter Outline at the beginning of each chapter. The Chapter Outline lists all the sections in the chapter. Next, look at the boldface heads that show you the main topics in each section. Finally, quickly read the first and last sentence of each paragraph.

Skim the first part of this chapter (pages 220–225). (a) What does the Chapter Outline tell you about the chapter? (b) List the main topics covered in the section "The New Government at Work." (c) What do you think the general idea of this section is?

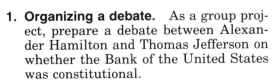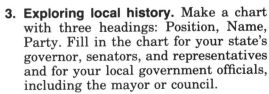

## ★ More to Do ★

1. **Organizing a debate.** As a group project, prepare a debate between Alexander Hamilton and Thomas Jefferson on whether the Bank of the United States was constitutional.

2. **Interviewing.** In small groups, prepare an interview with President Washington on his last day in office. Ask one person in the group to imagine he or she is George Washington. Find out which of Washington's achievements he values most and what he thinks lies ahead for the new nation.

3. **Exploring local history.** Make a chart with three headings: Position, Name, Party. Fill in the chart for your state's governor, senators, and representatives and for your local government officials, including the mayor or council.

4. **Making a speech.** When the election of 1800 was being decided in the House of Representatives, members had to choose between Aaron Burr and Thomas Jefferson. Imagine that you are a representative and write a speech to give in support of Aaron Burr as President.

# 11

# Age of Jefferson (1801–1816)

## Chapter Outline

**1** Jefferson Takes Office
**2** The Nation Doubles in Size
**3** Dangers at Sea
**4** War Fever
**5** The War of 1812
Readings, page 518

| 1800 | 1802 | 1804 | 1806 | 1808 | 1810 | 1812 | 1814 | 1816 |
|------|------|------|------|------|------|------|------|------|

**1803** Louisiana Purchase

**1804** Lewis and Clark set out

**1807** Embargo Act

**1812** War declared on Britain

**1814** War of 1812 ends

## About This Chapter

On March 4, 1801, Thomas Jefferson walked along the muddy streets of the new capital city. Washington, D.C., was still only half finished. The newly elected President was on his way to his inauguration. He deliberately kept the event simple. No guard of honor or servants accompanied him when he went inside the unfinished Capitol building. He took the oath of office and walked back to the boardinghouse where he was living.

Jefferson was the first President of the United States to take office in the new capital city. He was also the first Republican President. Federalists worried about how Jefferson would use his power. They soon found out what the new President and the new century would bring.

In fact, Jefferson did not see his election as his greatest success. For him, drafting the Declaration of Independence was more important. Once, some friends wanted to hold a public celebration for his birthday. Jefferson said, "The only birthday I ever commemorate is that of our Independence, the Fourth of July." As President, Jefferson tried to live up to the ideals of the Declaration.

After he left office, the next two Presidents, James Madison and James Monroe, carried on the traditions set down by Jefferson. His influence was so great that this period is often called the Age of Jefferson.

Study the time line above. Name two events that occurred after Jefferson took office.

During the War of 1812, the *Constitution* defeated the British frigate *Guerrière*. This painting celebrates that American victory.

# 1 Jefferson Takes Office

### Read to Learn

★ How did Jefferson treat the Federalists?

★ What were Jefferson's views on government?

★ Why was *Marbury* v. *Madison* an important case?

★ What do these words mean: democratic, laissez faire, judicial review?

Thomas Jefferson was a wealthy plantation and slave owner and a respected scholar. He had more than 6,000 books in his library at Monticello. He knew Greek, Latin, French, and Italian and was familiar with many Native American languages.

Even though Jefferson was a member of the upper class, he believed that his election was a victory for ordinary American citizens. In Europe, kings and nobles still ruled, but Jefferson was proud that the United States was a republic. He vowed to serve as President without fancy ceremonies. Once in office, Jefferson was determined to live up to his own principles.

## A More Democratic Style

As President, Thomas Jefferson was different from Washington or Adams. Because he wanted to represent ordinary citizens, Jefferson vowed to make the government more democratic.

Thomas Jefferson, third President of the United States, made many inventions. Among them was this polygraph machine. The machine copied a letter as the President wrote it. Jefferson wrote hundreds of letters. With this machine, he could keep a copy for his records.

*Democratic* means ensuring that all people have the same rights. Jefferson was determined to end the special privileges the rich and well-born enjoyed under the Federalists.

Jefferson's personal style matched his democratic beliefs. He preferred informal dinners to the formal parties held by Washington and Adams. He greeted people by shaking hands instead of bowing. European officials were shocked when Jefferson appeared in wrinkled clothes and slippers to receive them. By being informal, Jefferson was showing that the President was an ordinary person.

Federalists feared Jefferson's democratic beliefs. They knew that he supported the French Revolution, and they worried that he would lead a revolution in America. Also, they were afraid that he might punish them because they had used the Alien and Sedition acts to jail Republicans.

In his inaugural speech, Jefferson tried to ease these fears. He pointed out that although Republicans were in the majority, he would not treat the Federalists harshly. "The minority possess their equal rights, which equal law must protect," he stated. Americans must "unite with one heart and one mind." He concluded, "We are all Republicans, we are all Federalists."

## Old and New Programs

Jefferson's first job as President was to choose a cabinet that shared his views. He appointed his good friend, James Madison, as Secretary of State. Madison had worked closely with Jefferson to organize the Republican Party. The President chose Albert Gallatin as Secretary of the Treasury. Gallatin was a wizard with finances. Through careful management, he helped Jefferson reduce government expenses.

**A few changes.** As President, Jefferson kept some Federalist programs but changed others. On Gallatin's advice, Jefferson decided to keep the

Bank of the United States, which he once opposed. (See page 230.) He continued to pay off state debts and let many Federalists keep their government jobs. However, the President and Gallatin disliked the whiskey tax, so it was repealed.

Jefferson also let the Alien and Sedition acts expire, or run out. He freed citizens jailed under the acts and returned to the law that allowed immigrants to become citizens after five years in the country.

**Keeping government small.** Jefferson believed that the government should protect the rights of its citizens. After that, he believed, government should not interfere in people's lives. This idea is known as *laissez faire* (LEHS AY fehr), from the French term for "let alone." Jefferson put this idea into practice when he reduced the number of people in government and made the navy smaller.

Jefferson's policy of laissez faire was very different from Hamilton's view of government. Federalists, like Hamilton, wanted the government to promote trade, commerce, and manufacturing. They also wanted a strong army and navy.

## John Marshall and the Supreme Court

President Jefferson's programs were popular, and his Republican followers controlled Congress. But the Federalists remained powerful in the federal courts. Before leaving office in 1800, President John Adams appointed a number of new judges. Among them was John Marshall, the Chief Justice of the Supreme Court. So when Jefferson became President, he found John Marshall, a strong Federalist, at the head of the Supreme Court.

**The early court.** Although Jefferson and Marshall differed over politics, they were similar in some ways. Both men were well educated, bright, and owned plantations in Virginia. In fact, they were cousins. Both acted informally. Indeed, Marshall was absent-minded to the point that he sometimes even forgot to comb his hair.

In 1801, Marshall arrived in Washington. At the time, there was no Supreme Court building. The place where it was to be built was still a marsh covered with brambles. So the justices met in the basement of the Capitol.

The six justices kept mostly to themselves. They lived in the same small boardinghouse, ate together, and seldom went to parties. Members of Congress and other government officials scarcely knew them. In fact, Justice William Paterson and President Jefferson once traveled all day on the same stagecoach without either man recognizing the other!

***Marbury* v. *Madison.*** John Marshall strongly influenced the decisions

John Marshall served as Chief Justice of the Supreme Court for 34 years. During that time, he wrote more than 500 decisions. His ideas influenced the shape of the national government, which he believed should be more powerful than state governments.

of the Supreme Court for over 30 years. He made his most important decision in an 1803 case known as **Marbury v. Madison.**\*

The case—a complicated one—involved the Judiciary Act. Under this act, President Adams had appointed many new judges just before he left office. The Supreme Court decided *Marbury* v. *Madison* by striking down the Judiciary Act. The law, said the Court, was unconstitutional. Congress had no right to pass it.

The Court's decision, written by Chief Justice Marshall, set an important precedent. The decision established the right of the Supreme Court to judge any law made by Congress and to declare that law unconstitutional. The right of the Court to review laws is known as *judicial review.*

When Jefferson heard of the decision, he worried that the Supreme Court was growing too powerful. But Marshall used the Court's power carefully. Today, the Supreme Court still exercises the right of judicial review.

═══ **SECTION REVIEW** ═══

1. **Define:** democratic, laissez faire, judicial review.
2. How did Jefferson try to reassure the Federalists?
3. (a) Name two Federalist programs Jefferson did not change. (b) Describe one change he did make.
4. What branch of government did John Marshall influence?
5. **What Do You Think?** Why do you think Jefferson was afraid the Supreme Court might get too much power?

---

\*Every case brought before a court has two parties. One is the plaintiff, or person with a complaint. The other is the defendant, or person who must defend against the complaint. The plaintiff's name appears first, followed by the defendant's name. The v. means versus, or against.

# 2 The Nation Doubles in Size

### Read to Learn
★ Why was the Mississippi River important to western farmers?
★ How did the United States get Louisiana?
★ What lands did Lewis and Clark explore?
★ What do these words mean: continental divide?

The United States gained most of the land east of the Mississippi in 1783. Spain still owned the land to the west, known as Louisiana.\* Many American settlers looked eagerly at Louisiana. In 1803, President Jefferson took a step that doubled the nation in size and set it on a course of expansion for years to come.

### Control of the Mississippi

By 1800, almost one million Americans lived between the Appalachians and the Mississippi River. Most were farmers. The cheapest way to get their goods to markets on the east coast was to ship them down the Mississippi to New Orleans. Goods were stored in warehouses there until they could be loaded onto ships. Of course, farmers in the West were very concerned about who controlled the Mississippi and the port of New Orleans.

From time to time, Spain threatened to close New Orleans to Americans. In 1795, President Washington

---

\*In 1763, Spain gained control of the Mississippi River from France. It also gained lands west of the Mississippi, known as Louisiana.

sent Thomas Pinckney to Spain to find a way to keep the port open. Pinckney negotiated a treaty with Spain. In the **Pinckney Treaty,** Spain agreed to let Americans ship their goods down the Mississippi and store them in New Orleans. The treaty also settled a dispute over the northern border of Spanish Florida.

For a time, Americans sent their goods to New Orleans without problem. Then, in 1800, Spain signed a secret treaty with Napoleon Bonaparte of France. The Spanish gave Louisiana back to France. When President Jefferson learned about the treaty, he was alarmed. Napoleon was an amibitious empire builder. His armies were winning battles all across Europe. Jefferson was afraid that Napoleon might want to build an empire in North America as well as in Europe.

## Revolt in Haiti

Jefferson had reason to worry. Napoleon had plans to increase French power in America. He wanted to ship food from Louisiana to French islands in the West Indies. But his plan soon ran into trouble because of events in Haiti.*

Haiti was a French colony in the Caribbean. White French planters in Haiti grew rich from growing and exporting sugar. During the French Revolution, however, black slaves who worked the sugar plantations fought for their freedom. They were led by Toussaint L'Ouverture (too SAN loo vehr TYOOR). By 1801, Toussaint had forced the French out of Haiti.

Napoleon sent troops to regain control of Haiti. He expected to win easily, but the Haitians resisted fiercely. Many French soldiers died from yellow fever. Although Toussaint was taken prisoner, the French were unable to conquer the island.

*Haiti occupies the western half of Hispaniola, one of the islands Columbus explored.

In 1791, Toussaint L'Ouverture led slaves in Haiti in a revolt against French rule. After 13 years of fighting, L'Ouverture was captured. Although he died in a French prison, his followers won independence for Haiti in 1804.

## The Louisiana Purchase

Napoleon's troubles in Haiti benefited the United States. About the time that the French were losing in Haiti, President Jefferson sent Robert Livingston and James Monroe to France. Jefferson wanted to buy New Orleans from Napoleon to be sure that Americans could always use the city. The President told Livingston and Monroe to offer up to $10 million for the city.

The Americans talked to Napoleon's foreign minister, Talleyrand. At first, Talleyrand showed little interest in the offer. But then, French defeats in Haiti ruined Napoleon's dreams of empire in America. Also, Napoleon needed money to fight his wars in Europe. Suddenly, Talleyrand asked Livingston if the United States wanted to buy all of Louisiana, not just New Orleans.

Livingston and Monroe could hardly believe their ears. They did not have orders to buy all of Louisiana. But they knew Jefferson wanted control of the Mississippi. In the end, they agreed to pay the French $15 million for Louisiana. Neither the French nor the Americans consulted the various Indian nations who lived on the land about the purchase.

Jefferson was delighted when he heard the news. Like many other Americans, he was sure that Louisiana would help make the United States a great nation. He had one doubt, however. Did the Constitution give the President the right to buy land?

After much thought, he decided that the President did have the power to buy land because the Constitution allowed the President to make treaties. In 1803, the Senate agreed when it approved the *Louisiana Purchase.* The United States took control of vast new lands west of the Mississippi.

## Lewis and Clark Set Out

In 1803, Congress provided money for a team of explorers to study the newly bought land. Jefferson chose Meriwether Lewis, his Virginia neighbor and his private secretary, to head the team. Lewis asked another Virginian, William Clark, to join him. Lewis and Clark chose about 40 men to go with them.

Jefferson gave Lewis and Clark careful instructions. He asked them to map the country and make notes about the Native American peoples they met. They were to study the climate, wildlife, and mineral resources of the land. The President hoped that the explorers would find a route to the Pacific and develop trade with the Indians.

In May 1804, Lewis and Clark started up the Missouri River from St. Louis on a journey that would take them all the way to the Pacific. (Follow their route on the map at right.) At

first, progress was slow. The lower Missouri was full of tree limbs and stumps that snagged their boats. Also, they were traveling against the swift current. One night, the current tore away the riverbank where they were camping. The party had to scramble into their boats to avoid being washed downstream.

Lewis and Clark kept journals on their travels. They marveled at the broad, grassy plains that stretched "as far as the eye can reach." Everywhere, they saw "immense herds of buffalo, deer, elk, and antelopes." In their journals, they described flocks of pelicans on the river banks and prairie dogs digging burrows.

Lewis and Clark met people from many different Indian nations. They gave medals with the seal of the United States government to Indian leaders. The leaders often invited Lewis and Clark to their villages and had them carried on buffalo hides as a sign of friendship.

## Ahead to the Rockies

During the first winter, Lewis and Clark set up a camp with the Mandan Indians near Bismarck, North Dakota. The explorers planned to continue up the Missouri in the spring. But they worried about how they would cross the steep Rocky Mountains. Luckily, Sacajawea (sahk uh juh WEE uh), a Shoshone Indian, and her French Canadian husband were staying with the Mandans that winter. The Shoshones (shoh SHOH neez) lived in the Rocky Mountains, and Sacajawea offered to act as guide and interpreter.

In April 1805, the party traveled up the Missouri past the Yellowstone River. Lewis described the Great Falls of the Missouri as "the grandest sight I ever beheld." In the foothills of the Rockies, the country changed. Bighorn sheep ran along the high hills. The climate was drier. The sharp thorns of

Every map tells a story. Many maps in this book tell the story of explorers moving across the land and sea. See, for example, the routes of Dias and da Gama on page 57. Other maps show the movements of troops or ships during a war. See the battle maps on pages 182 and 186.

When Lewis and Clark set out in 1804, their job was to map the lands in the Louisiana Purchase.

1. **Study the map to see what it shows.** (a) What is the subject of this map? (b) What color shows the route of Lewis and Clark?

2. **Practice reading directions on the map.** To follow a route on a map, you need to determine in what direction or directions the route goes. Find the directional arrow that shows, N, S, E, and W. Sometimes, you need to combine directions when explorers travel in a direction between north and east. In this case, they are said to be traveling northeast (NE). They could also travel to the northwest (NW), southeast (SE), or southwest (SW). (a) In what direction did Lewis and Clark travel after they left St. Louis? (b) In what direction did they travel along the Columbia River?

3. **Describe movements on a map in terms of direction.** Maps like this one show movement. (a) Describe the directions in which Pike traveled during 1806 and 1807. (b) What city did he reach at the end of his trip?

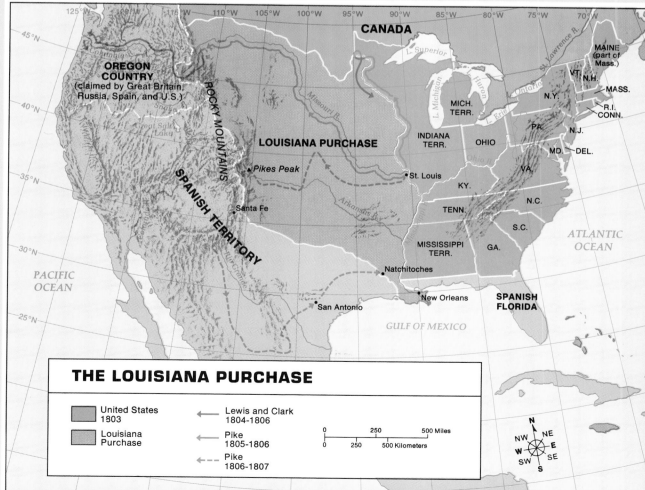

## THE LOUISIANA PURCHASE

- United States 1803
- Louisiana Purchase
- ← Lewis and Clark 1804-1806
- ← Pike 1805-1806
- ←-- Pike 1806-1807

0   250   500 Miles
0   250   500 Kilometers

Here, Lewis and Clark look out on the Great Falls of the Missouri River. With them are Sacajawea, their Native American guide, and York, Clark's black servant. Lewis and Clark's account of the animals and lands in the Louisiana Purchase created much enthusiasm back east.

prickly pears jabbed through the explorers' moccasins. Once, a grizzly bear chased Lewis when he was exploring alone.

As they neared the Rockies, Sacajawea recognized the lands of her people. One day, Lewis returned to camp with some Indian leaders. Sacajawea began "to dance and show every mark of the most extravagant joy." One of the men was her brother. Lewis and Clark bought horses from the Shoshones and found out from them the best route to follow across the mountains.

## On to the Pacific

In the Rockies, the explorers found rivers that flowed west toward the Pacific. They realized that they had crossed a continental divide. A *continental divide* is a mountain ridge that separates river systems. In North America, the continental divide is in the Rockies. Rivers east of the continental divide flow into the Mississippi and the Gulf of Mexico. West of the continental divide, rivers flow into the Pacific Ocean and Gulf of California.

Lewis and Clark found a large river flowing west. They built canoes and headed downstream until they reached the Columbia River.

In the Pacific Northwest, Lewis and Clark met the Nez Percé (NEHZ puhr SAY) Indians. The explorers wanted to learn about the Nez Percés, but every question had to go through four translators. First, their English words were translated into French for Sacajawea's husband. He then translated the French into Mandan. Sacajawea translated the Mandan into Shoshone. Then, a Shoshone who lived with the Nez Percés translated the question into Nez Percé. Of course, every answer went through the same process in reverse.

On November 7, 1805, Lewis and Clark reached their goal. Lewis wrote in his journal: "Great joy in camp. We are in view of the ocean, this great

Pacific Ocean which we have been so long anxious to see." On a nearby tree, Clark carved, "By Land from the U. States in 1804 & 5."

The trip back to St. Louis took another year. In 1806, Americans celebrated the news of the return of Lewis and Clark. The explorers brought back much valuable information about the Louisiana Purchase. They lost only one man from sickness. Except for one small battle, they got along peacefully with Native Americans in the West.

### Pike's Route West

Even before Lewis and Clark returned, another explorer, Zebulon Pike, set out from St. Louis. From 1805 to 1807, he explored the upper Mississippi River, the Kansas and Arkansas rivers, and parts of Colorado and New Mexico. On Thanksgiving Day 1806, Pike saw a tall mountain, today called Pikes Peak, in Colorado. Later, he headed into Spanish lands in the Southwest. The Spanish arrested him. In the end, Pike made his way home with news of the lands he had visited.

Many Indians lived in the lands that Lewis, Clark, and Pike visited. White settlers did not push onto these lands right away. But the area around New Orleans soon had a large enough white population to apply for statehood. In 1812, this area entered the Union as the state of Louisiana.

### SECTION REVIEW

1. **Locate:** Mississippi River, New Orleans, Haiti, Louisiana Purchase, Missouri River, Rocky Mountains, Columbia River, Pacific Ocean, Pikes Peak.
2. **Define:** continental divide.
3. (a) What was the purpose of the journey of Lewis and Clark? (b) How did Sacajawea help them?
4. What areas did Zebulon Pike explore?
5. **What Do You Think?** Why do you think Jefferson was both praised and criticized for the Louisiana Purchase?

# 3 Dangers at Sea

### Read to Learn

★ How was American trade threatened in the early 1800s?
★ Why did British warships seize American sailors?
★ Why were the Embargo and Nonintercourse acts unpopular?
★ What do these words mean: impressment, embargo?

Jefferson won popular support for the Louisiana Purchase. The nation was growing rapidly, and Americans were looking for new lands to settle. During this time, too, Americans were reaching out overseas. American traders looked for new markets. Yankee ships sailed to Europe, the West Indies, and even China.

### Yankee Traders

In the years after the Revolution, American trade grew rapidly. Ships sailed out of New England ports on voyages that sometimes lasted three years. When captains put into foreign ports, they kept a sharp lookout for trade goods and new markets in which to sell. Traders often took big risks, hoping for bigger profits in return. One clever trader sawed up the winter ice from New England ponds, packed it deep in sawdust, and carried it to India. There, he traded the ice for silks and spices.

In 1784, the *Empress of China* became the first American ship to trade with China. Before long, New England merchants built up a profitable trade with China. Yankee traders took ginseng, a plant that grew wild in New England, and exchanged it for Chinese silks and tea. The Chinese used the roots of the ginseng plant for medicines.

In the 1790s, Yankee ships sailed up the Pacific coast of North America. In fact, Yankee traders visited the Columbia River more than ten years before Lewis and Clark reached it by land. For a time, traders from Boston were so common in the Pacific Northwest that Native Americans called every white man "Boston." Traders bought furs from Native Americans. They then sold the furs for large profits in China.

## War With Tripoli

American trading ships ran great risks, especially in the Mediterranean Sea. For many years, the rulers of the Barbary States on the coast of North Africa attacked American and European ships. The United States and many European countries were forced to pay a yearly tribute, or bribe, to protect their ships from attack. (See the map below.)

The ruler of Tripoli, one of the Barbary States, wanted the United States to pay an even bigger bribe. When President Jefferson refused, Tripoli declared war on the United States. In response, Jefferson ordered American ships to blockade the port of Tripoli.

One of the American ships, the *Philadelphia,* ran aground near Tripoli. Tripoli pirates swarmed on board and imprisoned the crew. The pirates planned to use the *Philadelphia* to attack other ships. But a brave American officer, Lieutenant Stephen Decatur, had other plans. Late one night, Decatur and his crew sailed quietly into Tripoli harbor. They boarded the captured ship and set it on fire so that the pirates could not use it.

Meanwhile, a force of American marines marched 500 miles (800 km) across North Africa to make a surprise attack on Tripoli. The war with Tripoli lasted until 1805. In the end, the ruler of Tripoli signed a treaty promising to let American ships alone.

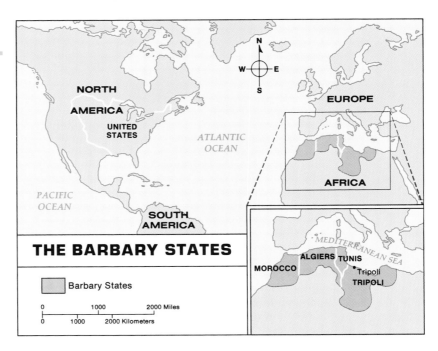

MAP SKILL President Jefferson wanted to end the practice of paying tribute to the Barbary States. Where were the Barbary States located?

THE BARBARY STATES

Barbary States

0     1000     2000 Miles
0   1000   2000 Kilometers

In a daring nighttime raid, Decatur boarded a captured ship in Tripoli harbor and set it on fire. Americans looked on Decatur as a national hero. Even the great British admiral, Lord Nelson, called Decatur's deed "the most . . . daring act of the age."

## More Troubles at Sea

During the early 1800s, American ships faced another problem at sea. In 1803, Britain and France went to war again. At first, Americans profited from the war. British and French ships were so busy fighting that they could not engage in trade. American merchants took advantage of the war to trade with both sides. As trade increased, American shipbuilders hurried to build new ships.

**Neutral ships are seized.** Then, Britain and France each tried to cut off trade to the other country. Americans claimed that they were neutral. But the warring countries ignored this claim as they had in the 1790s. (See page 227.) Napoleon seized American ships bound for England. At the same time, the British seized American ships carrying goods to and from France. Between 1805 and 1807, hundreds of American ships were seized.

**Impressment of American sailors.** Not only did Britain seize American ships, but it also took American sailors and forced them to serve on British ships. This practice was called *impressment*. The practice was common in Britain. For centuries, impressment gangs had raided villages and forced young men to serve in the navy.

In the early 1800s, many British sailors preferred to sail on American ships. They earned better wages, and conditions on American ships were less harsh. Once, the entire crew of a British ship that was docked at Norfolk, Virginia, deserted to join an American ship.

Because of the war with France, the British navy needed all the sailors it

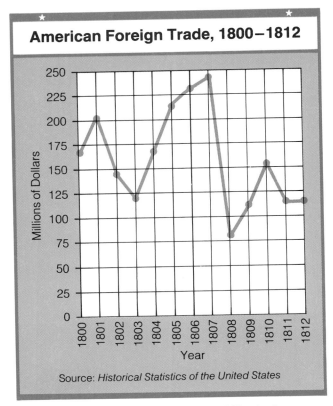

## American Foreign Trade, 1800–1812

Source: *Historical Statistics of the United States*

**GRAPH SKILL** In the early 1800s, trade was important to the new nation, especially to New Englanders. Why do you think trade was increasing up to 1807?

could find. Its warships began stopping and searching American merchant ships. If a British officer found English sailors on board a ship, he forced them off and made them serve in the British navy. If a sailor claimed to have become an American citizen, the officer impressed him anyway. "Once an Englishman, always an Englishman," the British claimed. Even worse, the British impressed thousands of American sailors.

One young American, James Brown, secretly sent a letter to his brother. "Being on shore one day in Lisbon, in Portugal," he wrote, "I was impressed by a gang and brought on board the [British ship] *Conqueror,* where I am still confined. Never have I been allowed to put my foot on shore since I was brought on board, which is now three years."

## Two Unpopular Acts

Americans were furious with the British for impressing their sailors and attacking their ships. Many wanted to declare war on Britain. Like Washing-

Americans resented the highhanded way in which British officers seized American sailors at sea. The British defended impressment by saying they were only taking deserters from their own navy. The British often ignored documents Congress gave sailors to prove they were American citizens.

In the early 1800s, the United States watched events in Europe with growing concern. As this 1805 cartoon shows, Americans feared that King George III of Britain and Napoleon Bonaparte of France were carving up the world. Napoleon controlled much of Europe. The British ruled the seas.

ton and Adams, President Jefferson wanted to avoid war. He knew that the small American navy could not match the powerful British fleet.

Instead, in 1807, he convinced Congress to pass the Embargo Act. An *embargo* is a ban on trade with another country. The *Embargo Act* forbade Americans to export or import any goods. Jefferson hoped that the embargo would hurt France and Britain because they would be unable to get badly needed goods. He could then offer to end the embargo if they would let Americans trade in peace.

Britain and France were hurt by the embargo. But Americans suffered even more. American sailors lost their jobs. Farmers were hurt because they could not ship wheat abroad. Docks in the South were piled high with cotton and tobacco. Ordinary citizens were unable to get imports such as sugar, salt, tea, and molasses.

The Embargo Act hurt New England merchants most, and they protested strongly. Finally, Jefferson admitted that the Embargo Act was a mistake. In 1809, Congress replaced it with the *Nonintercourse Act.* Under this act, Americans could trade with all nations except Britain and France. Also, if either Britain or France agreed to stop seizing American ships and sailors, the President could restore trade with that country.

Jefferson signed the Nonintercourse Act a few days before his second term ended. The year before, he had decided not to run for a third term as President. James Madison, his friend, ran and won an easy victory. When Madison took office in 1809, he hoped that Britain and France would soon give in to American pressure.

### SECTION REVIEW

1. **Define:** impressment, embargo.
2. (a) Why did Jefferson blockade Tripoli? (b) Describe one result of the war.
3. How did Britain anger the United States in the early 1800s?
4. (a) What was the purpose of the Embargo Act? (b) Why was it replaced?
5. **What Do You Think?** How do you think Jefferson's limits on trade hurt the American economy?

# 4 War Fever

**Read to Learn**

★ Why did the War Hawks want to fight Britain?

★ How did Tecumseh win the respect of the Indians?

★ What does this word mean: nationalism?

Like other Presidents, James Madison wanted to keep the nation out of war. But events at home and abroad proved to be beyond his control. France and Britain continued to seize American ships. By 1812, much of the nation had caught war fever.

## The War Hawks

In 1810, Napoleon promised to respect the rights of American ships. So Madison let Americans trade with France again. Britain refused to make a similar promise. So the embargo against Britain went on.

In Congress, feelings ran strongly against Britain. Only New Englanders wanted trade with Britain to be restored. Many representatives from the South and West wanted war with Britain. They were known as the *War Hawks.* The War Hawks had a strong sense of nationalism. *Nationalism* is pride in or devotion to one's own country. The War Hawks felt that Britain was insulting the United States by seizing American ships and sailors.

The most outspoken War Hawk was Henry Clay of Kentucky. Clay wanted war for two main reasons. He wanted revenge on Britain for attacking American ships. Also, he wanted an excuse to conquer Canada. "The militia of Kentucky are alone competent [able] to place Montreal and Upper Canada at your feet," Clay boasted to Congress.

## Westward Expansion

The War Hawks had yet another reason for wanting war with Britain. They claimed that Britain was arming Indians on the frontier and encouraging them to attack American settlers. In fact, this time it was not British meddling but rather American expansion that caused new fighting between Native Americans and settlers.

Under the Treaty of Greenville, Native Americans were forced to sell much of their Ohio land in 1795. (See page 229.) In 1803, Ohio was admitted to the Union. By then, thousands of settlers were pushing farther west into the Indiana Territory. These settlers began taking over Indian lands.

William Henry Harrison, governor of the Indiana Territory, supported the settlers' desire for land. Harrison looked down on Indians, calling them "wretched savages." In 1809, he tricked a few Indian leaders into signing a treaty. In it, they gave up 3 million acres for less than half a cent an acre.

## Tecumseh Takes a Stand

Many Native Americans were furious over this treaty. They claimed that the men who signed it did not have the right to sell the land. Among those angered by the sale were two Shawnee leaders: Tecumseh (tih KUM suh) and his brother, called the Prophet. The two men wanted to keep settlers from taking more Indian land.

**Strong leaders.** Tecumseh had fought at the Battle of Fallen Timbers. In the early 1800s, he organized many Native American nations into a confederation. The Prophet provided spiritual leadership for the confederation.

Tecumseh and the Prophet urged Native Americans to preserve their traditional ways. Many white customs, they said, were corrupting the Indian way of life. They took a strong stand against whiskey. White traders used gifts of whiskey to trick Indians into selling land and furs cheaply.

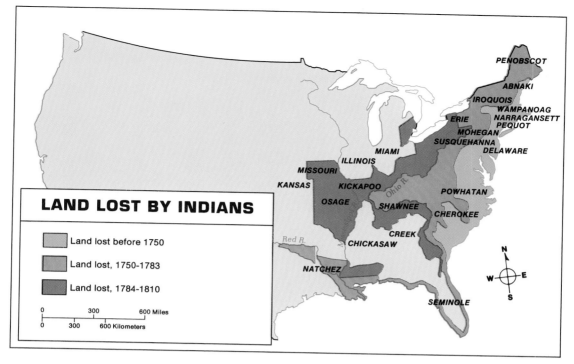

## LAND LOST BY INDIANS

Land lost before 1750

Land lost, 1750-1783

Land lost, 1784-1810

0    300    600 Miles

0    300    600 Kilometers

PENOBSCOT

ABNAKI

IROQUOIS

WAMPANOAG
NARRAGANSETT
PEQUOT

ERIE

MOHEGAN

SUSQUEHANNA

DELAWARE

MIAMI

ILLINOIS

MISSOURI

KANSAS

KICKAPOO

*Ohio R.*

POWHATAN

OSAGE

SHAWNEE

CHEROKEE

*Red R.*

CREEK

CHICKASAW

NATCHEZ

SEMINOLE

N
W    E
S

**MAP SKILL** As settlers moved west, they took over Indian lands. When did Indians in the East lose their lands? Which Native American groups in the West lost lands between 1784 and 1810?

Tecumseh earned the respect of Native Americans. He convinced them to unite against white settlers. "Until lately," he said, "there was no white man on this continent. . . . It all belonged to red men." The whites have "driven us from the great salt water, forced us over the mountains. . . . The way—and the only way—to check and to stop this evil is for all the red men to unite in claiming a common equal right in the land."

Even white leaders saw how much influence Tecumseh had among Native Americans. Harrison grudgingly admitted, "He is one of those uncommon geniuses which spring up occasionally to produce revolutions and overturn the established order of things."

**Battle of Tippecanoe.** Rivalries between Indian nations prevented Tecumseh from uniting all the Indians east of the Mississippi River. Still, white settlers were alarmed at his success. In 1811, they convinced Governor Harrison to march on Tecumseh's settlement at Tippecanoe Creek in Indi-

ana. At the time, Tecumseh was away meeting with Indian leaders to the south. His brother was in charge.

The Prophet decided to meet the danger by leading a surprise night attack on Harrison's troops. In the battle that followed, neither side won a real victory. But white people in the East celebrated the *Battle of Tippecanoe* as a major victory.

The next year, war between Britain and the United States appeared likely. Tecumseh went north to speak to the British in Canada. He offered to lead his Indian confederation against the Americans if war broke out.

## War Is Declared

The Battle of Tippecanoe marked the beginning of a long, deadly war between Native Americans and white settlers on the frontier. It also added fuel to the claim of the War Hawks that Britain was arming the Indians.

Using this claim, the War Hawks stepped up the pressure for war. They

Tecumseh, at left, and the Prophet, at right, called on Indian nations to stop selling land to the United States government. Tecumseh argued that the land belonged to all Indians and should not be divided or sold unless all agreed.

brought up other arguments, too. The United States must defend its rights at sea and end impressment. They urged Americans to conquer not only Canada but also Florida, which belonged to Spain, Britain's ally.

Finally, on June 18, 1812, President Madison gave in to the pressure. He asked Congress to declare war on Britain. Congress quickly agreed. Americans soon discovered that winning the war would not be as easy as they thought.

**SECTION REVIEW**

1. **Locate:** Ohio, Indiana Territory, Canada, Spanish Florida.
2. **Define:** nationalism.
3. What did the War Hawks hope to gain from a war with Britain?
4. (a) Who was Tecumseh? (b) What did he think the Indians should do to save their lands?
5. **What Do You Think?** Why do you think President Madison was unable to avoid war with Britain?

# 5 The War of 1812

**Read to Learn**

★ What were the major battles in the War of 1812?
★ How did the Indians help the British?
★ What issues did the peace treaty settle?

Despite the eagerness of the War Hawks, the nation was deeply divided over the war. People in the South and West generally supported the war. New Englanders mostly opposed it. British impressment hurt trade, but New Englanders knew that war would disrupt trade even more. They spoke with scorn of "Mr. Madison's war."

## The War at Sea

The nation was not ready for war. The American army was small and poorly trained. Its navy had only 16 ships fit to fight against the huge British navy. Yet Britain, too, had problems. It was locked in a deadly struggle with Napoleon in Europe and could spare few troops to defend Canada.

When the war began, Britain used its powerful navy to blockade American ports. It wanted to stop Americans from trading with other countries. The American navy was too small to break the blockade. Still, the Americans had several talented young captains who won stunning battles at sea.

One famous battle took place in August 1812. Captain Isaac Hull was in command of the *Constitution* when he saw a British frigate, the *Guerrière* (gair ee AIR), south of Newfoundland. For close to an hour, the two ships maneuvered into position. The *Guerrière* fired on the *Constitution* several times. Captain Hull ordered his sailors to hold their fire. When he finally got close enough, Hull bent over to shout to the sailors below, "Now boys, you may fire!" He bent over so forcefully that his trousers split at the seams!

The guns of the *Constitution* roared into action. They ripped large holes in the *Guerrière* and shot off both masts. When the smoke cleared, Hull asked the British captain if he had "struck" his flag—that is, surrendered by lowering his flag. The British captain was stunned by the attack. He could only reply: "Well, I don't know. Our mizzenmast is gone, our mainmast is gone. And, upon the whole, you may say we *have* struck our flag."

During the war, American ships won other victories at sea. Although these victories cheered Americans, they did little to help win the war.

## Fighting in the West

In 1812, the War Hawks demanded an invasion of Canada. They expected Canadians to welcome the chance to throw off British rule. They also thought that Americans could easily defeat the British troops in Canada.

The United States planned to invade Canada at three points: Detroit, Niagara Falls, and Montreal. To the surprise of the War Hawks, Canadians did not welcome the Americans. Instead, they fought back fiercely and forced Americans to retreat.

**Invasion of Canada.** In the West, William Hull led American forces from Detroit into Canada. The Canadians had only a few untrained troops there. To trick the Americans, General Isaac Brock paraded his soldiers in red cloaks to make Hull think that they were experienced British regulars. Tecumseh helped the Canadians by making raids on Hull's troops. As another trick, Brock allowed false "secret" messages to fall into American hands. One such message said that 5,000 Indians were helping him when, in fact, the number was far less.

Brock's tricks worked, and Hull retreated from Canada. The British followed him and captured Detroit. The Americans were unable to retake Detroit because the British controlled Lake Erie.

**The battle for Lake Erie.** In 1813, the Americans set out to win control of Lake Erie. Captain Oliver Hazard Perry had no fleet. So he designed and built his own ships. In September 1813, he sailed his tiny fleet into battle against the British.

During the battle, Perry's own ship was battered by the British and left helpless. Perry took his flag down and rowed over to another American ship. There, he hoisted the colors again and continued to fight. The battle ended with an American victory. Perry wrote his message of victory on the back of an envelope. "We have met the enemy and they are ours."

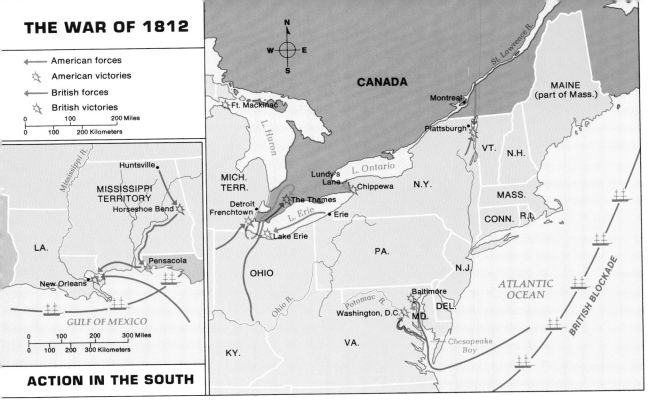

# THE WAR OF 1812

← American forces
☆ American victories
← British forces
☆ British victories

0 — 100 — 200 Miles
0 — 100 — 200 Kilometers

**ACTION IN THE SOUTH**

GULF OF MEXICO

0 — 100 — 200 — 300 Miles
0 — 100 — 200 — 300 Kilometers

**MAP SKILL** The War of 1812 was fought on several fronts. What battles took place in or near Canada? Which of these were American victories?

**Indian losses.** With Lake Erie in American hands, Tecumseh and the British were forced to abandon Detroit. General Harrison pursued them into Canada. At the *Battle of the Thames,* the Americans won a decisive victory. Tecumseh died in the fighting. With Tecumseh gone, the Indian confederation he had organized fell apart. Rivalries among the Indians led to more disasters.

The Creeks, Tecumseh's allies to the south, were divided over what to do. Some wanted to keep up the battle against white settlers. They were known as the Red Stick—a symbol for war—faction. During the fighting, both settlers and Indians committed brutal acts. Many were killed on both sides. A Tennessee officer, Andrew Jackson, took command of American forces in the Creek War.

In 1814, Jackson led his forces against the Creeks. With the help of the Cherokees, Jackson won a decisive victory at the *Battle of Horseshoe*

*Bend.* The battle ended the fighting for the moment. Once again, the Indians had to give up land to white settlers.

## Burning of Washington

In 1814, Britain and its allies finally defeated Napoleon. With the fighting over in Europe, Britain began sending its best troops to America. The British planned to invade the United States from Canada in the north and from New Orleans in the south. At the same time, they began raiding American cities along the east coast. (See the map above.)

British ships sailed into Chesapeake Bay in August 1814. They put troops ashore about 30 miles (48 km) from Washington. American troops met the British at Bladensburg, Maryland. President Madison rode out to watch, carrying a set of dueling pistols in case of trouble. What he saw disappointed him. The experienced British soldiers quickly scattered the poorly trained Americans. Washington was left undefended.

In the President's mansion, Dolley Madison anxiously waited for her husband to return. Her guard of soldiers disappeared. She scrawled a note to her sister Anna: "Will you believe it, my sister? We have had a battle or skirmish near Bladensburg and here I am still within sound of the cannon! Mr. Madison comes not. May God protect us. Two messengers covered with dust come to bid me fly. But here I mean to wait for him."

As British troops marched into the city, Dolley Madison gathered up important papers of the President and a fine portrait of George Washington. She fled south. The British captured the capital. They set fire to the President's mansion and other public buildings before leaving Washington.*

From Washington, the British marched north toward Baltimore. However, Baltimore was well defended, and the British were forced to give up the attack. (Read "The Star-Spangled Banner" on page 261.)

## Battle of New Orleans

Meanwhile, another British force was threatening the United States in the south. In late 1814, the British decided to attack New Orleans. From there, they hoped to sail up the Mississippi. But Andrew Jackson was waiting for them. Jackson had turned his frontier fighters into a strong army. He took Pensacola in Spanish Florida to keep the British from using it as a base. He then marched through Mobile and set up camp in New Orleans.

On Christmas Eve 1814, Jackson's troops surprised the British invaders outside New Orleans. After a brief battle, the Americans withdrew. They dug trenches to defend themselves. During

---

*When Washington was rebuilt after the fire, the President's mansion was given a coat of whitewash to cover the black charring. After that, it became known as the White House.

**AMERICANS WHO DARED**

### Dolley Madison

Dolley Madison influenced the social life of Washington for almost 50 years. Her career there began when her husband, James Madison, became Secretary of State to President Jefferson. She served as hostess for the widowed Jefferson. When James Madison was elected President, she held the first inaugural ball in Washington. Dolley Madison returned to the Capitol after the British burnt it and managed to entertain visitors as well as ever. Many times, her social skills helped to smooth over quarrels between political leaders.

the first week of January, the British tried to overrun Jackson's defenses. Then, on January 8, 1815, the British launched an all-out attack. In the battle that followed, the British bravely charged forward again and again. Over 2,000 redcoats fell before the deadly fire of American sharpshooters and cannons. Fewer than a dozen American lives were lost.

The *Battle of New Orleans* ended with a complete American victory. In parts of the country, Jackson became a

The bloodiest engagement of the War of 1812 was the Battle of New Orleans, shown here. Andrew Jackson's overwhelming victory made him a popular hero.

popular hero, second only to George Washington. However, Americans later learned that this bloody battle might have been avoided. It took place two weeks after the United States and Britain had signed a peace treaty in Europe.

## An End to the War

It took weeks for news to cross the Atlantic in the early 1800s. By late 1814, Americans knew that peace talks had begun. But no one knew how long they would last. While Jackson was preparing to fight the British at New Orleans, New Englanders were meeting to protest "Mr. Madison's war."

**The Hartford Convention.** In December 1814, delegates from several New England states met in Hartford, Connecticut. Most were Federalists. They disliked the Republican President and the war. The British blockade hurt New England trade. Also, many New

Englanders felt that the South and West would benefit if the nation won land in Canada and Florida. If new states were carved out of these lands, New England would lose influence.

Delegates to the *Hartford Convention* threatened to leave the Union if the war went on. While the convention debated what to do, news of the peace treaty arrived. With the war over, the Hartford Convention quickly ended.

**The peace treaty.** Peace talks took place in Ghent, Belgium. The *Treaty of Ghent* was signed on December 24, 1814. John Quincy Adams, one of the Americans there, summed up the treaty in these words: "Nothing was adjusted, nothing was settled." Both sides agreed to return to prewar conditions. The treaty did not say anything about impressment or neutral rights. But since Britain was no longer fighting France, these issues had faded.

Other issues, such as who would control the Great Lakes, were settled later through negotiation. In 1817, the

On September 13, 1814, Francis Scott Key was on board a British warship near Baltimore to negotiate the release of an American prisoner. That day, the British began their attack on Fort McHenry, the key to Baltimore's defense.

Key spent a sleepless night on deck. He watched British rockets exploding across the harbor. By dawn on September 14, the bombing had stopped. When the early morning fog lifted, Key was delighted to see that the American flag—the stars and stripes—still waved over Fort McHenry.

Soon after, Key wrote "The Star-Spangled Banner." The poem told the story of his night's watch. Before long, the poem was set to a popular tune and was sung widely. In 1931, Congress made it the national anthem of the United States. The poem begins:

> Oh, say, can you see by the dawn's early
>      light,
> What so proudly we hailed at the twilight's
>      last gleaming?
> Whose broad stripes and bright stars,
>      through the perilous fight,
> O'er the ramparts we watched were so
>      gallantly streaming?

And the rockets' red glare, the bombs
>      bursting in air,
> Gave proof through the night that our flag
>      was still there.
> Oh, say, does that star-spangled banner
>      yet wave
> O'er the land of the free and the home of
>      the brave?

★ How does Key's poem reflect his experiences?

United States and Britain signed the **Rush–Bagot Agreement.** It forbade warships on the Great Lakes. In 1818, the two countries agreed to set much of the border between Canada and the United States at 49°N latitude.

The War of 1812 did benefit the United States in some ways. Britain and other European nations were forced to treat the young republic with respect. Also, the success of heroes like Oliver Hazard Perry and Andrew Jackson gave Americans great pride in their country.

## SECTION REVIEW

1. **Locate:** Detroit, Montreal, Lake Erie, Horseshoe Bend, Washington, D.C., Baltimore, New Orleans, Hartford.
2. What unexpected problems did Americans face when they invaded Canada?
3. Why did many New Englanders oppose the war?
4. What did Dolley Madison rescue from Washington?
5. **What Do You Think?** Why do you think the Americans and British fought so hard for control of Lake Erie?

# Chapter 11 Review

## ★ Summary ★

President Thomas Jefferson, a Republican, kept some Federalist programs but changed others. In 1802, he doubled the size of the United States with the Louisiana Purchase. Lewis and Clark explored the newly acquired land.

In the early 1800s, American ships faced many dangers. The French and British ignored the rights of neutral ships. And the British seized American sailors. In 1812, President Madison gave in to pressure from the War Hawks and declared war on Britain.

During the War of 1812, the United States was unable to conquer Canada. There was fierce fighting on the frontier, where Indians tried to defend their lands against white settlers. Andrew Jackson's stunning victory at New Orleans took place two weeks after a peace treaty had been signed but before news of the treaty reached the United States.

## ★ Reviewing the Facts ★

**Key Terms.** Match each term in Column 1 with the correct definition in Column 2.

| Column 1 | Column 2 |
|---|---|
| 1. laissez faire | a. forcing American sailors to serve on British ships |
| 2. continental divide | b. mountain range that separates river systems |
| 3. impressment | c. devotion to one's country |
| 4. embargo | d. ban on trade with another country |
| 5. nationalism | e. let alone |

**Key People, Events, and Ideas.** Identify each of the following.

1. Albert Gallatin
2. John Marshall
3. *Marbury* v. *Madison*
4. Toussaint L'Ouverture
5. Meriwether Lewis
6. William Clark
7. Sacajawea
8. Embargo Act
9. War Hawks
10. Henry Clay
11. Tecumseh
12. Oliver Hazard Perry
13. Dolley Madison
14. Hartford Convention
15. Treaty of Ghent

## ★ Chapter Checkup ★

1. What precedent did John Marshall set for the Supreme Court?

2. Why did Americans want to control the Mississippi River? (b) How did the revolt in Haiti influence Napoleon's decision to sell Louisiana?

3. (a) Name three parts of the world that American trading ships visited in the early 1800s. (b) Why did President Jefferson blockade Tripoli in 1801?

4. (a) Why did British ships seize American sailors? (b) How did Jefferson try to stop France and Britain from seizing American ships?

5. Describe three causes of the War of 1812.

6. Explain why each of the following was important to Indians in the West: (a) the Prophet; (b) Battle of Tippecanoe; (c) Battle of Horseshoe Bend.

## ★ Thinking About History ★

1. **Understanding geography.** (a) How did the Louisiana Purchase affect the size of the United States? (b) What did the journey of Lewis and Clark prove? (c) How do you think these two events could have affected the view Americans had of their country?

2. **Taking a stand.** Do you think that Americans had good reason to invade Canada during the War of 1812? Explain your stand.

3. **Analyzing information.** Review the discussion of relations between white settlers and Indians on pages 92, 104–105, 156–157, 186–187, and 228–229. (a) How did these relations change over time? (b) Why do you think clashes continued to take place between these groups?

4. **Relating past to present.** Reread "The Star-Spangled Banner" on page 261. Why do you think this poem became the national anthem of the United States?

## ★ Using Your Skills ★

1. **Using visual evidence.** Study the picture on page 248. (a) Who is shown in the picture? (b) What part of the country are they exploring? (c) What geographical features are shown in the picture? (d) Why do you think it took the explorers almost a month to cross this river?

2. **Graph reading.** Study the graph on page 252. (a) What was the value of American foreign trade in 1807? (b) What was its value in 1812? (c) What event or events caused the change?

3. **Map reading.** Study the map on page 258. (a) What British victories are shown on this map? (b) What American victories are shown? (c) Where was the British blockade?

4. **Outlining.** Prepare an outline for Section 4 on pages 254–256. Then write a paragraph summarizing the events leading up to the War of 1812.

5. **Skimming a chapter.** Review the skill on skimming a chapter on page 239. Then practice skimming this chapter. (a) What are the main topics covered in this chapter? (b) What is the general idea of the section called "Dangers at Sea" (pages 249–253)?

## ★ More to Do ★

1. **Eyewitness reporting.** Prepare an eyewitness report from the point of view of an Indian meeting Lewis and Clark.

2. **Exploring local history.** Study the map on page 247 to determine what part of North America your state belonged to in 1803. Did the Lewis and Clark or the Pike expedition pass through your state? If so, draw the route of the expedition on an outline map of your state. Add to your map the locations of any local monuments to the explorers.

3. **Creating headlines.** Create headlines for newspapers supporting the War Hawks in the early 1800s.

4. **Writing a skit.** As a group project, prepare a short skit in which a British ship stops an American ship at sea. Have students imagine they are British officers planning to impress American sailors into the British navy.

5. **Researching.** Prepare a short biography of Dolley Madison. Explain why she is one of the best-known First Ladies.

CHAPTER

# 12

# The Nation
# Prospers (1790–1825)

## Chapter Outline

**1** The Industrial Revolution
**2** The Way West
**3** Changing Times
**4** America's Neighbors
Readings, page 523

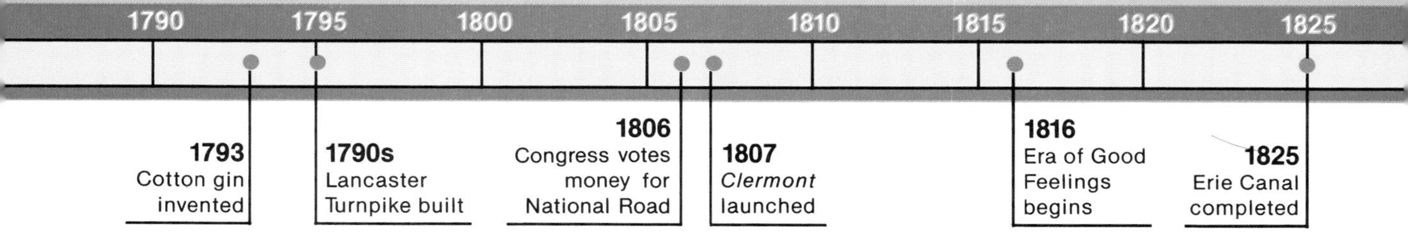

| 1790 | 1795 | 1800 | 1805 | 1810 | 1815 | 1820 | 1825 |
|------|------|------|------|------|------|------|------|

**1793**
Cotton gin
invented

**1790s**
Lancaster
Turnpike built

**1806**
Congress votes
money for
National Road

**1807**
*Clermont*
launched

**1816**
Era of Good
Feelings
begins

**1825**
Erie Canal
completed

## About This Chapter

After the War of 1812, thousands of Americans moved west. Many of the settlers were immigrants from Britain. Elias Pym Fordham, an Englishman, settled in Illinois. He wrote to friends in England about his new home.

The territory is "peopling so fast that very soon our country will be backed up," Fordham wrote. "Mr. Birkbeck is laying out a farm of 1,600 acres in the midst of his estate of 4,000 acres. My little estate lies on and between two small hills, from which descend several small streams that unite in the valley and flow on through the prairie."

Travel through the western lands was difficult. "I am going down the river in a boat," wrote Fordham. "I went down last autumn in two boats, in one of which I had two horses. To confess the truth, I nearly lost the boats and all the property. It was in the night and a most tremendous thunderstorm came on. The intervals between the flashes of lightning were so dark that we could not see some rocks, which we ran into and hung to all night."

In the early 1800s, America was changing in many ways. The Industrial Revolution was beginning. With the growth of industry, cities expanded rapidly. Many people left farms to work in the growing cities.

Study the time line above. Which events occurred after the War of 1812?

—264—

In the early 1800s, thousands of Americans moved west. The National Road, above, was sometimes jammed with people, wagons, and cattle.

# 1 The Industrial Revolution

## Read to Learn

★ What inventions helped start the Industrial Revolution?

★ How did the Industrial Revolution begin in America?

★ What was life like in the Lowell mills?

★ What do these words mean: spinning jenny, cotton gin, capitalist, factory system, interchangeable parts?

The early 1800s brought a new revolution to the United States. Unlike the revolution against British rule, this one had no battles and no fixed dates. Instead, it was a long, slow process that completely changed the way goods were produced.

## The Revolution Begins

The new revolution was called the Industrial Revolution. Before the Industrial Revolution, most goods were produced by hand, and most people were farmers. As the *Industrial Revolution* got under way, machines replaced hand tools, and new sources of power, such as steam and electricity, replaced human and animal power. During the Industrial Revolution, the economy shifted from farming to manufacturing, and people moved from farms to the cities.

**New ways to spin and weave.** The Industrial Revolution began in Britain in the mid-1700s. There, a series of inventions brought a revolution to the textile industry. The spinning of thread and weaving of cloth became mechanized. Before 1750, family members spun fibers into thread and wove it into cloth by hand in their homes. They used simple spinning wheels and hand looms. By the early 1800s, this system had changed.

In 1765, James Hargreaves developed the spinning jenny. With the *spinning jenny,* a person spun several threads at once, not just one thread as on a spinning wheel. In 1769, Richard Arkwright invented a machine that held 100 spindles of thread. This machine was too heavy to be operated by hand. So he used water power to turn it. The new machine was called the water frame.

Other inventions speeded up the process of weaving. In 1785, Edward Cartwright built a loom powered by water. Using this power loom, a worker could produce 200 times more cloth in a day than was possible before. In 1793, an American, Eli Whitney, gave a further boost to the textile industry. Whitney invented the *cotton gin,* a machine that speeded up the process of cleaning cotton fibers. (You will read more about the cotton gin in Chapter 15.)

**The factory system.** New machines like the water frame had to be set up near rivers because they needed running water to power them.* They were expensive to build. So most were owned by *capitalists,* people with capital, or money, to invest in business to make a profit. Early capitalists built spinning mills and hired hundreds of workers to run the machines.

The spinning mills were the beginning of a new system of production in Britain. Instead of spinning and weaving at home, people went to work in factories. The *factory system* brought workers and machines together in one place to produce goods. In factories, everyone had to work a certain number of hours each day. Workers were paid daily or weekly wages.

## Americans Build Factories

Britain led the way in the Industrial Revolution. In the late 1700s, Britain tried to keep its inventions secret from other countries. Parliament passed a law forbidding anyone from taking plans of Arkwright's water frame out of the country. It also said that factory workers could not leave the country.

Enforcing these laws was almost impossible, as Samuel Slater proved. Slater was a bright mechanic who worked in one of Arkwright's mills. He decided to seek his fortune in America, where several states were offering rewards for information about British inventions. Slater knew that British officials often searched the baggage of people sailing to America. So he memorized the design of Arkwright's mill before he sailed for New York in 1789.

In America, Slater heard that Moses Brown, a Quaker merchant, wanted to build a spinning factory in Rhode Island. Slater offered to help Brown. "If I do not make as good yarn as they do in England," he vowed confidently, "I will have nothing for my services, but will throw the whole of what I have attempted over the bridge." Brown hired him.

In 1790, Moses Brown opened his mill in Pawtucket, Rhode Island. It was the first factory in America. Slater worked hard to make the factory succeed. He improved on the machines he had worked with in Britain. In the winter, he was up before daybreak, chopping ice from the water wheel. Slater's wife Hannah helped, too. She developed a way to make stronger thread. Before long, other manufacturers were building mills, using Slater's ideas.

---

*Water flowing down a stream or a waterfall turned a water wheel that produced the power to run the machines.

Rivers powered the textile mills that sprang up across New England during the Industrial Revolution. Here, the building with the smokestack is one of the first American textile mills. Water power turned the wheels that ran machines in this early factory.

At first, American factories only spun threads. Weaving was still done on hand looms. By the early 1800s, Cartwright's power loom found its way to America.

## The Lowell Experiment

The War of 1812 gave a boost to American industry. Because the British were blockading the Atlantic coast, Americans started to make goods they had once imported from Europe.

During the war, a clever New England merchant named Francis Cabot Lowell improved on British textile mills. In Britain, spinning was done in one factory and weaving in another. Lowell decided to combine spinning and weaving under one roof.

In 1813, Lowell and several partners formed the *Boston Associates.* They raised about $1 million—a huge sum in those days—to build a textile factory in Waltham, Massachusetts. The new factory had all the machines needed to turn raw cotton into finished cloth. The machines were powered by water from the nearby Charles River.

**Life in the Lowell mills.** After Lowell's death, the Boston Associates built a factory town and named it after him. In 1821, Lowell, Massachusetts, was a village with only five farm families. By 1836, it was a bustling city of 18,000 people.

The Boston Associates hired young women from nearby farms to work in the Lowell mills. Young women often worked in factories in towns for a few years before they returned to the country to marry. They sent their wages home to help their parents.

At first, farm families hesitated to let their daughters go to work in the Lowell mills. To reassure parents, the Boston Associates built clean boarding-houses for their employees. They hired housemothers to run the houses. The company also planted thousands of shade trees, built churches, and made rules to protect the women.

In the early 1800s, conditions in the Lowell mills were much better than in most factories in Europe. As a result, the Lowell mills were seen by some as a symbol of progress brought about by the Industrial Revolution. But as the factory system spread, conditions grew worse and wages dropped.

**Children at work.** In the early factories, most workers were women and children. They could be paid less than men.

Children were especially useful in spinning factories. Because they were quick and small, they could easily scamper around machines to change the spindles. For his mill, Samuel Slater hired seven boys and two girls, ranging in age from 7 to 12.

Working hours were long—12 hours a day, 6 days a week. By today's standards, it seems cruel that those children worked such long hours. But in those days, most boys and girls worked long hours on the family farm. Therefore, farm families often let their children work in factories so that they could earn money needed at home.

## Interchangeable Parts

In the early 1800s, Eli Whitney came up with an idea that had a great impact on the way goods were produced. Most goods were produced by skilled workers. Whitney knew, for example, that a gunsmith spent many hours making the stock, barrel, and trigger of a rifle. Each rifle was slightly different from the next because each part was made by hand. If a rifle part broke, a gunsmith had to make a new part to fit that gun. This method of making and repairing goods was very slow.

Whitney's idea was to build machines that made each separate part of the gun. Every part would then be exactly alike. All the stocks would be the same size and shape. All the barrels would be the same length. If a trigger broke, it could easily be replaced with another machine-made trigger. Whitney introduced this idea of *interchangeable parts* in making guns. It was a big step forward. Interchangeable parts made it possible to put together and repair goods such as guns quickly.

The use of interchangeable parts spread slowly to other industries. Factories began to produce clocks, knives,

Before the Industrial Revolution, women had spun cloth at home. In the early 1800s, women did much of the work in the new textile factories. They were paid less than men for the same work.

As the new nation grew, Americans celebrated July 4th, or Independence Day, in many ways. By the early 1800s, people celebrated the Fourth with parades, picnics, and patriotic speeches. Symbols such as the American flag with its stars and stripes and the bald eagle became popular.

Americans chose the bald eagle as a symbol of the new republic because of its power. The bald eagle is found only in North America. It is not, in fact, bald but has white feathers on top of its head. Early settlers used the word bald because at a distance the eagle looked bareheaded without brown feathers on top.

Americans soon adopted other symbols. One was the Liberty Bell that was hung in the State House in Philadelphia in 1752. On one side, the bell has these words from the Bible: "Proclaim liberty throughout the land to all the inhabitants thereof." On July 8, 1776, the bell announced the first public reading of the Declaration of Independence.

Uncle Sam is another patriotic symbol. Uncle Sam was a real person—Samuel Wilson of Massachusetts. During the War of 1812, he supplied meat to the army and stamped each barrel U.S. When asked what the initials U.S. stood

for, one of Sam Wilson's employees replied, "Uncle Sam"—meaning Uncle Sam Wilson. The idea that food, uniforms, and other supplies came from Uncle Sam caught on. At first, Uncle Sam appeared in cartoons as a young man with stars and stripes on his shirt. Later, cartoonists drew him with the familiar gray hair, beard, top hat, and tailcoat we see today.

★ Why do you think symbols were important to the new nation?

pistols, locks, and other items with interchangeable parts.

## City Life

In the early 1800s, people moved to cities to work in factories. By today's standards, cities were small. A person could walk from one end of a city to the other in 30 minutes. Buildings were only a few stories high. Houses were built of wood, heated by fireplaces, and lit by lamps. As the factory system spread, cities grew.

**Dangers.** Growing cities had many problems. Fire was a constant threat. If a chimney caught fire, a blaze spread quickly from one wooden house to the next. In most cities, Americans set up volunteer fire departments. New York City had over 1,300 volunteers and 42 hand-drawn or horse-drawn engines. Volunteer fire companies competed fiercely to be first to the scene of a blaze. Sometimes, the rivalry between two companies was so fierce that they brawled in the street while the fire burned on.

Cities had other hazards. Dirt and gravel streets were muddy when it rained. Cities had no sewers, and garbage was thrown into the street. An English visitor to New York reported:

> The streets are filthy, and the stranger is not a little surprised to meet the hogs walking about in them, for the purpose of devouring the vegetables and trash thrown into the gutter.

Because people lived close together in cities, disease spread easily. Yellow fever and cholera epidemics raged through cities, killing hundreds.

**Advantages.** Despite these problems, cities had much to offer. There were plays to see and museums to visit. Circuses came from time to time. In the 1840s, city dwellers flocked to see hot air balloons carry a few daring passengers into the sky.

Fashions from Europe arrived first in the cities. In the early 1800s, most older American men still wore styles popular in colonial days, including wigs. Some younger men sported loose, full-length trousers instead of tight knee breeches. They wore their own hair, letting it curl down over the forehead. One critic complained that the new hair style looked "as if you had been fighting a hurricane backward."

Beginning in the 1790s, a revolution took place in women's fashion. The high-waisted, narrow lines of the French "Empire" style replaced the older style of full skirts and tightly laced dresses. In the 1840s, however, tight-waisted, restrictive clothing for women again became the fashion.

---

### SECTION REVIEW

1. **Define:** spinning jenny, cotton gin, capitalist, factory system, interchangeable parts.
2. (a) List three inventions of the Industrial Revolution. (b) Briefly explain how each changed the ways goods were produced.
3. How did Samuel Slater contribute to the Industrial Revolution in America?
4. Why were early workers in the factories mostly women and children?
5. **What Do You Think?** Why do you think capitalists were necessary to the Industrial Revolution?

# 2 The Way West

## Read to Learn
★ What routes did settlers take to move west?
★ How were roads improved?
★ Why were steamboats useful?
★ What do these words mean: turnpike, corduroy road, canal?

In the early 1800s, America was a nation on the move. Thousands of settlers headed west. As the nation grew, settlers needed ways to stay in touch with people in the East and transport their goods to market. As a result, Americans turned their attention to improving transportation.

## A Flood of Settlers

"Old America seems to be breaking up and moving westward," noted a visitor to the United States in 1817. At that time, the West was the land between the Appalachians and the Mississippi. Settlers had been moving west throughout the 1700s. Even during the Revolution, settlers continued to cross the Appalachians.

In the 1800s, the stream of pioneers heading west turned into a flood. By 1820, so many people had moved west that the population of most of the original 13 states had declined.

Crossing the Appalachian Mountains was hard for settlers. In 1750, however, Thomas Walker pioneered a route through a gap in the mountains near the Cumberland River. The *Cumberland Gap* was a natural gateway for settlers moving into Kentucky and Tennessee.

The rich, black soil of Alabama and Mississippi attracted settlers from Georgia and South Carolina. New Englanders, "Yorkers," and Pennsylvanians pushed into the Northwest Territory along several different routes. One route ran from Albany, New York, west along the Mohawk River through a gap in the Appalachians. (See the map on page 272.) Settlers then followed Indian trails west around Lake Erie. Some took boats across Lake Erie into Ohio.

Another route west was the Great Wagon Road through Pennsylvania that was built in colonial times. At the foothills of the Appalachians, settlers unloaded their wagons and used packhorses to carry their goods across the steep mountain trails to Pittsburgh. There, they loaded their goods onto large flatboats to carry them down the Ohio River into Indiana, Kentucky, and Illinois. Flatboats were well suited to the shallow rivers of the region. Even with a heavy load, they did not sink very deep.

With the flood of settlers, the western lands soon had enough people to apply for statehood. Between 1792 and 1819, eight new states joined the Union: Kentucky (1792), Tennessee (1796), Ohio (1803), Louisiana (1812), Indiana (1816), Mississippi (1817), Illinois (1818), and Alabama (1819).

## Improving the Roads

Settlers faced many hardships as they moved west. Among them was poor roads. What people called roads were little more than trails that were too narrow for even a single wagon. Trails often plunged through muddy swamps. Tree stumps stuck up through

### Daniel Boone

As a young man, Daniel Boone learned from Indians how to survive in the wilderness. Dressed in deerskins and carrying a tomahawk, hunting knife, and long rifle, he led pioneers west into Kentucky in 1769. Later, he led settlers along an old Indian path, renamed the Wilderness Road. Boone fought battles with the Indians to protect his new settlement of Boonesboro, Kentucky. In the 1800s, other settlers took the route Boone pioneered.

the road and broke axles on the wagons of careless travelers.

**Turnpikes.** Perhaps the best road in America was the *Lancaster Turnpike.* It was built in the 1790s between Philadelphia and Lancaster in Pennsylvania. The road was set on a bed of gravel, so rains drained off easily. It was topped with smooth, flat stones.

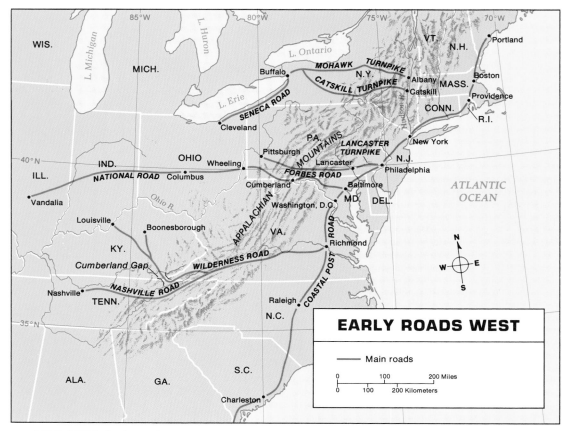

MAP SKILL In the early 1800s, settlers took new roads into the West. Private companies built turnpikes. The National Road was the first road built by the federal government. Today, the National Road is U.S. Highway 40. Through what states did the National Road run in the 1800s?

The Lancaster Turnpike was built by a private company. Other companies also built gravel and stone roads that helped improve travel. To pay for the roads, the companies collected tolls. At certain places along a road, a pole, called a pike, blocked the road. After a wagon paid a toll, the pike was turned aside. Roads with these pikes were called *turnpikes,* often shortened to pikes.

Gravel and stone roads were expensive to build. So many roads were made of logs instead. Such roads were called *corduroy roads* because the logs set side by side looked like corduroy cloth. Corduroy roads had fewer ruts and pot-holes than dirt roads, but they made for a very noisy and bumpy ride.

**Bridges.** A major problem in improving roads was bridging rivers. Stone bridges were expensive to build, but wooden ones rotted quickly. A Massachusetts carpenter finally designed a wooden bridge that could be built cheaply and easily. He found that putting a roof over a bridge protected it from the weather.

Covered bridges lasted four times longer than open ones. Soon, covered wooden bridges were being put up in many places. Today, a few covered bridges can still be seen on back roads in the East.

**The National Road.** Some states set aside money to improve roads and build new ones. In 1806, for the first time, Congress approved spending money to build a national road. The road was to run from Cumberland, Maryland, to Wheeling, Virginia.*

Because of the War of 1812, the National Road was not finished until 1818. Later, it was extended across Ohio and Indiana into Illinois. As each new part was built, settlers eagerly used it to drive their wagons west.

## The Sound of Steamboats

To settlers on the move, rivers were as useful as roads for transportation. In fact, floating downstream on a boat was often easier than traveling overland by wagon. The problem with river travel was moving upstream against the current. On parts of the Mississippi and Ohio rivers, the downstream current was very strong. Boats with sails could

---

*Today, Wheeling is in West Virginia.

beat their way upstream, but that was slow work. People sometimes used paddles or long poles to push boats upstream. Or they hauled them upstream from the shore with ropes. Yet none of these methods worked well.

**Fitch and Fulton.** The key to river travel by the 1800s was the steamboat. John Fitch, a Yankee from Connecticut, improved on steam engines that had been built in Britain. Fitch's steam engine turned paddle wheels that moved a boat upstream against the current.

Fitch tested his first steamboat on the Delaware River in 1787. At the time, the Constitutional Convention was meeting in Philadelphia. Fitch took several delegates for a ride on his new steamboat. Soon after, Fitch started a ferry service on the river. His business failed because few people used the ferry.

Twenty years later, Robert Fulton succeeded where Fitch had failed. Fulton grew up in Philadelphia and probably saw Fitch's steamboat. In 1807, he

Before new roads were built, travel was slow and uncomfortable. Tree stumps stuck up through the roads. The phrase "I'm stumped" may have come from coaches breaking down on these half-cleared tree stumps. At the far right of this picture, notice the corduroy road, where logs were set over marshy patches.

# Skill Lesson 12    Reading a Circle Graph

Circle graphs are one way of showing statistics. (See Skill Lesson 4 on page 81 and Skill Lesson 6 on page 140.) A circle graph is sometimes called a pie graph because it is divided into wedges, like a pie. Each wedge, or part, can be compared to every other part. A circle graph shows the relationship between each of the parts and the whole.

To compare information over time, two or more circle graphs can be used. A circle graph can also be used with a line or bar graph.

1. **Identify the information shown on the graphs.** (a) What year does the circle graph on the left show? (b) What do the colors represent? (c) What year does the circle graph on the right show? (d) What do the colors represent?

2. **Practice reading the graphs.** In a circle graph, you can compare any part with every other part or with the whole graph. The graph shows each part as a percentage of the whole. The whole graph is 100 percent. (a) What percent of the population lived in the North in 1800? (b) Which section of the country had the largest percent of the population in 1800? (c) Which section had the smallest percent of the population in 1800? (d) What percent of the population lived in the West in 1830? In the East? In the South?

3. **Interpret the information shown on the graphs.** Compare the two graphs. (a) Which section of the country gained the largest percent of the population between 1800 and 1830? (b) Which section of the country lost the greatest percent in this period? (c) Why do you think this section did not grow as fast as the West in this period? (d) Using your reading in the chapter and these graphs, make a generalization about what was happening to the population of the United States between 1800 and 1830.

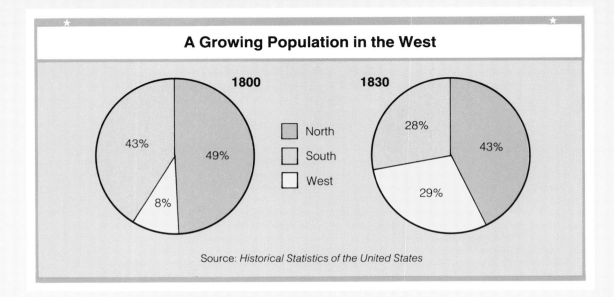

**A Growing Population in the West**

1800 — North 49%, West 43%, South 8%

1830 — North 43%, West 28%, South 29%

North / South / West

Source: *Historical Statistics of the United States*

— Canals

0     150     300 Miles

0     150     300 Kilometers

CANADA

MAINE

L. Champlain

VT.

N.H.

ERIE CANAL

CHAMPLAIN CANAL

N.Y.  Albany

Troy

MASS.

Buffalo

CONN.  R.I.

L. Ontario

L. Erie

Toledo

Cleveland

PA.

PENNSYLVANIA CANAL

New York

ILLINOIS AND MICHIGAN CANAL

Chicago

La Salle

Miami R.

Pittsburgh

N.J.

Philadelphia

WABASH AND ERIE CANAL

IND.

OHIO

Wabash R.

MIAMI AND ERIE CANAL

Cincinnati

OHIO AND ERIE CANAL

Potomac R.

CHESAPEAKE AND OHIO CANAL

MD.  DEL.

Washington, D.C.

ATLANTIC OCEAN

ILL.

Mississippi R.

Ohio R.

VA.

Richmond

Evansville

KY.

JAMES AND KANAWHA CANAL

N W E S

MAP SKILL The building of the Erie Canal set off an age of canal building across the new nation. Canals linked lakes and rivers and made inland travel easier. What is the longest canal shown on this map? In what direction does it run?

launched his steamboat, the *Clermont,* on the Hudson River. On his first run, Fulton took on passengers in New York City and headed upriver to Albany. The *Clermont* made the 300-mile (480 km) trip to Albany and back in just 62 hours. Within 3 months, the *Clermont* was making a profit for its owner.

**Western steamboats.** Fulton's success showed that a steamboat line could be profitable. Other steamboat lines quickly opened up river travel. Steamboats turned the Mississippi, Ohio, and Missouri rivers into busy routes for trade goods and travelers.

Western rivers were shallow compared with those in the East. They needed a special kind of boat. Henry Shreve, a pioneer steamboat captain, designed a flat-bottomed steamboat. It could carry heavy loads without getting stuck on sand bars.

By the 1830s, the booming of steamboat engines and the black smoke from their stacks were familiar sounds and sights along the Mississippi. At night, sparks lit up the sky as boats docked with a toot of the whistle. Although steamboats had comfortable cabins, they could be dangerous. Often, steam boilers exploded or sparks from smokestacks kindled raging fires. Even the best riverboat captains found themselves stuck on sand bars now and then.

## An Age of Canal Building

Rivers helped move people and their goods. Still, rivers did not exist everywhere they were needed. So Americans built canals to improve trade and travel. A *canal* is a channel dug and filled with water to allow ships to cross a stretch of land.

The first canals were only a few miles long. Some provided routes around waterfalls on a river. Others linked a river to a nearby lake. In the early 1800s, however, Americans began building longer canals.

**An ambitious plan.** One long canal was the *Erie Canal,* which connected the Hudson River with Lake Erie. (See the map above.) New Yorkers were eager to see this canal built. With it, goods could be moved across the Great Lakes and along the Mohawk and Hudson rivers into New York and back. New York City stood to gain much trade from the West. All the towns along the canal would prosper.

At first, many people thought that the plan was too ambitious. When a New Yorker told President Jefferson about it, the President remarked,

Canals helped link the West to the East in the early 1800s. Often, a team of horses dragged a boat along the canal, as you can see here. Boats had shelflike sleeping platforms for overnight passengers. During the day, passengers sat on top, ducking when a boat passed under a low bridge.

"Why, sir, you talk of making a canal 350 miles through the wilderness—it is little short of madness to think of it at this day!"

**The Erie Canal.** Governor DeWitt Clinton of New York disagreed. He convinced the state legislature to provide money for the canal. In 1817, workers began digging "Clinton's Ditch." Within a year, they had finished 69 miles (110 km) of the canal.

An immense task still remained to be done. To speed up the work, the canal builders invented new equipment. A machine was developed that could pull out nearly 40 tree stumps a day. In two places, the canal had to cross over rivers. Workers built stone aqueducts, or bridges, that carried the canal over the rivers.

When the Erie Canal was completed in 1825, trade flowed from the Great Lakes into New York. With the canal, shipping costs dropped, and travel time was greatly reduced. The canal helped make New York City the nation's leading center of commerce.

The success of the Erie Canal encouraged other states to build canals. As a result, canals helped link the nation together.

## SECTION REVIEW

1. **Locate:** Cumberland Gap, Kentucky, Tennessee, Alabama, Mississippi, Lake Erie, Ohio, Indiana, Illinois, Lancaster Turnpike, National Road, Erie Canal.
2. **Define:** turnpike, corduroy road, canal.
3. Describe one route settlers used to move west.
4. List three ways travel improved in the early 1800s.
5. **What Do You Think?** Why do you think the Erie Canal was such an important achievement?

# 3 Changing Times

**Read to Learn**

★ What was the Era of Good Feelings?
★ How did Congress help American industry after the War of 1812?
★ What do these words mean: dumping, protective tariff?

In the years after the War of 1812, many Americans were in a hopeful mood. The nation was growing and changing. New factories were built. Settlers were carving up western lands into new states. Changes were taking place in politics, too.

## An Era of Good Feelings

In 1816, a Republican President, James Madison, and a Republican majority in Congress firmly controlled the nation. By then, the Federalist Party was declining. Some Federalists joined the Republican Party. When Madison's second term ended, the Republicans nominated James Monroe to succeed him. Federalists chose Rufus King of New York. In the election, Monroe got 183 electoral votes and King only 34.

President Monroe belonged to the generation of Jefferson and Madison. He was over 60 years old when he took office. The new President still followed the fashions of the early 1800s. He powdered his hair and tied it back in a tail at a time when younger men wore their hair loose. He also preferred knee breeches and stockings to the full-length trousers of the new generation.

Still, Americans were fond of their old-fashioned President. Soon after taking office, Monroe toured New England, once the center of Federalist support. During the tour, New Englanders greeted Monroe so warmly that one Boston newspaper wrote about a new "Era of Good Feelings." When Monroe ran for a second term in 1820, no one ran against him. The easy Republican victory marked the end of the Federalist Party.

## Webster, Calhoun, and Clay

The disappearance of the Federalists did not mean an end to political differences. In Congress, a group of bright young leaders was taking center stage. They were Daniel Webster of Massachusetts, John C. Calhoun of South Carolina, and Henry Clay of Kentucky. Each came from a different section of the United States. All three played critical roles in Congress for more than 30 years.

Daniel Webster spoke for the North. He was one of the most powerful

Young Daniel Webster was a splendid speaker who could shed tears at will. As a New Englander, he opposed the War of 1812 in Congress. After the war, he backed measures to help trade and industry in New England.

speakers of his day, and he was proud of it. "He will not be outdone by any man, if it is within his power to avoid it," remarked a friend. His dark hair and eyebrows earned him the nickname of "Black Dan." Webster served as a representative in the House and later as a senator from Massachusetts.

John C. Calhoun spoke for the South. Like Webster, he served as a representative and a senator from his state. He, too, was a powerful speaker. He was trained at Yale College and always worked out his ideas clearly. Slim and handsome, he had deep-set eyes and a high forehead. His way of speaking was so intense that some people found themselves uncomfortable in his presence.

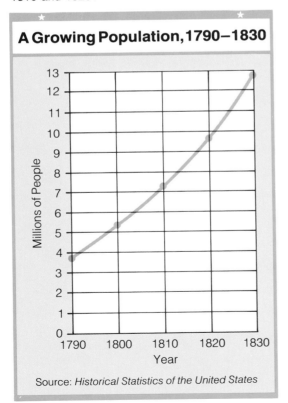

GRAPH SKILL The years after the War of 1812 were a time of economic growth. The nation's population grew, too, as this graph shows. About how much did the population increase between 1810 and 1820?

**A Growing Population, 1790–1830**

Source: *Historical Statistics of the United States*

In contrast, Henry Clay was full of charm and grace. Clay spoke for the West. As you read in Chapter 11, he was a War Hawk in 1812. Clay had simple, informal manners. He enjoyed staying up late at night to talk about politics or play cards. Like Webster and Calhoun, Clay's speeches could move people to laughter or tears.

## Help for American Industry

In the years after the War of 1812, congressmen like Webster, Calhoun, and Clay often debated economic issues. Despite the nation's physical growth, its economy faced severe problems. One problem was the absence of a national bank. Another was foreign competition.

**The second Bank of the United States.** The charter that set up the first Bank of the United States ran out in 1811. The Bank had loaned money and regulated the nation's money supply. Without it, the economy suffered. State banks made loans and issued money. But they put too much money into circulation, which caused prices to rise rapidly.

To solve the problem, Congress chartered the second Bank of the United States in 1816. By lending money to individuals and restoring order to the money supply, the Bank helped American businesses grow.

**Foreign competition.** American industry grew quickly between 1807 and 1814. First the Embargo Act and then the War of 1812 kept most British goods out of the United States. As a result, American manufacturers opened many new mills and factories.

In 1814, British goods again flooded into America. The British could make and sell goods more cheaply than Americans, who had to charge for building their new factories. As a result, American goods cost more. British manufacturers knew this. So they tried to put the new American factories out of business by dumping goods. *Dumping* means selling goods in another country at very low prices. Dumping caused dozens of New England businesses to fail. Angry factory owners turned to Congress for help.

**Tariff of 1816.** Congress responded by putting a high tariff on goods imported from Europe. The Tariff of 1816 increased tariffs to 25 percent. The increase made goods imported from Europe more expensive than American-made goods. (See the diagram at right.) This kind of tariff is called a *protective tariff* because it is meant to protect a country's industries from foreign competition.

The Tariff of 1816 sailed through Congress. In 1818 and 1824, Congress passed even higher tariffs. By then, some people, especially Southerners, began to resent the tariff. Southerners had built few factories, so the tariff did not help them. In fact, it forced them to buy more expensive American-made goods. John C. Calhoun became a bitter foe of the tariff. To Southerners like Calhoun, the tariff seemed to make northern manufacturers rich at the expense of the South.

## Clay's American System

As the debate over tariffs heated up, Henry Clay came up with a plan to help the economy of each section of the country. In 1824, he set out his ideas. Under Clay's *American System,* tariffs on imports would be kept high. High tariffs would help industry in the North expand. With wealth from expanding industry, Northerners would have the money to buy farm products from the West and South.

The other part of Clay's American System concerned internal improvements—the building of roads, bridges, and canals. Clay wanted Congress to spend money earned from the tariff on internal improvements. Such improvements, he said, would help the West and South by making it easier to ship goods to city markets.

Clay's American System was never really put into effect. Tariffs stayed

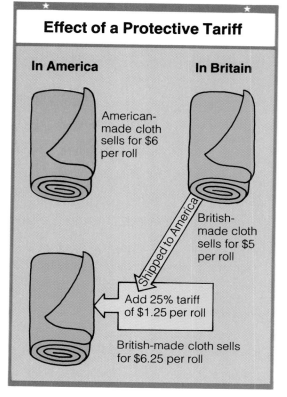

### Effect of a Protective Tariff

**In America**

American-made cloth sells for $6 per roll

**In Britain**

British-made cloth sells for $5 per roll

Shipped to America

Add 25% tariff of $1.25 per roll

British-made cloth sells for $6.25 per roll

DIAGRAM SKILL In 1816, the government passed a protective tariff to help American factory owners rather than to raise money. As this diagram shows, the tariff made British goods more expensive than American goods. Why do you think Southerners said that the tariff was unfair?

high, but Congress did not spend much money for internal improvements. Southerners found little to like in the American System. They did not support government building of roads and canals because the South could ship most goods by river.

### SECTION REVIEW

1. **Define:** dumping, protective tariff.
2. What section of the country did each of the following represent: (a) Daniel Webster; (b) John C. Calhoun; (c) Henry Clay?
3. Why did Congress pass the Tariff of 1816?
4. **What Do You Think?** What do you think were the major problems with Clay's American System?

# 4 America's Neighbors

**Read to Learn**

★ How did Canada achieve self-rule?
★ How did Latin American nations win independence?
★ What was the Monroe Doctrine?

As the United States grew and changed, so, too, did its neighbors to the north and south. To the north, Canada became an independent nation. To the south, the colonies of Spain and Portugal fought their own revolutions. These revolutions were inspired in part by the American Revolution. In this way, the United States served as an example to the nations around it.

## Canada Becomes a Nation

The population of Canada was a mix of Indian, French, and English. The first white settlers in Canada were French. In 1763, however, the British won Canada. During and after the American Revolution, thousands of Loyalists fled to Canada from the United States. They settled mainly in Nova Scotia, New Brunswick, Prince Edward Island, and the area north of the Great Lakes.

**A divided land.** French Canadians and English Canadians distrusted one another. They not only spoke different languages but practiced different religions. Most English settlers were Protestants. Most French settlers were Catholics.

In 1791, Britain decided to rule the two groups separately. It divided Canada into Upper and Lower Canada. Upper Canada included the area around the Great Lakes settled by English-speaking people. Lower Canada included the region along the St. Lawrence River settled by the French. Although each province had its own government, Britain made most of the important decisions for its colony.

During the early 1800s, Canadians grew discontent with British rule. In 1837, rebellions broke out. Britain did not want another revolution like the one in the 13 colonies. Lord Durham, the governor of Canada, recommended that Upper and Lower Canada be united. In a report to Parliament, he said that Canadians should be given control over local affairs. Britain would control only Canada's foreign affairs. The Durham Report became the basis for Canadian self-rule.

**The Dominion of Canada.** Canadians slowly gained control over their own affairs. In 1867, the provinces of Nova Scotia, New Brunswick, Ontario, and Quebec were joined into the *Dominion of Canada*. Later, Prince Edward Island, Manitoba, Alberta, Saskatchewan, and British Columbia joined the Dominion.

By slow and generally peaceful means, Canada became a nation. The govenment of Canada was similar to the British government. Canadians had an elected parliament and a prime minister. A governor general represented the British ruler but had little power.

## Revolutions in Latin America

To the south of the United States, Spanish colonists were eager for independence. They had many reasons to dislike Spanish rule. Most people had no say in government. The American and French revolutions encouraged the peoples of Latin America* to fight for control of their own affairs.

---

*Latin America refers to the parts of the Western Hemisphere where Latin languages such as Spanish, French, and Portuguese are spoken. It includes Mexico, Central and South America, and the West Indies.

**Simón Bolívar.** Perhaps the best known revolutionary leader was Simón Bolívar (see MOHN BAHL uh vuhr). He is often called the Liberator for his role in the Latin American wars of independence. Bolívar was born into a wealthy creole family in Venezuela. As a young man, he took up the cause of Latin American independence. "I will never allow my hands to be idle," he vowed, "nor my soul to rest until I have broken the shackles which chain us to Spain."

Bolívar visited the United States because he admired its form of government. When he returned to Venezuela, he led rebel armies in a long stuggle against Spain. In August 1819, Bolívar led an army on a daring march from Venezuela over the ice-capped Andes Mountains and into Colombia. There, he defeated the Spanish. Soon after, he became president of the independent Republic of Great Colombia. It included today's nations of Venezuela, Colombia, Ecuador, and Panama.

**José de San Martín.** Another daring leader was José de San Martín. He helped Argentina in its struggle for independence. Argentina won its freedom in 1816. San Martín also helped Chile, Peru, and Ecuador win their independence.

**Mexico wins independence.** During the early 1800s, Mexicans also fought for freedom from Spain. Among the heroes of these struggles were two priests: Miguel Hidalgo (hih DAL goh) and José Morelos (maw REH lohs).

In 1810, Father Hidalgo organized an army of Indians that freed several Mexican provinces. He then set up a government that outlawed slavery and returned land to the Indians. However, in 1811, Hidalgo was captured and executed by troops loyal to Spain. Morelos continued to fight for equal rights for all races and to give land to poor peasants. Wealthy Mexicans opposed his ideas and helped Spanish troops capture him.

Simón Bolívar, shown here, helped six Latin American nations win their freedom from Spanish rule. He accepted the title of Liberator but refused to exchange it for the title of king or emperor.

Mexicans finally won independence in 1821. A few years later, Mexican leaders wrote a constitution that made Mexico a republic.

## Other Nations Are Formed

In 1821, the people of Central America declared their independence from Spain. Two years later, they formed the United Provinces of Central America. It included today's nations of Nicaragua, Costa Rica, El Salvador, Honduras, and Guatemala.

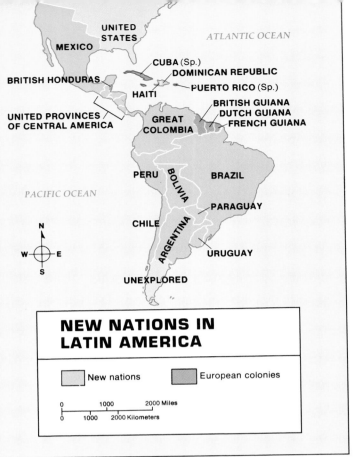

## NEW NATIONS IN LATIN AMERICA

| New nations | European colonies |

0   1000   2000 Miles
0  1000  2000 Kilometers

**MAP SKILL** The wars of independence in Latin America led to the creation of many new nations. Look at Central America on the map on page 580. What nations were carved out of the United Provinces of Central America?

The Portuguese colony of Brazil also won its independence—but without having to fight for it. Instead, the people asked Prince Pedro, son of the Portuguese king, to be their ruler. He accepted. In 1822, he declared Brazil's independence.

By 1825, most colonies in Latin America had thrown off European rule. Unlike the 13 colonies, however, the colonies of Latin America did not unite into a single country. Instead, they set up many different nations. One reason for this was geography. The Andes Mountains, for example, were a serious barrier to travel and communication. Also, the Spanish colonies were spread out over a huge area.

Like the United States, the new nations of Latin America faced many problems. They wanted to set up stable governments. But, as colonies, they had not been allowed to elect assemblies as the 13 American colonies had. So they had no experience in self-government. As a result, many of these nations were unable to achieve their goal of democratic rule.

## The United States Gains Florida

Although Spain lost many of its colonies, it held on to Puerto Rico, Cuba, and Florida. Many Americans thought that Florida should be added to the United States. As early as 1810, President Madison claimed West Florida, the land along the Gulf of Mexico.

Concern over Spanish Florida grew, especially among Southerners. Slaves from Georgia and other southern states often fled into Florida. Also, Creek and Seminole Indians in Florida raided settlements in Georgia. The Spanish did little to stop these raids. So in 1818, President Monroe sent Andrew Jackson into Florida to attack the Seminoles. Jackson's war against the Seminoles angered the Spanish. The United States replied that the Spanish had brought the trouble on themselves.

Because Spain was already fighting rebels in Mexico and elsewhere, it did not want war with the United States. John Quincy Adams, son of the second President of the United States, was Monroe's Secretary of State. Adams worked out a treaty with Spain that went into effect in 1821. In the *Adams–Onís Treaty,* Spain gave Florida to the United States in return for a payment of $5 million.

## The Monroe Doctrine

Even while Americans cheered the Adams–Onís Treaty, Monroe and Adams worried that European nations would interfere in North and South America. In 1815, Russia, Prussia, Austria, and France formed the Holy Alliance. Its aim was to crush any rev-

By the 1820s, the growth of American trade made shipbuilding even more important than it had been in colonial times. Here, Americans celebrate the launching of a new ship, *Fame.*

olution that sprang up in Europe. Monroe and Adams feared that members of the alliance might help Spain regain its old colonies. Russia also claimed lands on the Pacific coast of North America.

The British, too, worried about other European nations meddling in the affairs of North and South America. So they suggested that the United States and Britain issue a joint statement guaranteeing the freedom of the new nations of Latin America. Secretary of State Adams boldly advised Monroe to issue his own statement. Joining with the British, he warned, would make the United States appear "to come in as a [small] boat in the wake of the British man-of-war." Monroe agreed.

In a message to Congress in 1823, the President made a statement on foreign policy that is known as the *Monroe Doctrine.* The United States, he said, would not interfere in the affairs of European nations or European colonies in the Americas. In return, he warned European nations not to interfere with the newly independent nations of Latin America. The Monroe Doctrine also declared that the United States would oppose the building of any new colonies in the Americas.

Monroe's message showed that the United States was determined to keep Europeans out of the Western Hemisphere. In 1823, the United States did not have the power to enforce the Monroe Doctrine. However, Britain supported the Monroe Doctrine. Its powerful navy kept Europeans from trying to build new colonies in the Americas.

## SECTION REVIEW

1. **Locate:** Canada, Venezuela, Argentina, Chile, Peru, Colombia, Ecuador, Mexico, Nicaragua, Costa Rica, El Salvador, Honduras, Guatemala, Brazil.

2. (a) Why did Britain divide Canada in 1791? (b) What did Lord Durham recommend in his report to Parliament?

3. What role did each of the following play in Latin America: (a) Simón Bolívar; (b) José de San Martín; (c) Miguel Hidalgo?

4. How did Florida become part of the United States?

5. **What Do You Think?** Do you think the Monroe Doctrine is still important today? Why or why not?

# Chapter 12 Review

## ★ Summary ★

In the early 1800s, America was growing and changing. The Industrial Revolution brought the factory system and new machines to replace older ways of producing goods. New roads and canals and the use of steamboats helped improve transportation. To help the economy, Congress chartered the second Bank of the United States and passed a protective tariff.

America's neighbors struggled for independence during this period. Canada achieved self-rule through slow, peaceful means. In Latin America, however, Spanish colonies fought hard for their freedom. In 1823, the United States announced the Monroe Doctrine. It warned European nations to stay out of the affairs of the Western Hemisphere.

## ★ Reviewing the Facts ★

**Key Terms.** Match each term in Column 1 with the correct definition in Column 2.

**Column 1**
1. capitalist
2. factory system
3. canal
4. dumping
5. protective tariff

**Column 2**
a. selling goods in another country at very low prices
b. channel filled with water that lets ships cross land
c. person with money to invest in business to make a profit
d. tax to help home industries against foreign competition
e. way of bringing workers and machines together in one place to produce goods

**Key People, Events, and Ideas.** Identify each of the following.

1. Industrial Revolution
2. Eli Whitney
3. Samuel Slater
4. Francis Cabot Lowell
5. Lancaster Turnpike
6. John Fitch
7. Robert Fulton
8. Erie Canal
9. James Monroe
10. Era of Good Feelings
11. Tariff of 1816
12. American System
13. Simón Bolívar
14. Miguel Hidalgo
15. Adams–Onís Treaty

## ★ Chapter Checkup ★

1. (a) What industry was most affected by the inventions of the early Industrial Revolution? (b) How did the War of 1812 speed up the Industrial Revolution in America?

2. (a) Why did the Boston Associates hire women to work in the Lowell mills? (b) How did they try to attract women from farm families?

3. Explain how interchangeable parts improved the way goods were produced.

4. Explain how each of the following helped settlers moving west: (a) turnpikes; (b) steamboats; (c) Erie Canal.

5. (a) Why did northern manufacturers want a protective tariff? (b) How did Southerners respond to the tariff?

6. (a) Why did the United States fear that European nations might interfere in the Western Hemisphere? (b) What other nation supported the Monroe Doctrine? (c) Why was its support important?

## ★ Thinking About History ★

1. **Understanding the economy.** (a) How did the invention of new machines lead to the factory system? (b) Why were early factories set up near rivers?

2. **Relating past to present.** (a) Why were cities dangerous places to live in the early 1800s? (b) What advantages did they offer? (c) Do cities today still have the same dangers and advantages? Explain your answer.

3. **Understanding geography.** (a) How did geography make travel to the West difficult? (b) How did settlers overcome these difficulties?

4. **Comparing.** (a) Compare the way Canada won its independence to the way the Spanish colonies won theirs. (b) Suggest some reasons why their experiences were different.

## ★ Using Your Skills ★

1. **Map reading.** Study the map on page 272. (a) What city or cities in the West were located on major roads? (b) Describe one road that ran north–south. Name the city or state where the road began and where it ended. (c) What states did it cross?

2. **Reading for the main idea.** Each paragraph or group of paragraphs in this book has a main idea. The *main idea* is the generalization that underlies all the facts and examples. It ties them together. Often, the main idea is the topic sentence, or first sentence, of a paragraph. Facts are then given to support the main idea. Sometimes, the main idea is in the middle or end of a paragraph.

   Read the first paragraph on page 270 under the heading "A Flood of Settlers."

(a) What is the main idea of the paragraph? (b) What facts are given in that paragraph and the next one to support the main idea?

3. **Making a review chart.** Make a review chart with three vertical columns. Label the columns Inventor, Invention, and Importance. Then complete the chart by including all the inventors discussed in this chapter.

4. **Graph reading.** Study the graph on page 278. (a) What is the subject of the graph? (b) What was the population of the United States in 1800? 1820? 1830? (c) Compare this graph to the circle graphs on page 274. About how many people lived in the West in 1830?

## ★ More to Do ★

1. **Exploring local history.** Research and write a report about industries that developed in your local community during the early 1800s. Describe the effect the industries had on the way of life in the community.

2. **Eyewitness reporting.** Imagine that you are a reporter for an eastern newspaper and that you are traveling west with a family of settlers. Prepare an

article on the hardships of travel to send to your paper in the East.

3. **Building a model.** As a group project, build a model of an early steamboat.

4. **Researching.** Find out more about one of the leaders in the Latin American struggles for independence. Describe the leader's background, ideas, and efforts in the battle for freedom.

# Unit 4 Review

**Chapter 10** George Washington, the first President of the United States, guided the nation through its early years. During his second term, political parties took shape. Both Washington and Adams, the second President, managed to keep the United States out of foreign wars.

**Chapter 11** Thomas Jefferson had a more democratic style than the first two Presidents. During his time in office, the United States doubled in size. But British impressment of American sailors and the pressure of the War Hawks led President Madison into war in 1812.

**Chapter 12** The years after the War of 1812 were a time of change. The Industrial Revolution changed the way goods were made. Thousands of Americans moved west. New roads and canals were built to help the growing nation. Also, the nations of Latin America won their independence, and the United States warned European nations not to meddle in affairs of the Western Hemisphere.

★ **Unit Checkup** ★

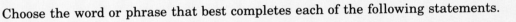

Choose the word or phrase that best completes each of the following statements.

1. Washington warned Americans against becoming involved in European affairs in the
   (a) Neutrality Proclamation.
   (b) Farewell Address.
   (c) Treaty of Greenville.

2. Hamilton's program to strengthen the economy included the
   (a) Alien and Sedition acts.
   (b) Tariff of 1816.
   (c) Bank of the United States.

3. Lewis and Clark explored the
   (a) Louisiana Purchase.
   (b) Northwest Territory.
   (c) Cumberland Gap.

4. One cause of the War of 1812 was the
   (a) burning of Washington.
   (b) attack on Fort McHenry.
   (c) impressment of American sailors.

5. Eli Whitney developed the
   (a) idea of interchangeable parts.
   (b) spinning jenny.
   (c) water frame.

★ **Building American Citizenship** ★

1. Newspapers influenced the growth of political parties in the 1790s by supporting one party or the other. Do you think newspapers play an important role in politics today? How? Why is freedom of the press important to a democratic government?

2. Thomas Jefferson supported such democratic beliefs as the rights and freedom of the individual. He once said, "The minority possess their equal rights, which equal law must protect." (See page 242.) How can a government elected by majority vote still protect the rights of a minority?

3. Why are good roads and transportation as important to the United States today as they were in the early 1800s?

# ★ Critical Thinking Skills ★

Time lines can be horizontal, as on pages 146 and 264. Or they can be vertical, like the one at right. Study this vertical time line. Then answer the following questions.

1. What Presidents are shown on the time line?
2. Who was President when the Embargo Act was passed?
3. Who was President during the War of 1812?
4. Did Madison become President before or after Jefferson?
5. Describe how each event on the time line affected relations between the United States and other nations.

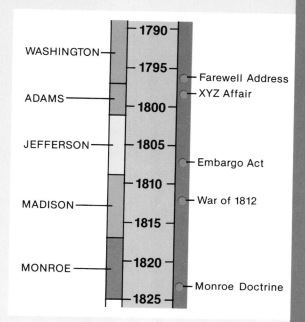

| | |
|---|---|
| | 1790 |
| WASHINGTON | |
| | 1795 |
| | — Farewell Address |
| ADAMS | — XYZ Affair |
| | 1800 |
| | |
| JEFFERSON | 1805 |
| | — Embargo Act |
| | 1810 |
| MADISON | — War of 1812 |
| | 1815 |
| | |
| MONROE | 1820 |
| | — Monroe Doctrine |
| | 1825 |

## History Writer's Handbook

### Selecting Supporting Information

Detail sentences in a one-paragraph answer give information to support the main idea. The information may be details, facts, examples, reasons, or incidents. The topic sentence often helps you decide what kind of information you need.

Look at the following topic sentence. *Hamilton's two-step plan for paying off the national debt and state debts may be described as follows.* The information you need is details about each step of Hamilton's plan. For example: *The national government would buy up the government's old bonds and issue new ones. The national government would also pay off debts owed by the states.*

Make sure you have enough information. Also make sure the information you select supports the main idea. Look at the following topic sentence. *Southerners resented the tariff of 1816 for two reasons.* The following information would not support the main idea. *In 1816, Congress passed a high tariff. In 1816, Congress chartered the second Bank of the United States.* Neither piece of information gives or explains a reason why Southerners resented the tariff of 1816. And the second piece of information does not even relate to the topic.

**Practice** Look at the following topic sentence for a one-paragraph answer. *Many Federalists favored war with France for two reasons.*

1. What kind of information should the detail sentences give?
2. Select information to include in the detail sentences. (See page 235.)

# Unit 5

# A GROWING NATION

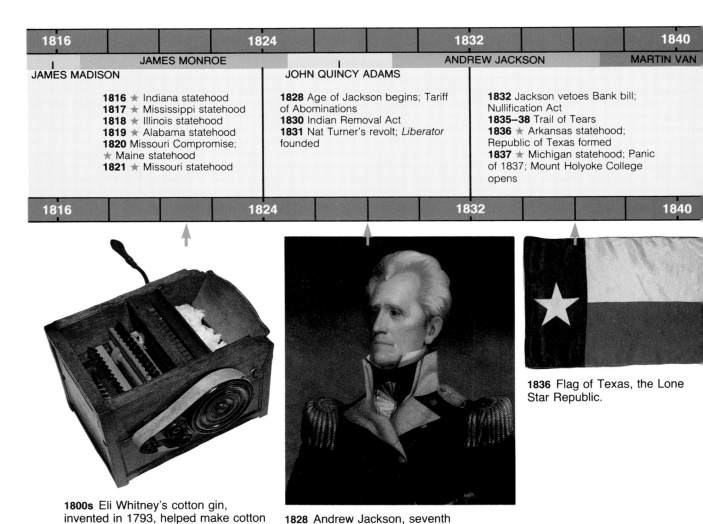

| 1816 | 1824 | 1832 | 1840 |
|------|------|------|------|

**JAMES MONROE**

JAMES MADISON

**JOHN QUINCY ADAMS**

**ANDREW JACKSON**

MARTIN VAN

**1816** ★ Indiana statehood
**1817** ★ Mississippi statehood
**1818** ★ Illinois statehood
**1819** ★ Alabama statehood
**1820** Missouri Compromise;
★ Maine statehood
**1821** ★ Missouri statehood

**1828** Age of Jackson begins; Tariff of Abominations
**1830** Indian Removal Act
**1831** Nat Turner's revolt; *Liberator* founded

**1832** Jackson vetoes Bank bill; Nullification Act
**1835–38** Trail of Tears
**1836** ★ Arkansas statehood; Republic of Texas formed
**1837** ★ Michigan statehood; Panic of 1837; Mount Holyoke College opens

| 1816 | 1824 | 1832 | 1840 |
|------|------|------|------|

**1836** Flag of Texas, the Lone Star Republic.

**1800s** Eli Whitney's cotton gin, invented in 1793, helped make cotton king in the South.

**1828** Andrew Jackson, seventh President of the United States.

UNIT OUTLINE

**CHAPTER** 13   Age of Jackson (1824–1840)

**CHAPTER** 14   Westward Ho! (1820–1860)

**CHAPTER** 15   Two Ways of Life (1820–1860)

**CHAPTER** 16   The Reforming Spirit (1820–1860)

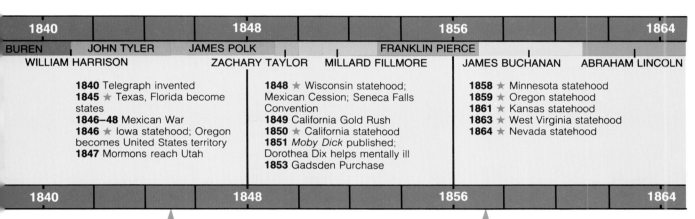

| 1840 | | | 1848 | | | 1856 | | | 1864 |
|---|---|---|---|---|---|---|---|---|---|

BUREN     JOHN TYLER     JAMES POLK       FRANKLIN PIERCE

WILLIAM HARRISON       ZACHARY TAYLOR   MILLARD FILLMORE     JAMES BUCHANAN    ABRAHAM LINCOLN

**1840** Telegraph invented
**1845** ★ Texas, Florida become states
**1846–48** Mexican War
**1846** ★ Iowa statehood; Oregon becomes United States territory
**1847** Mormons reach Utah

**1848** ★ Wisconsin statehood; Mexican Cession; Seneca Falls Convention
**1849** California Gold Rush
**1850** ★ California statehood
**1851** *Moby Dick* published; Dorothea Dix helps mentally ill
**1853** Gadsden Purchase

**1858** ★ Minnesota statehood
**1859** ★ Oregon statehood
**1861** ★ Kansas statehood
**1863** ★ West Virginia statehood
**1864** ★ Nevada statehood

| 1840 | | | 1848 | | | 1856 | | | 1864 |
|---|---|---|---|---|---|---|---|---|---|

**Mid-1800s** Settlers going west often traveled by boat along the upper Missouri River.

**Mid-1800s** Lucretia Mott, an abolitionist and crusader for women's rights.

CHAPTER

# 13

# Age of Jackson (1824–1840)

## Chapter Outline

**1** The People's Choice
**2** Jackson Takes Office
**3** Tests of Strength
**4** Jackson's Successors
Readings, page 529

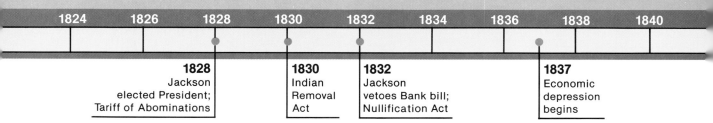

| 1824 | 1826 | 1828 | 1830 | 1832 | 1834 | 1836 | 1838 | 1840 |
|------|------|------|------|------|------|------|------|------|

**1828**
Jackson elected President; Tariff of Abominations

**1830**
Indian Removal Act

**1832**
Jackson vetoes Bank bill; Nullification Act

**1837**
Economic depression begins

## About This Chapter

Andrew Jackson was elected President in 1828. Jackson was a new kind of President. He was a self-made man and a frontiersman who was famous for his fearlessness. One story illustrates Jackson's grit.

Many years before he became President, Andrew Jackson served as a judge on the Tennessee frontier. One day, he faced an outlaw named Russell Bean. Bean had scared off the town sheriff by promising to shoot "the first skunk that came within ten feet." But when Andrew Jackson came roaring out of the courthouse, Bean changed his mind. "I looked [Jackson] in the eye and saw shoot," the outlaw explained. Bean decided to leave town rather than face Jackson's wrath.

Jackson made as strong a President as he had a judge. He faced a number of serious problems during his time in office. The President handled each crisis firmly. Because Jackson had such an influence on the country, the period from 1824 to 1840 is called the Age of Jackson.

During the Age of Jackson, the common people gained a new voice in politics. Farm hands, craftsworkers, small merchants, and other average Americans saw Jackson as one of them. Their votes made him President. The common people gave Andrew Jackson their loyal support throughout his years in office.

Study the time line above. What action did President Jackson take in 1832?

*Voting Day*, by George Bingham, catches the spirit of the Age of Jackson. By 1828, more people had a voice in government than ever before.

# 1 The People's Choice

### Read to Learn
★ Why was the election of 1824 disputed?
★ What plans did President Adams have for the nation?
★ How did democracy grow in the 1820s?
★ What do these words mean: suffrage, caucus, nominating convention?

Andrew Jackson, hero of many battles, was the people's choice for President in 1824. More people voted for Jackson than for any other candidate. But Jackson did not become President in 1824. How did this happen?

## The Election of 1824

In 1824, four men ran for President. All four were Republicans, but each drew support from different parts of the country. John Quincy Adams was most popular in the East. Henry Clay and Andrew Jackson had support in the West. William Crawford was favored in the South, but he was too ill to campaign much.

**The candidates.** John Quincy Adams of Massachusetts was the son of Abigail and John Adams, the second President. The younger Adams was a Harvard graduate and a talented diplomat. He helped end the War of 1812 and was Secretary of State under President James Monroe.

People admired Adams for his intelligence and strict morals. However, as a critic said, he was "hard as a piece of granite and cold as a lump of ice." This

John Quincy Adams was the first President to be photographed. He sat for this portrait in 1847, more than 20 years after he entered the White House.

coldness kept him from being well liked.

Henry Clay was Speaker of the House of Representatives. He was a skillful negotiator and helped work out important compromises in Congress. Clay was from Kentucky, a western state. But he was not nearly as popular as the other candidate from the West, Andrew Jackson.

To most Americans, Andrew Jackson was the hero of the Battle of New Orleans. He was also a fine example of a self-made man. He had risen from a poor boyhood to become a successful businessman. As a result, he won the support of self-made men everywhere, especially in the frontier areas of the West.

**Adams is elected.** The results of the 1824 election created a problem. Jackson won the popular vote. But none of the candidates won a majority of the electoral votes. Jackson led with 38 percent. Adams was second, Crawford third, and Clay fourth. Under the Constitution, the House of Representatives had to choose the President from the top three candidates. Clay could not be elected. But as Speaker of the House, he used his influence to help Adams.

With Clay's help, Adams was elected President. Soon after the election, President Adams named Henry Clay as Secretary of State. Angry Jackson supporters claimed that Adams and Clay had made a deal and stolen the election from Jackson. As Jackson rode home to Tennessee, he met an old friend. "Well, General," said the friend, "we did all we could for you here, but the rascals at Washington cheated you out of it."

"Indeed, my old friend," replied Jackson, "there was *cheating* and *corruption,* and *bribery,* too." In fact, nothing so dishonest had taken place. The election had been decided as the Constitution said. But Jackson and his followers were angry.

## Adams as President

John Quincy Adams had ambitious plans for the nation. Above all, the new President thought that the federal government should help the economy of the young republic grow.

**Plans for national growth.** President Adams wanted the government to pay for new roads and canals. He planned to set up a national university in Washington and build an observatory for astronomers. And he wanted the government to support projects to improve farming, manufacturing, trade, science, and the arts.

Adams' plans for national growth were not popular. Many people objected to spending federal money on such projects. Even the President's supporters found his many projects too costly. Congress approved money for a national road and for some canals. But it turned down all Adams' other plans.

**A bitter campaign.** Adams ran for reelection in 1828. This time, Andrew Jackson was his only opponent. Few issues were discussed during the campaign. Instead, it became a name-calling contest. Jackson supporters said that Adams had become President only because of the "corrupt bargain" with Clay in 1824.

Adams' supporters fought back. They called Jackson a murderer and handed out leaflets with coffins printed on them. Jackson had killed men in duels, they pointed out. Also, he had executed soldiers for deserting in battle. Some people even criticized Jackson's wife during the campaign.

Adams faced an uphill battle. His policies were unpopular, and even his background hurt him. Adams was seen as an aristocrat, a member of the upper class. A democratic spirit was sweeping the nation in the 1820s. Many people felt that aristocrats like Adams had run the nation long enough.

Jackson easily won the election. His supporters called his success a victory for the common people. By common people they meant farmers in the West and South and working people in the cities of the East.

## Growth of Democracy

The election of 1828 showed how America was changing. The nation was growing quickly. Three times more people voted in 1828 than in 1824. Many of the new voters lived in the frontier states between the Appalachians and the Mississippi River. Life on the frontier encouraged a democratic spirit. This spirit was reflected in the voting laws of the western states. Any white man over age 21 could vote.

**New voters.** The new voters in the western states were a rugged group of people. They often began life very poor. But through hard work, they prospered. Most white men in the West were on an equal footing. There were

fewer rich, old families than in the East. As a result, westerners thought that any honest, hard-working person could be successful.

There were also new voters in the East. Voting laws there were becoming more democratic. Several states dropped the requirement that voters own land. Thus, a large number of craftsworkers and shopkeepers won *suffrage,* the right to vote, for the first time. Despite these changes, many Americans still did not have the right to vote. They included women, Native

**MAP SKILL** In the election of 1828, Andrew Jackson won a clear majority of the popular and electoral vote. What part of the country supported John Quincy Adams?

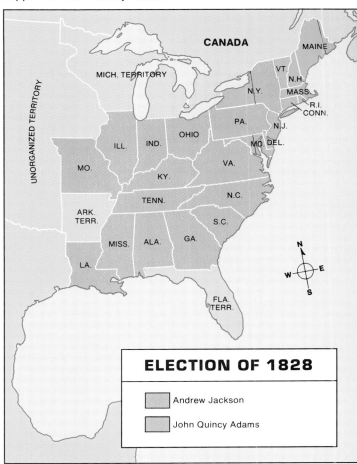

**ELECTION OF 1828**

Andrew Jackson

John Quincy Adams

# Spirit of America

## The People's President: Spirit of Democracy

When Andrew Jackson was sworn into office in March 1829, thousands of his supporters flooded the capital to cheer their hero. Many in the throng were rugged frontier people. After Jackson's swearing in, the crowd moved noisily to the White House for a party. One eyewitness wrote:

On their arrival at the White House, the . . . crowd clamored for refreshments and soon drained the barrels of punch. A great deal of china and glassware was broken, and the East Room was filled with a noisy mob. . . . Such a scene had never before been witnessed at the White House, and the aristocratic old Federalists saw, to their disgust, men whose boots were covered with the red mud of the unpaved streets standing on the satin-covered chairs to get a sight at the President of their choice.

Another eyewitness managed to get inside the crowded White House. She noted that "ladies fainted, men were seen with bloody noses." She added, with disapproval, "But it was the people's day, and the people's President, and the people would rule."

In the end, no one was badly hurt, but many were shocked. The party showed that a new kind of voter had chosen a new kind of President.

★ How do you think Andrew Jackson was different from "the aristocratic old Federalists"?

Americans, and most black Americans. Slaves had no political rights.

In the early years of the nation, most northern states allowed free blacks to vote. However, during the 1820s, most of these states took the vote away from free blacks. By 1830, blacks could vote only in a few New England states. To most white Americans at the time, it seemed natural that only white men took part in politics.

**New political parties.** By the late 1820s, new political parties had grown up. The Republican Party had been the major party for many years. But the differences between John Quincy Adams and Andrew Jackson showed a split in the Republican Party after 1824.

People who supported Adams and his plans for national growth called themselves National Republicans. Later, they took the name **Whigs.** Many business people in the East as well as some planters in the South were Whigs.

Jackson and his supporters formed a new party. They called themselves

*Democrats.* Most support for the Democratic Party came from frontier farmers and factory workers in the East.

**Choosing a candidate.** The new parties developed a more open way of choosing candidates for President. In the past, a few members of each party had held a *caucus,* or private meeting. At the caucus, party leaders chose the candidate. Many people thought that the system was undemocratic because very few people took part in it.

In the late 1820s, both political parties began holding *nominating conventions.* Delegates from all the states went to their party's nominating convention. The delegates then selected the party's candidate for President.

This gave people a more direct voice in choosing candidates. Today, the major political parties still hold conventions.

1. **Define:** suffrage, caucus, nominating convention.
2. Why was the election of 1824 decided in the House of Representatives?
3. How did frontier life encourage a democratic spirit?
4. What new political parties grew up in the late 1820s?
5. **What Do You Think?** Why do you think many people felt there was a "corrupt bargain" between Henry Clay and John Quincy Adams in 1824?

# 2 Jackson Takes Office

## Read to Learn

★ How did Andrew Jackson become a national leader?
★ Why did Jackson replace many officeholders?
★ Why did Jackson oppose a national bank?
★ What do these words mean: spoils system, kitchen cabinet, pet bank?

In March 1829, Andrew Jackson took office as the seventh President of the United States. Jackson was different from earlier Presidents. All of them had come from wealthy, powerful families in Virginia or New England. Jackson came from the West. He brought the spirit of the frontier to the office of President. His motto was "Let the people rule."

## Old Hickory

Jackson won the election of 1828 with the support of the common people. Like many of them, he was born in a log cabin. Jackson's parents moved from Ireland to the Carolina frontier two years before he was born. Young Andrew had to grow up quickly. His father died a few days before Andrew was born. His mother died when Jackson was 14 years old.

At age 13, Jackson fought in the American Revolution and was captured by the British. When ordered to clean a British officer's boots, Jackson proudly refused. The officer slashed Jackson's hand and face with a sword. Jackson bore the scars of these wounds for the rest of his life.

After the Revolution, Jackson studied law. He moved to the Tennessee frontier and built a successful law practice. Soon, he was rich enough to buy land and slaves. In 1796, Andrew Jackson was elected to the House of Representatives.

Jackson won national fame during the War of 1812. As commander of the United States forces, he defeated the British at New Orleans. To settlers on

This painting shows Andrew Jackson at the Battle of New Orleans. Although Jackson became one of the richest men in Tennessee, he was a hero to the common people. Jackson called himself "the direct representative of the American people."

the frontier, Jackson was also a hero of wars against the Indians. He defeated the Creek Indians at the Battle of Horseshoe Bend and forced them to give up millions of acres of land in Georgia and Alabama.

Jackson was a strong leader with a forceful personality. His enemies knew him as a fierce opponent. The Creeks that Jackson defeated called him Sharp Knife. But his own troops gave him a nickname that stuck. To them, he was as hard and tough as the wood of a hickory tree. They called him *Old Hickory.*

## Spoils to the Victor

Soon after Andrew Jackson took office, he fired many government employees. Some of these people had held their jobs since George Washington's time. The new President said that he was dismissing people who held their jobs as a privilege.

**The spoils system.** Jackson replaced officials with his own supporters. Some people saw this practice as a step toward greater democracy. They claimed it gave more people a chance to work in the government. Others disagreed. They said that Jackson gave jobs to loyal Democrats who helped elect him, not to people who could do the job well.

A Jackson supporter explained the practice this way: "To the victors belong the spoils." Spoils are profits or benefits. The practice of giving jobs to loyal supporters is called the *spoils system.* Politicians before Jackson had given jobs to supporters. But Jackson was the first President to do so on a large scale. After Jackson, the spoils system became an important part of American politics.

**Kitchen cabinet.** Jackson rewarded some of his supporters with cabinet jobs. Only Secretary of State Martin

Van Buren was really qualified for his post. As a result, Jackson seldom met with his official cabinet. Instead, he had a group of unofficial advisers. They included Democratic leaders and newspaper editors.

The group met in the White House kitchen and became known as the **kitchen cabinet.** The kitchen cabinet was made up of rough-and-ready men. They chewed tobacco and spat at the woodstove while they discussed politics. Despite their rough manners, these men were well informed. They kept Jackson up to date on the mood of the country.

## Jackson and the Bank

During Jackson's first term, a major political battle raged over the Bank of the United States. Like many people from the West, Jackson disliked the Bank. He thought that it had too much power. For example, the Bank regulated loans made by state banks. When the Bank's directors decided that state banks were making too many loans, it cut back the amount of money these banks could lend. This angered people in the South and West because they wanted to borrow money to buy land.

Jackson saw the Bank as a tool the rich used to help each other. He especially disliked Nicholas Biddle, president of the Bank since 1823. Biddle stood for everything Jackson and the Democrats mistrusted. He was rich and came from an aristocratic Philadelphia family.

**I will kill it!** Biddle worried that President Jackson might try to destroy the Bank. Two senators, Henry Clay and Daniel Webster, came up with a plan to save the Bank and defeat Jackson at the same time.

The Bank's charter did not have to be renewed until 1836. But Clay and Webster wanted the Bank to be an issue in the 1832 election. So they convinced Biddle to apply for renewal early. They were sure that most Americans supported the Bank. Thus, if Jackson vetoed the bill to renew the Bank's charter, he would lose popularity—and the election.

Clay pushed the recharter bill through Congress in 1832. Word that Congress had passed the bill reached Jackson when he was sick in bed. The President vowed, "The Bank . . . is trying to kill me, but I will kill it!"

**Jackson's veto.** When the Bank bill reached the President, he vetoed it at once. Jackson claimed that the Bank was unconstitutional. Earlier, the Supreme Court had ruled that the Bank was constitutional. In his veto message, Jackson challenged this ruling. He argued that only states, not the federal government, had the right to charter banks.

Republicans were sure that the President had blundered. To take advantage of the Bank issue, they chose Henry Clay to run against Jackson. When the votes were counted, however, the Republicans were stunned. Jackson

Whigs expected to beat Jackson in the election of 1832 because of the Bank issue. In this campaign cartoon, Jackson and Clay race toward the White House. As Jackson's horse stumbles on the Bank, Clay pulls ahead. In the end, however, Jackson won. Why do you think Jackson is swinging a club labeled "veto"?

Political cartoons can tell you a great deal about the past. For many years, cartoonists have tried to influence public feeling about important issues. To do so, they may exaggerate the facts. This is one reason why cartoons can often make a point more strongly than words can.

BORN TO COMMAND.

KING ANDREW THE FIRST.

Study the cartoon at left, which was published in the 1830s. Ask yourself what point about Andrew Jackson the cartoonist was trying to make. Then answer the following questions.

1. **Identify the symbols used in the cartoon.** Cartoons often use symbols. A *symbol* is something that stands for something else. For example, a skull and crossbones is a symbol for death. A dove is a symbol for peace. To understand a cartoon, you must know what its symbols mean.

   Figure out what the symbols in this cartoon stand for. (a) Who is pictured in the cartoon? (b) What is he holding in each hand? (c) What do these symbols stand for? (d) What is he wearing on his head? (e) What does this symbol stand for? (f) What is he standing on?

2. **Analyze the meaning of the symbols.** Use your reading of this chapter and the cartoon to decide what the symbols refer to. (a) What incident is probably referred to by the object in Jackson's left hand? (b) What event might the cartoonist have had in mind when he showed Jackson standing on the Constitution?

3. **Interpret the cartoon.** Draw conclusions about the cartoonist's point of view. (a) What do you think the cartoonist thought of President Jackson? Why? (b) How was the cartoonist trying to influence the public's attitude toward Jackson? (c) Does the cartoon give a balanced view of Jackson as President? Explain. (d) Study the painting of Jackson on page 296. Does the painting express an attitude toward Jackson different from that of the cartoon?

won by a large margin. Most voters stood solidly behind Jackson's veto of the Bank bill.

**Pet banks.** The Bank was due to close its doors in 1836. But Jackson wanted to send the Bank to an early grave. He ordered the Secretary of the Treasury, Roger Taney, to stop putting government money in the Bank. Instead, Taney put the money into state banks. These became known as *pet banks* because Taney and his friends owned shares in many of them. The loss of federal money crippled the Bank of the United States. When the Bank's charter ran out in 1836, Jackson's victory was complete.

═══ **SECTION REVIEW** ═══

1. **Define:** spoils system, kitchen cabinet, pet bank.
2. (a) What were the benefits of the spoils system? (b) What were its drawbacks?
3. Why did President Jackson dislike the Bank of the United States?
4. How did Clay and Webster make an election issue of the Bank?
5. **What Do You Think?** How do you think Andrew Jackson's background helped make him a strong President?

# 3 Tests of Strength

### Read to Learn

★ How did a high tariff cause a crisis in 1832?

★ Why were Native Americans forced off their land?

★ How did life become more democratic in the 1820s?

★ What do these words mean: nullification, states' rights, secede, discrimination?

The fight over the Bank increased Jackson's support among the people. By using the veto, Jackson showed that he was a strong President. In other tests of strength, Jackson took actions that made the office of the President more powerful.

## Debate Over Tariffs

Soon after Jackson won reelection in 1832, he faced another major crisis. The root of the crisis was a tariff bill passed by Congress in 1828. It was the highest tariff ever made law. Southerners called it the *Tariff of Abominations.* An abomination is something that is hated.

Like earlier tariffs, the tariff of 1828 helped manufacturers in the North by making European imports more expensive than American-made goods. (See page 279.) But the tariff hurt Southerners. They exported cotton to Europe and bought European-made goods in return. High tariffs made these imported goods more expensive for Southerners.

**Calhoun defends states' rights.** John C. Calhoun led the South's fight against the tariff. He used an idea Thomas Jefferson had developed for the Kentucky and Virginia resolutions. (See page 236.) Like Jefferson, Calhoun argued that a state had the right to cancel a federal law it considered unconstitutional. The idea of declaring a federal law illegal is called *nullification.*

Calhoun raised a serious issue. Did the states have the right to limit the power of the federal government? Or did the federal government have final say? Calhoun supported *states' rights,* the right of the states to limit the power of the federal government.

**Webster takes the floor.** Daniel Webster took a different position. In 1830, he attacked the idea of nullification on the Senate floor. If states had the right to nullify federal laws, he declared, the nation would be ripped apart. At the end of a long speech, his words rang out clearly: "Liberty and Union, now and forever, one and inseparable."

**A challenge to Jackson.** Many Southerners hoped that President Jackson would speak out for states' rights. After all, he was born in the South and lived in the West. In both sections, support for states' rights was strong. Also, Calhoun was Jackson's Vice President.

In 1830, Jackson and Calhoun attended a dinner party sponsored by southern congressmen. Several congressmen made toasts in favor of states' rights. Finally, it was Jackson's turn to make a toast. Everyone fell silent. Old Hickory raised his glass and turned to face Calhoun, the leading spokesman for states' rights. Jackson looked his Vice President in the eye and said, "Our Union—it must be preserved!"

The drama continued as Calhoun raised his glass. "The Union—next to our liberty, the most dear," he replied. The challenge was clear. Calhoun meant that the liberty of a state was more important than saving the Union.

The debate between supporters of states' rights and defenders of the Union would rage on for years. Because he disagreed with Jackson, Calhoun eventually resigned the office of Vice President. He then was elected senator from South Carolina.

## The Nullification Crisis

In 1832, the debate over states' rights heated up when Congress passed a new tariff. South Carolina responded by passing the Nullification Act. It declared that the tariffs of 1828 and 1832 were illegal. At the same time, the state prepared to defend itself. It threatened to *secede,* or withdraw, from the Union if challenged.

Jackson was furious when he heard the news from South Carolina. He said in private, "If one drop of blood be shed there in defiance of the laws of the United States, I will hang the first man of them I can get my hands on to the first tree I can find." Officially, the President was cooler. He supported a compromise tariff bill that Henry Clay suggested. The bill called for lower tariffs. At the same time, Jackson got Congress to pass a force bill. It allowed him to use the army, if necessary, to enforce the law.

Jackson's firm stand had its effect. No other state came forward to support South Carolina. Calhoun gave in and agreed to Clay's compromise tariff. South Carolina repealed the Nullification Act. Because of the President's

The determination of young John C. Calhoun shows clearly in this painting. When Calhoun entered Congress in 1812, fellow congressmen called him "the young Hercules." Hercules was a hero in Greek mythology who was famous for his superhuman strength.

strong leadership, the *Nullification Crisis* passed. Yet, troubling differences remained between the North and South. They would surface again in the years ahead.

## Tragedy for Native Americans

Jackson's stand on another issue had tragic results for Native Americans. Since Europeans first arrived in North America, they had steadily pushed Native Americans off the land. From New York to Florida, Indians were forced to move west. Indian leaders like Pontiac and Tecumseh tried to stop settlers from invading their lands. But their efforts ended in defeat.

**The Southeast Indians.** By the 1820s, only about 125,000 Indians still lived east of the Mississippi. Most belonged to the Creek, Chickasaw, Cherokee, Choctaw, and Seminole nations. The people of these five nations lived in the Southeast. Many had adopted the customs of white settlers. The Cherokees, for example, wrote their own constitution and published a newspaper.

Indians like the Cherokees wanted to live in peace with their white neighbors. But the rich land they owned in the Southeast was ideal for growing cotton. Land-hungry settlers wanted the land for themselves. President Jackson sympathized with the settlers. He believed that all Indians should move west of the Mississippi River.

**The Supreme Court rules.** Soon after Jackson took office, the state of Georgia claimed the right to seize Cherokee lands. The Cherokees went to court to defend their land. They signed a treaty with the federal government that protected their property. Therefore, they argued, Georgia did not have the right to take the land away. The Cherokee case reached the Supreme Court. Chief Justice John Marshall upheld the right of the Cherokees to keep their land.

### Sequoyah

Sequoyah (sih ᴋᴡᴏɪ uh), a Cherokee born in Tennessee, was a skilled hunter and trapper. After an accident crippled him, he worked for 12 years to create a written alphabet for his people. The alphabet had 86 symbols and used Greek, English, and Hebrew letters. In the 1820s, Cherokee children learned to read and write using Sequoyah's letters. The Cherokees also used his alphabet to write a constitution.

This time, President Jackson defended states' rights. He said that the federal government could not stop Georgia from moving the Indians. "John Marshall has made his decision," Jackson is reported to have said. "Now let him enforce it." The President then refused to use federal power to protect the Cherokees.

**Indian Removal Act.** Since the Supreme Court ruling was not enforced, the Indians had no protection. In 1830, Congress passed the *Indian Removal Act.* It stated that Native Americans had to move west of the Mississippi.

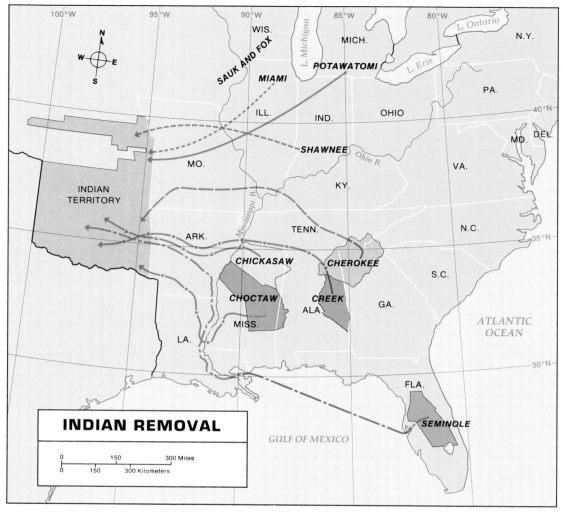

INDIAN REMOVAL

| 0 | 150 | 300 Miles |
| 0 | 150 | 300 Kilometers |

MAP SKILL In the 1830s, thousands of southeastern Indians were forced to march along the Trail of Tears. They had to move into the Indian Territory west of the Mississippi River. Besides the five southeastern nations, what other Indian peoples were forced to move west?

Most Americans had heard that the land there was a vast desert. So they did not mind turning the area over to the Indians.

## The Trail of Tears

The Cherokees and other Indian nations did not want to move west. But they had no choice. Between 1835 and 1838, the United States army forced them to leave at gunpoint. Their long, sad journey west became known as the *Trail of Tears.* One eyewitness described the scene:

The Cherokees are nearly all prisoners. They had been dragged from their homes and encamped at the forts and military places, all over the nation. In Georgia especially, multitudes were allowed no time to take anything with them except the clothes they had on. . . . The property of many has been taken and sold before their eyes for almost nothing.

The Indians marched hundreds of miles to lands they had never seen before. (See the map above.) They had little food and no shelter. Many children and older people perished. In all, about one quarter of the Indians died.

The Seminole Indians in Florida fought fiercely against removal. They were led by Chief Osceola. The Seminoles battled the United States army from 1835 to 1842. In the end, they were defeated. But the *Seminole War* was the costliest battle the United States fought to gain Indian lands. By 1844, only a few thousand Indians were left east of the Mississippi River.

## A Growing Spirit of Equality

During Jackson's two terms in the White House, changes begun earlier came into full swing. You have read how politics became more democratic in the 1820s. The democratic spirit also grew stronger in other ways. Americans talked and acted with a new spirit of equality.

In America, servants expected to be treated as equals. Butlers and maids refused to be called with bells, as was done in Europe. In fact, they did not like to be called servants at all. One coach driver complained that his employer "had had private meals every day and not asked him to the table." Americans were so keen on equality that Europeans found them downright rude.

The spirit of equality left out many Americans, however. The Indian Removal Act denied the most basic rights to Native Americans. Women could not vote or hold office. Their right to own property was limited. Black Americans actually lost rights in the 1820s. In both the North and South, free blacks faced growing discrimination, as you will read in Chapter 15. *Discrimination* is a policy or an attitude that denies equal rights to certain people. Despite the limits on equality, democracy grew during the Age of Jackson.

This painting by Mary Ann Thompson shows Cherokees on the Trail of Tears. More than 4,000 Cherokees died from freezing weather, disease, and cruel treatment on the long march west.

1. **Locate:** South Carolina, Georgia, Mississippi River.
2. **Define:** nullification, states' rights, secede, discrimination.
3. (a) What section of the country benefited most from high tariffs? (b) What section opposed high tariffs?
4. (a) Why did white settlers want to take over Indian lands in the Southeast? (b) How did the Cherokees try to defend their land?
5. **What Do You Think?** What do you think Andrew Jackson would have done if South Carolina had tried to secede from the United States during the Nullification Crisis?

# 4 Jackson's Successors

### Read to Learn
★ What caused the Panic of 1837?
★ How did William Henry Harrison become President?
★ What problems did John Tyler have as President?

Andrew Jackson did not run again in 1836. But he helped Vice President Martin Van Buren to follow him into the White House. When Van Buren took the oath of office, Jackson stood at his side. The crowd turned its gaze to the outgoing President, not Van Buren. As Old Hickory stepped down from the platform, a rousing cheer rose from the crowd. In that roar, the people expressed their loyalty to Andrew Jackson.

## The Panic of 1837

As Jackson's chosen successor, Martin Van Buren rode into office on a wave of popular support. But within two months of taking office, Van Buren faced the worst economic crisis the nation had known. The crisis is called the *Panic of 1837.*

**Causes.** The Panic of 1837 came about for several reasons. During the 1830s, the government sold millions of acres of public land in the West. Farmers bought some land, but speculators bought even more.

To pay for the land, speculators borrowed money from state banks, especially western banks. There was no national bank to restrict lending. As a result, state banks printed more and more paper money to meet the demand for loans. Often, the paper money was not backed by gold or silver.

In 1836, President Jackson had become alarmed at the wild speculation in land. To slow it down, he ordered that anyone buying public land had to pay with gold or silver, not with paper money. Speculators and others went to the state banks to exchange their paper money for gold and silver. But they found that the banks did not have gold and silver.

**Hard times.** Very quickly, the panic began. More and more people hurried to banks to try to get gold and silver for their paper money. In New York, one bank "was jammed with depositors crying 'Pay, pay!'" a witness said. Hundreds of banks failed. They had to lock their doors because they could not meet the demand.

About the same time, the price of cotton fell because of an oversupply. Cotton planters could not repay their bank loans. This caused more banks to fail. As a result, business slowed, and the nation moved into an economic depression.

The depression lasted three years. At its height, 90 percent of the nation's factories were closed. Thousands of people were thrown out of work. In some cities, hungry people broke into warehouses and stole food.

It was easy for people to blame Van Buren for the Panic of 1837. The President did not believe that the government should interfere with business, even during a depression. So Van Buren did little to ease the impact of the Panic. He did cut back expenses at the White House. When he entertained visitors, they were served simple dinners. But as the depression dragged on, Van Buren became less popular.

## Tippecanoe and Tyler Too

Even though Van Buren lost support, the Democrats nominated him to carry the party banner in 1840. The Whigs chose William Henry Harrison of Ohio. Harrison was well known as the hero of the Battle of Tippecanoe. (See page 259.) The Whigs named John Tyler as their candidate for Vice President. They used "Tippecanoe and Tyler too" as their campaign slogan.

The Whigs had learned a lot about campaigning from their old foe, Andrew Jackson. They wanted to win the votes of common people. So they presented Harrison as a simple Ohio farmer who lived in a log cabin. In fact, he came from a wealthy and powerful Virginia family. His father had been governor of Virginia and a signer of the Declaration of Independence.

Harrison won easily and forced the Democrats out of the White House for the first time in 12 years. The Whigs arrived in Washington with a clear-cut program. They wanted to set up a new Bank of the United States. They planned to spend federal money for roads, canals, and other improvements. And they wanted a high tariff. But the Whigs' hopes were soon dashed. After less than a month in office, President Harrison died of pneumonia.

John Tyler was the first Vice President to succeed a President who died in office. As President, his actions shocked and disappointed leaders of the Whig Party. Tyler had once been a

This campaign banner shows William Henry Harrison's log cabin symbol. During the campaign, Whigs tried new ways to stir up public support for their candidate. They held huge outdoor meetings and built log cabins in public places to get people to vote for Harrison.

Democrat. He disagreed with the Whigs on almost every issue. When Whigs in Congress passed a bill to recharter the Bank of the United States, Tyler vetoed it.

As a result, Tyler's whole cabinet resigned, except for Daniel Webster. The Whigs threw Tyler out of their party. Democrats were delighted with the Whigs' problem. "Tyler is heartily despised by everyone," reported one observer. "He has no influence at all." With few supporters, Tyler did little during his years in office.

### SECTION REVIEW

1. What did President Jackson do to stop land speculation in 1836?
2. What were the causes of the Panic of 1837?
3. How did the Whigs try to win the votes of common people in 1840?
4. Why were Whigs disappointed with John Tyler?
5. **What Do You Think?** What do you think President Van Buren could have done to ease the Panic of 1837?

# Chapter 13 Review

 **Summary**

In the 1820s, common people began to play a new role in government. In 1824, their choice for President was Andrew Jackson. Jackson was a Tennessee frontiersman, self-taught and self-made.

Jackson was not elected President until 1828. He took bold actions on several issues. Jackson undermined the national Bank. He kept South Carolina in the Union. And he allowed Indian removal despite a Supreme Court ruling against it.

Jackson's successor, Martin Van Buren, lost support because of the Panic of 1837. In 1840, Van Buren was beaten by William Henry Harrison. Harrison died after a month in office, leaving John Tyler to serve out an uneventful term.

 **Reviewing the Facts**

**Key Terms.** Match each term in Column 1 with the correct definition in Column 2.

**Column 1**
1. suffrage
2. caucus
3. states' rights
4. secede
5. discrimination

**Column 2**
a. private meeting to choose a candidate
b. right to vote
c. right of states to limit federal power
d. policy or attitude that denies equal rights to some people
e. withdraw

**Key People, Events, and Ideas.** Identify each of the following.

1. John Quincy Adams
2. Henry Clay
3. Whig
4. Democrat
5. Old Hickory

6. John C. Calhoun
7. Tariff of Abominations
8. Daniel Webster
9. Nullification Crisis
10. Indian Removal Act

11. Trail of Tears
12. Osceola
13. Seminole War
14. Martin Van Buren
15. Panic of 1837

 **Chapter Checkup**

1. (a) Describe President John Quincy Adams' plans for national growth. (b) Were his plans carried out? Explain.

2. Why were there many more voters in 1828 than in 1824?

3. (a) What political parties grew in the 1820s? (b) Who supported each party?

4. (a) What is a nominating convention? (b) How is it more democratic than a caucus?

5. What did each of the following do during the struggle over the Bank: (a) Nicholas Biddle; (b) Henry Clay; (c) Andrew Jackson.

6. (a) Why did South Carolina try to nullify the tariffs of 1828 and 1832? (b) How did President Jackson respond?

7. (a) Why did settlers want to force Indians to move west? (b) How did Andrew Jackson help them achieve their goal?

8. (a) Describe the causes of the Panic of 1837. (b) How did it affect the 1840 presidential election?

## ★ Thinking About History ★

1. **Relating past to present.** European visitors to the United States in the 1830s commented on the social and political equality of the people. (a) What groups of Americans gained more rights in the 1820s? (b) What groups of Americans have gained more rights since then?

2. **Expressing an opinion.** If Congress had approved the roads, canals, and other improvements planned by John Quincy Adams, the economy of the nation would have grown faster. Do you agree or disagree with this statement? Explain.

3. **Understanding the economy.** When the Bank of the United States limited lending in the 1820s, people in the West and South were hurt most. Why did people living near the frontier need to borrow money?

4. **Learning about citizenship.** During the Age of Jackson, how did common people play a more important role than ever before in American politics?

## ★ Using Your Skills ★

1. **Recognizing points of view.** Review Skill Lesson 5 on page 116. Then reread "The People's President" on page 294. (a) Do you think the first eyewitness supported Jackson? Why or why not? (b) Do you think the second eyewitness supported Jackson? Explain.

2. **Comparing.** Draw a chart with two columns and three rows. Label the columns John Quincy Adams and Andrew Jackson. Label the rows Family, Education, and Experience in Public Life. Fill out the chart. (a) What were the differences between Jackson and Adams? (b) How do the differences show the changes in American politics in the 1820s?

3. **Using a painting as a primary source.** Look at the painting on page 291. (a) What are the people in the picture getting ready to do? (b) What might the three men at right be talking about? (c) What groups of Americans are not shown in the painting? Why not?

4. **Placing events in time.** Study the time line on page 290. (a) When was the Tariff of Abominations passed? (b) When did South Carolina pass the Nullification Act? (c) What is the relationship between the two events?

## ★ More to Do ★

1. **Writing a letter.** Imagine that you are John C. Calhoun after the toast incident described on page 300. Write a letter of resignation to President Jackson explaining why you no longer wish to serve as his Vice President.

2. **Preparing a newspaper editorial.** Imagine that you are the editor of a Cherokee newspaper during the early 1830s. Write an editorial commenting on passage of the Indian Removal Act by Congress. Include a headline for your editorial.

3. **Exploring local history.** On an outline map of your state, mark the location of any cities, towns, monuments, parks, and other places named in memory of Andrew Jackson.

CHAPTER

# 14

# Westward Ho! (1820–1860)

## Chapter Outline

**1** Oregon Country
**2** The Lone Star Republic
**3** Looking Toward the West
**4** War With Mexico
**5** From Sea to Shining Sea
Readings, page 535

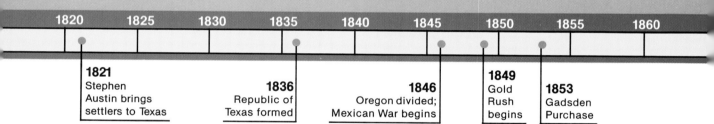

| 1820 | 1825 | 1830 | 1835 | 1840 | 1845 | 1850 | 1855 | 1860 |

**1821**
Stephen Austin brings settlers to Texas

**1836**
Republic of Texas formed

**1846**
Oregon divided; Mexican War begins

**1849**
Gold Rush begins

**1853**
Gadsden Purchase

## About This Chapter

From its beginning, America has been a nation on the move. The country began as a group of small colonies dotting the east coast. As these colonies grew, they slowly spread inland. After the Revolution, many Americans moved across the Appalachians. By the 1830s, they had carved up the land east of the Mississippi River.

Settlers continued to push west in the 1840s. They opened up lands in the West and the Southwest. In 1846, a New York newspaper editor named Horace Greeley published the article "To Aspiring Young Men." In it, Greeley offered this advice to young people: "If you have no family or friends to aid you . . . turn your face to the great West and there build up your home and fortune."

Greeley's advice exactly suited the spirit of the times. Soon, his statement was boiled down to the famous message "Go west, young man." And thousands upon thousands of American men and women rallied to the cry "Westward Ho!"

As more Americans moved west, the idea grew that the United States should expand all the way to the Pacific Ocean. During the 1840s, the nation added huge stretches of land to its area. Oregon, California, New Mexico, and Texas all became part of the United States. By 1850, the country reached from sea to sea.

Study the time line above. How long after Stephen Austin first led settlers into Texas did Texans establish the Republic of Texas?

—**308**—

In the mid-1800s, thousands of Americans headed west to find new opportunities. Here, pioneer families bed down after a long day on the trail.

# 1 Oregon Country

## Read to Learn

★ Who were the first American settlers in Oregon Country?
★ Why did Oregon fever sweep the United States?
★ What hardships did travelers on the Oregon Trail face?
★ What does this word mean: rendezvous?

By the 1820s, settlers had filled in much of the land east of the Mississippi. Americans continued to move west. However, few settled on the Great Plains between the Mississippi and the Rockies. Instead, they were drawn to lands farther west.

## Beyond the Rockies

In the early 1800s, people began to hear about a land beyond the Rocky Mountains called Oregon Country. At that time, *Oregon Country* meant the whole Pacific Northwest plus part of the Intermountain region and the Rockies. Today, this land includes the states of Oregon, Washington, Idaho, and parts of Montana and Canada. (See the map on page 310.)

**Land and climate.** The area once called Oregon Country has a varied climate and geography. Along the Pacific Coast, the land is fertile and gets lots of rain. Early white settlers found fine

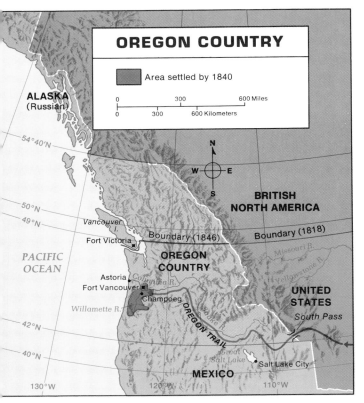

## OREGON COUNTRY

Area settled by 1840

ALASKA
(Russian)

54°40'N

50°N
49°N

PACIFIC
OCEAN

Vancouver I.
Fort Victoria
Boundary (1846)
Boundary (1818)

BRITISH
NORTH AMERICA

OREGON
COUNTRY

Astoria
Fort Vancouver
Champoeg
Willamette R.

42°N

40°N

Missouri R.
Yellowstone R.

UNITED
STATES

South Pass

OREGON TRAIL

Great
Salt Lake
Salt Lake City

MEXICO

130°W
120°W
110°W

**MAP SKILL** Oregon Country was the first area in the Far West to draw settlers from the United States. What two rivers did the Oregon Trail follow as it wound into Oregon Country?

farmland in the Willamette River valley and the lowlands around Puget Sound. Also, the Pacific Ocean keeps temperatures mild all year. Farther inland is a coastal mountain range that has dense forests. In the 1800s, these forests held bears and beavers that lured trappers to the West.

Between the coastal mountains and the Rockies is a high plateau. This Intermountain region is much drier than the coast and has scattered desert areas. Temperatures are also more extreme. At the eastern edge of Oregon Country were the Rocky Mountains. There, trappers found beavers and other valuable animals.

**Conflicting claims.** Several countries claimed Oregon in the early 1800s: the United States, Great Britain, Spain, and Russia. They paid

no attention to the rights of the Indians in Oregon.

The United States based its claim on the voyage of Robert Gray. A sea captain from Boston, Gray visited the coast of Oregon and named the Columbia River in 1792. The journey of Lewis and Clark through Oregon further supported American claims to the land.

John Jacob Astor, an American fur trader, sent a shipload of men and supplies around South America to Oregon in 1811. They built the town of Astoria at the mouth of the Columbia River. Astor's fur traders stayed only a short time, but they gave Americans another claim to Oregon.

The British claim to Oregon dated back to a visit by Sir Francis Drake in 1577. In the early 1800s, many British fur traders roamed Oregon. Britain also had Fort Vancouver, the only permanent outpost in Oregon. (See the map at left.)

In 1818, the United States and Britain agreed to occupy Oregon jointly. Citizens of both nations would have equal rights in Oregon. Spain and Russia had few settlers in the area. So they dropped their claims to Oregon.

### Mountain Men

In the early 1800s, a few hardy trappers followed Indian trails across the Rockies into Oregon. They wandered through the area, trapping furs and living off the land. The tough, lone adventurers were called *Mountain Men.*

Mountain Men were a colorful group. They dressed in shirts and trousers made of leather. Porcupine quills decorated their shirts. Around their neck hung a "possibles sack." Inside the sack were a pipe, some tobacco, a mold to make bullets, and other useful items.

**Living in the wild.** When game was plentiful, the trappers gorged themselves with food. They ate raw buffalo liver and gnawed buffalo steaks roasted over an open fire. During lean times, the trappers lived off the land as well as they could. "I have held my hands in an anthill until they were covered with ants, then greedily licked them off," recalled one Mountain Man. During harsh winters, Mountain Men often lived with Indians. In fact, they learned many of their survival methods from Indians.

In their hunt for furs, Mountain Men made many useful discoveries. Jedediah Smith found South Pass in Wyoming in 1823. This broad plateau offered an easy way to cross the Rocky Mountains. Manuel Lisa, a Spanish American trapper, led a trip up the Missouri River in 1807. He founded Fort Manuel, the first outpost on the upper Missouri.

**The rendezvous.** Through the fall and spring, Mountain Men tended their traps. In July, they came out of the wilderness. They met fur traders at a place chosen the year before, called the *rendezvous* (RAHN day voo), or get-together.

The rendezvous was a wild event. One Mountain Man described it as a time of "mirth, songs, dancing, shouting, trading, running, jumping, singing, racing, target-shooting, yarns, [and] frolic." After the first day, the Mountain Men bargained with the fur traders. Beaver hats were popular in the East and in Europe, so Mountain Men got a good price for their furs. But the traders charged high prices for the flour, bullets, and other supplies they hauled to the rendezvous.

In the late 1830s, the fur trade declined. Trappers killed so many beavers that the animals became scarce. Also, beaver hats went out of fashion. However, Mountain Men took on a new job—leading settlers across the rugged trails into Oregon.

## Early Settlers in Oregon

The first white Americans to build permanent homes in Oregon were missionaries. Marcus and Narcissa Whitman were among the first missionaries

### AMERICANS WHO DARED

### James Beckwourth

James Beckwourth was one of the best-known Mountain Men. Beckwourth, the son of a Virginia slave, headed west to escape slavery. He discovered a pass through the Sierra Nevada into California that was named for him. In 1856, Beckwourth added to his own legend by publishing his life story.

to reach Oregon. They had heard that Indians in Oregon were eager to accept Christianity. After the Whitmans married in 1836, their honeymoon was the seven-month journey to Oregon. Narcissa Whitman was one of the first white women to cross the Rocky Mountains.

The Whitmans built their mission near the Columbia River and began to work with the Cayuse (KĪ oos) Indians. Marcus Whitman was a doctor. Narcissa Whitman set up a mission school. Soon, other missionaries and settlers joined the Whitmans. As more settlers arrived and took over Indian lands, trouble arose with the Cayuses. Even worse, settlers brought diseases that often killed the Indians.

Narcissa Whitman, shown here, rejoiced when she and her husband finally reached the Columbia River valley in Oregon Country. "The beauty of this extensive valley," she wrote, "at this hour of twilight was enchanting and [turned] my mind from the fatigue under which I was laboring."

In 1847, tragedy struck the Whitmans' mission. An outbreak of measles among the settlers spread to the Cayuses. Dr. Whitman tended both white and Indian children, but many Cayuse children died. The angry Cayuses blamed the settlers for the disease. A band of Cayuses attacked the mission, killing the Whitmans and 12 others.

## The Oregon Trail

Despite the Whitmans' death, other bold pioneers set out on the long trek to Oregon. News about Oregon began to trickle back to the United States. There, farmers marvelled at stories of wheat that grew taller than a man and Oregon turnips five feet around. Stories like these touched off an outbreak of Oregon fever.

Oregon fever spread quickly. Soon, the trails west were clogged with pioneers. Beginning in 1843, wagon trains left every spring for Oregon. The route taken by these settlers was called the *Oregon Trail.* (See the map on page 320.)

Families planning to go west met at Independence, Missouri, in the early spring. Because most families had cattle or other animals, they camped outside town. When enough families had gathered, they formed a wagon train. Each wagon train elected leaders to make decisions along the trail.

## Life on the Trail

Wagon trains left Independence in May. The pioneers traveled quickly to reach Oregon before early October, when snow began to fall in the mountains. This meant that they had to cover 2,000 miles (3,200 km) on foot in 5 months. In the 1840s, traveling 15 miles a day was considered good time.

**Daily routine.** Families adapted quickly to life on the trail. At dawn, everyone woke to a bugle blast. Each person had a job to do. Young girls helped their mothers prepare breakfast. Men and boys harnessed the horses or oxen. By 6:00 A.M., the cry of "Wagons ho!" rang out on the plains.

The pioneers made a brief stop at noon for lunch. Then, they returned to the trail until 6:00 or 7:00 P.M. At night, the wagons were pulled in a circle. This kept the cattle from wandering off to find grass.

Pioneers often brought too much equipment. It was dangerous to ford streams and cross mountains with heavy wagons. To lighten the wagons, travelers threw away gear. Soon, the trails were littered with junk.

One traveler wrote home that the Oregon Trail was strewn with "large blacksmiths' anvils, ploughs, large grind-stones, baking ovens, kegs, barrels, harness, [and] clothing." Some

A diary is often a useful primary source because it tells you what the writer saw, heard, said, thought, and felt. It gives you firsthand information about people, places, and events. Because diaries are private, writers often say what they honestly think.

The excerpts below are from a diary kept by Amelia Stewart Knight. With her husband and children, she traveled the Oregon Trail in 1853. Her diary tells about the hardships the family faced on their way to a new life in Oregon.

1. **Identify the primary source.** (a) Who wrote the diary? (b) Under what conditions was it written? (c) Why do you think the writer wrote it?

2. **Analyze the information in the primary source.** Study the diary for information about how the writer lived.

(a) What does Knight say about hardships on the Oregon Trail? (b) Describe the geography of the area the Knight family traveled through. (c) What chores did Amelia Knight do? (d) What chores did the children do?

3. **Draw conclusions about the writer's point of view.** Decide how the writer felt about making the overland journey west. (a) How do you think Amelia Knight felt about the hardships of the journey? (b) How might keeping the diary have helped her face these hardships? (c) What personal qualities did a person need to make the journey? (d) Study the painting on page 309. What activities described in the diary can you see in the painting? (e) What other activities does the painting show?

---

 **Amelia Stewart Knight's Diary**

*Monday, April 18th*   Cold; breaking fast the first thing; very disagreeable weather; wind east cold and rainy, no fire. We are on a very large prairie, no timber to be seen as far as the eye can reach. Evening—Have crossed several bad streams today, and more than once have been stuck in the mud.

*Saturday, April 23rd*   Still in camp, it rained hard all night, and blew a hurricane almost. All the tents were blown down, and some wagons capsized. Evening—It has been raining hard all day; everything is wet and muddy. One of the oxen missing; the boys have been hunting him all day. (Dreary times, wet and muddy, and crowded in the tent, cold and wet and uncomfortable in the wagon. No place for the poor children.) I have been busy cooking, roasting coffee, etc. today, and have come into the wagon to write this and make our bed.

*Friday, May 6th*   We passed a train of wagons on their way back, the head man had drowned a few days before, in a river called the Elkhorn, while getting some cattle across. With sadness and pity I passed those who a few days before had been well and happy as ourselves.

*Friday, August 19th*   After looking in vain for water, we were about to give up, when husband came across a company of friendly Cayuse Indians, who showed him where to find water. The men and boys have driven the cattle down to water and I am waiting to get supper. We bought a few potatoes from an Indian, which will be a treat for our supper.

This painting shows a wagon train on the Oregon Trail fording the Platte River. At times, so many travelers crowded the trails west that the lead wagon of one train was just a few yards behind the last wagon in the train ahead.

travelers changed their dirty clothes for clean sets they found beside the trail. Pioneers also used the "plains library." They picked up a book, read it, and then left it beside the trail for later travelers to read.

**Hardships.** The long journey held many dangers. During the spring rains, travelers risked their lives floating wagons across swollen rivers. In the summer, they faced blistering heat on the plains. In the fall, they ran into early snow that blocked passes through the mountains. The greatest danger was illness. Cholera (KAHL er uh) and other diseases wiped out whole wagon trains.

**Indians.** As they moved west toward the Rockies, pioneers saw Indians often. At times, Indians attacked the whites trespassing on their land. More often, Indians traded with the travelers. Some pioneers depended on food they bought from Indians. One pioneer wrote: "Whenever we camp near any Indian village, we are no sooner stopped than a whole crowd may be seen coming galloping into our camp. The squaws do all the swapping."

Despite the hardships of the trip, more than 50,000 people reached Oregon between 1840 and 1860. Their wagon wheels cut so deeply into the plains that the ruts can still be seen today.

By the 1840s, Americans greatly outnumbered the British in Oregon. In 1818, the two nations had agreed to occupy Oregon jointly. However, many Americans began to feel that Oregon should be part of the United States. Arguments over the future of Oregon nearly led to war with Britain.

1. **Locate:** Oregon Country, Willamette River, Oregon Trail, Independence, South Pass.
2. **Define:** rendezvous.
3. What were Mountain Men looking for in the West?

4. Who were the first white Americans to build permanent homes in Oregon?
5. (a) Why did pioneers begin moving to Oregon Country? (b) What hardships did they face along the way?
6. **What Do You Think?** What qualities do you think Mountain Men needed to survive in the wilderness?

# 2 The Lone Star Republic

### Read to Learn
★ Who were the first settlers from the United States in Texas?
★ How did Texans win independence?
★ What problems did the Republic of Texas face?
★ What does this word mean: annex?

Even before pioneers began moving west along the Oregon Trail, other Americans were pushing into the Southwest. In the 1820s and 1830s, Americans settled on the fertile plains of central and southern Texas.

## Americans Settle in Texas

Since the early 1800s, American farmers had looked eagerly at Spanish lands in the Southwest. But Spain refused to let Americans settle in Texas until 1820. That year, Spain gave Moses Austin a land grant in Texas. But Austin died before he could set up a colony. His son, Stephen Austin, took up the work.

In 1821, Mexico gained its independence from Spain (see page 281). The new nation gladly let Stephen Austin lead settlers into Texas, its northern province. Only about 4,000 Mexicans lived in Texas. The Mexican government thought that the Americans would help develop the land. It also hoped that American settlers would help control Indian attacks.

Thousands of Indians lived in Texas. They included hunters such as the Comanches and Apaches as well as the Pueblos and other farming people. For 200 years, Spanish missionaries had tried to convert the Indians to Christianity. But they had little success. In fact, some Indian groups fiercely resisted the missionaries.

Mexico granted Austin and each settler 640 acres of land. The settlers agreed to become citizens of Mexico, obey its laws, and worship in the Catholic Church. Austin carefully chose 300 families to settle in Texas. He looked for hard-working people who could take care of themselves. In 1821, they began moving to Texas. Under Austin's wise leadership, the colony grew. By 1830, the number of Americans in Texas had reached 20,000.

Parts of Texas were ideal for cattle raising. Other parts had land good for growing cotton. Many Americans moved to Texas from the South. Some built large cotton plantations and brought in thousands of slaves to work the land.

## Problems With Mexico

Stephen Austin and his settlers had agreed to become Mexican citizens and Catholics. But other Americans flooding into Texas were Protestants. They spoke only a few words of Spanish, the

Stephen Austin seemed an unlikely pioneer. A sensitive and shy man, Austin enjoyed playing the flute and reading. But he was a man of action, too. In this painting, Austin reacts to news from a scout about a battle between Indians and settlers.

official language of Mexico, and they felt no loyalty to Mexico. Problems soon developed between settlers and the Mexican government.

In 1830, Mexico passed a law forbidding any more Americans to move to Texas. Mexico feared that the Americans wanted to make Texas part of the United States. In fact, the United States had already tried to buy Texas from Mexico.

The Mexican government also decided to make settlers obey laws that had been ignored for years. One law outlawed slavery in Texas. Another required Texans to worship in the Catholic Church. Texans resented the laws and the Mexican troops who came north to enforce them.

In 1832, General Antonio López de Santa Anna rose to power in Mexico. Two years later, Santa Anna threw out the Mexican constitution. Americans feared that Santa Anna might try to drive them out of Texas.

## The Fight for Independence

Americans in Texas believed that the time for action had come. In October 1835, Texans in the town of Gonzales (gon ZAH lehs) fought with Mexican troops. The Texans won. (See the map on page 317.) The fight at Gonzales is called "the Lexington of Texas," after the battle that began the American Revolution.

Two months after Gonzales, Texans forced Mexican troops out of San Antonio. News of the two Mexican defeats angered General Santa Anna. He marched north at the head of a large army, determined to crush the rebellion in Texas.

On March 2, 1836, Texans met in Washington-on-the-Brazos (BRAH zohs). There they declared their independence from Mexico. Texans set up the *Republic of Texas* and asked Sam Houston to command the army. Houston's army was small and untrained. So he decided to fall back as Santa Anna advanced.

**The Alamo.** At the same time that Texans were declaring their independence, a heroic fight was raging in San Antonio. There, 188 Texans, including both Americans and Mexicans, were trying to hold off Santa Anna's army. They took cover in the *Alamo,* an old Spanish mission. Thousands of Mexican troops surrounded the Alamo.

For 12 days, the Mexicans shelled the Alamo. The outnumbered Texans held out bravely. At last, on March 6, the Mexicans launched an all-out attack. Mexican soldiers poured over the walls of the old mission. In furious hand-to-hand fighting, all the defenders died. But hundreds of Mexican soldiers were killed in the battle. And the defenders of the Alamo had given Sam Houston time to organize his army. (See page 318.)

**Victory.** The slaughter at the Alamo both angered and inspired Texans. It brought a flood of volunteers into Sam Houston's army. They came from the United States as well as from Texas.

On April 21, 1836, Houston decided that the moment to attack had come. Santa Anna's army was camped near the San Jacinto (jeh SEEN toh) River. Texans charged into the Mexican camp, crying "Remember the Alamo!"

The ***Battle of San Jacinto*** lasted only 15 minutes. Texans killed 630 Mexicans and captured 700 more. The next day, Texans captured Santa Anna himself. They forced him to sign a treaty granting Texas its independence.

## The Republic of Texas

At the Battle of San Jacinto, Texans carried a flag with a single white star. After the battle, Texans began calling their nation the ***Lone Star Republic.*** They drew up a constitution like that of the United States and elected Sam Houston president.

**MAP SKILL** The Texas war of independence was brief but bloody. Three weeks after the Alamo defenders died, General Urrea of Mexico executed 300 Texans captured at Goliad. How do you think the events at the Alamo and Goliad affected Texans? Where did Texans finally defeat and capture General Santa Anna?

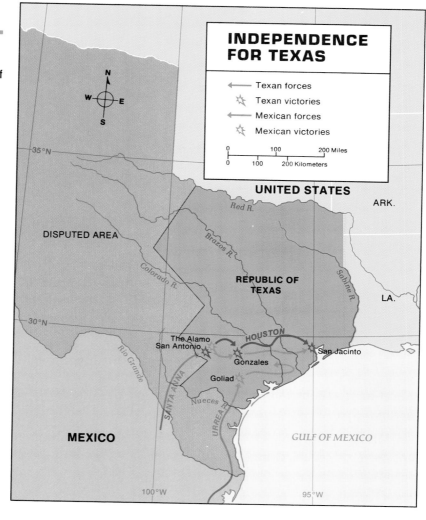

**INDEPENDENCE FOR TEXAS**

- ← Texan forces
- ☆ Texan victories
- ← Mexican forces
- ☆ Mexican victories

0    100    200 Miles
0  100   200 Kilometers

UNITED STATES

ARK.

Red R.

DISPUTED AREA

Brazos R.

Colorado R.

REPUBLIC OF TEXAS

Sabine R.

LA.

30°N

35°N

Rio Grande

SANTA ANNA

The Alamo
San Antonio

HOUSTON

Gonzales

San Jacinto

Goliad

URREA

Nueces R.

MEXICO

GULF OF MEXICO

100°W

95°W

William B. Travis commanded the Texans defending the Alamo. The group included the famous frontiersmen Jim Bowie and Davy Crockett as well as several women.

Travis wrote the following letter while he and his troops were trapped inside

the Alamo. He addressed it "To the People of Texas and all Americans in the world." Perhaps Travis realized that the defense of the Alamo would rally both Texans and Americans to fight for Texas independence.

> Fellow citizens and compatriots—I am besieged by a thousand or more of the Mexicans under Santa Anna. I have sustained a continual Bombardment and cannonade for 24 hours and have not lost a man. The enemy has demanded a surrender . . . otherwise the garrison are to be put to the *sword,* if the fort is taken. I have answered the demand with a cannon shot, and our flag still waves proudly from the walls.
>
> I shall never surrender or retreat. . . . I am determined to sustain myself as long as possible and die like a soldier who never forgets what is due to his honor and that of his country.
>
> VICTORY OR DEATH
> William Barret Travis

★ Why do you think the defenders of the Alamo fought to the death?

The new country faced huge problems. First, the government of Mexico did not accept the treaty signed by Santa Anna. Mexicans still considered Texas part of their country. Second, Texas was almost bankrupt. Sam Houston once gave a formal speech dressed in a blanket to show how badly Texas needed money. Most Texans hoped to solve these problems by becoming part of the United States.

In the United States, people were divided about whether to annex Texas. To *annex* means to add on. Southerners favored annexing Texas. Northerners were against it. At issue was slavery. Northerners knew that slave owners lived in Texas. Many Northerners opposed slavery and did not want to annex an area that allowed slavery. President Jackson also worried that annexing Texas would lead to war with Mexico. As a result, the United States refused to annex Texas.

Over the next ten years, the Lone Star Republic survived and prospered under Sam Houston's leadership. During the Panic of 1837, thousands of Americans moved to Texas. They went to find land and start businesses. Settlers from Germany and Switzerland swelled the population. By the 1840s, there were 140,000 people in Texas, including many Mexicans and black Americans.

Both free blacks and slaves had fought for Texas independence. After independence, however, slave owners wanted to drive free blacks out of the country. They claimed that free blacks caused unrest among the slaves. Despite pressure to leave, some free blacks stayed in Texas.

═══ SECTION REVIEW ═══

1. **Locate:** Republic of Texas, Mexico, San Antonio, Alamo, San Jacinto.
2. **Define:** annex.
3. (a) Why did Mexico at first encourage Americans to settle in Texas? (b) Why did Mexico stop allowing Americans to move to Texas?
4. (a) What problems did the Lone Star Republic face? (b) How did Texans hope to solve them?
5. **What Do You Think?** Why do you think events at the Alamo inspired Texans?

# 3 Looking Toward the West

## Read to Learn

★ What were the landforms and climate of the West?
★ Who were the first white settlers in the West?
★ How did the Spanish treat Native Americans in California?
★ What did Americans mean by the term Manifest Destiny?

In the 1840s, Americans began to talk about expanding the nation all the way to the Pacific Ocean. They looked with new interest toward California and the Southwest, both part of Mexico.

## The Southwest

The Southwest was part of Mexico in the 1840s. This huge region was known as the *New Mexico Territory.* It included most of New Mexico and Arizona as well as parts of Nevada, Utah, and Colorado. The capital of the territory was Santa Fe.

**Land and climate.** The Southwest is hot and dry. Thin grasses grow in some parts. Other parts are desert. Before the Spanish came, the Pueblos and Zuñis irrigated the land and farmed it. Other Indians, such as the Apaches and Yumas, were hunters.

A Spanish explorer, Juan de Oñate (oh NAH tay), traveled across New Mexico in 1598. He built the first white settlement at Santa Fe. When more Spanish settlers arrived, they set up huge sheep ranches. A few rich families owned the sheep ranches. Indians tended the herds.

**Santa Fe Trail.** Under the Spanish, Santa Fe became a busy trading town. However, Spain refused to let Americans settle in New Mexico. Only after Mexico won its independence were Americans welcome there.

William Becknell, a businessman and adventurer, was the first American to head for Santa Fe. Becknell set out from St. Louis in 1821, carrying tools and rolls of cloth. He led a group of traders on the long trip across the plains. When they reached Santa Fe, they found Mexicans eager to buy their goods. Other Americans soon followed Becknell's route from Independence to Santa Fe. The route became known as the *Santa Fe Trail.* (Trace the Santa Fe Trail on the map on page 320.)

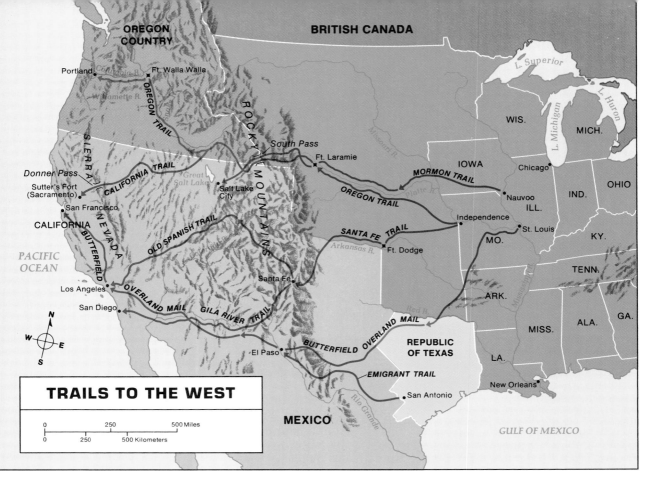

MAP SKILL Americans followed a number of trails to reach the West, as this map shows. Which overland trails ended in cities in California?

## California

Like New Mexico, California was part of Mexico in the early 1840s. Spain had claimed this land 100 years before English colonists built homes in Jamestown. As a result, Spanish culture shaped life in California.

**Land and climate.** California has a dramatic landscape. Two tall mountain ranges slice through the area. One hugs the coast. The other sits inland on the border of Nevada and Arizona. Between these two ranges is California's fertile central valley.

Northern California receives plenty of rain. In the south, water is scarce, and much of the land is desert. California enjoys mild temperatures all year, except in the high mountains.

**Spanish missions.** Spanish soldiers and missionaries built the first permanent European settlements in California. In 1769, Captain Gaspar de Portolá led a group of soldiers and missionaries up the Pacific coast. The chief missionary was Father Junípero Serra (hoo NEE peh roh SEHR rah).

Father Serra built his first mission at San Diego. He went on to build 20 other missions along the California coast. Each mission claimed the surrounding land and soon became self-sufficient. Spanish soldiers built forts near the missions.

**Treatment of Native Americans.** Soldiers forced local Indians to work for the missions. Resistance was limited because the California Indians were peaceful people. Also, they lived in small groups rather than large nations.

At the missions, Indians herded sheep and cattle and tended farmland. In return, they learned the Catholic religion and lived at the mission. Many missionaries were truly concerned with converting the Indians. However, life on the missions was hard. Thousands of Indians died from overwork and disease.

Life for Indians became even worse after Mexico won its independence from Spain. The Mexican government offered mission land to ranchers. Some ranchers cruelly mistreated the Indians. If Indians tried to run away, ranchers hunted them down. The harsh conditions had a deadly effect. Between 1770 and 1850, the number of Indians in California fell from 310,000 to 100,000.

## A Confident Nation

In the mid-1840s, only about 700 people from the United States lived in California. But more and more Americans were looking toward the West. Many heard tall tales about a pioneers' paradise in California. Also, Americans knew that their government had tried to buy California from Mexico several times. Officials were especially interested in the fine ports at San Diego and San Francisco.

**Manifest Destiny.** Americans felt confident in the 1840s. They believed that their democratic government was the best in the world. Many Americans wanted the United States to spread all the way across the continent.

In the 1840s, a New York newspaper coined a phrase for that feeling— *Manifest Destiny.* Manifest means

Spanish ranchers in North America lived an elegant life. Here, a hacendado, or landowner, and his wife ride out to greet visitors. Notice their rich clothing. Since hacendados lived many miles from their neighbors, they gave visitors a lavish welcome. One traveler commented on a feast he attended: "The dishes followed each other in such numbers that I am almost afraid to mention them."

clear or obvious. Destiny means something that is sure to happen. Americans who believed in Manifest Destiny thought that America was "obviously" meant to expand to the Pacific.

Manifest Destiny had another side, however. Some Americans thought they were better than Native Americans and Mexicans. For these Americans, racism justified taking over lands owned by Indians and Mexicans.

**Election of 1844.** Manifest Destiny played an important role in the election of 1844. The Whigs nominated Henry Clay for President. Clay was a famous and respected national leader. The Democrats chose a relative unknown, James Polk.

People soon knew Polk as the candidate who favored expansion. Polk demanded that California, New Mexico, Texas, and Oregon be added to the United States. The Democrats made Oregon a special issue. Even though Oregon was held jointly with Britain, they demanded the whole area all the way to its northern border at latitude 54°40′N. "Fifty-four forty or fight!" was their campaign slogan. Americans approved of Polk's goals, and he won the election.

### SECTION REVIEW

1. **Locate:** Santa Fe, Santa Fe Trail, San Diego.
2. What did William Becknell find when he arrived in Santa Fe?
3. Who were the first white settlers in California?
4. **What Do You Think?** Why do you think so many Americans believed in Manifest Destiny?

# 4 War With Mexico

### Read to Learn

★ How did Oregon become part of the United States?

★ Why did the United States go to war with Mexico?

★ How did Spanish and Indian cultures influence Americans?

★ What does this word mean: cede?

James Polk rode into the White House on a wave of support for expansion. The new President firmly believed in Manifest Destiny. To fulfill this dream, however, he faced a showdown with Britain and a war with Mexico.

## Expanding the Nation's Borders

By 1844, Americans were willing to reconsider the idea of annexing Texas. Expansionist feeling in the United States was running high, as Polk's election showed.

**Annexing Texas.** In 1844, Sam Houston signed a treaty of annexation with the United States, but the Senate refused to ratify it. Many people still feared that the treaty would lead to war with Mexico. Houston was disappointed. But he kept up hope and thought of a plan. To convince Congress to annex Texas, he let Americans think that Texas might become an ally of Britain. The trick worked. In March 1845, Congress passed a joint resolution admitting Texas to the Union.

Annexing Texas led at once to a dispute with Mexico. The dispute was over the southern border of Texas, now part of the United States. Texas said that its border was the Rio Grande. Mexico replied that the Nueces (noo AY says) River was the southern border of Texas. (See the map on page 324.)

**Oregon divided.** The dispute over the Texas border was not the only problem facing Polk when he took office in 1845. As he had promised in his campaign, Polk moved to gain control of Oregon. For a time, war between Britain and the United States seemed likely.

President Polk did not really want a war with Britain. So in 1846, he agreed to a compromise. Oregon was divided at latitude 49°N. Britain took the lands north of this line. The United States took the lands south of it and called them the Oregon Territory. This territory was later divided into three states. Oregon became a state in 1859, Washington in 1889, and Idaho in 1890.

## The Mexican War

In 1845, the United States and Mexico stood on the brink of war. Mexicans were furious when the United States annexed Texas. They had never accepted the independence of Texas. Also, they were afraid that Americans in California and New Mexico might rebel, as the Texans had done.

Americans, in turn, were angry with Mexico. President Polk offered to buy California and New Mexico from the Mexicans. But Mexico refused. Americans felt that Mexico was standing in the way of Manifest Destiny.

**American blood on American soil.** In January 1846, President Polk sent General Zachary Taylor to Texas. Taylor's mission was to cross the Nueces River and set up posts along the Rio Grande. Polk knew that Mexico claimed this land and that the move might push Mexico into war. In April 1846, Mexican troops crossed the Rio Grande and fought a brief battle with the Americans. Soldiers on both sides were killed.

President Polk claimed that Mexico had "shed American blood on American soil." He asked Congress to declare war on Mexico. Congress did as Polk wanted, but America was divided over the war. Many people in the South and West were eager to fight because they wanted more land. People in the North opposed the war. They saw it as a southern plot to add more slave states to the Union.

**Early battles.** When the *Mexican War* began, Americans attacked on several fronts. General Taylor crossed the Rio Grande into Mexico. He won several battles against the Mexican army. In February 1847, he defeated General Santa Anna at the Battle of Buena Vista. (See the map on page 324.)

Meanwhile, General Winfield Scott landed another American army at the Mexican port of Veracruz. After a long battle, the Americans took the city. Scott then marched toward Mexico City. He followed the same route taken by Hernando Cortés more than 300 years earlier.

**The Bear Flag Republic.** A third American army, led by General Stephen Kearny, headed west along the Santa Fe Trail. It reached San Diego in the fall of 1846. After several battles, Kearny took control of southern California.

Earlier, Americans in northern California had rebelled against Mexican rule. Captain John Frémont and a band of frontiersmen led the rebels. On June 15, 1845, they declared California an independent republic. The rebels raised a handmade flag showing a grizzly bear. They called their new nation the *Bear Flag Republic*. During the Mexican War, Frémont joined forces with the United States army.

## On to Victory

By 1847, the United States controlled all of New Mexico and California. Meantime, General Scott reached the outskirts of Mexico City. He hoped simply to walk into the Mexican capital. Instead, he had to fight a fierce battle. Young Mexican soldiers made a heroic last stand at Chapultepec (chah

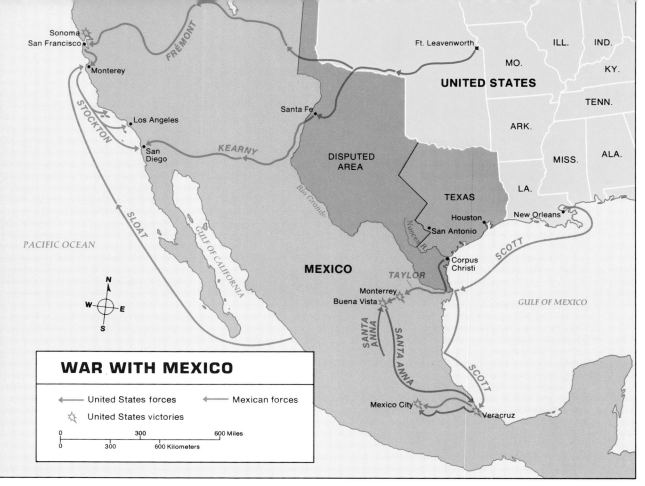

WAR WITH MEXICO

← United States forces    ← Mexican forces

✩ United States victories

0         300         600 Miles
0   300      600 Kilometers

**MAP SKILL** Fighting on the Texas border triggered the Mexican War. But the rest of the war took place in Mexico, as this map shows. Locate the two rivers that border the area disputed by Mexico and the United States at the start of the war. What are the two rivers?

POOL tuh pek), the fort that guarded Mexico City. Like the American defenders of the Alamo, the young Mexicans at Chapultepec fought to the last. Today, Mexicans still celebrate these young men as heroes.

**The peace treaty.** With the American army in Mexico City, the Mexican government had to make peace. In 1848, Mexico signed the Treaty of Guadalupe Hidalgo (gwah duh LOOP ay ih DAHL goh). Under the treaty, Mexico *ceded,* or gave, all of California and the New Mexico Territory to the United States. These lands were called the *Mexican Cession.* (See the map on page 326.) In return, the United States paid Mexico $15 million and agreed to respect the rights of Spanish-speaking people in the Mexican Cession.

**Gadsden Purchase.** A few years after the Mexican War, the United States completed its expansion across the continent. In 1853, it paid Mexico $10 million for a strip of land now in Arizona and New Mexico. The land was called the *Gadsden Purchase.* Americans rejoiced. Their dreams of Manifest Destiny had come true.

## Mexican and Indian Heritage

Texas and the Mexican Cession added vast new lands to the United States. In these new lands, Americans found a rich culture that blended Spanish and Indian traditions.

When English-speaking settlers flooded into the Southwest, they brought their own culture with them, including ideas about democratic government. At the same time, they learned much from the older residents of the area. Mexican Americans taught the newcomers, whom they called Anglos, how to irrigate the soil. They also showed the Americans how to mine silver and other minerals. Many Spanish and Indian words became part of the English language. They included stampede, buffalo, soda, and tornado.

Americans kept some Mexican laws. One law said that a husband and wife owned property jointly. In the rest of the United States, married women could not own property. Another law said that landowners could not cut off water to their neighbors. This law was important in the dry Southwest.

Americans often did not treat Mexican Americans and Indians well.

These older residents of the Southwest struggled to protect their traditions and rights. But Americans ignored old land claims. If Mexican Americans went to court to defend their property, they found that American judges rarely upheld their claims. "The Americans say they have come for our good," one Mexican American explained. "Yes, for all our goods."

## SECTION REVIEW

1. **Locate:** Rio Grande, Nueces River, Buena Vista, Veracruz, Mexico City, Mexican Cession, Gadsden Purchase.
2. **Define:** cede.
3. How did the United States gain the Oregon Territory?
4. What lands did the United States gain from the Mexican War?
5. **What Do You Think?** Why do you think Americans ignored the land claims of Mexican Americans?

# 5 From Sea to Shining Sea

## Read to Learn

★ Why did Mormons settle in Utah?
★ How did the Gold Rush change life in California?
★ Why did California have a mix of people?
★ What do these words mean: forty-niner, vigilante?

In 1848, the United States finally stretched "from sea to shining sea." The Stars and Stripes flew from the ports of New England to the sun-baked missions of San Diego. Restless pioneers soon headed into these lands to build homes and seek their fortunes.

## Mormons Move West

Among the early pioneers to settle in the Mexican Cession were the *Mor-* *mons*. The Mormons belonged to the Church of Jesus Christ of Latter Day Saints. The church was founded in the 1820s by Joseph Smith. Smith, a farmer who lived in upstate New York, won many followers.

**Early years.** Smith was an energetic and well-liked man. But some of his teachings angered non-Mormons. For example, at first Mormons believed in owning property in common. Smith also said that a man could have more than one wife.* The Mormons were forced to move from New York to Ohio, then to Missouri, and later to Illinois.

In the 1840s, the Mormons built the town of Nauvoo, Illinois, on the banks

---

*In 1890, Mormons gave up the practice of allowing a man to have more than one wife.

of the Mississippi River. The Mormons worked together for the good of their community. They ran successful farms and industries. By 1844, Nauvoo was the largest town in Illinois. Its clean streets were lined with neat brick houses.

However, the Mormons again had trouble with their neighbors. In 1844, a mob attacked Nauvoo and killed Joseph Smith. The Mormons quickly chose Brigham Young as their new leader. Young realized that the Mormons needed a home where they would be safe. He had read about a valley between the Rocky Mountains and the Great Salt Lake in Utah. Young decided that the isolated valley would make a safe home for the Mormons.

**An impossible task.** To move 15,000 men, women, and children from Illinois to Utah seemed an impossible task. Young relied on faith and careful planning to achieve his goal. In 1847, he led an advance party into the Great Salt Lake valley. For two years, Mormon wagon trains struggled across the plains and over the steep Rockies.

Once they reached Utah, the Mormons had to survive in the desert climate of the valley. Once again, Young proved to be a gifted leader. He planned an irrigation system to bring water to farms. Young also drew up plans for a large city, called *Salt Lake City,* to be built in the desert.

The Mormon settlement in Utah grew quickly. Like other white settlers,

MAP SKILL By 1848, the United States stretched all the way from the Atlantic to the Pacific Ocean. What area on the map was the last to become part of the United States? When was it added?

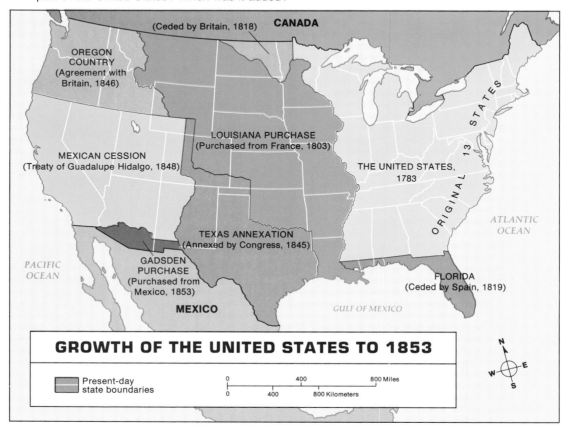

GROWTH OF THE UNITED STATES TO 1853

Mormons often suffered violence at the hands of their neighbors. Here, non-Mormons attack a Mormon settlement near Independence, Missouri, in 1833. The violence ruined the settlement, which Joseph Smith had hoped would one day be "the chief city in the Western Hemisphere."

Mormons took over thousands of acres of Indian land, usually without paying anything for it. Congress recognized Brigham Young as governor of the Utah Territory in 1850. Trouble broke out when non-Mormons moved to the area. In the end, peace was restored, and Utah became a state in 1896.

## The Gold Rush

While the Mormons were trekking into Utah, news reached the East that sent thousands of people hurrying along trails west. The news was the discovery of gold in California.

**Sutter's Mill.** John Sutter, a Swiss immigrant, was building a sawmill on the American River north of Sacramento in 1848. James Marshall was in charge of the job. One morning, Marshall saw a gleaming yellow rock in the river. He reached into the icy water and picked up the yellow lump. He held it in the sunlight. For a moment, Marshall could not speak. Then, a single word came to his lips: "Gold."

In a few days, news of the gold strike spread to San Francisco. Carpenters dropped their saws. Bakers left bread in their ovens. Schools emptied as teachers and students joined the rush to the gold fields. From California, the news sped eastward. Thousands of Americans caught gold fever. They spent their hard-earned savings to set out for the gold fields of California. The California Gold Rush had begun.

The Gold Rush drew people from all over the world in 1849. They were called *forty-niners*. If forty-niners had money, they traveled to California by sea because it was faster. But most traveled overland. Many passed through Salt Lake City. There, the Mormons prospered by selling food and horses to weary travelers. In 1849, more than 80,000 people made the long journey to California.

**Panning for gold.** At first, mining took little skill. The gold was near the surface of the earth. Miners used knives to dig for gold in riverbeds. Soon, they found a better way. They loaded gravel from the riverbed into a washing pan. They held the pan under water and swirled it gently. The river water washed away lighter gravel, leaving the heavier gold in the pan.

**MAP SKILL** During 1849 alone, some 80,000 people rushed to California. The population of San Francisco and other cities jumped. What cities were near to the gold mines in northern California?

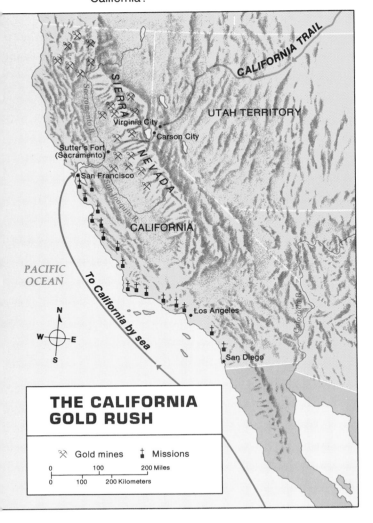

THE CALIFORNIA GOLD RUSH

Gold mines    Missions

0    100    200 Miles
0    100    200 Kilometers

Only a few miners struck it rich. Most went broke trying to make their fortunes. These people often had to leave the gold fields. Many found other jobs and helped to build up the economy of California.

**California joins the Union.** The Gold Rush changed life in California. Almost overnight, places like San Francisco grew from sleepy towns into bustling cities. The Gold Rush also created problems. Greed turned some forty-niners into criminals. Murders and robberies plagued many mining camps. To reduce crime, miners formed vigilance committees. *Vigilantes* (vihj uh LAN teez) dealt out punishment even though they had no legal power to do so. Sometimes, the accused criminal was lynched, or hanged, without a legal trial.

Californians realized that they needed a government to stop the lawlessness. In 1849, they drafted a state constitution. They then asked to be admitted to the Union. California's request created an uproar in the United States. The issue was whether the new state would allow slavery or not. You will read about this issue in Chapter 17. After much debate in Congress, California was finally admitted to the Union in 1850.

## A Mix of Peoples

California's population grew rapidly in the next few years. Most newcomers were white Americans. During the wild days of the Gold Rush, they often ignored the rights of other Californians.

**Native Americans.** Indians fared worst of all. Many were driven off their lands and died of starvation and disease. Others were murdered. In 1850, the Indian population in California was about 100,000. By the 1870s, there were only 17,000 Indians left in the state.

Forty-niners, like the men and woman here, worked hard to find gold. First, they used picks to break up a streambed. Then, they shoveled the mud and gravel into wooden placers such as the one in this photograph. The miners used water from the stream to wash away everything but the gold. Because it was heavier, gold stayed in the placer.

**Mexican Americans.** Often, Mexican Americans lost land they had owned for years. Many fought to preserve the laws and customs of their people. Jose Carillo (cah REE yoh) was from one of the oldest Mexican families in California. In part because of his efforts, the state's constitution was written in both Spanish and English.

**Chinese Americans.** Chinese settlers began coming to California in 1848. They were welcomed at first because California needed laborers. But when the Chinese staked claims in the gold fields, resentment grew. White miners often drove off the Chinese. But the Chinese stayed in California and helped the state grow.

**Black Americans.** Like other forty-niners, free blacks went to California hoping to strike it rich. Some did become wealthy. In fact, California had the wealthiest black population of any state by the 1850s. But blacks still faced discrimination. For example, Cal-

ifornia law denied blacks the right to testify against whites in court. In 1863, after a long struggle, blacks won the repeal of this law.

In spite of these problems, California thrived and grew. Settlers continued to pour into the state. By 1860, it had 100,000 citizens. The mix of peoples in California gave it a unique culture.

### SECTION REVIEW

1. **Locate:** Salt Lake City, Sutter's Mill, Sacramento, San Francisco.
2. **Define:** forty-niner, vigilante.
3. (a) Why did Brigham Young choose the Salt Lake River valley as the new home of the Mormons? (b) What hardships did the Mormons face when they reached Utah?
4. Describe what happened during the California Gold Rush.
5. **What Do You Think?** Why do you think the Mormon settlement in Utah was more orderly than mining camps in California?

# Chapter 14 Review

 **Summary**

During the mid-1800s, the nation grew rapidly. Settlers followed Mountain Men and missionaries into Oregon Country. In 1845, after a standoff with Britain, the United States took over part of Oregon.

In the 1820s, Americans began to move to Texas. In 1835, Texans rebelled against Mexico. They formed a republic in 1836. When Texas joined the Union in 1846, war with Mexico resulted. Mexico lost and gave up California and the Southwest.

In 1849, thousands of gold miners rushed to California. The population boom led California to join the Union in 1850.

 **Reviewing the Facts** ★

**Key Terms.** Match each term in Column 1 with the correct definition in Column 2.

| Column 1 | Column 2 |
|---|---|
| **1.** rendezvous | **a.** give |
| **2.** annex | **b.** someone who went to California during the Gold Rush |
| **3.** cede | **c.** add on |
| **4.** forty-niner | **d.** someone who punishes a suspected criminal even though he has no legal power to do so |
| **5.** vigilante | **e.** get-together |

**Key People, Events, and Ideas.** Identify each of the following.

**1.** Mountain Men
**2.** Narcissa Whitman
**3.** Oregon Trail
**4.** Stephen Austin
**5.** Antonio López de Santa Anna
**6.** Sam Houston
**7.** Alamo
**8.** Lone Star Republic
**9.** Santa Fe Trail
**10.** Junípero Serra
**11.** Manifest Destiny
**12.** James Polk
**13.** Bear Flag Republic
**14.** Mexican Cession
**15.** Joseph Smith

★ **Chapter Checkup**

**1.** (a) Why were many Americans attracted to the Oregon Country? (b) How did they travel there?

**2.** Explain how each of the following helped to open the West: (a) Mountain Men; (b) missionaries; (c) forty-niners.

**3.** Why did settlers in Texas rebel against the Mexican government?

**4.** (a) Describe the life of Indians on missions in California. (b) How did their lives change after Mexican independence?

**5.** How did the idea of Manifest Destiny influence the election of 1844?

**6.** List three ways older residents of the Southwest influenced American settlers.

**7.** (a) Why did the Mormons move west from Illinois? (b) Why did they choose to settle in the Great Salt Lake valley?

**8.** (a) Describe the mix of cultures in California after the Gold Rush. (b) How did the search for gold cause problems for some groups?

## Thinking About History

1. **Drawing a conclusion.** How was the defeat at the Alamo also a victory for Texans?

2. **Analyzing a quotation.** One army officer who fought against Mexico called the Mexican War "one of the most unjust ever waged by a stronger against a weaker nation." (a) What did he mean? (b) Do you agree or disagree with his statement? Explain.

3. **Understanding geography.** (a) What lands did the Mormons cross on their way from Illinois to the Great Salt Lake valley? (b) How did Mormons turn the desert into farmland?

4. **Relating past to present.** (a) Why do you think forty-niners were ready to risk their savings and their lives looking for gold in California? (b) Can you think of people today who take risks to make a fortune? Explain.

5. **Understanding the economy.** How do you think the Gold Rush helped to make settlements in the West grow?

## Using Your Skills

1. **Identifying immediate and long-range causes.** Wars and other events in history have both immediate and long-range causes. An *immediate cause* is an event that triggers a war. *Long-range causes* are problems or conflicts that build up over a period of time. Long-range causes of a war often create a mood of bad feeling between two countries. Review the events leading up to the Mexican War. (a) What was the immediate cause of war with Mexico? (b) What were the long-range causes?

2. **Making a review chart.** Make a review chart with three columns and four rows. Label the columns Oregon, Texas, and California. Label the rows First European Settlers, First Settlers From the United States, Date Became a Territory, and Date Became a State. Then complete the chart for the three areas.

3. **Map reading.** Study the map on page 324. (a) Who commanded the American troops that landed at Veracruz? (b) About how many miles is it from Veracruz to Mexico City? (c) What city in California did Kearny's troops capture?

4. **Placing events in time.** Study the time line on page 308. (a) When did the Mexican War begin? (b) How many years later did the Gold Rush begin? (c) Can you think of a way the first event affected the second?

## More to Do

1. **Writing a diary.** Imagine that you are a Mountain Man living in the Rocky Mountains in the 1830s. Write diary entries for seven days.

2. **Making a poster.** Make a poster to rally Texans to fight for independence from Mexico in March 1836.

3. **Exploring local history.** Write a report about any people who left your local area for the West during the 1830s or 1840s. If you live in the West, find out about people who arrived during this period.

4. **Drawing a cartoon.** Draw a cartoon about the Gold Rush to California.

5. **Researching.** Find out more about the Gadsden Purchase. Why did people want to purchase this area?

CHAPTER

# 15

# Two Ways of Life (1820–1860)

## Chapter Outline

**1** Industry in the North
**2** Life in the North
**3** The Cotton Kingdom
**4** Life in the South
Readings, page 541

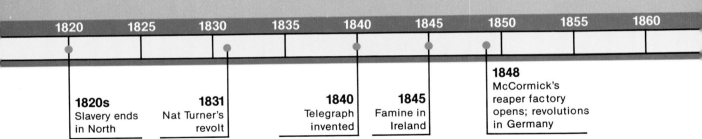

| 1820 | 1825 | 1830 | 1835 | 1840 | 1845 | 1850 | 1855 | 1860 |
|------|------|------|------|------|------|------|------|------|

**1820s**
Slavery ends
in North

**1831**
Nat Turner's
revolt

**1840**
Telegraph
invented

**1845**
Famine in
Ireland

**1848**
McCormick's
reaper factory
opens; revolutions
in Germany

## About This Chapter

The first half of the 1800s was a time of rapid change in America. In the North, factories sprang up in cities and villages. Factories brought a new way of life to the North. Cities grew, swollen by the arrival of immigrants from Europe.

One such immigrant was Jacob Lanzit. He came to America from Austria in the 1850s. To make a living, Lanzit tried various jobs. He sold cigars, peddled stationery, sewed clothing, and ran a dry goods store. Life in the New World was not as easy as Lanzit had hoped. "However," he wrote, "I can make a living. It is hard work, to be sure, but I am now in America; that means working."

Immigrants faced hardships, but had opportunities as well. Most made places for themselves in the bustling cities of the North. Jacob Lanzit went on to open his own printing shop and raise a family in New York City.

The South grew also, but in a different way. Few factories were built there. Farming, especially growing cotton, dominated southern life. Slavery spread as Southerners planted more land with cotton.

As the North and South grew, they developed distinct ways of life. To some people, the North and South seemed like two different countries.

Study the time line above. What event on the time line do you think encouraged people in Ireland to come to the United States?

Wealthy southern planters created an elegant way of life, as this painting of a plantation in Louisiana shows.

# 1 Industry in the North

### Read to Learn

★ What inventions helped the northern economy?

★ How did railroads help business?

★ What do these words mean: telegraph, clipper ship?

In the early 1800s, life was changing in the North. Factories were springing up on lands where cows once grazed. Peaceful New England towns were changed forever by the whir and clatter of new machines. Most Northerners still lived on farms. But more and more, the northern economy centered on manufacturing and trade.

## New Machines

The Industrial Revolution reached America in the early 1800s, as you read in Chapter 12. Inventions continued to spark the growth of new industries in the 1840s and 1850s. For example, Elias Howe patented a sewing machine in 1846. A few years later, Isaac Singer improved on Howe's sewing machine. He then advertised to increase demand for it.

The invention of the sewing machine had far-reaching effects. Factories were set up with hundreds of sewing machines. They produced dozens of shirts in the time it took a tailor to sew a few seams by hand.

**New farm tools.** Other inventions helped farmers. For example, John Deere invented a lightweight steel plow. In the past, plows were made of wood or iron. They were so heavy that they had to be pulled by slow-moving oxen. John Deere's plow was light enough for a horse to pull.

In 1848, Cyrus McCormick opened a factory in Chicago that made mechanical reapers. McCormick's reaper was a horse-drawn machine that mowed wheat and other grains. The new reaper could do the work of five people using hand tools.

Machines such as the reaper and steel plow helped farmers. Farmers produced more grain and needed fewer farm hands. As a result, thousands of farm workers left the countryside. Many took jobs in the new factories that were opening in cities and towns.

## Messages by Wire

Another invention gave Americans a new way to keep in touch. In 1840, Samuel F. B. Morse received a patent for his "talking wire," or telegraph. The *telegraph* was a machine that sent electrical signals along a wire. The signals were based on a code of dots and dashes. Each group of dots and dashes stood for a different letter of the alphabet. Later, this code was called the Morse code.

The telegraph was an instant success. Telegraph companies sprang up everywhere and strung thousands of miles of wire. Messages traveled over

**MAP SKILL** Farming, especially wheat and other grains, remained vital to the northern economy, as this product map shows. At the same time, industry became more important every year. Which states produced textiles? Which states had an important mining industry?

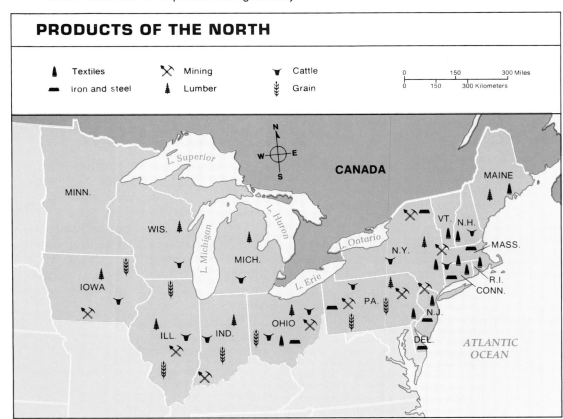

PRODUCTS OF THE NORTH

long distances in a matter of minutes. Newspaper reporters used telegraphs to wire in stories about major events such as the Mexican War. The telegraph helped business grow by making it easier for merchants to find out about the supply and price of goods.

### The Iron Horse

A further boost to the economy came as transportation improved. Americans continued to build new roads and canals. But the greatest change came with the railroad.

The first railroads had wood rails covered with a strip of iron. Horses pulled cars along the rails. Then, in 1829, the Stephenson family in England developed a steam-powered engine for pulling rail cars. The engine, called the *Rocket*, barreled along at 30 miles (48 km) per hour, an astonishing speed at the time. In America, people laughed at the noisy clatter of these "iron horses." Some were terrified by sparks that flew out of the engines, burning passengers' clothes and setting buildings on fire.

Many Americans believed that horse-drawn rail cars were safer and faster than steam-powered engines. In 1830, a race was held to settle the question.

A huge crowd gathered in Baltimore to watch a horse-drawn rail car race a steam engine called the *Tom Thumb*. One onlooker described the *Tom Thumb* as "a teakettle on a truck." When the race began, the horse labored to keep up with the chugging *Tom Thumb*. Suddenly, the steam engine broke down. The crowd cheered as the horse crossed the finish line first. But *Tom Thumb*'s defeat was not the end of the steam engine.

Engineers developed better rails and engines. Soon, private companies started building railroads. By the late 1850s, railroads connected the East to cities such as Chicago in the Midwest. Cities at hubs of the railroad network

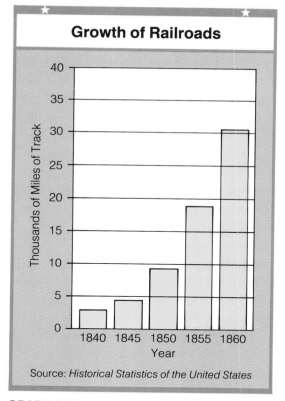

## Growth of Railroads

GRAPH SKILL Railroads expanded rapidly after 1840. The surge in railroad mileage came about mainly from track laid in the North and Midwest. Southerners did build thousands of miles of railroads, but they lagged behind Northerners. During which five-year period did the country's total railroad mileage pass 20,000 miles?

grew quickly. (See the map on page 369.)

### Golden Age of Sail

While railroads were boosting the economy on land, American ships were capturing much of the world's trade at sea. At busy seaports on the east coast, captains loaded their ships with wheat, cotton, lumber, furs, and tobacco.

Speed was the key to successful trade at sea. In 1845, an American named John Griffith launched the *Rainbow*, the first of the *clipper ships.* These elegant ships had tall masts and huge sails that caught every gust of wind. With their narrow hulls, they clipped swiftly through the water.

The most daring of all seafarers were whalers. In the 1850s, eight out of ten of the world's whaling ships sailed from New England. Many crew members were Americans. Others came from as far away as Portugal and Hawaii. Native Americans proved to be good harpooners. In a whaling port, it seemed that every language of the world could be heard.

Once at sea, crew members ignored differences in language and culture. They worked together as a team. When a whale was sighted, small rowboats went out from the ship. The harpooners stood in front. They threw harpoons with strong ropes tied to them. These stuck in the whale, which usually dove deep under the waves. The whale pulled rope out from the boats so fast that the crews had to pour water on it. Otherwise, friction would set the boats afire! When the whale resurfaced, it often dragged the boats for miles.

Slowly, the whale grew tired. Crews pulled in the ropes, drawing the boats closer to the huge animal. The harpooners stood once again. This time, they aimed sharp lances at the whale's heart. If they missed, the wounded whale might turn and crush the boats. If they struck true, the sea boiled red, and the whale died in minutes.

Whaling made many New England seaports prosper. Whale oil was sold as lamp fuel. Whalebone was used in umbrellas. Ambergris, found in male whales, was used in perfumes.

★ How do you think whaling affected the New England economy?

In the 1840s, shipbuilders like Donald McKay launched dozens of clipper ships. American clipper ships broke every speed record. They sailed from New York to Hong Kong in 81 days, flying past older ships that took 5 months to reach China. The speed of the clipper ships helped the United States win a large share of foreign trade during the 1840s and 1850s.

The triumph of the graceful clippers was short-lived. In the 1850s, clipper ships lost their advantage when the British launched the first ocean-going steamships. These sturdy iron vessels carried more cargo and traveled faster than clippers.

## An Expanding Economy

Northern industry grew steadily in the mid-1800s. In the 1830s, factories began to use steam power instead of water power.

Steam power helped the factory system to spread. It allowed manufacturers to build anywhere, not just near rivers. This was important because the best river sites had been taken in the North. Steam-driven machines were powerful and cheap to run. Soon, textile mills and other factories were using them.

With new machines, northern factory owners produced goods more cheaply and quickly than ever before. The low-priced goods found eager buyers. As demand increased, owners built larger factories. They hired dozens of workers to run machines.

Railroads also contributed to rapid industrial growth in the North. Railroads helped manufacturers ship raw materials and finished goods quickly and cheaply. They created new markets by opening up distant sections of the country to trade.

Railroads had an important effect on northern farming, too. Since colonial days, farmers in New England had scratched a living from poor, rocky soil. With the growth of railroads, farming in the richer soils of the West boomed. Western farmers shipped grain and other foods east by rail. As a result, New Englanders turned to manufacturing and trade.

## SECTION REVIEW

1. **Define:** telegraph, clipper ship.
2. List two inventions that helped farmers.
3. Why was the telegraph important?
4. How did railroads contribute to industrial growth in the North?
5. **What Do You Think?** Why do you think the Industrial Revolution caught on in the North?

# 2 Life in the North

### Read to Learn
★ What was life like for factory workers?
★ Why did workers organize unions?
★ What do these words mean: skilled worker, trade union, strike, unskilled worker, immigrant, famine, nativist, prejudice?

Most people in the North continued to live as farmers. However, life in the North was changing because of the growth of industry and cities.

## Working in Factories

Factories in the 1840s were different from the textile mills of the early 1800s. Owners built bigger factories and used steam-powered machines. They hired more workers to tend the machines. For these workers, wages remained low and hours long.

**A long day.** As the demand for workers grew, entire families signed on to work in factories. They needed the earnings of every member to pay for their food and housing.

A family's day began early—when the factory whistle sounded at 4:00 A.M. Father, mother, and children dressed in the dark before dawn and headed off to work. The whistle blew at 7:30 A.M. and again at noon to announce breakfast and lunch breaks. The day did not end until 7:30 P.M. when the final whistle sent workers home.

**Poor conditions.** During the long day, factory workers faced many dangers. Owners often paid little attention to bad working conditions. Few factories had windows or heating systems. The heat in summer was stifling. In winter, the cold contributed to sickness.

Poor lighting led to accidents. Also, machines had no safety devices. From time to time, workers' hands or arms were crushed by machines. Injured workers lost their jobs, and there was no insurance to make up for lost wages.

This painting shows a thriving New England town in the 1840s. Many small towns in the North had textile mills and other factories by this time. At first, factories drew their workers from men, women, and children living on nearby farms.

Despite the long hours and dangers, factory workers in America were better off than those in Europe. American workers could usually find jobs and earn regular wages. European workers often had no work at all.

## Workers Organize

Poor working conditions and low wages led workers to organize. The first to do so were skilled workers. *Skilled workers* were people who had learned a trade, such as carpenters and shoemakers. In the 1820s and 1830s, skilled workers in each trade banded together to form *trade unions*.

Trade unions called for a shorter work day, better wages, and safer working conditions. They sometimes pressed their demands by going on strike. In a *strike*, union workers refuse to do their jobs. But strikes were illegal in the United States. Strikers faced fines or jail sentences. And strike leaders were fired from their jobs.

Slowly, however, workers made progress. In 1840, they won a major victory when President Van Buren approved a 10-hour workday for government employees. Other workers still worked 12 to 15 hours a day. But they kept pressing their demands until they won the same hours as government workers. Workers celebrated another victory in 1842 when a Massachusetts court declared that they had the right to strike.

While skilled workers slowly won better pay, unskilled workers could not bargain for better wages. ***Unskilled workers*** did jobs that required little or no training. So they were easily replaced. As a result, employers were unwilling to listen to their demands for better pay.

## Women Speak Up

Thousands of women held jobs in factories. By the 1840s, conditions for women were getting worse at Lowell and other mills. For example, some mills charged fines if workers were late. They forbade women to talk on the job. Like men, women workers organized. They used strikes to protest cuts in wages and unfair work rules.

At first, few strikes succeeded. Employers fired strike leaders. They threatened to dismiss any workers who went on strike. Single women could return home to their families, but their pay was often badly needed. Married women knew that their children would suffer if they lost their jobs.

Sometimes, a strike succeeded. In 1831, mill workers in Exeter, New Hampshire, went on strike. They were protesting against an overseer who turned the clocks back every day. The women were working longer without getting extra pay. After they struck, the factory owner agreed to make the overseer stop the practice.

Despite many setbacks, women refused to remain silent. One group compared their struggle to the American Revolution: "As our fathers resisted . . . the lordly [greed] of the British, so we, their daughters, never will wear the yoke [of slavery] which has been prepared for us."

## A Flood of New Americans

Many of the new workers in the factories of the North were immigrants. An ***immigrant*** is a person who comes from his or her homeland and settles in another country. During the 1840s and 1850s, 4 million immigrants flooded into the United States.

**Potato famine.** In the 1840s, many immigrants came from Ireland. A disease rotted the potato crop in Europe in 1845. The loss of this crop caused a ***famine,*** or severe food shortage, especially in Ireland. Irish peasants depended on the potato. Without it, many starved.

Over 1.5 million Irish fled to America between 1845 and 1860. Most were too poor to buy farmland. So they settled in the cities where they landed. In

This engraving shows people on their way to work at a factory. Many of the workers carry their lunch in a basket or a lunch pail. Women and children often earned only one half or one third of what men earned for the same work.

New York City and Boston, thousands of Irish crowded into slums. They took any job they could find.

**Fleeing Germany.** Another group of immigrants came from Germany. Between 1850 and 1860, nearly one million Germans arrived in America. Many were fleeing from repression. In 1848, revolutions broke out in several parts of Germany. The rebels fought for democratic government. When the revolutions failed, thousands had to flee for their lives.

**Contributions.** Newcomers from many lands helped the American economy grow rapidly. Irish workers kept northern factories humming. Craftsworkers from Britain and Germany brought useful skills to America. Each group left its imprint on American life. Irish immigrants brought their lively music and dances. German immigrants brought the custom of decorating the Christmas tree. Immigrants from other nations enriched America with their language, foods, and customs.

## America for Americans

The flood of immigrants alarmed many Americans. Some Americans, called *nativists,* wanted to preserve the country for native-born white citizens. Nativists trumpeted the idea of "America for Americans" and favored laws to limit immigration. They also wanted to deny newcomers the right to vote until they had lived in America for 21 years. At the time, immigrants had to live here only 5 years to vote.

Nativists had many reasons for disliking immigrants. American workers resented immigrants because the newcomers worked for low pay. Other nativists disliked the newcomers because of prejudice. *Prejudice* is an unfavorable opinion about people who are of a different religion, race, or nationality. For example, some Protestants mistrusted Irish and German immigrants who were Catholics.

In the 1850s, nativists organized the *Know-Nothing Party.* This name came from the answer party members gave when asked about their activities. They replied, "I know nothing." In 1856, the Know-Nothing candidate for President won 21 percent of the popular vote. Soon after, the party died out.

## Free Blacks

Free blacks in the North faced worse prejudice than immigrants did. They had few rights. As one writer stated, black Americans were denied "the ballot-box, the jury box, the halls of legislature, the army, the public lands, the school, and the church."

Free blacks also faced discrimination on the job. One black carpenter was turned away by every furniture maker in Cincinnati. "At last," a study on free blacks reported, "he found a shop carried on by an Englishman, who agreed to employ him—but on entering the shop, the workmen threw down their tools and declared that he should leave or they would." As a result of prejudice, skilled blacks often took low-paying jobs as laborers.

Despite prejudice, some free blacks moved ahead. James Forten grew rich manufacturing sails. (See page 205.) Other blacks became lawyers, actors, and scientists.

### SECTION REVIEW

1. **Define:** skilled worker, trade union, strike, unskilled worker, immigrant, famine, nativist, prejudice.
2. (a) How did factory conditions get worse in the 1800s? (b) What benefits did early unions ask for?
3. (a) Where did most immigrants come from in the 1840s and 1850s? (b) Why did they leave their homelands?
4. What problems did free blacks face in the North?
5. **What Do You Think?** Why do you think most factory owners were happy to hire immigrants?

# 3 The Cotton Kingdom

**Read to Learn**

★ How did the cotton gin change the South?

★ Why was the South known as the Cotton Kingdom?

★ What industries grew in the South?

While factories sprouted up in towns and cities of the North, the South also enjoyed economic growth. Southerners shipped tons of tobacco, rice, and sugar to the North and to Europe. But one crop—cotton—came to dominate the southern economy.

## Eli Whitney's Invention

The Industrial Revolution greatly increased the demand for southern cotton. Textile mills in the North and in Britain could handle more and more cotton. At first, planters could not keep up with demand. They could grow plenty of cotton, but cleaning it took time.

Removing the seeds from the cotton fibers was a slow task. Planters badly needed a new way to clean cotton.

In 1793, Eli Whitney built the first cotton gin, a machine for cleaning cotton. (Gin was short for engine.) The cotton gin had two wooden rollers with thin wire teeth. When cotton was swept between the rollers, the wire teeth pulled the fibers clear of the seeds. (See the picture on page 288.)

The cotton gin was a simple but important invention. With a gin, one worker could do the work of 1,000 people cleaning cotton by hand. News of Whitney's invention spread quickly. In fact, thieves broke into his workshop to steal an early model. Because of the gin, Southerners grew more cotton.

## The Cotton Kingdom

Planters soon learned that land planted with cotton year after year

Harvesting cotton took long hours of backbreaking work. On most big plantations, a white overseer directed the work of slaves, as this painting by Mary Williams shows. Because cotton soon exhausted the soil, planters often sold their land and moved west. As planters moved westward in the 1800s, so did slavery.

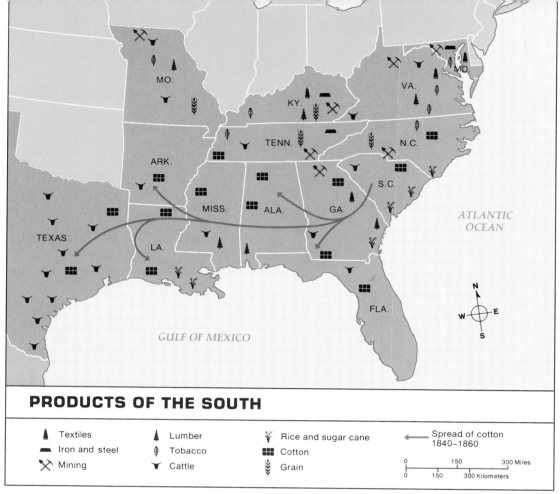

## PRODUCTS OF THE SOUTH

|  |  |
|---|---|
| ▲ Textiles | |
| ▬ Iron and steel | |
| ⚒ Mining | |
| 🌲 Lumber | |
| 🍃 Tobacco | |
| Y Cattle | |
| 🌾 Rice and sugar cane | |
| ▦ Cotton | |
| 🌾 Grain | |
| ← Spread of cotton 1840–1860 | |

0    150    300 Miles
0    150    300 Kilometers

**MAP SKILL** Southerners produced many different goods by the mid-1800s. Tobacco and rice were important crops. Livestock was a major source of income, too. But cotton overshadowed every other product of the South. To what areas did cotton growing spread between 1840 and 1860?

wore out. This forced them to find new land to cultivate.

After the War of 1812, planters headed west. They built farms on the fertile land of Alabama, Mississippi, and Louisiana. Some moved even farther west into Texas. Soon, cotton plantations stretched in a wide band from South Carolina and Georgia to Texas. This area became known as the *Cotton Kingdom.* (See the map above.)

Production boomed in the Cotton Kingdom. The boom helped the economy of the South and the nation as a whole. By the 1850s, the United States earned millions of dollars every year from cotton exports.

The increased demand for cotton had a tragic side, however. As the Cotton Kingdom spread, the demand for slaves grew. Slaves planted and picked the cotton. As slaves produced more cotton, planters earned the money to buy more land and more slaves.

The number of slaves in the South grew steadily after 1800. (See page 345.) Yet, most families owned no slaves at all. Of those who did, most had only one or two.

## Other Industries

Cotton was the major cash crop grown in the South. But tobacco, rice, and sugar cane were important money-making crops as well. Southerners also raised much of the nation's livestock. They shipped hogs and cattle to northern cities. Horses, oxen, and mules bred in the South pulled carts and dragged plows all around the nation.

The South took some steps to encourage industry. In the 1800s, Southerners built factories to process sugar and tobacco. They also built textile mills. William Gregg modeled his cotton mill in South Carolina on the Lowell mills in Massachusetts. Gregg built houses and gardens for his workers and schools for their children.

Even so, the South lagged far behind the North in industry. Wealthy Southerners put their money into land and slaves rather than factories. Southerners depended on the North and Europe for finished goods such as cloth and tools. Many resented this fact. One Southerner wrote that "slaveholders themselves are enslaved to the products of northern industry." Still, most Southerners were proud of their booming cotton industry. As long as cotton remained king, Southerners could look to the future with confidence.

## AMERICANS WHO DARED

### Eli Whitney

Eli Whitney grew up in Massachusetts at the time of the American Revolution. After college, Whitney spent time on a South Carolina plantation owned by Catherine Greene. One day, some planters complained that they needed a better way to clean cotton. Catherine Greene suggested they ask Whitney. Using odds and ends, Whitney built the first cotton gin in only 10 days.

## SECTION REVIEW

1. **Locate:** Alabama, Mississippi, Louisiana, Texas.
2. How did the cotton gin help planters?
3. Why did planters need more and more new land to cultivate?
4. What crops besides cotton were grown in the South?
5. **What Do You Think?** Why do you think the demand for cotton rose steadily in the 1800s?

# 4 Life in the South

## Read to Learn
★ How did white Southerners live?
★ How did free blacks live in the South?
★ What was life like for slaves?
★ What do these words mean: extended family?

The wealthiest Southerners were plantation owners. They lived off the unpaid labor of slaves. Most Southerners, however, did not own slaves. They had small farms and worked hard to provide for themselves.

## Southern Whites

White Southerners were divided into three groups. They were wealthy planters, farmers who worked their own land, and poor whites.

**Planters.** Planters were few in number, but their views and way of life dominated the South. A planter was someone who owned at least 20 slaves. Of the 5.5 million whites in the South, only 50,000 were planters in 1860. Still, planters had power over the lives of many people.

The richest planters built elegant homes and filled them with fine European furniture. They entertained lavishly, dressing and behaving like the nobility of Europe.

Planters had responsibilities, too. They had to make important decisions about when to plant and harvest their crops. Because of their wealth and influence, owners of large plantations often became political leaders. They devoted many hours to local and state politics. As a result, they hired men to oversee the work of slaves.

**Small farmers.** About 75 percent of southern whites were small farmers. These "plain folk," as they called themselves, owned land and perhaps one or two slaves. Unlike planters, plain folk usually worked in the cotton fields alongside their slaves.

Among small farmers, helping each other out was an important duty. "People who lived miles apart counted themselves as neighbors," wrote a farmer in Mississippi. "And in case of sorrow or sickness or need of any kind, there was no limit to the ready service neighbors provided."

**Poor whites.** A small group of poor whites clung to the bottom of the social ladder. They farmed but did not own land. Instead, they rented it. Many barely kept themselves and their families from starving.

Poor whites often lived in the hills and wooded areas of the South. They planted corn, potatoes, and other vege-

tables. Like their better-off neighbors, they herded cattle and pigs. Despite their difficult lives, poor whites enjoyed rights that were denied to free blacks and slaves.

## Southern Blacks

The black population of the South included free blacks and slaves. Although legally free, free blacks faced harsh discrimination. And slaves had no rights at all.

**Free blacks.** Many free blacks were descended from slaves freed during and after the Revolution. Others had bought their freedom or been granted it by their owners. But as the number of slaves grew, fewer earned their freedom. Slave owners did not like to have free blacks living near slaves. They thought free blacks encouraged slaves to rebel.

Still, by 1860, about 215,000 free blacks lived in the South. Many worked as servants and farm laborers. Some practiced skilled trades such as shoemaking.

Free blacks made valuable contributions to southern life. Norbert Rillieux (RIHL yoo), a free black in New Orleans, invented a machine that revolutionized sugar making. Henry Blair patented a seed planter.

Despite these successes, free blacks had difficult lives. They were denied basic rights, such as the right to vote or travel. Free blacks also feared being kidnapped and sold into slavery.

**Slaves.** By 1860, slaves made up one third of the population of the South. Most worked as field hands on cotton plantations. Men and women did backbreaking labor in the field. They cleared new land, planted, and harvested crops. Teenagers worked alongside adults in the fields. Children pulled weeds, picked insects from crops, and carried water to other workers.

Some slaves became skilled workers such as blacksmiths and carpenters. Planters often hired these skilled

Historians use graphs to show trends, or developments over time, as you learned in Skill Lesson 4 (page 81). Often, historians use two or more graphs to compare different kinds of information. They can compare a line graph and a circle graph. They can also use two line, bar, or circle graphs.

By comparing graphs, historians can often begin to draw conclusions about two or more developments. For example, suppose one graph shows an increase in population during a certain period. Another graph shows a decrease in disease for the same period. Historians looking at the graphs might think that population increased because disease decreased. They would need to know more information before they could be certain, however.

The graphs below are both line graphs. Each shows a trend that took place over a number of years. By comparing the two graphs and thinking about what you read in this chapter, you can draw conclusions about the two developments.

1. **Identify the information shown on the graphs.** (a) What is the title of the graph at left? (b) What is the title of the graph at right? (c) What do the numbers on the horizontal axis and vertical axis of the graph at left show? (d) What do the numbers on each axis of the graph at right show?

2. **Practice reading the graphs.** Notice that the numbers given on the vertical axis are in thousands. (a) About how many thousands of bales of cotton were produced in 1830? In 1860? (b) What was the slave population in 1830? In 1860?

3. **Compare the information shown on the graphs.** Use the graphs and your reading of this chapter to answer these questions. (a) Was there an upward or downward trend in cotton production between 1800 and 1860? (b) Was there an upward or downward trend in slave population in the same period? (c) How do you think the trend in cotton production is related to the trend in slave population?

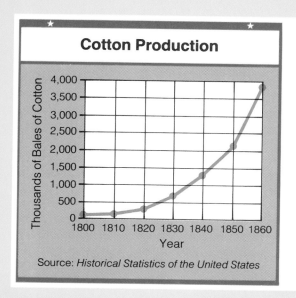

**Cotton Production**

Thousands of Bales of Cotton / Year

Source: *Historical Statistics of the United States*

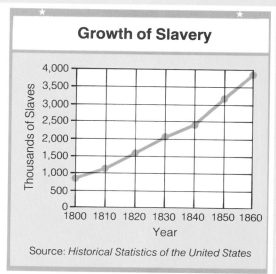

**Growth of Slavery**

Thousands of Slaves / Year

Source: *Historical Statistics of the United States*

workers out to other plantations. Some slaves worked in cities and lived almost as if they were free blacks. But their earnings belonged to their owners.

Older slaves, especially women, worked as servants in the planter's house. They cooked, cleaned, and did other chores under the supervision of the planter's wife.

## The Life of Slaves

The slave's life depended on individual owners. Some owners treated their slaves well. They made sure that their slaves had decent food, clean houses, and warm clothes. Other planters spent as little as possible to feed, clothe, and shelter slaves.

**Hard work.** Many planters were determined to get the most work possible from their slaves. As a result, slaves worked from sunup to sundown, as much as 16 hours a day. Frederick Douglass, an escaped slave, recalled his life under one harsh master:

> We were worked in all weathers. It was never too hot or too cold; it could never rain, blow, hail, or snow too hard for us to work in the field. Work, work, work. . . . The longest days were too short for him and the shortest nights too long for him.

Slaves sometimes suffered whippings and other cruel punishments. They had only one real protection against such treatment. Owners saw their slaves as valuable property. Therefore, most slave owners wanted to keep this human property healthy and productive.

**Slave families.** Keeping a family together was difficult for slaves. Because slaves were property, owners could buy and sell them at will. The law did not even recognize slave marriages or slave families. As a result, a husband and wife could be sold to different plantations. And children could be taken away from their parents and sold.

Nevertheless, family life provided a feeling of pride for slaves. Families gathered together during their precious time away from work. They kept small gardens. Parents and grandparents took care of children.

Slaves preserved some African customs. For example, grandparents, parents, children, aunts, uncles, and cousins formed a close-knit family group. This idea of an *extended family* had its roots in Africa. Slaves also handed down stories and songs to their children. In African cultures, parents taught children songs as a way to pass on their history and moral ideas.

Faith in God helped slaves cope with the harshness of daily life. Bible stories about how the ancient Israelites were freed from slavery inspired many slave songs. As they toiled in the fields, slaves sang about a coming day of freedom. One slave song, "Go Down, Moses," includes the lines:

> We need not always weep and moan,
>   Let my people go;
> And wear these slavery chains forlorn,
>   Let my people go.

## Resisting Slavery

Slaves actively fought against the system that denied them freedom. Some slaves resisted by breaking tools and destroying crops. Others pretended to be sick. Another way to resist was to run away. But escapes were seldom successful.

At times, slaves reacted with violence to the brutal system under which they lived. Denmark Vesey, a free black, planned a revolt in 1822. Vesey was betrayed before the revolt began. He and 35 others were executed.

In 1831, a slave preacher named Nat Turner led his followers through Virginia, killing more than 60 whites. Terrified whites hunted the countryside for Turner and his followers. They killed many innocent blacks before catching and hanging Turner.

Nat Turner's revolt increased southern fears of slave uprisings. But

These two pictures show the sorrow and the dignity of slave life. The slave auction at left shows a mother and her infant being sold in Missouri. Slave families were often broken up at auctions. The early photograph at right shows that some slave families succeeded in staying together. The grandparents, parents, and children in this family lived and worked together on a South Carolina plantation.

revolts were rare. Slaves had little chance to organize or arm themselves.

## Slave Codes

To keep control of the growing number of slaves, Southerners passed laws known as slave codes (see page 130). These laws were designed to keep slaves from rebelling or running away. Under the slave codes, slaves were not allowed outside after dark. They could not gather in groups of more than three or four. They could not leave their owner's land without a written pass. They could not own weapons.

Slave codes also made it a crime for slaves to learn to read and write. By limiting education for slaves, owners hoped to keep them from escaping. If slaves did escape, they had trouble finding their way north. Few runaway slaves could use maps or read train schedules.

Other laws were meant to protect slaves. For example, owners were forbidden to mistreat slaves. But slaves did not have the right to testify in court. So they could not bring charges against cruel owners.

As slavery grew, the economic ties between the North and South became stronger. Northern mill owners needed cotton from the South. And Southerners relied on goods from northern factories. Yet Americans saw that the two sections had different ways of life. Slavery seemed to be the key difference between them.

### SECTION REVIEW

1. **Define:** extended family.
2. Why did planters dominate southern life?
3. Describe the daily life of slaves.
4. How did Nat Turner's revolt affect white Southerners?
5. **What Do You Think?** How do you think denying education to slaves helped prevent escape attempts?

# Chapter 15 Review

 **Summary**

By the 1840s, the North and South were taking different paths. In the North, machines hummed inside new factories. People from farms and immigrants poured into cities to find jobs. As factory conditions got worse, men and women workers formed unions. They made few gains at first.

In the South, cotton growing spread, as did slavery. Most Southerners owned no slaves. Yet large planters dominated southern life and politics.

Slaves worked long hours for no pay, and slave codes made escape difficult. Family ties and religion eased some of the pain of slavery. Slavery was the key difference between the ways of life in the North and South.

 **Reviewing the Facts**

**Key Terms.** Match each term in Column 1 with the correct definition in Column 2.

| Column 1 | Column 2 |
|---|---|
| 1. trade union | **a.** someone who wanted to limit immigration |
| 2. strike | **b.** refusal by workers to do their jobs |
| 3. famine | **c.** unfavorable opinion about people of a different religion, race, or nationality |
| 4. nativist | **d.** organization of skilled workers |
| 5. prejudice | **e.** severe food shortage |

**Key People, Events, and Ideas.** Identify each of the following.

1. Isaac Singer
2. Cyrus McCormick
3. Samuel F. B. Morse
4. Donald McKay
5. Know-Nothing Party
6. Eli Whitney
7. Cotton Kingdom
8. Norbert Rillieux
9. Denmark Vesey
10. Nat Turner

★ **Chapter Checkup**

1. (a) What inventions improved farming in the 1830s and 1840s? (b) How did these inventions help factories grow?

2. (a) What inventions changed the way people kept in touch and traveled? (b) How did these inventions help the economy expand?

3. (a) How did clipper ships help the United States capture sea trade? (b) What cut short the age of clipper ships?

4. (a) How were conditions in factories changing by the 1840s? (b) How did factory workers respond to these changes?

5. (a) Why did immigration to the United States increase in the 1840s? (b) How did some native-born Americans respond?

6. (a) What was the Southern economy based on? (b) Why did slavery grow in the South through the mid-1800s?

7. (a) What were the three groups of white Southerners? (b) Which group was the most influential? Why?

8. (a) Why was family life important to slaves? (b) Why was it difficult for slave families to stay together?

## ★ Thinking About History ★

1. **Understanding geography.** A Norwegian farmer who came to the United States in the 1830s wrote, "Here in America, it is the railroads that build up the whole country." (a) How did railroads help the country grow? (b) What sections of the country did railroads help most?

2. **Relating past to present.** (a) How did the Industrial Revolution in the early 1800s change the way of life for many Northerners? (b) What major change is taking place in industry today? (c) How is it changing the way of life for many people?

3. **Learning about citizenship.** Why do you think Germans fleeing their country after 1848 wanted to come to the United States?

4. **Understanding the economy.** In the 1840s, a Southerner wrote this description of a southern gentleman: "See him with northern pen and ink, writing letters on northern paper, and sending them away in northern envelopes, sealed with northern wax, and impressed with a northern stamp." What point about the South do you think the writer was making?

## ★ Using Your Skills ★

1. **Placing events in time.** Study the time line on page 332. (a) When did slavery end in the North? (b) What event on the time line was a response to slavery in the South? (c) From your reading of the chapter, did the number of slaves in the South shrink or grow from 1820 to 1860?

2. **Comparing.** Review the descriptions of how free blacks lived in the North and South on pages 340 and 344. (a) In which section of the country did free blacks have more freedom? (b) Why do you think free blacks had more freedom there? (c) What basic rights were denied to free blacks in both sections?

3. **Using a painting as a primary source.** Study the painting on page 338. (a) What does the painting show? (b) How can you tell it was painted after 1800? (c) Do you think a painting of a town in the South would look different? Explain.

4. **Map reading.** Study the product maps on pages 334 and 342. (a) What products did both the North and South produce? (a) What products did the South alone produce? Why?

## ★ More to Do ★

1. **Preparing a report.** Write a report about the potato—where it was first grown, how it was used, and why it was important in Ireland. Use information from encyclopedias and books.

2. **Drawing a cartoon.** Draw a cartoon that either supports or criticizes the attitude of nativists toward immigrants in the 1850s.

3. **Writing a dialogue.** Write a dialogue between one Southerner who wants to invest in land to grow cotton and another Southerner who wants to build a textile mill.

4. **Exploring local history.** Prepare an oral report about the legal status of blacks in your local area during the 1850s.

# CHAPTER

# 16

# The Reforming
# Spirit (1820–1860)

## Chapter Outline

**1** Crusade Against Slavery
**2** Rights for Women
**3** Reform Marches On
**4** Creating an American Culture
Readings, page 546

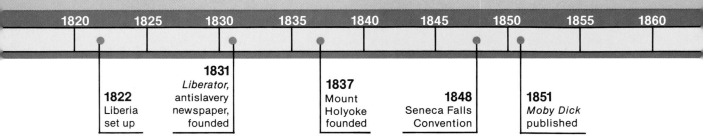

| 1820 | 1825 | 1830 | 1835 | 1840 | 1845 | 1850 | 1855 | 1860 |
|---|---|---|---|---|---|---|---|---|

**1822**
Liberia
set up

**1831**
*Liberator,*
antislavery
newspaper,
founded

**1837**
Mount
Holyoke
founded

**1848**
Seneca Falls
Convention

**1851**
*Moby Dick*
published

## About This Chapter

In the mid-1800s, a spirit of reform spread across the nation. People joined together to make others aware of America's problems and try to cure them. Some reformers called for better schools. Others tried to win basic rights for women. Many joined the movement to end slavery.

An important event in the antislavery movement came in 1829. That year, a free black named David Walker published his *Appeal to the Coloured Citizens of the World*. Walker urged slaves to throw off their chains by any means necessary. "Remember, Americans, that we must and shall be free," Walker warned. If slaves were not given their freedom, they would seize it by force, he threatened. "Will you wait until we shall,

under God, obtain our liberty by the crushing arm of power? Will it not be dreadful for you?" he asked white Americans.

Walker's book created a sensation in both the North and South. Many people, especially Southerners, were horrified by the threat of a slave revolt. Some Southerners refused even to listen to arguments against slavery from that point on.

Few antislavery reformers went as far as Walker did. Most hoped to end slavery gradually. Like other reformers, their goal was to make America a better place. In many cases, the efforts of these reformers succeeded.

Study the time line above. Which event do you think was an advance for the antislavery movement?

In the 1840s, more American children began going to school. Winslow Homer painted these schoolchildren playing a game called Snap the Whip.

# 1 Crusade Against Slavery

### Read to Learn

★ How did the antislavery movement grow?

★ What did antislavery groups do to help slaves?

★ How did Americans react to the antislavery crusade?

★ What do these words mean: abolition, underground railroad?

In the Age of Jackson, many Americans pointed proudly to the growth of democracy in their country. More people could vote and take part in government than before. But some Americans felt that democracy was still far from complete. Their voices rang out strongly against slavery. An English visitor summed up the problem slavery posed for Americans: "You will see them with one hand hoisting the cap of liberty, and with the other flogging their slaves."

## The Reforming Spirit

The idea that slavery was wrong grew out of two different backgrounds. One was political. The other was religious.

**Background.** The political reason for opposing slavery went back to the American Revolution. In the Declaration of Independence, Thomas Jefferson wrote that "all men are created equal." Yet many white Americans, including

Jefferson, did not think that the statement applied to slaves. Reformers felt that this situation had to change.

The second reason for opposing slavery was religious. Since colonial times, Quakers had spoken out against slavery. All men and women were equal in the eyes of God, they said. It was sinful for one human being to own another.

**Ending northern slavery.** In the North, other religious leaders followed the Quakers' example and opposed slavery. Preachers described the evils of slavery in vivid detail. Their sermons convinced many Northerners to take a stand. The campaign against slavery succeeded in the North. By 1804, all states from Pennsylvania north had promised to free slaves within their borders.

Slavery in the North ended without a big struggle. For one thing, there were only 50,000 slaves in the North in 1800, compared to nearly one million in the South. Even so, many whites worried about what would happen to the freed slaves.

**Liberia.** The *American Colonization Society* provided an answer. The society, founded in 1817, wanted to set up a colony in Africa for free blacks. In 1822, President Monroe helped the society establish *Liberia* in western Africa. Liberia was an independent nation in Africa. Its name comes from the Latin word for free.

Free blacks had mixed feelings about Liberia. Some believed that blacks should go to Africa because they would never have equal rights in America. But most blacks wanted to stay in America, their homeland. If free blacks left America, they said, slavery would grow stronger than ever.

At one meeting in Pittsburgh, blacks declared, "African colonization is a scheme to drain the better-informed part of the colored people out of these United States so that the chain of slavery may be riveted more tightly." In the end, only a few thousand blacks settled in Liberia.

## Call for Abolition

By the mid-1800s, the abolition movement was in full swing. *Abolition* means ending something completely. Abolitionists called for an end to slavery everywhere in the United States. Some supported a gradual end to slavery. They hoped that slavery would die out if it was kept out of the new western lands. Others insisted on an immediate end to slavery.

**Black abolitionists.** From the first, blacks played a major part in the abolition movement. Through lawsuits and petitions, blacks tried to abolish slavery. In the 1820s, Samuel Cornish and John Russwurm set up an antislavery newspaper, *Freedom's Journal.* They attacked slavery by publishing stories about the brutal treatment of slaves in the South. James Forten and other successful blacks gave generously to support this paper and other antislavery efforts.

**Frederick Douglass.** The best-known black leader was Frederick Douglass. Douglass had been born into slavery. He secretly taught himself to read, even though it was forbidden by the slave codes. Because he could not own books, Douglass picked through "the mud and filth of the gutter" to find pages from books.

In 1838, Douglass escaped from his owner in Maryland. He fled north to Massachusetts. There, Douglass attended an antislavery meeting. As he listened to the speakers, he felt that he must stand up and speak. In a powerful voice, he told the audience what freedom meant to a slave. Douglass made such a strong impression on the people at the meeting that he was asked to become a lecturer against slavery.

## William Lloyd Garrison

The most outspoken white abolitionist was a fiery young man from Boston, William Lloyd Garrison. In 1831, Garrison launched an antislavery newspaper, *The Liberator*. In the first issue, he told his readers that he would not rest until slavery ended. "I am in earnest. . . . I will not excuse—I will not retreat a single inch—AND I WILL BE HEARD." A year after starting *The Liberator,* Garrison organized the ***New England Anti-Slavery Society*** to press the crusade against slavery.

Garrison attracted other reformers to the cause. Theodore Weld, a minister, worked with Garrison in the 1830s. Weld added the zest of a religious crusade to antislavery meetings. In 1836, Theodore Weld married Angelina Grimké, a southern woman who despised slavery. They toured the North, convincing thousands to join the cause.

## The Underground Railroad

Abolitionists did more than write books and give speeches. Some risked prison and death by helping slaves escape from the South.

Brave men and women formed the underground railroad. This was not a real railroad. The ***underground railroad*** was a secret network of abolitionists. They worked together to help runaway slaves reach freedom in the North or Canada.

Free blacks and whites served as "conductors" on the underground railroad. Conductors guided escaping slaves to "stations" where they could sleep for the night. Some stations were the houses of abolitionists. Others were churches or even caves. Fleeing slaves hid in wagons that had false bottoms or under loads of hay. The trip was dangerous and difficult.

**AMERICANS WHO DARED**

### Frederick Douglass

Frederick Douglass escaped from slavery in Maryland. He became a famous abolitionist speaker in the North. On one occasion, he told an audience: "I expose slavery . . . because to expose it is to kill it. Slavery is one of those monsters of darkness to whom the light of truth is death. Expose slavery and it dies. . . . All the slaveholder asks of me is silence."

One daring conductor, Harriet Tubman, was an escaped slave herself. Tubman risked her life by returning 19 times to the South. She led hundreds of slaves to the North. On one of her last trips, Tubman led her aged parents to freedom.

Despite such efforts, the underground railroad could help only about 1,000 slaves a year to escape. Thus, only a few of the millions of southern slaves reached freedom along the underground railroad.

This painting shows a station on the underground railroad. The escaping slaves have traveled by wagon, hidden under a load of hay. Here, they are taken into a house by a white conductor.

## Responses to the Crusade

Abolitionists like William Lloyd Garrison were unpopular in both the North and South. Northern mill owners and bankers depended on cotton from the South. They saw Garrison's attacks on slavery as a threat to their prosperity. And many northern workers were afraid that freed slaves would come to the North and take their jobs by working for low wages.

In northern cities, mobs sometimes broke up antislavery meetings. They beat abolitionists and pelted them with stones. At times, these attacks backfired and won support for the abolitionists. One night, a Boston mob dragged Garrison through the streets at the end of a rope. A doctor who saw the attack wrote, "I am an abolitionist from this very moment."

The movement to end slavery made Southerners very uneasy. They accused abolitionists of preaching violence. David Walker's call for a slave revolt seemed to confirm the worst fears of the South. (See page 350.) Southern postmasters refused to deliver abolitionist newspapers. Many Southerners blamed Nat Turner's revolt in 1831 on Garrison. He had founded *The Liberator* only a few months before Turner's rebellion.

In response to the antislavery crusade, many slave owners defended slavery. One wrote that with good food, clothing, and houses, "the slaves will love their master and serve him cheerfully, diligently, and faithfully." Others argued that slaves were better off than northern workers who toiled in dusty, airless factories.

The antislavery movement grew in the 1840s and 1850s. It deepened the division between the North and South.

Even Southerners who owned no slaves felt that slavery had to be defended. To them, slavery was an essential part of the southern economy. Southerners tended to exaggerate northern support for the antislavery movement. They began to believe that Northerners wanted to destroy their way of life.

### SECTION REVIEW

1. **Define:** abolition, underground railroad.
2. Give two reasons why Americans opposed slavery.
3. (a) When did northern states end slavery? (b) Why did slavery there end without a big struggle?
4. (a) What was the goal of the American Colonization Society? (b) Why did many free blacks oppose colonization?
5. **What Do You Think?** Why do you think escaped slaves like Frederick Douglass made good antislavery speakers?

# 2 Rights for Women

## Read to Learn

★ What rights did women want in the mid-1800s?

★ Who were the leaders of the women's rights movement?

★ What did the Seneca Falls Convention achieve?

Both black and white women were active in the antislavery crusade. They held meetings, signed petitions, and wrote letters to Congress. As they worked to end slavery, women realized that they could make few changes because they lacked full social and political rights. As a result, many women abolitionists became crusaders for women's rights.

## Women's Rights Movement

In the 1800s, women had few political or legal rights. They could not vote or hold office. When a woman married, her property passed to her husband. If a woman held a job, her earnings belonged to her husband. A man also had the right to punish his wife as long as he did not seriously injure her.

**The Grimké sisters.** Women in the antislavery movement saw all too clearly how limited their rights were. Among the first to speak out on the subject were the Grimké sisters. Angelina and Sarah Grimké came from a slave-owning family in South Carolina. They grew to hate slavery and moved to the North to work for abolition. Their firsthand knowledge of slavery made them powerful speakers, and they drew large crowds in northern cities.

Some Northerners were shocked at the boldness of the Grimkés. Women rarely stood on stage and addressed an audience that included men. Preachers scolded the Grimkés. "When [a woman] assumes the place and tone of a man as a public reformer," warned several preachers, "her character becomes unnatural."

The Grimkés did not give up their crusade, however. Instead, Angelina Grimké answered critics in letters and pamphlets. She insisted on discussing women's rights as well as abolition: "What then can woman do for the slave, when she herself is under the feet of man and shamed into silence?"

**Sojourner Truth.** Black women also struggled for women's rights. Sojourner Truth was born into slavery in New York State. She ran away from her owner just before state law would have freed her. Truth was a spellbinding speaker. Once, she listened to a man claiming that women needed to be protected. Truth stood up and replied:

Sojourner Truth was born Isabella Baumfree in New York State. In 1827, she took her new name, claiming that God had sent her to tell the truth about slavery. Although she could not read, Truth was a powerful speaker for abolition and women's rights.

Nobody ever helps me into carriages, or over mudpuddles, or gives me any best place! And ain't I a woman? . . . I have borne thirteen children, and seen them most all sold off into slavery, and when I cried out with my mother's grief, none but Jesus heard me! And ain't I a woman?

**Others speak for equality.** Inspired by the Grimkés and Sojourner Truth, other women spoke up for women's rights. Many of these leaders came out of the antislavery movement. One group of women, including Lucretia Mott and Elizabeth Cady Stanton, traveled to London in 1840 for the World Antislavery Convention. When they arrived, they found that they were not welcome. Women were barred from the meeting!

After returning home, Mott and Stanton took up the cause of women's rights with new zeal. Mott was a Quaker minister and the mother of five children. A quiet speaker, her logic won the respect of many listeners. Elizabeth Cady Stanton was the daughter of a well-known New York judge. When she was growing up, clerks in her father's law office teased Stanton. They read her laws that denied basic rights to women. This teasing helped make Stanton a lifelong foe of inequality.

Another energetic organizer was Susan B. Anthony. She was ready to go anywhere at any time to speak for the cause. Even when an audience heckled her and threw eggs, Anthony always finished her speech. Anthony joined forces with Stanton and other women's rights leaders.

Elizabeth Cady Stanton, at left, and Susan B. Anthony, at right, dedicated their lives to the women's rights movement. Anthony was a superb organizer. In fact, one woman called her "the Napoleon of the movement," after the French military genius.

## The Seneca Falls Convention

Mott and Stanton decided to hold a national convention for women's rights. They wanted to draw attention to the problems women faced.

In 1848, the convention met in Seneca Falls, New York. At the *Seneca Falls Convention,* leaders of the women's rights movement voted on a plan of action. They called their plan the Declaration of Sentiments. It was modeled on the Declaration of Independence. The new declaration proclaimed, "We hold these truths to be self-evident: that all men and women are created equal."

The men and women at Seneca Falls approved resolutions demanding equality for women at work, school, church, and before the law. All the resolutions passed without a no vote, except for one. It demanded that women be allowed to vote in elections. Even the women at Seneca Falls hesitated to make this bold demand. In the

Many American women had little interest in the movement for women's rights. They were busy with traditional duties such as raising children, keeping house, and helping their husbands. As this print shows, getting produce from the farm to market was a task that needed the help of the whole family.

end, they approved the demand by a slim majority.

The Seneca Falls Convention marked the beginning of an organized women's rights movement. In the years after 1848, women worked for change in many areas. They won more legal rights in some states. New York State passed laws allowing women to keep property and earnings when they married. But progress was slow. Many men and women opposed the women's rights movement. The struggle for equal rights would be long.

## Improving Women's Education

A major concern of women at Seneca Falls was education. At the time, poor white and black women had little hope of even learning to read and write.

Middle class families could often afford to send their daughters to school. However, young women learned dancing and drawing, not mathematics or science, as young men did. Since women were expected to marry and take care of families, people thought that they did not need to learn such subjects.

Reformers like Emma Willard and Mary Lyon worked hard to improve education for women. Willard opened a high school for women in Troy, New York, that taught all subjects. Lyon spent years raising money to build Mount Holyoke Female Seminary. She avoided calling the school a college because many people thought that sending women to college was wrong. But Mount Holyoke, which opened in 1837, was the first women's college in America.

Twenty-nine medical schools refused to admit Elizabeth Blackwell because she was a woman. Friends advised her to take a man's name and clothing in order to reach her goal. Blackwell refused. Later, she was accepted at Geneva Medical College. In 1857, Blackwell set up a hospital for the poor in New York City.

Women also struggled to get an education in fields such as medicine. Elizabeth Blackwell applied to medical school at Geneva College in New York. She was accepted, even though most school officials thought that she would fail. To their surprise, Blackwell graduated first in her class. Many women had practiced medicine since colonial times, but Blackwell was the first woman doctor with a medical degree. She later set up the first nursing school in the United States.

At about the same time, a few men's colleges began to admit women. As women's education improved, women found jobs teaching, especially in grade schools.

## ═ SECTION REVIEW ═

1. What did women abolitionists realize about their rights?
2. Describe the role each of the following played in the women's rights movement: (a) Sojourner Truth; (b) Lucretia Mott; (c) Susan B. Anthony.
3. (a) What was the first women's college in the United States? (b) When did it open?
4. **What Do You Think?** Why do you think women at the Seneca Falls Convention modeled their declaration on the Declaration of Independence?

# 3 Reform Marches On

### Read to Learn
★ What reforms did Dorothea Dix seek?
★ How did public schools change in the 1800s?
★ What do these words mean: temperance movement?

The 1830s and 1840s were a busy period of reform. Hundreds of groups sprang up to urge improvements in everything from schools to prisons.

## Dorothea Dix

One Sunday in 1851, Dorothea Dix, a Massachusetts schoolteacher, was invited to read to prisoners in the local jail. When she entered the jail, Dix was horrified by what she found. A group of mentally ill people were locked up alongside the criminals. They were dressed in rags and kept in unheated cells. When Dorothea Dix left the jail, she decided she had to take action.

**Help for the mentally ill.** During the next 18 months, Dix visited every jail and asylum for the mentally ill in Massachusetts. In a report to the Massachusetts legislature, Dix listed the horrors she had seen. She told of inmates kept in "cages, closets, cellars, stalls, [and] pens." She pointed out that these people were ill and should be treated as patients, not criminals.

In response to her report, the legislature voted to improve care for the mentally ill. Dix took her crusade to many other states. In almost every one, her reports resulted in action to help the mentally ill.

**Prison reform.** Dix also criticized the horrible conditions in the prisons she visited. Prisoners were often stuffed into tiny, cold, damp rooms. Men, women, and children shared the same crowded quarters. If food was in short supply, prisoners went hungry unless they had money to buy meals from the jailers.

In the 1800s, people were jailed even for minor crimes such as owing money. In 1830, five out of six people in northern jails were debtors. Most owed less than $20. For more serious crimes, people suffered severe punishments such as whipping and branding.

Dorothea Dix's report to the Massachusetts legislature on the mentally ill pulled no punches. Dix wrote, "The condition of human beings, reduced to the extremist state of misery, cannot be told in softened language." Although her report shocked some legislators, it got quick action.

Reformers like Dix called for changes in the prison system. As a result, some states built new prisons housing one or two inmates to a cell. People convicted of minor crimes received shorter sentences. Cruel punishments were forbidden. And slowly, states stopped treating debtors as criminals.

## A Better Education

Reformers believed that all people needed an education. As more men won the right to vote, reformers felt they needed to be well informed.

However, few American children went to school before the 1820s. Where public schools existed, they were often old and run-down. Schools had little money for books. Teachers were poorly paid and trained. Students of all ages crowded together in a single room. Faced with a class of 80 students, many teachers worried more about controlling their students than teaching them.

**Growth of public schools.** In the 1820s, New York State led the way in public education. The state ordered every town to set up an elementary school. The new public schools were not totally free. Parents had to pay something for their children to attend. But it was a start. Before long, other states passed similar laws requiring towns to support public schools.

Horace Mann led the fight for public schools in Massachusetts. In 1837, Mann was put in charge of education in the state. He hounded legislators to provide money for new and better elementary schools. Under Mann's leadership, Massachusetts built new schools, extended the school year, and paid teachers better. The state also opened three colleges to train teachers.

Reformers in other states pressed their legislatures to follow the lead of Massachusetts. By the 1850s, most northern states had free, tax-supported elementary schools. Schools in the

South improved, but more slowly. In both the North and South, schooling stopped after eighth grade. There were very few public high schools.

**Schools for black Americans.** Free black children had little chance for an education. A few cities, such as Boston and New York, set up separate schools for black students. But these schools got less money than schools for white students. Even so, some blacks did get good educations. A few attended private colleges such as Harvard, Dartmouth, and Oberlin. In the 1850s, several colleges for black students opened in the North.

**Education for the disabled.** A few reformers worked to improve education for the physically disabled. In 1815, the Reverend Thomas Gallaudet (gal uh DEHT) set up a school for the deaf in Hartford, Connecticut. Gallaudet showed that deaf children could learn like other children. A few years later, Dr. Samuel Gridley Howe directed the first school for the blind. Howe invented a way to print books with raised letters. Blind students could read the letters by using their fingers.

## Fighting Demon Rum

In the 1800s, drinking alcohol was a widespread problem. At political rallies, weddings, and even funerals, men, women, and sometimes children drank alcohol. Often they drank heavily.

Reformers cried out against "demon rum." They linked alcohol to crime, the breakup of families, and mental illness. The campaign against drinking was called the *temperance movement.*

As new schools were built in the 1840s and 1850s, talented young women went into teaching. By 1860, most of the country's elementary school teachers were women. Why do you think women wanted to become teachers?

Some temperance groups wanted to persuade people to limit their drinking. Others demanded that states prohibit the sale of alcohol.

In the 1850s, Maine banned the sale of alcohol, and eight other states soon followed. However, many Americans opposed these laws, and most were repealed. Still, temperance crusaders pressed on. The movement gained new strength in the late 1800s.

Reform movements did much to improve life in America. Many states built new schools and provided better care for prisoners and the mentally ill. The public became more aware of the dangers of alcohol. Not all reforms succeeded. But in general, Americans had a renewed concern with improving society. And the work of Horace Mann, Dorothea Dix, and others paved the way for later reformers.

"Father, come home!" is the title of this engraving. It shows a young girl leading her father away from a barroom. The picture appeared in an 1854 best-seller exposing the evils of alcohol. The book led many drinkers to give up liquor and "come home" for good.

=== SECTION REVIEW ===

1. **Define:** temperance movement.
2. (a) List two problems Dorothea Dix uncovered. (b) What did she do to correct them?
3. Why did reformers feel that the growth of democracy made education even more important?

4. (a) Who led the fight for better public schools in Massachusetts? (b) What improvements in public education did Massachusetts make?
5. **What Do You Think?** What hopes do you think reformers in various movements shared? Why?

# 4 Creating an American Culture

**Read to Learn**

★ What themes did American writers use?
★ Which women writers enjoyed great popularity?
★ How did an American style of painting develop?

In the 1800s, writers and artists were creating a new vision of America. They broke free of European traditions and created styles that were truly American.

## American Writers

After 1820, American writers began to write stories with American themes. New York and Boston were home to many of the nation's writers.

**Early writers.** Washington Irving was the first American writer to become well known in Europe as well as America. Irving, a New Yorker, published his first works in the 1820s. His two most famous stories are "Rip Van Winkle" and "The Legend of Sleepy

Hollow." The stories appeared in a collection of stories called *The Sketch Book.* Both take place in the Hudson River valley north of New York City.

"Rip Van Winkle" is based on an old Dutch legend. Rip is a simple farmer in the days before the American Revolution. One day, he is put under a magic spell. He sleeps for 20 years. He awakes to find that his quiet village has changed into a bustling town. The town buzzes with talk about "rights of citizens—elections—members of congress—Bunker's Hill—heroes of seventy-six—and other words, which . . . bewildered Van Winkle." Readers appreciated the way Irving poked fun at Rip, who had slept through the entire American Revolution.

In the 1820s, James Fenimore Cooper began to publish a series of popular novels that were set on the American frontier. In *The Last of the Mohicans* and *The Deerslayer,* Cooper gave a romantic, or idealized, view of how whites and Indians got along. However, his stories were so full of exciting adventures that few readers cared whether they were true to life.

**Later novelists.** New England writers like Nathaniel Hawthorne often turned to historical themes. Hawthorne was descended from the Puritans of Salem, Massachusetts. America's Puritan past fascinated him. His best-known novel is *The Scarlet Letter,* published in 1850.

Herman Melville admired Hawthorne's works, and the two men became friends. In 1851, Melville published *Moby Dick,* which ranks among America's greatest novels. *Moby Dick* tells about a voyage of the *Pequod,* a whaling ship commanded by Captain Ahab. Ahab has vowed to kill the great white whale that bit off his leg years earlier. The novel had limited success in the 1800s. Today, however, this dramatic story of a whale hunt is seen as a symbolic struggle between good and evil.

In 1853, William Wells Brown published *Clotel,* a novel about slave life in America. Brown was America's first black novelist and the first black to earn his living as a writer.

**American poets.** John Greenleaf Whittier, a Quaker from Massachusetts, wanted to write poetry about early American history. But with the urging of his friend, William Lloyd Garrison, he found himself drawn to the antislavery cause. In many poems, Whittier sought to make people aware of the evils of slavery.

Of all American poets from this period, Walt Whitman is probably read more often today than any other. He published only one book of poems, *Leaves of Grass.* However, he added poems to this book over a period of 37 years. His bold, emotional language made his poetry different from any written before it. In his poems, Whitman praised America's land and celebrated the many different people that made America great.

## Emerson and His Circle

Perhaps the most widely read American writer in the mid-1800s was Ralph Waldo Emerson. In essays and poems, Emerson emphasized the importance of the individual. He believed that every person had an "inner light" that is part of God. Emerson urged people to rely on this inner light to guide their lives. In 1837, he composed his famous "Concord Hymn." It was dedicated to the first battle of the American Revolution.

Emerson influenced many writers, including Henry David Thoreau (THOR oh). Thoreau's best-known work is *Walden,* which tells about a year he spent living alone in a cabin in Massachusetts. Like Emerson, Thoreau thought that every person must judge what is right and wrong. He wrote: "If a man does not keep pace with his companions, perhaps it is because he hears a

# Arts in America
## Henry Wadsworth Longfellow

Henry Wadsworth Longfellow was America's best-loved poet during the 1800s. He based many of his poems loosely on events from America's past. For example, *The Song of Hiawatha* tells about an Indian chief who lived by Lake Superior in the 1600s. Another poem, *The Courtship of Miles Standish,* weaves its story around a leader of the Plymouth Colony in Massachusetts.

By writing about American themes, Longfellow deepened the feeling Americans had for their past. He also helped to create a sense of identity for Americans. Probably his most famous patriotic poem is "Paul Revere's Ride." The poem is set at the beginning of the American Revolution. It tells about the exciting ride Paul Revere made to alert colonists that British soldiers were on the march. The poem begins:

> Listen, my children, and you shall hear
> Of the midnight ride of Paul Revere,
> On the eighteenth of April, in Seventy-five;
> Hardly a man is now alive
> Who remembers that famous day and year.
> He said to his friend, "If the British march
> By land or sea from the town to-night,
> Hang a lantern aloft in the belfry arch
> Of the North Church tower as a signal light,—
> One, if by land, and two, if by sea;
> And I on the opposite shore will be,
> Ready to ride and spread the alarm
> Through every Middlesex village and farm,
> For the country folk to be up and to arm."

★ Why do you think Longfellow's poems appealed to Americans in the mid-1800s?

---

different drummer. Let him step to the music which he hears." Thoreau hated slavery and was a conductor on the underground railroad.

## Women Writers

Women writers published many books in the 1800s. Margaret Fuller, a friend of Emerson's, wrote *Woman in the Nineteenth Century.* This book strongly influenced the women's rights movement. Women also wrote many of the best-selling novels of the time. These novels often told about young women who gained wealth and happiness by honesty and self-sacrifice. Some novels were more true to life. They showed the hardship faced by widows and orphans.

Few of these novels are read today. But writers like Catharine Sedgwick and Fanny Fern earned far more money than Nathaniel Hawthorne or Herman Melville. In fact, Hawthorne complained bitterly about the success of women writers. "America is now wholly given over to a . . . mob of scribbling women," he once wrote.

## The Artists' View

Most American painters studied in Europe. Their paintings reflected European styles. Benjamin West was a portrait painter in Philadelphia in his youth. Later, he settled in London. West became famous for his historical paintings. In fact, King George III admired his work.

You will sometimes need to research information using books in the library. Every library has a card catalog. The card catalog helps you find the books you need quickly.

1. **Study the parts of the card catalog.** The *card catalog* is a set of drawers holding small cards. The cards are in alphabetical order. Every nonfiction, or factual, book has at least three cards. The author card lists the book by the author's last name. The title card lists the book by its title. The subject card lists the book by its subject—for example, Baseball or American history.

    You can tell what kind of card you are looking at by reading the top line. The top line will show either the author's last name, the title of the book, or the subject heading. Usually, author and title cards are kept together in one set of drawers. Subject cards are kept in another set of drawers.

    Look at Card A. (a) Is this an author, title, or subject card? (b) Who is the author of the book? (c) What is the title of the book? (d) What is the subject of the book?

2. **Practice using the call number.** Every card for a nonfiction book has a number in the top left corner. This is the call number of the book. The *call number* tells you where you will find the book on the library shelves. Each nonfiction book has its call number printed on the spine, or narrow back edge. Nonfiction books are arranged on the shelves in numerical order. The letters after the number are the first letters of the author's last name. Look at Card A. (a) What is the call number of the book? (b) What do the letters "Dul" printed below the call number mean?

3. **Use other cards in the card catalog.** Look at Cards B and C. (a) Is Card B an author, title, or subject card? (b) Is Card C an author, title, or subject card? (c) Why do the two cards have the same call number?

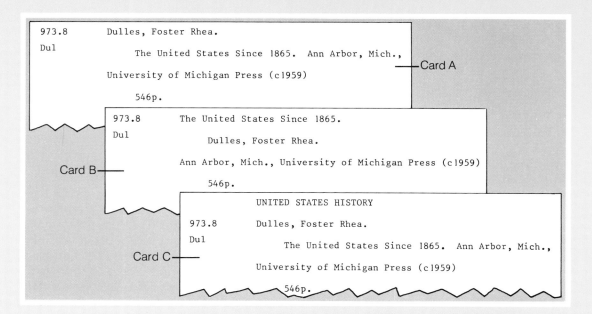

Card A
```
973.8      Dulles, Foster Rhea.
Dul
              The United States Since 1865.  Ann Arbor, Mich.,
University of Michigan Press (c1959)
          546p.
```

Card B
```
973.8      The United States Since 1865.
Dul
              Dulles, Foster Rhea.
          Ann Arbor, Mich., University of Michigan Press (c1959)
              546p.
```

Card C
```
              UNITED STATES HISTORY
973.8      Dulles, Foster Rhea.
Dul
              The United States Since 1865.  Ann Arbor, Mich.,
          University of Michigan Press (c1959)
              546p.
```

George Caleb Bingham captured the mood and details of life on the American frontier, as this painting, *Fur Traders Descending the Missouri,* shows. Bingham said that he painted so that "our social and political characteristics . . . will not be lost."

Many young American artists studied with West in London. They included Charles Wilson Peale, Gilbert Stuart, and John Singleton Copley. Both Peale and Stuart painted well-known portraits of George Washington.

By the mid-1800s, American artists began to develop their own style. The first group of artists to do so belonged to the **Hudson River School.** Artists like Thomas Cole and Asher Durand painted landscapes of the Hudson River and Catskill Mountains of New York.

Other American artists painted scenes of fertile farmlands and hard-working farm families. George Caleb Bingham was inspired by his native Missouri. Bingham's paintings show frontier life along the rivers that feed the great Mississippi.

Artists celebrated the vast American landscape. They expressed confidence in America and its future. This confidence was shared by reformers and by the thousands of Americans opening up new frontiers in the West.

### SECTION REVIEW

1. (a) List three American novelists. (b) Which American writer first became well known in Europe?
2. (a) Who wrote *Leaves of Grass?* (b) What is unusual about this book of poems?
3. What women writers were popular in the mid-1800s?
4. What did artists of the Hudson River School paint?
5. **What Do You Think?** Why do you think Americans only developed a style of painting in the mid-1800s?

# Chapter 16 Review

## ★ Summary ★

By the 1830s, reformers were busy trying to improve American life. Many joined the antislavery crusade. Northern abolitionists strongly attacked slavery. Some risked their lives to help slaves escape on the underground railroad.

Women abolitionists saw how their own rights were limited. In 1848, women's rights supporters held a convention at Seneca Falls. There, they drew up a list of demands. Other reformers called for more schools, improved care for the mentally ill, prison reform, and temperance.

At the same time, a new generation of writers and artists developed American themes. Together, the reformers, writers, and artists showed how the nation was maturing. Americans set out with confidence to cure the country's ills and to define what America was.

## ★ Reviewing the Facts ★

**Key Terms.** Match each term in Column 1 with the correct definition in Column 2.

| Column 1 | Column 2 |
|---|---|
| **1.** abolition | **a.** ending something completely |
| **2.** underground railroad | **b.** campaign against drinking |
| **3.** temperance movement | **c.** secret network of people who helped runaway slaves |

**Key People, Events, and Ideas.** Identify each of the following.

1. Liberia
2. Frederick Douglass
3. William Lloyd Garrison
4. Angelina Grimké
5. Sojourner Truth
6. Lucretia Mott
7. Seneca Falls Convention
8. Dorothea Dix
9. Horace Mann
10. Washington Irving
11. William Wells Brown
12. Walt Whitman
13. Margaret Fuller
14. Benjamin West
15. Hudson River School

## ★ Chapter Checkup ★

1. (a) What were the political roots of the antislavery movement? (b) What were the religious roots of the antislavery movement?

2. (a) Who were leaders of the abolition movement? (b) How did they try to end slavery?

3. (a) Why did some Northerners oppose the antislavery movement? (b) How did most white Southerners respond to the movement?

4. (a) How were women's rights limited in the 1800s? (b) What did women at the Seneca Falls Convention demand?

5. (a) What was the condition of public schools in the early 1800s? (b) How was education improved in the mid-1800s?

6. (a) How did opportunities for higher education for women change after 1820? (b) How did education for blacks change after 1820?

7. What theme did each of the following write about: (a) Washington Irving; (b) James Fenimore Cooper; (c) Walt Whitman?

8. What themes did American painters in the mid-1800s take up?

## ★ Thinking About History ★

1. **Relating past to present.** (a) How did antislavery leaders try to win support of the public? (b) How do reform leaders today try to win support for their causes?

2. **Understanding the economy.** By the mid-1800s, factories supplied many household items once made by hand. As a result, middle class women had more free time. (a) How does this fact help explain why some women became active reformers? (b) How does it explain why writers like Fanny Fern were so popular?

3. **Analyzing information.** American writers in the 1800s stressed the importance of the individual. How does the history of the United States help explain this emphasis on the individual?

4. **Learning about citizenship.** During the mid-1800s, Americans worked to reform many aspects of American life. (a) What new roles do you think women and black reformers took on? (b) How do you think the actions of abolitionists, women's rights supporters, and other reformers made Americans look at their society in a new way?

## ★ Using Your Skills ★

1. **Making a review chart.** Make a review chart with five columns and three rows. Label the columns Abolition, Women's Rights, Care for Mentally Ill, Prison Reform, and Education Reform. Label the rows Problems to Solve, Leaders, and Achievements. Then complete the chart. (a) According to the chart, how many people were leaders of more than one movement? (b) Which movement do you think achieved the most?

2. **Using a painting as a primary source.** Study the painting on page 360. (a) When was the painting done? (b) How does the classroom in the painting differ from a classroom today? (c) How is it similar?

3. **Placing events in time.** Study the time line on page 350. (a) When did William Lloyd Garrison begin publishing *The Liberator?* (b) When was the first women's college opened? (c) When was the Seneca Falls Convention held?

## ★ More to Do ★

1. **Inventing a story.** Imagine that you are a slave escaping to the North. Invent a story explaining why you are traveling alone.

2. **Writing a dialogue.** Write a dialogue between Sojourner Truth and the man she was answering in the incident described on pages 355 and 356.

3. **Drawing a cartoon.** Draw a cartoon criticizing the practice of putting debtors in prison.

4. **Writing a report.** Read Washington Irving's "Rip Van Winkle" or "The Legend of Sleepy Hollow." Write a report telling what happens in the story. What information does the story give about life in America?

5. **Exploring local history.** Write a report about efforts to reform slavery, women's rights, prisoners' rights, education, or mental health care in your local area during the mid-1800s.

# Unit 5 Review

**Chapter 13** Andrew Jackson became President in 1828. His bold actions made the office of President stronger. Despite conflicts, Jackson was a hero to common people just gaining a voice in politics.

**Chapter 14** America expanded quickly after 1820. Settlers moved to Texas and Oregon, which both became part of the United States in the mid-1840s. The Mexican War added California and the Southwest to the Union. By 1850, America stretched from sea to sea.

**Chapter 15** The North and South developed different ways of life through the mid-1800s. Industry and trade thrived in northern cities. In the South, the Cotton Kingdom spread and slavery grew.

**Chapter 16** By the 1830s, many reformers were working to improve America. Abolitionists tried to end slavery, women demanded basic rights, and other reformers sought to improve schools, prisons, and care for the mentally ill. New writers and artists helped shape American culture.

★ **Unit Checkup** ★

Choose the word or phrase that best completes each of the following statements.

1. President Martin Van Buren lost support because of the
   (a) Nullification Crisis.
   (b) Panic of 1837.
   (c) Indian Removal Act.

2. From 1818 to 1845, the United States occupied Oregon jointly with
   (a) Britain.
   (b) Russia.
   (c) France.

3. When Texans charged at the Battle of San Jacinto, they shouted,
   (a) "Fifty-four forty or fight!"
   (b) "Tippecanoe and Tyler too!"
   (c) "Remember the Alamo!"

4. Because of the potato famine of 1845, thousands of people came to America from
   (a) Germany.
   (b) Ireland.
   (c) France.

5. Helping free blacks move to Liberia was the goal of the
   (a) New England Anti-Slavery Society.
   (b) Seneca Falls Convention.
   (c) American Colonization Society.

★ **Building American Citizenship** ★

1. Many Irish and German immigrants came to the United States in the mid-1800s. (a) Why did nativists want to limit immigration? (b) What reasons do people today give for putting limits on immigration?

2. The black population of the 1800s included free blacks as well as slaves. (a) Why do you think free blacks worked to end slavery? (b) How do you think free blacks in the South felt about the antislavery movement?

3. Through family life, slaves passed on to their children pride in their history and moral ideas. Why do you think Americans today see family life as important to the nation?

# ★ Critical Thinking Skills ★

The map at right shows the growth of railroads between 1840 and 1860. Study the map. Then answer the following questions.

1. Were there more railroads in the North or South in 1840? In 1860?

2. (a) Which northern states had the most miles of railroad track in 1840? In 1860? (b) What can you conclude about the growth of the country's population?

3. Why do you think there were no railroads in western Virginia and eastern Kentucky?

4. Besides the railroads, what transportation advantages did Buffalo, Cleveland, Detroit, Chicago, and Milwaukee share?

5. How do you think the growth of factories in the North affected the building of railroads?

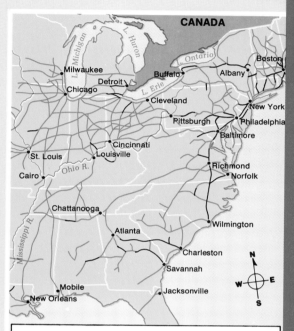

## GROWTH OF RAILROADS

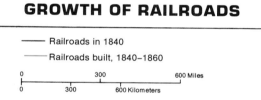

—— Railroads in 1840

—— Railroads built, 1840–1860

0 ___ 300 ___ 600 Miles
0 ___ 300 ___ 600 Kilometers

## ★ History Writer's Handbook ★

### Arranging Information for Comparison

Comparison order is arrangement of supporting information according to similarities and differences. One way to group the information is by subject.

Look at the following topic sentence: *The North's economy was different from the South's economy.* The subjects being compared are the economies of the North and South. In the detail sentences, first present all the information about one subject. For example: *The North's economy was based on manufacturing and trade. Northerners built new factories. They laid miles of railroad track.*

Then using a transition, present all the information about the other subject. Common transitions for differences include *but, however, in contrast, instead, on the contrary,* and *unlike.* Common transitions for similarities include *both, like, similarly,* and *similar to.*

**Practice** Write detail sentences about the South's economy.

# Unit 6

# THE NATION DIVIDED

| 1836 | 1844 | 1852 | 1860 |
|---|---|---|---|

MARTIN VAN BUREN   JOHN TYLER   JAMES POLK   FRANKLIN PIERCE   JAMES

ANDREW JACKSON   WILLIAM HARRISON   ZACHARY TAYLOR   MILLARD FILLMORE

**1836** ★ Arkansas statehood
**1837** ★ Michigan statehood

**1845** ★ Texas, Florida become states
**1846** ★ Iowa statehood
**1846–48** Mexican War
**1848** ★ Wisconsin statehood; Free Soil Party formed
**1850** Compromise of 1850; ★ California statehood

**1852** *Uncle Tom's Cabin* published
**1854** Kansas–Nebraska Act; Republican Party formed
**1858** ★ Minnesota statehood; Lincoln–Douglas debates
**1859** ★ Oregon statehood; raid on Harpers Ferry

| 1836 | 1844 | 1852 | 1860 |
|---|---|---|---|

**Mid-1800s** Southern planters at the New Orleans cotton market.

## CAUTION!!
## COLORED PEOPLE
### OF BOSTON, ONE & ALL,
You are hereby respectfully **CAUTIONED** and advised, to avoid conversing with the
### Watchmen and Police Officers of Boston,
For since the recent **ORDER OF THE MAYOR & ALDERMEN,** they are empowered to act as
## KIDNAPPERS
### AND
## Slave Catchers,
And they have already been actually employed in **KIDNAPPING, CATCHING, AND KEEPING SLAVES.** Therefore, if you value your **LIBERTY,** and the *Welfare of the Fugitives* among you, *Shun* them in every possible manner, as so many *HOUNDS* on the track of the most unfortunate of your race.
### Keep a Sharp Look Out for KIDNAPPERS, and have TOP EYE open.
*APRIL 24, 1851.*

**1851** Even in the North, free blacks and runaway slaves faced dangers, as this poster shows.

**1857** Dred Scott took his fight for freedom to the Supreme Court—and lost.

## UNIT OUTLINE

**CHAPTER** 17 The Coming of the War (1820–1860)

**CHAPTER** 18 The Civil War (1860–1865)

**CHAPTER** 19 The Road to Reunion (1864–1877)

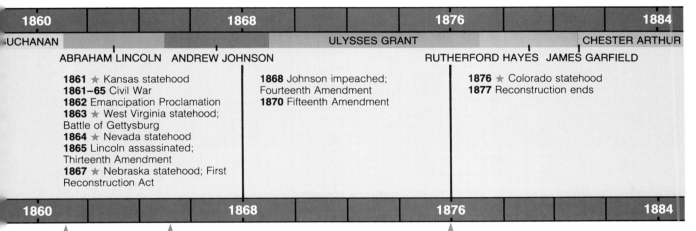

| 1860 | 1868 | 1876 | 1884 |
|---|---|---|---|

UCHANAN | ULYSSES GRANT | CHESTER ARTHUR

ABRAHAM LINCOLN ANDREW JOHNSON | RUTHERFORD HAYES JAMES GARFIELD

**1861** ★ Kansas statehood
**1861–65** Civil War
**1862** Emancipation Proclamation
**1863** ★ West Virginia statehood;
Battle of Gettysburg
**1864** ★ Nevada statehood
**1865** Lincoln assassinated;
Thirteenth Amendment
**1867** ★ Nebraska statehood; First
Reconstruction Act

**1868** Johnson impeached;
Fourteenth Amendment
**1870** Fifteenth Amendment

**1876** ★ Colorado statehood
**1877** Reconstruction ends

| 1860 | 1868 | 1876 | 1884 |
|---|---|---|---|

**1861–65** A Confederate drummer boy.

**1861–65** A lantern showing President Lincoln.

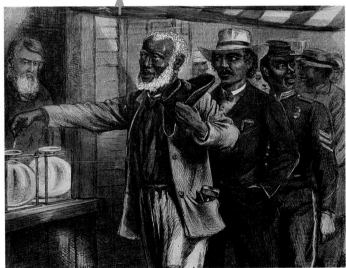

**1865–77** During Reconstruction, freedmen voted in the South.

CHAPTER

# 17

## The Coming of the War (1820–1860)

**Chapter Outline**

**1** Differences Over Slavery
**2** A Great Compromise
**3** Adding Fuel to the Fire
**4** A New Political Party
**5** The Union Is Broken
Readings, page 552

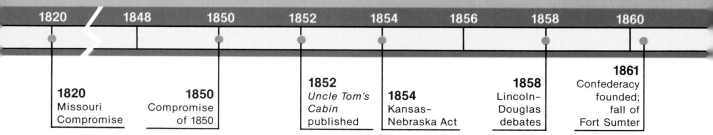

| 1820 | 1848 | 1850 | 1852 | 1854 | 1856 | 1858 | 1860 |
|------|------|------|------|------|------|------|------|

**1820**
Missouri
Compromise

**1850**
Compromise
of 1850

**1852**
*Uncle Tom's
Cabin*
published

**1854**
Kansas–
Nebraska Act

**1858**
Lincoln–
Douglas
debates

**1861**
Confederacy
founded;
fall of
Fort Sumter

## About This Chapter

By the mid-1800s, the issue of slavery sharply divided the North and South. Americans continued to move west into the Louisiana Purchase and then the Mexican Cession. As they did, the nation was forced to deal with this question: Should slavery be allowed in the new states carved out of the western territories? Northerners thought that new states should ban slavery and enter the Union as free states. Southerners thought that new states should allow slavery and join the Union as slave states.

The issue first arose when Missouri applied to join the Union as a slave state in December 1818. Northerners angrily objected to adding another slave state. They knew that another slave state would add to the power of the South in the Senate. A bitter debate erupted in Congress. Thomas Jefferson, then retired, wrote that "in the gloomiest moment of the revolutionary war I never had any [fears] equal to what I feel from this source." Jefferson said that the crisis over Missouri, "like a firebell in the night, awakened and filled me with terror."

Americans compromised on the slavery question at first. However, as time went on, feelings grew more heated, and compromise became more difficult.

Study the time line above. How many years passed between the Missouri Compromise and the Compromise of 1850?

In this painting, a slave family escapes from the South. When Northerners refused to return runaway slaves, an explosive situation developed.

# 1 Differences Over Slavery

## Read to Learn

★ How did the spread of slavery become an issue?

★ How did Congress compromise on the slavery question?

★ Why did some people form the Free Soil Party?

★ What do these words mean: sectionalism, popular sovereignty?

Louisiana was the first state created out of the Louisiana Purchase. Because slavery was well established there, Louisiana joined the Union as a slave state with little discussion in 1812. The issue of slavery in the West first came up in 1818. That year, Missouri's request to join the Union as a slave state caused an uproar.

## Debate Over Missouri

In 1818, there were 11 free states and 11 slave states. Each state had two senators. So there was a balance between the North and South in the Senate. If Missouri joined the Union as a slave state, the South would have a majority in the Senate. Northerners fought against letting Missouri in as a slave state. For months, Congress argued about what to do.

Finally, Senator Henry Clay proposed a plan that both the North and South accepted. During the debate over Missouri, Maine applied to become a state. Clay called for admitting Missouri as a slave state and Maine as a free state. Clay's plan was known as the

*Missouri Compromise.* It kept the number of slave and free states equal.

As part of the Missouri Compromise, Congress drew a line across the southern border of Missouri at latitude 36°30′N. Slavery was permitted in the Louisiana Purchase south of that line. But it was banned north of the line. Missouri itself was the only exception. (See the map on page 380.)

## Debate Over the Mexican Cession

The Missouri Compromise applied to the Louisiana Purchase only. In 1848, the Mexican War added vast lands in the West to the United States. Would slavery be allowed in the Mexican Cession?

**Wilmot Proviso.** Many Northerners opposed the war with Mexico, as you read in Chapter 14. They thought that the South wanted to push slavery into the West. Even before the Mexican War was over, a young congressman from Pennsylvania, David Wilmot, raised the slavery question. Wilmot called on Congress to outlaw slavery in any land won from Mexico. Southerners were furious. They argued that Congress had no right to outlaw slavery in the territories.

In 1846, the House passed Wilmot's measure, called the *Wilmot Proviso.* But the Senate defeated it. As a result, the question of slavery in the territories continued to be debated.

**Choosing sides.** In the 1840s, sectionalism grew stronger. *Sectionalism* means that people feel loyalty to their state or section instead of the whole country. Southerners were united by their support for slavery. To them, the North was a threat. Many Northerners saw the South as a foreign country where American rights and liberties did not exist.

As the debate over slavery in the West heated up, people found it harder not to take sides. Northern abolitionists demanded that slavery be abolished throughout the country. They

In the 1840s, abolitionists stepped up efforts to end slavery. William Whipper, shown here, was a wealthy black lumber merchant who lived in Pennsylvania. He was a leading abolitionist and an ally of William Lloyd Garrison.

insisted that slavery was morally wrong. By the 1840s, a growing number of Northerners agreed with them. Southern slave owners thought that slavery should be allowed in any territory. They also demanded that slaves who escaped to the North be returned to them. Many white Southerners went along with these ideas, even though they owned no slaves.

Between these extreme views were more moderate positions. Some moderates argued that the Missouri Compromise line should be extended across the Mexican Cession all the way to the Pacific. Any new state north of that line would be a free state. Any new state south of the line would be a slave state.

Other moderates supported the idea of popular sovereignty. *Popular sovereignty* means control by the people. In other words, the voters in a territory would decide whether or not to allow slavery. Slaves themselves, of course, could not vote.

**Free Soilers.** Debate over slavery in the territories led to the birth of a new political party. By 1848, many people in both the Whig and Democratic parties strongly opposed the spread of slavery. However, the leaders of both parties refused to take a stand on the question. They were afraid that the issue would split the nation.

Antislavery Whigs and Democrats met in Buffalo, New York, in 1848. They founded the *Free Soil Party.* Their slogan was "Free soil, free speech, free labor, and free men." The main goal of the new party was to stop the spread of slavery into the territories. Only a few Free Soilers were abolitionists who wanted to end slavery in the South.

## Election of 1848

Free Soilers named former President Martin Van Buren as their candidate for President in 1848. Democrats chose Senator Lewis Cass of Michigan.

Cass supported popular sovereignty. Whigs chose Zachary Taylor, hero of the Mexican War. Because Taylor was a slave owner from Louisiana, Whigs believed that he would win many votes in the South.

Taylor easily won the election. But Van Buren, the Free Soil candidate, won 10 percent of the popular vote. And 13 Free Soilers were elected to Congress. The strength of the Free Soilers after only three months of work showed that slavery was a hot political issue.

### SECTION REVIEW

1. **Locate:** Maine, Missouri, Missouri Compromise line.
2. **Define:** sectionalism, popular sovereignty.
3. Why did Missouri's request for statehood cause conflict in Congress?
4. Why was the Free Soil Party founded?
5. **What Do You Think?** How do you think the growth of the Free Soil Party showed that sectionalism was growing stronger?

# 2 A Great Compromise

### Read to Learn
* Why did the slavery question flare up again in 1850?
* How did the North and South again compromise?
* What law forced Northerners to help catch runaway slaves?
* What do these words mean: fugitive, civil war?

In 1850, the question of slavery in the West again divided the North and South. That year, California asked to join the Union as a free state. California was the first territory in the Mexican Cession to apply for statehood. Its request threatened the balance between free and slave states once more.

### Need for Compromise

Between 1821 and 1850, six states joined the Union. Michigan, Iowa, and Wisconsin joined as free states. Arkansas, Florida, and Texas came in as slave states. (See the diagram on page 377.) If California joined as a free state, the North would have a majority in the Senate. So Southerners angrily opposed admitting a free California. They also feared that more free states might be made out of the Mexican Cession. This would further upset the balance. Some Southerners even talked about seceding from the Union.

**Clay's plea.** In the midst of the crisis, Congress turned to Senator Henry Clay for help. Clay was known as the

Here, Senators debate the Compromise of 1850. At center, Henry Clay speaks to his fellow senators. Seated behind Clay, Daniel Webster rests his head on his hand. White-haired John C. Calhoun is the third person from the right. When the Senate at last reached a compromise, newspapers printed headlines such as "The Country Saved" and "Most Glorious News."

Great Compromiser because he had worked out the Missouri Compromise. In 1850, the 73-year-old senator was very ill. Still, he pleaded on the Senate floor for the North and South to compromise. If they failed to do so, Clay warned, the nation could fall apart.

**Calhoun's speech.** Senator John C. Calhoun of South Carolina prepared the southern reply to Clay. Like Clay, Calhoun was aging and ill. He knew that the debate over California was his last battle. Calhoun could not speak loudly enough to address the Senate. So he sat wrapped in a heavy cloak while another senator read his speech.

Calhoun was uncompromising. The slave system could not be changed, he said. Slavery must be allowed in the western territories. Calhoun also brought up the issue of slaves who escaped to the North. Calhoun wanted *fugitive,* or escaped, slaves returned to their owners in the South. Even more, Calhoun wanted Northerners to admit

that Southerners had a right to get their "property" back.

If the North could not agree to southern demands, Calhoun told the Senate, "let the states . . . agree to separate and part in peace. If you are unwilling we should part in peace, tell us so, and we shall know what to do." Calhoun meant that the South would secede from the Union.

**Webster for the Union.** A plea for unity came from Senator Daniel Webster of Massachusetts. Webster had been Henry Clay's rival for decades. But he stood firmly with Clay on the question of preserving the Union. Webster declared that he spoke to Congress "not as a Massachusetts man, not as a Northern man, but as an American."

Webster was upset by the talk of secession. "There can be no such thing as a peaceable secession," he said. The states could not separate without civil war. *Civil war* is a war between people of the same country.

Webster opposed the spread of slavery into the territories. And he demanded an end to the slave trade in Washington, D.C. But he thought that the South was right to ask for the return of escaped slaves.

## Compromise of 1850

In 1850, while the debate still raged, Calhoun died. His last words were: "The South! The South! God knows what will become of her!" President Taylor also died that summer. Taylor had opposed Clay's compromise plan. But the new President, Millard Fillmore, supported it. An agreement finally seemed possible.

Clay was now too sick himself to carry on. Senator Stephen Douglas of Illinois took up the effort. Douglas was smart and energetic. He guided each part of Clay's plan, called the Compromise of 1850, through Congress.

The *Compromise of 1850* had four main parts. First, California was admitted to the Union as a free state. Second, the rest of the Mexican Cession was divided into the New Mexico and Utah territories. In each territory, voters would decide the slavery question according to the idea of popular sovereignty. Third, the slave trade was banned in Washington, D.C. However, Congress declared that it had no right to ban the slave trade between slave states. Fourth, a strict fugitive slave law was passed.

The two sections reached a compromise. But neither side got all it wanted. Northerners were especially angry about the Fugitive Slave Law.

## Fugitive Slave Law

Most Northerners had ignored the old Fugitive Slave Law, passed in 1793. Fugitive slaves often lived as free blacks in northern cities.

The *Fugitive Slave Law of 1850* was more strict. The law said that all citizens had to help catch runaway slaves. Anyone who let a fugitive escape could be fined $1,000 and jailed for six months.

Even free blacks were threatened by the new law. Slave catchers kidnapped free blacks and claimed that they were fugitives. In addition, under the new law, a judge received $10 if a person was sent back to slavery but only $5 if a person was freed. Thus, for some judges, it paid to send blacks to the South, whether or not they were runaway slaves. Free or slave, blacks could not testify in their own defense.

GRAPH SKILL Southerners wanted the number of slave and free states to stay equal. This would keep a balance of power in the Senate. The North, with its large population, had a growing majority in the House of Representatives. How did the admission of California affect the balance between free and slave states?

### Balance of Free and Slave States

| Free States | Slave States |
|---|---|
| 1850 California | 1845 Texas |
| 1848 Wisconsin | 1845 Florida |
| 1846 Iowa | 1836 Arkansas |
| 1837 Michigan | 1821 Missouri |
| 1820 Maine | 1819 Alabama |
| 1818 Illinois | 1817 Mississippi |
| 1816 Indiana | 1812 Louisiana |
| 1803 Ohio | 1796 Tennessee |
| 1791 Vermont | 1792 Kentucky |
| Rhode Island | Virginia |
| New York | North Carolina |
| New Hampshire | South Carolina |
| Massachusetts | Maryland |
| Connecticut | Georgia |
| New Jersey | Delaware |
| Pennsylvania | |

Original 13 states

# Voices of Freedom

## The Play of the Century

In the 1850s, city people escaped from their cares in different ways. In New York, P. T. Barnum's American Museum offered 600,000 "curiosities," including wax figures and live animals. During the 1840s and 1850s, many people went to the theater. Shakespeare's plays were popular, and some American playwrights also met with success. A popular type of play was the melodrama. Melodramas were sensational, tragic stories of love and violence. One well-attended play featured a knife duel, a slave auction, and a steamship explosion.

Many Americans went to plays to forget about the country's worsening political mood. Yet the most popular play of the century had a powerful political message. It was a play based on *Uncle Tom's Cabin,* and its message was "Slavery is wrong!"

The Howards, a famous New York family of actors, gave 18 performances a week of *Uncle Tom's Cabin.* At the same time, 5 other versions of *Uncle Tom's Cabin* were playing in New York theaters.

The play had a major impact on how Northerners viewed slavery. Dramatic moments, like the escape of a slave and her child across the partly frozen Ohio River, won sympathy for slaves. And few playgoers left the theater with dry eyes after seeing the agony of Uncle Tom under Simon Legree's lash.

★ How do you think *Uncle Tom's Cabin* added to the tensions of the 1850s?

---

Southerners were happy with the Fugitive Slave Law, but Northerners hated it. They resented being forced to help capture runaway slaves and thus help slave owners. The sight of helpless people being chained, whipped, and shipped to a life of slavery horrified Northerners. Sometimes, mobs tried to rescue fugitives from their captors. Fights and riots broke out in several northern cities.

## Uncle Tom's Cabin

Northern outrage over the Fugitive Slave Law was inflamed by the novel *Uncle Tom's Cabin,* published in 1852. Harriet Beecher Stowe wrote it to show that slavery was evil and that the Fugitive Slave Law was unjust.

Stowe told the story of Uncle Tom, a kindhearted, aging slave. Uncle Tom's owners lose a lot of money and have to sell their land and slaves. A cruel planter, Simon Legree, buys Uncle Tom. Legree badly mistreats his slaves and finally kills Uncle Tom.

In its first year alone, 300,000 copies of *Uncle Tom's Cabin* were sold. The story was published in many different languages. A play based on the book was staged around the world.

Southerners claimed that *Uncle Tom's Cabin* did not give a true picture of slave life. Indeed, Stowe had seen little of slavery firsthand. Yet the book made people see slavery as a moral problem that touched everyone, not just a political question for Congress to settle. More Americans began to ask if it was right for one human being to own another human being. For this reason, *Uncle Tom's Cabin* was one of the most influential books in American history.

==== SECTION REVIEW ====

1. **Locate:** California, New Mexico Territory, Utah Territory.
2. **Define:** fugitive, civil war.
3. How did the Compromise of 1850 settle the question of slavery in California? In New Mexico and Utah?
4. How did the Fugitive Slave Law of 1850 differ from the one of 1793?
5. **What Do You Think?** Why do you think the Fugitive Slave Law of 1850 angered Northerners?

# 3 Adding Fuel to the Fire

### Read to Learn

★ How did slavery become an issue in 1854?

★ Why was Kansas a testing ground for popular sovereignty?

★ How did the Dred Scott decision affect Northerners and Southerners?

Americans hoped that the Compromise of 1850 would end the debate over slavery in the territories. But the Fugitive Slave Law and *Uncle Tom's Cabin* helped keep tensions high. Then, in 1854, the issue of slavery in the territories surfaced again.

## Kansas–Nebraska Act

In January 1854, Senator Stephen Douglas introduced a bill to set up a government for the Nebraska Territory. The Nebraska Territory stretched from Texas north to Canada and from Missouri west to Oregon. (See the map on page 380.)

Douglas wanted the territory organized so that a railroad could be built through it from Chicago to California. A railroad would open the West to settlers. It would also help Douglas' home state of Illinois by making Chicago the gateway to the West.

**Douglas' plan.** Douglas knew that Southerners would not agree to adding another free state to the Union. So he proposed dividing the Nebraska Territory into two territories, Kansas and Nebraska. The question of slavery in the two territories would be decided by popular sovereignty.

Douglas' bill, called the *Kansas–Nebraska Act,* seemed fair to many people. After all, the Compromise of 1850 applied popular sovereignty in New Mexico and Utah. But other people felt that Kansas and Nebraska were different. The Missouri Compromise had already banned slavery in those areas, they said. The Kansas–Nebraska Act would, in effect, undo the Missouri Compromise.

Southerners supported the Kansas–Nebraska Act. They were sure that Kansas would become a slave state because slave owners from Missouri would move west into Kansas. (See the map on page 380.)

President Franklin Pierce, a Democrat elected in 1852, also backed the bill. With the President's help, Douglas pushed the Kansas–Nebraska Act through Congress. He did not realize it at the time, but he had lit a fire under a powder keg.

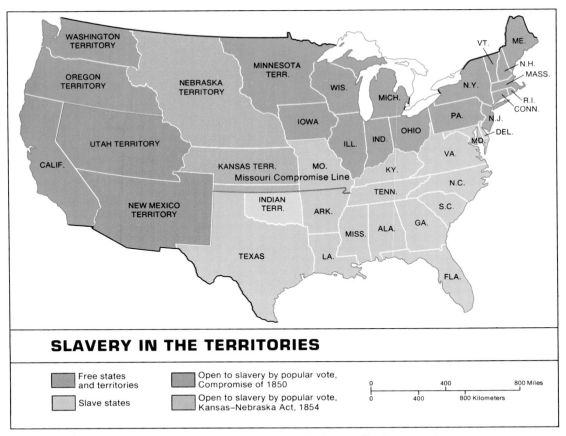

## SLAVERY IN THE TERRITORIES

- Free states and territories
- Slave states
- Open to slavery by popular vote, Compromise of 1850
- Open to slavery by popular vote, Kansas–Nebraska Act, 1854

0          400          800 Miles
0     400     800 Kilometers

MAP SKILL  The issue of slavery in the territories led to conflict between the North and South. In 1850, the North and South agreed to let voters in Utah and New Mexico decide the slavery question for themselves. What territories were opened to slavery in 1854?

**Northerners react.** Northern reaction to the Kansas–Nebraska Act was swift and angry. Opponents of slavery called the act a "criminal betrayal of precious rights." Now, slavery could spread to areas that had been free for over 30 years.

To protest the act, Northerners openly challenged the Fugitive Slave Law. Two days after the Kansas–Nebraska Act was passed, slave catchers in Boston seized Anthony Burns, an escaped slave. Citizens of Boston poured into the streets to keep Burns from being sent South. Two companies of soldiers had to stop the crowd from freeing Burns. Such incidents showed how deeply Northerners felt about slavery. Events in Kansas soon proved

that the slavery question could stir people to violence.

## Bleeding Kansas

In 1854, Kansas became the testing ground for popular sovereignty. Earlier, Kansas settlers had little interest in the question of slavery. Farmers went to Kansas from nearby states looking for cheap land. Few owned slaves. However, after passage of the Kansas–Nebraska Act, a new kind of settler began arriving in Kansas.

**Border Ruffians.** People from both the North and South wanted control of Kansas. Abolitionists helped more than 1,000 people move there from New England. Proslavery settlers moved into Kansas, too. Many were from Missouri. They wanted to make sure that New Englanders did not take over the territory. Proslavery bands from Missouri, called **Border Ruffians,** rode across the border. They battled with antislavery settlers.

**Two governments.** In 1855, Kansas held elections to choose a legislature. Hundreds of Border Ruffians rode to Kansas and voted illegally. They helped elect a proslavery legislature.

The new legislature quickly passed strict laws supporting slavery. One law said that people could receive the death penalty for helping slaves escape. Another made speaking out against slavery punishable by two years of hard labor.

Antislavery settlers refused to accept such laws. They elected their own governor and lawmakers. With two rival governments, Kansas was in chaos. Armed gangs roamed the land looking for trouble.

**Bloody battles.** In 1856, a drunken band of proslavery men raided the town of Lawrence, an antislavery stronghold. The raiders destroyed homes and smashed the presses of a Free Soil newspaper.

John Brown, a strong abolitionist, decided to strike back. Brown had moved to Kansas to help make it a free state. He claimed that God had sent him to punish supporters of slavery. After the attack on Lawrence, Brown rode with his four sons and two other men to the town of Pottawatomie (pot uh WOT uh mee) Creek. In the middle of the night, Brown and his followers dragged five proslavery settlers from their beds and murdered them.

The murders at Pottawatomie Creek caused more violence. Both sides fought fiercely. By late 1856, over 200 people had been killed. Newspapers called the territory **Bleeding Kansas.**

## Violence in the Senate

Even before Brown's attack, the battle over Kansas spilled into the Senate. A sharp-tongued abolitionist, Charles Sumner, took the Senate floor. In one speech, he blasted the actions of the proslavery legislature in Kansas. Then, Sumner viciously criticized his foes, especially Andrew Butler, an elderly senator from South Carolina.

Butler was not in the Senate on the day of Sumner's speech. But the next

In the 1850s, settlers for and against slavery battled one another in Kansas. This print shows the proslavery attack on Lawrence, where antislavery settlers lived. Why do you think the struggle in Kansas was later called a "mini civil war"?

Northern newspapers ran this picture of Preston Brooks beating Charles Sumner with a cane. The picture was intended to outrage Northerners. In the background, it shows southern senators laughing at the brutal act.

day, Congressman Preston Brooks, Butler's nephew, marched into the Senate chamber. Using a heavy cane, Brooks beat Sumner until he fell, bloody and unconscious, to the floor.

Many Southerners believed that Sumner got what he deserved. Brooks received hundreds of canes as gifts from Southerners who supported him. To Northerners, however, the brutal act was just one more proof that slavery led to violence.

## Dred Scott Decision

In 1857, a Supreme Court decision pushed the North and South further apart. The decision came in the Dred Scott case.

Dred Scott was a slave who lived in Missouri. Later, Scott moved with his owner to Illinois and then to Wisconsin, both free states. When his owner died, antislavery lawyers helped Scott file a lawsuit. They argued that since Scott had lived in free states, he should be a free man. Eventually, the case reached the Supreme Court.

The Court ruled that Scott could not file a lawsuit because, as a slave, he was not a citizen. The Court stated that slaves were property.

The Court went further. It ruled that Congress could not outlaw slavery in a territory. Only a state legislature could ban slavery, the Court said. As a result, the Missouri Compromise was unconstitutional.

Southerners rejoiced at the *Dred Scott decision.* It meant that slavery was legal except where a state voted to ban it. Northerners were shocked and angry. The Court's ruling made slavery legal in all the territories. Even Northerners who were not abolitionists felt that the Dred Scott decision was unjust.

### SECTION REVIEW

1. **Locate:** Kansas Territory, Nebraska Territory, Illinois.
2. How did the Kansas–Nebraska Act undo the Missouri Compromise?
3. Why did proslavery and antislavery forces move into Kansas?
4. What did the Dred Scott decision say?
5. **What Do You Think?** Why do you think the Dred Scott decision shocked Northerners?

—382—

# 4 A New Political Party

**Read to Learn**

★ What was the main goal of the Republican Party?
★ How did Abraham Lincoln become a national figure?
★ How did the raid on Harpers Ferry drive the North and South apart?
★ What does this word mean: arsenal?

Tension over the slavery question drove a wedge between the North and South. The wedge also split old political parties. Out of these divisions grew a new party.

## The Republican Party

In the mid-1850s, people who opposed slavery in the territories were looking for a political voice. The Free Soil Party had weakened. Whigs fought among themselves over the slavery question. Northern and southern Democrats were at odds with each other. Then, in 1854, a group of Free Soilers, northern Democrats, and antislavery Whigs met in Michigan. They formed a new political party, called the *Republican Party.*

The main goal of the Republicans was to keep slavery out of the western territories. Abolitionists supported the party, but they were still a minority. Most Republicans did not expect to end slavery in the South.

The Republican Party grew quickly. In 1856, Republicans chose John Charles Frémont as their candidate for President. Frémont was a frontiersman who had fought for California's independence. (See page 323.) He had never held office, but he opposed the spread of slavery.

Democrats chose James Buchanan of Pennsylvania. He had served as a senator and as Secretary of State. Many Democrats saw Buchanan as a "northern man with southern principles." They hoped that he would attract voters in both the North and South.

Buchanan won the election. However, the voting results alarmed the South. The new Republican Party made a strong showing. Frémont did very well in the North. He nearly won the election without the support of any southern state. Southerners felt that their influence was fading fast.

## Abraham Lincoln

Two years later, in 1858, the Illinois Senate race caught the attention of the whole nation. Senator Stephen Douglas was being challenged by Abraham Lincoln, a Republican. The race was important because most Americans thought that Douglas, a Democrat, would run for President in 1860.

Lincoln was not a national figure like Douglas. But he was well known in Illinois as a successful lawyer and politician. Lincoln had spent eight years in the Illinois legislature and then served as a congressman from Illinois.

People liked Lincoln because he was "just folks." He enjoyed swapping stories. Lincoln was known as a good, straightforward speaker. Even so, a listener once complained that he could not understand a speech of Lincoln's. "There are always some fleas a dog can't reach" was Lincoln's reply. Many people admired Lincoln for his honesty. Some called him Honest Abe.

Abraham Lincoln was born in the backwoods of Kentucky. Like many frontier people, his parents moved often in search of better land. They lived in Indiana and later in Illinois. Lincoln spent only a year in school as a child. But he taught himself to read and spent many hours reading by firelight.

After Lincoln left home, he set up a store in Illinois. He learned law on his own and began a career in politics. In 1858, Lincoln decided to run for the Senate because he strongly opposed the Kansas–Nebraska Act.

## Lincoln–Douglas Debates

During the Senate campaign, Lincoln challenged Douglas to a series of debates. People thought that Lincoln was foolish because Douglas was one of the greatest speakers in the nation. Douglas had a deep, confident voice. The senator stood only a little over five feet tall, but he seemed taller. People called him the Little Giant.

Abraham Lincoln, on the other hand, was more than six feet tall. He spoke in a high voice with a backwoods accent. He said "git" for "get" and "thar" for "there." He also had a slow, awkward walk.

**A house divided.** In the *Lincoln–Douglas Debates,* Douglas tried to make Lincoln seem like an abolitionist. Lincoln, in turn, tried to force Douglas to make proslavery statements. In one speech, Lincoln described the nation as "a house divided" over slavery. He warned that the "government cannot endure permanently half slave and half free." Douglas disagreed with Lincoln. He assured the audience that the North and South, free and slave, could get along.

Lincoln's "house divided" speech became famous. It was often quoted by people who wanted to show that Lincoln planned to abolish slavery in the South.

**Views on slavery.** In fact, Lincoln and Douglas were not so far apart on the slavery question. Douglas saw slavery as a political issue. He wanted to settle the question by popular sovereignty. Lincoln was dead set against slavery in the territories. He believed that blacks were entitled to "life, liberty, and the pursuit of happiness." Slavery was a "moral, social, and political wrong," he said. Even so, Lincoln was not an abolitionist. He had no wish "to interfere with the institution of slavery in the states where it exists."

Douglas won reelection to the Senate. But Abraham Lincoln became known to the nation during the campaign. His careful thinking and down-to-earth manner made him very popular. Two years later, Lincoln and Douglas would again be rivals for office. In the meantime, more bloodshed pushed the North and South further apart.

## Raid on Harpers Ferry

John Brown came into the national spotlight again in 1859. This time, Brown brought his campaign against

Abraham Lincoln debated Stephen Douglas, seated at left, seven times during the Senate race of 1858. Lincoln knew that many voters expected Douglas to be elected President in 1860. At one debate, Lincoln pointed to his own "poor, lean, lank face" and said, "Nobody has ever expected me to be President."

Sitting on his own coffin, John Brown rides to the gallows. Horace Pippin, a black artist, painted the scene based on his mother's description. She witnessed Brown's execution on December 2, 1859.

slavery to Virginia. In October, Brown and a group of followers raided the federal *arsenal,* or gun warehouse, at Harpers Ferry, Virginia. Brown planned to give weapons from the arsenal to slaves in the area. This, he hoped, would start a slave revolt.

Brown quickly gained control of the arsenal, but no slave uprising followed. Troops led by Colonel Robert E. Lee surrounded Brown and killed ten of his men. After a day of fighting, Brown was taken prisoner.

Most people in both the North and South thought that Brown's plan to start a slave revolt was insane. But Brown was calm during his trial. He sat quietly as the court found him guilty of murder and treason and sentenced him to death.

Because of the dignity he showed during his trial, Brown became a hero to many Northerners. Church bells rang on the morning of his execution. New Englanders sang a popular tune that began, "John Brown's body lies a mold'ring in the grave, but his soul is

marching on." Henry David Thoreau, the well-known writer, praised Brown as "a superior man."

To Southerners, the northern response to John Brown's death was outrageous. To criticize slavery was bad enough. But to sing the praise of a man who hoped to lead a slave revolt was intolerable! Many Southerners became convinced that the North wanted to destroy slavery and the South with it. The nation was poised for a violent clash.

## SECTION REVIEW

1. **Define:** arsenal.
2. What was the main goal of the new Republican Party?
3. Why did the Illinois Senate race in 1858 capture the attention of the American people?
4. (a) How did Northerners respond to John Brown's execution? (b) Why did this response anger Southerners?
5. **What Do You Think?** Why do you think the Republican Party did as well as it did in the election of 1856?

# 5 The Union Is Broken

### Read to Learn

★ Why did the election of 1860 make the South feel powerless?

★ Why did seven southern states secede from the Union?

★ What was the immediate cause of the Civil War?

Americans looked toward the election of 1860 with both hope and fear. The nation seemed to be tumbling toward disunion. People hoped that the election would somehow bind the nation together. But no candidate was able to unite Northerners and Southerners. Instead, the nation split along sectional lines.

## Election of 1860

The Democratic Party divided in two in 1860. Southern Democrats wanted the party to support slavery in the territories. But northern Democrats refused to do so. One exclaimed, "Gentlemen of the South, you mistake us—you mistake us! We will not do it!"

In the end, northern Democrats picked Stephen Douglas as their candidate for President. Southern Democrats met separately and chose John Breckinridge of Kentucky.

Some Democrats saw the split in their party as a danger signal for the country. They formed the Constitutional Union Party and chose John Bell of Tennessee to run for President. Bell simply wanted to keep the Union together.

Meanwhile, Republicans nominated Abraham Lincoln. The choice of Lincoln panicked Southerners. Many thought that Lincoln really was an abolitionist. After all, Lincoln had said that the country could not survive "half slave and half free." Did that not mean he wanted to end slavery? Lincoln's name was not even on the ballot in ten southern states.

Senator Douglas was sure that Lincoln would win the election. But Douglas believed that Democrats "must try to save the Union." He pleaded with southern voters to stay with the Union, no matter who was elected.

## The South Secedes

Lincoln carried the North and won the election. Southern votes did not affect the election at all. Northerners outnumbered Southerners and simply outvoted them. To Southerners, Lincoln's election meant that the South had lost its voice in national government. Southerners believed that the President, the Senate, and the House were now all set against their interests, especially slavery.*

Even before the election, the governor of South Carolina had written to other southern governors. If Lincoln was elected, he wrote, it was the duty of Southerners to quit the Union. With Lincoln in the White House, many Southerners felt that seceding from the Union was their only choice.

**Crittenden's last try.** Senator John Crittenden of Kentucky made a last effort to save the Union. In December 1860, he introduced a bill to extend the Missouri Compromise line to the Pacific. The bill did not please anyone. By this time, Southerners wanted to be free of the North. "I look upon the whole New England race as meddlers," wrote one Southerner.

South Carolina was the first state to secede. On December 20, 1860, delegates to a special convention in

---

*The North had a slight majority in the House and Senate. But Northerners did not have enough power to force the South to end slavery.

Maps can give you different kinds of information. (See Skill Lesson 1 on page 21.) Some maps give you special kinds of information. An election map shows the results of a presidential election.

Election maps are useful because they show which states each candidate won. Most election maps also have circle graphs to show what percent of the popular vote and electoral vote went to each candidate.

Use the election map and circle graphs below to learn more about the election of 1860.

1. **Decide what is shown on the map and graphs.** (a) What is the subject of the map? (b) What do the four colors stand for? (c) What does the graph at left show? (d) What does the graph at right show?

2. **Practice using information from the map and graphs.** Read the information on the map and graphs. (a) Which party won nearly all the northern states? (b) Which party won all the southern states? (c) What percent of the popular vote did the Republican Party receive? (d) What percent of the electoral vote did the Republican Party receive? (e) Who was the candidate of the Constitutional Union Party? (f) Did he win any states?

3. **Draw conclusions about the election.** Based on the map and graphs, draw conclusions about the election of 1860. (a) How does the map show that sectionalism was important in the election? (b) What did the election seem to show about the political voice of southern voters?

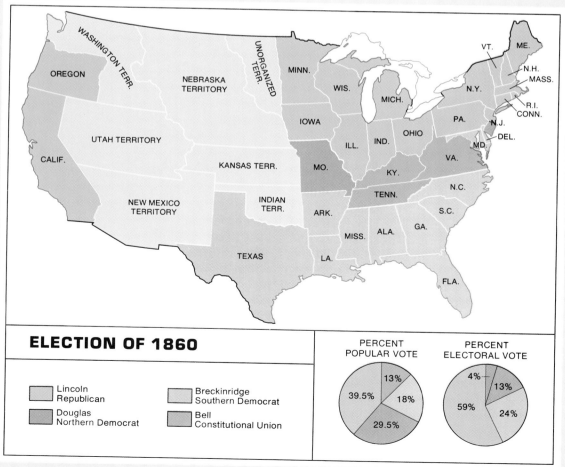

## ELECTION OF 1860

- Lincoln Republican
- Douglas Northern Democrat
- Breckinridge Southern Democrat
- Bell Constitutional Union

PERCENT POPULAR VOTE: 13%, 39.5%, 18%, 29.5%

PERCENT ELECTORAL VOTE: 4%, 13%, 59%, 24%

### Mary Boykin Chesnut

Mary Boykin Chesnut was born into a wealthy, slave-owning family in South Carolina. In February 1861, she began to keep a diary about the coming war. Early in 1861, Chesnut wrote that she dreaded "this break with so great a power as the United States, but I was ready and willing." She added, "Come what would, I wanted them to fight and stop talking."

Charleston voted for secession. "The state of South Carolina has resumed her position among the nations of the world," the delegates said. By February 1, 1861, six more southern states had seceded. (See the map on page 394.)

**The Confederacy.** In February 1861, the states that had seceded held a convention in Montgomery, Alabama. They formed a new nation and named it the *Confederate States of America.* Jefferson Davis of Mississippi was named president of the Confederacy.

Many Southerners were joyful and confident about the future. They believed that states had the right to secede. They did not think that the North would fight to keep the South in the Union. And if war did break out, Southerners were sure that they would win.

## Opening Shots

When Abraham Lincoln took office as President on March 4, 1861, he warned that "no state . . . can lawfully get out of the Union." At the same time, Lincoln promised that there would not be war with the South unless southern states started it. "We are not enemies, but friends. We must not be enemies," Lincoln told the South.

**Seizing federal forts.** However, the Confederacy had already begun seizing federal forts and arsenals. It felt that the Union, or federal, forts were a threat because the United States was now a foreign power.

President Lincoln faced a hard choice. Should he allow the Confederates to take over federal property? If he did, it would mean that states would have the right to leave the Union. Or should he use force to protect federal property? If Lincoln sent in troops, he risked losing the support of the four slave states that had not seceded. Such an action might also lose support in the North.

In March 1861, the Confederacy forced Lincoln to make a decision. By then, Confederate troops had taken over nearly all forts, post offices, and other federal buildings in the Confederacy. The Union held only three forts off the Florida coast and Fort Sumter in South Carolina.

**Fort Sumter is bombarded.** President Lincoln received word from the commander of *Fort Sumter* that food supplies were running low. The President sent a message to the governor of South Carolina. It said that only food would be shipped to Fort Sumter. Lincoln promised not to send any troops or weapons.

Confederate troops, in the foreground, fire cannons across Charleston Harbor at Fort Sumter. At top left is the flag of South Carolina. In the background, smoke rises from Fort Sumter, which flies the United States flag. When Northerners learned of the attack on Sumter, they rallied behind Lincoln and the Union. A New York paper declared, "Fort Sumter is lost, but the country is saved."

To the Confederacy, Fort Sumter was important because it guarded Charleston Harbor. The fort could not be left in Union hands. The Confederates asked for its surrender on April 12, 1861. Major Robert Anderson, the Union commander, would not give in. Confederate guns then opened fire. Major Anderson quickly ran out of ammunition. On April 13, he surrendered Fort Sumter.

Fort Sumter was nearly destroyed by Confederate cannons. But, amazingly, no one was injured. During the battle, people in Charleston flocked to the harbor to watch. To many, it was like a huge fireworks display. No one knew then that the fireworks marked the beginning of a war that would last four terrible years.

## SECTION REVIEW

1. Why did Lincoln's victory in 1860 alarm Southerners?
2. (a) When was the Confederacy formed? (b) Why did the Confederacy take over federal property?
3. Why did Lincoln hesitate to use force against the Confederacy?
4. **What Do You Think?** What do you think might have happened if Lincoln had sent troops to retake Fort Sumter?

# Chapter 17 Review

## ★ Summary ★

The issue of slavery in the territories led to conflict between the North and South. The Missouri Compromise settled the issue for a time. After the Mexican War, the North and South again argued about slavery, but compromised in 1850.

In 1854, the Kansas–Nebraska Act canceled the Missouri Compromise and an-gered Northerners. The Dred Scott decision further inflamed the North. John Brown's raid brought the nation to the edge of war.

After Lincoln's election in 1860, seven states seceded and formed the Confederacy. With the bombardment of Fort Sumter in April 1861, civil war had come.

## ★ Reviewing the Facts ★

**Key Terms.** Match each term in Column 1 with the correct definition in Column 2.

**Column 1**

1. sectionalism
2. popular sovereignty
3. fugitive
4. civil war
5. arsenal

**Column 2**

a. escaped slave
b. loyalty to state or section instead of country
c. control by the voters of a territory
d. warehouse for guns
e. fight between people of the same country

**Key People, Events, and Ideas.** Identify each of the following.

1. Missouri Compromise
2. Free Soil Party
3. Stephen Douglas
4. Compromise of 1850
5. Fugitive Slave Law of 1850
6. *Uncle Tom's Cabin*
7. Kansas–Nebraska Act
8. Bleeding Kansas
9. Dred Scott decision
10. Republican Party
11. Abraham Lincoln
12. Lincoln–Douglas Debates
13. John Brown
14. Confederate States of America
15. Fort Sumter

## ★ Chapter Checkup ★

1. What did the Missouri Compromise say about slavery?

2. (a) Why did the Mexican War raise the question of slavery in the territories? (b) What were two moderate plans to settle the question of slavery in the Mexican Cession?

3. List the four main parts of the Compromise of 1850.

4. (a) Why did Southerners want a strong fugitive slave law? (b) Why did Northerners object to the law?

5. (a) What was the Kansas–Nebraska Act? (b) How did it lead to violence?

6. (a) Why was the Republican Party formed? (b) What did it have in common with the Free Soil Party?

7. (a) What did the Dred Scott decision say about slavery in the territories? (b) Why did it dismay Northerners?

8. (a) Why did two Democrats run for President in 1860? (b) Why did seven states secede after Lincoln's victory?

## Thinking About History

1. **Drawing a conclusion.** The Compromise of 1850 banned the slave trade in Washington, D.C. Why do you think slave auctions in the nation's capital embarrassed many Americans?

2. **Learning about citizenship.** Many Southerners claimed that seceding from the Union was an idea justified by the Declaration of Independence. Study the Declaration of Independence, which begins on page 611. What parts of it could be used to justify secession?

3. **Analyzing information.** Review the discussion of tariffs on pages 279 and 299. (a) How do you think debates over tariffs added to differences between the North and South? (b) How might disagreement over tariffs have made the South more anxious about keeping power in the Senate?

4. **Relating past to present.** (a) Why do you think the Dred Scott decision had such a great impact on the nation? (b) Can you think of a recent Supreme Court decision that has had a major impact on America?

## Using Your Skills

1. **Map reading.** Study the map on page 380. (a) After the Missouri Compromise, what part of the Louisiana Purchase was slave? Free? (b) After the Compromise of 1850, what territories were opened to slavery by popular sovereignty? (c) After the Kansas–Nebraska Act of 1854, what territories were open to slavery by popular sovereignty?

2. **Using a painting as a primary source.** Study the painting on page 385. (a) What is the mood of the crowd pictured? (b) How can you tell the mood? (c) What is the black woman in the right corner doing? (d) Why might a black artist choose to paint this incident?

3. **Reading for the main idea.** Each paragraph or group of paragraphs in this book has a main idea. The main idea is the generalization that underlies all the facts and examples. Read the subsection called "Fugitive Slave Law" on pages 377–378. (a) What is the main idea of each paragraph? (b) Give two facts that support the main idea of each paragraph. (c) What is the main idea of the subsection?

## More to Do

1. **Exploring local history.** Use the map on page 380 and a blank map to show whether your state was affected by the Missouri Compromise, the Compromise of 1850, or the Kansas-Nebraska Act.

2. **Writing a dialogue.** Write a dialogue between supporters of Lincoln and Douglas during the debates of 1858.

3. **Drawing a political cartoon.** Draw a political cartoon that shows John Brown's execution from either the northern or southern point of view.

4. **Creating headlines.** Write two sets of headlines—one for a northern paper, one for a southern paper—about these incidents: the Dred Scott decision, the secession of South Carolina, and the bombarding of Fort Sumter.

CHAPTER

# 18

# The Civil War (1860–1865)

**Chapter Outline**

1 The Call to Arms
2 On the Battle Lines
3 Free at Last
4 Life in Wartime
5 The Tide Turns
Readings, page 559

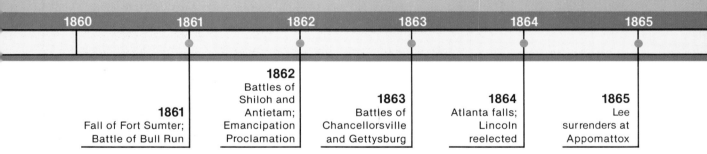

| 1860 | 1861 | 1862 | 1863 | 1864 | 1865 |
|------|------|------|------|------|------|

**1861**
Fall of Fort Sumter;
Battle of Bull Run

**1862**
Battles of
Shiloh and
Antietam;
Emancipation
Proclamation

**1863**
Battles of
Chancellorsville
and Gettysburg

**1864**
Atlanta falls;
Lincoln
reelected

**1865**
Lee
surrenders at
Appomattox

## About This Chapter

The Civil War stirred up strong passions. For Southerners, it was a war for independence, like the American Revolution. Northerners fought for an equally important goal—to save the Union.

Strong feelings about the justice of their cause were reflected in the songs of each side. Soldiers often sang to keep their spirits up before going into battle. A popular song in the South was "The Bonnie Blue Flag." One verse began:

Then here's to our Confed'racy,
Strong are we and brave,
Like patriots of old we'll fight
Our heritage to save.

Union soldiers had their own favorite songs. "The Battle-Cry of Freedom" included the rousing chorus:

The Union forever, hurrah! boys, hurrah!
Down with the traitor, up with the star,
While we rally round the flag, boys, rally once again,
Shouting the battle-cry of freedom.

With flags held high, soldiers on both sides marched off to war in 1860. They soon learned that war meant more than patriotic songs. More than half a million soldiers would die before the Civil War ended.

Study the time line above. What major southern city was captured in 1864?

More Americans died in the Civil War than in any other war. Many of those killed were young men, often teenagers.

# 1 The Call to Arms

### Read to Learn
★ How did the Civil War tear apart families and states?
★ What strengths and weaknesses did each side have?
★ How were Lincoln and Davis different as leaders?
★ What do these words mean: martial law?

The bombardment of Fort Sumter in April 1861 began the Civil War. As the war started, many American families had divided loyalties. Fathers joined the Union army while their sons volunteered to fight for the Confederacy. Mary Todd Lincoln, President Lincoln's wife, had three brothers who fought for the Confederacy. While General Robert E. Lee led Confederate soldiers, his favorite cousin fought for the Union.

## Choosing Sides

Feelings ran high in 1861. People in the Confederacy believed that they had a right to leave the Union. In fact, they called the conflict between the North and South the War for Southern Independence. President Lincoln and other Northerners believed just as strongly that the South had rebelled. Lincoln made it clear that he would do everything in his power to save the Union. Stephen Douglas summed up the way many people in the North felt: "There can be no neutrals in this war; only patriots—or traitors."

Both sides expected to win and to win quickly. Volunteers eagerly signed up, and recruits quickly filled both armies. During the spring of 1861, more than 100,000 men joined the Confederate army. More than 75,000 volunteers answered Lincoln's first call for troops.

Eight slave states were still part of the Union when Lincoln called for volunteers in April 1861. They were called the border states. Virginia,* North

Carolina, Arkansas, and Tennessee soon seceded and joined the Confederacy. (See the map below.)

Opinion was divided in the four border states that remained in the Union. Delaware stayed with the Union from the first. Kentucky and Missouri wavered between the North and South for several months. In the end, both remained in the Union.

Maryland was also divided. In April 1861, pro-Confederate mobs attacked Union troops in Baltimore. President Lincoln responded by declaring martial law in Maryland. *Martial law* means rule by the army instead of the elected government. Many people who sided with the South were arrested. Later, the Maryland legislature voted to remain in the Union.

---

*In the western part of Virginia, many people supported the Union. When Virginia seceded, the Westerners formed their own government. They joined the United States as West Virginia in 1863.

MAP SKILL In early 1861, eight slave states remained in the Union. Which border states eventually seceded?

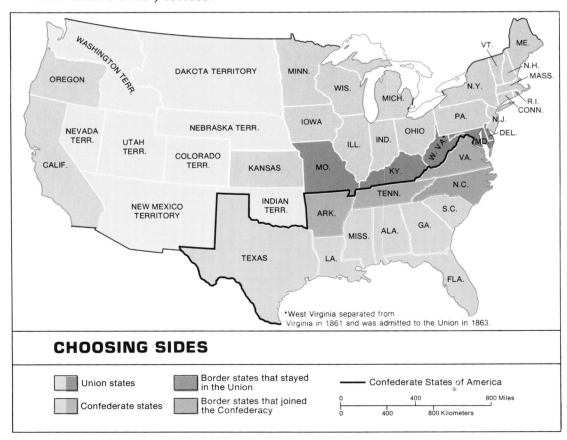

*West Virginia separated from Virginia in 1861 and was admitted to the Union in 1863.

## CHOOSING SIDES

Union states

Confederate states

Border states that stayed in the Union

Border states that joined the Confederacy

—— Confederate States of America

0    400    800 Miles
0   400   800 Kilometers

## Resources

Both sides had advantages and disadvantages as the war began. The South had the strong advantage of fighting a defensive war. If the North did not attack, the Confederacy would remain a separate country. Thus, it was up to the North to attack and defeat the Confederacy. "All we ask," Jefferson Davis said, "is to be left alone."

**The South.** Fighting a defensive war gave the South an important edge. Southerners were well aware that the North was threatening to invade their homeland. To defend their homes and families, southern soldiers were ready to fight to the bitter end.

Also, many southern men had skills that made them good soldiers. Hunting was an important part of southern life. Thus, young boys learned to ride horses and use guns. Wealthy young men often went to military schools. Southern graduates of West Point* were the most brilliant officers in the army before the war.

The South, however, had serious weaknesses. It had few factories to make guns and supplies. Before the war, Southerners bought such products from the North or from Europe. The South also had few railroads to move troops and supplies. The railroads they had often did not join one another. Tracks simply ran between two points and then stopped.

Also, the South had a small population. Only 9 million people lived there, compared to 22 million in the North. This meant that there were far fewer people in the South to fight and support a war effort than in the North. Besides, over one third of the people in the South were slaves.

**The North.** The North had almost four times as many free citizens as the South. Thus, it had a large source of volunteers. It also had many people to grow food and make supplies for its armies.

Industry was the North's greatest resource. Northern factories made 90 percent of the nation's manufactured goods. They supplied Union forces with guns, cannons, and ammunition. The North also had a broad railroad network. Almost 75 percent of the nation's rail lines were in the North. (See Skill Lesson 18 on page 396.)

The North had another important advantage over the South. It had a strong navy, while the South had almost no warships. The Union could use its navy to blockade the South and cut off its trade with Europe.

Still, the North had a hard military task. To bring the South back into the Union, northern soldiers had to conquer a huge area. Instead of defending their homes, they were invading unfamiliar land. Also, they needed training in basic fighting skills. Soldiers had to learn how to use weapons and how to survive far from home.

## Leadership

When the Civil War began, many people thought that the Confederate president, Jefferson Davis, was a better leader than Abraham Lincoln.

**Jefferson Davis.** Jefferson Davis was a West Point graduate. He had been an officer in the Mexican War. In addition, Davis served as Secretary of War under President Franklin Pierce. President Davis was respected for his honesty and courage.

However, Davis believed that he alone should direct military plans. He did not like to turn over details to others. When Davis made a decision, he "could not understand any other man coming to a different conclusion," as his wife put it. As a result, Davis wasted time worrying about small matters and arguing with advisers.

**Abraham Lincoln.** At first, some Northerners had doubts about the ability of Lincoln. He had little experience

---

*West Point, in New York State, is the site of the United States Military Academy. There, future army officers receive training.

A table is used to present information in a way you can understand quickly and easily. Tables often present numbers or statistics. The numbers are set up in columns and rows.

The table below compares the resources of the North and South in 1861. For both the North and South, the table shows the actual amount of the resource and the percent of the national total. Studying the table can help you understand why the North won the Civil War.

Use the following steps to read and interpret the table.

1. **Identify the information in the table.** Note that the resources in the table are measured in different ways. For example, population is measured in thousands of people. (a) What is the title of the table? (b) How is farmland measured in the table? (c) How is railroad track measured?

2. **Read the information in the table.** Note that the table has five columns. The first column shows what each resource is—farmland, factories, and so on. The second and third columns give the actual amount and percent of each resource that the North had. The fourth and fifth columns give the same information for the South. (a) What was the actual number of factories in the South? (b) What percent of the national total of factories did the South have? (c) What percent of the nation's railroad track did the North have?

3. **Compare the information in the table.** Use the table to compare the resources of the North and South. (a) Did the North or the South have more workers in industry? (b) How many acres of farmland did each side have? (c) In which resource did the South come closest to equaling the North?

4. **Interpret the information based on your reading.** Interpret the information in the table based on your reading of the chapter. (a) Which side had the advantage in each of the resources shown? (b) How might these advantages have helped that side during the war? (c) Which resource do you think was most important during the war? Explain your answer.

## Resources of the North and South, 1861

| Resources | North | | South | |
|---|---|---|---|---|
| | Number | Percent of Total | Number | Percent of Total |
| Farmland | 105,835 acres | 65% | 56,832 acres | 35% |
| Railroad Track | 21,847 miles | 71% | 8,947 miles | 29% |
| Value of Manufactured Goods | $1,794,417,000 | 92% | $155,552,000 | 8% |
| Factories | 119,500 | 85% | 20,600 | 15% |
| Workers in Industry | 1,198,000 | 92% | 111,000 | 8% |
| Population | 22,340,000 | 63% | 9,103,000 (3,954,000 Slaves) | 37% |

Source: *Historical Statistics of the United States*

in national politics or war. This lack of experience led him to make mistakes. But he learned from his errors. In time, Lincoln proved himself to be a patient but strong leader and a fine war planner.

Day by day, Lincoln gained the respect of those around him. Many liked his sense of humor. Lincoln could joke even when others criticized him. Secretary of War Edwin Stanton once referred to President Lincoln as a fool. When he heard, Lincoln commented: "Did Stanton say I was a fool? Then I must be one, for Stanton is generally right and he always says what he means." His ability to accept criticism helped Lincoln work well with others.

**Military leaders.** At the outbreak of war, army officers in the South had to make a choice. They could stay with the Union army and fight against their home states. Or, they could join the Confederate forces.

Robert E. Lee faced such a decision when his home state, Virginia, seceded. President Lincoln asked Lee to command the Union army. Lee refused.

"With all my devotion to the Union," Lee explained, "I have not been able to make up my mind to raise my hand against my relatives, my children, my home." Lee later became commander of the Confederate army.

Many of the army's best officers sided with the Confederacy. As a result, President Lincoln had trouble finding generals who could match the South's military leaders. He replaced several commanders before the Union began to win battles.

--- SECTION REVIEW ---

1. **Locate:** Virginia, Missouri, Kentucky, Maryland, Delaware.
2. **Define:** martial law.
3. (a) Which four states seceded after April 1861? (b) Which four slave states remained in the Union?
4. Why did many Southerners have skills that made them good soldiers?
5. **What Do You Think?** Why do you think the North's strengths would be more important in a long war than in a short war?

# 2 On the Battle Lines

### Read to Learn
* ★ What goals did each side have?
* ★ What battles took place early on?
* ★ How did the North achieve two of its three goals?

In both the North and South, tens of thousands of young men marched off to war to the cheers of family and friends. In the North, volunteers were urged "On to Richmond," the capital of the Confederacy. The cry in the South was "Forward to Washington!"

## Goals of the North and South

The Civil War had three major areas of combat: the East, the West,

and at sea. Union war goals involved all three areas.

First, the Union planned to blockade southern ports. This would shut off the South's trade with Europe. Second, in the West, the Union would try to take control of the Mississippi River. This would stop trade on the river and separate Arkansas, Texas, and Louisiana from the rest of the Confederacy. Third, in the East, Union generals hoped to seize Richmond and capture the Confederate government.

The South's goals were simple. It would fight a defensive war. Southerners hoped to wear out Union troops so that they would give up.

The South counted on European money and supplies to help end the war quickly. Cotton was important to the textile mills of England and other countries. Confederates were sure that Europeans wanted to ensure a supply of cotton for their mills.

## Fighting in the East

The North hoped for a quick victory, too. In July 1861, Union troops set out for Richmond, which was only about 100 miles (160 km) from Washington, D.C. They clashed with Confederate troops soon after they left. The battle took place near a small stream called Bull Run.

**Battle of Bull Run.** People from Washington gathered on a hilltop near Bull Run to watch the battle. There was a holiday feeling in the air. Many people carried picnic baskets. They expected to see Union troops crush the Confederates.

But Confederate troops did not turn and run. Under the firm leadership of General Thomas Jackson, they held their ground. Jackson earned the nickname Stonewall because he stood as firmly as a stone wall. In the end, it was Union troops that fled the battlefield. A congressman who watched the retreat said of the panicked Union soldiers:

Off they went . . . down the highway . . . across fields, towards the woods, anywhere, everywhere, to escape. The further they ran the more frightened they grew. . . . To enable them better to run, they threw away their blankets, knapsacks, canteens, and finally muskets, cartridge-boxes, and everything else.

Instead of pursuing, Confederate soldiers stopped to gather the equipment thrown down by Union troops. The *Battle of Bull Run* showed both sides that they needed to train their soldiers.

**An army in training.** After Bull Run, President Lincoln made General George McClellan commander of Union armies. McClellan was a superb organizer. He set out to whip the army into shape.

McClellan spent six months training his men. Since the Confederates were fighting a defensive war, little happened in the meantime. Newspapers in the North reported "all quiet along the Potomac" so often that the phrase became a joke. President Lincoln lost patience. He snapped, "If McClellan is not using the army, I should like to borrow it."

In March 1862, McClellan finally moved on Richmond. He and most of his troops went by steamboat from Washington down the Potomac River. (See the map on page 399.) The rest of the army stayed in Washington.

McClellan's troops landed on the peninsula between the York and James rivers. There, McClellan paused. General Lee learned that the Union army was near Richmond. He sent Stonewall Jackson to make a series of attacks near Washington. Because of these raids, troops could not be sent from Washington to help McClellan. When a Confederate cavalry slashed at McClellan's army, the Union general was forced to withdraw. Once again, there was a lull in the war in the East.

## War at Sea

The Union navy was far superior to that of the Confederacy. Early in the war, Union ships blockaded southern ports. At first, the Confederates used small ships to slip through the Union blockade. But traffic in southern ports eventually dropped by over 90 percent. The South desperately needed a way to break the Union blockade.

When the war began, the Union had abandoned the *Merrimac,* a warship, in Virginia. Confederates covered the *Merrimac* with iron plates four inches thick. Then they renamed it the *Virginia.* One afternoon in March 1862, the ironclad *Merrimac* defeated three Union ships. Their cannonballs bounced harmlessly off the *Merrimac*'s metal plates.

The Union had developed its own ironclad ship, the *Monitor.* The day after the Confederate victories, the *Monitor* attacked the *Merrimac* in Hampton Roads in Virginia. The Confederate ship boasted more firepower, but the *Monitor* moved more quickly. Neither ship seriously damaged the other, and both withdrew.

Ironclad ships changed naval warfare. Both sides rushed to build more of them. However, the South never mounted a serious attack against the Union navy. The Union blockade held throughout the war.

## Battle of Antietam

In September 1862, Robert E. Lee took the offensive. Lee believed that a victory in the North would weaken the Union's will to fight. He began to march north into Maryland. But luck was on the Union's side. A Confederate messenger lost General Lee's battle plans. When a Union soldier found the plans, he turned them over to General McClellan.

With Lee's whole battle plan before him, McClellan moved quickly. He attacked Lee's main force at Antietam (an TEET uhm) on September 17, 1862. In a daylong battle, over 24,000 Union and Confederate soldiers were killed or wounded.

Neither side won a victory at the ***Battle of Antietam.*** But when the sun rose the day after the battle, Union troops saw that Lee's soldiers had slipped away during the night. McClellan did not pursue Lee. Still, since Lee had withdrawn his forces, the North claimed victory.

## Campaign in the West

Until Antietam, the Union army had won few battles in the East. But Union forces had more success in

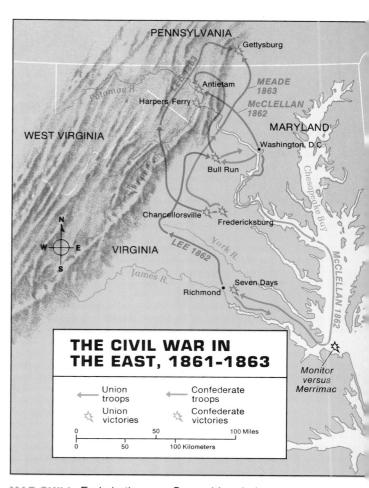

MAP SKILL  Early in the war, General Lee led the Confederate army from one victory to another in the East. Union forces at last claimed victory at the Battle of Antietam. What city in Virginia were Union forces trying to capture?

the West. There, the goal was to take control of the Mississippi River. General Ulysses S. Grant decided to attack Fort Henry and Fort Donelson in Tennessee. These two forts protected Confederate ships on tributaries of the Mississippi. Union troops captured the forts in February 1862. Grant then led his troops south toward the place where the Tennessee and Mississippi rivers join.

**Shiloh.**  In early April, Confederate forces surprised Grant near the town of Shiloh, Tennessee. Union troops won the bloody battle that followed.

The **Battle of Shiloh** was the first of the huge battles that became typical of the Civil War. One Confederate soldier wrote: "It was an awful thing to hear the sing of grape shot, the hum of cannon balls, and the roaring of the bomb shell. . . . O keep me out of such another fight!" More Americans died in one day at Shiloh than in the American Revolution, the War of 1812, and the Mexican War combined. Suddenly, it was clear that the war would not be quick or painless for either side.

**Winning the Mississippi.** After the capture of Shiloh, the Union gained control of river traffic on the northern Mississippi. In the meantime, the Union navy moved to take the southern part of the river. In April 1862, Union gunboats attacked and captured the port city of New Orleans. Other gunboats took Memphis, Tennessee. The Union was now in control of both ends of the great river. The South could no longer move supplies on the Mississippi.

But Union ships could not safely travel the river either. Confederates still controlled Vicksburg, Mississippi. Vicksburg sat on a high cliff overlooking the Mississippi. Cannons there could shell boats traveling between New Orleans and Memphis. (See the map on page 411.)

General Grant's forces tried again and again to take Vicksburg early in 1863. At last, Grant devised a brilliant trick. Skirting Vicksburg, he marched his troops east to Jackson, Mississippi. After taking that city by surprise, Grant turned around and attacked Vicksburg from the rear. The people of Vicksburg held out for six weeks. Finally, on July 4, 1863, the city fell.

The Union had achieved two of its goals. First, its naval blockade had shut off southern trade. Second, by tak-

As Union troops won victories in the South, they took over houses and plantations. The fine mansion shown here became a signaling station for the Union. From the platform on the roof, Union soldiers used flags to send messages to nearby troops.

ing control of the Mississippi River, the Union had split the Confederacy in two.

━━ SECTION REVIEW ━━

1. **Locate:** Washington, D.C., Richmond, Mississippi River, Tennessee River, Potomac River, Antietam, Shiloh, New Orleans, Vicksburg.

2. Why was the South fighting a defensive war?

3. What did both sides realize about their troops after the Battle of Bull Run?

4. What battles gave the Union control of the Mississippi River?

5. **What Do You Think?** How do you think news about bloody battles such as Shiloh affected men who were thinking of enlisting in the army?

# 3 Free at Last

### Read to Learn

★ Why did Lincoln free slaves in the Confederacy?

★ How did blacks help the Union?

★ What does this word mean: emancipate?

As the war dragged on, Northerners had to think carefully about why they were fighting. Their main purpose was to restore the Union. But abolitionists argued that the war must also rid the nation of slavery. By 1862, Lincoln and many other Northerners were willing to take this idea seriously.

After all, people asked, was slavery not at the root of the conflict between the North and South? Had thousands of northern boys died to bring a slaveholding South back into the Union? Questions such as these helped change the mood of Northerners.

## Emancipation Proclamation

The Civil War did not begin as a war against slavery. The Union included four slave states. President Lincoln did not want to take any action that might force these states to secede. Restoring the Union was his main goal. Lincoln had made this clear earlier: "If I could save the Union without freeing *any* slave, I would do it; and if I could save it by freeing *all* the slaves, I would

do it; and if I could do it by freeing some and leaving others alone, I would also do that."

**Broader goals.** In mid-1862, it seemed to Lincoln that he could save the Union only by broadening the goals of the war. He decided to free slaves living in the Confederacy. In the four loyal slave states, slaves would not be freed. Nor would slaves be freed in Confederate lands that had already been captured by the Union, such as New Orleans. Lincoln hoped that this action would weaken the South without angering slave owners in the Union.

Lincoln did not want people to think that freeing the slaves was a desperate action. So he waited for a Union victory before announcing his decision. The victory at Antietam gave him the chance he wanted.

**The Proclamation.** On September 22, 1862, Lincoln issued the *Emancipation Proclamation*. To *emancipate* means to set free. The Proclamation stated that all slaves in states still in rebellion would be free as of January 1, 1863. Since those states were not under Union control, no slaves were set free on that day. But as Union troops won control of areas, slaves were freed.

Still, the Emancipation Proclamation changed the purpose of the war. The abolition of slavery became a Union goal. The Proclamation won the

Blacks came from all over New England to join the 54th Regiment. Here, the regiment storms Fort Wagner on an island off South Carolina. Sergeant William Carney of the 54th won the Congressional Medal of Honor for his bravery during the attack.

Union the sympathy of people in Europe, especially workers. It became less likely that Britain or any other country would back the South. And the Proclamation prompted a wave of support for the Union from free blacks.

## Blacks for the Union

When the war began, free blacks in the North had tried to join the Union army. But federal laws kept them from becoming soldiers. So blacks signed up for noncombat tasks.

Meanwhile, Union troops pushed into the South. As they did, thousands of slaves flocked to their side. Some generals wanted to allow the former slaves to become soldiers and fight for the Union.

In the summer of 1862, Congress passed a law allowing blacks to join the army. Both free blacks and escaped slaves rallied to the Union cause. They formed all-black army units in many states. The new units had white commanders. And for more than a year, black soldiers received only half the pay of white soldiers. Even so, over 200,000 blacks fought with the Union during the war. About 68,000 were killed.

Massachusetts was one of the first states to organize all-black regiments. One of them, the 54th, attacked Fort Wagner near Charleston in the summer of 1863. The commander, most of the officers, and almost half the men were killed. The courage and devotion of the 54th Regiment won respect for black soldiers.

Both free blacks and escaped slaves made good soldiers. They went to war to restore the country, as other Union soldiers did. But they also fought to free their people. In a letter to President Lincoln, Secretary of War Stanton said that blacks "have proved themselves among the bravest of the brave, performing deeds of daring and shedding their blood with a heroism unsurpassed by soldiers of any other race."

## Blacks in the Confederacy

Slaves found it hard to hide their joy as news of the Emancipation Proclamation filtered into the South. One woman overheard the news just before she was to serve dinner. She asked to be excused so that she could get water from a nearby spring. Once she had reached the quiet of the spring, she shouted: "Glory, glory hallelujah to Jesus! I'm free! I'm free."

Even after the Proclamation, however, slaves had to work on plantations and in factories while whites were fighting. Because factory owners depended on them, slaves gained a few benefits. Some refused to work unless they were paid. Others stopped working if they were threatened with whippings or other punishments. Such "strikes" were often successful.

On many farms and plantations, slaves slowed down their work in the fields. This was one way to undermine the war effort. They knew that when Union troops captured an area, they would be freed.

## SECTION REVIEW

1. **Define:** emancipate.
2. (a) Why did Lincoln decide to emancipate the slaves? (b) Which slaves were freed by the Emancipation Proclamation?
3. (a) How did free blacks help the Union at first? (b) How did they help after 1862?
4. **What Do You Think?** How do you think the Emancipation Proclamation helped the Union war effort?

# 4 Life in Wartime

## Read to Learn
★ What was life like for soldiers during the Civil War?
★ How did each side pay for the war?
★ How did women contribute to the war effort?
★ What do these words mean: bounty, draft, habeas corpus, inflation, profiteer, tax-in-kind, civilian?

The Civil War touched the life of every American. It was not fought in some far-off land. The war took place on American soil, mainly in the South. Both armies were made up of Americans. And civilians, especially Southerners, suffered the many hardships of war.

## Johnny Rebs and Billy Yanks

Early in the war, soldiers on each side came up with nicknames for their enemy. Union troops wore blue uniforms. They were called blues or Billy Yanks, short for Yankees. Gray was the color of the Confederacy. Southern soldiers were called grays or Johnny Rebs, short for rebels.

**Becoming soldiers.** Troops on both sides were very young men. Most were under 21 years old. But war quickly changed raw recruits into tough veterans. Soldiers put in long hours drilling and marching. They slept on the ground in rain and snow. They scavenged for food, water, and firewood. Nothing hardened the "fresh fish," as new recruits were called, like combat. Boys of 18 learned to stand firm while cannon blasts shook the earth and bullets whizzed past their ears.

**Friend or foe.** At times, Rebs and Yanks could be friendly enemies. Before one battle, a Confederate hailed a Union soldier with "Say Yank, got something to trade?" After swapping Union coffee for southern tobacco, the soldiers shook hands. "Good luck, Yank!" said the Southerner. "I hope you won't get hurt in any of our fights."

**Deadly battles.** Soldiers returned to the horrors of combat quickly. New technology made Civil War battles deadly. Cone-shaped bullets replaced

Soldiers often sent photographs to their families to show how they looked in uniform. This photo shows a young Confederate private, Edwin Francis Jenson. Troops for both North and South were often no more than boys.

round musket balls. These bullets made rifles twice as accurate. New cannons could hurl exploding shells several miles. In any battle, one quarter or more of the soldiers were casualties. A casualty is a soldier who is killed or wounded.

In one battle, Union troops knew that they were facing almost certain death. Each soldier wrote his name on a slip of paper and pinned it to his uniform. The soldiers wanted their bodies to be identified when the battle was over.

**Other dangers.** Soldiers who were sick, wounded, or captured faced different horrors. Medical care in the field was crude. Surgeons cut off the arms and legs of wounded men. Many minor wounds became infected, and there were no medicines to fight infections. As a result, over half the wounded died. And disease killed more men than bullets did.

Prisoners of war on both sides suffered from disease and starvation. At Andersonville, a prison camp in Georgia, more than one Union prisoner out of three died. One prisoner wrote: "There is no such thing as delicacy here. . . . In the middle of last night I was awakened by being kicked by a dying man. He was soon dead. I got up and moved the body off a few feet, and again went to sleep to dream of the hideous sights."

## Support Dwindles

Some Northerners had opposed the war all along. Throughout the North, people were against fighting to keep the South in the Union. They were called *Copperheads.* Many people supported the war, but did not like the way Lincoln was managing it. And in the states where slavery existed, many people supported the South.

**The draft law.** Public support for the war dwindled as the fighting dragged on. To fill its armies, the North took new measures. From the start, the Union gave $100 *bounties,* or payments, to men who joined the army. Later, the bounty was raised to over $300. Even so, the Union was so desperate for soldiers that Congress passed a draft law in 1863. The *draft* required all males between 18 and 45 years old to serve in the military.

The draft law allowed a man to avoid going into the army by paying $300 or by hiring someone to serve in his place. This angered many common people. They called the war "a rich man's war and a poor man's fight." Many draftees deserted, or ran away.

**Riots in the North.** The draft law went into effect just two months after Lincoln signed the Emancipation Proclamation. As a result, some Northerners felt that they were being forced to fight to end slavery. Riots broke out in several cities. The worst riot, in New York City, lasted for four days in July 1863. White workers turned their

# Arts in America    **A Portrait of War**

As a boy, Mathew Brady was fascinated with photography, then a new process. While he was a teenager, Brady worked in a photographer's studio in New York. Later, he opened his own studios in New York and Washington. Brady became famous for his fine portraits of business and political leaders.

When the Civil War broke out, Brady was allowed to travel with Union troops. He and his assistants took over 3,500 pictures. Brady used his camera to make a lasting record of the Civil War.

★ Why do you think Brady wanted to photograph the Civil War?

This photograph shows President Lincoln and General McClellan on the battlefield at Antietam.

Between battles, soldiers spent weeks waiting in camp. One of Brady's assistants photographed this Union camp in Virginia.

anger against free blacks. They brutally murdered almost 100 blacks.

President Lincoln tried to stop anti-draft riots and other "disloyal practices." Several times, he denied *habeas corpus* (HAY bee uhs KOR puhs), the right to have a trial before being jailed. To those who protested his action, Lincoln quoted the Constitution. It gave him the right, he said, to deny people their rights "when in the cases of rebellion or invasion, the public safety may require it."

## States' Rights in the South

In the South, few people openly opposed the war. However, the Confederate constitution caused problems for Jefferson Davis. It guaranteed states' rights. Throughout the war, Davis had trouble getting the states to pay taxes and cooperate on military matters. Governor Joseph Brown of Georgia, for example, insisted that only Georgia officers command Georgia troops. At one point, Georgia threatened to secede from the Confederacy.

The South also had serious problems enlisting soldiers. The South had only 6 million white citizens. As early as 1862, the South passed a draft law. The law said that men who owned more than 20 slaves did not have to serve in the army. This caused much resentment among southern farmers and other plain folk.

Toward the end of the war, the South was unable to replace soldiers killed and wounded in battle. There simply were not enough white men to carry on the war. Robert E. Lee urged the Confederacy to let slaves serve as soldiers. Finally, the Confederacy agreed to Lee's plan. However, the war ended before any slaves put on gray uniforms.

## The Wartime Economy

Like all wars, the Civil War was very costly. Both sides had to find ways to pay for it. The war affected the economies of the North and South in different ways.

**The North.** President Lincoln did not want to raise taxes. He was afraid doing so might lessen support for the war. But the Union needed cash. So in 1861, Congress passed the nation's first income tax law. It required workers to pay a small part of their wages to the federal government. The North also raised millions of dollars more by selling bonds. People who bought bonds in effect lent money to the Union.

The North printed over $400 million in paper money during the war. People called these dollars "greenbacks" because of their color. With so much paper money in use, there was inflation. *Inflation* is a rise in prices as a result of an increase in the amount of money in circulation. With inflation, the dollar loses value. Since each dollar is worth less, merchants ask more for their goods. Between 1860 and 1862, prices for goods doubled in the North.

In some ways, the Civil War helped the northern economy. Because many farmers went off to fight, machines were used to plant and harvest. At least 165,000 reapers were sold during the war, compared to a few thousand a year before it. Farm production actually increased.

Wartime demand for clothing, shoes, guns, ammunition, and other supplies brought a boom to these industries. Some people made fortunes by profiteering. *Profiteers* overcharged the government for supplies desperately needed for the war.

**The South.** Like the North, the South had to raise money for the war. Its congress passed an income tax and a tax-in-kind. The *tax-in-kind* required farmers to turn over one tenth of their crops to the government. The South also printed paper money. It printed so much, in fact, that wild inflation resulted. By 1865, one Confederate dollar was worth only two cents in gold.

The southern economy suffered greatly because of the war. This was especially true of the cotton trade. Early in the war, Jefferson Davis stopped cotton shipments to Britain. He was sure that the British would side with the South in order to get cotton. But Britain was buying cotton from Egypt and India instead. By stopping the export of cotton, Davis only cut the South's income.

**Effect of blockade.** The Union blockade had a grim effect on the South. It created severe shortages for soldiers and for *civilians,* or people not in the army. For example, the South bought weapons in Europe, but the blockade kept most from being delivered. When Confederate troops won a battle, they had to scour the field to gather up guns and bullets. Southerners hurried to build weapons factories, but the shortages grew.

Even if supplies were available, they often did not reach the battlefronts. Union armies destroyed many railroad lines, and the South had few parts to make repairs. Breakdowns and delays became common on rail lines. Soldiers waited weeks for food and clothing.

## Women in the War Effort

Women played vital roles on both sides during the war. As men left for the battlefields, women took over jobs in industry, in teaching, and on farms. They held bake sales, donated jewelry, and organized fairs to raise money for medical supplies. Some women disguised themselves as soldiers and fought in battle. Others served as spies.

Many women hoped to help their army by working as nurses. Before the Civil War, women nurses were not allowed to take care of men. When war broke out, many women volunteered to care for wounded soldiers. Dorothea Dix was one of the most famous nurses in the North. Dix became superinten-

**AMERICANS WHO DARED**

### Mary Ann Bickerdyke

During the Civil War, Mary Ann Bickerdyke helped care for wounded Union soldiers. Her skill and energy won her the trust of the troops and the nickname "Mother Bickerdyke." Ulysses S. Grant and other generals had great respect for her. Once, she had an officer dismissed for neglecting his duty. The officer asked Major Sherman to help him get his post back. When Sherman learned that the officer had angered Mother Bickerdyke, he replied: "Oh, if it was Mother Bickerdyke, I can do nothing for you. She outranks me."

dent of nurses for the Union army. She set such strict rules for her nurses that some called her Dragon Dix. But Dix toiled day and night alongside the women she enlisted.

Clara Barton earned fame as a Civil War nurse and founder of the American Red Cross. She trained nurses, collected medical supplies, and served on the war front. Barton kept records on hundreds of soldiers. She was able to trace many who were missing. Sojourner

During the Civil War, there was work for every American. Here, women make bullets at an arsenal in Massachusetts. A Union soldier looks on.

Truth, the antislavery speaker, worked in Union hospitals and in camps for freed slaves. She also recruited black soldiers for the Union army.

In the South, Sally Louisa Tompkins opened a successful private hospital in Richmond, Virginia. When private hospitals were ordered to close, Tompkins was made a captain in the cavalry. This way, her hospital could stay open. Of the 1,333 patients treated in Tompkins' hospital, only 73 died—an excellent record for the time.

**SECTION REVIEW**

1. **Define:** bounty, draft, habeas corpus, inflation, profiteer, tax-in-kind, civilian.
2. (a) Why did support for the war decrease in the North? (b) What did each side do to get more soldiers?
3. Why did the Confederate constitution create problems for Jefferson Davis?
4. How did each side raise money for the war?
5. **What Do You Think?** Why do you think women found more opportunities to work outside the home during the war?

# 5 The Tide Turns

**Read to Learn**

★ How did the tide of war turn?
★ How did the Union try to break the South's will to fight?
★ Why did Lee surrender?

The Union claimed victory at Antietam in September 1862. But after Antietam, Robert E. Lee led the Confederate army to smashing victories over Union troops. These were gloomy days in the North. Few people realized that the tide of the war was about to turn.

## Later Battles

The war went well for the South in late 1862. In December, General Ambrose Burnside led Union troops against Robert E. Lee outside Fredericksburg, Virginia. Burnside ordered his men to charge six times across an

Robert E. Lee and Ulysses S. Grant differed as much in style as they did in politics. Lee was a perfect southern gentleman, well-dressed and dignified. Grant often wore wrinkled uniforms and appeared unshaven in public. Yet, Grant proved to be the only general who could win against the brilliant tactics of Lee.

open field. The Confederates had dug trenches along the field. From the trenches, they mowed down the Union soldiers. Southerners could hardly believe the bravery of the doomed Union troops. One wrote, "We forgot they were fighting us, and cheer after cheer at their fearlessness went up all along our lines."

**Battle of Chancellorsville.** Lee and Jackson outfought their Union foes once again at Chancellorsville, Virginia, in May 1863. But the victory brought an unexpected loss. A Confederate sentry fired at a soldier riding toward him at dusk. Instead of a Union soldier, the rider turned out to be Stonewall Jackson. Jackson died of blood poisoning several days later. Lee said sadly, "I have lost my right arm."

Yet with a victory behind him, Lee could not sit still. He led his troops through the Shenandoah Valley of Virginia into Pennsylvania. Lee hoped to take the Union forces by surprise and then turn south to capture Washington, D.C.

**Battle of Gettysburg.** By accident, some of Lee's men stumbled on Union troops at the small town of Gettysburg, Pennsylvania. Soon, both sides sent in reinforcements. From July 1 to July 3, over 150,000 soldiers fought outside the town. Union troops under General George Meade gained the high ground on the first day. The Confederates had to charge strong Union positions.

Failing to dislodge his enemy, Lee decided on a last-ditch gamble. He sent 15,000 troops, under General George Pickett, to attack the strongest Union position. *Pickett's Charge,* as the attack was called, fell back under deadly Union fire. Lee withdrew his shattered army into Virginia. The ***Battle of Gettysburg*** left over 40,000 dead and wounded. For the first time, Union troops had beaten Lee. The greater manpower and resources of the North at last were making a difference. The tide was turning in favor of the Union.

## The Gettysburg Address

When the soldiers who died at Gettysburg were buried, their graves stretched as far as the eye could see. On November 20, 1863, Northerners held a ceremony to dedicate this cemetery.

President Lincoln was invited to the ceremony, but he was not the main speaker. At the time, his popularity was at its lowest point. Lincoln waited while another speaker spoke for two hours. Then, the President stood up and spoke for just three minutes.

In his ***Gettysburg Address,*** Lincoln said that the Civil War tested whether a nation that believed "all men are created equal" could survive. He urged Americans to have the courage to overcome every challenge to their freedom.

Lincoln sat for this photograph just days before he made his speech at Gettysburg. The years of war seemed to increase Lincoln's patience, wisdom, and strength.

Looking at the thousands of graves, Lincoln told the audience:

> We here highly resolve that these dead shall not have died in vain—that this nation, under God, shall have a new birth of freedom—and that government of the people, by the people, for the people, shall not perish from the earth.

Few in the audience listened to Lincoln. Newspapers gave his speech little attention. Lincoln was dismayed by the lack of response. "It is a flat failure," he said of the speech. "The people are disappointed." But later generations have honored Lincoln for his brief speech at Gettysburg.

## Union Victories

After Gettysburg, Lincoln made Ulysses S. Grant the commander of Union forces. Grant had a plan for ending the war. He wanted to weaken the

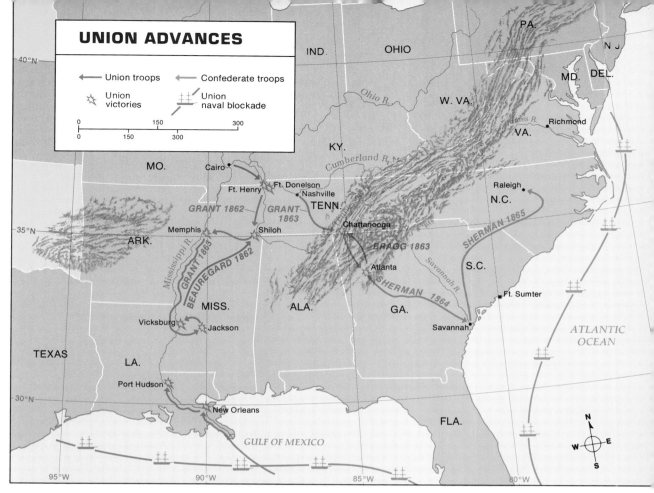

Union troops     Confederate troops

Union victories     Union naval blockade

0   150   300

0   150   300

40°N

IND.   OHIO   PA.   N.J.

MD.   DEL.

Ohio R.

W. VA.

James R.   Richmond

KY.   VA.

Cumberland R.

MO.   Cairo

Ft. Donelson

Ft. Henry   Nashville   Raleigh

GRANT 1862   GRANT 1863   TENN.   N.C.

35°N   Memphis   Shiloh   Chattanooga   SHERMAN 1865

ARK.   Mississippi R.   GRANT 1863   BRAGG 1863

BEAUREGARD 1862   Atlanta   Savannah R.   S.C.

MISS.   ALA.   SHERMAN 1964   Ft. Sumter

Vicksburg   Jackson   GA.   Savannah

TEXAS   LA.   ATLANTIC OCEAN

Port Hudson

30°N

New Orleans   FLA.

GULF OF MEXICO

N   W E   S

95°W   90°W   85°W   80°W

**MAP SKILL** Union forces in the West met success early in the war. From the West, Union troops under General Sherman pushed into Georgia and the Carolinas. What coastal city did Sherman capture after marching southeast from Atlanta?

South's ability to keep fighting. With 100,000 men, he drove south toward Richmond in May 1864.

At the same time, Grant sent General Philip Sheridan and his cavalry into the rich farmland of the Shenandoah Valley. He told Sheridan: "Leave nothing to invite the enemy to return. Destroy whatever cannot be consumed. Let the valley be left so that crows flying over it will have to carry their rations along with them." Sheridan obeyed. In the summer and fall, he destroyed farms and livestock throughout the valley.

**March to the sea.** Grant also sent General William Tecumseh Sherman on a march from Atlanta to the Atlantic Ocean. Like Sheridan, Sherman had orders to destroy everything useful to the South. After burning the city of Atlanta in September 1864, Union soldiers began their "march to the sea."

Sherman's men ripped up railroad tracks, built bonfires from the ties, and then melted and twisted the rails. They chopped telegraph wires into small pieces. They slaughtered livestock and burned everything that grew in the soil. They burned barns, homes, and factories. Looking over the destruction, Sherman said: "We have devoured the land. . . . To realize what war is one should follow in our tracks."

Grant, Sherman, and Sheridan had created a new kind of fighting, called total war. Because of it, civilians in the South suffered as much as soldiers.

**Lincoln is reelected.** But before these Union victories, Lincoln faced a reelection campaign. Many Northerners were unhappy about the war. Northern victory was uncertain. In August, Lincoln commented that his defeat in the upcoming election was "extremely probable."

The Democrats nominated George McClellan to run against Lincoln. Even though he had commanded the Union army, McClellan called for an immediate end to the war.

When Sherman took Atlanta in September, the picture got brighter for Lincoln. In October, Sheridan scored smashing victories in the Shenandoah Valley. These victories turned public opinion around. The popular vote was close, but Lincoln won reelection.

## Surrender at Appomattox

Grant had begun his drive to take Richmond in May 1864. Through the spring and summer, Grant fought a series of costly battles in Virginia against Lee. Both sides suffered terrible losses in the Wilderness, Cold Harbor, and other battles. (See the map at left.) Northerners read with horror that Grant lost 60,000 dead and wounded in a single month. Still, Grant pressed his attack. He knew that the Union could replace both men and supplies.

**Fall of Richmond.** On the other hand, Lee's army was shrinking. To prevent further losses, Lee dug in at the town of Petersburg, Virginia. Petersburg guarded the entrance to Richmond. Here, Grant kept the Southerners under siege for nine months. With a supply of fresh troops, Grant at last attacked Petersburg in March 1865. The town fell on April 3, and Grant captured Richmond the following day. But Jefferson Davis and his cabinet had slipped out of the city earlier.

President Lincoln insisted on visiting Richmond soon after its capture. Lincoln risked his life by walking through the smoldering streets of the city. The President told Southerners that they would be welcomed back into the Union.

**Lee surrenders.** Robert E. Lee and his army were trapped near a small

**MAP SKILL** The last battles of the war pitted Grant against Lee in Virginia. In spite of heavy losses, Grant attacked Lee again and again. Short of men and supplies, Lee at last surrendered at Appomattox Courthouse. Where did Grant hold Lee under siege for more than nine months?

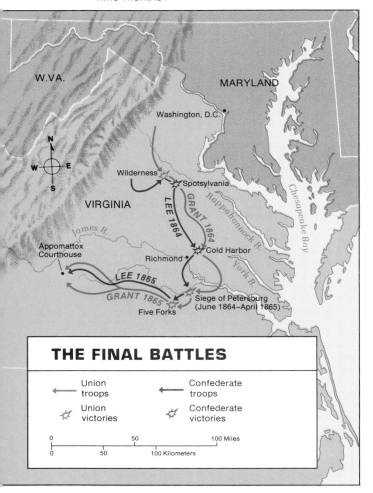

## THE FINAL BATTLES

← Union troops

← Confederate troops

☆ Union victories

☆ Confederate victories

0   50   100 Miles
0   50   100 Kilometers

Here, Confederate soldiers weep as they furl their flag for the last time. Defeat was bitter for the southern veterans. Many returned home to find farms and towns devastated by the war.

town in Virginia called *Appomattox Courthouse.* Lee knew that his men would be slaughtered if he ordered them to continue the fight. On April 9, 1865, Lee surrendered.

At Appomattox, Grant's terms of surrender were generous. Confederate troops had to turn over their rifles, but officers could keep their pistols. Troops who had horses could keep them. Grant knew that Southerners would need the animals for spring plowing. As the Confederates surrendered, Union soldiers began to cheer. Grant ordered them to be silent. "The war is over," he said. "The rebels are our countrymen again."

The Civil War made clear that no part of the United States could secede in peace. But putting the nation back together would be a difficult task. Abraham Lincoln's question at Gettysburg still had not been answered. Could a nation dedicated to the idea that "all men are created equal" survive?

### SECTION REVIEW

1. **Locate:** Fredericksburg, Gettysburg, Atlanta, Appomattox Courthouse.

2. Explain how the actions of each of these generals helped cripple the South's ability to fight: (a) Sheridan; (b) Sherman; (c) Grant.

3. What events helped Lincoln win reelection in November 1864?

4. How were Grant's terms of surrender to Lee generous?

5. **What Do You Think?** What do you think were the most important reasons for the defeat of the South?

# Chapter 18 Review

## ★ Summary ★

As the Civil War began, the North had three goals: to blockade southern ports, control the Mississippi River, and capture Richmond. The South planned to fight a defensive war.

At first, the war went badly for the Union. But in September 1862, the Union claimed victory at Antietam. President Lincoln used this victory to announce the Emancipation Proclamation. As of January 1, 1863, the war to restore the Union was also a war to end slavery.

In 1864, Grant and Lee fought a series of bloody battles in Virginia. Both sides suffered terrible losses. But only the North could replace its men and supplies. Richmond fell in April 1865, and Lee's army surrendered soon afterward.

## ★ Reviewing the Facts

**Key Terms.** Match each term in Column 1 with the correct definition in Column 2.

| Column 1 | Column 2 |
|---|---|
| 1. martial law | a. set free |
| 2. emancipate | b. rule by the army, not by the elected government |
| 3. habeas corpus | c. right to a trial before being jailed |
| 4. profiteer | d. law requiring men to serve in the military |
| 5. draft | e. someone who overcharges the government for war supplies |

**Key People, Events, and Ideas.** Identify each of the following.

1. Robert E. Lee
2. Battle of Bull Run
3. Ulysses S. Grant
4. Stonewall Jackson
5. George McClellan
6. Battle of Antietam
7. Emancipation Proclamation
8. Copperhead
9. Dorothea Dix
10. Sally Louisa Tompkins
11. Pickett's Charge
12. Battle of Gettysburg
13. Gettysburg Address
14. William Tecumseh Sherman
15. Appomattox Courthouse

## ★ Chapter Checkup

1. (a) What advantages did the South have when the war began? (b) What advantages did the North have?

2. Compare Abraham Lincoln and Jefferson Davis as leaders.

3. (a) What were the three war goals of the North? (b) How did the South hope to win the war?

4. (a) Why did the South expect to get help from Great Britain? (b) Give two reasons why Britain did not help the South.

5. (a) What battles did Grant win in the West? (b) Which war goals had the North achieved by July 1863?

6. Why did Lincoln handle the slave question with caution at first?

7. (a) How did the war affect the economy of the North? (b) How did it affect the economy of the South?

8. Why did Grant order Sherman's "march to the sea"?

## ★ Thinking About History ★

1. **Understanding the economy.** How did northern industry help the Union win the Civil War?

2. **Expressing an opinion.** Grant's policy of total war was wrong because it hurt civilians in the South as much as it hurt Confederate soldiers. Do you agree or disagree with this statement? Explain your answer.

3. **Drawing a conclusion.** Why did some people in the North and South criticize the Civil War as "a rich man's war and a poor man's fight"?

4. **Learning about citizenship.** Why do you think free blacks were eager to fight for the Union?

5. **Relating past to present.** (a) What advances in technology made Civil War battles deadly? (b) How would a modern war be even more deadly?

## ★ Using Your Skills ★

1. **Map reading.** Study the map on page 399. (a) What is the distance from Washington to Richmond? (b) Why do you think an army marching from Washington to Richmond would have to travel farther than the distance you measured?

2. **Identifying immediate and long-range causes.** Review the description of immediate and long-range causes on page 331. (a) What was the immediate cause of Lee's surrender at Appomattox Courthouse? (b) What were two long-range causes of Lee's surrender?

3. **Using a painting as a primary source.** Study the painting on page 400. (a) To which army do the soldiers belong? (b) What do you think the soldiers are doing with the pile of furniture at the right? (c) What do you think happened to the owners of the mansion? (d) What does this painting show about life in the South during the Civil War?

4. **Making a generalization.** Reread the section called "Blacks for the Union" on page 402. (a) List three facts about black efforts to help the Union. (b) Using the facts you listed, make a generalization about how blacks helped the Union.

## ★ More to Do ★

1. **Writing a diary.** Imagine that you are a southern plantation owner whose land and house are occupied by Union troops. Write several diary entries telling what happened when they arrived.

2. **Making a poster.** Make a poster encouraging men to enlist in the army of the Union or the Confederacy.

3. **Drawing a cartoon.** Draw a political cartoon criticizing the draft law of either the North or the South for excusing the rich.

4. **Researching a report.** Research a report on one of the women nurses mentioned in the chapter. (a) Did she work with an organization or on her own? (b) What did she do after the Civil War?

5. **Exploring local history.** Research to find out about any Civil War memorials in your state. Create a brochure that describes the memorials and encourages tourists to visit them.

CHAPTER

# 19

# The Road to Reunion (1864–1877)

## Chapter Outline

1 Restoring the Union
2 The President and Congress Clash
3 Changes in the South
4 A New Era in National Politics
Readings, page 566

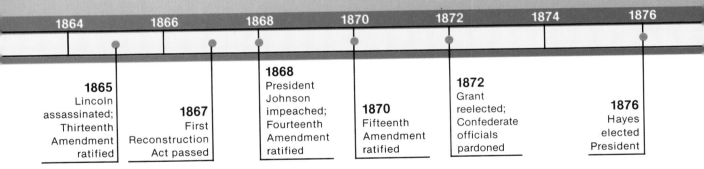

| 1864 | 1866 | 1868 | 1870 | 1872 | 1874 | 1876 |

**1865**
Lincoln assassinated; Thirteenth Amendment ratified

**1867**
First Reconstruction Act passed

**1868**
President Johnson impeached; Fourteenth Amendment ratified

**1870**
Fifteenth Amendment ratified

**1872**
Grant reelected; Confederate officials pardoned

**1876**
Hayes elected President

## About This Chapter

In 1865, the Civil War was over. Much of the South lay in ruins, and a whole way of life had ended. Amid the smoldering rubble of Atlanta and Richmond, black and white Southerners wondered about the future. How would the South rebuild its ruined cities, farms, and economy? What role would freed slaves play in southern society?

President Lincoln realized that one question was even more important: How would the North and South be reunited? In his second inaugural address, delivered in March 1865, Lincoln urged Northerners to forgive the South. "With malice toward none, with charity for all," the President said, "let us strive on to bind up the nation's wounds."

Many Northerners disagreed with Lincoln's plea for charity. They felt that the South had to be punished for causing the bloody Civil War. Some wanted Confederate leaders to stand trial for treason. Others wanted to break up southern plantations and give the land to freed slaves.

The years after the Civil War were difficult ones for the South. A bitter political struggle slowed recovery. But in the end, the South rebuilt its cities, economy, and society. The new shape of southern society lasted for almost a century.

Study the time line above. How many amendments to the Constitution were ratified in the period shown?

In 1865, Richmond and other southern cities lay in ruins. Southerners faced two challenges: rebuilding the South and rejoining the Union.

# 1 Restoring the Union

### Read to Learn

★ What was the condition of the South after the war?

★ How did Andrew Johnson become President?

★ Why did President Johnson and Congress clash?

★ What does this word mean: freedman?

Many soldiers who went to fight in the Civil War never returned home. The North lost many more soldiers than the South. However, the farms and cities of the North were hardly touched by the war. In the North, returning soldiers found industry booming and farms prospering. In the South, on the other hand, returning soldiers found devastated cities and farmlands.

### Conditions in the South

The problems facing the South were staggering. Two thirds of its railroad track had been destroyed. In some areas, 90 percent of all bridges were down. Farms and plantations were a shambles. Thousands of soldiers were disabled. Many southern cities had been destroyed. Much of Charleston, Richmond, Atlanta, and Savannah had been leveled.

After the war, a traveler in Tennessee described the Tennessee River valley. It consisted, he wrote, "for the most part of plantations in a state of semi-ruin, and plantations of which the ruin is for the present total and complete.... The trail of war is visible throughout the valley in burnt up [cotton] gin-houses, ruined bridges, mills, and factories."

The southern financial system was also wrecked. After the war, Confederate money was worthless. Many southern banks closed, and depositors lost all their money. People who had lent money to the Confederacy were never repaid.

Southern society had been changed forever by the war. No longer were there white owners and black slaves. When the war ended, nearly 4 million *freedmen,* or freed slaves, were living in the South. Most had no land, no jobs, and no education. Under slavery, they had been forbidden to own property and to learn to read and write. What would become of them? What rights would freedmen have?

## Early Plans for Reconstruction

President Lincoln was worried about rebuilding the South long before the war ended. Lincoln wanted to make it as easy as possible for the South to rejoin the Union. The quicker the nation was reunited, he thought, the faster the South could rebuild.

**Lincoln's plan.** Lincoln outlined a plan for Reconstruction as early as July 1863. *Reconstruction* refers to the period of the South's rebuilding, as well as the government program to rebuild it. Lincoln's plan called for 10 percent of the voters in each southern state to swear an oath of loyalty to the United States. After this was done, the state could form a new government. The new government then had to abolish slavery. When these three steps were taken, voters could elect members of Congress. The state could once again take part in the national government.

Many Republicans in Congress opposed Lincoln's *Ten Percent Plan.*

They thought that it was too generous toward the South. These Republicans passed their own plan for Reconstruction, called the *Wade–Davis Bill,* in July 1864. It required a majority of white men in the South to swear loyalty to the United States. It denied the right to vote or hold office to any Southerner who had volunteered to fight for the Confederacy.

**Freedmen's Bureau.** Lincoln refused to sign the Wade–Davis Bill because he felt that it was too harsh. Congress and the President did agree on one step, however. A month before Lee surrendered, Congress set up the Freedmen's Bureau with the support of Lincoln.

The *Freedmen's Bureau* provided food and clothing to former slaves. It sent agents into the South to set up schools. (See page 420.) The bureau provided medical care for over a million people. It also tried to find jobs for freedmen. Because so many Southerners were needy after the war, the bureau helped poor whites as well. One former Confederate was amazed to see "a Government which was lately fighting us with fire, and sword, and shell, now generously feeding our poor and distressed."

## Tragedy at Ford's Theater

President Lincoln hoped to convince Congress to support his Reconstruction plan. However, he never got the chance. On April 14, 1865, Lincoln went to Ford's Theater in Washington to see a play. Robert E. Lee had surrendered several days earlier.

As Lincoln watched the play, John Wilkes Booth crept into the President's box. Booth was a Southerner and a former actor. He blamed Lincoln for the South's crushing defeat in the war. Booth shot the President in the head. Lincoln died the next morning without ever regaining consciousness.

The nation had been joyous about the war ending. Now, millions were

Here, Lincoln's funeral procession winds through the streets of New York City. All along the route from Washington, D.C., to Illinois, huge crowds stood silently to pay their respects to the slain President.

plunged into mourning for Lincoln. When Northerners learned that Booth was from the South, they were furious. Many demanded that the South be punished for Lincoln's death. Booth fled the capital. He was caught and killed in a barn outside Washington.

## Johnson Is President

Vice President Andrew Johnson became President when Lincoln died. Johnson had been a Democratic senator from Tennessee. When Tennessee seceded in 1861, Johnson remained loyal to the Union. He was put on the Republican ticket in 1864 to win support from Democrats in the North. Like Andrew Jackson, Johnson had started out life poor. He was a fierce enemy of what he called southern aristocrats.

At first, Republicans in Congress thought that Johnson would support a strict Reconstruction plan, as they did. They were encouraged when Johnson said that "traitors must be made

impoverished." But the Republicans soon learned that they were wrong. Johnson's plan for Reconstruction was almost as mild as Lincoln's plan.

Johnson's plan called for a majority of the voters in each southern state to pledge loyalty to the United States. It also required each state to ratify the *Thirteenth Amendment.* The Thirteenth Amendment had been passed by Congress in 1864. It officially banned slavery throughout the country. Most southern states ratified the amendment, and it became part of the Constitution in December 1865.

## Conflict Over Readmission

The South had done as President Johnson asked. Therefore, in the winter of 1865, Johnson approved the new state governments that Southerners had set up. Voters in the South then chose senators and representatives. Many of those elected had been army officers and high officials under the

By 1869, some 600,000 freed slaves attended schools set up by the Freedmen's Bureau. For teachers, the schools relied mainly on volunteers from the North. About half the teachers were women. Many had been abolitionists before the war.

Teachers found both old and young students eager to learn. Grandmothers and granddaughters sat side by side in the classroom. Some schools stayed open nights so that sharecroppers could attend class after a day's work in the fields. One bureau agent in South Carolina wrote that the freed slaves "will starve themselves, and go without clothes, in order to send their children to school."

The Freedmen's Bureau laid the foundation for the South's public school system. It set up over 4,300 grade schools. The bureau created four universities for black students: Howard, Morehouse, Fisk, and Hampton Institute. The schools gave black students a chance to get a higher education. Many graduates became teachers. By the 1870s, blacks were teaching in grade schools throughout the South.

★ What do you think that the former slaves in the picture at left are learning to do?

Confederacy. Alexander Stephens, the former vice president of the Confederacy, was elected senator from Georgia.

Republicans in Congress were furious. They did not like the way President Johnson had handled the South. Under his plan, the very men who had led the South out of the Union were being elected to the House and Senate. Also, nowhere in the South had blacks been allowed to vote.

Congress met in December 1865. Republicans refused to allow the newly elected representatives from the South to take their seats. Instead, Republicans set up the Joint Committee on Reconstruction to draw up their own plan for dealing with the South. The stage was set for a showdown between Congress and the President.

=== **SECTION REVIEW** ===

1. **Define:** freedman.
2. How did the Freedmen's Bureau help former slaves and poor whites?
3. How was President Lincoln's Reconstruction plan different from the one proposed by Republicans in the Wade–Davis Bill?
4. (a) Why did some Republicans think Andrew Johnson supported a strict Reconstruction plan? (b) Were they right?
5. **What Do You Think?** Why do you think many Republicans were angry when Southerners elected former Confederate officials to Congress?

# 2 The President and Congress Clash

## Read to Learn

★ What rights did southern states deny freedmen?

★ What did Radical Republicans hope to do in the South?

★ Why was Andrew Johnson impeached?

★ What do these words mean: black code?

In the spring of 1866, the Joint Committee on Reconstruction heard reports on the southern governments formed under Johnson's plan. The committee was outraged at what it learned. Throughout the South, the committee found "evidence of an intense hostility to the federal Union, and an equally intense love of the late Confederacy."

## Black Codes

Southern states had ratified the Thirteenth Amendment, which ended slavery. However, white Southerners did not accept the idea of giving blacks real freedom. Throughout the South, legislatures passed *black codes.* These laws severely limited the rights of freedmen.

Black codes varied from state to state. However, all said that blacks could not vote, own guns, or serve on juries. Many allowed blacks to work only as servants or farm laborers. Some codes forced freedmen to sign contracts agreeing to work for a year at a time. Blacks who did not have contracts could be arrested and sentenced to work on a plantation or chain gang. This policy of forced labor was not much different from slavery.

Black codes were not as harsh as slave codes before the Civil War. For example, they gave blacks the right to own some kinds of property and to marry legally. But the codes were clearly meant to keep freedmen from gaining a political voice or achieving any economic power.

## Republicans React

Angry about the black codes and the election of Confederate officers, more Republicans turned against President Johnson. Those who took the lead in opposing him were called *Radical Republicans.* *

**Radical Republicans.** Congressman Thaddeus Stevens of Pennsylvania led the Radical Republicans in the House. Charles Sumner of Massachusetts was the Radical Republican voice in the Senate. Other Radical leaders included Senator Benjamin Wade and Congressman Henry Davis. They had sponsored the Wade–Davis Bill.

Radical Republicans had two main goals. They believed that rich southern planters had caused the Civil War. They wanted to make sure that these "aristocrats" did not regain power in the South. "Strip a proud nobility of their bloated estates," Thaddeus Stevens thundered, "send them forth to labor . . . and you will thus humble the proud traitors." Stevens, Sumner, and other Radicals also insisted on protecting the rights of freedmen.

**Moderate Republicans.** Radical Republicans never controlled Congress during Reconstruction. But they worked together with moderate Republicans. Moderates and Radicals had an important goal in common: keeping power. With Southerners barred from Congress, Republicans controlled both the House and Senate. Most Southerners were Democrats. If southern congressmen were seated, Republicans might lose their majorities.

Moderates agreed with Radical Republicans about some other goals as well. They wanted to keep a high tariff passed during the war. The tariff had

---

*A radical is a person who wants to make drastic changes in society.

You can find information in the library in many sources—books, encyclopedias, and magazines. In Skill Lesson 16 (page 364), you learned how to use the card catalog to find books in the library. Most libraries have several encyclopedias. Encyclopedias present useful overviews of many subjects. **Periodicals,** or magazines, offer up-to-date articles on many subjects.

1. **Find information in an encyclopedia.** Encyclopedias contain articles on many subjects. The articles are arranged in alphabetical order. Imagine that you are writing a report on President Andrew Johnson. Under JOHNSON, ANDREW, you would find the main article. It tells about his life and term in office. At the end of the article are **cross-references** that tell you which other articles in the encyclopedia have information about Andrew Johnson.

Using an encyclopedia in your classroom or school library, look up Andrew Johnson. Are there any cross-references at the end of the article? What other articles do the cross-references refer you to?

2. **Practice using the Readers' Guide.** The *Readers' Guide to Periodical Literature* is an index, or list, of articles that appear in popular magazines.

The *Readers' Guide* lists every article at least twice, once by the author's last name and again by the subject. Look at the sample from the *Readers' Guide* below at right. (a) What subject entry is shown? (b) How many articles are listed under the subject entry? (c) Which article appears under an author entry?

3. **Look for information in the Readers' Guide.** Each subject entry in the *Readers' Guide* tells you the title of the article and the author's name. It gives the title of the magazine in which the article appears, usually in an abbreviated form. The entry lists the volume number of the magazine, the page numbers of the article, and the date of the magazine. The date is also abbreviated. At the front of the *Readers' Guide* are lists that tell you what the abbreviations stand for.

Look at the sample from the *Readers' Guide.* (a) In which volume of *Aging* did the article "Candlelight and vintage years" appear? (b) On what page did the article appear? (c) In what magazine did the article "Fairness doctrine for the press" appear? (d) What was the date of the magazine in which the article "First Amendment" appeared? (e) What date do you think is indicated by the abbreviation Ag '77?

---

Volume: page number

Abbreviated magazine
title (Saturday Review)

Abbreviated date
(November 25, 1977)

FREEDMAN, Martha H.
Candlelight and vintage years. Aging  274:11
Ag '77

FREEDOM of the press
Fairness doctrine for the press? N. Cousins.
Sat R  5:4   N 12 '77

First Amendment;   A. Goldstein   Nat R   29:49-50
N 25 '77

wide support among northern industrialists. They also wanted to help freedmen. But moderates did not think that Congress should interfere too much with the affairs of the South.

## Congress Versus the President

Republicans first locked horns with President Johnson in 1866. In April, Congress passed the Civil Rights Act. This act gave citizenship to all blacks. By passing it, Congress hoped to combat black codes and protect the rights of black Americans. President Johnson vetoed the bill. But Republicans in Congress overrode the veto.

**The Fourteenth Amendment.** Some Republicans worried that the Supreme Court might find the Civil Rights Act unconstitutional. The Court had said in the Dred Scott decision of 1857 that blacks were not citizens. So Republicans proposed the Fourteenth Amendment to the Constitution.

The *Fourteenth Amendment* granted citizenship to all persons born in the United States. This included nearly all blacks. It also encouraged states to allow blacks to vote. It did so by threatening to take representatives away from states that did not let blacks vote. Republicans believed that freedmen would be able to defend their rights if they could vote.

Republicans tried to secure basic rights for southern blacks with the Fourteenth Amendment. But the country had far to go before most Americans would believe in racial equality. Republicans favored giving black Americans the vote. Yet most northern states still denied suffrage to blacks.

**Election of 1866.** Congress and the President clashed over the Fourteenth Amendment. President Johnson did not want states to ratify the amendment. None of the former Confederate states did, except Tennessee. Before the elections to Congress in November 1866, Johnson decided to take his case to the people. He urged voters to reject the Radical Republicans and stick with his Reconstruction plan.

Johnson traveled around the North, speaking against the Radical Republicans. The President was often heckled by his audience. Furious, Johnson yelled right back. This did not help his cause.

Before the elections, white mobs rioted in New Orleans, killing many freedmen. This convinced many Northerners that the government had to protect the freedmen from violence.

The President had misjudged the temper of the people. In the November election, voters sent large Republican majorities to both houses of Congress.

## Radical Reconstruction

With two-thirds majorities in both houses, the Republicans could override Johnson's veto. Johnson became the "dead dog of the White House," as one Republican noted. Republicans enacted their own Reconstruction program. The period that followed is often called *Radical Reconstruction.*

In March 1867, Congress passed the first *Reconstruction Act* over Johnson's veto. The Reconstruction Act threw out the southern state governments that had refused to ratify the Fourteenth Amendment—all the South except Tennessee. It divided the South into five military districts. Each district would be commanded by an army general. Only when the states did what Congress demanded could they rejoin the Union.

The Reconstruction Act required southern states to ratify the Fourteenth Amendment in order to rejoin the Union. Most important, the act stated that blacks must be allowed to vote in all southern states. At the same time, it took the vote away from former Confederate officials and army officers. This included about 10 percent of southern voters.

When elections were held to set up new state governments, many white

Southerners stayed away from the polls. They did so to show their disgust for northern interference. As a result, many Republicans were elected. They won control of the new governments.

Congress passed several Reconstruction acts, each over President Johnson's veto. However, it was Johnson's job to enforce the laws. Many Republicans feared that he would not do so. Therefore, Republicans tried to remove the President from office.

## The President on Trial

On February 24, 1868, the House of Representatives voted to impeach the President. As you have read, impeach means to bring an elected official to trial. According to the Constitution, the House can vote to impeach the President for "high crimes and misdemeanors." The case is tried in the Senate. The President is removed from office only if found guilty by two thirds of the senators. (See pages 629 and 636.)

Thaddeus Stevens read the charges against President Johnson on the Senate floor. During the trial, it became clear that the President was not guilty

of high crimes and misdemeanors. Charles Sumner admitted that the charges against Johnson were "political in character."

The final Senate vote was 35 to 19. This was one vote short of the two thirds needed to convict the President. Some Republicans refused to vote for conviction. They knew the President had not committed a crime. The Constitution did not intend a President to be dismissed because he disagreed with Congress, they believed. So the President thus served out the few months left in his term.

## Grant Takes Office

In 1868, Republicans nominated General Ulysses S. Grant as their candidate for President. Grant was the Union's greatest hero in the Civil War.

By election day in November 1868, most of the southern states had reentered the Union. All of the new southern governments allowed black Americans to vote. During the 1868 elections, about 700,000 southern blacks went to the polls. Nearly all voted for Grant, the Republican.

Republican politicians quickly realized an important fact. If blacks could vote in the North, they would help the Republicans win elections. In 1869, Republican congressmen proposed the *Fifteenth Amendment* to the Constitution. This amendment gave black Americans the right to vote in all states.

Some Republican politicians supported the amendment only because they were eager to win elections. But many other people remembered the great sacrifices made by black soldiers during the war. They felt that it was wrong to let blacks vote in the South but not the North. For these reasons, voters ratified the Fifteenth Amendment in 1870. Black Americans finally had the legal right to vote.

Spectators needed tickets to get into President Johnson's impeachment trial. During the trial, a northern senator waved the bloody shirt of a black beaten by whites. President Johnson was to blame for violence against blacks, the senator claimed. Despite the high emotions, Johnson was not convicted.

1. **Define:** black code.
2. How did black codes limit the freedom of blacks?
3. Who did Radical Republicans blame for the Civil War?
4. (a) What did Andrew Johnson ask voters to do in 1866? (b) Did the voters do as he asked? Explain.
5. **What Do You Think?** Why do you think that nearly all black voters supported the Republican Party during Reconstruction?

# 3 Changes in the South

### Read to Learn

★ Who controlled the South during Reconstruction?
★ What did Reconstruction governments accomplish?
★ How did Conservatives regain control of the South?
★ What do these words mean: scalawag, carpetbagger, sharecropper?

Before the Civil War, a small group of rich planters controlled politics in the South. During Reconstruction, southern politics changed. Many former Confederates could not vote, while blacks could. As a result, new groups dominated the Reconstruction governments.

## Governing the South

In the state governments formed during Reconstruction, the leaders of the old South had lost much of their influence. Instead, three other groups dominated the South during Reconstruction. These were white Southerners who supported the Republicans, Northerners who went South after the war, and freedmen.

**New governments.** Some white Southerners worked with the Republican governments. These Southerners were often business people. Many had not wanted to secede in 1860. They hoped to forget the war and get on with rebuilding the South. But many people in the South thought that any South-erner who worked with the Republicans was a traitor. They called these southern Republicans *scalawags,* a word used for an old, useless horse.

Another important group in the Reconstruction South was Northern-ers. White Southerners called these Northerners *carpetbaggers.* They said that carpetbaggers had left in a hurry to get rich in the South. They only had time to sling a few clothes into cheap cloth suitcases, called carpetbags.

Actually, Northerners went south for different reasons. Many were Union soldiers who had grown to love the fine land of the South. Some were teach-ers—often women—who wanted to help the South recover from the war. Others hoped to open businesses. Still others were reformers who wanted to help the freedmen. And some were for-tune hunters who hoped to profit dur-ing the rebuilding of the South.

**Blacks in office.** Blacks also had an active part in Reconstruction gov-ernments. As slaves, blacks had no voice at all in southern politics. Now, they were not only voting in large num-bers but also running for office and winning elections.

During Reconstruction, blacks were elected to be congressmen, mayors, and state legislators. Blanche Bruce and Hiram Revels won seats in the United States Senate. However, blacks did not control the Reconstruction South. Only in South Carolina did they make up a majority in the legislature.

During Reconstruction, blacks won election to both the House of Representatives and the Senate. In this painting, Robert Elliot, a black congressman from South Carolina, argues for a civil rights bill.

## Success and Failure

Reconstruction governments took important steps to rebuild the South. They built public schools for black as well as white children. Many states gave women the right to own property. They improved care of the mentally and physically handicapped. They rebuilt railroads, telegraph lines, bridges, and roads.

Improvements cost money. So Reconstruction governments passed steep taxes. Before the war, Southerners paid very low taxes. The new taxes created discontent among many Southern whites. So did corruption, which was widespread in the South.

Yet corruption was not limited to the governments of the South. Dishonesty plagued many state and local governments after the war, in both the North and South. Most southern officeholders during the period of Reconstruction served their states well and honestly.

## Resisting Reconstruction

Throughout Reconstruction, Southerners who had been powerful before the Civil War tried to regain control of southern politics. Nearly all were Democrats. These leaders, known as *Conservatives,* wanted the South to change as little as possible. Even so, they were willing to let blacks vote and hold a few offices, as long as whites stayed firmly in power.

However, many poor whites, as well as some leaders, took harsher action. These Southerners felt threatened by the millions of freedmen who now competed with them for land and power. They declared war on carpetbaggers, scalawags, and freedmen. As Senator Ben Tillman of South Carolina recalled:

> We reorganized the Democratic Party with one plank, and only one plank, namely, that "this is a white man's country, and white men must govern it." Under that banner we went to battle.

**The KKK.** Some Southerners organized secret groups to help them regain power. The most effective of these was the *Ku Klux Klan* (KKK). These groups worked to keep blacks and carpetbaggers out of office. White-sheeted klansmen claimed to be the ghosts of Confederate soldiers. They rode at night to the homes of black voters, shouting threats and burning wooden crosses. If threats did not work, the Klan used violence. Klan members murdered hundreds of blacks and their white allies.

**Response to terror.** Many moderate Southerners condemned the violence of the Klan. But they could do little to stop the Klan's reign of terror.

Blacks turned to the federal government for help. Black voters in Kentucky sent a letter to Congress that said, "We believe you are not familiar with the Ku Klux Klan's riding nightly over the country spreading terror wherever they go by robbing, whipping, and killing our people without provocation."

Congress tried to end the violence of the Klan. In 1870, Congress made it illegal to use force to keep people from voting. The laws did little to undo the damage already done. Some blacks risked their lives by voting and holding office. Many others stayed away from the ballot box.

## Life in the South

The South began to rebuild in spite of its political problems. The damage left by the war was repaired, but progress was very slow.

**Industry.** Between 1865 and 1879, the South laid 7,000 miles (11,200 km) of railroad track. The cotton industry recovered slowly. Not until 1880 did planters grow as much cotton as they had in 1860. The same year, 158 textile mills were operating. Other types of manufacturing also grew during and after Reconstruction. Birmingham, Alabama, became an important steelmaking city.

The KKK used threats and violence to try to end Republican rule in the South. This cartoon appeared in an Alabama newspaper. It warned carpetbaggers, pictured here as men from Ohio, to fear for their lives.

Still, the South lagged behind the rest of the nation in industry. In 1900, the South actually produced a smaller part of the nation's manufactured goods than it did in 1860.

**Freedmen.** Many freedmen left the plantations in the first months after the war ended. For them, moving away from their former owners was a way to prove that they were free. One woman told her ex-owner: "I must go. If I stay here, I'll never know I am free." But there were few opportunities for freedmen. Frederick Douglass noted bitterly that the freedman "was free from the old plantation, but he had nothing but the dusty road under his feet."

At the end of the war, some Radical Republicans talked about giving each freedman "40 acres and a mule." Radicals planned to get the land by breaking up large plantations. However, this never happened. Many freedmen ended up moving back to the same areas where they had been slaves.

**Agriculture.** Only a small group of planters had held on to their land and wealth during the war. During Reconstruction, these planters owned huge amounts of land. But they no longer had slaves to work the soil.

Many freedmen, as well as many poor whites, went to work for the large planters. They farmed the land owned by planters, using seed, fertilizer, and tools the planters provided. In return, they gave the landowners a share of the crop at harvest time. For this reason, these poor farmers were called *sharecroppers.*

Sharecroppers hoped to own their own land one day. But many faced a

After the Civil War, conditions were hard for both black and white Southerners. Families like this one fell deeply in debt and had to sell their land and homes. Often, they ended up as sharecroppers.

day-to-day struggle just to survive. Most sharecroppers were constantly in debt. They were doing well if they had enough food for themselves and their families.

Even large landowners faced hard times. Each spring, the landowners borrowed money from a bank for supplies. Sometimes, they got supplies on credit from a store owner. In the fall, the bank or store had to be paid back. Often, the harvest did not cover the whole debt. Thus, many landowners sank further and further into debt. Much of the South was locked into a cycle of poverty.

## SECTION REVIEW

1. **Define:** scalawag, carpetbagger, sharecropper.
2. What three groups dominated southern governments during Reconstruction?
3. How did Reconstruction governments help rebuild the South?
4. Why did many poor blacks and whites in the South become sharecroppers?
5. **What Do You Think?** How do you think the Ku Klux Klan helped Conservatives regain power in the South?

AMERICANS WHO DARED

### Parker Robbins

Parker Robbins was a free black born in North Carolina. When the Civil War came, he enlisted in the Union army. Robbins, shown in a Union officer's uniform, rose to the rank of sergeant major. After the war, Robbins helped frame the new constitution of North Carolina. Later, he was elected to Congress from his home state.

# 4 A New Era in National Politics

### Read to Learn

★ Why did Northerners lose interest in Reconstruction?
★ What happened in the election of 1876?
★ How did southern blacks lose power and rights after 1877?
★ What do these words mean: poll tax, literacy test, grandfather clause, segregation?

As the 1870s wore on, Conservative Democrats regained control of their state governments. At the same time, Northerners began to lose interest in the South.

### New Mood of the North

Radical Republicans were losing power in Congress during the 1870s. Thaddeus Stevens died in 1868, and Charles Sumner died in 1874. Many Northerners grew weary of efforts to change the South. They wanted to forget the Civil War. The South should be left alone, they believed.

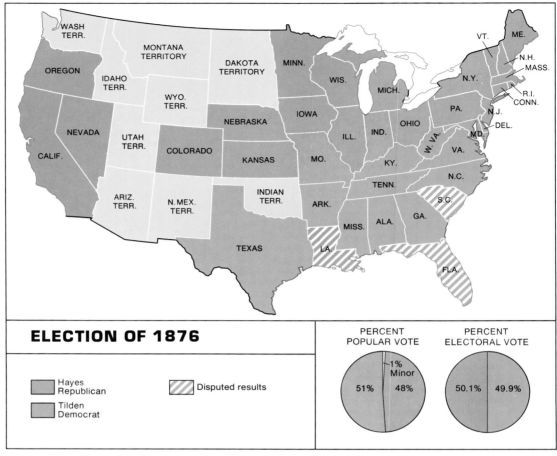

## ELECTION OF 1876

- Hayes
  Republican
- Tilden
  Democrat
- Disputed results

PERCENT POPULAR VOTE
51% 48% 1% Minor

PERCENT ELECTORAL VOTE
50.1% 49.9%

MAP SKILL In the election of 1876, Tilden won the popular vote. But a congressional committee gave the election to Hayes. In return, Hayes agreed to remove the last federal troops from the South. What three states were still occupied by federal troops in 1876?

One reason the Republicans lost support was corruption. President Grant appointed many friends to office. Some took advantage of their jobs by stealing money. Grant kept enough support to win reelection in 1872. But many Northerners lost faith in Republican leaders and policies.

Congress reflected the new mood of the North. In 1872, it passed a law pardoning Confederate officials. As a result, nearly all white Southerners could vote again. They voted solidly Democratic. The Republican state governments in the South fell, one by one. By 1876, only three states in the South were under Republican control: South Carolina, Florida, and Louisiana.

## Reconstruction Ends

The election of 1876 brought the end of Reconstruction. Democrats nominated Samuel Tilden, governor of New York, for President. Tilden was known as a reformer. He pledged to end corruption. Republicans chose Rutherford B. Hayes, governor of Ohio. Like Tilden, Hayes vowed to fight dishonesty in government.

When the votes were tallied, Tilden had 250,000 more popular votes than Hayes. But Tilden had only 184 electoral votes—one short of the number needed to become President. The election hinged on the votes of the three southern states still under Republican control. In each of these states, Tilden had won. But Republicans claimed that many people, especially blacks, had been kept from voting for Hayes. They said Hayes should have won the three states. In fact, they filed a second set of electoral votes—for Hayes.

Inauguration day drew near, and the country had no one to swear in as President. Congress appointed a special commission to settle the crisis. A majority of the commission members were Republican. So all the disputed votes went to Hayes.

Southern Democrats on the committee could have blocked the election of Hayes. But Hayes had agreed privately to end Reconstruction in the South. Once in office, Hayes removed all federal troops from South Carolina, Florida, and Louisiana. Reconstruction was over.

## A Century of Separation

After Hayes' election, white Conservatives tightened their grip on southern governments. Some groups continued to use terror against blacks who tried to vote or hold office. By the late 1880s, southern state governments had found other ways to keep blacks from voting.

**Limits on voting.** *Poll taxes* required voters to pay a fee each time they voted. Thus, poor freedmen could not afford to vote. *Literacy tests* often asked voters to read and explain a difficult part of the Constitution. Such tests were difficult for most freedmen, who had little education. However,

many southern whites were poor and illiterate, too. They also were kept from voting.

To permit more whites to vote, states passed *grandfather clauses*. If a voter's father or grandfather had voted in 1867, the voter was excused from the poll tax or literacy test. Since no southern blacks could vote in 1867, grandfather clauses kept many blacks from voting.

**Segregation.** As more blacks lost the vote during the 1890s, segregation became law. *Segregation* means separating people of different races. Southern states passed laws that separated blacks and whites in schools, churches, restaurants, theaters, trains, streetcars, playgrounds, hospitals, beaches, and even cemeteries. These were called *Jim Crow laws.*

Blacks fought segregation by challenging the laws in court. However, in 1896, the Supreme Court made the *Plessy* v. *Ferguson* decision. It allowed segregation as long as separate facilities for blacks and whites were equal. In fact, facilities for blacks were rarely equal.

Reconstruction was a time of both success and failure. Southerners, especially blacks, faced hard times for many years. But at last, all black Americans were citizens. And laws passed during Reconstruction became the basis of the civil rights movement almost 100 years later.

═══ SECTION REVIEW ═══

1. **Define:** poll tax, literacy test, grandfather clause, segregation.
2. (a) How did Hayes become President? (b) What did he agree to do in order to get southern support?
3. (a) What three states were important in the election of 1876? (b) Why?
4. How did segregation develop?
5. **What Do You Think?** Why do you think Northerners lost interest in the problems of the South in the 1870s?

# Chapter 19 Review

## ★ Summary ★

After the Civil War, Americans had to rebuild the ruined South and reunite the two sections of the nation. President Lincoln urged generosity toward the South. However, he was killed before his plan was adopted. Andrew Johnson was also ready to readmit the southern states quickly. But Republicans in Congress objected.

After the election of 1866, Republicans in Congress had enough votes to take over Reconstruction. Freedmen gained the right to vote, while some white Southerners lost it. Republican governments came to power. They took important steps to rebuild the South.

Northerners slowly lost interest in the problems of the South. By the mid-1870s, Democrats were in power in most of the South. Slowly, southern blacks were edged out of politics.

## ★ Reviewing the Facts ★

**Key Terms.** Match each term in Column 1 with the correct definition in Column 2.

| Column 1 | Column 2 |
|---|---|
| 1. freedman | a. farmer who pays part of a crop to the landowner |
| 2. carpetbagger | b. fee that voters pay at each election |
| 3. sharecropper | c. freed slave |
| 4. poll tax | d. separation of different races |
| 5. segregation | e. Northerner who went south during Reconstruction |

**Key People, Events, and Ideas.** Identify each of the following.

1. Ten Percent Plan
2. Wade–Davis Bill
3. Freedmen's Bureau
4. John Wilkes Booth
5. Andrew Johnson
6. Thirteenth Amendment
7. Radical Republicans
8. Thaddeus Stevens
9. Charles Sumner
10. Fourteenth Amendment
11. Fifteenth Amendment
12. Ulysses S. Grant
13. Ku Klux Klan
14. Samuel Tilden
15. Rutherford B. Hayes

## ★ Chapter Checkup ★

1. (a) What problems did the South face after the Civil War? (b) What problems did freedmen face?

2. (a) What was Lincoln's plan for readmitting southern states to the Union? (b) Why did some Republicans object to it?

3. (a) What did Radical Republicans want to achieve during Reconstruction? (b) Which goals did moderates agree with?

4. What were the main parts of the first Reconstruction Act?

5. (a) Why did Congress try to remove President Johnson from office? (b) Why did some Republicans vote against convicting the President?

6. What three groups dominated southern governments during Reconstruction?

7. List three reasons why Northerners went to the South after the Civil War.

8. How did Conservatives regain control of southern governments?

## ★ Thinking About History ★

1. **Expressing an opinion.** Congress had no right to interfere with the South after the Civil War. Do you agree or disagree with this statement? Explain.

2. **Relating past to present.** (a) What disagreement did Congress and President Johnson have during Reconstruction? (b) Can you think of a recent disagreement between Congress and the President? Explain.

3. **Analyzing a quotation.** After the Civil War, a Mississippi law said: "The Negro is free, whether we like it or not. . . . To be free, however, does not make him a citizen, or entitle him to social or political equality with the white man." (a) What does this law show about attitudes of southern whites toward freedmen? (b) What problems do you think freedmen in Mississippi faced as a result of this law?

4. **Learning about citizenship.** How did the amendments to the Constitution ratified during Reconstruction give black Americans a new role in government?

## ★ Using Your Skills ★

1. **Making a generalization.** Reread the discussion of the condition of the South after the Civil War (pages 417 and 418). (a) List three facts about the South after the war. (b) Using the facts you listed, make a generalization about the South after the war.

2. **Placing events in time.** Study the time lines on pages 370–371 and 416. (a) What year did the Civil War end? (b) What two events took place the same year?

3. **Understanding cause and effect.** Many events are connected by cause and effect. A cause is the reason that an event happened. An effect is the result of the cause. Read the three statements below. Decide which one is an effect and which two are causes. Then explain how the causes and the effect are connected.
   (a) Southern states passed black codes.
   (b) Southern states elected former Confederates to Congress.
   (c) Republicans opposed Johnson's plan to readmit southern states.

## ★ More to Do ★

1. **Interviewing.** As a group project, conduct interviews with students who imagine that they are freedmen living in the South after the Civil War. If possible, record the interviews and listen to the tape. Do you think the interviews give an accurate picture of life during Reconstruction? Explain.

2. **Drawing a cartoon.** Draw a political cartoon that criticizes the black codes passed in the South after the Civil War.

3. **Writing a letter.** Imagine that you are a Republican senator who voted against convicting Andrew Johnson in 1868. Write a letter to a friend explaining why you voted as you did.

4. **Exploring local history.** Prepare an oral report about life in your local area after the Civil War. If possible, locate photographs or written descriptions of the area during this time period.

# Unit 6 Review

**Chapter 17** Slavery in the western territories became an emotional issue in the late 1840s. At first, the North and South compromised. But events in the 1850s pushed the two sections further apart. When Abraham Lincoln was elected President in 1860, the South seceded. The Confederacy's bombardment of Fort Sumter signaled the start of the Civil War.

**Chapter 18** Both the North and South expected the war to end quickly, but the fighting dragged on. In 1862, President Lincoln announced the Emancipation Proclamation to weaken the South and broaden the war goals of the Union. By 1864, the greater resources of the North and Grant's plan of total war pushed the Union toward victory. In April 1865, Lee surrendered.

**Chapter 19** Republicans in Congress disagreed with Presidents Lincoln and Johnson about how to reconstruct the South. After 1866, Congress took charge. It divided the South into military districts and gave black Americans the vote. Republican governments came to power in the South. They were opposed by white Conservatives, who worked to regain control. By 1877, Republican control had ended in the South.

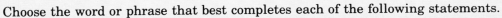

## ★ Unit Checkup ★

Choose the word or phrase that best completes each of the following statements.

1. The issue of slavery in the Mexican Cession was settled by the
   (a) Missouri Compromise.
   (b) Compromise of 1850.
   (c) Kansas–Nebraska Act.

2. Lincoln's election led to
   (a) the Dred Scott decision.
   (b) a raid on Harpers Ferry.
   (c) creation of the Confederacy.

3. The Union won its first major battle at
   (a) Bull Run.
   (b) Antietam.
   (c) Shiloh.

4. A plan of total war to break the South's will to fight was devised by
   (a) Sherman.
   (b) Grant.
   (c) Lincoln.

5. Lincoln outlined his ideas about Reconstruction in the
   (a) Ten Percent Plan.
   (b) Wade–Davis Bill.
   (c) Gettysburg Address.

## ★ Building American Citizenship ★

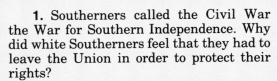

1. Southerners called the Civil War the War for Southern Independence. Why did white Southerners feel that they had to leave the Union in order to protect their rights?

2. During the Civil War, Frederick Douglass said that once a black American put on an army uniform, "no power on earth . . . can deny that he has earned the right to citizenship in the United States." Why do you think Douglass believed that blacks would win more rights after they had served in the army? Do you think Douglass was right?

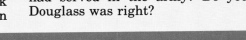

The cartoon at right was published during Reconstruction. Study the cartoon. Then answer the following questions.

1. Figure out what each person and thing in the cartoon stands for. (a) What does the woman stand for? (b) What does the carpetbag stand for? (c) Which President is pictured on top of the carpetbag?

2. (a) What is the woman in the cartoon walking on? (b) Why did the cartoonist show this?

3. (a) Why is the woman carrying the carpetbag? (b) Why are federal troops shown holding the carpetbag in place? (c) Why did the cartoonist show these things?

4. (a) What did the cartoonist think the North was doing to the South during Reconstruction? (b) Do you think the cartoonist was a Northerner or a Southerner?

5. Did the cartoonist exaggerate the facts in order to make a point? Explain.

## History Writer's Handbook

### Arranging Information to Show Cause and Effect

A **cause** is an event that produces an **effect,** another event. Often that effect becomes a cause. It produces still another event. To show this chain reaction, you would arrange supporting information in order of cause and effect.

Look at the following topic sentence. *The Missouri Compromise passed because Congress wanted to keep the number of free states and slave states equal.* You might arrange the events leading to the passage of the Missouri Compromise in cause-and-effect order. The following diagram of events shows the chain reaction of cause and effect.

( first event ) Missouri's request to join Union as a slave state
(causes) ↓

( second event ) Northern objections
(causes) ↓

( third event ) Henry Clay's proposal for compromise

Transitions to show cause and effect include *as a result, because, consequently, therefore, thus,* and *so.*

**Practice** Use the diagram to write detail sentences that support the topic sentence above. (See pages 373–374 for information.)

# A Look Ahead (1877–Present)

## Chapter Outline

1 The American Dream
2 Governing a Growing Nation
3 A Land of Opportunity
4 Becoming a World Power

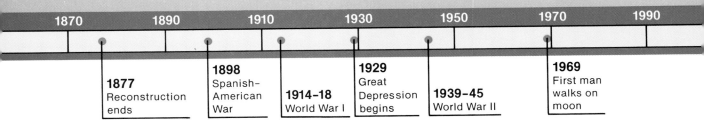

| 1870 | 1890 | 1910 | 1930 | 1950 | 1970 | 1990 |

**1877**
Reconstruction ends

**1898**
Spanish–American War

**1914–18**
World War I

**1929**
Great Depression begins

**1939–45**
World War II

**1969**
First man walks on moon

## About This Chapter

After the Civil War, the United States embarked on a period of rapid change. Industries sprang up, and cities expanded. America also became more involved in world affairs, entering World War I in 1917. A time of prosperity during the Roaring Twenties ended when the country was plunged into the Great Depression, which lasted throughout the 1930s. The United States played a vital role in World War II and emerged from the war as a world leader. Since World War II, Americans have continued to work toward fulfillment of the American dream.

Since 1886, one symbol of that dream has been the Statue of Liberty. Emma Lazarus wrote the poem carved at the base of the statue. It ends with these words, addressed to the world:

Give me your tired, your poor,
Your huddled masses yearning to breathe
free,
The wretched refuse of your teeming
shore.
Send these, the homeless, tempest-
tossed to me:
I lift my lamp beside the golden door!

America grew rapidly. The many people who came helped to build and strengthen the nation. This chapter presents an overview of developments in the United States since the Civil War. You will read about the American people, government, and economy and about the country's growing role in world affairs.

Study the time line above. When did the Great Depression begin?

—436—

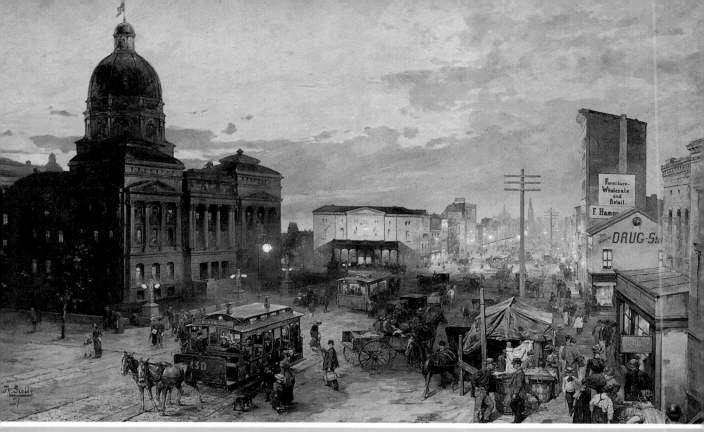

Bustling cities were characteristic of America's growth in the late 1800s. This painting shows downtown Indianapolis, Indiana, at sunset.

# 1 The American Dream

### Read to Learn

★ Why had people immigrated to America?

★ How have cities changed since the Civil War?

★ What new inventions have changed American life?

The United States has grown on the dreams of people coming to its shores from around the world. Since the first people crossed from Asia into Alaska, America has been a land of immigrants. Some, like the conquistadors from Spain, came for fame and glory. Many more came as farmers, traders, and trappers seeking "elbow room." They wanted good land and a chance to make a new start. Some came to find the freedom to worship as they pleased. Others were brought as slaves.

People of many cultures and many backgrounds have continued to come to America. All have contributed to the creation of a new people—Americans.

## A Land of Immigrants

Different waves of immigrants have come to the United States. In the 1880s, immigration rose sharply to almost half a million people a year. Many of the immigrants came from countries in Southern and Eastern Europe such as Italy, Poland, Russia, and Hungary. They included Jews escaping persecution in Eastern Europe as well as many Catholics.

The religious beliefs, customs, and languages of the newcomers were different from earlier immigrants. Many

Today, as in the past, hundreds of thousands of immigrants reach American shores each year. They come from all parts of the globe, and many apply for citizenship. At a vast ceremony held in the Orange Bowl in Miami in 1984, almost 10,000 immigrants became citizens at one time. Some showed their feelings about their new country by waving huge flags.

faced discrimination. In the 1920s, Congress limited the number of immigrants who could come from Europe.

In 1965, Congress revised the immigration laws so that more people could enter the country. Recently, many immigrants have come from Latin America and Asia. In 1986, Congress took steps to control illegal immigration. However, amnesty was granted to illegal aliens who had been in the country since January 1, 1982.

Each wave of immigrants has added to the richness of life in America. In the late 1800s and early 1900s, immigrants helped build America's railroads, subways, and factories. They brought their foods, songs, stories, and customs to America. Today, many ethnic groups weave rich and varied threads into the fabric of American culture.

## From Farms to Cities

In the past 100 years, American cities have grown dramatically. At the end of Reconstruction, less than one fourth of all Americans lived in cities in 1880. Between 1880 and 1900, the number of people living in cities doubled. By 1920, a majority of Americans lived in cities or suburbs.

The move to the cities changed American culture. Newspapers grew larger and became more interesting— even sensational. Huge department stores such as Macy's in New York offered goods of every type. Subways and trolleys whisked people from one side of town to the other. Professional sports, especially baseball, became popular pastimes.

Cities and suburbs continued to grow through the mid-1900s. Then, in the 1970s, the trend changed. For the first time since 1820, small towns and rural areas gained population faster than cities and suburbs. The older cities of the East and Midwest actually lost population. People left those regions and moved to the Sunbelt, as the states of the Southeast and Southwest are called. Many went in search of jobs. The sunny climate with mild winters also attracted people to the Sunbelt. By the 1980s, three of the ten largest cities in America were in Texas: Dallas, Houston, and San Antonio.

## A Musical Nation

Since colonial times, Americans have been known for their folk songs. As America changed, so did its music. In the early 1900s, a new kind of music, called jazz, was born in the South. It drew on the rhythms brought from West Africa to America by slaves. Black composers like Scott Joplin and "Jelly Roll" Morton were originators of jazz.

In the 1950s, another sound swept America—rock 'n' roll. Artists like Chuck Berry, Little Richard, and Bill Haley pioneered rock 'n' roll. Buddy

In the 1970s and 1980s, Americans moved south and west by the millions. Southern and western cities such as Houston grew dramatically. One lure was warmer winters, which mean more time outdoors and lower fuel bills. Another lure was more jobs, for industry was growing much faster in the Sunbelt than in other parts of the country.

Holly and Elvis Presley won huge followings among teenagers. But many parents complained that rock 'n' roll was noise, not music.

During the 1960s, 1970s, and 1980s, popular music took many forms. Americans of all ages and backgrounds enjoyed country and western, rhythm and blues, heavy metal, new wave, and jazz. Music superstars like Michael Jackson, Bruce Springsteen, and Tina Turner sold millions of albums each year.

## Technology and Culture

Inventions have also changed the shape of American culture. During the 1920s, radio stations began broadcasting all across the country. They brought news, sports, and entertainment into American homes. Today, radios and cassette recorders smaller than a credit card allow people to listen to music anywhere they go.

The first movie theaters opened in the early 1900s. Until 1927, movies were silent; that is, they had no sound track. Audiences read subtitles to follow the plot.

This 1937 mural, called *Comedy,* was painted by John Steuart Curry. Curry included familiar faces from movies and cartoons as well as portraits of popular radio personalities.

The first commercial television in the United States began in the late 1940s. In the 1950s, millions of Americans began buying television sets. Today, virtually every home has at least one set. Also, more people are buying VCRs, or video cassette recorders, which allow them to record programs or buy movies to watch at home.

Movies, radio, and television allow Americans to share experiences. They help shape our behavior and keep us informed. When candidates for President debate on television, for example, millions of Americans can watch and decide whom they will vote for.

Today, many Americans are also buying home computers. Parents use them to keep track of the family budget. Children use them to write their school papers. And the whole family enjoys computer games.

## America: Leader in Technology

In July 1969, American astronaut Neil Armstrong stepped out of a lunar landing craft onto the surface of the moon and said, "That's one small step for a man, one giant leap for mankind." Armstrong was the first person to walk on the moon.

Landing on the moon was only one of the space programs that helped make America the world leader in high technology. More recently, the United States has launched several space shuttles. Astronauts in the reusable shuttle

CHART SKILL This chart shows the Presidents from Reconstruction to the present. Who was President during World War I? World War II?

## Presidents of the United States, 1877–Present

| President | Dates | Major Events |
|---|---|---|
| Rutherford B. Hayes | 1877–1881 | End of Reconstruction |
| James A. Garfield | 1881 | American Federation of Labor founded |
| Chester A. Arthur | 1881–1885 | Civil Service Act |
| Grover Cleveland | 1885–1889 | Interstate Commerce Act; Statue of Liberty unveiled |
| Benjamin Harrison | 1889–1893 | Sherman Antitrust Act; rise of Populism |
| Grover Cleveland | 1893–1897 | *Plessy* v. *Ferguson* ruling |
| William McKinley | 1897–1901 | Spanish–American War |
| Theodore Roosevelt | 1901–1909 | Pure Food and Drug Act; NAACP founded |
| William H. Taft | 1909–1913 | Mexican Revolution; dollar diplomacy |
| Woodrow Wilson | 1913–1921 | Federal Reserve Act; World War I |
| Warren G. Harding | 1921–1923 | Teapot Dome scandal; Washington Naval Conference |
| Calvin Coolidge | 1923–1929 | Jazz Age; Lindbergh flies Atlantic |
| Herbert Hoover | 1929–1933 | Stock market crash; depression begins |
| Franklin D. Roosevelt | 1933–1945 | Great Depression; World War II |
| Harry S. Truman | 1945–1953 | Truman Doctrine; Korean War |
| Dwight D. Eisenhower | 1953–1961 | End of Korean War; launch of Sputnik |
| John F. Kennedy | 1961–1963 | Bay of Pigs; Cuban missile crisis |
| Lyndon B. Johnson | 1963–1969 | Civil Rights Act; Vietnam War |
| Richard M. Nixon | 1969–1974 | Visit to China; Watergate |
| Gerald R. Ford | 1974–1977 | Withdrawal from South Vietnam; Bicentennial |
| Jimmy Carter | 1977–1981 | Camp David Agreement; hostages in Iran |
| Ronald W. Reagan | 1981–1989 | Tax Reform Act passed; INF Treaty signed |
| George Bush | 1989– | War on drugs declared |

In 1969, United States astronauts Neil Armstrong and Edwin "Buzz" Aldrin landed on the moon and set up television cameras. Millions on earth watched on live television as the first humans hopped around in the moon's light gravity, collecting rock and soil samples.

perform many different tasks. They launch and repair satellites, do experiments, and make special medicines in the weightlessness of space.

For years, the United States has led the world in inventions. American scientists are still pioneers in such areas as computers, lasers, and advanced medical treatment. Successful breakthroughs in these areas have changed the way people live.

■ SECTION REVIEW ■

1. **Locate:** Italy, Poland, Russia, Hungary.
2. How were the immigrants of the late 1800s different from earlier immigrants?
3. What region of the country grew in population in the 1970s and 1980s?
4. How has the space shuttle been used?
5. **What Do You Think?** Why do you think America continues to be a haven for people from around the world?

# 2 Governing a Growing Nation

### Read to Learn

★ How have the civil rights of black Americans changed since the Civil War?
★ How did women win the right to vote?
★ Why did the federal government become more active in the 1930s?
★ What do these words mean: initiative, referendum, recall?

From 13 states along the Atlantic Ocean in 1776, the United States expanded 3,000 miles to the Pacific by 1848. Today, it reaches as far north as Alaska and as far west as the Hawaiian Islands in the Pacific. The American population has grown from 4 million to nearly 250 million. The government has also grown to meet the challenges of this development.

### More People Win the Right to Vote

In 1860, only white men age 21 or over had the right to vote in the United States. Today, however, all citizens over age 18 have the right to vote. Three constitutional amendments guarantee these rights.

**The Fifteenth Amendment.** The Fifteenth Amendment, ratified in 1870, stated that an adult male could not be prevented from voting because of his race. This officially extended the right to vote to black men. After Reconstruction, however, southern states passed laws to make it hard for blacks to vote. Other laws kept blacks and whites from associating in public places. In the North, too, blacks faced discrimination in many areas.

Black soldiers served gallantly in World War I and World War II. However, they were in segregated regiments. Not until 1948 was the military integrated, by order of President Truman. During the Korean War, blacks and whites fought side by side in the same regiments.

Beginning in the 1950s and 1960s, black Americans began to win more civil rights. The Reverend Martin Luther King, Jr., led nonviolent protests against segregation. His marches often met violent opposition. But that only increased his support.

In the 1960s, Congress passed civil rights laws to help end racial segregation and discrimination. The Voting Rights Act of 1964 protected blacks who wanted to register and vote. In 1964, only 35 percent of southern blacks were registered to vote. By 1969, almost 65 percent were registered. In 1984, Jesse Jackson became the first black to run for the Presidential nomination of a major party. Jackson tried again in 1988. His efforts encouraged many black Americans to vote.

**The Nineteenth Amendment.** Women won the right to vote when the Nineteenth Amendment was ratified in 1920. The struggle had been a long one. The Seneca Falls Convention in 1848 passed a resolution demanding suffrage for women. (See pages 356–357.) During the late 1800s and early 1900s, women's organizations worked to win

Beginning in the 1970s, the number of women in medicine and the sciences increased dramatically. This researcher works in the San Diego Zoo.

the vote. By 1919, women in many states could vote in state and local elections. The Nineteenth Amendment gave women the right to vote in Presidential elections as well.

During the 1960s, women won greater civil and economic rights. Federal laws made it illegal to favor men over women when hiring or paying wages. In the 1970s and 1980s, women made important gains in politics. The candidacy of Geraldine Ferraro for Vice President in 1984 reflected the growing strength of women in politics.

**The Twenty-sixth Amendment.** In March 1971, Congress passed the Twenty-sixth Amendment. This amendment guaranteed the right to vote to persons age 18 or older. It was ratified in less than 4 months. Soldiers as young as age 18 were fighting and dying in the Vietnam War. So there was widespread support for allowing 18-year-olds to vote.

## A Growing Role for Voters

As suffrage was extended to new groups, voters also gained new powers. In some states, voters today can introduce a bill to the legislature by collecting signatures on a petition. This is called an *initiative.* In a *referendum,* people vote directly on a bill. In some states, voters also have the power to remove a person from office in a *recall* election.

The initiative, referendum, and recall were ideas supported by reformers in the early 1900s. These reformers were called Progressives. Progressives also supported primary elections and direct election of senators. In a primary, voters from each political party decide who will be their party's candidate in the general election. Primaries meant that political bosses could no longer handpick candidates.

Originally, senators had been chosen by state legislatures. The Seventeenth Amendment, which was ratified in 1913, required the voters in each state to elect two senators.

## New Roles for Government

Since the 1800s, the responsibilities of the federal government have grown. Often, the government has stepped in to help or protect Americans. In the late 1800s, for example, reformers called on Congress to stop unfair actions by big business. Congress created the Interstate Commerce Commission, or ICC, in 1887. The ICC looked into complaints and took some big companies to court.

Government has become increasingly involved in our lives in this century. During the Great Depression of

The painter Isaac Soyer captured the soul-crushing despair of being out of work and out of hope during the Great Depression.

the 1930s, millions of workers were thrown out of work, and farmers lost their land. In 1932, when the depression was at its worst, Franklin Delano Roosevelt became President. With the help of Congress, he set up many new programs to relieve the suffering of the unemployed. The government also sponsored public works programs. These put unemployed men and women to work on projects such as building dams, schools, and parks.

Since the 1930s, government has been faced with other questions. Should it regulate the dangerous gases that pour from factory smokestacks? Should it protect consumers from foods and medicines that might be harmful? Should it inspect shops and factories to make sure they are safe for workers? The federal government now regulates each of these areas, as well as many others.

In the 1980s, Americans began to worry about the cost of enforcing such regulations and about the growing power of the federal government. Americans elected Ronald Reagan in 1980 and again in 1984 in part because he promised to reduce government regulation, cut taxes, and balance the budget. Yet the government continues to have an active role in many areas of American life.

## SECTION REVIEW

1. **Define:** initiative, referendum, recall.
2. What was the goal of the black civil rights movement of the 1950s and 1960s?
3. How did women win the right to vote?
4. How did the role of government expand in the 1900s?
5. **What Do You Think?** Why do you think people in the 1980s worried about government being too big?

# 3 A Land of Opportunity

### Read to Learn

★ How did railroads help industry grow?
★ How has the organization of business changed since the Civil War?
★ What types of jobs are more people working in today?
★ What do these words mean: corporation, monopoly?

After the Civil War, the American economy changed dramatically. In 1860, the United States was mostly a nation of farmers. By 1900, it had become a world leader in industry. Many factors contributed to this dramatic growth. Among the most important were a large and efficient transportation system, a flood of inventions, new ways of doing business, and a large and able work force.

## Transportation

Railroads were the key to rapid industrialization after the Civil War. During the war, Americans learned how important it was to be able to move equipment and products quickly from one place to another.

**The tie that binds.** After 1865, the railroad system expanded quickly. Railroad owners combined small lines into large systems. Cornelius Vanderbilt, for example, bought up all the rail lines between New York City and Chicago. This meant that goods loaded in Chicago rode on the same car of the New York Central Railroad all the way to New York City. As a result, the cost of shipping freight by rail dropped sharply.

In 1869, the first railroad to span the country was completed. Crews of the Union Pacific laid tracks from St. Louis, across the Great Plains and through the Rocky Mountains. Crews of the Central Pacific began in San Francisco and hacked through the granite peaks of the Sierra Nevada. The two crews met at Promontory Point, Utah.

By 1893, five more cross-country railroads spanned the nation. These railroads opened the West to settlement by cattle ranchers and farmers. As settlers from the East moved onto the Great Plains, war broke out with the Native Americans who lived there. In the end, the United States Army was victorious. The way of life of the Plains Indians came to an end as they were forced to move onto reservations.

The expanding rail system gave a boost to industry. Just building the railroads created a huge demand for coal, iron, steel, and lumber. And the railroads opened up new markets in towns and villages across the nation.

**Autos and airplanes.** In the 1900s, automobiles, trucks, and airplanes brought a new revolution to transportation. In 1900, cars were still novelties. Only 4,000 chugged along America's dirt roads. But Henry Ford developed an assembly line that made it possible to put cars together quickly and efficiently. This reduced the costs, so more people could afford a car. By 1920, over 9 million cars were on the roads. By the mid-1980s, that number had skyrocketed to over 320 million.

In 1903, two bicycle mechanics, Orville and Wilbur Wright, made history by building the first successful airplane. The first passenger airline in the United States began service in 1914. Airplanes were used during World War I (1914–1918). After the war, planes increasingly moved mail, freight, and passengers. During World War II (1939–1945), jet engines were first

By 1869, railroad tracks connected the west coast with the Midwest. Much of the back-breaking work of hacking out a railbed through the Sierra Nevada was done by crews of Chinese workers. The workers in this painting cheer one of the first trains along a track they have built.

developed. Today, jets carry goods and people to all parts of the world in record time. Wide-bodied jumbo jets carry 500 people at one time. Military jets fly faster than the speed of sound.

## Inventions Lead the Way

A flood of inventions in the late 1800s fueled the growth of American industry. Some inventions, such as the automobile, led to the creation of whole new industries. Others made it possible to produce vital goods more quickly and cheaply. For example, in the 1860s a new way to produce steel was developed. With the Bessemer process, as it was called, high-grade steel could be made much more cheaply than before.

Cheaper steel meant that steel rails could be used on the nation's railroads. They lasted 10 times longer than iron rails. Strong steel girders also made it possible to build skyscrapers, or buildings of 20 stories or more. Steel was used in smaller items such as nails, screws, needles, bolts, barrel hoops, and barbed wire. Today, steel remains an important material in cars, trucks, and buildings as well as in consumer goods such as stainless steel pans and tableware.

Many inventions in the late 1800s came from the laboratory of Thomas Alva Edison. Edison invented hundreds of new products, including the phonograph, sound motion picture, and the electric light bulb. He also developed the first electric power plant. Soon, streets, businesses, and houses were brightened by electric lights. Edison's laboratory was the first modern research laboratory. Today, many companies have huge research laboratories that produce thousands of inventions every year.

## New Ways of Doing Business

After the Civil War, Americans developed new ways to organize business. Earlier, most businesses had been small. Many were run by a single family. They often sold their products in neighboring villages, towns, and cities. In the late 1800s, the demand for products grew and so did businesses. Many of these larger businesses became corporations. A *corporation* is a business owned by investors who buy shares of stock.

The rapid growth of industry in the late 1800s caused problems, however. In many industries, single companies became large enough to force almost all other companies out of business. When one company gained control of a certain industry, it became a *monopoly.* Monopolies dominated steel, oil, and sugar production as well as other industries. Reformers in the late 1800s and early 1900s fought for government regulation of industry to prevent the abuses of monopolies. Many monopolies were broken up under Presidents Theodore Roosevelt, William Howard Taft, and Woodrow Wilson.

Today, government regulations prevent any one company from gaining a monopoly in an industry. Still, many modern companies are far larger than the monopolies of the late 1800s. Often, a single corporation owns a large number of smaller companies in many fields. For example, one conglomerate, as it is called, might own a bus company, a cosmetic company, a toy company, a frozen food company, and a football team.

## People Who Make the Economy Work

Industrial growth after the Civil War changed the way people worked. Many of the large new factories were dangerous places to work. They were poorly lighted and had few windows, so there was little fresh air. Textile workers inhaled dust and fibers. In steel mills, workers were only inches away from vats of melted steel.

To protest poor working conditions and long working hours, some workers

Computers have a wide variety of uses today. Here, computer-operated robots weld auto bodies in an assembly plant in Illinois.

joined together in labor unions. The first national union, the Knights of Labor, was founded in 1869. Early labor unions were unpopular with factory owners and much of the American public. Strikes in the late 1800s were sometimes broken up by police or army troops.

Slowly, unions won acceptance in many industries. In 1935, during the Great Depression, Congress passed a law making it legal for workers to form unions to bargain with factory owners. After that, labor unions grew quickly. By 1940, there were 9 million workers in unions. Large labor unions, like large corporations, became an accepted part of American business.

Today, economic changes are again affecting the work people do. In some industries, computers direct the operation of robots. Highly skilled workers program the computers and maintain the equipment. Yet new hazards are sometimes created as industries develop new chemicals. Often, the side effects of new products are not known for many years.

More people today are working in white collar and service jobs. They sell insurance, video cassette recorders, and automobiles. They program computers, repair washing machines, work in restaurants, service jetliners, and deliver newspapers.

Many American industries are also facing competition from companies in other countries. As a result, many of the products we buy are made overseas. American industries, in turn, are modernizing to meet the challenge of foreign competition.

## SECTION REVIEW

1. **Define:** corporation, monopoly.
2. (a) How did railroads open the West? (b) How did they help industry grow?
3. (a) How did monopolies develop in the late 1800s? (b) Why are there no monopolies today?
4. What did labor unions protest against in the late 1800s?
5. **What Do You Think?** Why do you think inventions are important to economic growth?

# 4 Becoming a World Power

## Read to Learn

★ Why did the United States take a more active role in world affairs?
★ What role did the United States play in the two world wars?
★ What foreign policy challenges has the United States faced since the end of World War II?

In the years after the Civil War, Americans found that they lived in a smaller world. The earth had not shrunk, of course. Advances in transportation and communication drew people closer together. By 1866, for example, an underwater telegraph cable sped news across the Atlantic

Ocean. Railroads and ocean-going steamers cut travel time on land and sea. Because of these and other changes, the United States became more involved in world affairs.

## An Active Role

When the 13 colonies first declared their independence, they were not a powerful nation. Washington, Jefferson, and other Presidents tried to keep the United States out of world affairs. They wanted the new nation to grow and prosper in peace.

After the Civil War, increased trade created new links between the United States and other nations. By then, the United States produced more food and manufactured goods than it needed. So Americans exported goods to foreign countries. Europe was the most important market. But trade with China, Japan, Korea, and the countries of Latin America grew also.

At the same time that American trade was growing, European countries were building empires in Africa and Asia. These empires increased the power and wealth of European nations. Americans feared that they would be squeezed out of many foreign markets.

In the 1890s, the United States itself gained territory overseas. For example, it annexed Hawaii in 1898. Hawaii had fine harbors for the American navy. From there, trading ships and navy ships could sail to Asia. This meant the United States could open and protect markets in Asia.

The Spanish–American War of 1898 also gave the United States new territories. The war broke out as a result of a dispute over Spanish actions in Cuba. American troops quickly defeated the Spanish. Under the peace treaty, the islands of Puerto Rico in the Caribbean and Guam and the Philippines in the Pacific became territories of the United States. Cuba became an independent nation.

## Relations With Latin America

In 1901, Theodore Roosevelt became President. His motto was "Speak softly, but carry a big stick." By this, he meant that the United States would strive for peace but not shy away from using force when necessary.

Roosevelt used the "big stick" in Latin America. Several European countries were trying to influence Venezuela and the Dominican Republic. Roosevelt reminded them that the Monroe Doctrine forbade foreign meddling in the region.

Throughout the 1900s, the United States has intervened in Latin America when Presidents felt it was necessary to protect American interests. For example, President William Howard Taft sent troops into Nicaragua and Honduras. President Woodrow Wilson sent marines to the island of Haiti. In 1984, President Ronald Reagan ordered troops to invade the tiny island of Grenada to protect American students living there.

## Two World Wars

In 1914, World War I broke out in Europe. At first, President Wilson kept the United States neutral. But in 1917, America entered the war on the side of Britain and its allies. When peace came the next year, many Americans wanted to return to the policy of staying out of world affairs. They were called isolationists.

In the 1930s, the nations of Europe again moved toward war. In Germany, Adolph Hitler rose to power. He ruled as a dictator, or leader with absolute power. In 1939, war broke out when Hitler invaded neighboring Poland. Italy and Japan sided with Hitler, forming the Axis powers. They fought against the Allies, including Britain, France, and the Soviet Union.

The United States stayed out of World War II until 1941. On December 7, 1941, the Japanese launched a surprise attack on Pearl Harbor in Hawaii. Congress then declared war on the Axis powers. After a long, bitter struggle, the Allies defeated Germany and Italy. The war against Japan did not end until American planes dropped atomic bombs on the Japanese cities of Hiroshima and Nagasaki.

## The United States as a World Power

Much of Europe had been severely damaged by World War II. To help it recover, the United States created the Marshall Plan. Under the plan, the United States gave billions of dollars to rebuild factories, railroads, and highways in Europe.

Soon after the war ended, the United States became concerned about the Soviet Union. The Soviet Union and the United States had been allies during World War II. After the war, however, the Soviets helped communists take power in Eastern European countries. To contain Soviet influence, the United States and the nations of Western Europe formed the North Atlantic Treaty Organization, or NATO.

Rivalry between the United States and the Soviet Union never broke out into armed conflict. But the tension and hostility between the two superpowers was known as the Cold War. In the late 1960s and the 1970s, relations between the Soviets and Americans improved somewhat. After a period of tension in the early 1980s, the United States and the Soviet Union agreed to begin new arms control negotiations. In 1987, the leaders of the two superpowers signed the INF Treaty that banned all medium-range nuclear missiles from Europe.

## Other Challenges

Since World War II, the United States has fought in two wars. From 1951 to 1954, American troops under United Nations command fought in Korea. In the 1960s and 1970s, American soldiers fought in Vietnam. Communist rebels were trying to overthrow the government of South Vietnam.

In 1961, East German authorities tried to stop East Berliners from fleeing into West Berlin by building a wall between the two sections of the city. To show American support for the free people of West Berlin, President Kennedy stood before the Berlin Wall in 1963 and declared in German to cheering thousands, "Ich bin ein Berliner" ("I am a Berliner").

In 1989, George Bush was elected President of the United States. President Bush and his wife, Barbara, are shown at left at his inauguration. At right are Vice President J. Danforth Quayle and his wife, Marilyn.

Many Americans, especially young people, protested against the Vietnam War. In the early 1970s, American troops finally returned home, but over 57,000 Americans had lost their lives in Southeast Asia.

In the Middle East, the United States has tried to bring about peace between its chief ally in the region, Israel, and Israel's Arab neighbors. Throughout the 1980s, fighting in Lebanon disrupted peace in the Middle East. Then in 1988, violence broke out in Israeli-occupied lands as Palestinians demanded self-rule.

Americans have also tried to help the peoples of the Third World. The Third World includes many countries in Africa, Asia, and Latin America that are beginning to industrialize. Most are very poor. The United States gives billions of dollars every year to help Third World nations develop their economies. But the problems of these countries are hard to solve.

The United States gives foreign aid in part because poverty can cause political problems. In poor countries, rebels often win the support of the people by promising to distribute the wealth more evenly. In Cuba, Fidel Castro led a successful revolution in 1959. When he won power, he angered the United States because he made Cuba a strong ally of the Soviet Union. Today, some Americans fear that the same thing may happen in Nicaragua and elsewhere in Central America.

As citizens of a superpower, Americans have many difficult problems to understand. People do not always agree on what action to take. Today, however, Americans no longer expect to return to the days when any country could think only about itself.

## SECTION REVIEW

1. **Locate:** China, Japan, Korea, Hawaii, Cuba, Puerto Rico, Germany, Soviet Union, Vietnam.

2. What territory did the United States acquire as a result of the Spanish–American War?

3. What was President Theodore Roosevelt's policy toward Latin America?

4. What role did the United States play in World War I and World War II?

5. **What Do You Think?** Why do you think the United States became a world power after World War II?

# Review

 **Reviewing the Facts**

**Key Terms.** Match each term in Column 1 with the correct definition in Column 2.

**Column 1**
1. initiative
2. referendum
3. recall
4. corporation
5. monopoly

**Column 2**
a. business owned by investors
b. process by which people vote directly on a bill
c. company that controls a certain industry
d. process allowing voters to introduce a bill
e. method of removing a person from office

 **Checkup**

1. (a) Why have immigrants come to America? (b) What have they contributed to American life?
2. How has technology affected American culture?
3. What groups of Americans have won the right to vote since the Civil War?
4. How has the power of the federal government changed since 1900?
5. In what ways have inventions changed the way Americans live and work?
6. Describe three ways the United States has become more active in world affairs since the Civil War.

 **Thinking About History**

1. **Relating past to present.** (a) What groups of people are immigrating to the United States today? (b) How are their reasons for coming similar to the reasons of the immigrants in the late 1800s? How are they different?
2. **Understanding the economy.** The growth of unions has slowed in the 1970s and 1980s. What changes in the way people work might help explain this?
3. **Understanding geography.** Why have events and developments in Latin America been especially important to the United States?

 **Using Your Skills**

1. **Using visual evidence.** Study the picture on page 443. (a) Who is shown in this painting? (b) What historical event is being illustrated? (c) How would you describe the mood of the people shown in the painting?
2. **Skimming a chapter.** Review the skill of skimming a chapter on page 239. Then skim this chapter. (a) What are the main topics in this chapter? (b) What is the general idea of the section "Becoming a World Power"?
3. **Ranking.** Make a list of ten events since the Civil War. Rank them from the one you think is most important to the one you think is least important.

# Readings and Other Sources

Unit 1    **The World of the Americas**    453

Unit 2    **Settling the New World**    470

Unit 3    **The Struggle for Independence**    493

Unit 4    **Strengthening the New Nation**    512

Unit 5    **A Growing Nation**    529

Unit 6    **The Nation Divided**    552

# Unit 1

## The World of the Americas

**Chapter**

# 1 The American Land (Prehistory–Present)

★ **1-1    America the Beautiful** ★

**Introduction**   The beauty and majesty of the American land has captured the imagination of people from the first Americans to Americans of the 1980s. In 1911, Katharine Lee Bates, a poet and professor of English at Wellesley College, wrote the words to this song, "America the Beautiful." In them she celebrated her country's beauty and its noble history.

**Vocabulary**   Before you read the selection, find the meaning of these words in a dictionary: spacious, alabaster.

O beautiful for spacious skies,
For amber waves of grain,
For purple mountain majesties
Above the fruited plain!
America! America!
God shed His grace on thee,
And crown thy good with
    brotherhood,
From sea to shining sea!

O beautiful for pilgrim feet,
Whose stern, impassion'd stress

A thoroughfare for freedom beat
Across the wilderness!
America! America!
God mend thine ev'ry flaw,
Confirm thy soul in self-control,
Thy liberty in law!


O beautiful for heroes proved,
In liberating strife,
Who more than self their country
    loved,
And mercy more than life!
America! America!
May God thy gold refine,
Till all success be nobleness,
And ev'ry gain divine!


O beautiful for patriot dream
That sees beyond the years
Thine alabaster cities gleam
Undimm'd by human tears!
America! America!
God shed His grace on thee,
And crown thy good with
    brotherhood,
From sea to shining sea!

**READING REVIEW** ★ ★ ★ ★ ★ ★

1. What virtue does the songwriter feel "crowns" all of America's other good points?
2. Some people have proposed that "America the Beautiful" be made the national anthem. (a) Do you agree? (b) What is the national anthem?
3. **Understanding geography.** List the physical regions of North America that are described in the song.

★ ★ ★ ★ ★ ★ ★ ★ ★ ★ ★ ★ ★ ★ ★ ★ ★ ★

## ★ 1-2 A European View of North America ★

**Introduction** Fur traders were the first Europeans to explore the heartland of North America and the Rocky Mountains to the west. In 1793, Alexander Mackenzie, a Scotsman, blazed a trading trail to the Rockies and across them to the Pacific. This selection from the journal Mackenzie kept on his trip describes the land as he approached the Rockies.

**Vocabulary** Before you read the selection, find the meaning of these words in a dictionary: strata, saline, ascending, precipice, verdure.

**May 9, 1793** The canoe was put into the water: her dimensions were 25 feet long within, exclusive of the curves of stem and stern, 26 inches hold, and 4 feet 9 inches beam. At the same time she was so light that two men could carry her on a good road three or four miles without resting.

In this slender vessel, we shipped provisions, goods for presents, arms, ammunition, and baggage, to the weight of 3,000 pounds, and an equipage of ten people, with two Indians as hunters and interpreters.

**May 10** Where the earth has given way, the face of the cliffs shows numerous strata, consisting of reddish earth and small stones, bitumen, and a grayish earth below which, near the water edge, is a red stone.

At half-past six in the afternoon the young men landed, when they killed an elk and wounded a buffalo. In this spot we formed our encampment for the night.

From the place which we quitted this morning, the west side of the river displayed a succession of the most beautiful scenery I had ever beheld.

The ground rises at intervals to a considerable height, and at every interval or pause in the rise, there is a very gently ascending space or lawn, which is alternated with abrupt precipices to the summit. This magnificent theater of nature has all the decorations which the trees and animals of the country can afford it. Groves of poplars in every shape vary the scene, and their intervals are enlivened with vast herds of elks and buffaloes—the former choosing the steeps and uplands and the latter preferring the plains. At this time the buffaloes were attended with their young ones, who were frisking about them.

The whole country displayed an exuberant verdure. The trees that bear a blossom were advancing fast to that delightful appearance, and the velvet rind of their branches, reflecting the oblique rays of a rising or setting sun, added a splendid gaiety to the scene, which no expressions of mine are qualified to describe. The east side of the river consists of a range of high land covered with the white spruce and the soft birch, while the banks abound with the alder and the willow. The water continued to rise and, the current being strong, we made a greater use of setting poles than paddles.

**May 12** The land on both sides of the river, during the two last days, is very much elevated, but particularly in the latter part of it. On the western side it presents in different places white, steep, and lofty cliffs. Our view being confined by these circumstances, we did not see so many animals as on the tenth. Between these lofty boundaries, the river becomes narrow, and in a great measure free from islands, for we had passed only four. The stream, indeed, was not more than from 200 to 300 yards broad, whereas before these cliffs pressed upon it, its breadth was twice that extent and sprinkled with islands.

**May 16** The land above the spot where we camped spreads into an extensive plain and stretches on to a very high ridge, which in some parts presents a face of rock but is principally covered with verdure and varied with the poplar and white birch tree.

The country is so crowded with animals as to have the appearance in some places of a stall yard, from the state of the ground and the quantity of dung which is scattered over it. The soil is black and light. We this day saw two grizzly and hideous bears.

**May 17** It froze during the night, and the air was sharp in the morning, when we continued our course, making good 11 miles during the forenoon. At two in the afternoon the Rocky Mountains appeared in light, with their summits covered with snow, bearing southwest by south. They formed a very agreeable object to every person in the canoe, as we attained the view of them much sooner than we expected.

Adapted from Alexander Mackenzie, *Voyage from Montreal on the River St. Laurence Through the Continent of North America to the Frozen and Pacific Oceans,* 1801.

## READING REVIEW ★ ★ ★ ★ ★ ★ ★

1. What animals did Mackenzie's party see on the journey toward the Rockies?
2. What means of transportation did Mackenzie use to make his trip west?
3. **Applying information.** How did the American land itself help Mackenzie's party on their journey?

★ ★ ★ ★ ★ ★ ★ ★ ★ ★ ★ ★ ★ ★ ★ ★ ★ ★

As explorers pushed westward across North America, they were struck by the variety and numbers of animals. This antelope is grazing on the northern plains.

**Introduction** Much of the United States has a climate with mild temperatures and enough rainfall to grow crops. The first Americans, like Americans for centuries since, used the warm sunshine and rain to grow food. The prayer to the sun printed below is from the Native American nation of the Havasupai.

**Vocabulary** Before you read the selection, find the meaning of this word in a dictionary: irrigate.

Sun, my relative
Be good coming out
Do something good for us.

Make me work,
So I can do anything in the garden
I hoe, I plant corn, I irrigate.

You, sun, be good going down at
    sunset

We lie down to sleep
I want to feel good.

While I sleep you come up.
Go on your course many times.
Make good things for us men.

Make me always the same as I am
    now.

From Leslie Spier, *Havasupai Ethnography* (New York: American Museum of Natural History, 1977).

**R E A D I N G   R E V I E W** ★ ★ ★ ★ ★ ★

1. What is the sun supposed to do in daytime?
2. What seems to have been a chief crop of the Havasupai?
3. **Relating past to present.** Do you think the sun is as important to Americans today as it was to the first Americans? Explain.

★ ★ ★ ★ ★ ★ ★ ★ ★ ★ ★ ★ ★ ★ ★ ★ ★ ★ ★

**Chapter**

# 2 The First Americans (Prehistory–1600)

**Introduction** Legends passed down from generation to generation are an important source of knowledge about early peoples in North America. By studying oral legends, you can learn about a group's culture. The legend printed here is from the Arapahos, who lived on the western plains. Today their descendants live mostly in Wyoming and Oklahoma.

**Vocabulary** Before you read the selection, find the meaning of these words in a dictionary: enclosure, windward, flint, tinder.

A man tried to think how the Arapahos might kill buffalo. He was a hard thinker who would go off for several days to fast and think. At last he dreamed that a voice spoke to him and told him what to do.

Going back to his people, he made an enclosure of trees set in the ground with willows wound between them. Then four runners who never tired were sent out to the windward of the herd of buffalo, two of them on each side of the herd. They drove the animals toward the enclosure and into it. Then the people drove the buffalo around inside until a heavy cloud of dust rose. Unable to see in the dust, the animals ran over the cliff and were killed.

At that time the people had nothing to cut their meat with. Another man took a buffalo shoulder blade and cut out a narrow piece of it with flint. This he sharpened until it was a good knife. He also made a knife from flint by flaking it into shape. All the people learned how to make knives.

This man made the first bow and arrows also. He made the first arrow point from the short rib of a buffalo. With his bow and four arrows, he went off alone and waited in the woods at a buffalo path. When a buffalo came along the path, he shot; the arrow disappeared in the body and the animal fell dead. Then he killed three others. He went back to camp and told his people: "Harness the dogs; there are four dead buffalo in the woods." Thereafter the Arapahos were able to get meat without driving the buffalo into an enclosure.

In the early days, people used the fire drill. A man, another hard thinker, went off alone to think. He learned that certain stones, when struck, would give a spark, and that this spark would light tinder. He gathered stones and filled a small horn with dry, soft wood. Then he went home.

His wife said to him, "Please make a fire." So he took out his horn and his flint stones, struck a spark, blew it, put grass on it, and soon, to the surprise of all who saw it, he had a fire.

The buffalo had a central place in the lives of Plains Indians. This Blackfoot shield is made of buffalo hide and shows a buffalo in the center.

Making a fire in this way was so much easier than using a fire drill that soon all the people did it.

These three men—the one who made the first enclosure for buffalo, the one who made the first knife and the first bow and arrows, and the one who showed people how to make fire easily—they were the men who brought our people to the condition in which they live now.

Adapted from *Indian Legends from the Northern Rockies*, by Ella E. Clark. Copyright © 1966 by the University of Oklahoma Press.

### READING REVIEW ★ ★ ★ ★ ★ ★ ★

1. (a) How did the Arapahos first kill buffalo? (b) What was the second method?
2. Why were the three men described in the legend important to the Arapahos?
3. **Using oral history.** What does the legend tell you about Arapaho life?

★ ★ ★ ★ ★ ★ ★ ★ ★ ★ ★ ★ ★ ★ ★ ★ ★ ★ ★ ★

---

## ★ 2-2  Prayer to the Young Cedar  ★

**Introduction** The peoples of the Northwest Coast, like all the early peoples of North America, had a close relationship with nature. Women used cedar bark to make baskets, clothes, and blankets. Before peeling the bark from a tree, a woman would say a prayer such as the one that follows.

**Vocabulary** Before you read the selection, find the meaning of this word in the dictionary: pity.

Among the things Northwest Coast Indians made from the cedar tree were canoes like the elaborately carved and painted one shown here. The Indians in the foreground are fishing for salmon.

Look at me, friend!
I come to ask for your dress,
For you have come to take pity on us;
For there is nothing for which you
  cannot be used, . . .
For you are really willing to give us
  your dress,
I come to beg you for this,
Long Life Maker,
For I am going to make a basket for
  lily roots out of you.
I pray you, friend, not to feel angry
On account of what I am going to do to
  you;
And I beg you, friend, to tell our
  friends about what I ask of you.
Take care, friend!

Keep sickness away from me,
So that I may not be killed by sickness
  or in war, O friend!

From *American Indian Prose and Poetry,* ed. Margot Astrov (New York: Capricorn Books, 1962). Copyright 1946 by Margot Astrov.

### READING REVIEW ★ ★ ★ ★ ★ ★ ★

1. What does the woman mean when she talks about the cedar's "dress"?
2. What is she going to do with the cedar's "dress"?
3. **Understanding other cultures.** Why do you think the woman prays to the tree before peeling its bark?

★ ★ ★ ★ ★ ★ ★ ★ ★ ★ ★ ★ ★ ★ ★ ★ ★ ★

## ★ 2-3    Keeping a Heritage Alive    ★

**Introduction** Much of what is known about the first Americans is based on the legends and stories kept alive by later generations. In this selection, Ohiyesa, a Sioux, tells how young boys learned the history of their people to keep it alive for future generations.

**Vocabulary** Before you read the selection, find the meaning of these words in a dictionary: systematic, instituted, confer, sustenance.

It is commonly supposed that there is no systematic education of their children among the people of this country. Nothing could be farther from the truth. All the customs of this people were held to be divinely instituted. Those in connection with the training of children were carefully followed and passed from one generation to the next.

The expectant parents jointly bent all their efforts to the task of giving the newcomer the best they could gather from a long line of ancestors. An expectant mother would often choose one of the greatest characters of her family and tribe as a model for her child. This hero was daily called to mind. She would gather from tradition all of his noted deeds and daring exploits, rehearsing them to herself when alone.

The Indians believed, also, that certain kinds of animals would confer peculiar gifts upon the unborn, while others would leave so strong an adverse impression that the child might become a monstrosity. A case of harelip was commonly blamed on the rabbit. It was said that a rabbit had charmed the mother and given to the baby its own features.

Scarcely was the young warrior ushered into the world when he was met by lullabies that speak of wonderful exploits in hunting and war. Those ideas which so fully occupied his mother's mind before his birth are now put into words by all about the child, who is as yet quite unresponsive to their appeals to his honor and ambition. He is called the future defender of his people, whose lives may depend upon his courage and skill. If the child is a girl, she is at once addressed as the future mother of a noble race.

In hunting songs, the leading animals are introduced. They come to the boy to offer their bodies for the sustenance of his tribe. The animals are re-garded as his friends and spoken of almost as tribes of people.

Very early, the Indian boy assumed the task of preserving and transmitting the legends of his ancestors and his race. Almost every evening a myth or a true story of some deed done in the past was narrated by one of the parents or grandparents, while the boy listened with parted lips and glistening eyes. On the following evening, he was usually required to repeat it. If he was not an apt scholar, he struggled long with his task. But, as a rule, the Indian boy is a good listener and has a good memory, so that the stories are tolerably well mastered.

This sort of teaching at once enlightens the boy's mind and stimulates his ambition. His idea of his own future career becomes a vivid and irresistible force.

Adapted from *Cry of the Thunderbird: The American Indian's Own Story,* Edited and with an Introduction and Commentary by Charles Hamilton. New Edition Copyright © 1972 by the University of Oklahoma Press.

### READING REVIEW ★ ★ ★ ★ ★ ★ ★

1. How did a mother call on the heritage of the people even before the baby was born?

2. How did a young boy learn about the history of his people?

3. **Relating past to present.** Compare the way young people today learn about their heritage with the way the young Sioux learned about theirs.

★ ★ ★ ★ ★ ★ ★ ★ ★ ★ ★ ★ ★ ★ ★ ★

★   **2-4   Founding the League of the Iroquois**   ★

**Introduction** About 1570, five Iroquois nations—the Mohawk, the Seneca, the Cayuga, the Oneida, and the Onondaga—formed the League of the Iroquois. They wanted to stop the fighting among the nations. According to legend, a Mohawk leader named Hiawatha helped found the league. Chief Elias Johnson relates the legend in this selection.

**Vocabulary** Before you read the selection, find the meaning of these words in a dictionary: tremble, habitation, annihilated.

Chapter 2

The council met. Hiawatha entered the assembly with even more than ordinary attention. Every eye was fixed upon him when he began to address the council in the following words.

"Friends and Brothers: You being members of many tribes, you have come from a great distance. The voice of war has aroused you up. You are afraid for your homes, your wives, and your children. You tremble for your safety. Believe me, I am with you. My heart beats with your hearts. We are one. We have one common object. We come to promote our common interest and to determine how this can be best done.

"To oppose those hordes of northern tribes, singly and alone, would prove certain destruction. We can make no progress in that way. We must unite ourselves into one common band of brothers. We must have but one voice. Many voices make confusion. We must have one fire, one pipe, and one war club. This will give us strength. If our warriors are united, they can defeat the enemy and drive them from our land; if we do this, we are safe.

"Onondaga, you are the people sitting under the shadow of the Great Tree, whose branches spread far and wide, and whose roots sink deep into the earth. You shall be the first nation, because you are warlike and mighty.

"Oneida, you, the people who recline your bodies against the Everlasting Stone that cannot be moved, shall be the second nation, because you always give good counsel.

"Seneca, you, the people who have your habitation at the foot of the Great Mountain and are overshadowed by its crags, shall be the third nation, because you are all greatly gifted in speech.

"Cayuga, you, whose dwelling is in the Dark Forest, and whose home is everywhere, shall be the fourth nation, becauses of your superior cunning in hunting.

"Mohawk, you, the people who live in the open country and possess much wisdom, shall be the fifth nation, because you understand better the art of raising corn and beans and making cabins.

"You five great and powerful nations, with your tribes, must unite and have one common interest, and no foe shall disturb or subdue you.

"And you of the different nations of the south, and you of the west, may place yourselves under our protection, and we will protect you. We earnestly desire the alliance and friendship of you all.

"If we unite in one band the Great Spirit will smile upon us, and we shall be free, prosperous, and happy; but if we shall remain as we are we shall earn his displeasure. We shall be enslaved, and perhaps annihilated forever.

"Brothers, these are the words of Hiawatha. Let them sink deep into your hearts. I have done."

A deep and impressive silence followed the delivery of this speech. On the following day the council again assembled to act on it. The union of the tribes into one confederacy was discussed and unanimously adopted.

Adapted from *Cry of the Thunderbird: The American Indian's Own Story,* Edited and with an Introduction and Commentary by Charles Hamilton. New Edition Copyright © 1972 by the University of Oklahoma Press.

## READING REVIEW ★ ★ ★ ★ ★ ★ ★ ★

1. What five nations did Hiawatha speak to?
2. Why did he urge them to unite?
3. **Making a review chart.** Make a chart with two columns. In the first column, list the five nations. In the second, describe the contribution Hiawatha thought each would make to the league.

★ ★ ★ ★ ★ ★ ★ ★ ★ ★ ★ ★ ★ ★ ★ ★ ★

**Introduction** The Incas developed farming methods that allowed them to grow ample food for all the people. The Sapa Incas, called the Inca in this selection, strictly controlled how the land was used and how food and clothing was distributed. In the early 1600s, Garcilaso de la Vega described how this was done. De la Vega was the son of an Inca princess and a Spanish army officer.

**Vocabulary** Before you read the selection, find the meaning of these words in a dictionary: torrid, arduous, arable, vassals, uncultivated.

The Incas had a sophisticated culture, as their farming methods show. Inca artists were also highly skilled. This silver alpaca was made by an Inca silversmith.

When the Inca had conquered a new province, he immediately sent engineers there, who were specialized in building canals for irrigation, in order to increase the corn acreage, which otherwise could not flourish in these torrid lands. In the same way, he irrigated the prairie lands, as may be seen today from the evidence of canals that still exist all over Peru. On the mountainsides, on the peaks, and on all rocky surfaces, they built terraces, sustained by stone walls, which they filled with light soil brought from elsewhere. These terraces grew wider from the top to the bottom of the slope, where some were as much as 240 acres in size.

These were arduous undertakings, but they made it possible to give the maximum development to the tiniest plots of barren land. Indeed, it often happened that they would build canals 15 to 20 leagues long to irrigate only a few acres of land.

Community records of landholdings were carefully kept up to date in all the provinces and villages, and arable land was divided into three parts: that belonging to the Sun, that of the Inca, and that of his vassals. This latter part was calculated to permit each village to provide for its own needs. In case there was an increase in population, the Inca reduced the surface of his own holdings. Thus it may be said that he kept for himself only that part that, without him, would have remained uncultivated. The major part of the terrace crops belonged to the king and to the Sun, which was only normal, inasmuch as it was the Inca who had had the terraces built.

Adapted from *The Royal Commentaries of the Inca Garcilaso de la Vega, 1539–1616*, ed. Alain Gheerbrant (New York: The Orion Press, 1961).

**READING REVIEW** ★ ★ ★ ★ ★ ★ ★

1. How did the Incas build terraces?
2. How did the Incas make sure that each village would have enough food?
3. **Understanding geography.** What geographical features of the Inca empire made it necessary for the Incas to build terraces and irrigate the land?

★ ★ ★ ★ ★ ★ ★ ★ ★ ★ ★ ★ ★ ★ ★ ★ ★ ★ ★

# Chapter 3 Europeans Explore America (1000-1650)

## ★ 3-1 Leif Ericson Explores Vinland ★

**Introduction** The story of Leif Ericson's trip to North America was passed on from generation to generation in Viking sagas such as this one. Sagas were the stories the Vikings told of their early leaders. They presented the facts of a story in a way that emphasized the romantic or noble aspects of a hero and his adventures.

**Vocabulary** Before you read the selection, find the meaning of these words in a dictionary: counsel, foster.

There was now much talk about voyages of discovery. Leif, the son of Eric the Red, of Brattahild, went to Biarni Heriulfson and bought the ship from him. He hired men for it, so that there were 35 men in all.

Now they sailed into the open sea with a northeast wind. They were days at sea before they saw land. They came to an island which lay to the east of the land. They went up and looked round them in good weather, and saw that there was dew upon the grass. And so it happened that they touched the dew with their hands and raised the fingers to the mouth. They thought that they had never before tasted anything so sweet.

After this they took counsel, and decided to remain there for the winter, and built large houses. There were many salmon in the river and in the lake, and larger salmon than they had seen before. The nature of the country was, as they thought, so good that cattle would not require house feeding in winter, for no frost came in the winter, and little did the grass wither there. Day and night were more equal than in Greenland, for on the shortest day

the sun was above the horizon from half past seven in the forenoon till half past four in the afternoon.

It happened one evening that a man of the party was missing. He was Tyrker the German. Leif took this much to heart, for Tyrker had been long with his father and him, and had loved Leif much in his childhood. Leif now took his people severely to task. He prepared to seek for Tyrker, and took 12 men with him. But when they had got a short way from the house, Tyrker came towards them and was joyfully received.

Then Leif said to him: "Why were thou so late, my foster father, and separated from the party?"

"I have not been much farther off, but still I have something new to tell of. I found vines and grapes."

"But is that true, my foster father?" said Leif.

"Surely it is true," Tyrker replied, "for I was raised in a land where there are many vines and grapes."

Now a cargo was cut down for the ship, and when the spring came they got ready and sailed away; and Leif gave the land a name after its qualities, and called it Vinland.

Adapted from *The Voyages of the Northmen to America*, 1877.

### READING REVIEW ★ ★ ★ ★ ★ ★ ★

1. What made Vinland an inviting place?
2. Leif Ericson named Vinland after what grew there. What else could a place be named for? Give an example.
3. **Analyzing a primary source.** How does this saga present Leif Ericson in a romantic or noble light?

★ ★ ★ ★ ★ ★ ★ ★ ★ ★ ★ ★ ★ ★ ★ ★ ★ ★

**Introduction** The stories Marco Polo told about his travels in Asia played a key role in inspiring Europeans to explore new and distant lands. Early explorers and geographers also turned to Marco Polo's accounts to help them in their ventures into these new lands. This selection is from accounts of his journeys in *The Book of Marco Polo.*

**Vocabulary** Before you read the selection, find the meaning of these words in a dictionary: sufficient, flax, gratification.

You must know that the city of Cambaluc has so many houses, and such a vast population inside the walls and outside, that it seems quite past all possibility. There is a suburb outside each of the 12 gates. These suburbs are so great that they contain more people than the city itself. In those suburbs live the foreign merchants and travelers who have come to bring presents to the emperor, or to sell articles at court, or because the city affords so good a mart to attract traders.

To this city also are brought articles of greater cost and rarity, and in greater abundance, than to any other city in the world. For people of every description, and from every region, bring things (including all the costly wares of India, as well as the fine and precious goods of Cathay [China] itself with its provinces).

As sample, I tell you, no day in the year passes that there do not enter the city 1,000 cartloads of silk alone, from which are made quantities of cloth of silk and gold, and of other goods. And this is not to be wondered at; for in all the countries around about there is no flax, so that everything has to be made of silk. It is true, indeed, that in some parts of the country there is cotton and hemp, but not sufficient for their wants. This, however, is not of much consequence, because silk is so abundant and cheap, and is a more valuable substance than either flax or cotton.

Round about this great city of Cambaluc there are some 200 other cities at various distances, from which traders come to sell their goods and buy others for their lords. And all find means to make their sales and purchases, so that the traffic of the city is passing great.

First and foremost, then, the document stated the city of Kinsay to be so great that it was 100 miles around. And there are in it 12,000 bridges of stone. For the most part they are so lofty that a great fleet could pass beneath them. And let no man marvel that there are so many bridges, for you see the whole city stands as it were in the water and surrounded by water, so that a great many bridges are required to give free passage about it.

Marco Polo's stories of wealth and luxury in Asia sparked interest among Europeans. This illustration of the wedding of Kublai Khan's son gives a sense of the splendor Polo described.

Inside the city there is a lake which has a compass of some 30 miles. All round it are built beautiful palaces and mansions, of the richest and most exquisite structure that you can imagine, belonging to the nobles of the city. In the middle of the lake are two islands, on each of which stands a rich, beautiful, and spacious building, furnished in such style as to seem fit for the palace of an emperor. And when any one of the citizens wanted to hold a marriage feast or to give any other entertainment, it used to be done at one of these palaces. And everything would be found there ready to order, such as silver plate, trenchers, and dishes, and whatever else was needful. The king made this provision for the gratification of his people and the place was open to everyone who desired to give an entertainment.

Adapted from *The Book of Ser Marco Polo*, introduction and notes by G. B. Parks (New York: Macmillan Publishing Co., Inc., 1929).

## READING REVIEW

1. What attracted so many people to the city of Cambaluc?
2. Why were so many garments made of silk in Asia?
3. **Understanding geography.** The names of the cities Marco Polo describes are now Khanbalik (Cambaluc) and Hangchow (Kinsay). Locate Hangchow on a world map. Use the scale to find how far Hangchow is from Venice, where Marco Polo began his journey.

---

## ★     3-3     Columbus Lands in America     ★

**Introduction** Today, October 12 is a national holiday. Each year on that day we celebrate Christopher Columbus's arrival in America. What was the first Columbus Day like? This selection, from Columbus's journal of his trip, gives a firsthand account of that day. The journal entry for the day records the first European impressions of Native Americans.

**Vocabulary** Before you read the selection, find the meaning of these words in a dictionary: hove to, standard, diverse, testimony, adjacent.

**Friday, October 12** The vessels were hove to, waiting for daylight; and on Friday they arrived at a small island called, in the language of the Indians, Guanahani.* The admiral went on shore in the armed boat, and Martin Alonso Pinzon and Vincente Yanez, his brother, who was captain of the *Niña*. The admiral took the royal standard, and the captains went with two banners of the green cross.

Having landed, they saw trees very green, and much water, and fruits of diverse kinds. The admiral called to the two captains. They said that they should bear faithful testimony that he, in presence of all, had taken possession of the said island for the king and for the queen.

Presently many people of the island assembled. What follows are the actual words of the admiral in his book of the first navigation and discovery of the Indies.

"I," he says, "wanted us to form a great friendship, for I knew that they were a people who could be more easily freed and converted to our holy faith by love than by force. So I gave to some of them red caps, and glass beads to put round their necks, and many other things of little value, which gave them great pleasure, and made them so much our friends that it was a marvel to see.

---

*Now Watling Island, it was named San Salvador by Columbus.

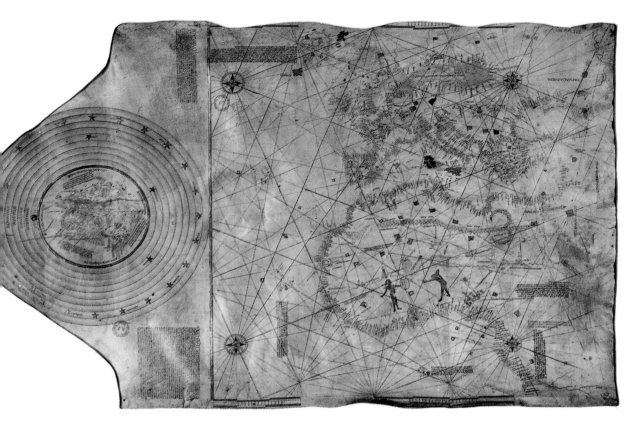

Historians think that this map, drawn on calfskin, may have been made by Christopher Columbus and taken along on the *Santa Maria* in 1492. The coastlines of Europe and Africa appear at right.

"They afterwards came to the ship's boats where we were, swimming and bringing us parrots, cotton threads in skeins, darts, and many other things. And we exchanged them for other things that we gave them, such as glass beads and small bells. In fine, they took all, and gave what they had with good will. It appeared to me to be a race of people very poor in everything.

"All I saw were youths, none more than 30 years of age. They are very handsome. Their hair is short and coarse, almost like the hairs of a horse's tail. They wear the hairs brought down to the eyebrows, except a few locks behind, which they wear long and never cut. They paint themselves black, and they are the color of the Canarians, neither black nor white. Some paint themselves white, others red, and others of what color they find. Some paint their faces, others the whole body, some only round the eyes, others only on the nose.

"They neither carry nor know of anything of arms, for I showed them swords, and they took them by the blade and cut themselves through ignorance. They have no iron, their darts being wands without iron, some of them having a fish's tooth at the end, and others being pointed in various ways.

"They are all of fair stature and size, with good faces, and well made. I saw some with marks of wounds on their bodies, and I made signs to ask what it was. And they gave me to understand that people from other adjacent islands came with the intention of seizing them, and that they defended themselves.

"They should be good servants and intelligent, for I saw that they quickly took in what was said to them. I believe that they would easily be made Christians, as it appeared to me that they had no religion. I will take, at the time of my departure, six of them for your Highnesses, that they may learn to speak. I saw no beast of any kind, except parrots, on this island."

The above is in the words of the admiral.

Adapted from *The Journal of Christopher Columbus*, 1893.

**READING REVIEW** ★ ★ ★ ★ ★ ★ ★

1. What was the first thing Columbus did when he landed?
2. Why did Columbus give the Indians beads and other trinkets?
3. **Drawing conclusions.** Columbus was trying to find the riches of Asia. How do you think this goal affected his attitude toward the Indians he found on Guanahani?

★ ★ ★ ★ ★ ★ ★ ★ ★ ★ ★ ★ ★ ★ ★ ★ ★

## ★ 3-4 Rescued by Indians ★

**Introduction** On November 6, 1528, Cabeza de Vaca and a party of about 80 men were shipwrecked on an island off the coast of Texas. The area was wild and unfamiliar. The men feared that the Indians who lived on the island might capture and kill them all. In this selection from his journal, de Vaca describes what happened.

**Vocabulary** Before you read the selection, find the meaning of these words in a dictionary: lament, sacrifice, victim.

I made the Indians understand by signs that our boat had sunk and three of our number had been drowned. The Indians, seeing what had befallen us and our state of suffering, sat down among us. From the sorrow and pity they felt, they all began to lament so earnestly that they might have been heard at a distance. They continued doing so for more than half an hour. It was strange to see these men, wild and untaught, howling like brutes over our misfortunes.

The cries having ceased, I talked with the Christians. I said that if it appeared well to them, I would beg these Indians to take us to their houses. Some, who had been in New Spain, replied that we ought not to think of it; for if they should do so, they would sacrifice us to their idols. But seeing no better course, and that any other led to a nearer and more certain death, I disregarded what was said and asked the Indians to take us to their dwellings. They indicated that it would give them delight.

Presently 30 men loaded themselves with wood and started for their houses, which were far off. We remained with the others until near night. Then, holding us up, they carried us with all haste. Because of the extreme coldness of the weather, they built four or five very large fires at intervals, and at each they warmed us. When they saw that we had regained some heat and strength, they took us to the next so swiftly that they hardly let us touch our feet to the ground.

In this manner we went as far as their village, where we found that they had made a house for us with many fires in it. An hour after our arrival, they began to dance and hold great rejoicing, which lasted all night, although for us there was no joy, festivity, nor sleep. We awaited the hour they should make us victims. In the morning they again gave us fish and roots, showing us such hospitality that we were reassured and lost somewhat the fear of sacrifice.

Adapted from "The Narrative of Alvar Nuñez Cabeca de Vaca," in *Spanish Explorers in the Southern United States,* ed. Frederick W. Hodge (New York: Barnes & Noble, 1959).

**READING REVIEW** ★ ★ ★ ★ ★ ★ ★

1. How did the Indians react to the sight of the shipwrecked Spaniards?
2. Who was reluctant to go to the Indians' houses? Why?
3. **Supporting generalizations.** List at least three things the Indians did that show they felt friendly towards the Spaniards.

★ ★ ★ ★ ★ ★ ★ ★ ★ ★ ★ ★ ★ ★ ★ ★ ★

## ★  3-5  Cartier and the Indians of Canada  ★

**Introduction** Explorer Jacques Cartier played a key role in the development of the two largest French Canadian cities—Québec and Montreal. During his time in North America, he also learned much about the culture of northern Indians. It was Cartier who first brought corn, one of the Indians' chief foods, to Europe. This selection, from a firsthand account of Cartier's second voyage to the New World, describes the visit to the site of Montreal.

**Vocabulary** Before you read the selection, find the meaning of these words in a dictionary: cunningly, chamber.

Cartier and other French explorers often traveled by canoe. When rapids appeared, the lightweight canoes could be portaged, or carried, to the next calm spot.

The next day very early in the morning, our captain very gorgeously attired himself. He caused all his company to be set in order to go to see the town of those people and a certain mountain that is somewhat near the city. We took with us three men of Hochelaga to bring us to the place. All along as we went we found the fairest and best country that possibly can be seen, full of great oaks under which the ground was all covered over with acorns.

We began to find large fields full of such corn as the country can yield. In the midst of those fields is the city of Hochelaga, placed near a great mountain. The mountain is tilled round about, very fertile. And on the top of it you may see very far. We named it Mount Royal. The city of Hochelaga is round, surrounded by timber.

There are in the town about 50 houses about 50 paces long and 12 or 15 broad. They are built all of wood, covered over with the bark of the wood as broad as any board, very finely and cunningly joined together. Within the houses, there are many rooms, lodgings, and chambers. In the middle of every one there is a great court, where they make their fire.

They have also on the top of their houses certain garrets, where they keep their corn to make their bread. They call it Carraconny. They have certain pieces of wood, made hollow, and on them, with mallets of wood, they beat their corn to powder. Then they make paste of it, and of the paste, cakes or wreaths. Then they lay them on a broad and hot stone, and cover it with hot stones. And so they bake their bread instead of in ovens.

Adapted from Richard Hakluyt, *The Third and Last Volume of the Voyages, Navigations, Traffiques, and Discoveries of the English Nation, 1600.*

## READING REVIEW ★ ★ ★ ★ ★ ★ ★

1. Describe the houses in Hochelaga.
2. How did the Indians of Hochelaga bake their corn bread?
3. **Understanding geography.** What kind of landform do you think the city of Montreal was named for? Explain.

★ ★ ★ ★ ★ ★ ★ ★ ★ ★ ★ ★ ★ ★ ★ ★ ★ ★ ★

---

## ★   3-6   Skills Needed in the New World   ★

**Introduction** Sailors skilled in the art of navigation were needed to guide explorers on their voyages to the New World. Once there, however, people with many other talents were needed if the explorers hoped to make a go of life in America. This selection contains a list compiled by the Englishman Richard Hakluyt of the various kinds of skilled workers he planned to include in an expedition to America.

**Vocabulary** Before you read the selection, find the meaning of these words in a dictionary: husbandmen, fortification, bulwarks, pike.

Sorts of men which are to go on this voyage

1. Men skillful in all mineral causes.
2. Fishermen, for sea fishings on the coasts, others for freshwater fishings.
3. Salt makers, to view the coast and see how rich the sea water there is.
4. Husbandmen, to view the soil and to decide what to till.
5. Vineyard men, to see how the soil may serve for the planting of vines.

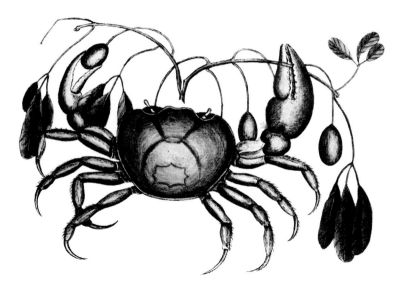

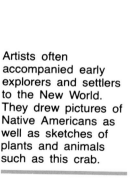

Artists often accompanied early explorers and settlers to the New World. They drew pictures of Native Americans as well as sketches of plants and animals such as this crab.

6. Men bred in the Shroff in South Spain, for discerning how olive trees may be planted there.

7. Others, for planting orange trees, fig trees, lemon trees, and almond trees.

8. Lime makers, to make lime for buildings.

9. Masons, carpenters, etc., for buildings there.

10. Brick makers and tile makers.

11. Men cunning in the art of fortification, that may choose places strong by nature to be fortified and that can plot out and direct workmen.

12. Choice spade men, to dig trenches cunningly and to raise bulwarks of earth for defense and offense.

13. Smiths, to forge the irons of the shovels and spades, and to make black bills and other weapons, and to mend many things.

14. Coopers, to make casks of all sorts.

15. Forgers of pikes' heads and of arrow heads, with Spanish iron and with all manner of tools to be carried with them.

16. Fletchers, to renew arrows, since archery prevaileth much against unarmed people and gunpowder may soon perish by setting on fire.

17. Bowyers also, to make bows there for need.

18. Makers of oars for boats and barges.

19. Shipwrights, to make barges and boats, and bigger vessels, if need be, to run along the coast and to pierce the great bays and inlets.

20. Turners, to turn targets [shields] of elm and tough wood for use against darts and arrows.

21. Tanners, to tan hides of buffs, oxen, etc.

22. Men skillful in burning of soap ashes and in making of pitch and tar and rosin to be fetched out of Prussia and Poland.

23. A skillful painter, to bring the descriptions of all beasts, birds, fishes, trees, towns, etc.

Adapted from John Brereton, *Discovery of the North Part of Virginia*, 1602.

### READING REVIEW ★ ★ ★ ★ ★ ★ ★

1. Name five types of equipment Hakluyt thought colonists would have to make.

2. (a) How does the last type of worker named differ from the rest? (b) Why did Hakluyt probably think this occupation was important?

3. **Building vocabulary.** Many common last names come from occupations. Use Hakluyt's list and a dictionary to find what these last names originally meant: Mason, Smith, Cooper, Fletcher, Turner.

★ ★ ★ ★ ★ ★ ★ ★ ★ ★ ★ ★ ★ ★ ★ ★ ★ ★

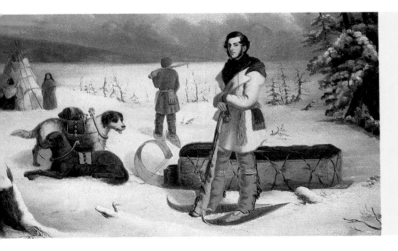

# Settling the New World

# 4 Planting Colonies (1530–1690)

## ★ 4-1 Hardships of the Atlantic Crossing ★

**Introduction** The men and women who made the first voyages across the Atlantic had to be hardy as well as brave. Conditions on board the early ships were grueling. This description of the crossing was written by Father Tomas de la Torre, a Spanish priest. De la Torre came to America in 1544 with Bartolomé de las Casas, the priest who tried to improve conditions among the Indians.

**Vocabulary** Before you read the selection, find the meaning of these words in a dictionary: habitat, entails, hardtack.

By the Grace of our Lord, on the morning of Wednesday, July 9, 1544, we hastily scrambled aboard the small boats that carried us out to the ships on which the remaining members of our order were booked for passage. Chief among us was the Bishop of Chiapas, the Very Reverend Bartolomé de las Casas. Having triumphed over the Council of the Indies, he came armed with royal authority to remedy the ills of the Indians and to free the slaves.

We soon realized that the sea was not man's natural habitat. Everyone became so seasick that nothing in the world could induce us to move from the spot where we lay.

A more befouled hospital and one so filled with the moans of the sick can hardly be imagined. Some sufferers were cooked alive in the heat below deck. The sun roasted others lying about the deck, where they were trod upon and trampled, and where they were so filthy that words cannot describe the scene. Bishop Las Casas gave the chickens he was bringing to the sufferers since the rest of us had not brought any.

To help those who are unfamiliar with life at sea understand something of the hardship and suffering that it entails, I shall set forth a few circumstances. First of all, a ship is a very narrow and stout prison from which no one can escape even if he wears no shackles or chains. Closely crowded in cramped quarters, heat and suffocation are unbearable. The deck floor is usually one's bed. And though some passengers brought soft mats, ours were small, hard, and thinly stuffed with dog hair.

The thirst that one endures is unbelievable, and it is increased by our fare of hardtack and salt beef. Water is measured out a half azumbre [about a liter] a day. An infinite number of lice eat one alive, and clothing cannot be washed because salt water shrinks it. Everywhere bad odors pervade the ship, especially below deck. These annoyances and many other hardships are very common in shipboard life.

Adapted from Fray Francisco Ximénez, *Historia de la Provincia de San Vicente de Chiapas y Guatemala de la Orden de Predicadores*, Prólogo del Lic. Antonio Villacorta, C., 3 vols., 1929.

**READING REVIEW** ★ ★ ★ ★ ★ ★

1. What did the diet of passengers on de la Torre's ship consist of?

2. (a) Why, according to de la Torre, was de las Casas making this trip to America? (b) What does de la Torre seem to think of de las Casas? (c) How can you tell?

3. **Summarizing.** Briefly, what were the things that made the Atlantic crossing unpleasant?

★ ★ ★ ★ ★ ★ ★ ★ ★ ★ ★ ★ ★ ★ ★ ★ ★ ★

---

## ★ 4-2   A Description of Mexico City   ★

**Introduction**  The Spanish colonies in the New World were the first European settlements to flourish here. By the mid-1500s, New Spain boasted cities, universities, and printing presses. The new colonial cities were especially impressive. In part, this was because they were often built on the sites of the great cities of the Aztecs and Incas. This description is of Mexico City, which was built on the foundations of the ancient Aztec capital, Tenochtitlan. It comes from a description by an English trader, Henry Hawks, who visited New Spain in 1567.

**Vocabulary**  Before you read the selection, find the meaning of these words in a dictionary: victuals, divers.

Mexico is a great city. It has more than 50,000 households. There are not over 5,000 or 6,000 houses of Spaniards. All the others are the people of the country, which live under the Spaniards' laws. There are in this city stately buildings and many monasteries of friars and nuns which the Spaniards have made. The building of the Indians is somewhat beautiful outwardly, and within full of small rooms, with very small windows. This city stands in the middle of a great lake. And the water goes through all or most of the streets. There come small boats, which they call canoes. In them they bring all things necessary, such as wood and coals, and grass for their horses, stones and lime to build, and corn.

This city is subject to many earthquakes, which often cast down houses and kill people. This city is very well provided with water to drink and with all manner of victuals, such as fruits, fish, bread, hens and capons, guinea cocks and hens, and all other fowl. There are in this city every week three fairs or markets, which are attended by many people, Spaniards as well as the people of the country. There are in these fairs or markets all manner of things that may be invented to sell, and in especial things of the country.

Toward the north from Mexico, there are many silver mines. There is more silver found in these mines toward the north than there is in any other parts. These mines are commonly upon great hills and stony ground, very hard to work.

Out of some of the mines the Indians find a certain kind of earth of divers colours, wherewith they paint themselves in times of their dances and other pastimes which they use.

In this country of Nova Hispania, there are also mines of gold, although the gold be commonly found in rivers or very near rivers. And now in these days there is not so much gold found as there has been before.

There are many great rivers and great store of fish in them, not unlike our kinds of fish. And there are great woods and as fair trees as may be seen of divers sorts, especially fir trees, that may mast any ship that goes upon the sea, oaks and pineapples, and another tree which they call mesquite. It bears a fruit like a peapod, very sweet, which the wild people gather and keep all the year and eat instead of bread.

There is a great number of beasts or cattle in the country of Cibola, which were never brought there by the Spaniards but breed naturally in the country. They are like our oxen, saving that they have long hair like a lion and short horns, and they have upon their shoulders a bunch like a camel, which is higher than the rest of their body. They are very wild and swift in running. They call them the beasts or cattle of Cibola.

Adapted from Richard Hakluyt, *Principal Navigations*, 1589.

READING REVIEW ★ ★ ★ ★ ★ ★ ★

1. What animal is Hawks describing at the end of this passage?
2. What evidence is there in Hawks's description that Indian and Spanish influences mixed in the culture of New Spain?
3. **Comparing.** Compare Mexico City, as described here, with the ancient Aztec capital of Tenochtitlan, described in Chapter 2.

★ ★ ★ ★ ★ ★ ★ ★ ★ ★ ★ ★ ★ ★ ★ ★ ★ ★ ★ ★

---

★  **4-3    Marquette and Joliet**  ★

**Introduction** French traders in Canada heard stories of a great river to the south and west from the Indians with whom they traded. In 1673, the French colonial government asked Father Jacques Marquette and Louis Joliet to try to find this "Mississippi," the Indian word meaning "great river." Marquette knew several Indian languages, and Joliet was a skilled mapmaker. This selection is from the report Father Marquette wrote of their trip.

**Vocabulary** Before you read the selection, find the meaning of these words in a dictionary: league, reconnoiter, token.

The first nation that we came to was that of the Folle Avoine [Menominee]. I told these people of my design to go and discover remote nations, in order to teach them the mysteries of our holy religion. They were greatly surprised to hear it and did their best to prevent me from going. They told me that I would meet nations who would never show mercy to strangers, but break their heads without any cause; and that war was kindled between various peoples who lived along our route. This exposed us to the further danger of being killed by the bands of warriors who are ever in the field.

They also said that the great river was very dangerous; that it was full of horrible monsters, which ate men and canoes together; that there was even a demon who barred the way and swallowed up all who ventured to approach him; finally, that the heat was so bad in these countries that it would inevitably cause our death.

I thanked them for the good advice that they gave me, but told them that I could not follow it because the salvation of souls was at stake. For that I would be delighted to give my life.

Thus we left the waters flowing to Quebec, 400 or 500 leagues from here, to float on those that would take us through strange lands.

Finally on June 25 we saw on the water's edge some tracks of men, and a narrow and somewhat beaten path leading to a fine prairie. We stopped to examine it; and, thinking that it was a road which led to some village, we resolved to go and reconnoiter it.

Monsieur Joliet and I undertook this investigation—a rather hazardous one for two men who exposed themselves alone to the mercy of an unknown people. We silently followed the narrow path. After walking about two leagues, we discovered a village on the bank of a river. Then we heartily commended ourselves to God, and, after asking His aid, we went farther without being seen. We approached so near that we could even hear the savages talking. We therefore decided that it was time to reveal ourselves. This we did by shouting with all our energy, and stopped without going any farther. On hearing the shout, the savages quickly came out of their cabins. Having recognized us as Frenchmen, especially when they saw a black gown— or, at least, having no cause to distrust us since we were only two men and had given them notice of our arrival— they named four old men to come and speak to us.

Two of these old men bore tobacco pipes, finely decorated and adorned with various feathers. They walked

French settlers followed in the path blazed by explorers such as Marquette and Joliet. As this picture shows, it took brave, hardy men and women to adapt to the rugged life on the cold Canadian frontier.

slowly and raised their pipes toward the sun without saying a word. Finally, when they had drawn near, they stopped to look at us attentively. I spoke to them first and asked who they were. They replied that they were Illinois; and as a token of peace, they offered us their pipes to smoke. They afterward invited us to enter their village, where all the people impatiently awaited us.

Adapted from *The Jesuit Relations and Allied Documents*, ed. Reuben Gold Thwaites, 1900.

## READING REVIEW · · · · · · ·

1. What dangers did the Menominee Indians warn the two Frenchmen about?
2. How did the Indians whom Marquette and Joliet met show that they meant the Frenchmen no harm?
3. **Making inferences.** Why did Father Marquette make this dangerous trip and take such risks as going alone into the Indian village?

* * * * * * * * * * * * * * * * * *

**Introduction** After the rough first years of the Jamestown colony, when all but 60 of 900 settlers died, conditions gradually began to improve. Yet life in Virginia was still far from easy. Those who lived outside Jamestown faced great difficulties—shortages, illness, loneliness. Richard Frethorne describes this life in a letter he wrote to his parents in England in 1623. His life was especially difficult because he came to America as an indentured servant. (See page 117.)

**Vocabulary** Before you read this selection, find the meaning of these words in a dictionary: rogue, victuals, redeem, entreat.

Loving and kind father and mother:

My most humble duty remembered to you, hoping in God of your good health. This is to let you understand that I, your child, am in a most heavy case because of the nature of the country, which causes much sickness. When we are sick there is nothing to comfort us. Since I came out of the ship, I never ate anything but peas and loblollie (that is, water gruel). As for deer or venison, I never saw any since I came into this land. There is indeed some fowl. But we are not allowed to go and get it. We must work hard both early and late for a mess of water gruel and a mouthful of bread and beef.

We live in fear of the enemy every hour; we are but 32 to fight against 3,000 if they should come. And the nearest help that we have is 10 miles from us. When the rogues overcame this place the last time they slew 80 persons.

I have nothing to comfort me. I have nothing at all—no, not a shirt to my back but two rags, nor no clothes but one poor suit, nor but one pair of shoes, one pair of stockings, and one cap. My cloak was stolen by one of my own fellows. And to his dying hour, he would not tell me what he did with it. Some of my fellows saw him take butter and beef out of a ship, which my cloak, I doubt not, paid for.

I am not a quarter as strong as I was in England, and all is for want of victuals. I tell you that I have eaten more in one day in your home than I have here in a week. You have given more than my day's allowance to a beggar at the door.

If you love me you will redeem me suddenly, for which I do entreat and beg. And if you cannot get the merchants to redeem me for some little money, then for God's sake get a gathering or ask some good folks to lay out some little sum of money in meal and cheese and butter and beef. The answer of this letter will be life or death to me.

Your loving son,
Richard Frethorne
Virginia
3rd April, 1623

Adapted from Richard Frethorne, letter to his father and mother, 1623, in *The Records of the Virginia Company of London,* ed. Susan M. Kingsbury (New York: AMS Press, 1935).

**READING REVIEW** ★ ★ ★ ★ ★ ★ ★

1. What does Richard Frethorne ask his father to do for him?
2. What does Frethorne dislike most about his life in America?
3. **Comparing points of view.** (a) How did Richard Frethorne's experience with native Americans and his attitude toward them differ from that of Marquette? (b) How would you explain the difference?

★ ★ ★ ★ ★ ★ ★ ★ ★ ★ ★ ★ ★ ★ ★ ★ ★ ★ ★

**Introduction** Indians helped the Pilgrims survive in Plymouth. This friendly relationship between Indians and English was largely due to the good will of people on both sides. These passages are from a journal written by William Bradford, first governor of Plymouth Colony, and Edward Winslow, one of the colony's founders. Their journal is the only firsthand account of the Pilgrims' first weeks in America.

**Vocabulary** Before you read the selection, find the meaning of these words in a dictionary: rendezvous, carriage.

**Friday, March 16**

There presented himself a savage, which caused an alarm. He very boldly came all alone and along the houses straight to the rendezvous where we met him.

He greeted us in English and bade us welcome, for he had learned some broken English amongst the Englishmen that came to fish along the coast.

Samoset [the Indian] was a man free in speech, so far as he could express his mind, and of a seemly carriage. We questioned him of many things. He was the first savage we could meet withal.

These people are ill affected towards the English because of Hunt, a master of a ship, who deceived the people, and carried 20 away and sold them for slaves.

**Thursday, March 22**

About noon we met again about our public business, but we had scarce been an hour together but Samoset came again with Squanto, who was one of the 20 captives carried away by Hunt. He had been in England and could speak a little English. They brought with them some few skins of trade, and some red herrings newly taken and dried. After an hour their King came. Then we made a treaty of peace, which was:

1. That neither he nor any of his should do hurt to any of our people.

2. And if any of his did hurt to any of ours, he should send the offender that we might punish him.

3. If any did unjustly war against him, we would aid him; if any did war against us, he should aid us.

4. He should go to his neighbors to tell them of this, that they might not wrong us, but might be likewise included in the conditions of peace.

Many different Native American nations lived in North America when the Pilgrims and other Europeans arrived. This painting shows several Indians who have just sighted a European ship on the Hudson River. Such sights must have seemed alien and frightening at first.

5. That when their men came to us, they should leave their bows and arrows behind them, as we should do our muskets when we came to them.

So after all was done, the Governor conducted him to the brook, and there they embraced each other and he departed.

*Adapted from William Bradford and Edward Winslow, A Relation or Journal of the beginnings and proceedings of the English Plantation at Plimoth in New England by certaine English Adventurers, 1622.*

**READING REVIEW** ★ ★ ★ ★ ★ ★ ★

1. How did Samoset learn English?
2. What had happened to Squanto in the past that made his friendliness toward the Pilgrims surprising?
3. **Analyzing a primary source.** (a) In the peace treaty, what did the Indians agree to do that would benefit the English? (b) What did the English agree to do that would benefit the Indians? (c) Which side gained the most from the treaty?

★ ★ ★ ★ ★ ★ ★ ★ ★ ★ ★ ★ ★ ★ ★ ★ ★ ★

## ★ 4-6 What to Take to the New World ★

**Introduction** Many colonists had a hard time in America because they were not well prepared for their new life. They were used to a wide variety of available goods and services. Yet early colonists had to take with them or make themselves everything they would need in their new life.

The Reverend Francis Higginson decided to do what he could to help future colonists. In 1630, he published a book that contained this checklist of things to take to the New World.

**Vocabulary** Before you read the selection, find the meaning of these words in a dictionary: firkin, ell, frowers, trencher, kine.

*Victuals for a whole year for a man, and so after the rate for more*
8 bushels of meal
2 bushels of peas
2 bushels of oatmeal
1 gallon of aqua-vita
1 gallon of oil
2 gallons of vinegar
1 firkin of butter
   *Apparel*
1 Monmouth cap
3 falling bands
3 shirts
1 waistcoat
1 suit of canvas

1 suit of frieze
1 suit of cloth
3 pair of stockings
4 pair of shoes
2 pair of sheets
7 ells of canvas, to make a bed and bolster
1 pair of blankets
1 coarse rug
   *Arms*
1 armor, complete
1 long piece
1 sword
1 belt
1 bandoleer
20 pound of powder
60 pound of lead
1 pistol and goose shot
   *Tools*
1 broad hoe
1 narrow hoe
1 broad axe
1 felling axe
1 steel handsaw
1 whipsaw
1 hammer
1 spade
2 augers
4 chisels
2 piercers, stocked
1 gimlet
1 hatchet
2 frowers
1 handbill

1 grindstone
1 pickaxe
nails, of all sorts
    *Household Implements*
1 iron pot
1 kettle
1 frying pan
1 gridiron
2 skillets
1 spit
wooden platters
dishes
spoons
trenchers
    *Spices*
sugar
pepper
cloves
mace
cinnamon
nutmegs, fruit

Also, there are diverse other things necessary to be taken over to this plantation, [such] as books, nets, hooks and lines, cheese, bacon, kine, goats, etc.

Adapted from *Chronicles of the First Planters of the Colony of Massachusetts Bay*, ed. Alexander Young, 1846.

## READING REVIEW ★ ★ ★ ★ ★ ★ ★

1. A bushel equals 32 quarts. How much oatmeal did Reverend Higginson assume a man would eat in a week?
2. What other important items do you think should have been included in the list?
3. **Classifying information.** Under which heading would Higginson have listed the following items: flour, salt, rope, towels, bucket?

★ ★ ★ ★ ★ ★ ★ ★ ★ ★ ★ ★ ★ ★ ★ ★ ★

Chapter

# 5 English Colonies Take Root (1630–1750)

## ★ 5-1 A Slave's Ballad on an Indian Attack ★

**Introduction** In 1621, Pilgrims and Indians sat down together for the first Thanksgiving. Yet not long afterwards, this friendly beginning had given way to open hostility. New Englanders started to claim Indian land, and the Indians struck back in revenge. These attacks could be unexpected and frightening. The 1746 attack on the village of Deerfield, Massachusetts, was typical. One of the best descriptions of the event is the account given by Lucy Terry, a black slave. Terry wrote this account in the form of a ballad.

**Vocabulary** Before you read the selection, find the meaning of these words in a dictionary: ambush, valiant.

A 1704 Indian attack on Deerfield, Massachusetts, is shown in this painting. The town was destroyed and at least 50 colonists were killed.

August 'twas the twenty-fifth
Seventeen hundred forty-six
The Indians did in ambush lay
Some very valiant men to slay.
Twas nigh unto Sam Dickinson's mill
The Indians there five men did kill
The names of whom I'll not leave out.
Samuel Allen like a hero fought
And though he was so brave and bold
His face no more shall we behold.
Eleazer Hawks was killed outright
Before he had time to fight
Before he did the Indians see
Was shot and killed immediately.
Oliver Amsden he was slain
Which caused his friends much grief
    and pain.
Simeon Amsden they found dead
Not many rods off from his head.
Adonijah Gillet we do hear
Did lose his life which was so dear.
John Saddler fled across the water
And so escaped the dreadful slaughter.
Eunice Allen see the Indians coming

And hoped to save herself by running
And had not her petticoats stopt her
The awful creatures had not cotched her
And tommyhawked her on the head
And left her on the ground for dead.
Young Samuel Allen, Oh! lack-a-day
Was taken and carried to Canada.

Adapted from Lucy Terry, "A Slave Report in Rhyme on the Indian Attack on Old Deerfield, August 25, 1746."

## READING REVIEW ★ ★ ★ ★ ★ ★ ★

1. What kind of weapons did the Indians use?
2. It seems that entire families were involved in the attack. Describe the fate of the Allens in your own words.
3. **Using a poem as a primary source.** What sort of relationship do you think Lucy had with her owners and with the other white families in Deerfield? Base your answers on evidence in the ballad.

★ ★ ★ ★ ★ ★ ★ ★ ★ ★ ★ ★ ★ ★ ★ ★ ★ ★ ★

## ★ 5-2 Witchcraft in Massachusetts? ★

**Introduction** Not only uneducated people took part in the Salem witch hunt. Even the best-educated of Puritans believed in the devil and the possibility that he used ordinary men and women to do his work. Increase Mather was one of the intellectual leaders of the Massachusetts Bay Colony. Yet in 1684, Mather wrote a pamphlet warning his fellow citizens that the devil was at work in their midst. This selection is taken from that pamphlet.

**Vocabulary** Before you read the selection, find the meaning of these words in a dictionary: disquieted, bodkin, vanity, conjurer.

In the year 1679, the house of William Morse, in Newberry in New England, was strangely disquieted by a demon. After those troubles began, he did, by the advice of friends, write down the particulars of those unusual accidents. And the account which he gives thereof follows:—

On December 8, in the morning, there were five great stones and bricks by an invisible hand thrown in at the west end of the house while the man's wife was making the bed. The bedstead was lifted up from the floor, and the bedstaff flung out of the window, and a cat was hurled at her. A long staff danced up and down in the chimney; a burnt brick and a piece of weatherboard were thrown in at the window.

In another evening, they went to bed undressed because of their late disturbances, and the man, wife, and boy presently felt themselves pricked. Upon searching, they found in the bed a bodkin, a knitting needle, and two sticks pointed at both ends. The man received also a great blow on his thigh and on his face, which fetched blood. And while he was writing, a candlestick was twice thrown at him; and a great piece of bark fiercely smote him; and a pail of water turned up without hands.

On December 26, the boy barked like a dog, and clucked like an hen; and after long being kept from speaking, said: "There's Powel, I am pinched." His tongue likewise hung out of his mouth so as that it could by no means be forced in till his fit was over, and then he said 'twas forced out by Powel.

Neither were there many words spoken by Satan all this time. Only once, having put out their light, they heard a scraping on the boards and then a piping and drumming on them, which was followed with a voice singing, "Revenge! Revenge! Sweet is revenge!" And they, being terrified by it, called upon God. Suddenly, with a mournful note, there were six times uttered such expressions as, "Alas! me knock no more! Me knock no more!" And now all ceased.

Thus far is the story concerning the demon of William Morse's house in Newberry. The true reason for these strange disturbances is as yet not certainly known. Some did suspect Morse's wife to be guilty of witchcraft.

One of the neighbors took apples which were brought out of that house, and put them into the fire—upon which, they say, their houses were much disturbed. I shall not here enlarge upon the vanity and superstition of such experiments, reserving that for another place.

Others were apt to think that a seaman, by some suspected to be a conjurer, set the devil to work thus to disquiet Morse's family. Or it may be some other thing, as yet kept hid in the secrets of Providence.

Adapted from Increase Mather, "An Essay for the Recording of Illustrious Providences," 1684.

## READING REVIEW ★ ★ ★ ★ ★ ★

1. Describe three of the events reported to be the work of a demon for which there could be a logical or scientific explanation.

2. (a) Does Mather think he is superstitious? (b) Do you think he is? Support your answers with evidence from the selection.

3. **Drawing conclusions.** What do you think might have happened to a woman named Powel at the time of the Salem witchcraft trials? Why?

★ ★ ★ ★ ★ ★ ★ ★ ★ ★ ★ ★ ★ ★ ★ ★ ★ ★ ★

Two New England colonies, Connecticut and Rhode Island, were set up by people who were discontent with life in Massachusetts Bay. Thomas Hooker, shown here moving to the Connecticut River Valley, thought that there should be limits on the power of the government.

**Introduction** The Dutch were eager for settlers to come to the colony of New Netherland and transform its vast expanses into productive farmland. Some wealthy people were lured by the promise of a large tract of land in return for starting a small private colony. Others, awed by the scope of such an undertaking, needed more encouragement. So in 1650, the Secretary of New Netherland, Cornelius Van Tienhoven, wrote a report that gave detailed advice on how to go about founding a colony in New Netherland. This selection is from that report.

**Vocabulary** Before you read the selection, find the meaning of these words in a dictionary: felled, palisades, hamlet, wainscot, spars.

Those who are obliged to work in the colonies ought to sail from this country in March or at the latest in April, so as to be able to plant garden vegetables, maize, and beans, and also to

Much work was required before settlers could even begin to build or plant crops. One way of clearing land is shown here. First, strips of bark were cut around the trees to kill them. When dead, they were cut down. Finally, the stumps were burned.

use the whole summer in clearing land and building cottages as I shall hereafter describe.

All, then, who arrive in New Netherland must immediately set about preparing the soil, so as to be able, if possible, to plant some winter grain. The trees are usually felled from the stump, cut up and burnt in the field, except such as are suitable for building—for palisades, posts, and rails. The farmer, having thus begun, must try every year to clear as much new land as he possibly can and sow it with such seed as he considers suitable.

It is not necessary that the farmer should take up much livestock in the beginning, since clearing land and other work do not permit him to save much hay or to build barns for stabling. One pair of draft horses or a yoke of oxen is necessary to take the planks for buildings or rails from the land to the place where they are to be set. The farmer can get all sorts of cattle in the course of the second summer, when he will have more leisure to cut and bring home hay and also to build barns and houses for men and cattle.

Before beginning to build it will above all things be necessary to select a well-located spot, either on some river or bay, suitable for the settlement of a village or hamlet. This is to be properly surveyed and divided into lots, with good streets according to the situation of the place. This hamlet can be fenced all around with high palisades or long boards and closed with gates, which is advantageous in case of attack by the natives.

Those in New Netherland and especially in New England, who have no means to build farmhouses at first, should dig a square pit in the ground, cellar fashion, six or seven feet deep and as long and as broad as they think proper. They should case the earth inside with wood all around the wall, and line the wood with the bark of trees or something else, to prevent the caving in of the earth. They should floor this cellar with plank and wainscot it overhead for a ceiling, raise a roof of spars, and clear up and cover the spars with bark or green sods—so that they can live dry and warm in these houses with their entire families for two, three, and four years.

The wealthy and principal men in New England, in the beginning of the colonies, began their first dwelling houses in this fashion for two reasons: firstly, in order not to waste time building, and secondly, in order not to discourage poorer laboring people whom they brought over in numbers from the fatherland. In the course of three or four years, when the country became adapted to agriculture, they built themselves handsome houses, spending on them several thousands.

Adapted from Cornelius Van Tienhoven, "Information Relative to Taking Up Land in New Netherland," in *The Documentary History of the State of New York,* ed. E. B. O'Callaghan, Vol. IV, 1851.

### READING REVIEW ★ ★ ★ ★ ★ ★

1. What sort of houses did Van Tienhoven encourage colonists to build at first?
2. Why does he recommend this type of housing?
3. **Understanding chronology.** In what order did Van Tienhoven suggest colonists undertake the following tasks: planting a garden, clearing land, building a house, buying cattle, preparing palisades and fence rails?

★ ★ ★ ★ ★ ★ ★ ★ ★ ★ ★ ★ ★ ★ ★ ★ ★ ★

## ★ 5-4 Bacon Rebels ★

**Introduction** The first rebellion of colonists against a British governor was that led by a fiery young Virginian, Nathaniel Bacon, in 1676. Bacon complained that the government had not helped the colonists defend themselves against Indian attacks, despite repeated promises to do so. Their patience exhausted, Bacon and his followers decided to take matters into their own hands. The result was fierce and frightening violence. This selection was written by a member of the Virginia legislature who witnessed much of the rebellion firsthand.

**Vocabulary** Before you read the selection, find the meaning of these words in a dictionary: redoubt, proclamation, procrastination.

In these frightful times the most exposed small families withdrew into our houses, which we fortified with palisades and redoubts. Neighbors joined their labors, taking their arms into the fields and setting sentinels. No man stirred out of doors unarmed. Indians were sighted, three, four, five, or six in a party, lurking throughout the whole land. Yet (what was remarkable) I rarely heard of any houses burnt, nor ever of any corn or tobacco cut up, or other injury done, besides murders, except the killing of a very few cattle and swine.

Frequent complaints of bloodshed were sent to Sir William Berkeley, the governor, from the heads of the rivers, which were often answered with promises of assistance.

The people at the heads of James and York Rivers grew impatient at the many slaughters of their neighbors. They rose for their own defense, choosing Mr. Bacon for their leader.

During these delays, with people often slain, the officers and 300 men, led by Mr. Bacon, met. They discussed the danger of going without a commission* on the one part, and the continual murders of their neighbors on the other part, and came to this resolution: to prepare themselves with supplies for a march, but in the meantime, to send again for a commission. If one could not be obtained by a certain day, they would proceed, commission or no commission.

This day ended and no commission came. So they marched into the wilderness in quest of these Indians. After this the Governor sent his proclamation, denouncing all rebels who should not return within a limited time. Most obeyed. But Mr. Bacon with 57 men proceeded until their provisions were near spent, without finding enemies. Then coming near a fort of friendly Indians, on the other side of the James River, they offered payment for provisions which these Indians kindly promised to give them on the morrow. But the Indians put them off with promises until the third day when they had eaten their last morsels. And now 'twas suspected these Indians had received private messages from the Governor which were the causes of these procrastinations. That evening a shot from the place they left on the other side of the river killed one of Mr. Bacon's men. This made them believe that those in the fort had sent for other Indians to come behind them and cut them off.

Thereupon they set fire to the palisades, stormed and burnt the fort and cabins, and (with the loss of three English) slew 150 Indians.

Adapted from *Beginning, Progress and Conclusion of Bacon's Rebellion in Virginia,* reprinted 1897.

---

*A commission refers to the official right to undertake certain actions, in this case to fight the Indians.

Bacon and his followers came from the recently settled backcountry of Virginia. Conditions in the wild and rugged backcountry were very different from those in the older coastal settlements. The failure of the colonial government to understand the differences helped create the frustration that led to Bacon's rebellion.

## READING REVIEW ★ ★ ★ ★ ★ ★ ★

1. What had Indians done to anger the colonists?

2. What led Bacon to attack the Indians he did?

3. **Expressing an opinion.** (a) Do you think Bacon's actions were justified? Explain. (b) Why do you think the Indians were attacking the settlers?

★ ★ ★ ★ ★ ★ ★ ★ ★ ★ ★ ★ ★ ★ ★ ★ ★ ★

**Introduction** Many colonists sympathized with Nathaniel Bacon's hostility towards the Indians they met in the New World. Others, however, saw the Indians as a friendly, even a noble people. Robert Beverley lived in Virginia at the same time as Bacon. Yet he had a very different attitude towards the same Indian nations that Bacon attacked. This selection is from a book Beverley wrote about Virginia.

**Vocabulary** Before you read the selection, find the meaning of these words in a dictionary: retinue, diverted, boisterous, melancholy.

The Indians are of the middling and large stature of the English. They are straight and well-proportioned, having the cleanest and most exact limbs in the world. They are so perfect in their outward frame that I never heard of one single Indian that was either dwarfish, crooked, bandy-legged, or otherwise misshapen.

Their color, when they are grown up, is a chestnut brown and tawny, but much lighter in their infancy. Their skin comes afterward to harden and grow blacker, by greasing and sunning themselves. They have generally coal black hair, and very black eyes. Their women are generally beautiful, possessing shape and features agreeable enough, and wanting no charm but that of education.

The men wear their hair cut after several fanciful fashions, sometimes greased and sometimes painted. The great men, or better sort, preserve a long lock behind for distinction. They pull their beards out by the roots with mussel shells. The women wear the hair of the head very long, either hanging at their backs, or brought forward in a single lock, bound up with a band of wampum or beads. Sometimes also they wear it neatly tied up in a knot behind. It is commonly greased, and shining black, but never painted.

They have a remarkable way of entertaining all strangers, which is performed after the following manner. First, the king or queen, with a guard and a great retinue, march out of the town, a quarter or half a mile, carrying mats. When they meet the strangers, they invite them to sit down upon those mats. Then they pass the ceremony of the pipe. They fill that pipe with the best tobacco they have, and then present it to the strangers, and smoke out of the same after them. Afterward, having spent about half an hour in serious conversation, they get up all together and march into the town.

Here the first compliment is to wash the courteous traveler's feet. Then he is entertained by a great number of attendants. After this he is diverted with antique Indian dances, performed both by men and women, and accompanied with great variety of wild music.

Their sports and pastimes are singing, dancing, instrumental music, and some boisterous games which are performed by running, catching, and leaping upon one another.

Their singing is not the most charming that I have heard. It consists much in raising the voice and is full of slow melancholy accents. However, I must admit even this music contains some wild notes that are pleasant.

Their dancing is performed either by few or a great company, but without much regard either to time or to steps. The first of these is by one or two persons, or at most by three. In the meanwhile, the company sit about them in a ring upon the ground, singing outrageously and shaking their rattles.

The other is performed by a great number of people, the dancers themselves forming a ring. Each has his rattle in his hand, or what other thing he fancies most, as his bow and arrows or his tomahawk. They also dress themselves up with branches of trees or some other strange costume.

Adapted from Robert Beverley, *The History of Virginia in Four Parts*, 1705.

**READING REVIEW** ★ ★ ★ ★ ★ ★ ★

1. What does Beverley think of the Indians' appearance?

2. How do the Indians of Virginia welcome strangers?

3. **Making inferences.** Beverley is not hostile to the Indians. But does he respect them? Explain.

★ ★ ★ ★ ★ ★ ★ ★ ★ ★ ★ ★ ★ ★ ★ ★ ★

## ★ 5-6 Contract of an Indentured Apprentice ★

**Introduction** Indentured servants agreed to work for a certain period of time in return for payment of their passage to America. Such arrangements were also made by colonists who wished to learn a particular craft or trade. These young people, called apprentices, would agree to work for a master craftsworker for a number of years in exchange for being taught that person's trade. This contract between an apprentice cordwainer, or leatherworker, and his master is typical of such agreements of indenture. The obligations of both people involved are spelled out in detail.

**Vocabulary** Before you read the selection, find the meaning of these words in a dictionary: consent, matrimony.

This indenture witnesses that William Matthews, son of Marrat of the city of New York, does voluntarily and of his own free will and by the consent of his mother put himself as an apprentice cordwainer to Thomas Windover.

He will serve from August 15, 1718, until the full term of seven years be completed and ended. During all of this term, the said apprentice shall faithfully serve his said master, shall faithfully keep his secrets, and gladly obey his lawful commands everywhere.

He shall do no damage to his said master, nor see any done by others without giving notice to his said master. He shall not waste his said master's goods nor lend them unlawfully to any. He shall not contract matrimony within the said term.

At cards, dice, or any other unlawful game, he shall not play with his own goods or the goods of others. Without permission from his master, he shall neither buy nor sell during the said term. He shall not absent himself day or night from his master's service without his permission, nor visit alehouses, but in all things he shall behave himself as a faithful apprentice toward his master all during his said term.

The said master, during the said term, shall, by the best means or methods, teach or cause the said apprentice to be taught the art or mystery of a cordwainer. He shall find and provide unto the said apprentice meat, drink, clothing, lodging, and washing fit for an apprentice. During the said term, every night in winter he shall give the apprentice one quarter of schooling. At the end of the said tèrm, he shall provide him with a decent new suit of clothes, four shirts, and two neckties.

Adapted from *Collections of the New York Historical Society for the Year 1909*, 1910.

READING REVIEW ★ ★ ★ ★ ★ ★ ★

1. In what ways did William Matthews's contract limit his actions?
2. Young Matthews's master owed him food, clothing, and lodging. What else did he owe his apprentice?

3. **Analyzing a primary source.** An indentured worker had to serve his master and obey him. Yet such a worker could still be said to be free. What lines in the contract support this fact?

★ ★ ★ ★ ★ ★ ★ ★ ★ ★ ★ ★ ★ ★ ★ ★ ★

# Chapter 6 Life in the Colonies (1630–1775)

## ★ 6-1 A Young Girl of Colonial Boston ★

**Introduction** By the 1700s, life in Boston was livelier and more leisurely than it had been for the earlier Puritan settlers. Yet Puritan influence remained strong. Seeing to the proper development of their minds and souls was still a priority with Bostonians. This selection is from the diary kept by an 11-year-old Boston girl in the mid–1700s. In it, Anna Green Winslow gives a glimpse of what life was like for a young girl.

**Vocabulary** Before you read the selection, find the meaning of these words in a dictionary: disabled, flax, exert.

**January 4, 1772** I was dressed in my yellow coat, my black bib & apron, my shoes, the cap my Aunt Storer presented me with (blue ribbons on it) & a very handsome locket in the shape of a heart she gave me. And I would tell you that for the first time they all liked my dress very much.

**January 11** I have attended my school every day this week except Wednesday afternoon. I made a visit to Aunt Suky, & was dressed just as I was to go to the ball. I heard Mr. Thacher preach our lecture last eve-

ning. I remember a great deal of the sermon, but don't have time to put it down.

**February 9** I am disabled by a sore on my fourth finger & something like one on my middle finger from using my own pens. But altho' my right hand is in bandages, my left is free. My aunt says it will be a nice opportunity when it improves to learn to spin flax. I am pleased with the proposal & aim at present to exert myself for this purpose. I hope, when two or at most three months are past, to give

Young girls in the colonies spent much time at handiwork such as sewing, spinning, and knitting. Many made elaborate embroidered samplers to demonstrate their skill with a needle. Samplers were typical of the practical forms of art that developed in the colonies. This sampler was made in Connecticut in the 1700s.

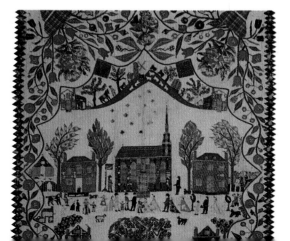

you a visible demonstration of my skill in this art, as well as several others.

I have read my Bible to my aunt this morning (as is the daily custom) & sometimes I read other books to her.

**February 21** My Grandmamma sent Miss Deming, Miss Winslow, & I one eighth of a dollar apiece for a New Year's gift. I have made the purchase I told you of a few pages ago, that is, last Thursday I purchased with my aunt Deming's leave a very beautiful white feather hat. I have long been saving my money to buy this hat.

**February 22** I have spun 30 knots of linen and mended a pair of stockings for Lucinda, read a part of the *Pilgrim's Progress,* copied part of my text journal.

Played some, laugh'd enough, & I tell aunt it is all human nature, if not human reason.

Adapted from *Diary of Anna Green Winslow.*

**READING REVIEW** ★ ★ ★ ★ ★ ★

1. What place do clothes have in Anna's life? How does her attitude toward clothes compare with that of an 11-year-old girl today?

2. What role does Anna think playing, talking, and laughing should have in people's lives?

3. **Analyzing a primary source.** What evidence is there in Anna's diary that her family still feels that the life of the mind and of the soul are important?

★ ★ ★ ★ ★ ★ ★ ★ ★ ★ ★ ★ ★ ★ ★ ★ ★ ★ ★ ★ ★ ★

---

## ★  6-2    A Critical View of Philadelphia    ★

**Introduction** For the most part, people who settled in the Middle Colonies enjoyed a comfortable life. Travelers remarked especially on the agreeableness of life in Philadelphia, the region's largest city. But at least one observer had a less than flattering response to Philadelphia. A Scottish doctor, Alexander Hamilton, traveled to several colonial cities in 1744. This selection is from his account of his travels.

**Vocabulary** Before you read the selection, find the meaning of these words in a dictionary: regularity, obstinate, perpetual, nonresistance, traffic.

At my entering the city, I observed the regularity of the streets. But at the same time the majority of the houses were mean and low and much decayed, the streets in general not paved, very dirty, and covered with rubbish.

**Thursday, June 7** I noticed one example of industriousness as soon as I got up and looked out my window, and that was the shops open at 5 in the morning.

**Friday, June 8** I dined at a tavern with a very mixed company of different nations and religions. There were Scots, English, Dutch, Germans, and Irish; there were Roman Catholics, Church men, Presbyterians, Quakers, Methodists, Seventh-Day men, Moravians, Anabaptists, and one Jew. The whole company consisted of 25 planted round an oblong table in a great hall well-stocked with flies.

**Saturday, June 9** The market in this city is perhaps the largest in North America. The street where it stands, called Market Street, is large and spacious, composed of the best houses in the city.

They have but one public clock here which strikes the hour but has neither hands nor dial plate. It is strange that they should want such an ornament and convenience in so large a place, but the chief part of the community are Quakers, who seem to shun ornament in their public buildings as well as in their apparel or dress.

The Quakers are the richest and the people of greatest interest in the government. Their House of Assembly is chiefly composed of them. They have the character of an obstinate, stiff-necked generation and are a perpetual trouble to their governors.

Here is no public storehouse of arms nor any method of defense, either for city or province, in case of the invasion of an enemy. This is owing to the obstinacy of the Quakers in maintaining their principle of nonresistance.

I never was in a place so populous where public diversions were found so little. There is no such things as assemblies of the gentry among them, for either dancing or music. Their chief employ, indeed, is trade and mercantile business, which turns their thoughts from these innocent amusements, for the most part so agreeable and entertaining to the young, and indeed, in the opinion of moderate people, so helpful in the improvement of politeness, good manners, and humanity.

Adapted from Alexander Hamilton, *Itinerarium*, 1907.

The influence of cultures other than the English was strongest in the Middle Colonies. This was especially true in New York, which had been a Dutch colony for years.

**READING REVIEW** ★ ★ ★ ★ ★ ★ ★

1. Name three things about Philadelphia that Hamilton admires.
2. What does Hamilton dislike about the Quakers?
3. **Recognizing a point of view.** Hamilton is dismayed to find that Philadelphia has no "public amusements." What does he say in defense of such amusements?

★ ★ ★ ★ ★ ★ ★ ★ ★ ★ ★ ★ ★ ★ ★ ★ ★ ★ ★ ★ ★

---

## ★  6-3    A Slave Describes the Middle Passage  ★

**Introduction**  The horrors endured by slaves on the Middle Passage from Africa to the New World can be most keenly realized by hearing them described firsthand. One slave who eventually wrote an account of his experiences was Gustavus Vasa. Vasa was captured by white slave traders when he was only 11. Young Vasa was industrious, however. After several years he was able to buy his freedom and acquire an education. This selection is from his autobiography.

**Vocabulary**  Before you read the selection, find the meaning of these words in a dictionary: indulge, flog, loathsome.

When I was carried on board I was immediately handled and tossed up, to see if I were sound, by some of the crew. I was now persuaded that I had got into a world of bad spirits, and that they were going to kill me.

I was not long allowed to indulge my grief. I was soon put down under the decks. There, with the stench and crying together, I became so sick and low that I was not able to eat, nor had I the least desire to taste anything. But soon, to my grief, two of the white men offered me something to eat. On my refusing to eat, one of them held me fast by the hands and tied my feet, while the other flogged me severely.

I feared I should be put to death because the white people looked and acted, as I thought, in so savage a manner. I had never seen among any people such instances of brutal cruelty. And this was not only shown towards

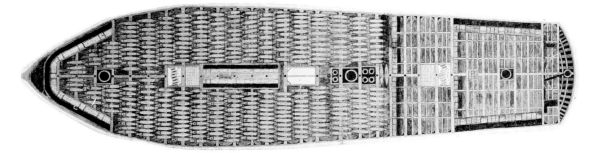

This diagram of the inside of a slave ship shows a loading plan for squeezing as many chained men and women as possible into the available space. Such severe overcrowding was but one part of the inhuman treatment slaves received on the Middle Passage.

us blacks, but also to some of the whites themselves. One white man in particular I saw flogged so unmercifully with a large rope that he died because of it; and they tossed him over the side as they would have done a brute. This made me fear these people the more.

The stench of the hold while we were on the coast was so intolerably loathsome that it was dangerous to remain there for any time. The closeness of the place and the heat of the climate, added to the number in the ship, which was so crowded that each had scarcely room to turn himself, almost suffocated us.

One day, when we had a smooth sea and moderate wind, two of my wearied countrymen, who were chained together, preferring death to such a life of misery, somehow made through the nettings and jumped into the sea. Immediately another quite dejected fellow, who on account of his illness was allowed to be out of irons,

also followed their example. And I believe many more would very soon have done the same if they had not been stopped by the ship's crew, who were instantly alarmed. There was such a noise and confusion among the people of the ship to stop and get the boat to go after the slaves. Two of the wretches were drowned, but they got the other, and afterwards flogged him unmercifully for preferring death to slavery.

Adapted from Gustavus Vasa, *The Interesting Narrative of the Life of Olandah Equiano or Gustavus Vasa, Written by Himself,* 1793.

### READING REVIEW ★ ★ ★ ★ ★ ★ ★

1. What did the white traders do that especially aroused Vasa's fear?
2. Why did several of the slaves jump overboard?
3. **Drawing conclusions.** Why do you think the traders tried to keep the slaves alive, yet at the same time treated them so poorly?

★ ★ ★ ★ ★ ★ ★ ★ ★ ★ ★ ★ ★ ★ ★ ★ ★ ★

---

### ★  6-4    Getting an Education in Virginia    ★

**Introduction** Except among the wealthy, schooling was often hard to come by in the middle and southern colonies. This selection, from the autobiography of Devereux Jarratt, tells of the problems faced by both those who wanted to learn and those who wanted to teach. Yet the selection also tells how the love of learning triumphs over great odds.

Vocabulary Before you read the selection, find the meaning of these
words in a dictionary: scrawl, rhetoric,
harrowed.

At 8 or 9 years old, I was sent to an English school in the neighborhood. And I continued to go to one teacher and another as opportunity arose, though not without great interruptions, till I was 12 or 13. In this time I learned to read the Bible and to write a sorry scrawl, and acquired some knowledge of arithmetic. With this small fund, I left school.

By the time I was 18 or 19, I wished for more knowledge, especially in figures. My friends, I dare say, thought me a scholar—but I knew better. I had not gone far in arithmetic, and was very superficial in the rules I had been hurried through. To understand figures well we reckoned the height of learning. Philosophy, rhetoric, logic, etc. we never heard of. There were no books on such subjects among us. Arithmetic was all and all. To acquire this, I borrowed a plain book. And while the horse, with which I harrowed or ploughed, was grazing an hour or two at noon, I frequently spent the time studying that book. And being now of an age for better discovering the nature of things, I made greater progress in the real knowledge and use of figures in one month than I had done in years while at school. But I had no thought, then, of becoming a teacher. Yet, while at the plough or ax, I seemed out of my element. Neither of these, as time showed, was the business for which I was designed.

I was so well skilled in the division of crops that, you may be sure, the fame of my learning sounded far. One Jacob Moon, living in Albemarle county, about 100 miles from New Kent, had also heard how learned I was. He sent me word that he should be glad to employ me as a schoolmaster, and supposed I might get as many pupils in his neighborhood as would make it worth my while to set up a school. I readily agreed. We soon entered on the business of raising a school. But I quickly discovered that the number of pupils would be far short of what I had been made to expect.

I opened my little school, though the promised income, as might be foreseen, would scarce afford me clothing of the coarsest sort. However, I was content with a little which I could call my own.

Adapted from Devereux Jarratt, *The Life of Devereux Jarratt,* 1806.

## READING REVIEW

1. What did Jarratt think was the most important school subject?
2. Why do you think Jarratt was content as a teacher, even though his income was very small?
3. **Expressing an opinion.** Jarratt says he learned more about figures in one month as an adult than he had in years in school. Do you agree with the saying "Education is wasted on the young"? Why or why not?

## ★ 6-5 Advice on Entering College ★

**Introduction** New Englanders took education seriously, and none more so than the select few who went on to college, often at the age of 13 or 14. This selection is from a letter written by Thomas Shepard, a Massachusetts minister, to his son who was about to enter Harvard College.

**Vocabulary** Before you read the selection, find the meaning of this word in a dictionary: vanity.

  **Chapter 6**

Dear Son,

Remember the end of this turn of your life—your coming into the College. It is to fit you for the most glorious work which God can call you to—the holy ministry.

Remember that though you have spent your time in the vanity of childhood sports and laughter, little minding better things, now, when it is time to enter the College, God and man expect you should put away childish things. So you may not be weary in the work God sets you about, remember these rules.

1. Single out two or three scholars who are most godly, learned, and studious to help you in your studies. Get into the acquaintance of some of your equals, to spend some time with them often discussing the things you hear and read and learn; and also grow acquainted with some that are your superiors, of whom you may often ask questions and from whom you may learn more than by your equals only.

2. Let not your studies be pursued in a disorderly way; but keep a fixed order of studies suited to your own genius and circumstances of things. Fix your course and the season for each kind of study, and allow no other matters or persons to interrupt you.

3. Let difficult studies have the strength and flower of your time and thoughts; and therein allow no difficulty to pass unresolved. But either by your own labor or by asking others, or by both, master it before you pass from it.

4. Choose to confess your ignorance in any matter so that you may be instructed by your tutor or another rather than continue in your ignorance.

5. Suffer not too much to be spent and broken away in visits. Let them be such as may be for your profit in learning some way or other.

Your father,
T. Shepard

Adapted from letter from the Reverend Mr. Thomas Shepard to his son, 1672, in *Publications of the Colonial Society of Massachusetts*, 1913.

## READING REVIEW ★ ★ ★ ★ ★ ★ ★

1. What was the purpose of a college education, according to the letter?
2. According to Shepard, what is the chief purpose of friends in college?
3. **Summarizing.** Rewrite in your own words the five instructions Shepard gives to his son.

★ ★ ★ ★ ★ ★ ★ ★ ★ ★ ★ ★ ★ ★ ★ ★ ★

## ★ 6-6 The Wisdom of Benjamin Franklin ★

**Introduction** Benjamin Franklin was one of the first of this country's many self-made men. Although poor as a boy and lacking much formal schooling, Franklin became one of the most respected men in the world. Franklin learned much in the course of his life about what makes for success. He summed up many of his ideas in brief sayings that people could remember easily. Some are printed here.

**Vocabulary** Before you read the selection, find the meaning of these words in a dictionary: bestir, industry, hinder, frugality, saucy, suppress.

God helps them that help themselves.

But dost thou love life, then do not waste time, for that is the stuff life is made of.

How much more than is necessary do we spend in sleep, forgetting that the sleeping fox catches no poultry, and that there will be sleeping enough in the grave.

Early to bed and early to rise, makes a man healthy, wealthy, and wise.

So what means wishing and hoping for better times? We may make these times better if we bestir ourselves.

At the working man's house, hunger looks in but dares not enter, for industry pays debts.

God gives all things to industry.

Work while it is called today, for you know not how much you may be hindered tomorrow.

Never leave that till tomorrow which you can do today.

So much for industry, my friends, and attention to one's own business; but to this we must add frugality, if we would make our industry more certainly successful. A man may, if he knows not how to save as he gets, keep his nose all his life to the grindstone and die not worth a penny at last.

If you would be wealthy, think of saving as well as of getting.

Away, then, with your expensive follies, and you will not then have so much cause to complain of hard times, heavy taxes, and chargeable families.

You may think, perhaps, that a little tea, or a little punch now and then, diet a little more costly, clothes a little finer, and a little entertainment now and then can be no great matter; but remember, a small leak will sink a great ship.

Many a one, for the sake of finery on the back, have gone with a hungry belly, and half starved their families.

Pride is as loud a beggar as want, and a great deal more saucy.

When you have bought one fine thing, you must buy ten more that your appearance may be all of a piece. It is easier to suppress the first desire than to satisfy all that follow it.

For age and want save while you may; no morning sun lasts a whole day.

Get what you can, and what you get hold; tis the stone that will turn all your lead into gold.

Adapted from Benjamin Franklin, "The Way to Wealth," 1758.

## READING REVIEW ★ ★ ★ ★ ★ ★ ★

1. What is Franklin's policy on spending money on extravagances? Do you agree with him?

2. What reasons does Franklin give for avoiding even one small fine or extravagant item?

3. **Understanding the economy.** What are the two main principles that Franklin says will lead to wealth?

★ ★ ★ ★ ★ ★ ★ ★ ★ ★ ★ ★ ★ ★ ★ ★ ★ ★ ★

Benjamin Franklin made many lasting contributions to American life. For example, he started the colonies' first fire department in Philadelphia.

**Introduction** By the mid–1700s, the colonists had begun to develop a culture of their own. How did life in this new land transform Europeans into a new breed of men and women called Americans? One of the first people to try to answer this question was a Frenchman named Michel–Guillaume Jean de Crèvecoeur. Crèvecoeur had settled in New York and traveled extensively in the colonies in the 1760s. This selection is from his impressions of what he saw.

**Vocabulary** Before you read the selection, find the meaning of these words in a dictionary: servile, haughty, resurrection, epoch, freeholder, vagrant.

The American is a new man, who acts upon new principles. From servile dependence, poverty, and useless labor, he has passed to work of a very different nature, rewarded by an ample living. This is an American.

A European, when he arrives, very suddenly alters his scale. Two hundred miles used to appear a very great distance; it is now but a trifle. He no sooner breathes our air than he forms schemes and begins projects he never would have thought of in his own country. Thus Europeans become Americans.

Let me select one as an example of the rest. He is hired. He goes to work and works moderately. Instead of being employed by a haughty person, he finds himself with his equal. His wages are high. If he behaves with decency and is faithful, he is cared for, and becomes, as it were, a member of the family. He begins to feel the effects of a sort of resurrection. Until now he had not lived, but simply vegetated. He now feels himself a man because he is treated as such.

Judge what a change must arise in the mind and thoughts of this man. He begins to forget his former servitude and dependence. His heart begins to swell and glow. This first swell inspires him with those new thoughts which make a man an American.

He looks around and sees many a prosperous person who but a few years before was as poor as himself. This encourages him much. He begins to form some little scheme, the first he ever formed in his life.

He is encouraged, he has gained friends. He is advised and directed, he feels bold, he purchases some land.

What an epoch in this man's life! He is become a freeholder, from perhaps a German peasant. He is now an American. Instead of being a vagrant, he has a place of residence. And for the first time in his life, he counts for something. For until now he has been a nothing.

This great change has a double effect. It snuffs out all his old European attitudes. He forgets that servility which poverty had taught him. If he is a good man, he forms schemes of future prosperity. He proposes to educate his children better than he has been educated himself. He feels a desire to labor he never felt before.

Adapted from Michel–Guillaume Jean de Crèvecoeur, *Letters from an American Farmer*, 1782.

**READING REVIEW** ★ ★ ★ ★ ★ ★

1. According to Crèvecoeur, what had life been like for people in Europe before they came to America?

2. What was it about life in America that caused colonists to work hard and make plans for their future?

3. **Relating past to present.** Today, poverty is a problem in parts of America, especially in some of our larger cities. If Crèvecoeur were alive today, what do you think he might propose as a solution to poverty?

★ ★ ★ ★ ★ ★ ★ ★ ★ ★ ★ ★ ★ ★ ★ ★

# Unit 3

# The Struggle for Independence

**Chapter**

# 7 Crisis in the Colonies (1745–1775)

★ **7-1 Friendship With the Mohawks** ★

**Introduction** English settlers often had conflicts with Native Americans. Unlike French fur traders, English settlers cleared and farmed the land. This threatened the Indian way of life. One English trader, William Johnson, won the respect of the Indians. He convinced the Mohawks to support the English in their struggle with the French. This painting shows a meeting between Johnson and the Mohawks.

**READING REVIEW** ★ ★ ★ ★ ★ ★

1. Does this appear to be a friendly meeting? Explain.
2. What do you suppose the buildings on either side of the house are for?
3. **Using visual evidence.** What can you conclude about relations between the English and the Mohawks from this painting?

★ ★ ★ ★ ★ ★ ★ ★ ★ ★ ★ ★ ★ ★ ★ ★ ★ ★

**Introduction**   In 1753, young George Washington was sent on a mission to warn the French to pull back their forces from the Ohio Valley. Washington's account of the trip reveals much about both French and English attitudes towards the Indians who were caught in the middle of the struggle between the two great European nations. This selection is from Washington's report to the governor of Virginia.

**Vocabulary**   Before you read the selection, find the meaning of these words in a dictionary: dispatch, complaisant.

**Wednesday, October 31, 1753** I was appointed by the Honorable Robert Dinwiddie, Governor of Virginia, to visit and deliver a letter to the commandant of the French forces on the Ohio.

**November 25** About three o'clock this evening the Half-King Jeskakate came to town. I went up and invited him privately to my tent and asked him to relate some of the particulars of his journey to the French commandant, and reception there, also to give me an account of the ways and distance.

**November 26** As I had orders to make all possible dispatch, I told him that my business would not allow delay. He told me that he could not consent to our going without a guard for fear some accident should befall us. Accordingly he gave orders to King Shingiss, who was present, and two men of their nation to be ready to set out with us next morning.

We set out about nine o'clock with the Half-King, White Thunder, and the Hunter.

**December 7** At eleven o'clock we set out for the fort. We were prevented from arriving there till the eleventh by excessive rains, snows, and bad traveling through many mires and swamps.

**December 12** I prepared early to meet the French commander.

I asked the commander by what authority he had made prisoners of several of our English subjects. He told me that the country belonged to them; that no Englishman had a right to trade upon those waters; and that he had orders to make every person prisoner who tried it.

**December 15** The commandant ordered a plentiful store of provisions to be put on board our canoe. He appeared to be extremely complaisant, though he was using every plan which he could invent to set our own Indians against us. He tried to prevent their going till after our departure, using presents, rewards, and everything which could be suggested by him or his officers. I can't say that ever in my life I suffered so much anxiety as I did in this affair.

**December 16** The French were not slack in their inventions to keep the Indians this day also, but I urged and insisted that the Half-King set off with us as he had promised.

Adapted from *The Writings of George Washington*, ed. Worthington C. Ford, 1889.

**R E A D I N G   R E V I E W** ★ ★ ★ ★ ★ ★ ★

1. What gesture did the Half-King make to Washington that showed his concern?

2. How did the French commander justify the arrest of several Englishman?

3. **Analyzing a primary source.** What evidence is there in Washington's report that both the French and the British used the Indians for their own purposes?

★ ★ ★ ★ ★ ★ ★ ★ ★ ★ ★ ★ ★ ★ ★ ★ ★

**Introduction** The battle on the Plains of Abraham was one of the great battles of history. Not only did its outcome determine whether Canada was to be British or French. It also pitted against each other two great generals —Englishman James Wolfe, just 32 years old, and a French nobleman, the Marquis de Montcalm. This selection about the encounter is from *Montcalm and Wolfe,* written by historian Francis Parkman in 1884.

**Vocabulary** Before you read the selection, find the meaning of these words in a dictionary: detachment, infantry, ardor, fugitive.

Montcalm had passed a troubled night. At daybreak he heard the sound of cannon above the town. He had sent an officer nearer Quebec, with orders to bring him word at once should anything unusual happen. But no word came, and about six o'clock he mounted and rode there.

Montcalm was amazed at what he saw. He had expected a detachment, and he found an army. Full in sight before him stretched the lines of Wolfe: the close ranks of the English infantry, a silent wall of red. Fight he must, for Wolfe was now in a position to cut off all his supplies. Montcalm's men were full of ardor, and he resolved to attack before their ardor cooled. He spoke a few words to them in his keen, strong way.

"I remember very well how he looked," one of the Canadians, then a boy of eighteen, used to say in his old age. "He rode a black or dark bay horse along the front of our lines, brandishing his sword, as if to excite us to do our duty. He wore a coat with wide sleeves, which fell back as he raised his arm, and showed the white linen of the wristband."

Wolfe himself was everywhere. How cool he was and how his followers loved him. It was toward ten o'clock when, from the high ground on the right of the line, Wolfe saw that the crisis was near. The French came on rapidly, uttering loud shouts, and firing as soon as they were within range. The British advanced a few rods, then halted and stood still.

When the French were within 40 paces, the word of command rang out, and a crash of musketry answered all along the line. When the smoke rose, a miserable sight was revealed: the ground was strewn with dead and wounded. The advancing French stopped short and turned into a frantic mob.

The order was given to charge. Wolfe himself led the charge. A shot shattered his wrist. He wrapped his handkerchief about it and kept on. Another shot struck him, and he still advanced, when a third lodged in his breast. He staggered, and sat on the ground. Lieutenant Brown, of the grenadiers, one Henderson, a volunteer in

The nobility with which General James Wolfe died on the Plains of Abraham quickly became legendary. His last moments were celebrated by artists as well as historians. This painting, Benjamin West's *Death of General Wolfe,* was done in 1770.

the same company, and a private soldier carried him in their arms to the rear. He begged them to lay him down. They did so, and asked if he would have a surgeon. "There's no need," he answered. "It's all over with me. Go, one of you, to Colonel Burton," ordered the dying man. "Tell him to march Webb's regiment down to Charles River, to cut off their retreat from the bridge." Then, turning on his side, he murmured, "Now, God be praised, I will die in peace!" and in a few moments his gallant soul had fled.

Montcalm, still on horseback, was carried with the tide of fugitives towards the town. As he approached the walls a shot passed through his body. He kept his seat; two soldiers supported him, one on each side, and led his horse through the St. Louis gate. On the open space within, among the excited crowd, were several women, drawn, no doubt, by eagerness to know the result of the fight. One of them recognized him, saw the streaming blood, and shrieked, "Oh my God! my God! The Marquis is killed!" "It's nothing, it's nothing," replied the dying man. "Don't be troubled for me, my good friends."

Adapted from Francis Parkman, *Montcalm and Wolfe*, 1884.

## READING REVIEW ★ ★ ★ ★ ★ ★ ★

1. Why was Montcalm surprised when he arrived at Quebec?

2. According to Parkman, why did Montcalm decide he had to fight Wolfe?

3. **Supporting generalizations.** (a) Based on this account, how would you describe each of the two men? (b) Support your generalization with specific examples.

★ ★ ★ ★ ★ ★ ★ ★ ★ ★ ★ ★ ★ ★ ★ ★ ★ ★

## ★ 7-4 Indians Treat Captives With Kindness ★

**Introduction** English colonists did much to provoke the anger of Native Americans. Many, such as Pontiac and those he led, eventually fought back. Yet even in the midst of open hostility, many Indians remained friendly towards the colonists. In this selection, William Smith reports that the Indians he fought against in Pontiac's War treated the English prisoners they had taken more like guests than like enemy captives.

**Vocabulary** Before you read the selection, find the meaning of these words in a dictionary: torrents, provisions, persisted.

They delivered up their beloved captives with the utmost reluctance. They shed torrents of tears over them, recommending them to the care and protection of the French commanding officer. Their regard for the prisoners continued all the time they remained in camp. They visited from day to day and brought them corn, skins, and horses, accompanied with other presents and all the marks of the most sincere and tender affection.

Nay, they did not stop there. When the army marched, some of the Indians asked for and obtained leave to accompany their former captives all the way to Fort Pitt, and employed themselves in hunting and bringing provisions for them on the road.

A young Mingo carried this still further. A young woman of Virginia was among the captives, to whom he had formed so strong an attachment as to call her his wife. He ignored all warnings of the great danger to which he exposed himself by approaching the frontiers. He followed her, at the risk of being killed by the surviving relations of many unfortunate persons who had been captured or scalped by those of his nation.

Among the children who had been carried off young and had long lived with the Indians, it is not to be expected that any marks of joy would appear on being restored to their parents or relatives. They had been accustomed to look upon the Indians as the only connections they had. And they had been tenderly treated by them and spoke their language. Therefore, it is no wonder that they parted from the savages with tears. But it must not be denied that there were even some grown persons who showed an unwillingness to return.

Adapted from William Smith, *An Historical Account of an Expedition Against the Ohio Indians, in the Year 1764, Under the Command of Henry Bouquet, Esq.*

### READING REVIEW ★ ★ ★ ★ ★ ★ ★

1. What did the Indians do that showed their affection for their prisoners?
2. How did the children react to being united with their parents? Why?
3. **Relating cause and effect.** What effect did the Indians' treatment have on the colonists who were their prisoners?

★ ★ ★ ★ ★ ★ ★ ★ ★ ★ ★ ★ ★ ★ ★ ★ ★ ★

## ★  7-5  Paul Revere on the Boston Massacre  ★

**Introduction**  Copies of Paul Revere's engraving of the Boston Massacre, shown here, did much to arouse colonists' anger toward the British. One reason for its powerful effect was a poem Revere wrote to accompany his illustration. Both the poem and the picture presented the massacre in a way that emphasized the gruesomeness of what the British had done. Revere's poem follows on page 498. The words P--n and C---st are thinly disguised names of two of the British involved in the incident.

**Vocabulary**  Before you read the selection, find the meaning of these words in a dictionary: hallowed, aught, appease, venal, execrations.

# Unhappy Boston!

Unhappy Boston! see thy sons deplore
Thy hallowed walks besmeared with
    guiltless gore:
While faithless P--n and his savage
    bands
With murderous hatred stretch their
    bloody hands;
Like fierce barbarians grinning o'er
    their prey
Approve the slaughter and enjoy the
    day.
If scalding drops, from rage, from an-
    guish wrung,
If speechless sorrow laboring for a
    tongue,
Or if a weeping world can aught ap-
    pease
The weeping ghosts of victims such as
    these;
The patriots' flowing tears for each are
    shed,
A glorious tribute which embalms the
    dead.
But know, Fate summons to that awful
    goal,

Where justice strips the murderer of
    his soul:
Should venal C---st, the scandal of the
    land,
Snatch the relentless villain from her
    hand,
Keen execrations on this plate in-
    scribed
Shall reach a judge who never can be
    bribed.

Adapted from Paul Revere, "Bloody Boston," in Burton
Stevenson, *Poems of American History,* 1908.

### READING REVIEW ★ ★ ★ ★ ★ ★ ★

1. What feelings and attitudes does the poem say the British had at the time of the Boston Massacre?

2. According to this poem, what role did the colonists play in the massacre?

3. **Recognizing propaganda.** Propaganda is the promotion or distortion of information in favor of a particular cause. What about the way Revere describes the Boston Massacre makes his poem qualify as propaganda?

★ ★ ★ ★ ★ ★ ★ ★ ★ ★ ★ ★ ★ ★ ★ ★ ★ ★ ★ ★ ★

## ★ 7-6 Philadelphia's Tea Protest ★

**Introduction** The Boston Tea Party is well known. Yet other colonial cities also took bold measures against the Tea Act of 1773. This letter was sent by angry colonists in Philadelphia to the captain of a British tea ship. In it they threatened, among other things, to tar and feather* the captain if he should land his cargo.

**Vocabulary** Before you read the selection, find the meaning of these words in a dictionary: combustible, pitch, diabolical, gauntlet, decant.

---

*Tarring and feathering was a measure frequently used by colonists to strike back at British officials. Hot tar was poured over the victim, often burning him badly. Then feathers were stuck in the tar to give him the appearance of a giant chicken, and so humiliate him.

Sir:

We are informed that you have unwisely taken charge of a quantity of tea which has been sent out by the East India Company as a trial of American virtue and resolution.

Now, your cargo, on your arrival here, will most assuredly bring you into hot water. As you are perhaps a stranger to these parts, we have concluded to advise you of the present situation of affairs in Philadelphia. Thus, you may stop short in your dangerous errand. You can secure your ship against the rafts of combustible matter which may be set on fire and turned loose against her. And more than all this, you may preserve your own person from the pitch and feathers that are prepared for you.

In the first place, we must tell you that the Pennsylvanians are, to a man, passionately fond of freedom, the birthright of Americans, and at all events are determined to enjoy it.

That they sincerely believe no power on the face of the earth has a right to tax them without their consent.

That, in their opinion, the tea in your custody is designed by the ministry to enforce such a tax, which they will undoubtedly oppose.

You are sent out on a diabolical service. And if you are so foolish and stubborn as to complete your voyage by bringing your ship to anchor in this port, you may run such a gauntlet as will cause you in your last moments most heartily to curse those who have made you the dupe of their greed and ambition.

What think you, Captain, of a halter around your neck—ten gallons of liquid tar decanted on your head—with the feathers of a dozen wild geese laid over that to enliven your appearance?

Only think seriously of this—and fly to the place from whence you came—fly without hesitation—without the formality of a protest—and above all, Captain Ayres, let us advise you to fly without the wild geese features.

Your friends to serve,
The Committee of Tarring and Feathering

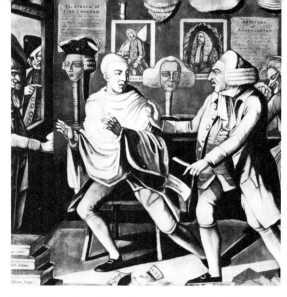

Colonists enjoyed a chance to see the British humiliated. This cartoon shows a surprised British officer being thrown out of a barber shop, wigless and half-shaven. The barber had refused to finish the shave when he discovered that his customer was a British official.

Adapted from Frederick D. Stone in *Pennsylvania Magazine of History and Biography,* 1891.

## READING REVIEW ★ ★ ★ ★ ★ ★

1. What did the Philadelphians threaten to do to the captain's ship?
2. Why did they oppose the importation of the captain's tea?
3. **Drawing conclusions.** (a) What does this letter tell you about colonial feelings toward the British? (b) Do you think Captain Ayres brought his tea into Philadelphia?

★ ★ ★ ★ ★ ★ ★ ★ ★ ★ ★ ★ ★ ★ ★ ★ ★

Chapter

# 8 The American Revolution (1775–1783)

## ★ 8-1 Glory on Bunker Hill ★

**Introduction** American troops were proud of the showing they made in the Battle of Bunker Hill. Although they lost the battle, they had shown that they could hold their own against the British. The glory that soldiers found on Bunker Hill became the subject of this popular song.

**Vocabulary** Before you read the selection, find the meaning of these words in a dictionary: veteran, sire.

# The Sword of Bunker Hill

He lay upon his dying bed;
His eye was growing dim,
When with a feeble voice he call'd
His weeping son to him:
"Weep not, my boy!" the veteran said,
"I bow to Heaven's high will,—
But quickly from yon antlers bring
The Sword of Bunker Hill;
But quickly from yon antlers bring
The Sword of Bunker Hill."

The sword was brought, the soldier's
    eye
Lit with a sudden flame;
And as he grasped the ancient blade,
He murmured Warren's name:
Then said, "My boy, I leave you gold,—
But what is richer still,
I leave you, mark me, mark me now—
The Sword of Bunker Hill;
I leave you, mark me, mark me now—
The Sword of Bunker Hill.

"'Twas on that dread, immortal day,
I dared the Briton's band,
A captain raised this blade on me—
I tore it from his hand;
And while the glorious battle raged,
It lightened freedom's will—
For boy, the God of freedom blessed
The Sword of Bunker Hill;

For, boy, the God of freedom blessed
The Sword of Bunker Hill.

"Oh, keep the sword!"—his accents
    broke—
A smile—and he was dead!
His wrinkled hand still grasped the
    blade
Upon that dying bed.
The son remains; the sword remains—
Its glory growing still—
And twenty millions bless the sire,
And Sword of Bunker Hill;
And twenty millions bless the sire,
And Sword of Bunker Hill.

A Revolutionary War song.

**READING REVIEW** ★ ★ ★ ★ ★ ★ ★

1. How did the dying soldier come to own the sword of Bunker Hill?
2. What did the soldier mean when he said to his son that the sword of Bunker Hill was "richer than gold"?
3. **Using a song as historical evidence.** The songwriter says "the God of freedom blessed the Sword of Bunker Hill." What attitudes about the war can you infer from this statement?

★ ★ ★ ★ ★ ★ ★ ★ ★ ★ ★ ★ ★ ★ ★ ★ ★ ★

---

## ★ 8-2    How the Declaration Was Written    ★

**Introduction** The Declaration of Independence is one of the most important documents in our country's history. Americans celebrate its signing yearly, on July 4. Yet its origins are humble, little different from those of many other papers written by committees. In this letter written later in his life, Boston patriot John Adams gives us an insider's view of how the Declaration came to be.

**Vocabulary** Before you read the selection, find the meaning of these words in a dictionary: felicity, explicit, oratory, philippic, hackneyed.

You inquire why so young a man as Mr. Jefferson was placed at the head of the committee for preparing a Declaration of Independence? I answer: Mr. Jefferson came into Congress in June

1775 and brought with him a reputation for literature, science, and a happy talent of composition. Writings of his were handed about, remarkable for the peculiar felicity of expression. Though a silent member in Congress, he was so prompt, frank, explicit, and decisive upon committees and in conversation—not even Samuel Adams was more so—that he soon seized upon my heart. And upon this occasion I gave him my vote and did all in my power to convince the others.

The subcommittee met. Jefferson proposed to me to make the draft. I said, "I will not." "You should do it." "Oh! no." "Why will you not? You ought to do it." "I will not," I replied. "Why?" "Reasons enough." "What can be your reasons?" "Reason first, you are a Virginian, and a Virginian ought to appear at the head of this business. Reason second, I am obnoxious, suspected, and unpopular. You are very much otherwise. Reason third, you can write ten times better than I can." "Well," said Jefferson, "if you are decided, I will do as well as I can." "Very well. When you have drawn it up, we will have a meeting."

A meeting we accordingly had, and looked the paper over. I was delighted with its high tone and the flights of oratory with which it abounded, especially that concerning Negro slavery, which, though I knew his Southern brethren would never allow to pass in Congress, I certainly never would oppose. There were other expressions which I would not have inserted if I had drawn it up, particularly that which called the king a tyrant. I thought this too personal, for I never believed George to be a tyrant in disposition and in nature. I always believed him to be deceived by his advisers on both sides of the Atlantic, and cruel in his official capacity only. I thought the expression too passionate, and too much like a scolding, for so grave and solemn a document. But I do

After debating Jefferson's proposed Declaration of Independence for two days, Congress voted to accept it. This painting shows that historic occasion.

not now remember that I made or suggested a single alteration.

We reported it to the committee of five. It was read, and I do not remember that Franklin or Sherman criticized anything. We were all in haste. Congress was impatient and the document was reported, as I believe, in Jefferson's handwriting, as he first drew it. Congress cut off about a quarter of it, as I expected they would. But they cut some of the best of it, and left all that was objectionable, if anything in it was. I have long wondered that the original draft had not been published. I suppose the reason is the vehement philippic against Negro slavery.

As you justly observe, there is not an idea in it but what had been hackneyed in Congress for two years before. The substance of it is contained in the declaration of rights and the violation of those rights in the Journals of Congress in 1774. Indeed, the essence of it is contained in a pamphlet, voted and printed by the town of Boston, before the first Congress met, composed by James Otis, as I suppose, in one of his lucid intervals, and pruned and polished by Samuel Adams.

Adapted from *The Works of John Adams*, 1850.

1. According to Adams, where did Jefferson get the ideas in the Declaration of Independence?
2. Why did Adams want Jefferson to write the draft of the Declaration of Independence?

3. **Drawing conclusions.** Adams does not say explicitly what was cut from Jefferson's first version of the Declaration. Yet he gives enough clues that you should be able to figure out one of the cut sections. What was this?

★ ★ ★ ★ ★ ★ ★ ★ ★ ★ ★ ★ ★ ★ ★ ★ ★ ★

## ★ 8-3 A Loyalist Is Tarred and Feathered ★

**Introduction** The treatment suffered by Loyalists at the hands of their fellow colonists was often harsh. One popular means of harrassment was tarring and feathering. The letter below, written by Ann Hulton, a Loyalist woman from Boston, gives a particularly graphic account of a tarring and feathering.

**Vocabulary** Before you read the selection, find the meaning of this word in a dictionary: magistrate.

The most shocking cruelty was exercised a few nights ago upon a poor old man, one Malcolm. A quarrel was picked with him. He was afterward taken and tarred and feathered. There's no law that knows a punishment for the greatest crimes beyond what this is, of cruel torture. And this instance exceeds any other before it. He was stripped naked on one of the severest cold nights this winter. His body was covered all over with tar, then with feathers. His arms were dislocated in tearing off his clothes. He was dragged in a cart, with thousands attending, some beating him with clubs and knocking him out of the cart, then in again. They gave him several severe whippings, at different parts of the town. This spectacle of horror and sportive cruelty went on for about five hours.

The unhappy wretch they say behaved with the greatest bravery. When under torture they demanded of him to curse his masters, the king, governors, etc., which they could not make him

do. He still cried, "Curse all traitors." They brought him to the gallows and put a rope about his neck saying they would hang him. He said he wished they would, but that they could not for God was above the Devil.

They owe him a grudge for some things, particularly, he was with Governor Tryon in the Battle with the Regulators. The Governor has declared that he was of great service to him in that affair, by his courageous spirit encountering the greatest dangers.

Governor Tryon had sent him a gift of ten guineas just before this inhuman treatment. He has a wife and family and an aged father and mother who, they say, saw the spectacle which no indifferent person can mention without horror.

These few instances among many serve to show the wretched state of government and the barbarisms of the times. There's no magistrate that dare stop the outrages. No person is secure.

Adapted from Ann Hulton, *Letters of a Loyalist: Lady Ann Hulton* (Cambridge, Mass.: Harvard University Press, 1927).

1. What did the Patriots hope to achieve by this tarring and feathering?
2. Why was Malcolm in particular singled out to be a victim?
3. **Supporting generalizations.** (a) What attitude does Ann Hulton express toward the Patriot movement? (b) Do you think the evidence she cites is strong enough to support her conclusion?

★ ★ ★ ★ ★ ★ ★ ★ ★ ★ ★ ★ ★ ★ ★ ★ ★ ★

**Introduction** Without the help of the Marquis de Lafayette and the French, the colonists might not have won their fight for freedom. The young Marquis who led the French troops was an extraordinary man—enthusiastic, idealistic, warm, and brave. He was just 20 years old when he came over to help Washington in 1777. This letter, written to his wife shortly after his arrival in the colonies, gives much insight into American life as well as into Lafayette's character.

**Vocabulary** Before you read the selection find the meaning of these words in a dictionary: prevail, higgling, adieu.

Charleston, June 19, 1777

My last letter to you, my dear love, has informed you that I arrived safely in this country, after having suffered a little from seasickness during the first weeks of the voyage.

I will now tell you about the country and its inhabitants. They are as agreeable as my enthusiasm had painted them. Simplicity of manners, kindness, love of country and of liberty, and a delightful equality everywhere prevail. The wealthiest man and the poorest are on a level. Although there are some large fortunes, I challenge anyone to discover the slightest difference between the manners of these two classes respectively toward each other.

I first saw the country life at the house of Major Benjamin Huger. I am now in the city, where everything is very much after the English fashion, except that there is more simplicity, equality, friendliness, and courtesy here than in England. The city of Charleston is one of the handsomest and best built, and its inhabitants among the most agreeable, that I have ever seen. The American women are very pretty, simple in their manners, and exhibit a neatness which is everywhere cultivated even more studiously than in England.

What most charms me is that all the citizens are like brothers. In America there are no poor, nor even what we call peasantry. Each individual has his own honest property and the same rights as the most wealthy landowner. The inns are very different from those of Europe. The host and hostess sit at table with you and do the honors of a comfortable meal. And on going away you pay your bill without higgling.

Considering the pleasant life I lead in this country, my sympathy with the people, which makes me feel as much at ease in their society as if I had known them for 20 years, the similarity between their mode of thinking and my own, and my love of liberty and of glory, one might suppose that I am very happy. But you are not with me; my friends are not with me; and there is no happiness for me far from you and them. I am impatient beyond measure to hear from you.

The night is far advanced, and the heat dreadful. I am devoured by insects; so, you see, the best countries have their disadvantages. Adieu.

Lafayette

Adapted from Marquis de Lafayette, "Letter to his Wife," June 19, 1777, in *America Visited*, ed. Edith I. Coombs (New York: Book League of America, 1946).

**R E A D I N G   R E V I E W** ★ ★ ★ ★ ★ ★ ★

1. How does Lafayette describe American women?

2. What does Lafayette like most about life in the colonies?

3. **Analyzing a primary source.** What clues are there in this letter about why Lafayette decided to support the colonists' cause?

★ ★ ★ ★ ★ ★ ★ ★ ★ ★ ★ ★ ★ ★ ★ ★ ★

**Introduction** Many Native Americans may have wanted to stay neutral in the conflict between Britain and the colonies. But this was not always easy to do. Both sides pressured the Indians to support them. George Washington wrote this letter to the Passamaquoddy Indians of Maine, urging them to support the colonial cause.

**Vocabulary** Before you read the selection, find the meaning of these words in a dictionary: allies, covenant, councilor.

Brothers of Passamaquodai:

I am glad to hear by Major Shaw that you accepted the chain of friendship which I sent you last February at Cambridge and that you are determined to keep it bright and unbroken. When I first heard that you refused to send any of your warriors to my assistance when called upon by our brother of St. Johns, I did not know what to think. I was afraid some enemy had turned your hearts against me. But I am since informed that all your young men were hunting, which was the reason of their not coming. This has made my mind easy. And I hope you will always in future join with your brothers of St. Johns and Penobscott when required.

Brothers, I have a piece of news to tell you which I hope you will attend to. Our enemy the King of Great Britain tried to stir up all the Indians from Canada to South Carolina against us. But our brothers of the six nations and their allies the Shawanese and Delawares would not listen to the advice of the messengers sent among them. They kept fast hold of our covenant chain. The Cherokees and the southern tribes were foolish enough to listen to them and to take up the hatchet against us. Upon this our warriors went into their country and burnt their houses, destroyed their corn, and forced them to sue for peace.

Now brothers, never let the king's wicked councilor turn your hearts against me and your brothers of this country, but bear in mind what I told you last February and what I told you now.

In token of my friendship I send you this from my army on the banks of the great River Delaware this 24th day of December, 1776.

George Washington

Adapted from George Washington, "Letter to the Passamaquoddy," December 24, 1776.

**R E A D I N G   R E V I E W** ★ ★ ★ ★ ★ ★ ★

1. What was Washington worried about?
2. Why did colonists burn Cherokee homes and destroy their crops?
3. **Relating cause and effect.** What do you think Washington's motive was for telling the story of the Cherokees in this letter?

★ ★ ★ ★ ★ ★ ★ ★ ★ ★ ★ ★ ★ ★ ★ ★ ★ ★

★　8-6　A Slave's Support for the Patriots　★

**Introduction** The brilliant young slave Phillis Wheatley was widely known for her fine poems, many of which supported the colonists' struggle against Britain. Wheatley had been brought from Africa as a child. She had long supported the demand for liberty, as this poem written in 1773 shows.

Vocabulary  Before you read the selection, find the meaning of these
words in a dictionary: grievance, unre-
dressed, wanton, tyranny, sway.

To the Right Honourable William, Earl
of Dartmouth, His Majesty's Principal
Secretary of State for North America,
and company.

No more America in mournful strain
Of wrongs, and grievance unredress'd
    complain,
No longer shall thou dread the iron
    chain,
Which wanton Tyranny with lawless
    hand Has made,
And which it meant to enslave the
    land.

Should you, my lord, while you pursue
    my song,
Wonder from when my love of Freedom
    sprung,
Whence flow these wishes for the com-
    mon good,
By feeling hearts alone best under-
    stood,
I, young in life, by seeming cruel fate
Was snatched from Afric's fancied
    happy seat:
What pangs excruciating must molest,
What sorrows labour in my parent's
    breast?
Steeled was the soul and by no misery
    moved
That from a father seized his babe be-
    loved.

Most blacks, both slave and free, supported the
Patriots in their revolt against Britain. During the
course of the war, about 5,000 blacks fought for
the Patriot cause. This portrait of a free black
sailor was done in 1779.

Such, such my case. And can I then
    but pray
Others may never feel tyrannic sway?

Adapted from Phillis Wheatley, *Poems on Various
Subjects*, 1773.

### R E A D I N G  R E V I E W ★ ★ ★ ★ ★ ★ ★

1. What do you think the poet means when
she talks of "the iron chain" which is
"meant to enslave the land"?

2. What experience is she referring to when
she talks of being "snatched from Afric's
. . . happy seat"?

3. **Using a poem as a primary source.**
What reason does Wheatley give here for
supporting the Patriots' cause?

★ ★ ★ ★ ★ ★ ★ ★ ★ ★ ★ ★ ★ ★ ★ ★ ★

## ★  8-7  An Eyewitness at Yorktown  ★

**Introduction**  The surrender of General Cornwallis at Yorktown, Virginia,
did not actually end the Revolution. It
would be a while before the British
would agree to negotiate terms for
peace. Yet both sides were keenly
aware of the significance of the event.
British pride and morale had been dealt
a severe blow—perhaps a mortal one.

This account of the surrender is from
the diary of Dr. James Thacher, a Massachusetts doctor who served as a
surgeon in the colonial army.

**Vocabulary**  Before you read the selection, find the meaning of these
words in a dictionary: chagrin, mortification, sullen, divested.

This print gives a sense of the festive air with which colonists greeted Cornwallis's surrender at Yorktown. American troops are shown in green, French forces in blue, and the British in red. The yellow piles represent the weapons of the British.

October 19, 1781

This is to us a most glorious day; but to the English, one of bitter chagrin and disappointment.

At about twelve o'clock, the combined army was arranged and drawn up in two lines extending more than a mile in length. The Americans were drawn up in a line on the right side of the road, and the French occupied the left.

The Americans were not all in uniform, nor was their dress so neat. Yet they exhibited an erect, soldierly air, and every face beamed with satisfaction and joy. The crowd of spectators from the country was enormous—in point of numbers probably equal to the military—but universal silence and order prevailed.

It was about two o'clock when the captive army advanced through the line formed for their reception. Every eye was prepared to gaze on Lord Cornwallis, the object of peculiar interest. But he disappointed our anxious expectations. Pretending illness, he made General O'Hara his substitute as the leader of his army.

The British army was conducted into a large field, where it was intended they should ground their arms. The royal troops, while marching through the line formed by our army, exhibited a decent and neat appearance as respects arms and clothing. Their commander had opened his store and directed every soldier to be furnished with a new suit prior to the surrender.

But in their line of march we remarked a disorderly and unsoldierly conduct. Their step was irregular and their ranks frequently broken. But it was in the field, when they came to the last act of the drama, that the spirit and pride of the British soldier was put to the severest test. Here their mortification could not be concealed. Some of the platoon officers appeared to be exceedingly chagrined when given the word, "Ground arms." And I am a witness that they performed this duty in a very unofficerlike manner, and that many of the soldiers showed a sullen temper, throwing their arms on the pile with violence, as if determined to render them useless.

After having grounded their arms and divested themselves of their equipment, the captive troops were conducted back to Yorktown.

Adapted from James Thacher, *Military Journal During the American Revolution*, 1854.

### READING REVIEW ★ ★ ★ ★ ★ ★ ★

1. How did the American and French troops look at the surrender ceremonies?
2. What in the appearance or behavior of the British showed their feelings.?
3. **Making inferences.** (a) What was the official reason for Cornwallis's absence from the ceremonies? (b) What does Thacher think of this reason? (c) Why do you think Cornwallis was absent?

★ ★ ★ ★ ★ ★ ★ ★ ★ ★ ★ ★ ★ ★ ★ ★ ★ ★

## Chapter 9 Creating a Government (1776–1790)

### ★ 9-1 The Articles of Confederation ★

**Introduction** After declaring their independence, the new states were wary of a strong national government. The first constitution they approved, the Articles of Confederation, guaranteed certain powers to the states and restricted those granted to the new national government. Selections from the articles appear here.

**Vocabulary** Before reading the selection, find the meaning of these words in a dictionary: sovereignty, confederation.

**Article I.** The style of this confederacy shall be "The United States of America."

**Article II.** Each state retains its sovereignty, freedom, and independence. Every power and right which is

In the days of the Articles of Confederation, settlers headed west in large numbers. Indians grew alarmed as settlers occupied land that had been theirs. The Iroquois chief called Cornplanter, shown here, wrote several letters to General Washington protesting the situation.

not expressly delegated to the United States in Congress assembled.

**Article III.** The said states hereby enter into a firm league of friendship with each other, for their common defense, the security of their liberties, and their mutual and general welfare. They agree to bind themselves to assist each other against all attacks made upon them, or any of them, on account of religion, trade, or any other pretense whatever.

Adapted from *Articles of Confederation*, 1781.

**R E A D I N G   R E V I E W** ★ ★ ★ ★ ★ ★ ★

1. What powers and rights did the articles grant to the states?
2. What were the purposes for which the new confederation was formed?
3. **Ranking.** (a) What reason for forming a confederation seems to have been most important to those who wrote the Articles? (b) What in the recent history of the states might account for this?

★ ★ ★ ★ ★ ★ ★ ★ ★ ★ ★ ★ ★ ★ ★ ★ ★ ★ ★

---

## ★   9-2   No Taxation Without Representation   ★

**Introduction** Southern delegates to the Constitutional Convention wanted to include slaves in their population count so that the South could have more representatives in Congress. Yet slaves had no political rights. Many northerners felt that this was unfair. But some northern governments had exploited blacks in a similar fashion. In Massachusetts, for example, blacks could not vote, but free blacks had to pay taxes. This situation was corrected in 1783, largely as a result of a petition written by Paul Cuffe, a free black. This selection is from Cuffe's petition.

**Vocabulary** Before you read the selection, find the meaning of these words in a dictionary: petition, estate, depressed.

The petition of several poor Negroes and mulattoes who live in the town of Dartmouth humbly shows that, being chiefly of the African race and by reason of long bondage and hard slavery, we have been deprived of the profits of our labor or the advantage of inheriting estates from our parents as our neighbors the white people do. And some of us have not long enjoyed our own freedom. Yet of late, we have been and now are taxed.

We understand that, if continued, this will reduce us to a state of beggary whereby we shall become a burden to others if this is not stopped by the intervention of your justice and power.

Your petitioners further show that we believe ourselves to be wronged, in that while we are not allowed the privilege of freemen of the state, having no vote or influence in the election of those that tax us, yet many of our color (as is well known) have cheerfully entered the field of battle in the defense of the common cause.

We most humbly request therefore that you would take our unhappy case into your serious consideration and in your wisdom and power grant us relief from taxation while under our present depressed circumstances.

Adapted from a manuscript in the Archives Division, Massachusetts Historical Society.

**R E A D I N G   R E V I E W** ★ ★ ★ ★ ★ ★ ★

1. Why did Cuffe feel that it was unjust to tax blacks?
2. What does Cuffe say will eventually happen if blacks are forced to pay taxes?
3. **Understanding economic ideas.** Why, according to Cuffe's petition, did blacks suffer more severe financial hardship than whites after the Revolution?

★ ★ ★ ★ ★ ★ ★ ★ ★ ★ ★ ★ ★ ★ ★ ★ ★ ★ ★

**Introduction** Some of the great strengths of our Constitution came out of the compromises made. As a result, however, few delegates were happy with all parts of the document. In an attempt to stir up enthusiasm, Benjamin Franklin made this speech to convention delegates on the day they gathered to sign the Constitution.

**Vocabulary** Before you read the selection, find the meaning of these words in a dictionary: constituents, integrity, unanimously.

Mr. President, I confess that there are several parts of this Constitution which I do not at present approve. But I am not sure I shall never approve them. For, having lived long, I have experienced many instances of being obliged, by better information or fuller consideration, to change my opinions. The older I grow, the more apt I am to doubt my own judgment, and to pay more respect to the judgment of others.

In these sentiments, sir, I agree to this Consitution, with all its faults, if they are such, because I think a general government is necessary for us.

I doubt, too, whether any other convention would be able to make a better constitution. For, when you assemble a number of men to have the advantage of their joint wisdom, you inevitably assemble with those men all their prejudices, their passions, their errors of opinion, their local interests, and their selfish views. From such an assembly can a perfect production be expected? It therefore astonishes me, sir, to find this Constitution approaching so near to perfection as it does. Thus I consent, sir, to this Constitution, because I expect no better, and because I am not sure that it is not the best.

The opinions I have of its errors I sacrifice to the public good. I have never whispered a syllable of them abroad. If every one of us, in returning to our constituents, were to report the objections he has to it, and try to gain partisans in support of them, we might prevent its being generally received. Much of the strength and efficiency of any government, in securing happiness for the people, depends on the general opinion of the goodness of the government, as well as of the wisdom and integrity of its governors.

I hope, therefore, that for our own sakes, as a part of the people, and for the sake of future generations, we shall act heartily and unanimously in recommending this Constitution wherever our influence may extend.

Adapted from James Madison, *Debates in the Federal Convention, 1840*.

### READING REVIEW ★ ★ ★ ★ ★ ★ ★

1. Why did Franklin think that this was the best possible Constitution?
2. Did Franklin think the delegates should tell the public of their doubts? Why or why not?
3. **Learning about citizenship.** (a) Why did Franklin say that it was important for delegates to unite in supporting the Constitution? (b) How might the principle Franklin puts forth here apply to our country today?

★ ★ ★ ★ ★ ★ ★ ★ ★ ★ ★ ★ ★ ★ ★ ★ ★

The framers of the Constitution hoped that the document would help strengthen and unify the new country. Another measure they took to help achieve this goal was adopting a national symbol—the powerful bald eagle.

**Introduction** The Constitutional Convention met just a year after Daniel Shays led a revolt of Massachusetts farmers. When Massachusetts called its convention to vote on ratifying the new Constitution, many farmers opposed it. Some, however, such as Jonathan Smith, favored the new Constitution. This selection is from the speech Smith made at the state convention.

**Vocabulary** Before you read the selection, find the meaning of these words in a dictionary: anarchy, tyranny, standard, reap.

Mr. President, I am a plain man, and get my living by the plow. I am not used to speak in public, but I beg your leave to say a few words to my brother plow-joggers in this house.

I have lived in a part of the country where I have known the worth of good government by the want of it. There was a black cloud that rose in the east last winter, and spread over the west. It brought on a state of anarchy and that led to tyranny. People that used to live peaceably, and were before good neighbors, got distracted, and took up arms against government. People took up arms. And if you went to speak to them, you had the musket of death presented to your breast. They would rob you of your property, threaten to burn your houses, oblige you to be on your guard night and day. Alarms spread from town to town, families were broken up, the tender mother would cry, O my son is among them!

Our distress was so great that we should have been glad to snatch at anything that looked like a government. Had any person that was able to protect us come and set up his standard, we should all have flocked to it, even if it had been a monarch, and that monarch might have proved a tyrant. So that you see that anarchy leads to tyranny.

Now, Mr. President, when I saw this Constitution, I found that it was a cure for these disorders. It was just such a thing as we wanted. I got a copy of it and read it over and over. I had been a member of the convention to form our own state constitution, and had learnt something of the checks and balances of power; and I found them all here. I formed my own opinion, and was pleased with this Constitution.

Some gentlemen say, don't be in a hurry, take time to consider, and don't take a leap in the dark. I say, take things in time—gather fruit when it is ripe. There is a time to sow, and a time to reap. We sowed our seed when we sent men to the federal convention. Now is the harvest. Now is the time to reap the fruit of our labor. And if we don't do it now, I am afraid we never shall have another opportunity.

Adapted from Jonathan Elliot, *The Debates on the Federal Constitution*, 1836.

When the last votes needed for ratification finally came in, New York City celebrated with a huge parade. This is the banner that was carried by the Society of Pewterers.

1. According to Smith, how would anarchy lead to tyranny?
2. What reason does Smith give for adopting the Constitution now?

3. **Making inferences.** Why did Smith believe that the present Constitution would be a "cure" for disorders such as Shays' Rebellion?

★ ★ ★ ★ ★ ★ ★ ★ ★ ★ ★ ★ ★ ★ ★ ★ ★ ★ ★

## ★ 9-5 An Antifederalist Argues His Case ★

**Introduction** People opposed adoption of the Constitution for many reasons. Some were simply wary of adopting such an important document too quickly without giving it enough thought. The following statement of this objection is from an anonymous contribution to a New York newspaper.

**Vocabulary** Before you read the selection, find the meaning of these words in a dictionary: illustrious, anarchy, frugality.

As far as I am able to determine, these are the main arguments in favor of the new Constitution.

1. That the men who formed it were wise and experienced; that they were an illustrious band of patriots and had the happiness of their country at heart; that they were four months deliberating on the subject; and therefore it must be a perfect system.

2. That if the system be not received, this country will be without any government, and, as a result, will be reduced to a state of anarchy and confusion; and in the end a government will be imposed upon us, not the result of reason and reflection, but the result of force.

With respect to the first, it will be readily seen that it leaves no room for any investigation of the merits of the proposed Constitution. For if we are to infer the perfection of this system from the characters and abilities of the men who formed it, we may as well accept it without any questions.

In answer to the second argument, I deny that we are in immediate danger of anarchy. Those who are anxious to bring about a measure will always tell us that the present is the critical moment. Tyrants have always made use of this plea, and nothing in our circumstances can justify it.

The country is in profound peace, and we are not threatened by invasion from any quarter.

It is true, the regulation of trade and a provision for the payment of the interest of the public debt is wanting; but no immediate commotion will rise from these. Time may be taken for calm discussion.

Individuals are just recovering from the losses sustained by the late war. Industry and frugality are taking their station and banishing idleness and wastefulness. Individuals are lessening their private debts, and several millions of the public debt is paid off by the sale of western territory.

There is no reason, therefore, why we should hastily and rashly adopt a system which is imperfect or insecure.

Adapted from *New York Journal and Weekly Register*, November 8, 1787.

## READING REVIEW ★ ★ ★ ★ ★ ★

1. According to the author, what are the two main reasons for support of the Constitution? State them in your own words.

2. How does the author answer the argument that anarchy would result if the Constitution is not ratified?

3. **Comparing points of view.** (a) How does this author's view of the need to act quickly differ from Jonathan Smith's? (b) What might explain the difference?

★ ★ ★ ★ ★ ★ ★ ★ ★ ★ ★ ★ ★ ★ ★ ★ ★ ★ ★

# Unit 4

# Strengthening the New Nation

# 10 The First Presidents (1789–1800)

★ **10-1   The First President Becomes a Legend**   ★

**Introduction**  George Washington was a legend in his own time. The plain, unadorned facts of his life were themselves the stuff of legend. Yet, early on, people began to tell stories about Washington that colored the truth in order to glorify him still further. One of the books that did most to transform the real-life George Washington into a national folk hero was the biography written by Mason Weems, a parson and bookseller. This well-known story comes from Weems's book.

**Vocabulary**  Before you read the selection, find the meaning of these words in a dictionary: vile, barbarously, anecdote, immoderately.

Never did the wise Ulysses take more pains with his beloved son Telemachus, than did Mr. Washington with George, to inspire him with an early love of truth. "Truth, George," said he, "is the loveliest quality of youth. I would ride 50 miles, my son, to see the little boy whose heart is so honest and his lips so pure that we may depend on every word he says. O how lovely does such a child appear in the eyes of everybody!"

"Pa," said George very seriously, "do I ever tell lies?"

"No, George, I thank God you do not, my son; and I rejoice in the hope you never will. At least, you shall never, from me, have cause to be guilty of so shameful a thing. Many parents, indeed, even force their children to this vile practice, by barbarously beating them for every little fault. Hence, on the next offense, the little terrified creature slips out a lie just to escape the rod! But as to yourself, George, you know I have always told you and now tell you again that, whenever by accident you do anything wrong, which must often be the case as you are but a poor little boy yet, without experience or knowledge, never tell a falsehood to conceal it. But come bravely up, my son, like a little man, and tell me of it. And instead of beating you, George, I will but the more honor and love you for it, my dear."

The following anecdote is a case in point. It is too valuable to be lost and too true to be doubted.

When George was about six years old, he was made the wealthy owner of a hatchet! Like most little boys, he was immoderately fond of it and was constantly going out chopping everything that came in his way.

One day, in the garden, he unluckily tried the edge of his hatchet on the body of a beautiful young English cherry tree, which he barked so terribly that I don't believe the tree ever got the better of it.

The next morning, the old gentleman, finding out what had happened to his tree—which, by the by, was a great favorite—came into the house and, with much warmth, asked for the mischievous one responsible. Presently, George and his hatchet made their appearance.

"George," said his father, "do you know who killed that beautiful little cherry tree yonder in the garden?"

This was a tough question, and George staggered under it for a mo-ment. But he quickly recovered himself, and looking at his father, he bravely cried out, "I can't tell a lie, Pa; you know I can't tell a lie. I did cut it with my hatchet."

"Run to my arms, you dearest boy," cried his father with joy, "run to my arms. Glad am I, George, that you killed my tree, for you have paid me for it a thousandfold. Such an act of heroism in my son is worth more than a thousand trees."

Adapted from Mason L. Weems, *The Life of Washington*, 1800.

### READING REVIEW ★ ★ ★ ★ ★ ★ ★

1. According to Weem's story, why are many children forced to begin to lie?

2. What moral lesson is Weems trying to teach with this story?

3. **Using fiction as historical evidence.** (a) Historians agree that Parson Weems made up this story. What evidence can you find to support this conclusion? (b) What can you learn from Weem's story about people's feelings toward George Washington in 1800?

★ ★ ★ ★ ★ ★ ★ ★ ★ ★ ★ ★ ★ ★ ★ ★ ★

## ★  10-2  Washington Advises Neutrality  ★

**Introduction** George Washington's term as President established many precedents for the new nation. One of the most important was the policy of neutrality in foreign affairs. Washington set this precedent by keeping the United States out of wars among the countries of Europe. In this selection from his Farewell Address, he makes it clear that he believes future generations of Americans should continue to remain neutral.

**Vocabulary** Before you read the selection, find the meaning of these words in a dictionary: habitual, disposes, illusion, deluded.

Observe good faith and justice towards all nations. Cultivate peace and harmony with all.

In carrying out such a plan, nothing is more essential than that permanent, habitual hatred against particular nations and passionate attachments for others should be excluded. In place of them, just and friendly feelings towards all should be cultivated. Hatred of one nation for another disposes each more readily to offer insult and injury, to lay hold of slight causes of anger, and to be haughty and headstrong when accidental or minor occasions of dispute occur.

So likewise a passionate attachment of one nation for another produces a variety of evils. Sympathy for the favorite nation helps create the illusion of an imaginary common interest in cases where no real common interest exists. It introduces into one the hatreds of the other. And it betrays the former into a participation in the quarrels and wars of the latter, without adequate cause. And it gives to ambitious, corrupted, or deluded citizens (who devote themselves to the favorite nation) an easy chance to betray, or sacrifice the interests of, their own country without hatred, sometimes even with popularity.

Europe has a set of primary interests which to us have no or a very remote relation. Hence she must be engaged in frequent controversies, the causes of which are essentially foreign to our concerns. Therefore, it must be unwise for us to involve ourselves by artificial ties in the ordinary combinations and collisions of her friendships or hatreds.

Adapted from George Washington, "Farewell Address," September 17, 1796.

Americans were eager to find patriotic symbols for their new nation. George Washington soon came to be one such symbol. This painting shows two other symbols: the flag and Miss Liberty.

### READING REVIEW ★ ★ ★ ★ ★ ★ ★

1. What does Washington say are the dangers of too strong an attachment to another nation?
2. What does he say are the dangers of too strong a dislike of another nation?
3. **Relating past to present.** To what degree do you think Washington's advice on foreign policy is still valid?

★ ★ ★ ★ ★ ★ ★ ★ ★ ★ ★ ★ ★ ★ ★ ★

## ★ 10-3 Jefferson Opposes the National Bank ★

**Introduction** Early on, the leaders of the new nation began separating into the two camps that would soon become the Federalist and Republican parties. One of the first issues to separate them was that of the national bank. The two men who became leaders of the rival parties, Alexander Hamilton and Thomas Jefferson, locked horns in legendary dispute over the bank. To help him make up his own mind about the bank proposal, President Washington asked Hamilton and Jefferson to give him written defenses of their positions. This selection is from Jefferson's paper.

**Vocabulary** Before you read the selection, find the meaning of these words in a dictionary: delegate, enumerate, proprietors, commerce, welfare, execution.

I consider the foundation of the Constitution to be laid on this ground—that all powers not delegated to the United States by the Constitution nor prohibited by it to the states are reserved to the states, or to the people. To take a single step beyond the boundaries thus specially drawn around the powers of Congress is to take possession of a boundless field of power no longer capable of being defined.

The incorporation of a bank and the powers assumed by this bill have not, in my opinion, been delegated to the United States by the Constitution.

**I.** They are not among the powers specially enumerated in the Constitution. For these are:

1. "A power to lay taxes for the purpose of paying the debts of the United States." But no debt is paid by this bill nor any tax laid.

2. "To borrow money." But this bill neither borrows money nor insures the borrowing of it. The proprietors of the bank will be just as free as any other money-holders to lend or not to lend their money to the public.

3. "To regulate commerce with foreign nations and among the states and with the Indian tribes." To erect a bank and to regulate commerce are very different acts.

**II.** Nor are they within either of the general phrases, which are the two following:

1. "To lay taxes to provide for the general welfare of the United States." They are not to do anything they please to provide for the general welfare, but only to lay taxes for that purpose.

2. "To make all laws necessary and proper for carrying into execution the enumerated powers." But they can all be carried into execution without a bank. A bank, therefore, is not necessary and consequently not authorized by this phrase.

It has been much urged that a bank will give great ease or convenience in the collection of taxes. Suppose this were true. Yet the Constitution allows only the means which are "necessary," not those which are merely "convenient," for effecting the enumerated powers. If such a freedom of construction is allowed to this phrase as to give any nonenumerated power, it will go to every one. Therefore it was that the Constitution restrained them to the necessary means—that is to say, to those means without which the grant of the power would be worthless.

Adapted from Thomas Jefferson, "Opinion on the Constitutionality of the Bank," February 15, 1791.

**READING REVIEW** ★ ★ ★ ★ ★ ★

1. Explain in your own words Jefferson's idea of a necessary law.
2. (a) What does Jefferson think of as the foundation, or basic principle, of the Constitution? (b) What does he think will happen if the basic principle is not held to?
3. **Making inferences.** Based on Jefferson's paper, list two arguments that were probably being made in favor of the constitutionality of a national bank.

★ ★ ★ ★ ★ ★ ★ ★ ★ ★ ★ ★ ★ ★ ★ ★ ★

With the growth of political parties, election day became an important public event. In this painting, the whole town has turned out for an election.

---

## ★ 10-4 Hamilton Supports the Bank ★

**Introduction** Alexander Hamilton was widely respected for his gifts as a writer as well as for his creative political thinking. This defense of a national bank, which Hamilton wrote for Washington, is regarded as one of his most brilliant works. His plan for a national bank to help solve the financial problems of the new nation was a bold and original one.

**Vocabulary** Before you read the selection, find the meaning of these words in a dictionary: liberal, latitude, criterion.

Through this manner of reasoning about the right to use all the means required for the exercise of the specified powers of the government, it is objected that none but necessary and proper means are to be used. And Jefferson maintains that no means are to be considered as necessary but those without which the grant of the power would be worthless.

It is essential to the being of the national government that so mistaken an idea of the meaning of the word "necessary" should be exploded.

Necessary often means no more than needful, useful, or helpful to. And this is the true sense in which it is to be understood as used in the Constitution. It was the intent of the Convention to give a liberal latitude to the exercise of the specified powers.

To understand the word as the Secretary of State does would be to depart from its obvious and popular sense and to give it a restrictive function, an idea never before entertained.

It would be to give it the same force as if the word "absolutely" or "indispensably" had been used before it.

The degree in which a measure is necessary can never be a test of the legal right to adopt it. That must be a matter of opinion. The relation between the measure and the end must be the criterion of constitutionality, not the more or less of necessity or usefulness.

If the end be clearly included within any of the specified powers, and if the measure have an obvious relation to that end and is not forbidden by any particular provision of the Constitution, it may safely be said to come within the scope of the national government.

Adapted from *The Works of Alexander Hamilton*, ed. J.C. Hamilton, 1864.

### R E A D I N G   R E V I E W ★ ★ ★ ★ ★ ★ ★

1. What does Hamilton say the Constitutional Convention intended when it specified the powers it gave to Congress? Explain in your own words.

2. How could Hamilton use the argument in this selection to support a national bank?

3. **Analyzing conflicting opinions.** (a) How does Hamilton's interpretation of the word "necessary" differ from Jefferson's? (b) Give an example of a means one man would consider necessary, the other not necessary, to accomplish a certain end. You may use situations from everyday life.

★ ★ ★ ★ ★ ★ ★ ★ ★ ★ ★ ★ ★ ★ ★ ★ ★ ★

---

## ★ 10-5    A Song to Unite Americans ★

**Introduction** Party rivalry between Republicans and Federalists reached a peak with the passing of the Alien and Sedition acts. Many people were worried that the disputes between the two parties would undermine the strength of the new nation. Joseph Hopkinson, a Philadelphia lawyer, decided to do what he could to reunite his squabbling fellow citizens. He wrote a song for a friend who was a singer. The song, "Hail Columbia," was designed to stir patriotic feelings. It was an immediate hit. President John Adams rose and applauded the first night he heard it.

**Vocabulary** Before you read the selection, find the meaning of these words in a dictionary: valor, altar.

Hail Columbia, happy land
Hail ye heroes, heav'n-born band
Who fought and bled in freedom's cause
Who fought and bled in freedom's cause
And when the storm of war was gone

Enjoyed the peace your valor won.
Let independence be your boast
Ever mindful what it cost
Ever grateful for the prize
Let its altar reach the skies.

*Chorus*
Firm united let us stand
Rallying round our liberty
As a band of brothers joined
Peace and safety we shall find.

Joseph Hopkinson, "Hail Columbia," 1798.

### R E A D I N G   R E V I E W ★ ★ ★ ★ ★ ★ ★

1. What is Hopkinson referring to with the words "freedom's cause"?

2. Why do you think the songwriter makes such extensive references to America's wartime experiences?

3. **Using a song as historical evidence.** What is the message of the chorus of the song?

★ ★ ★ ★ ★ ★ ★ ★ ★ ★ ★ ★ ★ ★ ★ ★ ★ ★

# Chapter 11 Age of Jefferson (1801–1816)

## ★ 11-1 The First Republican President ★

**Introduction** Thomas Jefferson's first inaugural address gave Americans a clear idea of what they could expect from their first Republican President. In this selection from his speech, he spells out what he believed to be the essential principles of the government of the United States. Another key message of Jefferson's speech was his wish to make peace with the Federalists.

**Vocabulary** Before you read the selection, find the meaning of these words in a dictionary: social intercourse, domestic, pretensions.

Friends and Fellow Citizens:

During the contest of opinion through which we have passed, the liveliness of discussions has sometimes worn an aspect which might make a strong impression on strangers unused to thinking freely and to speaking and writing what they think. But this being now decided by the voice of the nation, all will, of course, unite in common efforts for the common good. All, too, will bear in mind this sacred principle, that though the will of the majority is in all cases to prevail, the minority possesses their equal rights, which equal law must protect, and to violate would be oppression. Let us, then, fellow citizens, unite with one heart and one mind. Let us restore to social intercourse that harmony and affection without which liberty and even life itself are but dreary things.

We have called by different names brothers of the same principle. We are all Republicans, we are all Federalists.

As I am about to enter, fellow citizens, on the exercise of duties which involve everything dear and valuable to you, it is proper you should understand what I think are the essential principles of our government: equal and exact justice to all men, of whatever state or persuasion, religious or political; peace, trade, and honest friendship with all nations, entangling alliances with none; the support of the state governments in all their rights, as the most able administrations for our domestic concerns; absolute willingness to abide by the decisions of the majority; encouragement of agriculture, and of trade as its handmaid; freedom of religion; freedom of the press; trial by juries impartially selected.

I go, then, fellow citizens, to the post you have assigned me. I have no pretensions to that high confidence you placed in our first and greatest revolutionary character, whose outstanding services had entitled him to the first place in his country's love and destined for him the fairest page in the volume of faithful history. I ask so much confidence only as may give firmness and effectiveness to the legal administration of your affairs. I shall often go wrong through defect of judgment. When right, I shall often be thought wrong by those whose positions will not command a view of the whole ground. I ask your indulgence for my own errors and your support against the errors of others.

Adapted from Thomas Jefferson, "First Inaugural Address," 1801.

**READING REVIEW** ★ ★ ★ ★ ★ ★ ★ ★

1. Why does Jefferson think the Federalists should be treated with respect?
2. With which of the essential principles of government listed by Jefferson might Federalists have disagreed?

3. **Drawing conclusions.** In the last paragraph, Jefferson refers at length to someone whom he does not name. (a) Who is he talking about? (b) What is his attitude toward this person?

★ ★ ★ ★ ★ ★ ★ ★ ★ ★ ★ ★ ★ ★ ★ ★ ★ ★ ★

## ★ 11-2 The Shoshones Meet Lewis and Clark ★

**Introduction** Although relations between white Americans and western Indians quickly became hostile, they began with a spirit of friendship and trust on both sides. When Meriwether Lewis and William Clark journeyed west in 1804, they relied heavily on the help of the Shoshone Indians. This selection is an account by a Shoshone of the Indians' first impressions of Lewis and Clark and their party.

**Vocabulary** Before you read the selection, find the meaning of these words in a dictionary: tranquil, doleful, forebodings, pilfering.

The Shoshones had camped in the mountains because of fears of the Blackfeet, who possessed firearms. After several moons, however, this state of tranquil happiness was interrupted by the unexpected arrival of two strangers. They were unlike any people we had seen before, fairer than ourselves, and clothed with skins unknown to us.

They gave us things like solid water, which was sometimes brilliant as the sun and which sometimes showed us our own faces. Nothing could equal our wonder and delight. We thought them the children of the Great Spirit. But we were destined to be again overwhelmed with fear, for we soon discovered that they were in possession of the identical thunder and lightning that had proved in the hands of our foes to be so fatal to our happiness.

Many of our people were now terrified, fearing that they were allied with our enemies the Blackfeet. This opinion was strengthened when they asked us to go and meet their friends. At first this was denied. But a speech from our beloved chief, who told us that it was best to be friendly to people so terribly armed, convinced most of our warriors to follow him to their camp. As they disappeared over a hill in the neighborhood of our village, the women set up a doleful yell, which was equivalent to bidding them farewell forever. This did anything but raise their drooping spirits.

Lewis and Clark were often helped by Native Americans on their trip west. They spent one winter with the Mandans who lived in villages along the Missouri River much like the one shown here. The Mandans' boats were made of buffalo hide stretched over willow frames.

After such dismal forebodings, imagine how agreeably they were disappointed when, upon arriving at the strangers' camp, they found, instead of an overwhelming force of enemies, a few strangers like the two already with them. The strangers treated them with great kindness and gave them many things that had not existed before even in their dreams.

Our eagle-eyed chief discovered from the carelessness of the strangers with regard to their things that they were unacquainted with theft. This led him to caution his followers against pilfering any article whatever. His instructions were strictly obeyed. Mutual confidence was thus established. The strangers accompanied him back to the village, and there was peace and joy in the lodges of our people.

Adapted from W. A. Ferris, *Life in the Rocky Mountains,* ed. Paul C. Phillips (Denver: The Old West Publishing Co., 1940).

READING REVIEW ★ ★ ★ ★ ★ ★ ★

1. What common objects did the author of this account have in mind when he spoke of "solid water"? Of "thunder and lightning"?

2. What was the Shoshone chief's original motive for agreeing to go with the white men?

3. **Relating cause and effect.** (a) Why did the Shoshones come to trust the white men? (b) What did the Shoshones do that helped the white men trust them?

★ ★ ★ ★ ★ ★ ★ ★ ★ ★ ★ ★ ★ ★ ★ ★ ★ ★ ★ ★

## ★ 11-3 Sympathy for Impressed Americans ★

**Introduction** One cause of the War of 1812 was the impressment of American sailors by the British. Whether people wanted war or not, most agreed that this practice was an outrage. Even some of the British sympathized with impressed Americans. This description of impressment was written by a British sailor, Captain Basil Hall, who had witnessed impressment firsthand. His ship, the *Leander*, had stopped and searched a number of American vessels for "British" seamen.

**Vocabulary** Before you read the selection, find the meaning of these words in a dictionary: annoyance, indignation, indignities.

There was another circumstance of still more serious annoyance to the Americans. I need hardly mention that I refer to the impressment of those seamen whom we found serving on board American merchant ships but who were known to be or supposed to be British subjects.

To place the full annoyance of these matters in a light to be viewed fairly by English people, let us suppose that the Americans and French were to go to war and that England for once remained neutral—an odd case, I admit, but one which might happen.

Imagine that the American squadron, employed to blockade the French ships in Liverpool, were short-handed. And expecting action any day, it had become an object of great concern with them to get their ships manned. And suppose, likewise, that it were perfectly well known to all parties that on board every English ship arriving or sailing from the port there were several American citizens. But they called themselves English and had in their possession "protections," or certificates to that effect. These were sworn to in regular form but were well known to be false. Things being in this situation, imagine that the American men-of-war, off the English port, were then to fire at and stop every ship. Then, besides overhauling her papers and

**Readings** —520—

cargo, they were to take out any seaman whom they had reason or said they had reason to consider an American citizen, or whose country they guessed from dialect or appearance. I wish to know with what degree of patience this would be submitted to in England.

I merely wish to put the general case broadly before our own eyes so that we may bring it distinctly home to ourselves and then see whether or not the Americans had reason for their indignation. The truth is that they had very good reason to be annoyed. Now, let us be frank with our rivals and ask ourselves whether the Americans would have been worthy of our friendship, or even of our hostility, had they tamely submitted to indignities which, if passed upon ourselves, would have roused the whole country into a towering passion of nationality.

Adapted from Captain Basil Hall, *Fragments of Voyages and Travels*, 1831.

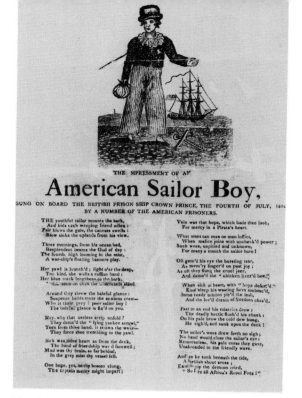

The impressment of American sailors by the British made people furious. This song was written to give a vivid picture of the plight of an impressed sailor.

**READING REVIEW**  ★ ★ ★ ★ ★ ★

1. What methods were used to determine a sailor's nationality?

2. What would Hall have thought of Americans if they had gone along with impressment?

3. **Making inferences.** (a) From Hall's account, what can you infer about the legal status of many British sailors who worked on American ships? (b) How did this affect his opinion of the practice of impressment?

★ ★ ★ ★ ★ ★ ★ ★ ★ ★ ★ ★ ★ ★ ★ ★ ★ ★ ★

---

## ★ 11-4 Tecumseh Protests Land Sale ★

**Introduction** Tecumseh was one of the Native Americans' greatest leaders. He was loved by people of many Indian nations and respected by many white Americans as well. Tecumseh cared passionately about the welfare of his people. Yet, although he was willing to fight on behalf of his fellow Indians, Tecumseh was not a warlike man. He tried first to secure their rights by peaceful means. This selection is from a speech Tecumseh made to Governor William Henry Harrison of Indiana Territory. Harrison had recently tricked several Indians into selling much of their land.

**Vocabulary** Before you read the selection, find the meaning of these words in a dictionary: obliterate, traverse, encroaching.

I would not then come to Governor Harrison to ask him to tear the treaty and to obliterate the landmark. But I would say to him: Sir, you have liberty to return to your own country.

The being within, communing with past ages, tells me that until lately there was no white man on this continent. It then all belonged to red men, children of the same parents, placed on it by the Great Spirit that made them to keep it, to traverse it, to enjoy its productions, and to fill it with the same race—once a happy race, since made miserable by the white people, who are never contented but always encroaching.

The way—and the only way—to check and to stop this evil is for all the red men to unite in claiming a common equal right in the land as it was at first and should be yet. For it never was divided but belongs to all for the use of each. That no part has a right to sell even to each other much less to strangers—those who want all and will not do with less.

The white people have no right to take the land from the Indians, because they had it first. It is theirs. They may sell, but all must join. Any sale not made by all is not valid. The late sale is bad. It was made by a part only. Part do not know how to sell. It requires all to make a bargain for all.

All red men have equal rights to the unoccupied land. There cannot be two occupants in the same place. The first excludes all others. It is not so in hunting or traveling, for there the same ground will serve many, as they may follow each other all day. But the camp is stationary, and that is occupancy. It belongs to the first who sits down on his blanket or skins which he has thrown upon the ground. Till he leaves it, no other has a right.

Adapted from *The Library of Oratory*, ed. C. M. Depew, 1902.

**READING REVIEW** ★ ★ ★ ★ ★ ★ ★

1. How does Tecumseh describe white people?

2. Tecumseh would not completely exclude white settlers from Indian land. Under what circumstances would he allow them?

3. **Finding the main idea.** (a) What is the main reason Tecumseh opposes the recent sale? (b) What other reason does he have for opposing it?

★ ★ ★ ★ ★ ★ ★ ★ ★ ★ ★ ★ ★ ★ ★ ★ ★ ★ ★

---

## ★ 11-5  Henry Clay Defends War With Britain ★

**Introduction** Even after the War of 1812 had begun, many Americans continued to oppose it. Easterners especially objected to the attempt to conquer Canada. Congressman Henry Clay worked hard to win support for the war. In 1813, Clay made this speech to Congress defending the war and the contest in Canada.

**Vocabulary** Before you read the selection, find the meaning of these words in a dictionary: instigated, judicious, humane, maxim.

What cause, Mr. Chairman, which existed for declaring the war has been removed? Indian hostilities, which were before secretly instigated, are now openly encouraged. The practice of impressment is unceasingly insisted upon. Yet the administration has given the strongest demonstration of its love of peace. An honorable peace is attainable only by an efficient war. My plan would be to call out the ample resources of the country, give them a judicious direction, prosecute the war with the utmost vigor, strike wherever we can reach the enemy, at sea or on land, and negotiate the terms of a peace.

The gentleman from Delaware sees in Canada no object worthy of conquest. Other gentlemen consider the invasion of that country as wicked and unjustifiable. Its inhabitants are represented as unoffending, connected with those of the bordering states by a thousand tender ties, interchanging acts of kindness and all the rituals of good neighborhood. Canada innocent! Canada unoffending! Is it not in Canada that the tomahawk of the savage has been molded into its deathlike form? Is it not from Canadian storehouses that those supplies have been issued which nourish and sustain the Indian hostilities?

The gentlemen would not touch the continental provinces of the enemy nor, I presume, for the same reason, her possessions in the West Indies. The same humane spirit would spare the seamen and soldiers of the enemy. The sacred person of His Majesty must not be attacked, for the learned gentlemen on the other side are quite familiar with the maxim that the king can do no wrong.

Indeed, sir, I know of no person on whom we may make war upon the principles of the honorable gentlemen, except Mr. Stephen, the celebrated author of the Orders in Council, or the Board of Admiralty, who authorize and regulate the practice of impressment.

Adapted from *Annals of Congress*, 12 Cong., 2 sess. 1811–1813.

**R E A D I N G   R E V I E W** ★ ★ ★ ★ ★ ★

1. What does Clay say is the best way to achieve peace?

2. Why, according to Clay, are some people reluctant to pursue a war against Canada?

3. **Summarizing.** Clay uses two arguments to prove that opposition to the war is wrong. Summarize the second of his arguments in your own words.

★ ★ ★ ★ ★ ★ ★ ★ ★ ★ ★ ★ ★ ★ ★ ★ ★ ★

**Chapter**

# 12 The Nation Prospers (1790–1825)

★    **12-1    Pros and Cons of Factory Life**    ★

**Introduction**  Working conditions in early factories were a subject of much debate. This imaginary conversation is from an issue of *The Lowell Offering*, a journal published by the young women who worked in the Lowell mills. In it, the workers themselves discuss some of the pros and cons of factory life.

**Vocabulary**  Before you read the selection, find the meaning of these words in a dictionary: degrading, contemptuously, derogatory.

**Miss S:** I am very happy to see you this evening, Miss Bartlett, for I have something particular to say to you. Now do tell me if you still hold to your decision to return to your factory employment.

**Miss B:** I do. I have no objection, neither have I heard any sufficiently strong to stop me.

**Miss S:** The idea that it is degrading, in the opinion of many, would be objection enough for me.

**Miss B:** By whom is factory labor considered degrading? It is by those

One common complaint about the early factories was of cramped, crowded working conditions. This drawing shows conditions in a book bindery.

who believe all labor degrading—by those who contemptuously speak of the farmer, the mechanic, the printer, the seamstress, and all who are obliged to toil—by those who seem to think the condition of labor excludes all the capacities of the mind and the virtues of humanity.

**Miss S:** There are objections to factory labor which serve to render it degrading. For instance, to be called and to be dismissed by the ringing of a bell savors of slavery and cannot help but be destructive to self-respect.

**Miss B:** In almost all kinds of employment it is necessary to keep regular established hours. Because we are reminded of those hours by the ringing of a bell, it is no argument against our employment. Our engagements are voluntarily entered into with our employers. However derogatory to our dignity and liberty you may consider factory labor, there is not a tinge of slavery existing in it.

**Miss S:** It cannot be denied that some females guilty of immoralities find their way into the factories and boardinghouses. The example and influence of such must be harmful and result in the increase of vice.

**Miss B:** We know that some objectionable characters occasionally find a place among those employed in factories. But, my dear Miss S, did you ever know or hear of a class of people among whom wrong of any description was never known?

**Miss S:** O, no!

**Miss B:** Then, if in one case the guilt of a few has not corrupted the whole, why should it in the other?

**Miss S:** You will not acknowledge that factory labor is degrading or that it is productive of vice, but you must admit that it fosters ignorance. When there are so many hours out of each day devoted to labor, there can be no time for study and improvement.

**Miss B:** It is true that too large a portion of our time is confined to labor. But a factory girl's work is neither hard nor complicated. She can go on with perfect regularity in her duties while her mind may be actively employed on any other subject. Our well-worn libraries, evening schools, crowded churches, and sabbath schools prove that factory workers find leisure to use the means of improvement.

Adapted from *The Lowell Offering*, 1833.

### READING REVIEW ★ ★ ★ ★ ★ ★ ★

1. What three objections does Miss S make about factory life?
2. How does Miss B answer the claim that factory work fosters ignorance?
3. **Expressing an opinion.** Do you think the arguments made by Miss B or Miss S are more convincing? Why?

★ ★ ★ ★ ★ ★ ★ ★ ★ ★ ★ ★ ★ ★ ★ ★ ★ ★

**Introduction**  Many of the new forms of transportation developed in the 1800s were more than fast and efficient. They often had an air of excitement and glamor about them as well. Certainly the steamboats that traveled the Mississippi did. In this selection from *Life of the Mississippi*, Mark Twain describes the fascination steamboats held for him and his neighbors in the town where he grew up.

**Vocabulary**  Before you read the selection, find the meaning of these words in a dictionary: packet, transpired, drayman, gilded, gingerbread.

When I was a boy, there was but one permanent ambition among my comrades in our village on the west bank of the Mississippi River. That was to be a steamboatman.

One day, a cheap, gaudy packet arrived upward from St. Louis and another downward from Keokuk. Before these events, the day was glorious with expectancy; after they had transpired, the day was a dead and empty thing. Not only the boys but the whole village felt this.

After all these years, I can picture that old time to myself now, just as it was then. A film of dark smoke appears. Instantly a Negro drayman lifts up the cry, "S-t-e-a-m-boat acomin'!" and the scene changes! All in a twinkling, the dead town is alive and moving. Drays, carts, men, boys, all go hurrying from many quarters to a common center, the wharf. Assembled there, the people fasten their eyes upon the coming boat as upon a wonder they are seeing for the first time.

And the boat is rather a handsome sight, too. She is long and sharp and trim and pretty. She has two tall, fancy-topped chimneys, with a gilded device of some kind swung between them, and a fanciful pilothouse, all glass and "gingerbread." The paddle boxes are gorgeous with a picture or with gilded rays above the boat's name. There is a flag gallantly flying from the jackstaff. The pent steam is screaming through the gauge cocks.

The captain lifts his hand, a bell rings, the wheels stop. Then they turn back, churning the water to foam, and the steamer is at rest. Then such a scramble as there is to get aboard and to get ashore, and to take in freight and to discharge freight, all at one and the same time. And such yelling and cursing as the mates accompany it all with!

Ten minutes later the steamer is under way again, with no flag on the jackstaff and no black smoke spewing from the chimneys. After ten more minutes the town is dead again.

Adapted from Mark Twain, *Life on the Mississippi*, 1874.

**R E A D I N G   R E V I E W** ★ ★ ★ ★ ★ ★ ★

1. What effect did the arrival of a steamboat have on a small river town?
2. What details in this passage would support the statement that Mississippi steamboats had a glamorous and romantic air about them?
3. **Understanding geography.** Using a map of the United States and the clues in this selection, find the approximate location of the town Twain grew up in.

★ ★ ★ ★ ★ ★ ★ ★ ★ ★ ★ ★ ★ ★ ★ ★ ★ ★ ★

Steamboats played a key role in the economic growth of the South. Planters used them to ship cotton and other goods to market easily. By the mid-1800's, steamboats were an important feature of life in the bustling port of New Orleans, shown here.

## ★ 12-3 A Southerner Objects to the Tariff ★

**Introduction** Many farmers objected to the protective tariffs of 1816 and 1818. They resented the fact that the government was helping industry and not helping agriculture. They also resented having to pay more for manufactured goods. The tariff issue added to the growing distrust between the nation's industrialists, located mainly in the North, and its farmers in the South and West. This selection is from a speech made by Virginia congressman John Randolph against the Tariff of 1816. Randolph was known for his fiery language.

**Vocabulary** Before you read the selection, find the meaning of these words in a dictionary: cultivators, exotic, speculator, opulence.

It comes down to this: whether you, as a planter, will consent to be taxed in order to hire another man to go to work in a shoemaker's shop or to set up a spinning jenny. For my part I will not agree to it. No, I will buy where I can get products cheapest. I will not agree to lay a duty on the cultivators of the soil to encourage exotic products. After all, we should only get much worse things at a much higher price. Why pay a man much more than the value for it to work up our own cotton into clothing, when, by selling my raw material, I can get my clothing much better and cheaper from Dacca? How does the honorable gentleman have a right to be supported by the earnings of the others?

The cultivators bear the whole brunt of the war and taxation and remain poor, while the others run in the ring of pleasure and fatten upon them. The cultivators not only pay all but fight all, while the others run. The manufacturer is the citizen of no place or any place. The cultivator has his property, his lands, his all, his household goods to defend. The commercial speculators live in opulence, whirling in coaches, and indulging in palaces. Even without your aid, the cultivators are no match for them. Alert, vigilant, enterprising, and active, the manufacturing interest are collected in masses, ready to associate at a moment's warning for any purpose of general interest to their body. Do but ring the fire bell, and you can assemble all the manufacturing interest of Philadelphia in 15 minutes.

The cultivators, the patient drudges of the other orders of society, are now waiting for your resolution. For on you it depends, whether they shall be left further unhurt or be, like those in Europe, reduced and subjected to another squeeze from the hard grasp of power. Sir, I am done.

Adapted from *Annals of Congress*, 14 Cong., 1 sess., 1815–1816.

## READING REVIEW ★ ★ ★ ★ ★ ★ ★

1. What specific reasons does Randolph give for objecting to the tariff?

2. (a) What is Randolph's view of manufacturers in general? (b) How does he view farmers?

3. **Distinguishing fact from opinion.** Randolph exaggerates his case to make his point. Name at least two statements he makes that are probably not factual.

★ ★ ★ ★ ★ ★ ★ ★ ★ ★ ★ ★ ★ ★ ★ ★ ★

## ★ 12-4 Monroe Doctrine Declared ★

**Introduction** In his Farewell Address, George Washington urged America to stay out of the affairs of other nations. By 1823, however, President James Monroe saw a need to qualify Washington's policy of neutrality. The United States would not stand idly by if European nations tried to interfere in the affairs of North or South America. Monroe made this speech to Congress setting forth the new policy, which soon came to be known as the Monroe Doctrine.

**Vocabulary** Before you read the selection, find the meaning of these words in a dictionary: comport, impartial, candor, dependencies.

The occasion has been judged proper for asserting, as a principle in which the rights and interests of the United States are involved, that the American continents, by the free and independent condition which they have assumed and maintain, are henceforth not to be considered as subjects for future colonization by any European powers.

Of events in that quarter of the globe with which we have so much intercourse and from which we derive our origin, we have always been anxious and interested spectators. The citizens of the United States cherish sentiments the most friendly in favor of the liberty and happiness of their fellow men on that side of the Atlantic. In the wars of the European powers in matters relating to themselves, we have never taken any part, nor does it comport with our policy so to do. It is only when our rights are invaded or seriously menaced that we resent injuries or make preparation for our defense.

With the movements in this hemisphere, we are of necessity more immediately connected, and by causes which must be obvious to all enlightened and impartial observers. The political system of the European powers is essentially different in this respect from that of America. We owe it, therefore, to candor and to the friendly relations existing between the United States and those powers to declare that we should consider any attempt on their part to extend their system to any portion of this hemisphere as dangerous to our peace and safety. With the existing colonies or dependencies of any European power we have not interfered and shall not interfere. But with the governments who have declared their independence and maintained it, and whose independence we have, on great consideration and on just principles, acknowledged, we could not view any intervention for the purpose of oppressing them, or controlling in any other manner their destiny, by any European power in any other light than as the demonstration of an unfriendly disposition toward the United States.

Adapted from *The Monroe Doctrine*, 1823.

### READING REVIEW ★ ★ ★ ★ ★ ★ ★

1. Why, according to Monroe, should the American continents no longer be open to European colonization?
2. Under what circumstances would the United States oppose European involvement in the affairs of South America?
3. **Relating past to present.** Under what circumstances might a President today use the Monroe Doctrine?

★ ★ ★ ★ ★ ★ ★ ★ ★ ★ ★ ★ ★ ★ ★ ★

## ★ 12-5 Americans Sing Praises of Home ★

**Introduction** In the early decades of America's growth, singing was one of the main forms of popular entertainment. The songs Americans of this era liked best were often sentimental. They praised the virtues of simple, familiar things. One of the great favorites was "Home, Sweet Home," which appears here. The words were written by Howard Payne, an actor and playwright who never had a home of his own.

**Vocabulary** Before you read the selection, find the meaning of these words in a dictionary: hallow, exile.

Mid pleasures and palaces though we
    may roam,
Be it ever so humble, there's no place
    like home!
A charm from the skies seems to hal-
    low us there,
Which, seek through the world, is ne'er
    met with elsewhere.
    *Chorus*
Home! home! sweet, sweet home!
There's no place like home! There's no
    place like home.

I gaze on the moon as I tread the drear
    wild,

And feel that my mother now thinks of
    her child;
As she looks on that moon from our
    own cottage door,
Through the woodbine whose fragrance
    shall cheer me no more.

An exile from home, splendor dazzles
    in vain;
Oh, give me my lowly thatched cottage
    again;
The birds singing gaily, that came at
    my call;
Give me them, and that peace of mind,
    dearer than all.

John Howard Payne, "Home, Sweet Home," 1823.

### READING REVIEW

1. What sort of home does this song sing the praises of?
2. Which verse of "Home, Sweet Home" would a newcomer to one of America's growing cities probably relate to best?
3. **Using a song as historical evidence.** The decades after the War of 1812 were a time of growth and change for Americans. What does the popularity of a song such as "Home, Sweet Home" tell us about people's reaction to change?

★ ★ ★ ★ ★ ★ ★ ★ ★ ★ ★ ★ ★ ★ ★ ★

# A Growing Nation

Chapter

# 13 Age of Jackson (1824–1840)

---

## ★ 13-1 The Election of 1824 ★

**Introduction** The election of 1824 showed the changes that had begun to take place in America. The country was growing and expanding. Its population was growing and becoming more diverse. In 1824, four different Republican candidates ran for President. Each was popular with a different group of Americans. The vote was so close that the House of Representatives had to choose a President from among the top three candidates in the electoral college vote. These circle graphs show how the votes were distributed.

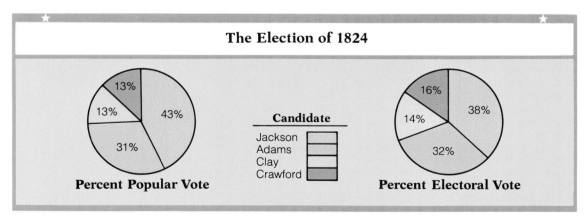

**The Election of 1824**

**Candidate**

Jackson
Adams
Clay
Crawford

**Percent Popular Vote**

**Percent Electoral Vote**

**READING REVIEW** ★ ★ ★ ★ ★ ★ ★ ★

1. (a) Which candidates won a greater percentage of electoral votes than popular votes? (b) Which won a smaller percentage?

2. Which three candidates were the ones the House of Representatives had to choose among?

3. **Using graphs.** (a) Who won the largest percentage of electoral votes? (b) Why did he not win the election?

★ ★ ★ ★ ★ ★ ★ ★ ★ ★ ★ ★ ★ ★ ★ ★ ★ ★ ★

**Introduction** Andrew Jackson owed much of his celebrated strength of character to his mother. Elizabeth Jackson was widowed at a young age. Singlehandedly, she saw her young sons through the horrors of smallpox and the American Revolution. She also nursed imprisoned American soldiers during the Revolution. In the course of this work, she caught a fever and died. In her last hours, she wrote this letter to her young son Andrew.

**Vocabulary** Before you read the selection, find the meaning of these words in a dictionary: steadfast, obsequious, imposition.

Dear Andrew,

If I should not see you again, I wish you to remember and treasure up some things I have already said to you. In this world, you will have to make your own way. To do that, you must have friends. You can make friends by being honest, and you can keep them by being steadfast. You must keep in mind that friends worth having will in the long run expect as much from you as they give to you.

To forget an obligation or be ungrateful for a kindness is a crime. Men guilty of it sooner or later must suffer the penalty.

In personal conduct, always be polite, but never obsequious. No one will respect you more than you respect yourself. Avoid quarrels as long as you can without yielding to imposition. But sustain your manhood always.

Never wound the feelings of others. If ever you have to defend your feelings or your honor, do it calmly. If angry at first, wait till your anger cools before you proceed.

Love,
Mother

Adapted from *Letters in American History,* by H. Jack Lang. Copyright © 1982 by H. Jack Lang. Used by permission of Harmony Books, a division of Crown Publishers, Inc.

**READING REVIEW** ★ ★ ★ ★ ★ ★ ★

1. What advice did Elizabeth Jackson give her son about friends?
2. What standard political practice begun by Jackson seems rooted in his mother's advice?
3. **Ranking.** (a) Which parts of his mother's advice seem to have had the greatest effect on Jackson? (b) Which seem to have had the least?

★ ★ ★ ★ ★ ★ ★ ★ ★ ★ ★ ★ ★ ★ ★ ★ ★ ★ ★

Andrew Jackson thought of himself as a friend of the common people. During the Age of Jackson, more people than ever before became involved in the nation's political life. This painting shows a variety of spectators in a country courtroom.

**Introduction**  The debate over the Tariff of Abominations grew into a debate over the right of a state to override the federal government. John C. Calhoun became the leader of those who took the "states' rights" position. This selection is from a speech he gave against a tariff passed in 1832.

**Vocabulary**  Before you read the selection, find the meaning of these words in a dictionary: encroach, revenue, sovereignty, discord, despotism.

We, the people of South Carolina, have declared the act of Congress to alter the tariff on imports to be unconstitutional and therefore null and void.

We hold it to be a very imperfect idea of the duty which each state agreed to in ratifying the Constitution to suppose that a state should simply not exercise the powers delegated to the federal government. This is an important duty. But there is another duty no less important—to resist the government, should it encroach on the reserved powers.

That the protective tariff system included in the act is, in fact, unconstitutional we hold to be certain. And it is under this deep and solemn conviction that we have acted.

It has not been claimed, nor is it now, that there is in the Constitution any positive grant of power to protect manufactures. Nor can it be denied that frequent attempts were made at the Constitutional Convention to obtain the power and that they all failed.

Its advocates claim to derive this power from the right "to lay and collect taxes, duties, imposts, and excises" or from that "to regulate commerce." Yet the claim plainly rests on the assumption that the power to impose duties may be applied not only to raise revenue or regulate commerce but also to protect manufactures.

That such a power is not granted by the Constitution we hold to be certain. It has become an instrument in the hands of the powerful to oppress the weaker. It must, ultimately, concentrate all power in the federal government and abolish the sovereignty of the states. Discord, corruption, and, eventually, despotism must follow, if the system is not resisted.

Adapted from *Works of John C. Calhoun*, ed. Richard K. Crallé, 1856.

### R E A D I N G   R E V I E W ★ ★ ★ ★ ★ ★ ★

1. What major argument does Calhoun use to support the right of a state to declare a federal law null and void?
2. According to Calhoun, why were the tariffs of 1828 and 1832 unconstitutional?
3. **Using diagrams.** Review the diagram of the separation of powers on page 206. (a) Give two examples of delegated powers. (b) Give two examples of reserved powers. (c) Why did Calhoun think the protective tariffs threatened the separation of powers?

★ ★ ★ ★ ★ ★ ★ ★ ★ ★ ★ ★ ★ ★ ★ ★ ★

**Introduction**  Senator Daniel Webster of Massachusetts opposed Calhoun and the South Carolinians. Webster argued that the supreme power of the land lay with the federal government, not with the states. Webster expressed his views in a series of speeches made in response to Senator Robert Hayne of

South Carolina. This selection is from one of these speeches. Hayne was a member of the antitariff group that Calhoun came to lead.

**Vocabulary** Before you read the selection, find the meaning of these words in a dictionary: sovereign, agency, discretion, sanctioned, dissevered, fraternal.

This leads us to inquire into the origin of this government and the source of its power. Whose agent is it? Is it the creature of the state legislatures or the creature of the people? It is, sir, the people's Constitution, the people's government. The states are, unquestionably, sovereign, so far as their sovereignty is not affected by this supreme law. But the state legislatures, as political bodies, however sovereign, are yet not sovereign over the people.

The people, then, sir, erected this government. They gave it a Constitution. In that Constitution they have spelled out the powers which they bestow on it. But, sir, they have not stopped here. If they had, they would have accomplished but half their work.

Sir, the very chief end, the main design, for which the whole Constitution was framed and adopted was to establish a government that should not be obliged to act through state agency or depend on state opinion and state discretion. The people had had quite enough of that kind of government under the Confederacy.* Under that system, Congress could only recommend. Their acts were not of binding force till the states had adopted and sanctioned them.

Are we in that condition still? Sir, if we are, then vain will be our attempt to maintain the Constitution under which we sit. But, sir, the people have wisely provided, in the Constitution itself, a proper, suitable means for settling questions of constitutional law. Congress established, at its very first session, a way to bring all questions of constitutional power to the final decision of the Supreme Court. It then, sir, became a government.

I have thus stated the reasons for my dissent to the doctrines which have been advanced and maintained. This is a subject of which my heart is full. Since it concerns nothing less than the union of the states, it is of most vital and essential importance to the public happiness. It is to that union we owe our safety at home and our dignity abroad. It is to that union that we are chiefly indebted for whatever makes us most proud of our country.

When my eyes shall be turned to behold, for the last time, the sun in heaven, may I not see him shining on the broken and dishonored fragments of a once glorious union. May I not see him shining on states disserved, discordant, belligerent. May I not see him shining on a land torn by civil war or drenched, it may be, in fraternal blood! Let my last feeble and lingering glance, rather, behold the gorgeous flag of the republic, bearing for its motto that sentiment dear to every true American heart—liberty and union, now and forever, one and inseparable!

Adapted from *Congressional Debates*, 21 Cong., 1 sess., 1830.

### READING REVIEW ✶ ✶ ✶ ✶ ✶ ✶

1. Who does Webster say is the supreme source of power in the United States?
2. What does Webster imply would happen to the country if states' rights arguments were allowed to hold sway?
3. **Defending a point of view.** Write a paragraph defending either the position of federal sovereignty or that of states' rights. Use Webster's or Calhoun's arguments or your own.

✶ ✶ ✶ ✶ ✶ ✶ ✶ ✶ ✶ ✶ ✶ ✶ ✶ ✶ ✶ ✶

---

*Webster is referring to the Articles of Confederation.

**Introduction** One of Andrew Jackson's goals as President was to move all Native Americans west of the Mississippi River. Jackson was willing to go to great lengths to accomplish this goal. He wrote this letter to the Seminole Indians, advising them to move west voluntarily. In it, Jackson gave a hint of the measures he was prepared to use if the Seminoles refused to leave. The Seminoles did refuse to go. The bloody seven-year-long Seminole War that followed showed that the President meant business.

**Vocabulary** Before you read the selection, find the meaning of these words in a dictionary: counsel, annuities.

My Children—

I am sorry to have heard that you have been listening to bad counsel. You know me. You know that I would not deceive nor advise you to do anything that was unjust or harmful. Open your ears and attend to what I shall now say to you. They are the words of a friend and the words of truth.

The white people are settling around you. The game has disappeared from your country. Your people are poor and hungry. All this you have known for some time. I tell you that you must go and that you will go. Even if you had a right to stay, how could you live where you now are? You have sold all your country. You have not a piece as large as a blanket to sit down upon. What is to support yourselves, your women, and children?

The tract you have given up will soon be surveyed and sold. Immediately afterwards, it will be occupied by a white population. You will soon be in a state of starvation. You will be forced to rob and plunder the property of our citizens. You will be resisted, punished, perhaps killed.

Now is it not better peaceably to move to a fine, fertile country, occupied by your own kindred, where you can raise all the necessities of life, and where game is yet abundant? The annuities payable to you and the other arrangements made in your favor will make your situation comfortable. They will enable you to increase and improve.

If, therefore, you had a right to stay where you now are, still every true friend would advise you to move. But you have no right to stay, and you must go. I am very desirous that you should go peaceably and voluntarily. You shall be comfortably taken care of and kindly treated on the road. When you arrive in your new country, supplies will be issued to you for a year so that you can have ample time to provide for your future support.

But in case some of your rash young men should forcibly oppose your arrangements for removal, I have ordered a large military force to be sent among you. I have directed that one-third of your people, as provided for in

The Seminole Indians fiercely resisted President Jackson's order to move west. Chief Osceola, shown here, led them in their struggle.

the treaty, be removed during the present season. If you listen to the voice of friendship and truth, you will go quietly and voluntarily. But should you listen to the bad birds that are always flying about you and refuse to move, I have then directed the commanding officer to remove you by force. This will be done. I pray the Great Spirit, therefore, to incline you to do what is right.

Your friend,
A. Jackson

Washington, February 16, 1835

Adapted from "President Andrew Jackson's Letter to the Seminoles," in *History of the Indian Wars*, ed. Henry Trumbull, 1841.

## READING REVIEW ★ ★ ★ ★ ★ ★ ★

1. According to Jackson, why should the Seminoles leave?
2. If the Seminoles refuse to leave, what does Jackson warn them he would do?
3. **Expressing an opinion.** Jackson signs this letter "Your friend." Do you think Jackson was the Seminoles' friend? Why or why not?

★ ★ ★ ★ ★ ★ ★ ★ ★ ★ ★ ★ ★ ★ ★ ★ ★ ★

## ★ 13-6 A Campaign Song ★

**Introduction** During the Age of Jackson, American politics changed in many ways. New, strong leaders emerged in all sections of the country. New parties were born. Most important, more people began to vote and become involved in politics. As a result, campaigns became more colorful and elaborate, designed to reach more of the new voters. These lyrics are from a song written especially for the election of 1840.

**Vocabulary** Before you read the selection, find the meaning of these words in a dictionary: faction, fain, swindler, impudent, knavery.

A stands for Adams, whose administration
  Was like a dead weight on the neck of the nation.
B stands for Banks, and also for Biddle,
  Their tune they must alter or hang up their fiddle.
C stands for Clay, for the potter unfit,
  He ne'er can be molded to honor a bit.
D stands for Dollars, half Dollars, and Dimes,

Then speedily give us good hard-money times.
E stands for Eagle, our country's proud bird,
  He soars where the thunder of battle is heard.
F stands for the Federal faction, who fain
  Would be lords o'er the poor and skin them for gain.
G stands for the Game which the bank swindlers play,
  But the people have called for a reckoning day.

. . . . . . . . . . . . . . . .

I stands for the Impudent lies that are told
  By the aristocratic party, those liars of old.
J stands for Jackson, who never would flinch
  Nor yield to the foes of this country an inch.
K stands for Knavery of every kind;
  Examine the banks and enough of't you'll find.

Adapted from "The Alphabetical Song," 1840.

**READING REVIEW** ★ ★ ★ ★ ★ ★ ★

1. Who does the song imply was responsible for the depression that began in 1837?
2. What is meant by the line "Then speedily give us good hard-money times"?

3. **Drawing conclusions.** (a) What party would you say the writer of this song belonged to? (b) What parts of the song lead you to make this conclusion? Explain your answer.

★ ★ ★ ★ ★ ★ ★ ★ ★ ★ ★ ★ ★ ★ ★ ★ ★

Chapter

# 14 Westward Ho! (1820–1860)

## ★ 14-1 Camp Life in the Rockies ★

**Introduction** Life for the Mountain Men who opened the Oregon Country for later settlers was rough and often difficult. Yet these men's simple ways had an appealing side. This description of life among the Mountain Men was written by Osborne Russell, a trapper and hunter who came to Oregon Country in 1834.

**Vocabulary** Before you read the selection, find the meaning of this word in a dictionary: comprised.

I joined Mr. Bridger's company, who were passing the winter on Blackfoot Creek. Mr Bridger's men killed plenty of bulls, but they were so poor that their meat was perfectly blue. Yet this was their only article of food, as bread and vegetables were out of the question in the Rocky Mountains.

It would doubtless be amusing to a disinterested spectator to witness the process of cooking poor bull meat. On going through the camp at any time in the day, heaps of ashes might be seen with the fire burning on the summit. An independent-looking individual, who is termed a camp kicker, sits with a "two-year-old club" in his hand watching the pile with much impatience. At length, he pokes over the ashes with his club to work loose a great mass of meat. When he hits it with his club, it bounds five or six feet from the ground like a huge ball of gum rubber. This operation, frequently repeated, shakes loose the ashes clinging to the meat and prepares it for carving. He then drops his club and draws his butcher knife, calling to his comrades, "Come Major, Judge, Squire, Dollar, Pike, Cotton, and Gabe, won't you take a lunch of Simon?"

Mountain men looked forward to trips to frontier forts where they traded pelts for supplies. They also enjoyed the chance to swap stories with fellow trappers. This painting is of Fort Walla Walla in Oregon Country.

We passed away the time very agreeably. Our only employment was to feed our horses, kill buffalo, and eat—that is to say, the trappers. The camp keepers' business in winter quarters is to guard the horses, cook, and keep fires. We all had snug lodges made of dressed buffalo skins. In the center we built a fire. Each lodge generally comprised about six men.

The long winter evenings were passed away by collecting in some of the most spacious lodges and having debates and arguments or spinning long yarns until midnight, in perfect good humor. I for one will cheerfully confess that I have derived no little benefit from the frequent arguments and debates held in what we termed "The Rocky Mountain College."

At the summer rendezvous at Green River, we found the hunting parties all assembled waiting for the arrival of supplies from the States. Some were gambling at cards, some playing the Indian game of "hand," and others horse racing. Here and there could be seen small groups collected under shady trees relating the events of the past year, all in good spirits and health, for sickness is a stranger seldom met with in these regions.

Adapted from Osborne Russell, *The Journal of a Trapper, or, Nine Years in the Rocky Mountains*, 1914.

**READING REVIEW** ★ ★ ★ ★ ★ ★ ★

1. Describe the job of a camp kicker.
2. (a) What did the Mountain Men do for entertainment in the winter? (b) At their summer rendezvous?
3. **Supporting generalizations.** What evidence is there in this account that Russell enjoyed life as a trapper?

★ ★ ★ ★ ★ ★ ★ ★ ★ ★ ★ ★ ★ ★ ★ ★ ★ ★ ★

## ★ 14-2 A Defense of the Texas Struggle ★

Many Texans were ready to go to war with Mexico because they had grown to love their new land. Settlers had poured years of work into building farms such as the one shown here.

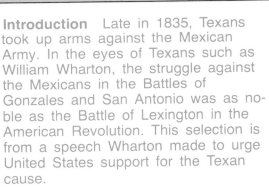

**Introduction** Late in 1835, Texans took up arms against the Mexican Army. In the eyes of Texans such as William Wharton, the struggle against the Mexicans in the Battles of Gonzales and San Antonio was as noble as the Battle of Lexington in the American Revolution. This selection is from a speech Wharton made to urge United States support for the Texan cause.

**Vocabulary** Before you read the selection, find the meaning of these words in a dictionary: despotism, simultaneously, indignation, smitten.

You have now seen, gentlemen, that our constitution has been violated illegally and totally destroyed. You have seen that, added to this, our governor has been imprisoned and our legislature disbanded. Now, mark the patience of the people of Texas! Even after all these outrages on their rights, they did not rise in arms and make an appeal to the god of battles for justice and righting of their wrongs. They still hoped that the Mexican nation would have the firmness and patriotism to crush this military despotism.

In this hope, they were cruelly deceived. In the month of September last, a Mexican armed schooner appeared off our coast and declared all of our ports in a state of blockade. Simultaneously with this, General Coss invaded our territory by land. About the same time, a military force was sent to the colonial town of Gonzales to demand of the inhabitants a surrender of their arms. This demand was refused with the promptness and indignation of freemen. A battle immediately ensued on the 28th September last, which ended in the defeat and hasty retreat of the Mexican forces.

Gonzales was then the Lexington of our struggle. And the same cry for liberty, which from the blood of the slain at Lexington and Bunker's Hill rose to high Heaven and penetrated every corner of this land, flew with electrical rapidity after the battles of Gonzales and St. Antonio.

The inhabitants promptly responded to its call. They felt now that the rod of oppression had smitten sufficiently severe. They could no longer submit without giving up forever the glorious name of freemen. Accordingly, they rallied around the standard of their country. All were alive with the spirit of "76."

Adapted from an address delivered by William Wharton, April 26, 1836.

### READING REVIEW ★ ★ ★ ★ ★ ★

1. How does Wharton show that Mexico was threatening the colony of Texas?
2. Why did the Texans lose patience and take up arms against Mexico?
3. **Making inferences.** How was the struggle of the Texans against Mexico similar to the American Revolution?

★ ★ ★ ★ ★ ★ ★ ★ ★ ★ ★ ★ ★ ★ ★ ★ ★ ★ ★

## ★ 14-3 Prudencia Higuera's Brass Buttons ★

**Introduction** By the mid-1800s, the Spanish had been in California for several generations. Some had established large, prosperous ranches. Then, in the early 1800s, settlers from the United States began to arrive. In this selection, Prudencia Higuera, daughter of a Spanish rancher, gives her impressions of the first encounter with these settlers.

**Vocabulary** Before you read the selection, find the meaning of this word in a dictionary: interpreter.

In the autumn of 1840, my father lived near what is now called Pinole Point in Contra Costa County, California. I was then about 12 years old. I remembered the time because it was then that we saw the first American vessel that traded along the shores of San Pablo Bay.

The captain soon came with a small boat and two sailors. One was a Frenchman who knew Spanish very well and who acted as interpreter. The captain asked my father to get into the boat and go to the vessel. Mother was much afraid to let him go, as we all thought the Americans were not to be trusted unless we knew them well. We feared they would carry my father off and keep him a prisoner. Father said, however, that it was all right. He went and put on his best clothes, gay with silver braid. We all cried and kissed him goodbye, while Mother clung about his neck and said we might never see him again.

Then the captain told her: "If you are afraid, I will have the sailors take him to the vessel while I stay here until he comes back. He ought to see all the goods I have or he will not know what to buy." After a little, my mother let him go with the captain. We stood on the beach to see them off.

He came back the next day bringing four boatloads of cloth, axes, shoes, fish lines, and many new things. My brother had traded some deerskins for a gun and four toothbrushes, the first ones I had ever seen. I remember that we children rubbed them on our teeth till the blood came. We concluded that, after all, we liked best the bits of pounded willow root that we used for brushes before.

After the ship sailed, my mother and sisters began to cut out new dresses, which the Indian women sewed. On one of mine, Mother put some big brass buttons about an inch across with eagles on them. How proud I was! I used to rub them hard every day to make them shine, using the toothbrush.

Then our neighbors, who were 10 or 15 miles away, came to see all the things we had bought. One girl offered me a beautiful black colt she owned for six of the brass buttons. But I continued for a long time to think more of those buttons than of anything else I possessed.

Adapted from *As I Saw It: Women Who Lived the American Adventure*, copyright © 1978 by Cheryl G. Hoople. A Dial Books for Young Readers book. Reprinted by permission of E.P. Dutton, a division of New American Library.

### READING REVIEW ★ ★ ★ ★ ★ ★ ★

1. Why was Prudencia's mother afraid to let her father go to the Americans' ship?
2. (a) What American device was new to the Spanish? (b) How did Prudencia finally use it?
3. **Drawing conclusions.** What sort of attitude do you think Prudencia and her family had towards Americans after this first meeting?

★ ★ ★ ★ ★ ★ ★ ★ ★ ★ ★ ★ ★ ★ ★ ★ ★

## ★ 14-4 America's Manifest Destiny ★

**Introduction** In the 1840s, more and more Americans looked eagerly toward the rich and beautiful lands of the Southwest. Yet this territory belonged to Mexico. To explain why the United States should own this land, John L. O'Sullivan developed the idea of manifest destiny. This selection is from a newspaper article O'Sullivan wrote in 1845.

**Vocabulary** Before you read the selection, find the meaning of these words in a dictionary: inevitable, irreversible, preposterous, irresistible, dominion, spontaneous.

It is time now for opposition to the annexation of Texas to cease. It is time for the common duty of patriotism to the country to succeed. Or if this claim will not be recognized, it is at least time for common sense to bow with decent grace to the inevitable and the irreversible.

The pretense that the annexation has been unrightful and unrighteous is wholly untrue and unjust to ourselves. If Texas became peopled with an American population, it was on the express invitation of Mexico herself. The invitation was accompanied with guarantees of state independence and the maintenance of a federal system similar to our own. What, then, can be more preposterous than all this clamor by Mexico against annexation as a violation of any rights of hers, any duties of ours?

Nor is there any just foundation for the charge that annexation is a great proslavery measure calculated to increase and keep alive that institution. Slavery had nothing to do with it. Opinions were and are greatly divided, in both the North and South, as to the influence to be exerted by the annexation on slavery and the slave states.

California will, probably, next fall away. Distracted Mexico never can exert any real governmental authority over such a country. The Anglo-Saxon foot is already on California's borders. Already, the advance guard of the irresistible army of Anglo-Saxon emigration has begun to pour down upon it. It is armed with the plough and the rifle. It marks its trail with schools and colleges, courts and representative halls, mills and meeting houses. A population will soon be in actual occupation of California, over which it will be idle for Mexico to dream of dominion. They will necessarily become independent. All this without interference by our government, without responsibility of our people—in the natural flow of events, the spontaneous working of principles.

Adapted from *United States Magazine and Democratic Review*, 1845.

### READING REVIEW ★ ★ ★ ★ ★ ★ ★

1. (a) How does O'Sullivan justify the annexation of Texas? (b) What role does he say slave states had in it?
2. What Mexican territory does O'Sullivan say will be the next to fall to the United States?
3. **Expressing an opinion.** (a) Do you agree that America had a "manifest destiny" to expand across the continent? (b) Why or why not?

★ ★ ★ ★ ★ ★ ★ ★ ★ ★ ★ ★ ★ ★ ★ ★

## ★ 14-5 Black Opposition to the Mexican War ★

**Introduction** From its beginning, the war with Mexico was controversial. Many Southerners and Westerners supported the war. Many Northerners, both white and black, opposed it. They feared that the acquisition of Mexican territory would lead to the extension of slavery. This editorial, about the news of the American victory in 1848, was written by Frederick Douglass, a black leader of the antislavery movement.

**Vocabulary** Before you read the selection, find the meaning of these words in a dictionary: barbarous, unoffending, plunder, hypocritical, pretense.

PEACE! PEACE! PEACE!
The shout is on every lip and published in every paper. The joyful news is told in every quarter with enthusiastic delight. We are such an exception to the great mass of our fellow countrymen, in respect to everything else, and we have been so accustomed to

In the final offensive of the Mexican War, Major General Winfield Scott captured Mexico City. This painting shows his army entering the city.

hear them rejoice over the most barbarous outrages committed upon an unoffending people, that we find it difficult to unite with them in their jubilation at this time. We believe that by peace they mean plunder.

In our judgment, those who have all along been loudly in favor of a vigorous prosecution of the war, and announcing its bloody triumphs with apparent delight, have no sincere love of peace and are not now rejoicing over peace, but plunder. They have succeeded in robbing Mexico of her territory. And they are rejoicing over their success under the hypocritical pretense of a regard for peace. Had they not succeeded in robbing Mexico of the most important and most valuable part of her territory, many of those now loudest in their cries of favor for peace would be loudest and wildest for war— war to the knife.

Our soul is sick of such hypocrisy. That an end is put to the wholesale murder in Mexico is truly just cause for rejoicing. But we are not the people to rejoice. We ought rather blush and hang our heads for shame. In the spirit of profound humility, we should beg pardon for our crimes at the hands of a god whose mercy endures forever.

Adapted from Frederick Douglass, editorial in *North Star*, March 17, 1848.

## READING REVIEW ★ ★ ★ ★ ★ ★ ★

1. What does Douglass mean when he says Americans are celebrating plunder rather than peace?
2. (a) Who does Douglass blame for the war? (b) How do you know?
3. **Applying information.** Why might a former slave like Douglass have sympathized with the Mexicans?

★ ★ ★ ★ ★ ★ ★ ★ ★ ★ ★ ★ ★ ★ ★ ★

---

## ★ 14-6 Louise Clappe Strikes Gold ★

**Introduction** After the discovery of gold at Sutter's Mill in January 1848, thousands rushed to the California gold fields. Among this group of eager gold seekers were Louise and Fayette Clappe. They settled in a wild mining town called Rich Bar. Louise Clappe described her new life in letters to her sister, such as this one.

**Vocabulary** Before you read the selection, find the meaning of these words in a dictionary: erroneous, specimens.

November 25, 1851

Nothing of importance has happened since I last wrote you, except that I have become a miner. I can truly say I am sorry I "learned the trade," for I wet my feet, tore my dress, spoilt a pair of new gloves, nearly froze my fingers, got an awful headache, took cold, and lost a valuable pin in this, my labor of love.

Of lady gold-washers in general—it is a common habit with people residing in towns in the vicinity of the "diggings" to make up parties to those places. Each woman of the company will exhibit on her return at least $20 of ore, which she will gravely inform you she has just "panned out" from a single basinful of the soil. This, of course, gives strangers a very erroneous idea of the average richness of gold-bearing dirt.

I myself thought (now don't laugh) that one had but to stroll gracefully along romantic streamlets on sunny afternoons, with a parasol and white kid gloves perhaps, and to stop now and then to admire the scenery, and carelessly rinse out a small panful of yellow sand in order to fill one's workbag with the most beautiful and rare specimens of the precious mineral. Since I have been here, I have discovered my mistake—and also the secret of the brilliant success of former gold-washers.

The miners are in the habit of flattering the vanity of their fair visitors by scattering a handful of "salt" (which, strange to say, is exactly the color of gold dust) through the dirt before the dainty fingers touch it. The dear creatures go home with their treasures, firmly believing that mining is the prettiest pastime in the world.

To be sure, there are now and then "lucky strikes." Once a person took $256 out of a single basinful of soil. But such luck is as rare as the winning of a $100,000 prize in a lottery. We are acquainted with many here whose gains have never amounted to much more than "wages"—that is, from $6 to $8 a day. A "claim" which yields a man a steady income of $10 per day is considered very valuable.

Adapted from letter written by Louise Amelia "Dame Shirley" Clappe, November 25, 1851 (published 1854–1855).

### READING REVIEW ★ ★ ★ ★ ★ ★ ★

1. According to Louise Clappe, how likely was it that a person could strike it rich panning for gold?
2. (a) What trick played by one miner on another is described in this letter? (b) How common do you suppose such tricks were?
3. **Comparing.** How was the work of mining different from the way Louise Clappe had first imagined it?

★ ★ ★ ★ ★ ★ ★ ★ ★ ★ ★ ★ ★ ★ ★ ★ ★ ★ ★

# Chapter 15 Two Ways of Life (1820–1860)

## ★ 15-1 At Work on a Clipper ★

**Introduction** With the invention of swift clipper ships, American shipping came into its own. To pass the time while they worked, and to keep their movements in rhythm, sailors on board the clippers sang sea chanteys. This chantey was popular not only with sailors but with the many California-bound passengers who sailed the clippers during the Gold Rush.

**Vocabulary** Before you read the selection, find the meaning of this word in a dictionary: tinker.

Come all ye young fellers that follow the
    sea
With a ho ho, blow the man down
Now just pay attention and listen to me
Give me some time to blow the man down

Speedy clipper ships enabled the United States to become a leader in trade with China. This painting shows the trading posts of six nations at Canton about 1800.

Aboard the *Black Baller* I first served my
time
With a ho ho, blow the man down
But on the *Black Baller* I wasted my time
Give me some time to blow the man down

We'd tinkers and tailors and sailors and
all
With a ho ho, blow the man down
That sailed for good seamen aboard the
*Black Ball*
Give me some time to blow the man down

Now when the *Black Baller's* preparin'
for sea
With a ho ho, blow the man down
You'd bust your sides laughin' at sights
that you see
Give me some time to blow the man down

But when the *Black Baller* is clear of the
land
With a ho ho, blow the man down
Old kicking Jack Williams gives ev'ry
command
Give me some time to blow the man down

Adapted from the song "Blow the Man Down," 1849.

### READING REVIEW

1. According to the song, what occupations
did men leave to go to work at sea?
2. How was life on shipboard different in
port from the way it was at sea?
3. **Using a song as historical evidence.**
Life on board ship is often thought to be
glamorous or romantic. What image of a
sailor's life does this song present?

---

## ★ 15-2 Life in a Mill in 1832 ★

**Introduction** In the 1820s, New England textile industries hired many young, unmarried women to work in their factories. As the demand for cheap labor increased, wages dropped and conditions worsened. Some citizens began to protest this growing problem. One of those who spoke out was Seth Luther. The following selection is taken from an address he gave in 1832.

**Vocabulary** Before you read the selection, find the meaning of these words in a dictionary: vice, broach, climax.

We see the system of manufacturing praised to the skies. Senators, representatives, owners, and agents of cotton mills use all means to keep out of sight the evils growing up under it. In cotton mills, cruelties are practiced, excessive labor required, and education neglected. Vice is on the increase. Yet they are called "the palaces of the poor."

A member of the United States Senate seems to be extremely pleased with cotton mills. He says, "Who has not been delighted with the clockwork movements of a large cotton manufactory?" He says the women work in large airy apartments, well warmed. They are neatly dressed, with ruddy complexions and happy faces. They mend the broken threads and replace the exhausted balls or broaches. And at stated periods they go to and return from their meals with a light and cheerful step.

While on a visit to that pink of perfection, Waltham, I remarked that the females moved with a very light step. Well they might, for the bell rang for them to return to the mill from their homes 19 minutes after it had rung for them to go to breakfast. Some of these females boarded the largest part of half a mile from the mill.

The grand climax is that, at the end of the week, after working like slaves for 13 or 14 hours every day, according to the Senators, "they enter the temples of God on the Sabbath and thank him for all his benefits. The

American System above all, he says, requires a peculiar outpouring of gratitude. We do not believe there can be a single person who ever thanked God for permission to work in a cotton mill.

Adapted from Seth Luther, *Address*, 1836.

## READING REVIEW ★ ★ ★ ★ ★ ★ ★

1. What specific practices does Luther mention as examples of the hardship of factory life?

2. Luther scoffed at the term "palaces of the poor," used to describe factories. What did people mean by this term?

3. **Relating cause and effect.** Why do you think a senator would give such a glowing report on life in factories?

★ ★ ★ ★ ★ ★ ★ ★ ★ ★ ★ ★ ★ ★ ★ ★ ★ ★

Iron works, as well as textile mills, were important to northern industry in the mid-1800s. The Excelsior Iron Works, shown here, was located in New York State.

## ★ 15-3 A Violent Reaction to Foreign-Born Voters ★

**Introduction** As more and more immigrants arrived in the United States, prejudice against them grew. In 1855, some citizens of Louisville, Kentucky, who opposed the right of foreign-born Americans to vote, used violence to keep them from the polls. These nativist Americans worked through the Know-Nothing Party. This description of the election day events is from the *Louisville Courier*.

**Vocabulary** Before you read the selection, find the meaning of these words in a dictionary: farce, intimidation, pursuance, gauntlet, pillaged.

We passed, yesterday, through the forms of an election. Never, perhaps, was a greater farce, or as we should term it tragedy, enacted. Hundreds and thousands were prevented from voting by direct acts of intimidation. The city, indeed, was, during the day, in possession of an armed mob. The base passions of the mob were aroused to the highest pitch by the fiery appeals of the newspaper and the popular leaders of the Know-Nothing Party.

On Sunday night, large detachments of men were sent to the First and Second Wards to see that the polls were properly opened. These men discharged the important trusts committed to them in such manner as to commend them forever to the admiration of outlaws. They opened the polls. They provided ways and means for their own party to vote. They buffed and bullied all who could not show the sign. They in fact converted the election into a perfect farce, without one redeeming feature.

By daybreak, the polls were taken possession of by the Know-Nothing Party. In pursuance of their planned game, they used every strategy to hinder the vote of every man who could not show to the "guardians of the polls" his soundness on the K. N. question. In the Sixth Ward a party of bullies were masters of the polls. We saw two foreigners driven from the polls, forced to run a gauntlet, beaten unmercifully, stoned, and stabbed.

In the afternoon, a number of houses, chiefly German coffee houses, were broken into and pillaged. After dusk, a row of frame houses on Main Street between Tenth and Eleventh was set on fire. These houses were chiefly tenanted by Irish. When any of the tenants ventured out to escape the flames, they were immediately shot down.

We are sickened with the very thought of the men murdered and houses burned and pillaged that signaled the victory yesterday. No fewer than 20 corpses form the trophies of this wonderful achievement.

Adapted from an article in the *Louisville Courier*, August 6, 1855.

## READING REVIEW ★ ★ ★ ★ ★ ★

1. What means did the Know-Nothings use to intimidate foreign-born voters?

2. According to the article, what ethnic groups were the chief victims of the Know-Nothings' violence?

3. **Distinguishing fact from opinion.** (a) Which parts of the article are statements of opinion? (b) Give two examples of facts in the article.

★ ★ ★ ★ ★ ★ ★ ★ ★ ★ ★ ★ ★ ★ ★ ★

## ★ 15-4 Inventing the Cotton Gin ★

**Introduction** The invention of the cotton gin revolutionized the cotton industry of the South. The machine was eventually able to clean as much cotton a day as 1,000 slaves could clean by hand. Eli Whitney invented the cotton gin shortly after he graduated from college. In this letter written to his parents, Whitney tells how he came to build the first gin.

**Vocabulary** Before you read the selection, find the meaning of these words in a dictionary: advantageous, enjoining.

New Haven
Sept. 11th, 1793
Dear Parent,

I presume, sir, you want to hear how I have spent my time since I left college. It is my duty to inform you, and I should have done it before this time.

I went from New York with the family of the late Major General Greene to Georgia. I went immediately with the family to their plantation. I expected to spend four or five days and then proceed into Carolina to take the school, as I have mentioned in former letters.

During this time I heard much said of the extreme difficulty of ginning cotton, that is, separating it from its seeds. There were a number of very respectable gentlemen at Mrs. Greene's who all agreed that if a machine could be invented which would clean the cotton more efficiently, it would be a great thing both to the country and to the inventor.

I involuntarily happened to be thinking on the subject and struck out a plan of a machine in my mind. In about ten days I made a little model. I was offered 100 guineas for it if I would give up all right and title to it. I decided to give up my school and turn my attention to perfecting the machine. I made one with which one man will clean ten times as much cotton as he can in any other way before known.

How advantageous this business will eventually prove to me, I cannot say, but think I had better pursue it rather than any other business into which I can enter.

I wish you, sir, not to show this letter nor communicate anything of its contents to anybody except my brothers and sister, enjoining it on them to keep the whole a profound secret.

With respect to Mama, I am, kind Parent,

Your most obedient Son,
Eli Whitney, Junior

Adapted from a letter of Eli Whitney, Jr., to his father, September 11, 1793.

**READING REVIEW** ★ ★ ★ ★ ★ ★ ★

1. (a) What had Eli Whitney planned to do after college? (b) What effect did the invention of the cotton gin have on his plans?
2. Why do you think Whitney wanted his family to keep this letter a secret?
3. **Relating past to present.** (a) What recent invention has had as profound an effect on people's lives as the cotton gin had on the lives of Southern planters? (b) In what way or ways has this invention changed our lives?

★ ★ ★ ★ ★ ★ ★ ★ ★ ★ ★ ★ ★ ★ ★ ★ ★ ★

Here, several slaves use an early cotton gin to clean cotton. In the front of the machine, you can see the row of teeth that pulled the cotton from the seeds.

---

## ★  15-5  Memories of a Slave Auction  ★

**Introduction** One of the most degrading events in the lives of slaves was the slave auction. At an auction, the slaves were paraded and poked as though they were horses or cattle. Many were separated from husband, wife, children, or other loved ones. In this selection, Solomon Northrup, an ex-slave, describes an auction that took place in New Orleans in 1841.

**Vocabulary** Before you read the selection, find the meaning of these words in a dictionary: barter, paroxysm, afflicted, beseeching.

In the first place, we were required to wash thoroughly and those with beards to shave. We were then conducted into a large room in the front part of the building to which the yard was attached, in order to be properly trained before the admission of customers.

The men were arranged on one side of the room, the women at the other. The tallest was placed at the head of the row, then the next tallest, and so on in the order of their respective heights. Freeman, owner of the slave-pen, charged us to remember our places. He ordered us to appear smart and lively, sometimes threatening us. During the day, he exercised us in the art of "looking smart" and of moving to our places with exact precision.

Next day many customers called to examine Freeman's "new lot." The latter gentleman was very talkative, dwelling at much length upon our several good points and qualities. He would make us hold up our heads and walk briskly back and forth, while customers would feel of our hands and arms and bodies, turn us about, ask us what we could do, make us open our mouths and show our teeth, precisely as a jockey examines a horse which he is about to barter for or purchase. Scars upon a slave's back were considered evidence of a rebellious or unruly spirit and hurt his sale.

During the day, a number of sales were made. All the time the trade was going on, Eliza was crying aloud, and wringing her hands. She begged the man not to buy her son Randall unless he also bought herself and her daughter Emily. She promised, in that case, to be the most faithful slave that ever lived. The man answered that he could not afford it. Then Eliza burst in a paroxysm of grief, weeping mournfully. Freeman turned round to her, savagely, with his whip in his uplifted hand, ordering her to stop her noise or he would flog her. All the frowns and threats of Freeman could not wholly silence the afflicted mother. She kept on begging and beseeching them not to separate the three. But it was of no avail. The man could not afford it. The bargain was agreed upon, and Randall must go alone. Then Eliza ran to him, embraced him passionately, kissed him again and again, and told him to remember her—all the while her tears falling in the boy's face like rain.

"Don't cry, mama. I will be a good boy. Don't cry," said Randall, looking back, as they passed out of the door.

It was a mournful scene indeed. I would have cried myself if I had dared.

Adapted from Solomon Northrup, *Twelve Years a Slave*, 1853.

## READING REVIEW ★ ★ ★ ★ ★ ★ ★

1. Why were the slaves examined for scars by prospective buyers?
2. Why were Eliza and Randall separated?
3. **Comparing.** How, according to Northrup, was a slave auction like an animal auction?

★ ★ ★ ★ ★ ★ ★ ★ ★ ★ ★ ★ ★ ★ ★

Chapter

# 16 The Reforming Spirit (1820–1860)

## ★  16-1  A Daring Escape to Freedom  ★

**Introduction**  The history of the Underground Railroad abounds in dramatic stories. The slaves who escaped to freedom and the people who helped them risked their lives. One story was that of the escape from Georgia of Ellen and William Craft, a young slave couple. This letter by a fellow fugitive slave, abolitionist William Wells Brown, tells their story.

**Vocabulary**  Before you read the selection, find the meaning of these words in a dictionary: precedent, advocate.

One of the most interesting cases of the escape of fugitives from American slavery that has ever come before the American people has just occurred, under the following circumstances. William and Ellen Craft, man and wife, lived with different masters in the state of Georgia. Ellen is so near white that she can pass without suspicion for a white woman. Her husband is much darker. He is a mechanic. By working nights and Sundays, he laid up money enough to bring himself and his wife out of slavery.

Their plan was without precedent. But though unusual, it was the means of getting them their freedom. Ellen dressed in man's clothing and passed as the master, while her husband passed as the servant. In this way they traveled from Georgia to Philadelphia. On their journey, they put up at the best hotels where they stopped. Neither of them can read or write. And Ellen, knowing that she would be called upon to write her name at the hotels, tied her right hand up as though it was lame, which proved of some service to her.

In Charleston, South Carolina, they put up at the hotel which Governor McDuffie and John C. Calhoun generally make their home. Yet these distinguished advocates of the "peculiar institution" say that the slaves cannot take care of themselves. They arrived in Philadelphia in four days from the time they started.

They are very intelligent. They are young, Ellen 22 and William 24 years of age. Ellen is truly a heroine.

Yours truly,
William W. Brown

Adapted from *The Liberator*, January 12, 1849.

## READING REVIEW ★ ★ ★ ★ ★ ★

1. What did the Crafts have to do before they could even try to escape to freedom?
2. (a) How did Ellen cover up the fact that she could not write? (b) Why would it have been dangerous for people to discover that she could not write?
3. **Analyzing a primary source.** Wells states that both McDuffie and Calhoun believed that slaves cannot take care of themselves. Why do you think Brown mentions this fact?

★ ★ ★ ★ ★ ★ ★ ★ ★ ★ ★ ★ ★ ★ ★ ★ ★

An attempted escape was extremely risky for slaves. Yet to many the chance of freedom made the risk worthwhile. The faces of these runaway slaves who realize they may be free at last show how much freedom could mean.

**Introduction** As the campaign against slavery heated up, more Southerners began to defend the institution. This selection contains two arguments made by Southerners. Thomas Dew was a professor at William and Mary College in Virginia, and George McDuffie was governor of South Carolina.

**Vocabulary** Before you read the selection, find the meaning of these words in a dictionary: inevitably, conducive, sanction, servile, attributes.

## Thomas Dew

Let us now look a moment to the slave, and consider his position. Mr. Jefferson has described him as hating rather than loving his master. We assert again that Mr. Jefferson is not borne out by the fact. We are well convinced that there is nothing but the relations of husband and wife, parent and child, or brother and sister which produces a closer tie than the relation of master and servant. We do not hesitate to affirm that, throughout the whole slave-holding country, the slaves of a good master are his warmest, most constant, and most devoted friends. They have been accustomed to look up to him as their supporter, director, and defender. Everyone acquainted with southern slaves knows that the slave rejoices in the prosperity of his master.

A merrier being does not exist on the face of the globe than the Negro slave of the United States. They are happy and contented, and the master is much less cruel than is generally imagined. Why then, since the slave is happy and happiness is the great object of all animated creation, should we attempt to disturb his contentment by planting in his mind a vain and indefinite desire for liberty—a something which he cannot understand and which must inevitably dry up the very sources of his happiness?

## George McDuffie

No human institution, in my opinion, is more clearly consistent with the will of God than slavery. And no one of his laws is written in more legible characters than that which consigns the African race to this condition as more conducive to their own happiness than any other with which they might meet. Whether we consult the sacred Scriptures or the lights of nature and reason, we shall find these truths as abundantly apparent as if written with a sunbeam in the heavens. Under both the Jewish and Christian branches of our religion, slavery existed with the wholehearted sanction of its prophets, its apostles, and finally its great Author. The ancient Hebrew fathers themselves, those chosen men of God, were slaveholders.

That the African Negro is destined by God to occupy this condition of servile dependence is not less clear. They have all the qualities that fit them for slaves and not one of those that would fit them to be freemen. Until the "African can change his skin," it will be in vain to attempt, by any human power, to make freemen of those whom God has doomed to be slaves.

Adapted from Thomas R. Dew, *Review of the Debate in the Virginia Legislature of 1831 and 1832*, 1832, and George McDuffie, message to the Legislature of South Carolina, *Journal of the General Assembly of the State of South Carolina*, 1835.

### READING REVIEW ★ ★ ★ ★ ★ ★ ★

1. What is the main argument Thomas Dew makes in defense of slavery?
2. George McDuffie argues that it is the will of God that the American institution of slavery exists. What are the two principal reasons he gives for believing this?
3. **Comparing points of view.** Compare the attitudes toward slavery expressed here with the attitude expressed by Solomon Northrup in Reading 15-5.

★ ★ ★ ★ ★ ★ ★ ★ ★ ★ ★ ★ ★ ★ ★ ★

**Introduction** In the 1800s, women began not only to demand equal rights with men under the law. They also began to question the attitudes that kept the sexes unequal. Elizabeth Cady Stanton traced much of women's dependence on men to the way in which young girls were raised. Stanton herself had raised seven children. In this speech to a woman's convention held in Akron, Ohio, she proposes a very different approach to raising girls.

**Vocabulary** Before you read the selection, find the meaning of these words in a dictionary: self-reliance, drone.

Dear Friends: The great work before us is the education of those just coming on the stage of action. Begin with the girls of today, and in 20 years we can revolutionize this nation. The childhood of woman must be free and unrestrained.

The girl must be allowed to romp and play, climb, skate, and swim. Her clothes must be more like those of the boy—strong, loose-fitting garments, thick boots, etc.—so that she may be out at all times and enter freely into all kinds of sports. Teach her to go alone, by night and day, if need be, on the lonely highway or through the busy streets of the crowded city.

The manner in which all courage and self-reliance is educated out of the girl, her path portrayed with dangers and difficulties that never exist, is sad indeed. Better, far, suffer occasional insults or die outright than live the life of a coward or never move without a protector. The best protector any woman can have, one that will serve her at all times and in all places, is courage. This she must get by her own experience.

The girl must early be impressed with the idea that she is to be "a hand,

not a mouth"—a worker, not a drone—in the great hive of human activity. Like the boy, she must be taught to look forward to a life of self-dependence and to prepare herself early for some trade or profession.

Do you think women thus educated would long remain the weak, dependent beings we now find them? By no means. Depend upon it, as educated capitalists and skilled laborers, they would not be long in finding their true level in political and social life.

Adapted from Elizabeth C. Stanton, Susan B. Anthony, and Matilda J. Gage, *History of Woman Suffrage,* 1881-1922.

**READING REVIEW** ★ ★ ★ ★ ★ ★ ★

1. How did Elizabeth Cady Stanton propose to develop courage in young girls?
2. Why did she think it important for women to have courage?
3. **Relating past to present.** (a) To what degree have Stanton's proposals for the education of girls been put into practice today? (b) To what degree do today's young women have the attitudes toward life Stanton proposed?

★ ★ ★ ★ ★ ★ ★ ★ ★ ★ ★ ★ ★ ★ ★ ★ ★

Elizabeth Cady Stanton devoted much of her life to working for greater equality for women. She was also a busy wife and mother. Here she is shown with one of her seven children.

**Introduction** Americans on the frontier shared the nation's growing concern with education. Although poor and struggling, the settlers in a new area often worked hard to scrape together the money and materials needed to build a school and hire a teacher for their children. One-room country schoolhouses, such as the one shown in this painting by Winslow Homer, soon became commonplace.

**READING REVIEW** ★ ★ ★ ★ ★ ★ ★ ★ ★ ★ ★ ★ ★ ★ ★ ★ ★ ★

1. Judging by this painting, what kind of equipment did teachers and students in country schools have to work with?
2. What would you say is the age range of the children in this classroom?
3. **Using visual evidence.** Based on the painting, how would you describe education in a one-room school?

★ ★ ★ ★ ★ ★ ★ ★ ★ ★ ★ ★ ★ ★ ★ ★ ★ ★ ★ ★ ★ ★ ★ ★ ★ ★ ★ ★

**Introduction**  Some writers of the 1800s celebrated their country's past and its way of life. Others warned their fellow citizens of potential dangers they saw in American habits and attitudes. Henry David Thoreau was a writer of the second type. In *Walden*, a book he wrote about a year he spent living in the woods, Thoreau urged Americans not to get too caught up in the growing complexity of life.

**Vocabulary**  Before you read the selection, find the meaning of these words in a dictionary: marrow, Spartan, superficial, unwieldy, elevation.

I went to the woods because I wished to live deliberately, to face only the essential facts of life, and to see if I could not learn what it had to teach, and not, when I came to die, discover that I had not lived. I did not wish to live what was not life. Living is so dear. I wanted to live deep and suck out all the marrow of life, to live sturdily and Spartanlike.

Our life is frittered away by detail. An honest man has hardly need to count more than his ten fingers, or in extreme cases he may add his ten toes, and lump the rest. Simplicity, simplicity, simplicity! I say, let your affairs be as two or three, and not a hundred or a thousand. Instead of a million, count half a dozen, and keep your accounts on your thumbnail. Simplify, simplify. Instead of three meals a day, if it be necessary eat but one, and instead of a hundred dishes, five. And reduce other things in proportion.

The nation itself, with all its so-called internal improvements, which, by the way, are all external and superficial, is just such an unwieldy and overgrown establishment. It is cluttered with furniture and tripped up by its own traps, ruined by luxury and heedless expense, by lack of calculation and a worthy aim. And the only cure for it, as for them, is in a stern and more than Spartan simplicity of life and elevation of purpose.

It lives too fast. Men think that it is essential that the nation have commerce, and export ice, and talk through a telegraph, and ride 30 miles an hour. But whether we should live like baboons or like men is a little uncertain. If we do not forge rails and devote days and nights to the work, but go to tinkering upon our lives to improve them, who will build railroads? And if railroads are not built, how shall we get to heaven in season? But if we stay at home and mind our business, who will want railroads?

Adapted from Henry David Thoreau, *Walden*, 1849.

**READING REVIEW** ★ ★ ★ ★ ★ ★

1. (a) What are two examples Thoreau gives of how to simplify life? (b) What others can you think of?

2. What is Thoreau's opinion of the industrial culture growing up around him?

3. **Making generalizations.** What would Thoreau say is the purpose of life?

★ ★ ★ ★ ★ ★ ★ ★ ★ ★ ★ ★ ★ ★ ★ ★ ★ ★

In the 1800s, writers and painters portrayed both the simplicity and the grandeur of the American landscape. This view of Mt. Whitney was painted by Albert Bierstadt.

# Unit 6

# The Nation Divided

Chapter

# 17 The Coming of the War (1820–1860)

★     **17-1**     **A Question of Slavery in the West**     ★

**Introduction** In 1846, Pennsylvania Congressman David Wilmot proposed that Congress prohibit slavery in any territory won from Mexico. His proposal touched off a great debate. This selection is from Wilmot's proposal, called the Wilmot Proviso.

**Vocabulary** Before you read the selection, find the meaning of these words in a dictionary: unmolested, integrity, concession.

Sir, the issue now presented is not whether slavery shall exist unmolested where it now is, but whether it shall be carried to new and distant regions, now free, where the footprint of a slave cannot be found. This, sir, is the issue. Upon it I take my stand, and from it I cannot be frightened or driven by idle charges of abolitionism. I ask not that slavery be abolished. I demand that this government preserve the integrity of free territory against the aggressions of slavery.

Sir, I was in favor of the annexation of Texas. The democracy of the North, almost to a man, went for annexation. Yes, sir, here was an empire larger than France given up to slavery. Shall further concessions be made by the North? Shall we give up free territory? Never, sir, never, until we ourselves are fit to be slaves.

But, sir, we are told that the joint blood and treasure of the whole country being spent in this acquisition,* therefore it should be divided and slavery allowed to take its share. Sir, the South has her share already.

Adapted from *Appendix to the Congressional Globe*, 1847.

**READING REVIEW** ★ ★ ★ ★ ★ ★ ★

1. What is Wilmot's attitude toward slavery in the states where it already exists?
2. (a) According to Wilmot, why do some people favor allowing slavery in the newly acquired Mexican territory? (b) How does he counter their argument?
3. **Finding the main idea.** State the main idea of the first paragraph.

★ ★ ★ ★ ★ ★ ★ ★ ★ ★ ★ ★ ★ ★ ★ ★ ★

*He is referring to the Mexican War.

**Introduction** The 1850 Senate debate over Henry Clay's proposed compromise on slavery was one of the most tense in American history. Senator John C. Calhoun, long a champion of the South, warned that the Union was in terrible danger. Because Calhoun was gravely ill, his speech was read by Senator James Mason of Virginia. This selection is from Calhoun's speech.

**Vocabulary** Before you read the selection, find the meaning of these words in a dictionary: indispensable, consistently, concession, submission.

How can the Union be preserved? To give a satisfactory answer to this mighty question, it is indispensable to have an accurate and thorough knowledge of the nature and the character of the cause by which the Union is endangered.

It is a great mistake to suppose that disunion can be effected by a single blow. The cords which bound these states together in one common union are far too numerous and powerful for that.

Disunion must be the work of time. It is only through a long process that the cords can be snapped, until the whole fabric falls asunder. Already the agitation of the slavery question has snapped some of the most important and has greatly weakened all the others.

If the agitation goes on, the same force, acting with increased intensity, will finally snap every cord. Then nothing will be left to hold the states together except force.

So the question again recurs—how can the Union be saved? To this I answer, there is but one way by which it can be—and that is by adopting such measures as will satisfy the states belonging to the southern section so that they can remain in the Union consistently with their honor and their safety.

The South asks for justice, simple justice, and less she ought not to take. She has no compromise to offer but the Constitution and no concession or surrender to make. She has already surrendered so much that she has little left to surrender.

For over a quarter of a century, John C. Calhoun and Daniel Webster had been powerful figures in the United States Senate. The debate over slavery in 1850 was their last. Compare these photographs with those of the younger Calhoun and Webster on pages 277 and 300.

But can this be done? Yes, easily. The North has only to will it to accomplish it—to do justice by conceding to the South an equal right in the acquired territory. The North has to do her duty by causing the laws relative to fugitive slaves to be faithfully fulfilled. It has to cease agitation on the slave question. And it has to provide for the insertion of a provision in the Constitution which will restore to the South, in substance, the power she possessed of protecting herself.

But will the North agree to this? It is for her to answer the question. But, I will say, she cannot refuse, if she has half the love of the Union which she professes to have. At all events, the responsibility of saving the Union rests on the North, and not on the South.

If you, who represent the stronger portion, cannot agree to settle these questions on the broad principle of justice and duty, say so. Let the states we both represent agree to separate and part in peace. If you are unwilling that we should part in peace, tell us so. We shall know what to do when you reduce the question to submission or resistance.

Adapted from *Works of John C. Calhoun*, ed. Richard K. Cralle, 1856.

### READING REVIEW ★ ★ ★ ★ ★ ★ ★

1. (a) What does Calhoun believe is the only way to save the Union? (b) Whose responsibility is it?
2. Why, according to Calhoun, should the South not compromise with the North?
3. **Making inferences.** What do you think Calhoun is hinting at when he says that if the North is unwilling to let the South part in peace "we shall know what to do"?

★ ★ ★ ★ ★ ★ ★ ★ ★ ★ ★ ★ ★ ★ ★ ★ ★ ★ ★

### ★  17-3    A Plea to Preserve the Union    ★

**Introduction** Probably the best-known speech of the great Senate debate of 1850 was made by Daniel Webster of Massachusetts. Webster had been known for decades as one of the most powerful speakers in the Senate. For much of that time he had used his public speaking talents to win support for the North. However, after hearing Calhoun's address to the Senate, Webster was determined to do what he could to preserve the Union. Webster spoke for over three hours, with hardly a glance at his notes. This selection is from his speech.

**Vocabulary** Before you read the selection, find the meaning of these words in a dictionary: crimination, recrimination, grievances, injunction, dissolution, eminently.

Mr. President, I wish to speak today not as a Massachusetts man, nor as a northern man, but as an American. I shall speak today for the preservation of the Union. Hear me for my cause.

Mr. President, in the excited times in which we live, there is found to exist a state of crimination and recrimination between the North and the South. There are lists of grievances produced by each. Those grievances, real or supposed, alienate the minds of one portion of the country from the other. I see no solid grievance—no grievance presented by the South—but the want of a proper regard to the injunction of the Constitution for the delivery of fugitive slaves.

There are also complaints of the North against the South. The first and gravest is that the North adopted the Constitution recognizing the existence of slavery in the states and recognizing the right, to a certain extent, of representation of the slaves in Congress, under circumstances which do not now exist. The North complains that, instead of slavery being regarded as an evil, as it was then—an evil which all hoped would be extinguished gradually—it is now regarded by the South as an institution to be cherished and preserved and extended—an institution which the South has already extended to the utmost of her power by the acquisition of new territory.

Mr. President, I should much prefer to have heard, from every member of this floor, declarations of opinion that this Union should never be dissolved than the declaration of opinion that, under the pressure of any circumstances, such a dissolution was possible. I hear with pain and anguish and distress the word secession, especially when it falls from the lips of those who are eminently patriotic.

Secession! Peaceable secession! Sir, your eyes and mine are never destined to see that miracle. Peaceable secession is an utter impossibility.

Is the great Constitution under which we live here—covering this whole country—is it to be thawed and melted away by secession, as the snows on the mountain melt under the influence of a vernal sun—disappear almost unobserved, and die off? No, sir! No, sir! I will not state what might produce the disruption of the states, but, Sir, I see it as plainly as I see the sun in heaven—I see that disruption must produce such a war as I will not describe.

Adapted from *Congressional Globe*, 31 Cong., 1 sess., 1849–1850.

### READING REVIEW ★ ★ ★ ★ ★ ★ ★

1. What grievance of the South does Webster feel is a solid one?
2. What grievance of the North does he mention?
3. **Analyzing a primary source.** Why is Webster upset by talk of secession?

★ ★ ★ ★ ★ ★ ★ ★ ★ ★ ★ ★ ★ ★ ★ ★ ★ ★ ★

## ★  17-4    The Suffering of Uncle Tom    ★

**Introduction** Harriet Beecher Stowe's novel *Uncle Tom's Cabin* led many people to question the morality of slavery and roused others to call for its abolition. In fact, the book's influence was so great that, when President Lincoln finally met Mrs. Stowe during the Civil War, he is said to have greeted her: "So, you're the little lady who made this big war!" In this selection from the book, Simon Legree tries to make Tom tell him where some fugitive slaves are hiding.

**Vocabulary** Before you read the selection, find the meaning of these words in a dictionary: despotic, paroxysm, vehemence.

"Now, Quimbo," said Legree, as he stretched himself down in the sitting room, "you jest go and walk that Tom up here, right away! The old cuss is at the bottom of this yer whole matter. I'll have it out of his old black hide, or I'll know the reason why!"

Tom heard the message with a forewarning heart, for he knew all the plans of the fugitives' escape and the place of their present concealment. He knew the deadly character of the man he had to deal with and his despotic power. But he felt strong in God to meet death, rather than betray the helpless.

"Ay, ay!" said Quimbo, as he dragged Tom along. "Ye'll cotch it, now! See how ye'll look, now, helpin' Mas'r's niggers to run away! See what ye'll get!"

"Well, Tom!" said Legree, walking up and seizing him grimly by the collar of his coat. Legree spoke through his teeth in a paroxysm of determined rage. "Do you know I've made up my mind to KILL you?"

"It's very likely, Mas'r," said Tom, calmly.

"I have," said Legree, with grim, terrible calmness, "done—just—that—thing, Tom, unless you'll tell me what you know about these yer gals!"

"I han't got nothing to tell, Mas'r," said Tom, with a slow, firm, deliberate utterance.

"Do you dare to tell me, ye old black Christian, ye don't know?" said Legree.

Tom was silent.

---

Under the new Fugitive Slave Law, free blacks and runaway slaves in the North could be captured and returned to former masters. Antislavery forces printed posters such as this one to alert northern blacks of this danger.

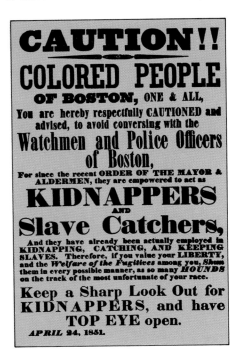

CAUTION!!
COLORED PEOPLE
OF BOSTON, ONE & ALL,
You are hereby respectfully CAUTIONED and advised, to avoid conversing with the
Watchmen and Police Officers of Boston,
For since the recent ORDER OF THE MAYOR & ALDERMEN, they are empowered to act as
KIDNAPPERS
AND
Slave Catchers,
And they have already been actually employed in KIDNAPPING, CATCHING, AND KEEPING SLAVES. Therefore, if you value your LIBERTY, and the Welfare of the Fugitives among you, Shun them in every possible manner, as so many HOUNDS on the track of the most unfortunate of your race.
Keep a Sharp Look Out for KIDNAPPERS, and have TOP EYE open.
APRIL 24, 1851.

"Speak!" thundered Legree, striking him furiously. "Do you know anything?"

"I know, Mas'r. But I can't tell anything. I can die!"

Legree drew in a long breath. Suppressing his rage, he took Tom by the arm. Approaching his face almost to him, Legree said in a terrible voice, "Hark 'e, Tom! Ye think, 'cause I've let you off before, I don't mean what I say. But this time, I've made up my mind and counted the cost. I'll count every drop of blood there is in you and take 'em, one by one till ye give up!"

Tom looked up to his master and answered, "Mas'r, if you was sick, or in trouble, or dying, and I could save ye, I'd give ye my heart's blood. And if taking every drop of blood in this poor old body would save your precious soul, I'd give 'em freely, as the Lord gave his for me. O, Mas'r! Don't bring this great sin on your soul! It will hurt you more than 'twill me! Do the worst you can. My trouble'll be over soon, but if ye don't repent, yours won't never end!"

Like a strange snatch of heavenly music heard in the lull of a storm, this burst of feeling made a moment's blank pause. Legree stood aghast and looked at Tom.

It was but a moment. There was one hesitating pause, and the spirit of evil came back with sevenfold vehemence. Legree, foaming with rage, smote his victim to the ground.

Adapted from Harriet Beecher Stowe, *Uncle Tom's Cabin*, 1852.

### READING REVIEW ★ ★ ★ ★ ★ ★ ★

1. Why was Legree threatening to kill Tom?
2. Why did Tom refuse to answer Legree's questions?
3. **Using fiction as historical evidence.** Tom's final remarks to Legree reflect an argument people often made against slavery. Explain that argument in your own words.

★ ★ ★ ★ ★ ★ ★ ★ ★ ★ ★ ★ ★ ★ ★ ★ ★ ★

## ★   17-5   The Dred Scott Decision: A Black View   ★

**Introduction**  How did blacks react to the Dred Scott decision, which declared that slaves were property and that even free blacks could not be citizens of the United States? Frederick Douglass, a leading black antislavery speaker, responded in this speech made at an abolitionist rally.

**Vocabulary**  Before you read the selection, find the meaning of these words in a dictionary: scandalous, edict.

You will readily ask me how I am affected by this devilish decision. My answer is, and no thanks to the slaveholding wing of the Supreme Court, my hopes were never brighter than now. I have no fear that the national conscience will be put to sleep by such an open, glaring, and scandalous tissue of lies as that decision is and has been over and over shown to be.

The Supreme Court of the United States is not the only power in this world. It is very great, but the Supreme Court of the Almighty is greater. Such a decision cannot stand. We can appeal from man to God. All that is merciful and just, on earth and in heaven, will despise this edict.

If it were at all likely that the people of these free states would tamely submit to this judgment, I might feel gloomy and sad over it. And possibly it might be necessary for my people to look for a home in some other country. But as the case stands, we have nothing to fear. In one point of view, we, the abolitionists and colored people, should meet this decision, unlooked for and monstrous as it appears, in a cheerful spirit. This very attempt to blot out forever the hopes of an enslaved people may be one necessary link in the chain of events leading to the downfall and complete overthrow of the whole slave system.

Adapted from *Two Speeches by Frederick Douglass*, 1857.

### READING REVIEW ★ · ★ · ★ · ★

1. With what spirit did Douglass greet the Dred Scott decision?
2. What reason did he give for adopting this attitude?
3. **Making inferences.**  What do you think Douglass meant when he said the decision might be "one necessary link in the chain of events leading to the complete overthrow of the slave system"?

★ ★ ★ ★ ★ ★ ★ ★ ★ ★ ★ ★ ★ ★ ★ ★ ★

## ★   17-6   Singing the Praises of John Brown   ★

**Introduction**  One of the events that helped push North and South toward war was John Brown's attempt to start a slave revolt in Harpers Ferry, Virginia. Brown and his raid became the subject of one of the most rousing Union songs to come out of the Civil war. "John Brown's Body" was sung by many Union troops marching to early battles. Later on in the war, the tune was used for the song "Battle Hymn of the Republic."

**Vocabulary**  Before you read the selection, find the meaning of this word in a dictionary: traitor.

John Brown's body lies amold'ring in
  the grave,
John Brown's body lies amold'ring in
  the grave,
John Brown's body lies amold'ring in
  the grave,
His soul goes marching on!

*Chorus*
Glory, glory! Hallelujah! Glory, glory!
  Hallelujah!
Glory, glory! Hallelujah! His soul is
  marching on.

He captured Harpers Ferry with his
  nineteen men so true,
And he frightened old Virginia till she
  trembled through and through;
They hung him for a traitor, themselves the traitor crew,
But his soul is marching on!

John Brown died that the slave might
  be free,
John Brown died that the slave might
  be free,
John Brown died that the slave might
  be free,
But his soul goes marching on!

Adapted from a traditional song.

**READING REVIEW** ★ ★ ★ ★ ★ ★ ★

1. What did John Brown do that "frightened old Virginia"?
2. Why does the song call those who hung Brown traitors?
3. **Using a song as historical evidence.** What do you think the song is referring to when it says Brown's "soul is marching on"?

★ ★ ★ ★ ★ ★ ★ ★ ★ ★ ★ ★ ★ ★ ★ ★ ★ ★

## ★ 17-7 Mississippi Secedes From the Union ★

**Introduction** Mississippi was one of the first southern states to secede from the Union. This selection is the formal declaration of secession. In it, the state's political leaders spell out the reasons for their decision to leave the Union.

**Vocabulary** Before you read the selection, find the meaning of these words in a dictionary: sovereign, compact, enticed, incendiary, insurrection, aggrieved.

The constitutional Union was formed by the several states in their separate sovereign capacity for the purpose of mutual advantage and protection. The several states are distinct sovereignties, whose supremacy is limited only so far as the same has been delegated by voluntary compact to a federal government. When that government fails to accomplish the ends for which it was established, the parties to the compact have the right to resume such delegated powers.

The institution of slavery existed prior to the formation of the federal Constitution and is recognized by its letter. All efforts to reduce its value or lessen its duration by Congress or any of the free states is a violation of the compact of union and is destructive of the ends for which it was established. But in defiance of the principles of the Union thus established, the people of the northern states have assumed a revolutionary position towards the southern states.

They have enticed our slaves from us and by state intervention obstructed and prevented their return under the fugitive slave law.

They declare in every manner in which public opinion is expressed their determination to exclude from admittance into the Union any new state that tolerates slavery in its constitution.

They have sought to create discord in the southern states by incendiary publications.

They encourage a hostile invasion of a southern state to excite insurrection, murder, and plunder.

Therefore, the Legislature of the State of Mississippi resolves that the secession of each aggrieved state is the proper remedy for these injuries.

Adapted from *Laws of Mississippi*, 1860.

### READING REVIEW ★ ★ ★ ★ ★ ★ ★

1. According to the declaration, when does a state have the right to take back the powers it has given to the federal government?

2. Why, according to the declaration, is any antislavery action a violation of the national compact of union?

3. **Drawing conclusions.** What event do you think the declaration is referring to when it mentions "a hostile invasion of a southern state to excite insurrection"?

★ ★ ★ ★ ★ ★ ★ ★ ★ ★ ★ ★ ★ ★ ★ ★ ★ ★ ★

When the southern states seceded from the Union, they set up the Confederate States of America. Shown here are Confederate President Jefferson Davis, seated third from left, and his cabinet. General Robert E. Lee is at center.

# Chapter 18 The Civil War (1860–1865)

## ★ 18-1 The Bonnie Blue Flag ★

**Introduction** An early Confederate flag showed a white star on a solid blue background. This song was written by Harry McCarty in honor of that flag.

**Vocabulary** Before you read the selection, find the meaning of these words in a dictionary: treachery, impelled.

We are a band of brothers
  And native to the soil,
Fighting for the property
  We gained by honest toil;
And when our rights were threatened,
  The cry rose near and far —

"Hurrah for the Bonnie Blue Flag
  That bears the single star!"

  *Chorus*
Hurrah! hurrah!
For Southern rights, hurrah!
Hurrah for the Bonnie Blue Flag
That bears the single star.

As long as the Union
  Was faithful to her trust,
Like friends and like brothers
  Both kind were we and just;
But now, when Northern treachery
  Attempts our rights to mar,
We hoist on high the Bonnie Blue Flag
  That bears the single star.

First gallant South Carolina
    Nobly made the stand,
Then came Alabama,
    Who took her by the hand;
Next quickly Mississippi,
    Georgia and Florida,
All raised on high the Bonnie Blue Flag
    That bears the single star.

And here's to old Virginia —
    The Old Dominion State —
With the young Confed'racy,
    At length has linked her fate.
Impelled by her example,
    Now other states prepare
To hoist on high the Bonnie Blue Flag
    That bears the single star.

Then here's to our Confed'racy,
    Strong are we and brave,
Like patriots of old we'll fight
    Our heritage to save.
And rather than submit to shame,
    To die we would prefer;

So cheer for the Bonnie Blue Flag
    That bears the single star.

Then cheer, boys, cheer;
    Raise the joyous shout,
For Arkansas and North Carolina
    Now have both gone out;
And let another rousing cheer
    For Tennessee be given,
The single star of the Bonnie Blue Flag
    Has grown to be eleven.

Adapted from *Rebel Rhymes and Rhapsodies*, 1864.

**READING REVIEW** ★ ★ ★ ★ ★ ★ ★

1. What were the first four states to join the Confederacy?
2. According to the song, what was the Confederacy fighting for?
3. **Understanding geography.** Locate the states mentioned in the song on the map on page 394.

★ ★ ★ ★ ★ ★ ★ ★ ★ ★ ★ ★ ★ ★ ★ ★ ★ ★ ★ ★

## ★ 18-2 Encouraging Union Soldiers ★

**Introduction** For many of the Union recruits, army life was a new and often frightening experience. One of their chief sources of encouragement was the support of their mothers, sisters, wives, and sweethearts. This poem shows the passionate patriotism of Phoebe Cary, a Union woman.

**Vocabulary** Before you read the selection, find the meaning of these words in a dictionary: host, vision, fancy, smite.

Rouse, freeman, the foe has arisen,
    His hosts are abroad on the plain;
And, under the stars of your banner,
    Swear never to strike it again!

O, fathers, who sit with your children,
    Would you leave them a land that
    is free?

Turn now from their tender caresses,
    And put them away from your knee.

O, brothers, we played with in childhood,
    On hills where the clover bloomed
    sweet;
See to it that never a traitor
    Shall trample them under his feet.

O, lovers, awake to your duty
    From visions that fancy has nursed;
Look not in the eyes that would keep you;
    Our country has need of you first.

And we, whom your lives have made
    blessed,
    Will pray for your souls in the fight
That you may be strong to do battle
    For Freedom, for God, and the Right.

We are daughters of men who were
    heroes;
    We can smile as we bid you depart;

But never a coward or traitor
    Shall have room for a place in our
    heart.

Then quit you like men in the conflict,
    Who fight for their home and their
    hand;
Smite deep, in the name of Jehovah,
    And conquer, or die where you
    stand.

Adapted from *Lyrics of Loyalty*, 1864.

**READING REVIEW** ★ ★ ★ ★ ★ ★ ★

1. What argument does Cary use to encourage fathers to fight?
2. How do you think Cary would react to reports that her brother had retreated under fire?
3. **Using a poem as a primary source.** According to this poem, what were Union soldiers fighting to defend?

★ ★ ★ ★ ★ ★ ★ ★ ★ ★ ★ ★ ★ ★ ★ ★ ★ ★

## ★ 18-3     Lee Takes Pity on a Union Soldier     ★

**Introduction** A number of soldiers on both sides were keenly aware that they were fighting against their brothers. Confederate General Robert E. Lee was one of those who always had deep respect for the brave men who fought on both sides, as the following account by a Union soldier shows.

**Vocabulary** Before you read the selection, find the meaning of these words in a dictionary: exposure, taunted.

I was at the battle of Gettysburg myself, and an incident occurred there which changed my views of the southern people. I had fought and cursed the Confederates desperately. I could see nothing good in any of them. The last day of the fight I was badly wounded. A ball shattered my left leg. I lay on the ground not far from Cemetery Ridge. As General Lee ordered his retreat, he and his officers rode near me. As they came along, I recognized him. Though faint from exposure and loss of blood, I raised up my hands, looked Lee in the face, and shouted as loudly as I could, "Hurrah for the Union!"

The general heard me, looked, stopped his horse, dismounted, and came toward me. I confess that I at first thought he meant to kill me. But as he came up, he looked down at me with such a sad expression upon his face that all fear left me. He extended his hand to me. Looking right into my eyes, he said, "My son, I hope you will soon be well."

If I live a thousand years, I shall never forget the expression on General Lee's face. There he was, defeated, retiring from a field that had cost him

One of the Confederacy's greatest strengths was its generals. In addition to Robert E. Lee, the South had the services of such brave and inspiring leaders as General Stonewall Jackson. Jackson is shown here overseeing manoeuvers at the Battle of Bull Run.

and his cause almost their last hope. And yet he stopped to say words like those to a wounded soldier of the opposition who had taunted him as he passed by! As soon as the General had left me, I cried myself to sleep there upon the bloody ground!

Adapted from *A Civil War Treasury of Tales, Legends and Folklore*, ed. B.A. Bodkin (New York: Random House, Inc., 1960).

## ★ 18-4    The Battle of Antietam    ★

**Introduction** People at home learned about the fighting by reading newspaper articles written by reporters who traveled with the armies. Often these reporters risked their lives. This account of the Battle of Antietam was written by George Washburn Smalley, war correspondent for the *New York Tribune*.

**Vocabulary** Before you read the selection, find the meaning of these words in a dictionary: rapidity, canopied, tumult, flanked, unfaltering.

Battlefield of Sharpsburg
Wednesday evening, Sept. 17, 1862

Fierce and desperate battle between 200,000 men has raged since daylight. Finally, at four o'clock, McClellan sent simultaneous orders to Burnside and Franklin. McClellan was to advance and carry the batteries in his front at all hazards and any cost. Burnside was to carry the woods next in front of him to the right, which the Rebels still held.

Burnside obeyed most gallantly. Getting his troops well in hand, he sent a portion of his artillery to the front. He advanced them with rapidity and the most determined vigor, straight up the hill in front, where the Rebels had maintained their most dangerous battery.

The next moment the road in which the Rebel battery was planted was canopied with clouds of dust swiftly descending into the valley. Underneath was a tumult of wagons, guns, horses, and men flying at speed down the road. The hill was carried, but could it be held?

There is a halt. The Rebel left gives way and scatters over the field. The rest stand fast and fire. More infantry comes up. Burnside is outnumbered, flanked, compelled to yield the hill he took so bravely. His position is no longer one of attack. He defends himself with unfaltering firmness, but he sends to McClellan for help.

Looking down into the valley where 15,000 troops are lying, McClellan turns a half-questioning look on Fitz John Porter, who stands by his side, gravely scanning the field. They are Porter's troops below, fresh and impatient to share in this fight. But the same thought is passing through the minds of both generals: "They are the only reserves of the army. They cannot be spared."

Burnside's messenger rides up. His message is "I want troops and guns. If you do not send them I cannot hold my position for half an hour." McClellan turns and speaks very slowly: "Tell General Burnside that this is the battle of the war. He must hold his ground till dark at any cost."

The sun is already down. Not half an hour of daylight is left. None suspected how near was the peril of defeat. But the Rebels halted instead of pushing on. Before it was quite dark, the battle was over. Only a solitary gun of Burnside's thundered against the enemy. Presently this also ceased, and the field was still.

Adapted from *New York Daily Tribune*, September 20, 1862.

**READING REVIEW** ★ ★ ★ ★ ★ ★ ★ ★

1. Why did General McClellan refuse to send Porter's troops to help Burnside?
2. How was Burnside able to carry out the order to "hold his ground at any cost"?
3. **Building vocabulary.** General Burnside was famous for his dashing side whiskers, which were named "sideburns" after him. Find out who these styles are named for: pompadour, cardigan, bowler.

★ ★ ★ ★ ★ ★ ★ ★ ★ ★ ★ ★ ★ ★ ★ ★ ★ ★

## ★ 18-5 Issuing the Emancipation Proclamation ★

**Introduction** When the Emancipation Proclamation was issued, the North was fighting for the abolition of slavery as well as for preserving the Union. This new goal won the North much support, especially from free blacks, abolitionists, and many Europeans. This painting by A. A. Lamb shows the mood of many Northerners at the time.

**READING REVIEW** ★ ★ ★ ★ ★ ★ ★ ★ ★ ★ ★ ★ ★ ★ ★ ★ ★ ★ ★ ★ ★ ★

1. (a) What group of people is at the left? (b) Who is carrying the proclamation?
2. What symbols of the Union does the artist use?
3. **Using visual evidence.** (a) Why do you think Lamb painted this picture? (b) How would his purpose have affected what he painted?

★ ★ ★ ★ ★ ★ ★ ★ ★ ★ ★ ★ ★ ★ ★ ★ ★ ★ ★ ★ ★ ★ ★

# ★ 18-6  A Southern Woman Takes Over at Home ★

**Introduction**  Southern women had an especially hard time during the war. Nearly every able-bodied man enlisted in the army, leaving the women to manage farms and plantations. Women in the South also had to deal with the serious troubles of the Confederate economy—the severe shortages of clothing and food. This selection is from an account of the war years by Victoria Clayton, who was married to a wealthy Alabama planter and lawyer.

**Vocabulary**  Before you read the selection, find the meaning of these words in a dictionary: ingenuity, laborious.

While my husband was at the front doing active service, I was at home struggling to keep the family comfortable. We were blockaded on every side. We could get nothing from without, so we had to make everything at home.

It became necessary for every home to be supplied with spinning wheels and the old-fashioned loom, in order to manufacture clothing for the members of the family. This was no small undertaking. I knew nothing about spinning and weaving cloth. I had to learn myself and then to teach the Negroes. Fortunately for me, most of the Negroes knew how to spin thread, the first step towards cloth-making. Our work was hard and continuous.

Our ladies would attend services in the church of God dressed in their homespun goods. They felt well pleased with their appearances—indeed, better pleased than if they had been dressed in silk of the finest fabric.

We made good warm flannels and other articles of apparel for our soldiers. Every woman learned to knit socks and stockings for her household, and many of the former were sent to the army.

Being blockaded, we were obliged to put our ingenuity to work to meet the demands on us as heads of families. Some things we could not raise—for instance, the accustomed necessary luxury of every home: coffee. So we went to work to hunt up a substitute. Various articles were tried, but the best of all was the sweet potato.

I entrusted the planting and cultivation of the various crops to old Joe. He had been my husband's nurse in infancy, and we always loved and trusted him. I kept a gentle saddle horse, and occasionally, accompanied by Joe, would ride over the entire plantation on a tour of inspection.

We were required to give one-tenth of all that was raised to the government. There being no educated white person on the plantation except myself, it was necessary that I attend to the gathering and measuring of every crop and the delivery of the tenth to the government authorities. This tenth we gave cheerfully, and we often wished we had more to give.

My duties were numerous and often laborious. And this was the case with the typical southern woman.

Adapted from Victoria V. Clayton, *White and Black Under the Old Regime*, 1899.

## READING REVIEW ★ ★ ★ ★ ★ ★ ★

1. What new skills did Victoria Clayton learn in order to cope with the shortages created by the war?
2. Clayton says her duties were numerous. What new duties did she have to take on in her husband's absence?
3. **Making inferences.** (a) What sort of relationship did there seem to be between Victoria Clayton and the slaves her family owned? (b) How can you tell? (c) Can you get a complete picture of life at home in the South during the war from this account? Explain.

★ ★ ★ ★ ★ ★ ★ ★ ★ ★ ★ ★ ★ ★ ★ ★ ★ ★ ★

**Introduction** On April 9, 1865, Robert E. Lee and Ulysses S. Grant met at Appomattox Courthouse to arrange for the surrender of Confederate troops. The day was one of deep feeling and high drama. It brought together two of the greatest leaders to emerge from the war. This selection is from Grant's *Personal Memoirs*.

**Vocabulary** Before you read the selection, find the meaning of these words in a dictionary: foe, valiantly, humiliation, cavalry, artillery, paroles.

What General Lee's feelings were I do not know. It was impossible to say whether he felt inwardly glad that the end had finally come, or felt sad over the results and was too manly to show it. Whatever his feelings, they were entirely concealed from my observation. But my own feelings, which had been quite jubilant on the receipt of his letter, were sad and depressed. I felt like anything rather than rejoicing at the downfall of a foe who had fought so long and valiantly.

General Lee was dressed in a full uniform which was entirely new. He was wearing a sword of considerable value. In my rough traveling suit, the uniform of a private with the straps of a lieutenant-general, I must have contrasted very strangely with a man so handsomely dressed.

We soon fell into a conversation about old army times. He remarked that he remembered me very well in the old army. I told him that of course I remembered him perfectly. After the conversation had run on in this style for some time, General Lee called my attention to the object of our meeting.

When I put my pen to the paper, the thought occurred to me that the officers had their own private horses and effects, which were important to them but of no value to us. I also thought it would be an unnecessary humiliation to ask them to deliver their sidearms.

General Lee appeared to have no objections to the terms first proposed. When he read over that part of the terms about sidearms, horses, and private property of the officers, he remarked, with some feeling, I thought, that this would have a happy effect upon his army.

Then, General Lee remarked to me that in their army, the men of the cavalry and artillery owned their own horses. Would these men be permitted to keep their horses? I told him that, as the terms were written, they would not.

I then said to him that I took it that most of the men in the ranks were small farmers. The whole country had been so raided by the two armies that it was doubtful whether they would be able to put in a crop to carry themselves and their families through the next winter without the aid of the horses they were then riding. I would, therefore, instruct the officers I left behind to receive the paroles of his troops to let every man of the Confederate army who claimed to own a horse or mule take the animal to his home. Lee remarked again that this would have a happy effect.

Adapted from Ulysses S. Grant, *Personal Memoirs*, 1886.

**R E A D I N G   R E V I E W** ★ ★ ★ ★ ★ ★ ★

1. How did General Grant feel about the surrender?
2. Why did Grant decide to allow the confederate soldiers to keep their horses?
3. **Defending an opinion.** (a) How would you describe the attitudes of Grant and Lee at this meeting? (b) What evidence supports your opinion? (c) What other information would be useful?

★ ★ ★ ★ ★ ★ ★ ★ ★ ★ ★ ★ ★ ★ ★ ★ ★

# Chapter 19 The Road to Reunion (1864–1877)

## ★ 19-1 A Planter Faces the Future ★

**Introduction** After the Civil War, many Southerners returned home to devastation. Many of the planters who had dominated southern society found their homes and crops in ruins. In this selection, Susan Dabney Smedes tells how her father coped with life after the war.

**Vocabulary** Before you read the selection, find the meaning of these words in a dictionary: contrivances, desolate, chivalrous.

My father, Thomas Dabney, was at Burleigh when he heard of General Lee's surrender. On the day the news reached him, he called his son to him. They rode together to the field where the Negroes were at work. He informed them of the news that had reached him and that they were now free. His advice was that they should continue to work the crop as they had been doing. At the end of the year they should receive such pay for their labor as he thought just.

From this time till January 1, 1866, no apparent change took place among the Burleigh Negroes. Those who worked in the fields went out as usual and cultivated and gathered in the crops. In the house, they went about their customary duties. We expected them to go away or to demand wages or at least to give some sign that they knew they were free. But except that they were very quiet and serious, we saw no change in them. At Christmas such compensation was made them for their services as seemed just. Afterward fixed wages were offered and accepted.

My father had come home to a house stripped of nearly every article of furniture and to a plantation stripped of the means of cultivating any but a small proportion of it. A few mules and one cow were all that was left of the stock. We had brought a few pieces of common furniture from Georgia, and a very few necessary articles were bought. In the course of time, some homemade contrivances and comforts relieved the desolate appearances of the rooms. But no attempt was ever made to refurnish the house.

He owned nothing that could be turned into money without great sacrifice but five bales of cotton. There were yet two sons and two daughters to be educated. He decided to get a tutor for them and to receive several other pupils in his house in order to make up the salary. The household was put on an economical footing. The plantation Negroes were hired to work in the fields, and things seemed to promise more prosperous days.

His chivalrous nature had always revolted from the sight of a woman doing hard work. He determined to spare his daughters all such labor as he could perform. General Sherman had said that he would like to bring every southern woman to the washtub. "He shall never bring my daughters to the washtub," Thomas Dabney said. "I will do the washing myself." And he did it for two years. He was in his seventieth year when he began to do it.

When he was 70 years of age, he decided to learn to grow a garden. He had never performed manual labor, but he now applied himself to learn to hoe as a way of supplying his family with vegetables. With the labor of those aged hands, he made a garden that was the best ordered that we had ever seen at Burleigh. He made his garden, as he did everything that he undertook, in the most painstaking manner, neglecting nothing that could insure success. The rows in that garden were models of exactness and neatness.

The garden was on the top of a long, high hill. In a time of drought or if he had set out anything that needed watering, he toiled up that long, steep hill with bucket after bucket of water. That garden supplied the daily food of his family nearly all the year round. He planted vegetables in such quantities that it was impossible to eat them all. So he sold barrels of vegetables in New Orleans.

He showed with pride what he had done by his personal labor in gardening and in washing. He placed the clothes on the lines as carefully as if they were meant to hang there always. He said that he had never seen snowier ones. And it was true.

At the end of the hard day's work he would say sometimes: "General Sherman has not brought my daughters to the washtub. I could not stand that."

Southerners on the home front had endured great hardships. When General Sherman marched through Georgia, his men looted and burned everything in their path. Many Southerners, like those shown here, left ruined homes and fled in terror.

Adapted from Susan Dabney Smedes, *Memorials of a Southern Planter*, 1887.

## READING REVIEW ★ ★ ★ ★ ★ ★ ★

1. How did Thomas Dabney's former slaves react to the news that they were free?
2. Why did Dabney wash clothes rather than allow his daughters to do it?
3. **Drawing conclusions.** In what ways was Thomas Dabney's life after the Civil War different from his life before the war?

★ ★ ★ ★ ★ ★ ★ ★ ★ ★ ★ ★ ★ ★ ★ ★ ★ ★

## ★ 19-2 From the Black Codes ★

**Introduction** The black codes, passed by southern states in order to control the activity of newly freed slaves, were the cause of great controversy. The codes guaranteed freedmen certain rights. Yet, at the same time, these laws undermined many new and hardwon freedoms. These are articles from the black codes of Mississippi.

**Vocabulary** Before you read the selection, find the meaning of these words in a dictionary: probate, apprentice, minor, corporeal, vagrant.

It shall be the duty of all sheriffs, justices of the peace, and other civil officers of the several counties in this state, to report to the probate courts of their respective counties semiannually all freedmen, free negroes, and mulattoes under the age of 18 who are orphans, or whose parent or parents have not the means or who refuse to provide for and support them. It shall be the duty of the probate court to apprentice the minors to some competent and suitable person on terms the court may direct. The former owner of the minors shall be preferred when, in the opinion of the court, he or she is a suitable person for that purpose.

In the management and control of the apprentices, the master or mistress shall have the power to inflict such moderate corporeal punishment as a father or guardian is allowed to inflict on his or her child.

All freedmen, free Negroes, and mulattoes in this state over the age of 18 years found with no lawful employment or business, or found unlawfully assembling themselves together, in either the day or the night, and all white persons assembling with freedmen, free Negroes or mulattoes, or usually associating with them on terms of equality, shall be deemed vagrants. On conviction of vagrancy, they shall be fined.

All freedmen, free Negroes, and mulattoes may sue and be sued in all the courts of law of this state. They may acquire personal property by descent or purchase and may dispose of the property in the same manner and to the same extent that white persons may.

Adapted from *Laws of the State of Mississippi, Passed at a Regular Session of the Mississippi Legislature*, 1865.

**READING REVIEW** ★ ★ ★ ★ ★ ★ ★

1. What rights did the Mississippi black codes grant to the newly freed slaves?
2. Why might the black code law on vagrants be considered harsh?
3. **Summarizing.** Describe in your own words the black code policy on apprenticing young blacks.

★ ★ ★ ★ ★ ★ ★ ★ ★ ★ ★ ★ ★ ★ ★ ★ ★ ★ ★

---

## ★ 19-3  A Former Slave on Reconstruction  ★

**Introduction**  Freedmen responded to their new freedom in many ways. Some left their old plantations immediately. Others, however, remained on close terms with their former owners. This account is ex-slave Katie Rowe's memory of the first years after the Civil War.

**Vocabulary**  Before you read the selection, find the meaning of these words in a dictionary: pestering, ruction.

When we git back to Monroe to the old place, we git a big surprise. Old Master cut it up in chunks and put us out on it on the halves. But he had to sell part of it to git the money to git us mules and tools and food to run on. Then after a while he had to sell some more. He seem like he git old mighty fast.

About that time they was a lot of people coming into that country from the North. They kept telling us that the thing for us to do was to be free, and come and go where and when we please.

They try to git us to go and vote. But none of us folks took much stock by what they say. Old Master tell us plenty times to mix in the politics when the young-uns git educated and know what to do.

Some of the blacks who work for the white folks from the North act pretty uppity and big. They come pestering round the dance places and try to talk up ructions amongst us, but it don't last long.

The Ku Kluckers start riding round at night, and they pass the word that the blacks got to have a pass to go and come and to stay at the dances. They have to git the pass from the white folks they work for. Passes writ from the northern people wouldn't do no good. That the way the Kluckers keep the blacks in line.

They wasn't very bad 'cause the blacks round here wasn't bad. But I hear plenty git whupped in other places 'cause they act up and say they don't have to take off their hats in the white stores and such.

Any black who behave hisself and don't go running round late a night and drinking never had no trouble with the Kluckers.

Adapted from "Recollections of Katie Rowe of Arkansas," in B. A. Botkin, *Lay My Burden Down* (Chicago: University of Chicago Press, 1945).

**READING REVIEW** ★ ★ ★ ★ ★ ★ ★ ★

1. How did Katie Rowe's owner treat his slaves after the war?
2. How did Rowe seem to feel toward her owner?
3. **Using oral history.** Rowe says any black who behaved himself did not have trouble with the Ku Klux Klan. What was her idea of a former slave behaving himself or herself?

★ ★ ★ ★ ★ ★ ★ ★ ★ ★ ★ ★ ★ ★ ★ ★ ★ ★

## ★  19-4    Winning and Losing the Right to Vote   ★

**Introduction**  During Reconstruction, freedmen voted in large numbers. By the 1880s, however, threats of violence from groups like the Ku Klux Klan, as well as new laws, stopped most blacks from voting in the South. These two drawings illustrate the change.

**READING REVIEW** ★ ★ ★ ★ ★ ★ ★ ★ ★ ★ ★ ★ ★ ★ ★ ★ ★ ★ ★ ★ ★ ★

1. (a) Which of the drawings represents the situation in the late 1880s? (b) What evidence supports your answer?
2. The caption for the drawing on the right says, "Everything points to a Democratic victory this fall." What do you think the artist meant by that?
3. **Using visual evidence.**  What can you learn about the voting rights of blacks by studying these two drawings?

★ ★ ★ ★ ★ ★ ★ ★ ★ ★ ★ ★ ★ ★ ★ ★ ★ ★ ★ ★ ★ ★ ★ ★ ★

**Land Claims
in North America, 1783**

- United States — 27%
- Britain — 14%
- Spain — 45%
- France — 10.5%
- Unexplored — 3%
- Disputed — .5%

# REFERENCE SECTION

Historical Atlas 572

Geographic Atlas 580

The Fifty States 588

Gazetteer of American History 589

A Chronology of American History 594

Connections With American Literature 598

Presidents of the United States 600

Glossary 605

Pronunciation Key 605

The Declaration of Independence 611

Exploring Our Living Constitution 615

The Constitution of the United States
of America 628

An Overview of Citizenship 650

Index 654

# North America Before 1500

The first Americans discovered a land of endless diversity when they traveled across North America. The land itself ranges from lush coastal plains to high rugged mountain peaks, from deep forest to barren desert. As the earliest Americans spread across the two continents, they learned to use the land and what it offered. Hundreds of different cultures developed. The map at right shows some of these cultures. Study the map, chart, and illustrations. Then answer these questions:

1. Which Indian nations were part of the Southwest cultural group?
2. Which illustrations represent Indian nations found in the Middle America cultural group?
3. Why would the spirit of the sun be important to the Bella Coola in the winter?
4. What geographic characteristics of the Eastern Woodlands are shown in the picture of the Algonquin village?
5. Review what you learned about Native American cultures in Chapter 2. Then study the chart at right. Which pictures show the influence of climate or geography on the culture of the groups shown on the map?

Mayan women were skilled weavers. Here, one end of a loom is attached to the woman's waist and the other to a tree.

## Environment of Early American Cultures

| Culture Group | Environment |
|---|---|
| Far North | Very short summers; long cold winters |
| Northwest Coast | Mild, rainy; dense forests |
| California-Intermountain | Mild and rainy along coast; dry and hot in deserts; cold winters in mountains |
| Southwest | Very hot and dry in desert |
| Great Plains | Hot summers; cold winters; little rainfall |
| Eastern Woodlands | Hot summers; cold winters; dense forests |
| Southeast | Humid summers; mild winters |

This ancient bowl was found on the Hopi Mesa. The ring around the edge is called a lifeline. The Anasazi woman making the bowl left an opening in the ring because her life was not yet complete.

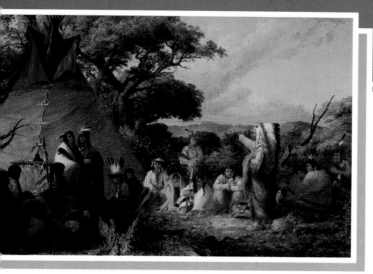

Although from the 1800s, this painting shows some ways of life on the Plains that had changed little. Note the hides used for the tipi.

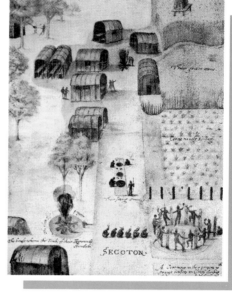

The Bella Coola used this wooden mask of the sun spirit during winter religious ceremonies.

This scene of an Algonquin village, painted in 1585, shows life much as it was before Europeans arrived.

NATIVE AMERICAN CULTURES

Present-day state boundaries

0        500        1000 Miles
0    500    1000 Kilometers

TLINGIT
ESKIMO
FAR NORTH
BEAVER
CREE
BELLA COOLA
NORTHWEST COAST
CHIPPEWA
BLACKFEET
ALGONQUIN
HURON
NEZ PERCÉ
IROQUOIS
COOS
CROW
MANDAN
EASTERN WOODLANDS
PACIFIC OCEAN
POMO
CALIFORNIA-INTERMOUNTAIN
CHEYENNE
GREAT PLAINS
MIAMI
DELAWARE
ATLANTIC OCEAN
SHOSHONE
ARAPAHO
SHAWNEE
HOPI
NAVAJO
PUEBLO
OSAGE
CHEROKEE
SOUTHWEST
COMANCHE
SOUTHEAST
NATCHEZ
APACHE
SEMINOLE
GULF OF MEXICO
MIDDLE AMERICA
MAYA
AZTEC

Daring explorers sought adventure, wealth, and glory in North America as early as the late 1400s. Settlers soon followed. Some came in search of a better life. Many came looking for religious freedom. By 1753, English colonies flourished along the Atlantic coast. The Spanish had set up missions and towns in the Southwest. French forts lined the Mississippi River in Louisiana and the Great Lakes in New France. The map at right shows European land claims in 1753. Competition for land in North America led to war between England and France the following year, in 1754. Study the map, graph, and pictures. Then answer these questions:

1. Which nation claimed land along the Mississippi in 1753?

2. How did geographic location make conflict between France and England likely?

3. Based on the pictures, which European settlers were probably the greatest threat to Native Americans? Why?

4. Compare the map with the one on page 156. How would the wedges in the circle graph change between 1753 and 1763?

This Spanish mission at El Paso was founded in 1659. It became a gateway for Spanish settlers in the Southwest.

Settlers in Pennsylvania turned dense forests into productive farmland. This prosperous farm grew up during the mid-1750s.

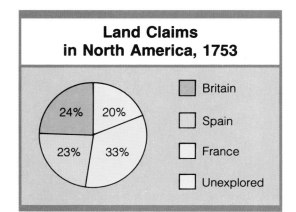

## Land Claims in North America, 1753

24%   20%
23%   33%

☐ Britain
☐ Spain
☐ France
☐ Unexplored

French trappers traveled far along roaring rivers. Their fur trade with Indian nations was the basis of French claims in North America.

New York was a thriving colonial port town in the mid-1750s.

*The New England Primer* was used in schools and homes in the English colonies. It illustrates the strong influence of religion among colonists.

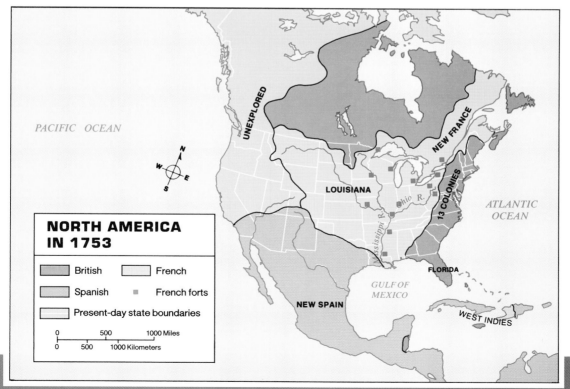

## NORTH AMERICA IN 1753

- British
- Spanish
- Present-day state boundaries
- French
- ■ French forts

0    500    1000 Miles
0    500    1000 Kilometers

PACIFIC OCEAN

UNEXPLORED

NEW FRANCE

LOUISIANA

Ohio R.

13 COLONIES

ATLANTIC OCEAN

Mississippi R.

FLORIDA

NEW SPAIN

GULF OF MEXICO

WEST INDIES

# North America in 1783

A new nation was born when the American colonists defeated Britain in the American Revolution. The United States had begun as 13 colonies wedged between the Appalachian Mountains and the Atlantic coast. In 1783, it stretched west to the Mississippi, north to Canada and the Great Lakes, and south to Florida. As settlers moved west across the Appalachians, they took along the ideals of liberty that had given birth to the country.

The French had lost their claims to land in North America during the French and Indian War. But most of the continent was still claimed by the Spanish and the British. Study the map, graph, and pictures. Then answer the questions below.

1. What nation claimed the land west of the United States in 1783?

2. Which nation claimed the largest portion of North America in 1783?

3. (a) Based on the map, which European nations might have been a threat to settlers near Fort Snelling? (b) What other groups did settlers probably consider a threat? Why?

4. What do you think American settlers would do when they reached the Mississippi River? Why?

Paul Revere made this silver bowl in 1768 at the beginning of the American colonists' struggle for liberty.

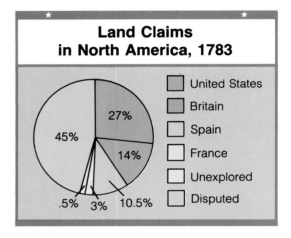

**Land Claims in North America, 1783**

- United States
- Britain
- Spain
- France
- Unexplored
- Disputed

45%
27%
14%
.5%  3%  10.5%

Although most of North America was claimed by the United States or European nations, Native Americans lived throughout the land. In northern areas, such as Canada, snowshoes helped hunters move easily on snow.

Settlers used flatboats to move goods along the rivers of the western part of the new nation, as this painting from the 1800s shows.

After 1783, American settlers moved west in a steady stream. The army built forts to protect them. Fort Snelling, shown here, was built on the northwest frontier on the Mississippi River.

To the west of the new nation, Spanish settlers were building thriving towns and rancheros, or ranches.

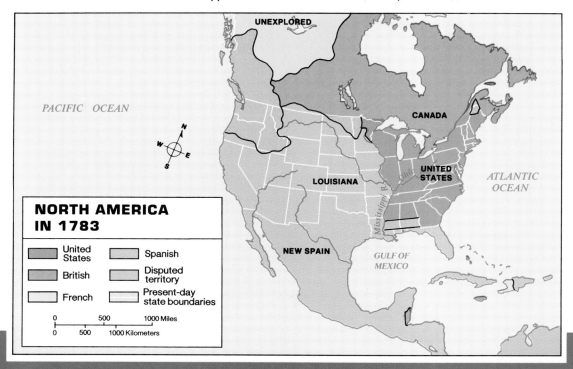

PACIFIC OCEAN

UNEXPLORED

CANADA

LOUISIANA

UNITED STATES

ATLANTIC OCEAN

NEW SPAIN

GULF OF MEXICO

Mississippi R.

Ohio R.

**NORTH AMERICA IN 1783**

- United States
- British
- French
- Spanish
- Disputed territory
- Present-day state boundaries

0   500   1000 Miles
0   500   1000 Kilometers

# Growth of the United States to 1853

By 1853, the United States stretched from sea to sea. The nation acquired huge tracts of land through purchase, treaty, and war. This land, far from being empty, was home to many different peoples. They included Native Americans who had lived there long before Europeans arrived. Many Mexicans also had found themselves in a foreign land after the Mexican War. Plus, adventurers from all over the world had come in search of gold. The expansion of the country was to offer great opportunities and difficult challenges in the years ahead. Territorial expansion is shown on the map at right. Study the map, the graph, and the pictures. Then answer these questions:

1. (a) When did the Oregon Country become part of the United States? (b) Which picture best illustrates the trip to Oregon?

2. (a) What was the last addition to the United States shown on the map? (b) What cultural heritage was probably strongest in that area?

3. (a) Based on the graph, during which period was the most land added to the United States? (b) Which pictures help you understand the geography and culture of those areas?

Settlers began moving toward Oregon in the early 1800s. At first, they traveled by covered wagons. Later, railroads would crisscross the country.

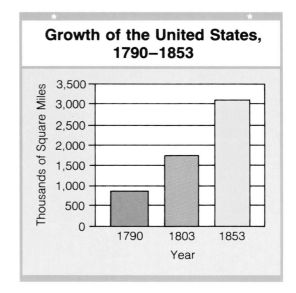

**Growth of the United States, 1790–1853**

*Thousands of Square Miles*

| | |
|---|---|
| 3,500 | |
| 3,000 | |
| 2,500 | |
| 2,000 | |
| 1,500 | |
| 1,000 | |
| 500 | |
| 0 | |

1790    1803    1853

Year

This painting of a horse race shows the influence of Mexican culture in areas the United States acquired from Mexico. This cultural influence has remained strong in Texas and other areas of the Southwest.

These Sioux are playing lacrosse, a game that settlers learned from Indians. As settlers moved onto the Plains, the lives of Indians changed forever.

The discovery of gold in California attracted people from all over the world. Miners such as these spread out in search of priceless treasure.

In the early 1800s, canals, such as the Erie Canal, became part of a vast system of transportation.

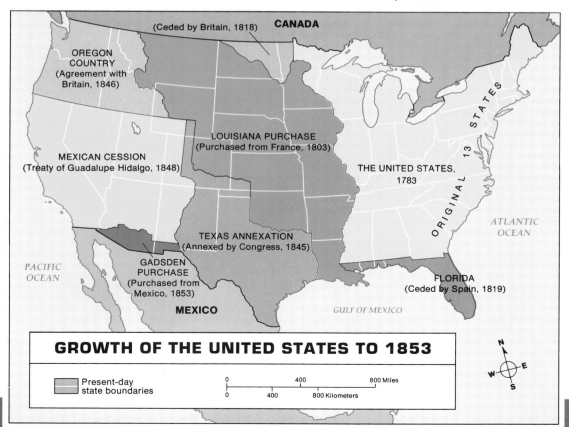

CANADA

OREGON COUNTRY (Agreement with Britain, 1846)

(Ceded by Britain, 1818)

LOUISIANA PURCHASE (Purchased from France, 1803)

MEXICAN CESSION (Treaty of Guadalupe Hidalgo, 1848)

THE UNITED STATES, 1783

ORIGINAL 13 STATES

TEXAS ANNEXATION (Annexed by Congress, 1845)

PACIFIC OCEAN

GADSDEN PURCHASE (Purchased from Mexico, 1853)

MEXICO

ATLANTIC OCEAN

FLORIDA (Ceded by Spain, 1819)

GULF OF MEXICO

**GROWTH OF THE UNITED STATES TO 1853**

Present-day state boundaries

0   400   800 Miles
0   400   800 Kilometers

N
W   E
S

ARCTI

GREENLAND
(Denmark)

Svalbard Is.
(Norway)

ALASKA
(U.S.)

Yukon

CANADA

Reykjavik ★ ICELAND

NORWAY

FINLAND

Helsinki ★

SWEDEN

Lenin

Mosc

Kiev

NORTH

AMERICA

Mackenzie

EUROPE
(see inset map)

Montreal
Ottawa ★

FRANCE

San Francisco ★

Chicago ★

Colorado

UNITED STATES

Ohio

New York ★

Washington, D.C.

SPAIN

ITALY

TURM

Azores
(Port.)

NORTH

Houston ●

Mississippi

New Orleans ●

BERMUDA
(U.K.)

Algiers ★

Tunis ★

NORTH

PACIFIC

OCEAN

MEXICO

Rabat ★

MOROCCO

TUNISIA

THE
BAHAMAS

Havana ★

NORTH

ATLANTIC OCEAN

Canary Is.
(Spain)

ALGERIA

LIBYA

MIDDL
EAST

W. SAHARA
(Morocco)

(see inset map

EGYPT

Mexico City ★

CUBA

DOMINICAN
REPUBLIC

Port-au-Prince ★

Puerto Rico (U.S.)

ST. CHRISTOPHER AND NEVIS

MAURITANIA

MALI

NIGER

AFRICA

CHAD

SUDAN

GUATEMALA

BELIZE

JAMAICA

HAITI

Santo
Domingo

ANTIGUA & BARBUDA

DOMINICA

SENEGAL

Nouakchott ★

Niamey ★

N'Djamena ★

C. AFR.
REP.

Guatemala ★

HONDURAS

ST. LUCIA

CAPE VERDE

Dakar ★

Bamako ★

BURKINA

FASO

NIGERIA

EL SALVADOR

San Salvador ★

Tegucigalpa

BARBADOS

GAMBIA

GUINEA-BISSAU

TOGO

San José ★

Managua ★

NICARAGUA

GRENADA

ST. VINCENT & THE GRENADINES

Conakry ★

GUINEA

Lagos ★

BENIN

CAMEROON

COSTA RICA

Panamá ★

TRINIDAD
& TOBAGO

SIERRA LEONE

IVORY
COAST

Lomé

Porto-
Novo

Bangui ★

PANAMA

VENEZUELA

Caracas ★

GUYANA

Monrovia ★

LIBERIA

Freetown ★

Abidjan ★

GHANA

Yaoundé ★

EQ. GUINEA

UGANDA

Georgetown ★

Paramaribo

SURINAME

SÃO TOMÉ AND PRÍNCIPE

Libreville ★

GABON

Kampala ★

KE

Bogotá ★

COLOMBIA

FR. GUIANA
(France)

CONGO

RWANDA

Nairobi ★

Galápagos Is
(Ecuador)

Negro

Equator

ZAIRE

Brazzaville ★

Kinshasa ★

BURUNDI

TANZA

ECUADOR

Quito ★

SOUTH

CABINDA
(Angola)

Da

Amazon

Madeira

AMERICA

Luanda ★

PERU

BRAZIL

ANGOLA

MALAWI

Lima ★

ZAMBIA

Lilongwe ★

SOUTH

BOLIVIA

Brasília ★

Lusaka ★

Ha

São Francisco

ZIMBABWE

PACIFIC OCEAN

La Paz ★

Sucre ★

NAMIBIA

MOZAMBI

São Paulo ●

Rio de Janeiro ●

SOUTH

Windhoek ★

BOTSWANA

PARAGUAY

Asunción ★

ATLANTIC OCEAN

WALVIS BAY
(S. Africa)

Gaborone ★

ia

Pretoria ★

SWAZII

CHILE

URUGUAY

Maseru ★

LESOTH

Santiago ★

Buenos Aires ★

Montevideo ★

Cape Town ★

SOUTH
AFRICA

ARGENTINA

Falkland Is.
(U.K.)

S. Georgia
(Falkland Is.)

N

W ⊕ E

S

---

## EUROPE

| 0 | 250 Miles |
| 0 | 250 Kilometers |

NORWAY

Oslo ★

Stockholm ★

N.
IRELAND

SWEDEN

Dublin ★

IRELAND

UNITED
KINGDOM

DENMARK

Copenhagen ★

London ★

Amsterdam

NETH.

Berlin ★

POLAND

Warsaw ★

U.S.S.R.
(SOVIET
UNION)

BELGIUM

Brussels ★

Bonn ★

E. GERMANY

Prague ★

Paris ★

LUX.

W.
GER.

LIECH.

CZECHOSLOVAKIA

Vienna ★

Budapest ★

FRANCE

Bern ★

SWITZ.

ANDORRA

ITALY

AUS.

HUNGARY

ROMANIA

PORT.

SPAIN

Belgrade ★

Bucharest ★

Lisbon ★

Madrid ★

MONACO

SAN
MARINO

Danube

YUGOSLAVIA

BULGARIA

Rome ★

ALBANIA

Sofia ★

Tirané ★

MEDITERRANEAN

SEA

GREECE

Athens ★

TURKEY

★ MALTA

ANTARCTICA

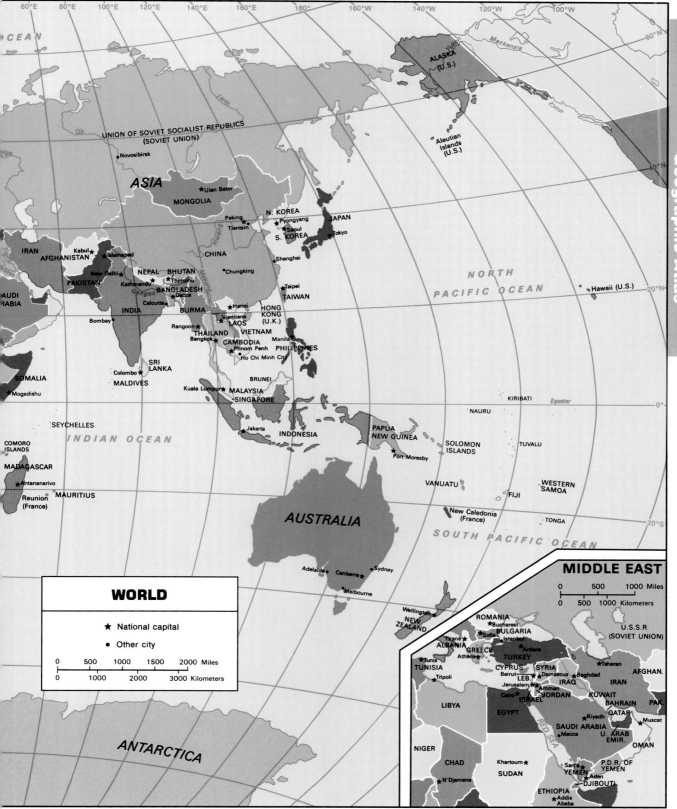

60°E 80°E 100°E 120°E 140°E 160°E 180° 160°W 140°W 120°W 100°W

60°N
40°N
20°N
0°
20°S

OCEAN

Ob

UNION OF SOVIET SOCIALIST REPUBLICS
(SOVIET UNION)

•Novosibirsk

Lena

Yukon

Mackenzie

ALASKA
(U.S.)

ASIA

•Ulan Bator
MONGOLIA

Aleutian
Islands
(U.S.)

IRAN
AFGHANISTAN
Kabul
★Islamabad
PAKISTAN
New Delhi★

NEPAL BHUTAN
Kathmandu★ ★Thimphu
BANGLADESH
Calcutta• ★Dacca

•Peking
Tientsin★

CHINA

Huang

•Chungking

N. KOREA
Pyongyang★
Seoul★
S. KOREA

JAPAN
Tokyo★

Shanghai•

NORTH

PACIFIC OCEAN

•Hawaii (U.S.)

AUDI
RABIA

Ganges

INDIA

Bombay•

BURMA
Rangoon•

Taipei•
TAIWAN

Mekong

Hanoi★
Vientiane★
LAOS
THAILAND VIETNAM
Bangkok★
CAMBODIA
★Phnom Penh
Ho Chi Minh City•

HONG
KONG
(U.K.)

Manila•
PHILIPPINES

SOMALIA
•Mogadishu

SRI
Colombo• LANKA
MALDIVES

Kuala Lumpur★
MALAYSIA
SINGAPORE

BRUNEI

SEYCHELLES

INDIAN OCEAN

Jakarta•
INDONESIA

PAPUA
NEW GUINEA
Port Moresby★

KIRIBATI
Equator

NAURU

SOLOMON
ISLANDS

TUVALU

COMORO
ISLANDS

MADAGASCAR
★Antananarivo

Reunion MAURITIUS
(France)

VANUATU

FIJI

WESTERN
SAMOA

New Caledonia
(France)

TONGA

AUSTRALIA

SOUTH PACIFIC OCEAN

Adelaide• Canberra★ •Sydney
•Melbourne

Wellington★
NEW
ZEALAND

ANTARCTICA

## MIDDLE EAST

0        500      1000 Miles

0     500    1000 Kilometers

ROMANIA
•Bucharest
BULGARIA
Tiranë★ ★Sofia
ALBANIA •Istanbul
GREECE ★Ankara
Athens• TURKEY
★Tunis
TUNISIA CYPRUS SYRIA
Beirut• Damascus★ ★Baghdad
Tripoli• LEB. IRAQ
Jerusalem★ ★Amman
Cairo★ ISRAEL JORDAN KUWAIT
EGYPT

U.S.S.R.
(SOVIET UNION)

★Teheran
AFGHAN.
IRAN
PAK.

LIBYA

BAHRAIN
QATAR
Riyadh★
SAUDI ARABIA
•Mecca U. ARAB
EMIR.

Muscat•

OMAN

NIGER

CHAD
•N'Djamena

Khartoum★
SUDAN

RED SEA

San'a★
YEMEN
Aden•

ETHIOPIA
Addis
Ababa•

P.D.R. OF
YEMEN

DJIBOUTI

130°W   125°W   120°W   115°W   110°W   105°W   100°W

Pacific Time Zone

Mountain Time Zone

CANADA

Central Time Zone

50°N

45°N

Seattle
Spokane
Olympia
**WASHINGTON 1889**

Portland
Salem
Eugene
**OREGON 1859**

• Great Falls

Helena ★ **MONTANA 1889**

• Billings

**IDAHO 1890**
★ Boise

Pocatello •

**WYOMING 1890**

• Casper

Minot •
Grand Forks

**NORTH DAKOTA 1889**
Bismarck •

**SOUTH DAKOTA 1889**
Rapid City •   ★ Pierre

Sioux Falls

40°N

Sacramento ★
Reno •
★ Carson City
San Francisco •
• Oakland
• San Jose

**NEVADA 1864**

Great Salt Lake

Ogden •
★ Salt Lake City

**UTAH 1896**

Cheyenne
★

★ Denver
Colorado Springs •

**COLORADO 1876**

**NEBRASKA 1867**

Lincoln •

**KANSAS 1861**

Wichita •

35°N

**CALIFORNIA 1850**

Las Vegas •

Los Angeles •
Long Beach •
Salton Sea
San Diego •

PACIFIC OCEAN

**ARIZONA 1912**

★ Phoenix

Tucson •

★ Santa Fe

• Albuquerque

**NEW MEXICO 1912**

Las Cruces •

El Paso •

**OKLAHOMA 1907**
Oklahoma City ★

Dallas •
Ft. Worth •

**TEXAS 1845**

Austin ★

San Antonio •

30°N

120°W   115°W   110°W   105°W

**Hawaii–Aleutian Time Zone**

160°W   155°W

Honolulu ★   **HAWAII 1959**

PACIFIC OCEAN

20°N

0   50   100 Miles
0   50 100 150 Kilometers

50°N   170°E

**Hawaii–Aleutian Time Zone**

PACIFIC OCEAN

180°   170°W   160°W

SOVIET UNION

**Alaska Time Zone**

Arctic Circle

140°W

130°W

Fairbanks •

**ALASKA 1959**

Anchorage •

BERING SEA

Gulf of Alaska

Juneau ★

CANADA

**Pacific Time Zone**

60°N

25°N

**MEXICO**

0   200   400 Miles
0   200   400   600 Kilometers

100°W

—582—

THE UNITED STATES

★ Capital city

● Other city

**1787** Year of admission to the Union

━━ Boundaries of time zones

| 0 | 100 | 200 | 300 Miles |
| 0 | 100 200 | 300 | 400 Kilometers |

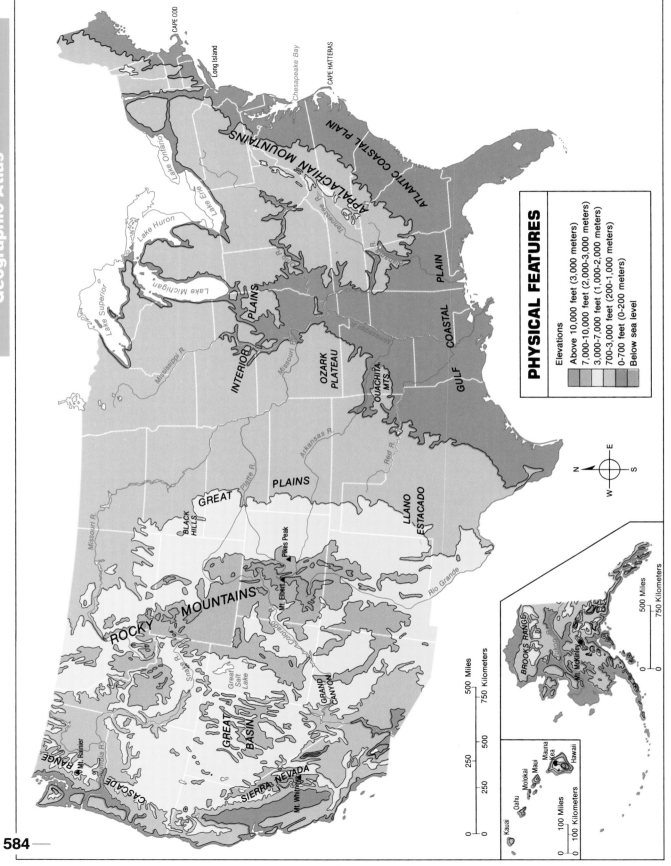

## PHYSICAL FEATURES

**Elevations**

Above 10,000 feet (3,000 meters)
7,000-10,000 feet (2,000-3,000 meters)
3,000-7,000 feet (1,000-2,000 meters)
700-3,000 feet (200-1,000 meters)
0-700 feet (0-200 meters)
Below sea level

CAPE COD
Long Island
Chesapeake Bay
CAPE HATTERAS

APPALACHIAN MOUNTAINS
ATLANTIC COASTAL PLAIN

Lake Ontario
Lake Erie
Lake Huron
Lake Superior
Lake Michigan

Tennessee R.

GULF COASTAL PLAIN

INTERIOR PLAINS

OZARK PLATEAU

OUACHITA MTS.

Mississippi R.
Missouri R.
Arkansas R.
Red R.

Platte R.

GREAT PLAINS

BLACK HILLS

LLANO ESTACADO

Pikes Peak
Mt. Elbert

ROCKY MOUNTAINS

Rio Grande

Colorado R.

Snake R.

Columbia R.

Great Salt Lake

GRAND CANYON

GREAT BASIN

SIERRA NEVADA

Mt. Whitney

CASCADE RANGE

Mt. Rainier

N E S W

250    500    750 Kilometers
0    250    500 Miles

BROOKS RANGE

Yukon R.

Mt. McKinley

0    750 Kilometers
0    500 Miles

Kauai
Oahu
Molokai
Maui
Mauna Kea
Hawaii

0    100 Kilometers
0    100 Miles

—584—

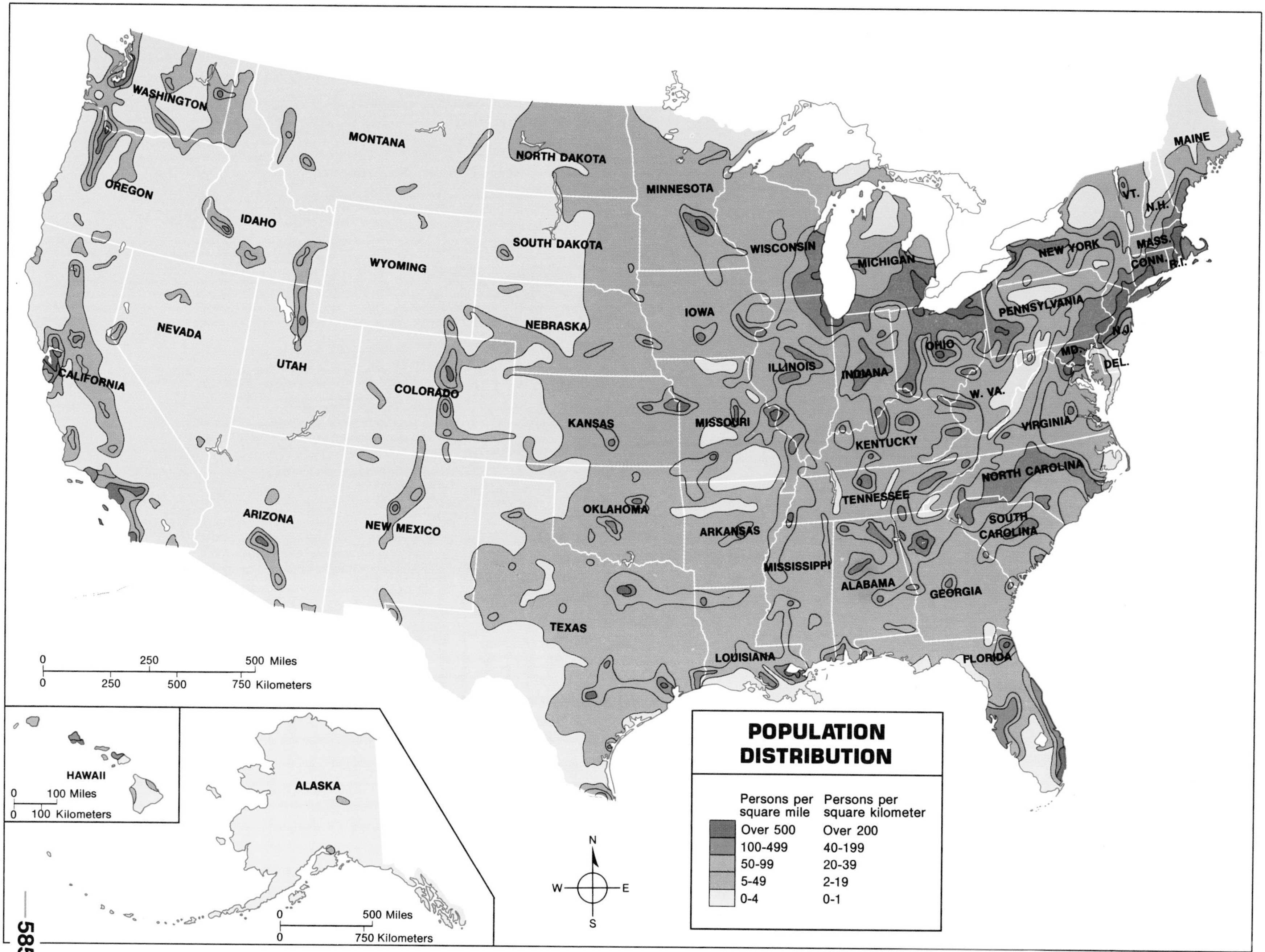
POPULATION DISTRIBUTION
Persons per square mile
Persons per square kilometer
Over 500
Over 200
100-499
40-199
50-99
20-39
5-49
2-19
0-4
0-1
WASHINGTON
OREGON
CALIFORNIA
NEVADA
IDAHO
MONTANA
WYOMING
UTAH
ARIZONA
COLORADO
NEW MEXICO
NORTH DAKOTA
SOUTH DAKOTA
NEBRASKA
KANSAS
OKLAHOMA
TEXAS
MINNESOTA
IOWA
MISSOURI
ARKANSAS
LOUISIANA
WISCONSIN
ILLINOIS
MICHIGAN
INDIANA
OHIO
KENTUCKY
TENNESSEE
MISSISSIPPI
ALABAMA
GEORGIA
FLORIDA
SOUTH CAROLINA
NORTH CAROLINA
VIRGINIA
W. VA.
MD.
DEL.
N.J.
PENNSYLVANIA
NEW YORK
CONN.
R.I.
MASS.
VT.
N.H.
MAINE
ALASKA
HAWAII
0
250
500 Miles
0
250
500
750 Kilometers
0
100 Miles
0
100 Kilometers
0
500 Miles
0
750 Kilometers
N
S
E
W

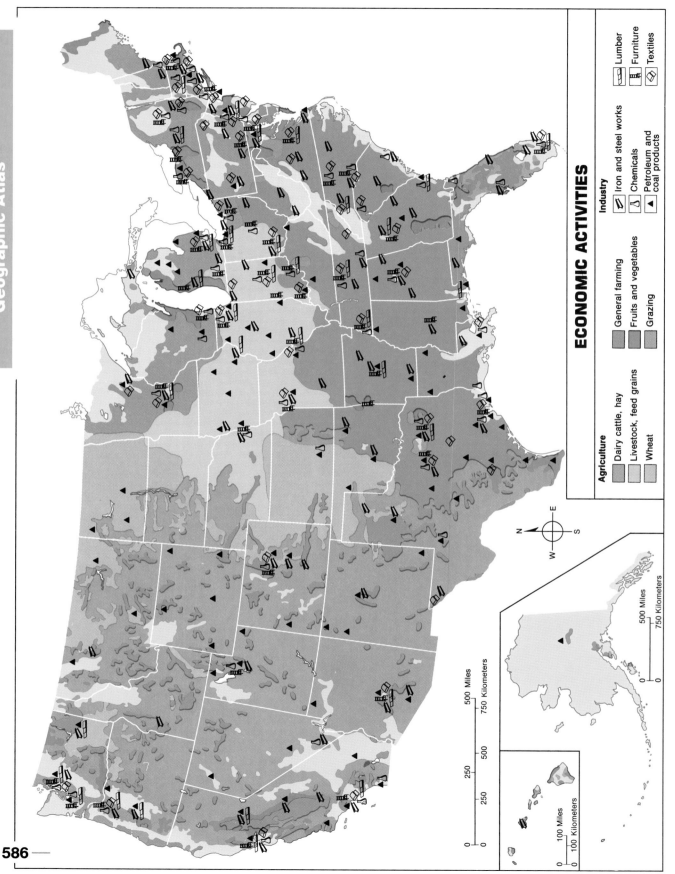

# ECONOMIC ACTIVITIES

**Agriculture**

Dairy cattle, hay

Livestock, feed grains

Wheat

General farming

Fruits and vegetables

Grazing

**Industry**

Iron and steel works

Chemicals

Petroleum and coal products

Lumber

Furniture

Textiles

N  W  E  S

0    250    500    750 Kilometers
0    250    500 Miles

0    100 Miles
0    100 Kilometers

0    500 Miles
0    750 Kilometers

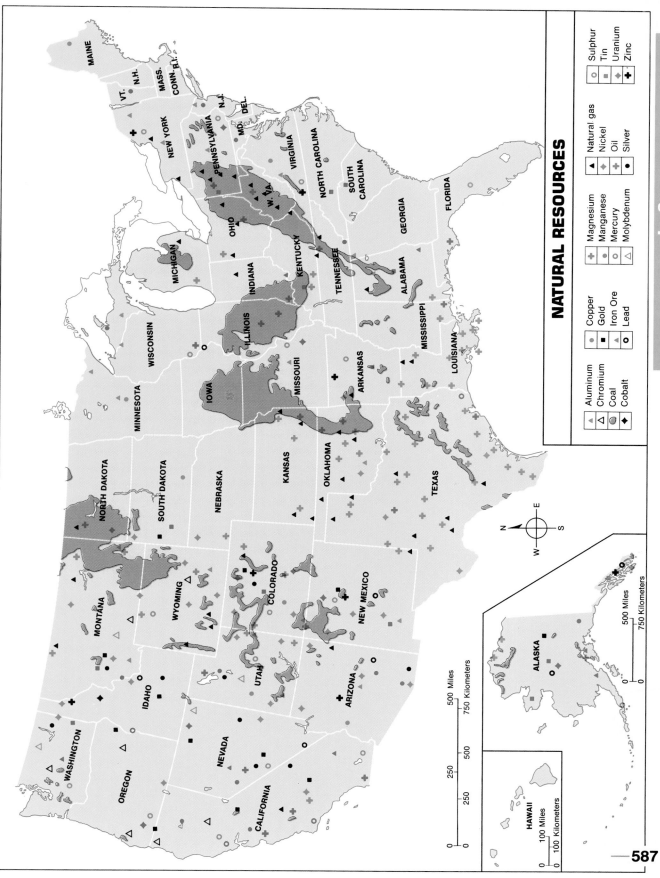

## NATURAL RESOURCES

**Aluminum** ◄  **Copper** ●  **Magnesium** ✚  **Natural gas** ◄  **Sulphur** ○
**Chromium** △  **Gold** ■  **Manganese** ●  **Nickel** ✦  **Tin** ■
**Coal** ●  **Iron Ore** ◄  **Mercury** ○  **Oil** ✚  **Uranium** ✦
**Cobalt** ✦  **Lead** ○  **Molybdenum** △  **Silver** ●  **Zinc** ✚

Geographic Atlas

—587—

# The Fifty States

| State | Date of Entry to Union (Order of Entry) | Area in Square Miles | Population (1985) | Number of Representatives in House | Capital | Largest City |
|---|---|---|---|---|---|---|
| Alabama | 1819 (22) | 51,705 | 4,004,435 | 7 | Montgomery | Birmingham |
| Alaska | 1959 (49) | 591,004 | 514,819 | 1 | Juneau | Anchorage |
| Arizona | 1912 (48) | 114,000 | 3,086,827 | 5 | Phoenix | Phoenix |
| Arkansas | 1836 (25) | 53,187 | 2,345,431 | 4 | Little Rock | Little Rock |
| California | 1850 (31) | 158,706 | 25,816,590 | 45 | Sacramento | Los Angeles |
| Colorado | 1876 (38) | 104,091 | 3,253,425 | 6 | Denver | Denver |
| Connecticut | 1788 (5) | 5,018 | 3,160,280 | 6 | Hartford | Bridgeport |
| Delaware | 1787 (1) | 2,044 | 605,711 | 1 | Dover | Wilmington |
| Florida | 1845 (27) | 58,664 | 11,071,358 | 19 | Tallahassee | Jacksonville |
| Georgia | 1788 (4) | 58,910 | 5,878,225 | 10 | Atlanta | Atlanta |
| Hawaii | 1959 (50) | 6,471 | 1,050,270 | 2 | Honolulu | Honolulu |
| Idaho | 1890 (43) | 83,564 | 1,004,071 | 2 | Boise | Boise |
| Illinois | 1818 (21) | 56,345 | 11,502,433 | 22 | Springfield | Chicago |
| Indiana | 1816 (19) | 36,185 | 5,489,287 | 10 | Indianapolis | Indianapolis |
| Iowa | 1846 (29) | 56,275 | 2,894,273 | 6 | Des Moines | Des Moines |
| Kansas | 1861 (34) | 82,277 | 2,453,581 | 5 | Topeka | Wichita |
| Kentucky | 1792 (15) | 40,409 | 3,747,769 | 7 | Frankfort | Louisville |
| Louisiana | 1812 (18) | 47,751 | 4,553,903 | 8 | Baton Rouge | New Orleans |
| Maine | 1820 (23) | 33,265 | 1,158,539 | 2 | Augusta | Portland |
| Maryland | 1788 (7) | 10,460 | 4,342,562 | 8 | Annapolis | Baltimore |
| Massachusetts | 1788 (6) | 8,284 | 5,764,125 | 11 | Boston | Boston |
| Michigan | 1837 (26) | 58,527 | 8,992,766 | 18 | Lansing | Detroit |
| Minnesota | 1858 (32) | 84,402 | 4,199,749 | 8 | St. Paul | Minneapolis |
| Mississippi | 1817 (20) | 47,689 | 2,623,069 | 5 | Jackson | Jackson |
| Missouri | 1821 (24) | 69,697 | 5,004,162 | 9 | Jefferson City | St. Louis |
| Montana | 1889 (41) | 147,046 | 826,933 | 2 | Helena | Billings |
| Nebraska | 1867 (37) | 77,355 | 1,606,779 | 3 | Lincoln | Omaha |
| Nevada | 1864 (36) | 110,561 | 933,451 | 2 | Carson City | Las Vegas |
| New Hampshire | 1788 (9) | 9,279 | 980,841 | 2 | Concord | Manchester |
| New Jersey | 1787 (3) | 7,787 | 7,509,625 | 14 | Trenton | Newark |
| New Mexico | 1912 (47) | 121,593 | 1,446,347 | 3 | Santa Fe | Albuquerque |
| New York | 1788 (11) | 49,108 | 17,676,828 | 34 | Albany | New York |
| North Carolina | 1789 (12) | 52,669 | 6,178,329 | 11 | Raleigh | Charlotte |
| North Dakota | 1889 (39) | 70,703 | 692,027 | 1 | Bismarck | Fargo |
| Ohio | 1803 (17) | 41,330 | 10,763,309 | 21 | Columbus | Cleveland |
| Oklahoma | 1907 (46) | 69,956 | 3,427,371 | 6 | Oklahoma City | Oklahoma City |
| Oregon | 1859 (33) | 97,073 | 2,680,087 | 5 | Salem | Portland |
| Pennsylvania | 1787 (2) | 45,308 | 11,895,301 | 23 | Harrisburg | Philadelphia |
| Rhode Island | 1790 (13) | 1,212 | 958,151 | 2 | Providence | Providence |
| South Carolina | 1788 (8) | 31,113 | 3,321,520 | 6 | Columbia | Columbia |
| South Dakota | 1889 (40) | 77,116 | 705,027 | 1 | Pierre | Sioux Falls |
| Tennessee | 1796 (16) | 42,144 | 4,723,332 | 9 | Nashville | Memphis |
| Texas | 1845 (28) | 266,807 | 16,384,800 | 27 | Austin | Houston |
| Utah | 1896 (45) | 84,899 | 1,684,942 | 3 | Salt Lake City | Salt Lake City |
| Vermont | 1791 (14) | 9,614 | 529,396 | 1 | Montpelier | Burlington |
| Virginia | 1788 (10) | 40,767 | 5,642,183 | 10 | Richmond | Norfolk |
| Washington | 1889 (42) | 68,138 | 4,366,248 | 8 | Olympia | Seattle |
| West Virginia | 1863 (35) | 24,231 | 1,968,989 | 4 | Charleston | Charleston |
| Wisconsin | 1848 (30) | 56,153 | 4,792,115 | 9 | Madison | Milwaukee |
| Wyoming | 1890 (44) | 97,809 | 534,744 | 1 | Cheyenne | Casper |
| District of Columbia | | 69 | 621,251 | 1 (nonvoting) | | |

| Self-Governing Areas, Possessions, and Dependencies | Area in Square Miles | Population (1980) | Capital |
|---|---|---|---|
| Puerto Rico | 3,515 | 3,196,520 | San Juan |
| Guam | 209 | 105,821 | Agana |
| U.S. Virgin Islands | 132 | 95,591 | Charlotte Amalie |
| American Samoa | 77 | 32,395 | Pago Pago |

This gazetteer, or geographical dictionary, lists places of importance to American history. The approximate latitude and longitude is given for cities, towns, and other specific locations. See Skill Lesson 3 (page 56), Using Latitude and Longitude. After the description of each place, there are usually two numbers in parentheses. The first number refers to the text page where you can find out more about the place. The second number is *italicized* and refers to a map (*m*) where the place is shown.

---

# A

**Alabama** 22nd state. Nicknamed the Heart of Dixie or the Cotton State. (p. 578, *m572–73*)

**Alamo** (29°N/99°W) Spanish mission and fort in San Antonio, Texas. After Texans defending the fort were killed by Mexican soldiers in 1836, "Remember the Alamo" became the battle cry of Texans in their struggle for independence. (p. 316, *m317*)

**Alaska** 49th state. Largest in size but the least populated of the 50 states. (p. 578, *m572–73*)

**Albany** (43°N/74°W). Capital of New York State. Called Fort Orange by the Dutch of New Netherland. (p. 47, *m572–73*)

**Andes** Rugged mountain chain in South America. (p. 26, *m45*)

**Antietam** (39°N/78°W) Creek in Maryland. Site of a Union victory in 1862. (p. 399, *m399*)

**Appalachian Mountains** Stretch from Georgia to Maine and Canada. Heavily forested and a barrier to colonial expansion. (p. 23, *m136*)

**Appomattox Courthouse** (37°N/79°W) Small town in Virginia where Lee surrendered to Grant on April 9, 1865. (p. 412, *m411*)

**Arizona** 48th state. Nicknamed the Grand Canyon State. (p. 578, *m572–73*)

**Arkansas** 25th state. Nicknamed the Land of Opportunity. (p. 578, *m572–73*)

**Atlanta** (34°N/84°W) Capital and largest city of Georgia. Burned by Sherman in 1864 before his "march to the sea." (p. 411, *m411*)

**Atlantic Ocean** World's second largest ocean. (p. 22, *m21*)

**Atlantic Plain** Part of the coastal plain in the eastern United States. (p. 25, *m24*)

# B

**Badlands** Dry region of South Dakota. (p. 25)

**Baltimore** (39°N/77°W) Port city in Maryland. (p. 99, *m112*)

**Bering Sea** Narrow sea between Asia and North America. Scientists think a land bridge existed here during the last ice age. (p. 20, *m21*)

**Boston** (42°N/71°W) Seaport and industrial city in Massachusetts. U.S.S. *Constitution*, retired in 1897, can be seen in the Boston Navy Yard. (p. 100, *m102*)

**Brazil** Largest country in South America. Became independent in 1822. (p. 27, *m570–71*)

**Breed's Hill** (42°N/71°W) Overlooks Boston Harbor. Site of fighting during the Battle of Bunker Hill. (p. 174, *m175*)

**Breuckelen** (41°N/74°W) Dutch settlement in New Netherland. Now called Brooklyn. Located in New York. (p. 87, *m87*)

**Buena Vista** (26°N/101°W) Site of an American victory in the Mexican War. (p. 323, *m324*)

**Buffalo** (43°N/79°W) Industrial city in New York State on Lake Erie. Free Soil Party was founded there in 1848. (p. 375, *m572–73*)

**Bull Run** (39°N/78°W) Small stream in Virginia. Site of Confederate victories in 1861 and 1862. (p. 398, *m399*)

**Bunker Hill** (42°N/71°W) Overlooks Boston Harbor. Was fortified by Americans, then abandoned in favor of nearby Breed's Hill in 1775. Site of an early battle during the Revolution. (p. 173, *m175*)

# C

**Cahokia** (39°N/90°W) Fur-trading post in southwestern Illinois in the 1700s. Captured by George Rogers Clark in 1778 during the Revolution. (p. 187, *m186*)

**California** 31st state. Nicknamed the Golden State. Ceded to the United States by Mexico in 1848. (p. 578, *m572–73*)

**Canada** Northern neighbor of the United States. Made up of 10 provinces: Ontario, Quebec, Nova Scotia, New Brunswick, Alberta, British Columbia, Manitoba, Newfoundland and Labrador, Prince Edward Island, and Saskatchewan. (p. 150, *m570–71*)

**Cape Bojador** (26°N/16°W) Located at the bulge of West Africa. (p. 56, *m57*)

**Cape Cod** (42°N/70°W) Located on the coast of Massachusetts. Pilgrims on the *Mayflower* landed here. (p. 94, *m94*)

**Cape Horn** (56°S/67°W) Southern tip of South America. Magellan rounded this cape in 1520. (p. 60, *m61*)

**Cape of Good Hope** (34°S/18°E) Southern tip of Africa. Dias rounded this cape in 1488. (p. 55, *m57*)

**Caribbean Sea** Tropical sea in the Western Hemisphere. Dotted with islands of the West Indies. Since 1823, United States has tried to exclude foreign powers from the region. (p. 22, *m58*, *m570–71*)

**Central America** Part of North America that lies between Mexico and South America. (p. 27, *m570–71*)

**Central Plains** Eastern part of the Interior Plains. Once covered with tall prairie grasses. Now a productive farming region with many cities. (p. 24, *m24*)

**Chancellorsville** (38°N/78°W) Site of a Confederate victory in 1863. (p. 409, *m411*)

**Charleston** (33°N/80°W) City in South Carolina. Spelled Charles Town in colonial days. (p. 110, *m112*)

**Chesapeake Bay** Large inlet of the Atlantic Ocean in Virginia and Maryland. (p. 90, *m94*)

**Chicago** (42°N/88°W) Second largest city in the United States. Developed as a railroad and meatpacking center in the late 1800s. (p. 24, *m572–73*)

**China** Country in East Asia. Visited by Marco Polo in the 1200s. Now the world's most populous country. (p. 48, *m570–71*)

**Colorado** 38th state. Nicknamed the Centennial State. (p. 578, *m572–73*)

**Columbia River** Chief river of the Pacific Northwest. (p. 247, *m247*)

**Concord** (43°N/71°W) Village near

Gazetteer

Boston, Massachusetts. Site of the first battle of the American Revolution in April 1775. (p. 163, *m169*)

**Connecticut** One of the 13 original states. Nicknamed the Constitution State or the Nutmeg State. (p. 578, *m572–73*)

**Costa Rica** Country in Central America. Won independence from Spain in 1821. (p. 281, *m570–71*)

**Cotton Kingdom** In the 1850s, many plantations worked by slaves produced cotton in this region. Stretched from South Carolina to Georgia and Texas. (p. 342, *m342*)

**Cowpens** (35°N/82°W) Located in South Carolina. Site of a decisive American victory in 1781 during the Revolution. (p. 191, *m191*)

**Croatoan Island** Place where Roanoke settlers may have moved between 1587 and 1590. (p. 89, *m94*)

**Cuba** (22°N/79°W) Island country in the Caribbean. Gained independence from Spain in 1898. (p. 79, *m570–71*)

**Cumberland Gap** (37°N/84°W) Pass in the Appalachian Mountains near the border of Virginia, Kentucky, and Tennessee. (p. 271, *m272*)

**Cuzco** (14°S/72°W) Inca capital located high in the Andes Mountains of Peru. (p. 44, *m45*)

# D

**Dallas** (33°N/97°W) City in Texas. Located on the Interior Plains. (p. 24, *m572–73*)

**Delaware** One of the 13 original states. Nicknamed the First State and the Diamond State. (p. 578, *m572–73*)

**Delaware River** Flows into the Atantic Ocean through Delaware Bay. (p. 105, *m94*)

**Detroit** (42°N/83°W) Capital of Michigan. (p. 257, *m572–73*)

**District of Columbia** Located on the Potomac River. Seat of the federal government of the United States. (p. 578, *m572–73*)

# E

**East Indies** Islands in Southeast Asia. Now part of Indonesia. Source of cloves and spices in the 1500s and 1600s. (p. 51, *m570–71*)

**Ecuador** Country in South America. (p. 82, *m570–71*)

**El Paso** (32°N/106°W) City on the Rio Grande in Texas. Settled by Spanish. (p. 83, *m572–73*)

**El Salvador** Country in Central America. Won independence from Spain in 1821. (p. 281, *m570–71*)

**England** Part of Great Britain. (p. 53, *m570–71*)

**Equator** Line of latitude labeled 0°. Separates the Northern and Southern hemispheres. (p. 27, *m57*)

**Erie Canal** Linked the Mohawk River with Buffalo and Lake Erie. Built between 1817 and 1825. (p. 275, *m275*)

**Europe** Smallest of the world's continents. (p. 48, *m570–71*)

# F

**Florida** 27th state. Nicknamed the Sunshine State. (p. 578, *m572–73*)

**Fort McHenry** (39°N/77°W) Located in Baltimore Harbor. British bombardment there in 1814 inspired Francis Scott Key to write "The Star-Spangled Banner." (p. 261)

**Fort Orange** (43°N/74°W) Dutch name for Albany, New York. (p. 86, *m87*)

**Fort Oswego** (44°N/76°W) British fort and fur-trading post. Located on Lake Ontario. (p. 153, *m182*)

**Fort Pitt** (40°N/80°W) British name for Fort Duquesne after its capture from the French in 1758. (p. 154, *m186*)

**Fort Sumter** (33°N/80°W) Guarded the entrance to Charleston Harbor in South Carolina. Confederates fired the first shots of the Civil War there in 1861. (p. 393, *m411*)

**Fort Ticonderoga** (44°N/74°W) French, then British, fort at the south end of Lake Champlain. Captured by Ethan Allen and his Green Mountain Boys in 1775. (p. 173, *m176*)

**France** Country in Western Europe. First ally of the United States. (p. 53, *m570–71*)

**Fredericksburg** (38°N/78°W) Located in eastern Virginia. Site of a Confederate victory in 1862. Now part of Fredericksburg and Spotsylvania County Battlefields Memorial National Military Park. (p. 409, *m411*)

# G

**Gadsden Purchase** Land purchased from Mexico in 1853. Now part of Arizona and New Mexico. (p. 324, *m326*)

**Georgia** One of the 13 original states. Nicknamed the Peach State or the Empire State of the South. (p. 578, *m572–73*)

**Gettysburg** (40°N/77°W) Small town in southern Pennsylvania. Site of a Union victory in 1863 and

Lincoln's famous Gettysburg Address. (p. 410, *m411*)

**Goliad** (29°N/97°W) City in Texas near San Antonio. After Mexicans executed 300 Texans there in 1836, "Remember Goliad" became a battle cry during the Texan war for independence. (p. 317, *m317*)

**Gonzalez** (97°N/30°W) City in Texas near San Antonio. Site of the first Texan victory over Mexico in 1835. Called "the Lexington of Texas." (p. 316, *m317*)

**Great Britain** Island nation of Western Europe. Includes England, Scotland, Wales, and Northern Ireland. (p. 151, *m570–71*)

**Great Lakes** Group of five freshwater lakes in the heart of the United States. (p. 26, *m24*)

**Great Plains** Western part of the Interior Plains. Once grazed by large herds of buffalo. Now an important ranching and wheat-growing region. (p. 24, *m24*)

**Great Salt Lake** Vast salt lake in Utah. (p. 23, *m572–73*)

**Great Wagon Road** Early pioneer route across the Appalachians to Pittsburgh and the Ohio Valley. (p. 128, *m130*)

**Greenland** World's largest island. Colonized by Vikings in the 10th century. (p. 48, *m570–71*)

**Guam** (14°N/143°E) Island in the Pacific Ocean. Territory of the United States. Acquired from Spain in 1898. (p. 578, *m570–71*)

**Guatemala** Country in Central America. Gained independence from Spain in 1821. Mayas built an advanced civilization there over 3,000 years ago. (p. 27, *m570–71*)

**Gulf of Mexico** Body of water along the southern coast of the United States. (p. 25, *m24*)

**Gulf Plain** Part of the coastal plain lowland that lies along the Gulf of Mexico. (p. 25, *m24*)

# H

**Haiti** Country in the West Indies. Won independence from France in the early 1800s. (p. 57, *m570–71*)

**Harpers Ferry** (39°N/78°W) Town in West Virginia. Abolitionist John Brown raided the arsenal there in 1859. (p. 385, *m399*)

**Hawaii** Newest of the 50 states. Nicknamed the Aloha State. (p. 578, *m572–73*)

**Hispaniola** (18°N/73°W) Island in the Caribbean that Columbus visited on his first voyage. Occupied today by the Dominican Republic and Haiti. (p. 57, *m58*)

**Hudson Bay**   Large inlet of the Arctic Ocean. Named for the explorer Henry Hudson. (p. 68, *m66*)

**Hudson River**   Largest river in New York State. Explored by Henry Hudson in 1609. (p. 67, *m87*)

# I

**Iceland** (65°N/20°W)   Island nation in the north Atlantic Ocean. Settled by Vikings in the ninth century. (p. 49, *m570–71*)

**Idaho**   43rd state. Nicknamed the Gem State. Acquired by the United States as part of Oregon Country. (p. 578, *m572–73*)

**Illinois**   21st state. Nicknamed the Inland Empire. Settled as part of the Northwest Territory. (p. 578, *m572–73*)

**Independence** (37°N/96°W)   City in western Missouri. Starting point of the Oregon Trail in the 1840s. (p. 312, *m320*)

**India**   Country in South Asia. World's second most populated country after China. (p. 53, *m570–71*)

**Indiana**   19th state. Nicknamed the Hoosier State. Settled as part of the Northwest Territory. (p. 578, *m572–73*)

**Indian Ocean**   Separates Africa from India. (p. 55, *m57*)

**Interior Plains**   Region of the central United States that stretches from the Rockies to the Appalachians. (p. 23, *m24*)

**Intermountain Region**   Rugged and mostly dry region from the Rocky Mountains to the Sierra Nevada and coastal mountains of the western United States. (p. 23, *m24*)

**Iowa**   29th state. Nicknamed the Hawkeye State. Acquired by the United States as part of the Louisiana Purchase. (p. 578, *m572–73*)

**Isthmus of Panama**   Narrow strip of land joining North and South America. (p. 22, *m61*)

# J

**Jackson** (32°N/90°W)   City in western Mississippi. Captured by Grant in 1863. (p. 400, *m411*)

**Jamestown** (37°N/77°W)   First successful English colony in North America. (p. 76, *m112*)

# K

**Kansas**   34th state. Nicknamed the Sunflower State. Acquired by the United States as part of the Louisiana Purchase. (p. 578, *m572–73*)

**Kaskaskia** (38°N/90°W)   French, then British, fur-trading post on an island in the Mississippi River. Captured by George Rogers Clark in 1778. First state capital of Illinois. (p. 187, *m186*)

**Kentucky**   15th state. Nicknamed the Bluegrass State. Was the first area west of the Appalachians to be settled by early pioneers. (p. 578, *m572–73*)

# L

**Lake Champlain** (45°N/73°W)   Borders New York and Vermont. Part of the water route connecting the Hudson and St. Lawrence rivers. Fort Ticonderoga is at the southern end. (p. 173, *m175*)

**Lake Erie**   One of the five Great Lakes. Shared by the United States and Canada. (p. 26, *m24*)

**Lake Huron**   One of the five Great Lakes. Shared by the United States and Canada. (p. 26, *m24*)

**Lake Michigan**   Only one of the Great Lakes located wholly within the United States. (p. 26, *m24*)

**Lake Ontario**   One of the five Great Lakes. Shared by the United States and Canada. (p. 26, *m24*)

**Lake Superior**   Highest and farthest inland of the five Great Lakes. Shared by the United States and Canada. (p. 26, *m24*)

**Latin America**   Name for those parts of the Western Hemisphere where Latin languages such as Spanish, French, and Portuguese are spoken. Includes Mexico, Central and South America, and the West Indies. (p. 282, *m282*)

**Lexington** (42°N/71°W)   Site of the first clash between minutemen and British troops in 1775. Now a suburb of Boston. (p. 169, *m169*)

**Line of Demarcation**   Line drawn by the Pope in 1494. Divided the non-Christian world between Spain and Portugal. (p. 60, *m61*)

**Lone Star Republic**   Another name for the Republic of Texas (1836–1845). (p. 317, *m317*)

**Louisbourg** (46°N/60°W)   Fort built by France on Cape Breton Island in eastern Canada. Changed hands several times between France and Britain. (p. 154, *m154*)

**Louisiana**   18th state. Nicknamed the Pelican State. First state created out of the Louisiana Purchase. (p. 578, *m572–73*)

**Louisiana Purchase**   Region between the Mississippi River and the Rocky Mountains purchased from France in 1803. (p. 245, *m247*)

# M

**Maine**   23rd state. Nicknamed the Pine Tree State. Originally part of Massachusetts. Maine gained separate statehood in 1820 under the terms of the Missouri Compromise. (p. 578, *m572–73*)

**Maryland**   One of the 13 original states. Nicknamed the Old Line State or the Free State. (p. 578, *m572–73*)

**Massachusetts**   One of the 13 original states. Nicknamed the Bay State or the Old Colony. (p. 578, *m572–73*)

**Massachusetts Bay Colony**   Founded by the Massachusetts Bay Company and settled by Puritans. (p. 100, *m102*)

**Mexican Cession**   Lands acquired by the United States from Mexico under the Treaty of Guadalupe Hidalgo in 1848. (p. 324, *m326*)

**Mexico**   Southern neighbor of the United States. Gained independence from Spain in 1821. (p. 23, *m570–71*)

**Mexico City** (19°N/99°W)   Capital of Mexico. Was the capital of New Spain. Site of the ancient Aztec city of Tenochtitlan. (p. 82, *m78*)

**Michigan**   26th state. Nicknamed the Great Lake State or the Wolverine State. Settled as part of the Northwest Territory. (p. 578, *m572–73*)

**Minnesota**   32d state. Nicknamed the North Star State or the Gopher State. Most of it was acquired by the United States as part of the Louisiana Purchase. (p. 578, *m572–73*)

**Mississippi**   20th state. Nicknamed the Magnolia State. (p. 578, *m572–73*)

**Mississippi River**   Second longest river in the United States. Links the Great Lakes with the Gulf of Mexico. (p. 25, *m24*)

**Missouri**   24th state. Nicknamed the Show Me State. Acquired by the United States as part of the Louisiana Purchase. (p. 578, *m572–73*)

**Missouri Compromise line**   Line drawn across the Louisiana Purchase at latitude 36° 36′N to divide free states from slave states. (p. 374, *m380*)

**Missouri River**   Longest river in the United States. Rises in the northern Rocky Mountains and joins the Mississippi River near St. Louis. (p. 20, *m24*)

**Montana**   41st state. Nicknamed the Treasure State. Acquired in part by the United States through the Louisiana Purchase. (p. 578, *m572–73*)

**Montreal** (46°N/74°W)  Major city in Canada. Located on the St. Lawrence River. Settled by the French. (p. 155, *m154*)

# N

**National Road**  Early road to the Old West. Now part of U.S. Highway 40. (p. 272, *m272*)

**Nebraska**  37th state. Nicknamed the Cornhusker State. Acquired by the United States as part of the Louisiana Purchase. (p. 578, *m572–73*)

**Nevada**  36th state. Nicknamed the Sagebrush State or the Battle Born State. Acquired by the United States at the end of the Mexican War. (p. 578, *m572–73*)

**New Amsterdam** (41°N/74°W)  Settlement founded by the Dutch on Manhattan Island. Now called New York City. (p. 86, *m87*)

**New England**  Name for the region that today includes the states from Maine to Connecticut. (p. 98, *m102*)

**Newfoundland** (48°N/57°W)  Island at the mouth of the St. Lawrence River. Part of Canada. (p. 66, *m66*)

**New France**  Colony established by France in North America. (p. 84, *m85*)

**New Hampshire**  One of the 13 original states. Nicknamed the Granite State. (p. 578, *m572–73*)

**New Jersey**  One of the 13 original states. Nicknamed the Garden State. (p. 578, *m572–73*)

**New Mexico**  47th state. Nicknamed the Land of Enchantment. Acquired by the United States at the end of the Mexican War. (p. 578, *m572–73*)

**New Netherland**  Dutch colony on the Hudson River. Conquered by the English and renamed New York in 1664. (p. 83, *m87*)

**New Orleans** (30°N/90°W)  Port city in Louisiana near the mouth of the Mississippi River. Settled by the French in the 1600s. Site of a battle between American and British forces in 1815. (p. 84, *m85*)

**New Spain**  Area ruled by Spain for 300 years. Included Spanish colonies in West Indies, Central America, and North America. (p. 77, *m78*)

**New Sweden**  Swedish colony on the Delaware River. Founded about 1640. Taken over by the Dutch in 1655, then by the English in 1664. Now part of Pennsylvania, New Jersey, and Delaware. (p. 87, *m87*)

**New York**  One of the 13 original states. Nicknamed the Empire State. (p. 578, *m572–73*)

**New York City** (41°N/74°W)  Port city at the mouth of the Hudson River. Founded by the Dutch as New Amsterdam. First capital of the United States. (p. 126, *m127*)

**Nicaragua**  Country in Central America. Won independence from Spain in 1821. (p. 281, *m570–71*)

**North America**  World's third largest continent. Separated from South America by the Isthmus of Panama. (p. 20, *m570–71*)

**North Carolina**  One of the 13 original states. Nicknamed the Tar Heel State or the Old North State. (p. 578, *m572–73*)

**North Dakota**  39th state. Nicknamed the Sioux State or the Flickertail State. Acquired by the United States as part of the Louisiana Purchase. (p. 578, *m572–73*)

**Northwest Territory**  Name for lands north of the Ohio River and east of the Mississippi River. Acquired by the United States by the Treaty of Paris in 1783. (p. 200, *m201*)

**Nova Scotia**  Province of eastern Canada. Early French, then British colony. (p. 83, *m85*)

**Nueces River**  Claimed by Mexico as the southern border of Texas in the Mexican War. (p. 322, *m324*)

# O

**Ohio**  17th state. Nicknamed the Buckeye State. Settled as part of the Northwest Territory. (p. 578, *m572–73*)

**Ohio River**  Important transportation route. Begins at Pittsburgh and joins the Mississippi River at Cairo. (p. 20, *m24*)

**Oklahoma**  46th state. Nicknamed the Sooner State. Acquired by the United States as part of the Louisiana Purchase. (p. 578, *m572–73*)

**Oregon**  33rd state. Nicknamed the Beaver State. Acquired by the United States as part of Oregon Country. (p. 578, *m572–73*)

**Oregon Country**  Located in the Pacific Northwest. Claimed by the United States, Britain, Spain, and Russia. (p. 309, *m326*)

**Oregon Trail**  Overland route from Independence on the Missouri River to the Columbia River valley. (p. 309, *m310*)

# P

**Pacific Northwest**  Stretches from Alaska to northern California along the west coast of North America. (p. 27)

**Pacific Ocean**  World's largest ocean. (p. 22, *m21*)

**Pennsylvania**  One of the 13 original states. Nicknamed the Keystone State. (p. 578, *m572–73*)

**Peru**  Country in South America. Gained independence from Spain in 1821. (p. 27, *m570–71*)

**Philadelphia** (40°N/75°W)  Major port and chief city in Pennsylvania. Second capital of the United States. (p. 108, *m107*)

**Philippine Islands** (14°N/125°E)  Group of islands in the Pacific Ocean off the east coast of Asia. Magellan was killed there. (p. 61, *m570–71*)

**Pikes Peak** (39°N/105°W)  Located in the Rocky Mountains of central Colorado. Named for Zebulon Pike, who reached it in 1806. (p. 249, *m247*)

**Plymouth** (42°N/71°W)  New England colony founded in 1620 by Pilgrims. Absorbed by the Massachusetts Bay Colony in 1691. (p. 76, *m102*)

**Portugal**  Country in western Europe. In the 1400s, sailors set out from there to explore the coast of Africa. (p. 53, *m570–71*)

**Potomac River**  Forms part of the Maryland–Virginia border. Flows through Washington, D.C., and into Chesapeake Bay. (p. 90, *m94*)

**Prime Meridian**  Line of longitude labeled 0°. (p. 56, *m57*)

**Princeton** (40°N/75°W)  Located in New Jersey. Site of an American victory during the Revolution. (p. 182, *m182*)

**Puerto Rico** (18°N/67°W)  Island in the Caribbean Sea. Acquired from Spain after the Spanish–American War. Now a self-governing commonwealth of the United States. (p. 58, *m570–71*)

# Q

**Quebec City** (47°N/71°W)  Located in eastern Canada on the St. Lawrence River. Founded in 1608 by the French explorer Samuel de Champlain. Captured by the British in 1759. (p. 83, *m85*)

# R

**Republic of Texas**  Independent nation set up by American settlers in Texas. Lasted from 1836 to 1845. (p. 316, *m317*)

**Rhode Island**  One of the 13 original states. Nicknamed the Little Rhody or the Ocean State. (p. 578, *m572–73*)

**Richmond** (38°N/78°W) Located on the James River. Capital of the Confederacy. (p. 397, *m191*)

**Rio Grande** Forms the border between the United States and Mexico. (p. 26, *m317*)

**Roanoke Island** (36°N/76°W) Located off the coast of North Carolina. Site of the "lost colony" founded in 1587. (p. 88, *m94*)

**Rocky Mountains** Stretches from Alaska to New Mexico through the western United States. Barrier to travel in pioneer days. (p. 23, *m24*)

# S

**Sacramento** (39°N/122°W) Capital of California. Developed as a Gold Rush boom town. (p. 327, *m572–73*)

**Sagres** (37°N/9°W) Town facing the Atlantic at the tip of Portugal. In the 1400s, Prince Henry the Navigator set up an informal school for sailors there. (p. 53, *m57*)

**St. Augustine** (30°N/81°W) City in Florida. Founded by Spain in 1565. Oldest European settlement in the United States. (p. 83, *m78*)

**St. Lawrence River** Waterway leading from the Great Lakes to the Atlantic Ocean. Forms part of the border between the United States and Canada. (p. 26, *m85*)

**Salt Lake City** (41°N/112°W) Largest city in Utah. Founded in 1847 by Mormons. (p. 23, *m572–73*)

**San Antonio** (29°N/99°W) City in southern Texas. Chief Texas settlement in Spanish and Mexican days. Site of the Alamo. (p. 83, *m317*)

**San Diego** (33°N/117°W) City in southern California. Founded as a Spanish mission. (p. 320, *m320*)

**San Francisco** (38°N/122°W) City in northern California. Boom town of the 1848 California Gold Rush. (p. 23, *m320*)

**San Jacinto River** Flows across southeastern Texas into Galveston Bay. Site of a Texan victory in 1836. (p. 317, *m317*)

**Santa Fe** (35°N/106°W) Capital of New Mexico. First settled by the Spanish. (p. 83, *m320*)

**Santa Fe Trail** Overland trail from Independence to Santa Fe. Opened in 1821 after Mexico gained independence from Spain. (p. 319, *m320*)

**Saratoga** (43°N/75°W) City in eastern New York. Also called Saratoga Springs. The American victory there in 1777 was a turning point in the Revolution. (p. 181, *m182*)

**Savannah** (32°N/81°W) Oldest city in Georgia. Founded in 1733. (p. 112, *m132*)

**Shiloh** (35°N/88°W) Site of a Union victory in 1862. Located on the Tennessee River. (p. 399, *m411*)

**Sierra Nevada** Mountain range mostly in California. (p. 23, *m24*)

**Songhai** Ancient West African kingdom. (p. 54, *m57*)

**South America** World's fourth largest continent. Part of the Western Hemisphere. (p. 22, *m570–71*)

**South Carolina** One of the 13 original states. Nicknamed the Palmetto State. (p. 578, *m572–73*)

**South Dakota** 40th state. Nicknamed the Coyote State or the Sunshine State. Acquired by the United States as part of the Louisiana Purchase. (p. 578, *m572–73*)

**Spain** Country in southwestern Europe. Columbus sailed from Spain in 1492. (p. 53, *m570–71*)

**Spanish Florida** Part of New Spain. Purchased by the United States in 1821. (p. 112, *m85*)

**Strait of Magellan** (53°S/69°W) Narrow water route at the tip of South America. (p. 22, *m61*)

# T

**Tennessee** 16th state. Nicknamed the Volunteer State. Gained statehood after North Carolina ceded its western lands to the United States. (p. 578, *m572–73*)

**Tennessee River** Tributary of the Ohio River. (p. 25, *m411*)

**Tenochtitlan** (19°N/99°W) Capital of the Aztec empire. Now part of Mexico City. (p. 42, *m45*)

**Texas** 28th state. Nicknamed the Lone Star State. Proclaimed independence from Mexico in 1836. Was a separate republic until 1845. (p. 578, *m572–73*)

**Tikal** (17°N/90°W) Ancient Maya city. (p. 42, *m45*)

**Timbuktu** (17°N/3°W) City on the southern edge of the Sahara Desert. Flourished as a center of trade and learning. (p. 54, *m57*)

# U

**Utah** 45th state. Nicknamed the Beehive State. Settled by Mormons. (p. 578, *m572–73*)

# V

**Valley Forge** (40°N/76°W) Winter headquarters for the Continental Army in 1777–1778. Located near Philadelphia. (p. 183, *m182*)

**Venezuela** Country in South America. Part of the Republic of Greater Colombia from 1819 to 1930. (p. 218, *m570–71*)

**Veracruz** (19°N/96°W) Port city in Mexico on the Gulf of Mexico. (p. 323, *m324*)

**Vermont** 14th state. Nicknamed the Green Mountain State. First new state to join the Union after the Revolution. (p. 578, *m572–73*)

**Vicksburg** (42°N/86°W) Located on a high cliff overlooking the Mississippi River. Site of a Union victory in 1863. (p. 400, *m411*)

**Vincennes** (39°N/88°W) City in Indiana. Settled by the French. British fort there was captured by George Rogers Clark in 1779. (p. 187, *m186*)

**Virginia** One of the 13 original states. Nicknamed the Old Dominion. (p. 578, *m572–73*)

**Virgin Islands** (18°N/64°W) Territory of the United States. Purchased from Denmark in 1917. (p. 578)

# W

**Washington** 42nd state. Nicknamed the Evergreen State. (p. 578, *m572–73*)

**Washington, D.C.** (39°N/83°W) Capital of the United States since 1800. Called Federal City until it was renamed for George Washington in 1799. (p. 234, *m258*)

**Washington-on-the-Brazos** (30°N/96°W) Town in Texas near Houston. Texans signed their declaration of independence from Mexico there in 1836. (p. 316, *m317*)

**Western Hemisphere** Western half of the world. Includes North and South America. (p. 22)

**West Indies** Islands in the Caribbean Sea. Explored by Columbus in 1492. (p. 47, *m570–71*)

**West Virginia** 35th state. Nicknamed the Mountain State. Separated from Virginia early in the Civil War. (p. 578, *m572–73*)

**Willamette River** Flows across fertile farmlands in northern Oregon to join the Columbia River. (p. 310, *m310*)

**Wisconsin** 30th state. Nicknamed the Badger State. Settled as part of the Northwest Territory. (p. 578, *m572–73*)

**Wyoming** 44th state. Nicknamed the Equality State. (p. 578, *m572–73*)

# Y

**Yorktown** (37°N/76°W) Town in Virginia near the York River. Site of a decisive American victory in 1781. (p. 189, *m191*)

**Gazetteer**

# A Chronology of American History

This chronology includes some of the most important events and developments in American history. It can be used to trace developments in the areas of government and citizenship, exploration and invention, American life, and the world of ideas.

| | Government and Citizenship | Explorers and Inventors |
|---|---|---|
| **Prehistory–1499** | Mayas, Aztecs, Incas build empires in Americas<br>Crusades for Holy Land begin<br>Rulers build strong nations in Europe | Mayas develop accurate calendar<br>Incas use quinine to treat malaria<br>Columbus sails to America<br>Vasco da Gama reaches India |
| **1500–1599** | Cortés defeats Aztecs<br>Pizarro captures Inca capital<br>Spanish pass Laws of the Indies<br>English colony set up at Roanoke | Spanish explore North America<br>Magellan's expedition circles globe<br>Cartier sails up St. Lawrence River<br>Drake sails around world |
| **1600–1649** | House of Burgesses set up in Virginia<br>Mayflower Compact signed<br>Massachusetts Bay Colony founded<br>Fundamental Orders of Connecticut written | Joint stock companies finance English settlements in North America<br>Champlain founds Quebec<br>West Indian tobacco brought to Virginia |
| **1650–1699** | France claims Louisiana<br>Glorious Revolution in England<br>Town meetings held in New England | Marquette and Joliet explore Mississippi River<br>La Salle reaches Mississippi delta |
| **1700–1749** | Georgia founded<br>Carolinas divided into two colonies<br>English settlers move into Ohio Valley | Indigo developed as cash crop<br>Benjamin Franklin invents Franklin stove |
| **1750–1799** | French and Indian War<br>Intolerable Acts passed<br>Declaration of Independence signed<br>American Revolution<br>Constitution ratified | Fitch launches first steam-powered boat<br>Slater sets up textile mills in New England<br>Eli Whitney invents cotton gin |

| Changes in American Life | The World of Ideas | |
|---|---|---|
| Agriculture develops in Americas<br>Great Serpent Mound built<br>Trade between Europe and Asia<br>  expands | Mayas develop system of writing<br>Aztecs build Tenochtitlan<br>Renaissance begins in Europe | **Prehistory–<br>1499** |
| Native American population of<br>  Spanish America declines<br>French develop fishing and fur trading<br>  in North America | Spanish convert Native Americans to<br>  Christianity<br>Universities open in Spanish America<br>John White paints in North America | **1500–<br>1599** |
| Spanish, French, Dutch, and English<br>  colonists adapt to life in New World<br>John Smith helps Jamestown survive<br>Slavery introduced in Virginia | Religious toleration granted in<br>  Maryland<br>Harvard College founded<br>First public schools set up in<br>  Massachusetts | **1600–<br>1649** |
| Navigation Acts passed<br>New England becomes trade and<br>  shipbuilding center | Quakers seek religious freedom in<br>  Pennsylvania<br>College of William and Mary founded | **1650–<br>1699** |
| Triangular trade flourishes<br>Plantations expand in South<br>Growth of port cities | Yale College founded<br>*Poor Richard's Almanac* published<br>Great Awakening begins in colonies | **1700–<br>1749** |
| Proclamation of 1763<br>Parliament passes Sugar, Quartering,<br>  Stamp, and Townshend acts<br>Colonies boycott British goods<br>Northwest Ordinance takes effect | Thomas Paine writes *Common Sense*<br>Phillis Wheatley publishes poetry<br>Northern states ban slave trade<br>National capital designed and built | **1750–<br>1799** |

| | Government and Citizenship | Explorers and Inventors |
|---|---|---|
| **1800–1824** | Louisiana Purchase<br>War of 1812<br>Missouri Compromise passed<br>Monroe Doctrine | Lewis and Clark expedition<br>Steamboats improved<br>Eli Whitney develops interchangeable parts |
| **1825–1849** | Age of Jackson<br>Indian Removal Act passed<br>Texas wins independence<br>Oregon divided along 49th parallel | Erie Canal opened<br>Mechanical reaper, steel plow, and telegraph developed<br>Railroads expand |
| **1850–1874** | Compromise of 1850<br>Civil War<br>Emancipation Proclamation<br>Indian wars on Great Plains | Passenger elevator, sleeping car, and air brake invented<br>Bessemer process developed<br>Transcontinental railroad completed |
| **1875–1899** | Battle of Little Bighorn<br>Populist Party formed<br>Sherman Antitrust Act passed<br>Spanish–American War | Refrigeration developed<br>Telephone, phonograph, and incandescent light bulb invented<br>First skyscraper built |
| **1900–1924** | Progressive Movement<br>Roosevelt Corollary<br>World War I<br>Fourteen Points<br>United States rejects Treaty of Versailles | Panama Canal built<br>Airplane invented<br>Assembly line introduced<br>Electric appliances become widespread |
| **1925–1949** | New Deal<br>World War II<br>Truman Doctrine and Marshall Plan<br>NATO created | Lindbergh flies across Atlantic<br>Antibiotics developed<br>Atomic bomb developed<br>First computers invented |
| **1950–1974** | Korean War<br>Civil Rights Act passed<br>Watergate affair<br>Vietnam War | *Explorer 1* launched into orbit<br>American astronauts land on moon<br>Nuclear power plants built<br>Vaccines increase life expectancy |
| **1975–Present** | Camp David Agreement on Middle East<br>Sandra Day O'Connor appointed to Supreme Court | Computers and microsurgery advance medicine<br>Space shuttle flights<br>*Voyager 1* passes Saturn |

| Changes in American Life | The World of Ideas | |
|---|---|---|
| Henry Clay's American System<br>Industry spreads in North<br>Cotton growing expands in South<br>Antislavery movement grows | "The Star-Spangled Banner" written<br>First trade unions set up<br>Hudson River School of painting<br>Washington Irving becomes well-known<br>  writer | 1800–<br>1824 |
| California Gold Rush<br>Temperance movement develops<br>*The Liberator* founded<br>Seneca Falls Convention | Mormon Church founded<br>Idea of Manifest Destiny takes hold<br>Mount Holyoke becomes first women's<br>  college in United States | 1825–<br>1849 |
| Thirteenth Amendment ends slavery<br>Homestead Act passed<br>Cattle and mining boom in West<br>Knights of Labor founded | *The Scarlet Letter* published<br>Free public education spreads in<br>  North<br>*Uncle Tom's Cabin* published | 1850–<br>1874 |
| Frontier closes<br>Trusts established<br>Immigration grows<br>Cities expand rapidly | Newspapers expand circulation<br>Progressive education movement<br>American Realists school of painting<br>Reformers expose problems of cities | 1875–<br>1899 |
| Muckrakers expose social problems<br>Pure Food and Drug Act passed<br>NAACP formed<br>Women work in war industries | Women win right to vote<br>Jazz Age<br>Harlem Renaissance<br>Commercial radio begins<br>Hollywood becomes world movie<br>  capital | 1900–<br>1924 |
| Bull market on Wall Street<br>Great Depression<br>Wartime production ends depression<br>Internment of Japanese Americans | Writers and photographers describe<br>  effects of depression<br>*The Grapes of Wrath* published<br>WPA sponsors artistic projects | 1925–<br>1949 |
| Rapid expansion of suburbs<br>Civil rights movement<br>Great Society programs | Rock 'n' roll becomes popular<br>Television age begins<br>New emphasis on equal rights for all<br>  Americans | 1950–<br>1974 |
| Increase of women in work force<br>Move to Sunbelt<br>Americans enjoy higher standard of<br>  living | Computers and lasers revolutionize<br>  entertainment and communications<br>Physical fitness becomes popular<br>Concern for environment spreads | 1975–<br>Present |

# Connections With American Literature

| TOPIC | AUTHOR | WORK | GENRE |
|---|---|---|---|
| **UNIT 1 THE WORLD OF THE AMERICAS** | | | |
| Peoples of the Desert, pages 34–35 | Zuñi Indians | The Girl Who Hunted Rabbits | myth |
| Peoples of North America, pages 36–41 | Tewa Indians | Song of the Sky Loom | myth |
| Peoples of North America, pages 36–41 | Ella E. Clark | The Origin of Fire | myth |
| Peoples of North America, pages 36–41 | Bernard DeVoto | The Indian All Around Us | essay |
| Eastern Woodlands, pages 40–41 | Iroquois Indians | The Iroquois Constitution | document |
| Aztecs, page 42 | Juliet Piggott | Popocatepetl and Ixtlaccihuatl | myth |
| Spain joins the Search, pages 55–57 | Joaquin Miller | Columbus | poem |
| **UNIT 2 SETTLING THE NEW WORLD** | | | |
| Fur Trappers and Traders, pages 83–84 | James Fenimore Cooper | The Deerslayer The Pathfinder | novels |
| King Philip's War, page 105 | Mary Rowlandson | Captivity Narrative | biography |
| New Netherland, pages 105–106 | Washington Irving | Rip Van Winkle | tale |
| The New England Way of Life, pages 121–125 | Henry Wadsworth Longfellow | The Village Blacksmith | poem |
| The New England Way of Life, pages 121–125 | Nathaniel Hawthorne | Feathertop | short story |
| A New American Culture, pages 134–135 | Robert Frost | The Gift Outright | poem |
| Benjamin Franklin, pages 136–137 | Benjamin Franklin | Poor Richard's Almanac | book |
| **UNIT 3 THE STRUGGLE FOR INDEPENDENCE** | | | |
| The British Are Coming! pages 168–169 | Ralph Waldo Emerson | Concord Hymn | poem |
| Paul Revere's Ride, page 168 | Henry Wadsworth Longfellow | Paul Revere's Ride | poem |
| Fighting Begins, pages 173–177 | Esther Forbes | Johnny Tremain | novel |
| The Voice of *Common Sense,* pages 177–178 | Thomas Paine | Common Sense | pamphlet |
| The Declaration of Independence, pages 178–179 | Thomas Jefferson | The Declaration of Independence | document |
| The Winter at Valley Forge, page 184 | Maxwell Anderson | Valley Forge | play |
| Women in the Revolution, pages 188–189 | Phillis Wheatley | To the Right Honourable William, Earl of Dartmouth | letter |

| TOPIC | AUTHOR | WORK | GENRE |
|---|---|---|---|
| **UNIT 4 STRENGTHENING THE NEW NATION** | | | |
| Washington's Farewell Address, page 229 | George Washington | Farewell Address | speech |
| Election of 1800, page 237 | Edward Everett Hale | The Man Without a Country | short story |
| Benjamin Banneker, page 237 | Benjamin Banneker | Letter to Thomas Jefferson | letter |
| The Nation Doubles in Size, pages 244–249 | Carl Sandburg | Paul Bunyan of the North Woods | folk tale |
| The Nation Doubles in Size, pages 244–249 | Rosemary Carr Benét | Johnny Appleseed | folk tale |
| The War at Sea, page 257 | Oliver Wendell Holmes | Old Ironsides | poem |
| The Sound of Steamboats, pages 273–275 | Mark Twain | Life on the Mississippi | auto- biography |
| Webster, Calhoun, and Clay, pages 277–278 | Stephen Vincent Benét | The Devil and Daniel Webster | short story |
| **UNIT 5 A GROWING NATION** | | | |
| The Trail of Tears, pages 302–303 | Walt Whitman | Osceola | poem |
| The Lone Star Republic, pages 315–319 | Adrien Stoutenburg | Davy Crockett | folk tale |
| The Life of Slaves, page 346 | Paul Laurence Dunbar | Sympathy | poem |
| The Underground Railroad, page 353 | Ann Petry | Harriet Tubman: Guide to Freedom | biography |
| Sojourner Truth, pages 355–356 | Sojourner Truth | Ain't I a Woman? | speech |
| American Writers, pages 361–362 | Nathaniel Hawthorne | The Snow Image The Great Stone Face | short stories |
| Emerson and His Circle, pages 362–363 | Ralph Waldo Emerson | Self-Reliance | essay |
| **UNIT 6 THE NATION DIVIDED** | | | |
| Webster for the Union, pages 376–377 | John Greenleaf Whittier | Ichabod | poem |
| On the Battle Lines, pages 397–401 | John Greenleaf Whittier | Barbara Frietchie | poem |
| Shiloh, pages 399–400 | Ray Bradbury | The Drummer Boy of Shiloh | short story |
| The Gettysburg Address, page 410 | Abraham Lincoln | Gettysburg Address | speech |
| Tragedy at Ford's Theater, pages 418–419 | Walt Whitman | O Captain! My Captain! | poem |
| Conditions in the South, pages 423–424 | Arna Bontemps | Southern Mansion | poem |

Connections With Literature

# Presidents of the United States

1

**1. George Washington** (1732–1799)
Years in office: 1789–1797
No political party
Elected from: Virginia
Vice Pres.: John Adams

**2. John Adams** (1735–1826)
Years in office: 1797–1801
Federalist Party
Elected from: Massachusetts
Vice Pres.: Thomas Jefferson

2

**3. Thomas Jefferson** (1743–1826)
Years in office: 1801–1809
Democratic Republican Party
Elected from: Virginia
Vice Pres.: Aaron Burr, George Clinton

3

**4. James Madison** (1751–1836)
Years in office: 1809–1817
Democratic Republican Party
Elected from: Virginia
Vice Pres.: George Clinton,
          Elbridge Gerry

4

**5. James Monroe** (1758–1831)
Years in office: 1817–1825
Democratic Republican Party
Elected from: Virginia
Vice Pres.: Daniel Tompkins

**6. John Quincy Adams** (1767–1848)
Years in office: 1825–1829
National Republican Party
Elected from: Massachusetts
Vice Pres.: John Calhoun

5

6

**7. Andrew Jackson** (1767–1845)
Years in office: 1829–1837
Democratic Party
Elected from: Tennessee
Vice Pres.: John Calhoun,
          Martin Van Buren

**8. Martin Van Buren** (1782–1862)
Years in office: 1837–1841
Democratic Party
Elected from: New York
Vice Pres.: Richard Johnson

7

8

Presidents

—600—

9

**9. William Henry Harrison*** (1773–1841)
Years in office: 1841
Whig Party
Elected from: Ohio
Vice Pres.: John Tyler

10

**10. John Tyler** (1790–1862)
Years in office: 1841–1845
Whig Party
Elected from: Virginia
Vice Pres.: none

11

**11. James K. Polk** (1795–1849)
Years in office: 1845–1849
Democratic Party
Elected from: Tennessee
Vice Pres.: George Dallas

**12. Zachary Taylor*** (1784–1850)
Years in office: 1849–1850
Whig Party
Elected from: Louisiana
Vice Pres.: Millard Fillmore

12

**13. Millard Fillmore** (1800–1874)
Years in office: 1850–1853
Whig Party
Elected from: New York
Vice Pres.: none

13

**14. Franklin Pierce** (1804–1869)
Years in office: 1853–1857
Democratic Party
Elected from: New Hampshire
Vice Pres.: William King

14

**15. James Buchanan** (1791–1868)
Years in office: 1857–1861
Democratic Party
Elected from: Pennsylvania
Vice Pres.: John Breckinridge

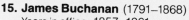

**16. Abraham Lincoln**** (1809–1865)
Years in office: 1861–1865
Republican Party
Elected from: Illinois
Vice Pres.: Hannibal Hamlin,
                  Andrew Johnson

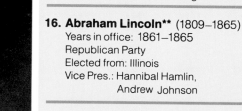

15

16

Presidents

*Died in office     **Assassinated     ***Resigned

17

### 17. Andrew Johnson (1808–1875)
Years in office: 1865–1869
Republican Party
Elected from: Tennessee
Vice Pres.: none

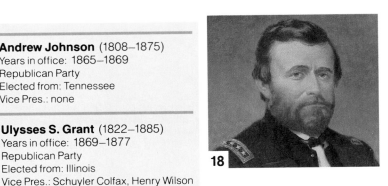

18

### 18. Ulysses S. Grant (1822–1885)
Years in office: 1869–1877
Republican Party
Elected from: Illinois
Vice Pres.: Schuyler Colfax, Henry Wilson

### 19. Rutherford B. Hayes (1822–1893)
Years in office: 1877–1881
Republican Party
Elected from: Ohio
Vice Pres.: William Wheeler

### 20. James A. Garfield** (1831–1881)
Years in office: 1881
Republican Party
Elected from: Ohio
Vice Pres.: Chester A. Arthur

19

20

### 21. Chester A. Arthur (1830–1886)
Years in office: 1881–1885
Republican Party
Elected from: New York
Vice Pres.: none

### 22. Grover Cleveland (1837–1908)
Years in office: 1885–1889
Democratic Party
Elected from: New York
Vice Pres.: Thomas Hendricks

### 23. Benjamin Harrison (1833–1901)
Years in office: 1889–1893
Republican Party
Elected from: Indiana
Vice Pres.: Levi Morton

### 24. Grover Cleveland (1837–1908)
Years in office: 1893–1897
Democratic Party
Elected from: New York
Vice Pres.: Adlai Stevenson

22

24

21

23

**Presidents**

**25**

**25. Willam McKinley\*\*** (1843–1901)
Years in office: 1897–1901
Republican Party
Elected from: Ohio
Vice Pres.: Garret Hobart,
Theodore Roosevelt

**26**

**26. Theodore Roosevelt** (1858–1919)
Years in office: 1901–1909
Republican Party
Elected from: New York
Vice Pres.: Charles Fairbanks

**27**

**27. William Howard Taft** (1857–1930)
Years in office: 1909–1913
Republican Party
Elected from: Ohio
Vice Pres.: James Sherman

**28. Woodrow Wilson** (1856–1924)
Years in office: 1913–1921
Democratic Party
Elected from: New Jersey
Vice Pres.: Thomas Marshall

**28**

**29. Warren G. Harding\*** (1865–1923)
Years in office: 1921–1923
Republican Party
Elected from: Ohio
Vice Pres.: Calvin Coolidge

**29**

**30. Calvin Coolidge** (1872–1933)
Years in office: 1923–1929
Republican Party
Elected from: Massachusetts
Vice Pres.: Charles Dawes

**30**

**31. Herbert C. Hoover** (1874–1964)
Years in office: 1929–1933
Republican Party
Elected from: California
Vice Pres.: Charles Curtis

**32. Franklin D. Roosevelt\*** (1882–1945)
Years in office: 1933–1945
Democratic Party
Elected from: New York
Vice Pres.: John Garner, Henry Wallace,
Harry S. Truman

**31**

**32**

**Presidents**

\*Died in office    \*\*Assassinated    \*\*\*Resigned

33

34

**33. Harry S. Truman** (1884–1972)
Years in office: 1945–1953
Democratic Party
Elected from: Missouri
Vice Pres.: Alben Barkley

**34. Dwight D. Eisenhower** (1890–1969)
Years in office: 1953–1961
Republican Party
Elected from: New York
Vice Pres.: Richard M. Nixon

**35. John F. Kennedy\*\*** (1917–1963)
Years in office: 1961–1963
Democratic Party
Elected from: Massachusetts
Vice Pres.: Lyndon B. Johnson

35

**36. Lyndon B. Johnson** (1908–1973)
Years in office: 1963–1969
Democratic Party
Elected from: Texas
Vice Pres.: Hubert Humphrey

36

**37. Richard M. Nixon\*\*\*** (1913–      )
Years in office: 1969–1974
Republican Party
Elected from: New York
Vice Pres.: Spiro Agnew, Gerald R. Ford

37

**38. Gerald R. Ford** (1913–      )
Years in office: 1974–1977
Republican Party
Elected from: Michigan
Vice Pres.: Nelson Rockefeller

38

**39. Jimmy Carter** (1924–      )
Years in office: 1977–1981
Democratic Party
Elected from: Georgia
Vice Pres.: Walter Mondale

39

**40. Ronald W. Reagan** (1911–      )
Years in office: 1981–1989
Republican Party
Elected from: California
Vice Pres.: George Bush

40

**41. George Bush** (1924–      )
Years in office: 1989–
Republican Party
Elected from: Texas
Vice Pres.: Dan Quayle

41

\*Died in office      \*\*Assassinated      \*\*\*Resigned

# Glossary

This glossary defines all vocabulary words and many important historical terms and phrases. These words and terms appear in dark slanted type the first time they are used in the text. The page number after each definition refers to the page on which the word or phrase is first discussed in the text. For other references, see the Index.

## Pronunciation Key

When difficult names or terms first appear in the text, they are respelled to aid pronunciation. A syllable in SMALL CAPITAL LETTERS receives the most stress. The key below lists the letters used for respelling. It includes examples of words using each sound and showing how they would be respelled.

| Symbol | Example | Respelling |
|--------|---------|------------|
| a | hat | (hat) |
| ay | pay, late | (pay), (layt) |
| ah | star, hot | (stahr), (haht) |
| ai | air, dare | (air), (dair) |
| aw | law, all | (law), (awl) |
| eh | met | (meht) |
| ee | bee, eat | (bee), (eet) |
| er | learn, sir, fur | (lern), (ser), (fer) |
| ih | fit | (fiht) |
| ī | mile | (mīl) |
| ir | ear | (ir) |
| oh | no | (noh) |
| oi | soil, boy | (soil), (boi) |
| oo | root, rule | (root), (rool) |
| or | born, door | (born), (dor) |
| ow | plow, out | (plow), (owt) |

| Symbol | Example | Respelling |
|--------|---------|------------|
| u | put, book | (put), (buk) |
| uh | fun | (fuhn) |
| yoo | few, use | (fyoo), (yooz) |
| ch | chill, reach | (chihl), (reech) |
| g | go, dig | (goh), (dihg) |
| j | jet, gently, bridge | (jeht), (JEHNT lee), (brihj) |
| k | kite, cup | (kīt), (kuhp) |
| ks | mix | (mihks) |
| kw | quick | (kwihk) |
| ng | bring | (brihng) |
| s | say, cent | (say), (sehnt) |
| sh | she, crash | (shee), (krash) |
| th | three | (three) |
| y | yet, onion | (yeht), (UHN yuhn) |
| z | zip, always | (zihp), (AWL wayz) |
| zh | treasure | (TREH zher) |

## A

**abolition** act of ending something completely. (p. 352)

**Act of Toleration** (1649) law that gave religious freedom to all Christians in Maryland. (p. 110)

**Adams–Onís Treaty** agreement by which Spain gave Florida to the United States in return for $5 million. (p. 282)

**adobe** sun-dried clay brick. (p. 34)

**alien** foreigner. (p. 236)

**Alien Act** (1798) law that allowed the President to expel foreigners thought to be dangerous to the country. (p. 236)

**almanac** book containing calendars and other useful information. (p. 136)

**amend** change. (p. 213)

**American Colonization Society** group founded in 1817 that wanted to set up a colony for free blacks in Africa. (p. 352)

**annex** add on, such as territory. (p. 318)

**Antifederalist** person opposed to the Constitution during the ratification debate in 1787. (p. 211)

**apprentice** person who learns a trade or craft from a master craftsman. (p. 135)

**archaeologist** scientist who studies evidence left by early people. (p. 33)

**arsenal** gun warehouse. (p. 385)

**Articles of Confederation** first American constitution. (p. 198)

**astrolabe** instrument used by sailors to figure out their latitude at sea. (p. 54)

## B

**backcountry** area in western Maryland and Virginia along the Appalachian Mountains. (p. 128)

**Bear Flag Republic** country set up in 1845 by Americans in California. (p. 323)

**bill** proposed law. (p. 208)

**Bill of Rights** first ten amendments to the Constitution of the United States of America. Ratified in 1791. (p. 213)

**black code** set of laws that limited the rights of freedmen. Passed by southern legislatures after the Civil War. (p. 421)

**blockade** shutting off of a port to keep people or supplies from moving in or out. (p. 177)

**bond** certificate that promises to pay the holder a sum of money plus interest on a certain date. (p. 223)

**Boston Associates** group of capitalists who built textile factories in Massachusetts. (p. 267)

**Boston Massacre** shooting of five Bostonians by British soldiers on March 5, 1770. (p. 163)

**Boston Tea Party** protest by a group of Bostonians who dressed as Indians and threw tea into Boston Harbor. (p. 166)

**bounty** payment. Given to men who joined the Union army. (p. 404)

**boycott** refuse to buy certain goods or services. (p. 159)

**Breadbasket Colonies** name for the Middle Colonies because they exported so much grain. (p. 126)

**burgess** representative to the colonial assembly of Virginia. (p. 92)

# C

**cabinet** group of officials who head government departments and advise the President. (p. 222)

**canal** channel dug and filled with water to allow ships to cross a stretch of land. (p. 275)

**capital** money raised for a business venture. (p. 90)

**capitalist** person with money to invest in business to make a profit. (p. 266)

**caravel** ship with a steering rudder and triangular sails. (p. 54)

**carpetbagger** name for a Northerner who went to the South during Reconstruction. (p. 425)

**cash crop** surplus of food sold for money on the world market. (p. 126)

**caucus** private meeting of political party leaders. (p. 295)

**cavalry** troops on horseback. (p. 184)

**cede** give up. (p. 324)

**century** 100-year period. (p. 167)

**charter** document giving certain rights to a person or company. (p. 89)

**checks and balances** system set up by the Constitution in which each branch of the federal government has the power to check, or limit, the actions of other branches. (p. 208)

**civilian** person not in the military. (p. 407)

**civil war** war between people of the same country. (p. 376)

**climate** average weather of a place over a period of 20 or 30 years. (p. 26)

**clipper ship** fastest sailing ship of the 1840s and 1850s. (p. 335)

**colony** group of people settled in a distant land who are ruled by the government of their native land. (p. 58)

**committee of correspondence** group of colonists who wrote letters and pamphlets protesting British rule. (p. 163)

**compromise** settlement in which each side gives up some of its demands in order to reach an agreement. (p. 204)

**Compromise of 1850** agreement over slavery that admitted California to the Union as a free state, allowed popular sovereignty in New Mexico and Utah, banned slave trade in Washington, D.C., and passed a strict fugitive slave law. (p. 377)

**Confederate States of America** nation formed by the states that seceded from the Union in 1860 and 1861. (p. 388)

**conquistador** Spanish word for conqueror. (p. 62)

**constitution** document that sets out the laws and principles of a government. (p. 197)

**Constitutional Convention** meeting of delegates from 12 states who wrote a constitution for the United States in 1787. (p. 202)

**continental divide** mountain ridge that separates river systems. (p. 248)

**Copperhead** Northerner who opposed fighting to keep the South in the Union. (p. 404)

**corduroy road** log road. (p. 272)

**corporation** business owned by investors who buy shares of stock. (p. 446)

**cotton gin** invention of Eli Whitney's that speeded up the cleaning of cotton fibers. (p. 266)

**coureur de bois** (koo RUHR duh BWAH) French phrase meaning runner of the woods. (p. 83)

**creole** descendant of Spanish settlers who was born in the Americas. (p. 79)

**Crusades** series of wars fought by Christians to conquer the Holy Land. (p. 51)

**culture** way of life of a given people. (p. 33)

# D

**Daughters of Liberty** group of colonial women who joined together to protest the Stamp Act and protect colonial liberties. (p. 160)

**decade** 10-year period. (p. 167)

**Declaration of Independence** (1776) document that stated the colonies had become a free and independent nation. (p. 178)

**Declaratory Act** (1776) British law that allowed Parliament to tax the colonists. (p. 159)

**democratic** ensuring that all people have the same rights. (p. 242)

**discrimination** policy or attitude that denies equal rights to certain people. (p. 303)

**draft** law requiring men of a certain age to serve in the military. (p. 404)

**Dred Scott decision** Supreme Court decision in 1857. Stated that slaves were property, not citizens. (p. 382)

**drought** long dry spell. (p. 35)

**due process** right of every citizen to the same fair rules in all cases brought to trial. (p. 213)

**dumping** selling goods in another country at very low prices. (p. 278)

# E

**economic depression** period when business activity slows, prices and wages fall, and unemployment rises. (p. 201)

**electoral college** group of electors from each state that meets every four years to vote for the President and Vice President. (p. 208)

**elevation** height. (p. 22)

**emancipate** set free. (p. 401)

**Emancipation Proclamation** (1863) declaration issued by Lincoln that freed slaves in the Confederacy. (p. 401)

**embargo** ban on trade with another country. (p. 253)

**emigrate** leave one's country and settle elsewhere. (p. 100)

**encomienda** (ehn koh mee EHN dah) right to demand taxes or labor from Native Americans living in the Spanish colonies. (p. 79)

**enumerated article** any of the goods that Parliament said colonists could sell only to England. (p. 113)

**execute** carry out. (p. 198)

**executive branch** part of a government that carries out the laws. (p. 203)

**export** trade good sold outside a country. (p. 113)

**extended family** close-knit family group that includes grandparents, parents, children, aunts, uncles, and cousins. (p. 346)

# F

**fact** something that actually happened and can be proved. (p. 232)

**factory system** method of producing goods that brings workers and machines together in one place. (p. 266)

**famine** severe shortage of food. (p. 339)

**Farewell Address** George Washington's advice to his fellow citizens when he left office in 1796. (p. 229)

**federalism** sharing of power between the states and the national government. (p. 206)

**Federalist** supporter of the Constitution in the ratification debate in 1787. Favored a strong national government. (pp. 211, 231)

**feudalism** system of rule by lords who owed loyalty to their king. (p. 50)

**Fifteenth Amendment** constitutional amendment that gave black Americans the right to vote in all states. (p. 424)

**First Continental Congress** meeting of delegates from 12 colonies in September 1774. (p. 166)

**forty-niner** person who went to California during the Gold Rush in 1849. (p. 327)

**Fourteenth Amendment** constitutional amendment that granted citizenship to all persons born in the United States. Encouraged states to allow blacks to vote. (p. 423)

**Frame of Government** document that set up the government of the Pennsylvania colony. (p. 107)

**freedman** freed slave. (p. 418)

**Freedmen's Bureau** government agency that helped freed slaves. (p. 418)

**Free Soil Party** political party founded in 1848 by antislavery Whigs and Democrats. (p. 375)

**French and Indian War** conflict between the French and British in North America. Fought from 1754 to 1763. (p. 151)

**fugitive** runaway, such as an escaped slave in the 1800s. (p. 376)

**Fugitive Slave Law of 1850** law that required citizens to help catch runaway slaves. (p. 377)

**Fundamental Orders of Connecticut** system of laws in the colony of Connecticut that limited the powers of the government. (p. 101)

# G

**General Court** representative assembly in the Massachusetts Bay Colony. (p. 101)

**gentry** highest social class in the colonies. (p. 135)

**geography** physical features, climate, plants, animals, and resources of a region. (p. 19)

**Gettysburg Address** speech given by Lincoln in 1863 at this Civil War battle site in Pennsylvania. (p. 410)

**glacier** thick sheet of ice. (p. 19)

**grandfather clause** law passed by southern states after the Civil War. Excused a voter from a poll tax or literacy test if his father or grandfather had voted in 1867. Kept most blacks from voting. (p. 431)

**Great Awakening** religious movement in the colonies in the 1730s and 1740s. (p. 137)

**Great Compromise** Roger Sherman's plan at the Constitutional Convention for a two-house legislature. Settled differences between large and small states. (p. 204)

**Great Migration** movement of thousands of English settlers to the Massachusetts Bay Colony. (p. 100)

**Green Mountain Boys** group of patriots from Vermont. Led by Ethan Allen. Captured Fort Ticonderoga in 1775. (p. 174)

# H

**habeas corpus** right to have charges filed or a trial before being jailed. (p. 406)

**Hartford Convention** meeting of New Englanders who opposed the War of 1812. (p. 260)

**hill** raised part of the earth's surface. Less steep than a mountain. (p. 22)

**hogan** Navajo house built of mud plaster and supported by wooden poles. (p. 39)

**House of Burgesses** representative assembly in colonial Virginia. (p. 92)

**House of Representatives** lower house of Congress. Each state is represented according to the size of its population. (p. 204)

**Hudson River School** group of artists who painted Hudson River and Catskill Mountains landscapes. (p. 365)

# I

**igloo** Eskimo house made of snow and ice. (p. 36)

**immigrant** person who comes from his or her homeland to settle in another country. (p. 339)

**impeach** bring charges against an official such as the President. (p. 210)

**import** trade good brought into a country. (p. 113)

**impressment** act of seizing men from a ship or village and forcing them to serve in the navy. Practiced by the British in the 1700s and 1800s. (p. 251)

**indentured servant** person who signed a contract to work for a certain length of time in exchange for passage to the colonies. (p. 117)

**Indian Removal Act** (1830) law that forced Native Americans to move west of the Mississippi. (p. 301)

**Industrial Revolution** process whereby machines replaced hand tools, and new sources of power, such as steam and electricity, replaced human and animal power. Caused a shift from farming to manufacturing. (p. 265)

**inflation** economic cycle in which the value of money falls and the prices of goods rise. (p. 406)

**initiative** procedure that allows voters to introduce a bill by collecting signatures on a petition. (p. 442)

**interchangeable parts** identical parts of a tool or instrument that are made by machine. Such parts can be easily assembled or replaced. (p. 268)

**Intolerable Acts** laws passed by Parliament in 1774 to punish colonists in Massachusetts for the Boston Tea Party. (p. 166)

**irrigate** bring water to an area such as farmland. (p. 27)

**isthmus** narrow strip of land. (p. 22)

# J

**Jay's Treaty** (1795) agreement to stop British attacks on American merchant ships and settle other differences between the two nations. (p. 227)

**joint stock company** private company that sold shares to investors to finance trading voyages. (p. 90)

**judicial branch** part of a government that decides if laws are carried out fairly. (p. 203)

**judicial review** right of the Supreme Court to review laws passed by Congress and declare them unconstitutional. (p. 244)

**Judiciary Act** (1789) law that organized the federal court system into district and circuit courts. (p. 222)

# K

**Kansas–Nebraska Act** (1854) law that divided Nebraska into two territories. Provided that the question of slavery in the territories would be decided by popular sovereignty. (p. 379)

**Kentucky and Virginia Resolutions** (1798, 1799) declarations that states had the right to declare a law unconstitutional. (p. 236)

**King Philip's War** conflict between English settlers and Indians in Massachusetts in 1675. (p. 105)

**kitchen cabinet** group of unofficial advisers to President Andrew Jackson. (p. 297)

**Know-Nothing Party** political party organized by nativists in the 1850s. (p. 340)

**Ku Klux Klan** secret group first set up in the South after the Civil War. Members terrorized blacks and other groups they hated. (p. 427)

# L

**laissez faire** French term meaning let alone. Referred to the idea that government should not interfere in people's lives. (p. 243)

**Land Ordinance of 1785** law that set up a system for settling the Northwest Territory. (p. 200)

**Laws of the Indies** laws that governed Spanish colonies in the New World. (p. 78)

**League of the Iroquois** council of the five nations of the Iroquois. (p. 41)

**legislative branch** part of a government that passes laws. (p. 203)

**legislature** group of people with power to make laws for a country or colony. (p. 115)

**Lincoln–Douglas Debates** series of political debates between Abraham Lincoln and Stephen Douglas in 1858. (p. 384)

**literacy test** examination to see if a person can read and write. (p. 431)

**long house** Iroquois dwelling. (p. 40)

**Loyalist** colonist who stayed loyal to Great Britain during the American Revolution. (p. 179)

# M

**Magna Carta** document that guaranteed rights to English nobles in 1215. (p. 92)

**magnetic compass** Chinese invention brought to Europe by the Arabs. Showed which direction was north. (p. 54)

**Manifest Destiny** belief of many Americans in the 1840s that the United States should own all the land between the Atlantic and Pacific oceans. (p. 321)

**manor** part of a lord's holding in the Middle Ages. Included a village or several villages and the surrounding lands. (p. 50)

**martial law** rule by the military. (p. 394)

**Mayflower Compact** agreement signed by Pilgrims before landing at Plymouth. (p. 94)

**mercantilism** economic theory that a nation's strength came from building up its gold supplies and expanding its trade. (p. 113)

**mestizo** person in the Spanish colonies of mixed Spanish and Indian background. (p. 79)

**Mexican War** conflict between the United States and Mexico over Texas. Lasted from 1846 to 1848. (p. 323)

**Middle Ages** period in Europe from about 500 to 1350. (p. 50)

**Middle Passage** ocean trip from Africa to the Americas in which thousands of slaves died. (p. 131)

**militia** army of citizens who serve as soldiers in an emergency. (p. 169)

**minuteman** volunteer who trained to fight the British in 1775. (p. 168)

**mission** religious settlement. Run by Catholic priests and friars in the Spanish colonies. (p. 78)

**Missouri Compromise** (1820) plan proposed by Henry Clay to keep the number of slave and free states equal. Admitted Missouri as a slave state and Maine as a free state. (p. 374)

**monopoly** company that completely controls the market of a certain industry. (p. 446)

**Monroe Doctrine** policy statement of President James Monroe in 1823. Warned European nations not to interfere with the newly independent nations of Latin America. (p. 283)

**Mormon** member of the Church of Jesus Christ of Latter Day Saints. (p. 325)

**Mound Builders** group of Native Americans who built thousands of huge earth mounds from eastern Oklahoma to the Atlantic. (p. 34)

**mountain** high, rugged land usually at least 5,000 feet above sea level. (p. 22)

**Mountain Men** trappers who followed Indian trails across the Rockies into Oregon in the early 1800s. (p. 310)

# N

**national debt** money a government owes. (p. 223)

**nationalism** pride in or devotion to one's country. (p. 254)

**Native American** descendant of people who reached America thousands of years ago. (p. 36)

**nativist** person who wanted to limit immigration and preserve the United States for native-born white Americans. (p. 340)

**navigation** practice of plotting a course at sea. (p. 53)

**Navigation Acts** series of laws passed in the 1600s that governed trade between England and its colonies. (p. 113)

**neutral** choosing not to fight on either side in a war. (p. 186)

**Neutrality Proclamation** (1793) Washington's statment that the United States would remain neutral in the war between France and other European nations. (p. 227)

**New England Anti-Slavery Society** group organized by William Lloyd Garrison to end slavery. (p. 353)

**New Jersey Plan** William Paterson's plan for the new government presented to the Constitutional Convention. (p. 204)

**nominating convention** meeting at which a political party selects its candidate for President. (p. 295)

**nonimportation agreement** promise of colonial merchants and planters to stop importing goods taxed by the Townshend Acts. (p. 160)

**Northwest Ordinance** (1787) law that set up a government for the Northwest Territory. Set up a way for new states to be admitted to the United States. (p. 200)

**nullification** idea of declaring a federal law illegal. (p. 299)

**Nullification Crisis** tense situation created by South Carolina when it declared the tariffs of 1828 and 1832 illegal. (p. 301)

**nullify** cancel, such as a law. (p. 236)

# O

**Olive Branch Petition** letter sent to King George III by the Continental Congress asking him to repeal the Intolerable Acts. (p. 174)

**override** overrule. Congress can override a President's veto if two thirds of both houses vote to do so. (p. 210)

# P

**Panic of 1837** economic crisis in which hundreds of banks failed. (p. 304)

**Patriot** colonist who supported the American Revolution. (p. 179)

**patroon** rich landowner in the Dutch colonies. (p. 105)

**peninsular** person sent from Spain to rule the Spanish colonies. (p. 78)

**pet bank** state bank used by President Jackson and Roger Taney for government money. (p. 299)

**Pickett's Charge** Confederate attack led by General George Pickett at the Battle of Gettysburg. (p. 410)

**pictograph** picture that represents an object. (p. 42)

**Pilgrims** group of English people who went to the New World in search of religious freedom. (p. 92)

**Pinckney Treaty** (1795) agreement between the United States and Spain to keep the port of New Orleans open. (p. 245)

**plain** broad area of fairly level land. (p. 22)

**Plan of Union** Benjamin Franklin's plan to unite the colonies in 1754. (p. 153)

**plantation** large estate farmed by many workers. (p. 79)

**plateau** area of mostly high, level land usually at least 2,000 feet (600 m) above sea level. (p. 22)

**poll tax** fee paid by a voter in order to vote. (p. 431)

**popular sovereignty** practice of allowing each territory to vote whether to allow slavery. (p. 374)

**population** number of people living in a place. (p. 153)

**potlatch** ceremonial dinner among some Native Americans of the Northwest Coast. (p. 37)

**precedent** act or decision that sets an example for others to follow. (p. 221)

**prejudice** unfavorable opinion about people who are of a different religion, race, or nationality. (p. 340)

**presidio** fort that housed soldiers in the Spanish colonies. (p. 78)

**primary source** firsthand information about people or events of the past. (p. 43)

**Proclamation of 1763** British law that forbade colonists to settle west of a line along the Appalachian Mountains. (p. 157)

**profiteer** person who takes advantage of an emergency to make money. (p. 406)

**proprietary colony** English colony in which the king gave land to one or more proprietors in exchange for a yearly payment. (p. 106)

**protective tariff** tax placed on goods from another country. (p. 279)

**Protestant Reformation** movement in the 1500s to reform the Catholic Church. (p. 68)

**public school** school supported by taxes. (p. 134)

**pueblo** Spanish word for village or town. (p. 35)

**Pueblos** group of Native Americans who lived in the Southwest. (p. 38)

**Puritans** group of English Protestants who wanted to purify the practices of the Church of England. Settled in Massachusetts. (p. 100)

# Q

**Quakers** Protestant group founded by George Fox. Settled in Pennsylvania. (p. 107)

**Quartering Act** (1766) law that required colonists to pay for the housing of British soldiers. (p. 161)

**Quebec Act** (1774) law that set up a government for Canada and protected the rights of French Catholics. (p. 166)

# R

**racism** belief that one race is superior to another. (p. 130)

**Radical Reconstruction** period after the Civil War when Republicans controlled Congress and passed harsh laws affecting the South. (p. 422)

**Radical Republicans** group of Republicans in Congress who wanted to protect the rights of freedmen in the South and keep rich southern planters out of power. (p. 421)

**ratify** approve. (p. 192)

**recall** special election that allows voters to remove an elected official from office. (p. 442)

**referendum** process by which people can vote directly on a bill. (p. 442)

**relief** on a map, difference in height of land. Shown by using special colors. (p. 21)

**Renaissance** period from 1350 to 1600 in which Europeans made great advances. (p. 52)

**rendezvous** French word for a get-together. Annual meeting of Mountain Men where they traded furs for supplies. (p. 311)

**repeal** cancel. (p. 159)

**representative government** system of government in which voters elect representatives to make laws for them. (p. 92)

**republic** nation in which voters choose representatives to govern them. (p. 205)

**Republican Party** political party formed in 1854 by a group of Free Soilers, northern Democrats, and antislavery Whigs. (p. 383)

**royal colony** English colony directly under the king's control. (p. 107)

**Rush–Bagot Agreement** (1817) agreement between the United States and Britain that forbade warships on the Great Lakes. (p. 261)

# S

**scalawag** white Southerner who supported Radical Republicans. (p. 425)

**secede** withdraw. (p. 300)

**sectionalism** strong sense of loyalty to a state or section instead of to the whole country. (p. 374)

**sedition** stirring up of rebellion against a government. (p. 236)

**Sedition Act** (1798) law that allowed citizens to be fined or jailed for criticizing public officials. (p. 236)

**segregation** separation of people of different races. (p. 431)

**Seminole War** conflict between the Seminole Indians and the United States Army. Lasted from 1835 to 1842. (p. 303)

**Senate** upper house of Congress. Each state is represented by two senators. (p. 204)

**Seneca Falls Convention** meeting at which leaders of the women's rights movement voted on a plan for achieving equality. (p. 356)

**separation of powers** system in which each branch of government has its own powers. (p. 207)

**serf** peasant who had to stay on the manor where he or she was born. (p. 50)

**sharecropper** farmer who works land owned by another and gives the landowner part of the harvest. (p. 428)

**Shays' Rebellion** (1786) revolt of Massachusetts farmers whose farms were being seized for debt. (p. 201)

**skilled worker** person with a trade, such as a carpenter, a printer, or a shoemaker. (p. 338)

**slave code** series of laws that controlled behavior of slaves and denied them basic rights. (p. 130)

**Sons of Liberty** group of colonial men who joined together to protest the Stamp Act and protect colonial liberties. (p. 160)

**Spanish Armada** large fleet sent by Spain against England in 1558. (p. 69)

**speculator** person who invests in a risky venture in hopes of making a large profit. (p. 224)

**spinning jenny** invention that let a person spin several threads at once. (p. 266)

**spoils system** practice of giving government jobs to loyal supporters. Used by the winning political party after an election. (p. 296)

**Stamp Act** (1765) law passed by Parliament that taxed legal documents, newspapers, almanacs, playing cards, and dice. (p. 159)

**states' rights** idea that individual states had the right to limit the power of the federal government. (p. 299)

**statistics** facts in number form. (p. 81)

**stockade** high fence made of wooden posts. Built by colonists to protect settlements from Indian attacks. (p. 92)

**stocks** wooden frames with holes for the arms and legs. Used to punish people found guilty of crimes. (p. 123)

**strike** organized work stoppage by union workers in order to win better pay or working conditions. (p. 338)

**subsistence farmer** person who grew enough for his or her own needs. (p. 121)

**suffrage** right to vote. (p. 293)

**Sugar Act** (1764) law passed by Parliament that taxed molasses. (p. 158)

**surplus** extra, such as food. (p. 121)

**Swamp Fox** nickname for the Patriot Francis Marion of South Carolina. (p. 190)

# T

**tariff** tax. Placed on goods brought into a country. (p. 225)

**Tariff of Abominations** name given by Southerners to the Tariff of 1828. (p. 299)

**tax-in-kind** tax paid with goods rather than money. (p. 406)

**Tea Act** (1773) law passed by Parliament that let the British East India Company sell tea directly to colonists. (p. 164)

**telegraph** machine that sends electrical signals along a wire. Invented by Samuel F. B. Morse in 1840. (p. 334)

**temperance movement** campaign against the sale or drinking of alcohol. (p. 360)

**tenant farmer** person who works land owned by another. Tenant pays rent to the landowner. (p. 127)

**Ten Percent Plan** Lincoln's plan for Reconstruction whereby southern states could be readmitted to the Union. (p. 418)

**Thanksgiving** day set aside by the Pilgrims to give thanks to God for a good harvest. (p. 95)

**Thirteenth Amendment** constitutional amendment that banned slavery in the United States. (p. 419)

**Three Fifths Compromise** agreement of delegates to the Constitutional Convention that three fifths of the slaves in any state be counted in that state's population. (p. 204)

**tidewater** coastal plain such as the Atlantic coast of the Southeast. (p. 130)

**time line** chart showing the relationship between events with dates marked on a line. (p. 167)

**toleration** willingness to let others have their own beliefs. (p. 102)

**Townshend Acts** (1767) laws passed by Parliament that taxed goods such as glass, paper, silk, lead, and tea. (p. 160)

**trade union** association of workers formed to win better wages and working conditions. (p. 338)

**Trail of Tears** forced march of the Cherokee Indians to lands west of the Mississippi. (p. 302)

**traitor** person who betrays his or her country. (p. 178)

**Treaty of Ghent** (1814) peace treaty between the United States and Britain that ended the War of 1812. (p. 260)

**Treaty of Greenville** (1795) treaty between the United States and 12 Indian nations of the Northwest Territory. (p. 229)

**Treaty of Paris** (1763) agreement between the British and French that ended the French and Indian War. (p. 155)

**triangular trade** series of colonial trade routes between New England, the West Indies, Europe, and Africa. (p. 139)

**tributary** branch of a river. (p. 25)

**turnpike** road built by a private company. Charged tolls to those using it. (p. 272)

# U

**unconstitutional** not permitted by the constitution of a nation. (p. 236)

**underground railroad** secret network of people who helped runaway slaves reach freedom in the North or Canada. (p. 353)

**unskilled worker** person who does a job that requires little special training. (p. 339)

# V

**veto** reject. Under the Constitution, the President can veto a bill passed by Congress. (p. 210)

**viceroy** official who rules an area in the name of a king or queen. (p. 77)

**vigilante** person who deals out punishments without holding a trial. Formed in western mining camps to reduce crime. (p. 328)

**Vikings** seagoing people from Scandinavia. (p. 49)

**Virginia Company** joint stock company that received a charter from King James I to start a colony. (p. 89)

**Virginia Plan** plan of government presented by Edmund Randolph and James Madison to the Constitutional Convention. (p. 203)

# W

**Wade–Davis Bill** Reconstruction plan passed by Republicans in Congress in July 1864. Vetoed by Lincoln. (p. 418)

**War Hawks** members of Congress who wanted war with Britain in 1812. (p. 254)

**weather** condition of the air at any given time and place. (p. 26)

**Whiskey Rebellion** (1794) revolt of farmers to protest the tax on whiskey. (p. 225)

**Wilmot Proviso** proposed law of Congressman David Wilmot to outlaw slavery in any land won from Mexico. (p. 374)

**writ of assistance** legal document that let a British customs officer inspect a ship's cargo without giving any reason for the search. (p. 160)

# X

**XYZ Affair** (1797) incident when French agents asked American ambassadors in Paris for a bribe. (p. 235)

# Y

**Yankee** name for New England merchant who won a reputation for always getting a good buy. (p. 139)

# The Declaration of Independence

On June 7, 1776, the Continental Congress approved the resolution that "these United Colonies are, and of right ought to be, free and independent States." Congress then appointed a committee to write a declaration of independence. The committee members were John Adams, Benjamin Franklin, Robert Livingston, Roger Sherman, and Thomas Jefferson.

Jefferson actually wrote the Declaration, but he got advice from the others. On July 2, Congress discussed the Declaration and made some changes. On July 4, 1776, it adopted the Declaration of Independence in its final form.

The Declaration is printed in black. The headings have been added to show the parts of the Declaration. They are not part of the original text. Annotations, or explanations, are on the tan side of the page. Page numbers in the annotations show where a subject is discussed in the text. Hard words are defined in the annotations.

When in the course of human events it becomes necessary for one people to dissolve the political bands which have connected them with another and to assume, among the powers of the earth, the separate and equal station to which the laws of nature and of nature's God entitle them, a decent respect to the opinions of mankind requires that they should declare the causes which impel them to the separation.

**dissolve:** break **powers of the earth:** other nations **station:** place **impel:** force

The colonists feel that they must explain to the world the reasons why they are breaking away from England.

## The Purpose of Government Is to Protect Basic Rights

We hold these truths to be self-evident, that all men are created equal; that they are endowed by their Creator with certain unalienable rights; that among these are life, liberty, and the pursuit of happiness. That, to secure these rights, governments are instituted among men, deriving their just powers from the consent of the governed; that, whenever any form of government becomes destructive of these ends, it is the right of the people to alter or to abolish it, and to institute a new government, laying its foundation on such principles, and organizing its powers in such form, as to them shall seem most likely to effect their safety and happiness. Prudence, indeed, will dictate that governments long established should not be changed for light and transient causes; and, accordingly, all experience hath shown that mankind are more disposed to suffer, while evils are sufferable, than to right themselves by abolishing the forms to which they are accustomed. But when a long train of abuses and usurpations, pursuing invariably the same object, evinces a design to reduce them under absolute despotism, it is their right, it is their duty, to throw off such government and to provide new guards for their future security. Such has been the patient sufferance of these colonies, and such is now the necessity which constrains

**endowed:** given **unalienable rights:** so basic that they cannot be taken away **secure:** protect **instituted:** set up **deriving:** getting **alter:** change **effect:** bring about

People set up governments to protect their basic rights. Governments get their power from the consent of the governed. If a government takes away the basic rights of the people, the people have the right to change the government.

**prudence:** wisdom **transient:** temporary, passing **disposed:** likely **usurpations:** taking and using powers that do not belong to a person **invariably:** always **evinces a design to reduce them under absolute despotism:** makes a clear plan to put them under complete and unjust control **sufferance:** endurance **constrains:** forces **absolute tyranny:** harsh and unjust government **candid:** honest

People do not change governments for slight reason. But they are forced to do so when a government becomes tyrannical. King George III has a long record of abusing his power.

them to alter their former systems of government. The history of the present King of Great Britain is a history of repeated injuries and usurpations, all having, in direct object, the establishment of an absolute tyranny over these States. To prove this, let facts be submitted to a candid world:

## Wrongs Done by the King

He has refused his assent to laws the most wholesome and necessary for the public good.

He has forbidden his governors to pass laws of immediate and pressing importance, unless suspended in their operation till his assent should be obtained; and, when so suspended, he has utterly neglected to attend to them.

He has refused to pass other laws for the accommodation of the large districts of people, unless those people would relinquish the right of representation in the legislature: a right inestimable to them and formidable to tyrants only.

He has called together legislative bodies at places unusual, uncomfortable, and distant from the depository of their public records, for the sole purpose of fatiguing them into compliance with his measures.

He has dissolved representative houses, repeatedly for opposing, with manly firmness, his invasions on the rights of the people.

He has refused, for a long time after such dissolutions, to cause others to be elected: whereby the legislative powers, incapable of annihilation, have returned to the people at large for their exercise; the state remaining, in the meantime, exposed to all the danger of invasion from without and convulsions within.

He has endeavored to prevent the population of these States; for that purpose, obstructing the laws for naturalization of foreigners, refusing to pass others to encourage their migration hither, and raising the conditions of new appropriations of lands.

He has obstructed the administration of justice by refusing his assent to laws for establishing judiciary powers.

He has made judges dependent on his will alone for the tenure of their offices and the amount and payment of their salaries.

He has erected a multitude of new offices and sent hither swarms of officers to harass our people and eat out their substance.

He has kept among us, in time of peace, standing armies, without the consent of our legislatures.

He has affected to render the military independent of, and superior to, the civil power.

He has combined with others to subject us to a jurisdiction foreign to our Constitution and unacknowledged by our laws, giving his assent to their acts of pretended legislation—

For quartering large bodies of armed troops among us;

For protecting them by a mock trial from punishment for

---

**assent:** approval   **relinquish:** give up
**inestimable:** too great a value to be
measured   **formidable:** causing fear

This part of the Declaration spells out three sets of wrongs that led the colonists to break with Britain.

The first set of wrongs is the king's unjust use of power. The king has refused to approve laws that are needed. He has tried to control the colonial legislatures.

**depository** central storehouse
**fatiguing:** tiring out   **compliance:**
giving in   **dissolved:** broken up
**annihilation:** total destruction
**convulsions:** disturbances

The king has tried to force colonial legislatures into doing his will by wearing them out. He has dissolved legislatures (such as those of New York and Massachusetts. See pages 162, 166).

**endeavored:** tried   **obstructing:**
blocking   **naturalization:** process of
becoming a citizen   **migration:**
moving   **hither:** here   **appropriations:**
grants   **obstructed the administration
of justice:** prevented justice from being
done   **judiciary powers:** system of law
courts   **tenure:** term (of office)   **erected:**
set up   **multitude:** large number   **swarms:**
huge crowds   **harass:** cause trouble
**render:** make

Among other wrongs, he has refused to let settlers move west to take up new land. He has prevented justice from being done. Also, he has sent large numbers of customs officials to cause problems for the colonists.

**jurisdiction:** authority   **quartering:** housing   **mock:** false

The king has joined with others, meaning Parliament, to make laws for the colonies. The Declaration then lists the second set of wrongs— unjust acts of Parliament.

any murders which they should commit on the inhabitants of these States;

For cutting off our trade with all parts of the world;

For imposing taxes on us without our consent;

For depriving us, in many cases, of the benefit of trial by jury;

For transporting us beyond seas to be tried for pretended offences;

For abolishing the free system of English laws in a neighboring province, establishing therein an arbitrary government, and enlarging its boundaries, so as to render it at once an example and fit instrument for introducing the same absolute rule into these colonies;

For taking away our charters, abolishing our most valuable laws, and altering, fundamentally, the powers of our governments;

For suspending our own legislatures and declaring themselves invested with power to legislate for us in all cases whatsoever.

He has abdicated government here by declaring us out of his protection and waging war against us.

He has plundered our seas, ravaged our coasts, burnt our towns, and destroyed the lives of our people.

He is, at this time, transporting large armies of foreign mercenaries to complete the works of death, desolation, and tyranny already begun with circumstances of cruelty and perfidy scarcely paralleled in the most barbarous ages, and totally unworthy, the head of a civilized nation.

He has constrained our fellow citizens, taken captive on the high seas, to bear arms against their country, to become the executioners of their friends and brethren, or to fall themselves by their hands.

He has excited domestic insurrections amongst us and has endeavored to bring on the inhabitants of our frontiers, the merciless Indian savages, whose known rule of warfare is an undistinguished destruction of all ages, sexes, and conditions.

In every stage of these oppressions, we have petitioned for redress in the most humble terms; our repeated petitions have been answered only by repeated injury. A prince whose character is thus marked by every act which may define a tyrant is unfit to be the ruler of a free people.

Nor have we been wanting in attention to our British brethren. We have warned them, from time to time, of attempts made by their legislature to extend an unwarrantable jurisdiction over us. We have reminded them of the circumstances of our emigration and settlement here. We have appealed to their native justice and magnanimity, and we have conjured them, by the ties of our common kindred, to disavow these usurpations, which would inevitably interrupt our connections and correspondence. They, too, have been deaf to the voice of justice and consanguinity. We must, therefore, acquiesce in the necessity which denounces our separation, and hold them, as we hold the rest of mankind, enemies in war, in peace, friends.

**imposing:** forcing **depriving:** taking away **transporting us beyond the seas:** sending colonists to England for trial **neighboring province:** Quebec **arbitrary government:** unjust rule **fit instrument:** suitable tool **invested with power:** having the power

During the years leading up to 1776, the colonists claimed that Parliament had no right to make laws for them because they were not represented in it. Here, the colonists object to recent laws of Parliament such as the Quartering Act (page 166) and the blockade of colonial ports (page 177) that cut off their trade. They also object to Parliament's claim that it had the right to tax them without their consent.

**abdicated:** given up **plundered:** robbed **ravaged:** attacked **mercenaries:** hired soldiers **desolation:** misery **perfidy:** falseness **barbarous:** uncivilized **constrained:** forced **brethren:** brothers **domestic insurrections:** internal revolts

Here, the Declaration lists the third set of wrongs—warlike acts of the king. Instead of listening to the colonists, the king has made war on them. He has hired soldiers to fight in America (page 177).

**oppressions:** harsh rule **petitioned:** asked **redress:** relief **unwarrantable jurisdiction over:** unfair authority **magnanimity:** generosity **conjured:** called upon **common kindred:** relatives **disavow:** turn away from **consanguinity:** blood relationships, kinship **acquiese** agree **denounces:** speaks out against

During this time, colonists have repeatedly asked for relief. But their requests have brought only more suffering. They have appealed to the British people but received no help. So they are forced to separate.

# Colonies Declare Independence

We, therefore, the representatives of the United States of America, in general Congress assembled, appealing to the Supreme Judge of the world for the rectitude of our intentions, do, in the name and by the authority of the good people of these colonies, solemnly publish and declare, that these united colonies are, and of right ought to be, free and independent states: that they are absolved from all allegiance to the British Crown, and that all political connection between them and the state of Great Britain is, and ought to be, totally dissolved; and that, as free and independent states, they have full power to levy war, conclude peace, contract alliances, establish commerce, and to do all other acts and things which independent states may of right do. And, for the support of this declaration, with a firm reliance on the protection of Divine Providence, we mutually pledge to each other our lives, our fortunes, and our sacred honor.

---

## Signers of the Declaration of Independence

**John Hancock,** President    **Charles Thomson,** Secretary

**New Hampshire**
Josiah Bartlett
William Whipple
Matthew Thornton

**Massachusetts**
Samuel Adams
John Adams
Robert Treat Paine
Elbridge Gerry

**Rhode Island**
Stephen Hopkins
William Ellery

**Connecticut**
Roger Sherman
Samuel Huntington
William Williams
Oliver Wolcott

**New York**
William Floyd
Philip Livingston
Francis Lewis
Lewis Morris

**New Jersey**
Richard Stockton
John Witherspoon
Francis Hopkinson
John Hart
Abraham Clark

**Delaware**
Caesar Rodney
George Read
Thomas McKean

**Pennsylvania**
Robert Morris
Benjamin Rush
Benjamin Franklin
John Morton
George Clymer
James Smith
George Taylor
James Wilson
George Ross

**Maryland**
Samuel Chase
William Paca
Thomas Stone
Charles Carroll

**Virginia**
George Wythe
Richard Henry Lee
Thomas Jefferson
Benjamin Harrison
Thomas Nelson, Jr.
Francis Lightfoot Lee
Carter Braxton

**North Carolina**
William Hooper
Joseph Hewes
John Penn

**South Carolina**
Edward Rutledge
Thomas Heyward, Jr.
Thomas Lynch, Jr.
Arthur Middleton

**Georgia**
Button Gwinnett
Lyman Hall
George Walton

Declaration of Independence

# Exploring Our Living Constitution

## You and the Constitution

To appreciate how the Constitution of the United States affects you, imagine for a moment that it never existed. The United States might still be the loose confederation of highly independent, squabbling states it was in 1787. Some of the states might even have broken away and declared themselves separate nations.

Suppose that you plan to visit a friend in a neighboring state. Without the Constitution, you might need a passport to enter the state. Or the state might deny you entry because of your race or religion.

Now suppose that you send a letter to your local newspaper strongly criticizing your governor. Without the Constitution, the newspaper might reject your letter because it only prints articles that the state government approves. The governor might order your arrest and imprisonment without the benefit of a trial.

The Constitution affects you personally. It protects your freedom to express your opinions and criticize your leaders. It defends your choice of religion and guarantees you equal opportunity under the law, whatever your race, sex, or national background. Most important of all, it allows you to make your own choices about how you will live your life.

The 200th anniversary of the Constitution in 1987 was cause for joyous celebrations. But it also led Americans to reflect on the meaning and importance of the Constitution. Having existed for two centuries, with only 26 formal changes, the Constitution was sometimes taken for granted.

## Contents of the Constitution

| Original Constitution | Page |
|---|---|
| **Preamble** | 628 |
| **Article** | |
| 1   The Legislative Branch | 628 |
| 2   The Executive Branch | 634 |
| 3   The Judicial Branch | 636 |
| 4   Relations Among the States | 637 |
| 5   Amending the Constitution | 638 |
| 6   National Supremacy | 639 |
| 7   Ratification | 639 |

| Bill of Rights | Page |
|---|---|
| **Amendment** | |
| 1   Freedoms of Religion, Speech, Press, Assembly, and Petition | 640 |
| 2   Right to Bear Arms | 640 |
| 3   Lodging Troops in Private Homes | 640 |
| 4   Search and Seizure | 640 |
| 5   Rights of the Accused | 641 |
| 6   Right to Speedy Trial by Jury | 641 |
| 7   Jury Trial in Civil Cases | 641 |
| 8   Bail and Punishment | 642 |
| 9   Powers Reserved to the People | 642 |
| 10   Powers Reserved to the States | 642 |

| Additional Amendments | Page |
|---|---|
| **Amendment** | |
| 11   Suits Against States | 642 |
| 12   Election of President and Vice-President | 642 |
| 13   Abolition of Slavery | 643 |
| 14   Rights of Citizens | 643 |
| 15   Voting Rights | 644 |
| 16   The Income Tax | 645 |
| 17   Direct Election of Senators | 645 |
| 18   Prohibition of Alcoholic Beverages | 645 |
| 19   Women's Suffrage | 646 |
| 20   Presidential Terms; Sessions of Congress | 646 |
| 21   Repeal of Prohibition | 647 |
| 22   Limit on Number of President's Terms | 647 |
| 23   Presidential Electors for District of Columbia | 648 |
| 24   Abolition of Poll Tax in National Elections | 648 |
| 25   Presidential Succession and Disability | 648 |
| 26   Voting Age | 649 |

Exploring Our Constitution

## Impact of the Constitution on You

**How much do you know about the Constitution and its impact on your life? Do you know that you**

★ are protected from working under the age of 14?

★ are guaranteed a minimum wage when you do work?

★ are entitled to hear criminal charges brought against you and have a lawyer represent you?

★ have a right to a hearing if you are suspended from school?

★ can have your purse or locker searched if school officials have a reasonable suspicion that you have done something wrong?

★ are allowed to pursue a peaceful political protest in school?

★ have greater freedom of speech and press outside school than inside school?

**CHART SKILL** The Constitution affects your life in many ways. Name two ways that it impacts on your working rights. Name one way that it impacts on your rights at school.

The Constitution was the first attempt in history to design a national government on paper. More important, the document contained ideas that were considered revolutionary at the time. For example, it held that a society could exist without being divided into nobles and common people. It also held that a stable government could be based on elections, not heredity.

To some people, this new experiment in government was bold and reckless. Yet, the Constitution has remained the framework of our government for over 200 years. And it has become the basis of the constitutions of more than 160 other nations.

The Constitution is a success because it is flexible. That is, it can be adapted to changing conditions. The framers knew that they had not produced a perfect document. They also realized that the nation would grow. So they provided the means to change the Constitution. The framers did not make it easy to make changes, but they did make it possible. You will learn more about changing the Constitution on page 626.

# Five Principles of the Constitution

★     ★

You know that you must obey the law. But do you know that the President must also? There are no exceptions to that rule under the Constitution. It applies to every person and to every group. This is so because the Constitution has guaranteed that the nation is dedicated to the rule of law.

In the pages that follow, you will look at five principles basic to the Constitution: popular sovereignty, limited government, federalism, separation of powers, and checks and balances. See the chart on page 617.

As you can see from the contents of the Constitution on page 615, the Constitution includes a preamble, or opening statement, 7 articles, and 26 amendments. Because the Constitution is only a framework, it does not spell out in detail how to apply the basic principles of government. Since 1787, therefore, Americans have debated about the principles as well as how the government should work. As you look at the basic principles of the Constitution, think about how they help protect your way of life.

*Exploring Our Constitution*

—616—

## Principles of the Constitution

| Principle | Definition |
| --- | --- |
| Popular sovereignty | Principle of government in which the people hold the final authority or power |
| Limited government | Principle that the government is not all powerful but can do only what the people say it can do |
| Federalism | Division of power between the national government and the state governments |
| Separation of powers | Division of the operations of the national government into three branches, each with its own powers and responsibilities |
| Checks and balances | Means by which each branch of the national government is able to check, or control, the power of the other two branches |

**CHART SKILL** The Constitution is based on five principles. According to the principle of popular sovereignty, who holds the final power in government? Which principle calls for dividing power between the national government and the state governments?

## Popular Sovereignty Means the People Rule

Popular sovereignty is a term that means that the people hold the final authority, or ruling power. The framers of the Constitution believed in this principle. They also held that a contract exists between the people and the government. The government receives the power to rule from the people. In return, the government provides certain guarantees for the people.

**We, the people.** The Preamble of the Constitution contains both ideas—popular sovereignty and a contract between the government and its people. "We, the people," it begins. The "people" then list the purposes of the government they are establishing. These include "to form a more perfect Union, establish justice, insure domestic tranquillity, provide for the common defense, promote the general welfare, and secure the blessings of liberty to ourselves and our posterity."

The rest of the Constitution spells out the powers that the people give to the government to carry out its purposes. The Constitution also limits the power of government. It says what the government may not do.

**The people vote.** The Constitution guarantees the people a democratic government. But the people exercise their ruling power indirectly. They do not make the laws themselves. Instead, they elect representatives to make laws. At the same time, they hold these representatives responsible for the acts of government.

Americans today have the right to vote for members of the House of Representatives (Article 1, Section 2) and for members of the Senate (Amendment 17). The people also elect the members of the electoral college. The electors, in turn, choose the President (Article 2, Section 1).

When the Constitution was ratified, or approved, only white men over age 21 who owned property could vote.

As the chart below shows, other Americans have won the right to vote since then. Today, if you are a citizen, you are eligible to vote at age 18.

★ How do the American people carry out their right to rule themselves?

## ISSUES FOR TODAY

Every election day, the polls are open from early morning until late evening. But often, fewer than one half of the eligible voters show up to vote. Many people offer the excuse that they are not registered. That is, they have not signed up in advance of the election as required by state law.

States have the right under the Constitution to set voting requirements. They require voter registration to prevent people from voting more than once in the same election. In the past, some people used another person's name in order to vote a second time.

Voters have to register only once unless they move or fail to vote for a long period. Yet, many Americans think registration is a bother. Some reformers want to end registration entirely. Others want to make it easier. They propose registration by mail or at the polls on election day. Or perhaps, they suggest, officials could make home visits to register citizens.

★ Do you think registration reform would increase the number of people who vote? Explain.

CHART SKILL The right to vote has expanded since the Constitution first went into effect. Who could vote in 1789? In 1971? Which amendment granted women the right to vote?

### The Right to Vote

| Year | People Allowed to Vote |
| --- | --- |
| 1789 | White men over age 21 who meet property requirements (state laws) |
| Early 1800s–1850s | All white men over age 21 (state laws) |
| 1870 | Black men (Amendment 15) |
| 1920 | Women (Amendment 19) |
| 1961 | People in the District of Columbia in presidential elections (Amendment 23) |
| 1971 | People over age 18 (Amendment 26) |

## The Government's Power Should Be Limited

The authors of the Constitution remembered well what life had been like under British rule. They knew that most Americans feared a strong government because of their experiences with the British king.

No one wanted to give up the rights gained by fighting the American Revolution. Yet, the failures of the Articles of Confederation made it clear that the new government had to be powerful. How could the framers achieve a balance between guaranteed rights and a strong government? The answer was limited government, or a government by law.

**Limits on power.** As the law of the land, the Constitution limits the powers of government to those granted by the people. It clearly states the powers of Congress and the President and describes the role of the judiciary. In this way, you and every other citizen know exactly what powers the federal government has. In addition, the Constitution spells out the powers denied to the national government and to the state governments.

The most important limits on government are set out in the Bill of Rights. In these amendments, the Constitution guarantees the individual freedoms of the people. One of these amendments also gives the states or the people any powers not specifically granted to the national government.

As you have read, the principle of popular sovereignty limits the government. As you read about the other principles of government, you will see that they help limit any part of the government from gaining too much power.

### ISSUES FOR TODAY

Recently, the growing federal debt has gained nationwide attention. Legislators and the President have struggled to find a solution.

According to the Constitution, only Congress can authorize spending. In 1985, Congress passed a law requiring itself to limit spending. But some people urge a stronger measure. They want an amendment requiring a balanced budget. A balanced-budget amendment would forbid the government from spending more money than it takes in.

Supporters of the amendment think that it would force the government to face the issue of the national debt and make budget cuts. For them, ending the debt is important to the future of the country.

Opponents of the amendment fear that it will limit the ability of the government to deal with economic crises. During a slowdown in the economy, the government's income drops. But at the same time, more people are out of work and need aid. If the budget must be balanced, Congress would have to cut spending just when the nation might need it most.

★ How would a balanced-budget amendment limit the government?

## Federalism Results in a Sharing of Power

When the 13 colonies became the 13 states, they did not want to give much power to the central government. As a result, the government under the Articles of Confederation was weak. It took Shays' Rebellion to convince some people that they needed a stronger government. (See page 201.)

**Framers choose federalism.** The framers of the Constitution were faced with a real problem. They had to balance the need for a stronger central government with the stubborn resistance of many people to such a measure. Their solution was to base the new government on the principle of federalism.

Federalism is a system of government in which power is divided between the national government and the state governments. This system set up a strong national authority to deal with national issues. At the same time, it gave the states the authority to govern their own citizens.

The Constitution delegates, or assigns, some powers to the national, or federal, government. Other powers are reserved to the states. Still other powers, sometimes called concurrent powers, are shared by the national and state governments. The chart on page 620 shows how powers are divided under federalism.

**The national government.** The powers of the national government include those given specifically to Congress or to the President. The power to tax, to coin money, and to declare war are among the powers granted to Congress in Article 1, Section 8. Amend-

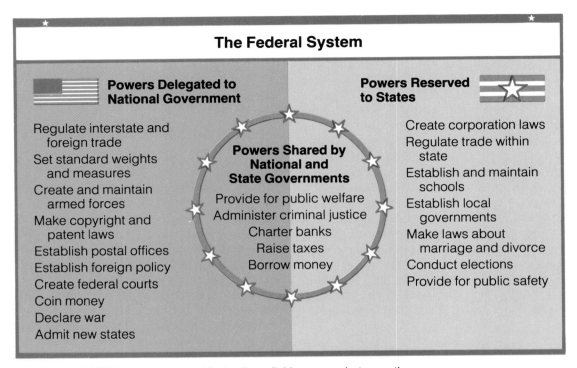

## The Federal System

**Powers Delegated to National Government**

Regulate interstate and foreign trade

Set standard weights and measures

Create and maintain armed forces

Make copyright and patent laws

Establish postal offices

Establish foreign policy

Create federal courts

Coin money

Declare war

Admit new states

**Powers Shared by National and State Governments**

Provide for public welfare

Administer criminal justice

Charter banks

Raise taxes

Borrow money

**Powers Reserved to States**

Create corporation laws

Regulate trade within state

Establish and maintain schools

Establish local governments

Make laws about marriage and divorce

Conduct elections

Provide for public safety

**CHART SKILL** The system of federalism divides power between the national government and the state governments. Name two powers reserved to the states. Who has the power to raise taxes?

ment 16 adds the power to impose an income tax. Article 2, Section 2, describes the powers of the President. These include being commander in chief of the army and navy, granting reprieves and pardons, and making treaties with the advice and consent of the Senate.

The framers knew that they could not foresee what life would be like in the future. So Article 1, Section 8, Clause 18, gives Congress the power "to make all laws which shall be necessary and proper" to carry out its functions. This so-called "elastic clause" has allowed Congress to deal with changing conditions. For example, Congress has passed laws regulating the airline industry, television, and genetic engineering.

**Protection of the states.** The Constitution protects the rights of the states. In addition to having all powers

not specifically granted to the national government, the states are guaranteed other rights. All states must be treated equally. And each state must respect the laws of the others.

If a dispute should arise between the national government and a state, however, there is no doubt where the final authority lies. The Constitution is the "supreme law of the land." The federal courts settle disputes between the states and the national government.

★ The age at which a person can legally marry is different in New York and Louisiana. But a person legally married in Louisiana is considered legally married in New York. Why?

## ISSUES FOR TODAY

How well does the principle of federalism work? In general, the state governments and the federal government cooperate. But clashes can occur. In the 1970s, there was a severe oil shortage. To help solve the problem, the federal government passed a law reducing the speed limit on interstate highways to 55 miles (80 km) per hour. Reduced speeds, Congress claimed, would save millions of gallons of gas as well as thousands of lives.

Many states followed suit. They reduced speed limits on state and local highways, which they alone control. But some states, mainly in the West, resisted the change. They argued that travel over the huge distances in their states would take too long at the slower speeds and therefore would increase the costs of moving goods.

The federal government tried to force the states to reduce their speed limits. It threatened to cut off federal dollars for building and repairing highways. Before long, the states gave in. But the federal government's threats to cut budgets in order to get its way caused bitterness.

★ Do you think the federal government should be able to cut funds to force states to follow national policy? Explain.

## Separation of Powers Further Limits the Government

Separation of powers is the division of the national government into three branches, each with its own powers and responsibilities. When the framers set up the government this way, it was a novel experiment. At the time, nearly every government in Europe was a monarchy. The king or queen made the laws, enforced the laws, and appointed the judges to interpret the laws. This system was efficient, but it was also dangerous.

**Three branches.** The Constitution prevents one person or agency from having all the power. The first three articles set up three branches of government. See the chart below. The leg-

CHART SKILL The Constitution set up three branches of government. Each branch has its own powers. Who heads the executive branch? What is the role of the legislative branch?

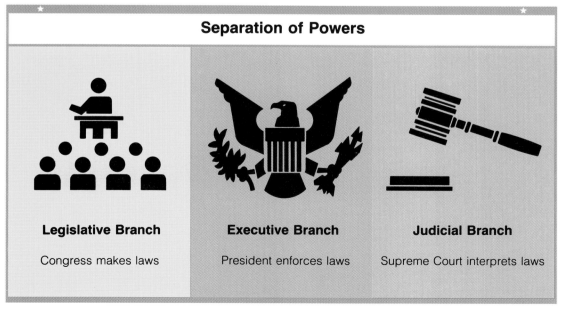

**Separation of Powers**

**Legislative Branch**

Congress makes laws

**Executive Branch**

President enforces laws

**Judicial Branch**

Supreme Court interprets laws

islative branch (Article 1) makes the laws. The executive branch (Article 2) enforces the laws. And the judicial branch (Article 3) interprets and explains the laws of the United States.

The House of Representatives and the Senate make up the legislative branch, called Congress. The President heads the executive branch and appoints advisers and other officials to oversee the operations of the government. The Supreme Court and other federal courts make up the judicial branch.

**More safeguards.** The framers did not fear only the concentration of power. They also distrusted the judgment of the masses. Suppose the people were swayed to vote for tyrants worse than any monarch? Separation of powers was an added safeguard. It made it difficult, if not impossible, for any one group to control all three branches of government.

Little was left to chance. For example, you probably have seen advertisements for candidates on television. Have you ever wondered who can be a candidate? The Constitution includes specific requirements about who can run for office. It also details the selection process for members of each branch of government. (See the chart below.)

★ How do you think European history affected the framers' decision to set up a separation of powers?

CHART SKILL The Constitution details the number, length of term, method of selection, and requirements of officeholders in the three branches of government. What are the requirements for the President? A senator? Which officeholders are elected directly by the voters?

## Federal Officeholders

| Office | Number | Term | Selection | Requirements |
|---|---|---|---|---|
| Representative | At least 1 per state; based on state population | 2 years | Elected by voters of congressional district | Age 25 or over Citizen for 7 years Resident of state in which elected |
| Senator | 2 per state | 6 years | Original Constitution— elected by state legislature Amendment 17— elected by voters | Age 30 or over Citizen for 9 years Resident of state in which elected |
| President and Vice-President | 1 | 4 years | Elected by electoral college | Age 35 or over Natural-born citizen Resident of U.S. for 14 years |
| Supreme Court judge | 9 | Life | Appointed by President with approval of Senate | No requirements in Constitution |

No one can seriously claim that separation of powers is an efficient way to run a government. In fact, one historian, James MacGregor Burns, calls the separation of powers "a deadlock of democracy." By that, he refers to the standstill that occurs when the President and Congress disagree on what should be done.

For example, in the 1980s, both the President and Congress saw the need to balance the federal budget. Both agreed that spending had to be cut. They disagreed, however, on where to make cuts. While they argued, the huge government debt ballooned. It threatened the nation's economy.

In today's fast-changing world, the government must make difficult decisions. Failure of the President and Congress to act can pose a real danger. But some people argue that the bargaining that goes on between the President and Congress is important to democratic government. It prevents any one branch from becoming too powerful.

★ Do you think that the benefits of a separation of powers outweigh the need for immediate action? Explain your answer.

## Checks and Balances Protect Against Tyranny

Federalism and separation of powers are only two of the ways the Constitution limits the government. The framers went a step further and gave each branch of government the means to check, or control, the power of the other two branches. They hoped that this system of checks and balances would keep any one branch from gaining too much power.

**Examples.** How does the system of checks and balances work? The chart on page 624 shows some of the checks the President, the Congress, and the Supreme Court have on each other. For example, the President can check Congress by vetoing a bill, or proposed law. The Supreme Court, in turn, can check the President and Congress by declaring a law unconstitutional.

Judicial review, or the right of the Supreme Court to decide if a law is constitutional, is not stated directly in the Constitution. It is implied, however, in Article 3, Section 2. In the case of *Marbury* v. *Madison,* an early Supreme Court decision interpreted that clause to give the Supreme Court the right of judicial review (see page 244).

As the chart shows, Congress has several checks on the power of the President. For example, the Senate must approve many of the President's appointments. It must also approve treaties signed by the President. In addition, Congress can override a presidential veto so that a bill can become a law without the President's signature.

**Need for compromise.** The system of checks and balances often requires the President and Congress to reach compromises. This is especially true when the President and the majority of the members of Congress are from different political parties. If the President threatens to veto a bill in Congress, the lawmakers might decide to change parts of the bill to make it more acceptable. In the same way, the President might choose a person for a cabinet position or judgeship whom the Senate is likely to approve.

★ What might result if the President could not veto bills or Congress could not override a veto?

Do the nine black-robed justices on the Supreme Court hold too much power? Your answer to that question will probably depend on whether you agree with the decisions the Court has made.

Exploring Our Constitution

## System of Checks and Balances

| Executive Branch (President) | Checks on the Legislative Branch | Checks on the Judicial Branch |
|---|---|---|
| | Can propose laws<br>Can veto laws<br>Can call special sessions of Congress<br>Makes appointments<br>Negotiates foreign treaties | Appoints federal judges<br>Can grant pardons to federal offenders |

| Legislative Branch (Congress) | Checks on the Executive Branch | Checks on the Judicial Branch |
|---|---|---|
| | Can override President's veto<br>Confirms executive appointments<br>Ratifies treaties<br>Appropriates money<br>Can impeach and remove President | Creates lower federal courts<br>Can impeach and remove judges<br>Can propose amendments to overrule judicial decisions<br>Approves appointments of federal judges |

| Judicial Branch (Supreme Court) | Check on the Executive Branch | Check on the Legislative Branch |
|---|---|---|
| | Can declare executive actions unconstitutional | Can declare acts of Congress unconstitutional |

**CHART SKILL** Through the system of checks and balances, each branch of government has checks, or controls, on the power of the other branches. Name one check that the President has on Congress. How can the Supreme Court check Congress?

In recent years, the Supreme Court has dealt with many troubling legal issues. For example, it has ruled on cases involving busing to desegregate schools, the rights of people under age 18 to freedom of speech, and the death penalty.

Supreme Court justices vow to uphold the Constitution. But their interpretations can, and do, vary. A Supreme Court decision requires a majority vote of the nine justices. In a 5–4 decision, the opinion of only one justice affects the outcome of the case.

Various groups have called for changes in the way the Supreme Court operates. For example, some argue that it should take more than five justices to declare a law unconstitutional.

★ Do you think declaring a law unconstitutional should require the vote of at least six justices? Explain.

# Protection of Individual Liberties

What does the Constitution mean to most Americans? First and foremost, it is the document that protects their individual, or civil, rights and liberties. These include freedom of religion, speech, press, assembly, and petition. Protection of rights is central to the Constitution. As you have read, the principles of the Constitution came out of the framers' personal experiences. They had seen injustice done, and they sought to prevent it.

**Guarantees of liberty.** The framers wanted to create a government that would protect the rights and freedoms of the people. Thomas Jefferson had stated the following in the Declaration of Independence:

> We hold these truths to be self-evident, that all men are created equal, and that they are endowed by their Creator with certain inalienable Rights, that among these are Life, Liberty, and the pursuit of Happiness.

The new government was designed to fulfill all these promises of equality and liberty.

The original Constitution safeguarded some rights by forbidding or limiting government actions that might affect those rights. Article 6, Section 3, for example, says that "no religious test shall ever be required as a qualification to any office or public trust under the United States."

Some people, however, did not think that the Constitution provided enough protection for their individual rights. Several states refused to approve the Constitution until they were promised that a bill of rights would be added. See page 615 for the amendments in the Bill of Rights.

**Ideas of liberty grow.** Individual liberties are not limited to those specifically named in the Constitution. Amendment 9 states that the people have rights beyond those discussed in the Constitution. Today, Americans believe that individual liberties include the right to free, quality education, to safe working conditions, and to equal job opportunities.

Until this century, many Americans were denied the protections of the Constitution. Even though Amendment 13 (1865) ended slavery and Amendment 14 (1868) defined the rights of citizens, black Americans faced discrimination. Only after years of struggle have blacks won equal protection under the law. Women and other minority groups also have struggled to gain equal protection and equal rights.

CHART SKILL Amendment 1 of the Constitution guarantees some basic individual liberties. Name two freedoms it protects. Which freedom allows you to hold and attend meetings?

## Liberties Protected by the First Amendment

Freedom of the Press

Freedom of Religion

Freedom of Petition

Freedom of Assembly

Freedom of Speech

Since the 1960s, federal courts have interpreted Amendment 14 to mean that state and local governments must abide by the guarantees of the Bill of Rights. For example, a state cannot deny a person a speedy trial or impose cruel and unusual punishments. Applying the guarantees of the Bill of Rights to state governments has been a giant step toward protection of individual liberties.

★ How has the protection of individual liberties expanded since the signing of the original Constitution?

### ISSUES FOR TODAY

"I can say whatever I want," argues a citizen. "I have rights." Right? Wrong. The constitutional guarantees of individual liberties are not absolute. That is, even though you have the right to freedom of speech, you do not have the right to say anything at any time. For example, you do not have the right to deliberately lie about a person. Similarly, even though you have religious freedom, you cannot commit a crime in the name of religion.

People often turn to the courts when their rights come into conflict with the rights of others. Again and again, the Supreme Court has been called on to interpret and apply the Constitution.

Consider the case of *Hazelwood School District* v. *Kuhlmeier et al*. The principal of Hazelwood East refused to allow the school newspaper to publish an article. He said that the article violated the right to privacy of certain families. The school journalists claimed that the principal's decision violated their rights to freedom of speech and press. Lawyers for the school district argued that the newspaper was a school activity and, therefore, could be regulated by the principal.

In 1988, the Supreme Court agreed that the issue was not freedom of speech but the right of the school to control education. The school, it ruled, could censor the newspaper.

★ How would you interpret this statement: Your right to swing your fist ends where my nose begins?

# Changing the Constitution

★ ★

The framers of the Constitution wanted to set up a lasting government, and they succeeded. They wrote a constitution that we recognize today as a living document. That is, its basic principles have survived for over 200 years. At the same time, it has adapted to tremendous change.

**The amendment process.** The framers provided formal methods to amend, or change, the Constitution. Article 5 describes two ways to propose amendments and two ways to ratify amendments. See the chart on page 627.

The amendment process guarantees that changes will not be made

lightly. Since 1789, more than 9,000 amendments have been proposed in Congress. Only 26 have made it through the ratifying process. Of those, 10 were in the Bill of Rights passed in 1791.

**Informal changes.** The Constitution has stayed up to date through many informal changes. The framers outlined the structure of the government. But they left it to future generations to fill in the details. Informal changes have been made by laws passed in Congress (see page 224), treaties (see page 246), court decisions (see page 243), customs and practices of political parties (see page 295), and

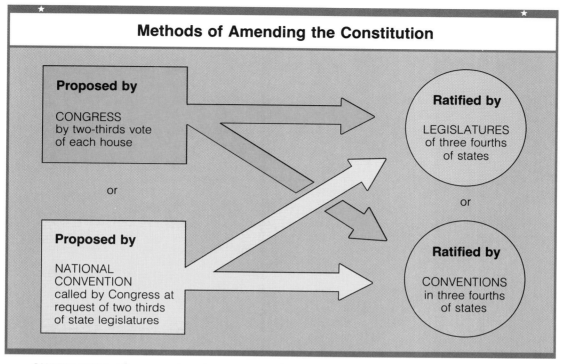

## Methods of Amending the Constitution

**Proposed by**

CONGRESS
by two-thirds vote
of each house

or

**Proposed by**

NATIONAL
CONVENTION
called by Congress at
request of two thirds
of state legislatures

**Ratified by**

LEGISLATURES
of three fourths
of states

or

**Ratified by**

CONVENTIONS
in three fourths
of states

**CHART SKILL** The amendment process requires proposal and ratification. Name one way to propose an amendment. Name one way to ratify an amendment.

rules of government agencies.

"I do not think we are more inspired, have more wisdom, or possess more virtue than those who will come after us," said George Washington. Believing this, the framers of the Constitution kept the document brief and kept their language general. In this way, the Constitution has been able to adapt to the challenges of an ever-changing world.

★ Why do you think only 26 amendments have been ratified?

### ISSUES FOR TODAY

Many Americans are unhappy with the workings of the political process. They suggest changing the Constitution to make the government more democratic and efficient. Some proposals for amendments to the Constitution are listed below. Read the proposals

and think about which principle of the Constitution is involved.

The Constitution should be amended to:

- Allow for a direct national vote on a major issue.
- Limit the amount of money candidates can spend on political campaigns.
- Abolish the electoral college and let citizens vote directly for the President.
- Give the President one six-year term.
- Repeal the two-term limit on the President.
- Give members of the House of Representatives longer terms.
- ★ Choose one of the proposals and explain why you would or would not support an amendment.

# The Constitution of the United States of America

The Constitution is printed in black. The titles of articles, sections, and clauses are not part of the original document. They have been added to help you find information in the Constitution. Some words or lines are crossed out because they have been changed by amendments or no longer apply. Annotations, or explanations, are on the tan side of the page. Page numbers in the annotations show where a subject is discussed in the text. Hard words are defined in the annotations.

The Preamble describes the purpose of the government set up by the Constitution. Americans expect their government to defend justice and liberty and provide peace and safety from foreign enemies.

## Preamble

We, the people of the United States, in order to form a more perfect Union, establish justice, insure domestic tranquillity, provide for the common defense, promote the general welfare, and secure the blessings of liberty to ourselves and our posterity, do ordain and establish this Constitution for the United States of America.

## Article 1. The Legislative Branch

The Constitution gives Congress the power to make laws. Congress is divided into the Senate and House of Representatives.

### Section 1.   A Two-House Legislature

All legislative powers herein granted shall be vested in a Congress of the United States, which shall consist of a Senate and House of Representatives.

### Section 2.   House of Representatives

**Clause 1** *Electors* refers to voters. Members of the House of Representatives are elected every two years. Any citizen allowed to vote for members of the larger house of the state legislature can also vote for members of the House.

**1. Election of Members**   The House of Representatives shall be composed of members chosen every second year by the people of the several states, and the electors in each state shall have the qualifications requisite for electors of the most numerous branch of the state legislature.

**Clause 2** A member of the House of Representatives must be at least 25 years old, an American citizen for 7 years, and a resident of the state he or she represents.

**2. Qualifications**   No person shall be a Representative who shall not have attained to the age of twenty-five years, and been seven years a citizen of the United States, and who shall not, when elected, be an inhabitant of that state in which he shall be chosen.

**Clause 3** The number of representatives each state elects is based on its population. An **enumeration,** or census, must be taken every ten years to determine population. Today, the number of representatives in the House is fixed at 435.

This is the famous Three Fifths Compromise worked out at the Constitutional Convention (page 204). **Persons bound to service** meant indentured servants. **All other persons** meant slaves. All free people in a state were counted. However, only three fifths of the slaves were included in the population count. This three fifths clause became meaningless when slaves were freed by the Thirteenth Amendment.

**3. Determining Representation**   Representatives and direct taxes shall be apportioned among the several states which may be included within this Union, according to their respective numbers which shall be determined by adding to the whole number of free persons, including those bound to service for a term of years, and excluding Indians not taxed, three-fifths of all other persons. The actual enumeration shall be made within three years after the first meeting of the Congress of the United States, and within every subsequent term of ten years, in such manner as they shall by law direct. The number of Representatives shall not exceed one for every 30,000, but each state shall have at least one Representative; and until such enumeration shall be made, the state of New Hampshire shall be entitled to choose three; Massachusetts, eight; Rhode Island and Providence Plantations, one; Connecticut, five; New York, six; New Jersey, four; Pennsylvania, eight;

Delaware, one; Maryland, six; Virginia, ten; North Carolina, five; South Carolina, five; and Georgia, three.

**4. Filling Vacancies**   When vacancies happen in the representation from any state, the executive authority thereof shall issue writs of election to fill such vacancies.

**5. Selection of Officers; Power of Impeachment**   The House of Representatives shall choose their Speaker and other officers; and shall have the sole power of impeachment.

## Section 3.   The Senate

**1. Selection of Members**   The Senate of the United States shall be composed of two Senators from each state chosen by the legislature thereof, for six years, and each Senator shall have one vote.

**2. Alternating Terms; Filling Vacancies**   Immediately after they shall be assembled in consequence of the first election, they shall be divided as equally as may be into three classes. The seats of the Senators of the first class shall be vacated at the expiration of the second year, of the second class at the expiration of the fourth year, and of the third class at the expiration of the sixth year, so that one-third may be chosen every second year; and if vacancies happen by resignation, or otherwise, during the recess of the legislature of any state, the executive thereof may make temporary appointments until the next meeting of the legislature, which shall then fill such vacancies.

**3. Qualifications**   No person shall be a Senator who shall not have attained to the age of thirty years, and been nine years a citizen of the United States, and who shall not, when elected, be an inhabitant of that state for which he shall be chosen.

**4. President of the Senate**   The Vice-President of the United States shall be president of the Senate, but shall have no vote, unless they be equally divided.

**5. Election of Senate Officers**   The Senate shall choose their other officers, and also a president *pro tempore,* in the absence of the Vice-President, or when he shall exercise the office of the President of the United States.

**6. Impeachment Trials**   The Senate shall have the sole power to try all impeachments. When sitting for that purpose, they shall be on oath or affirmation. When the President of the United States is tried, the Chief Justice shall preside; and no person shall be convicted without the concurrence of two-thirds of the members present.

**7. Penalties Upon Conviction**   Judgment in cases of impeachment shall not extend further than to removal from office, and disqualification to hold and enjoy any office of honor, trust, or

**Clause 4**   *Executive authority* means the governor of a state. If a member of the House leaves office before his or her term ends, the governor must call a special election to fill the seat.

**Clause 5**   The House elects a speaker. Today, the speaker is usually chosen by the party that has a majority in the House. Also, only the House has the power to *impeach,* or accuse, a federal official of wrongdoing.

**Clause 1**   Each state has two senators. Senators serve for six-year terms. The Seventeenth Amendment changed the way senators were elected.

**Clause 2**   Every two years, one third of the senators run for reelection. Thus, the makeup of the Senate is never totally changed by any one election. The Seventeenth Amendment changed the way of filling *vacancies,* or empty seats. Today, the governor of a state chooses a senator to fill a vacancy that occurs between elections.

**Clause 3**   A senator must be at least 30 years old, an American citizen for 9 years, and a resident of the state he or she represents.

**Clause 4**   The Vice President presides over Senate meetings, but he or she can only vote to break a tie.

**Clause 5**   *Pro tempore* means temporary. The Senate chooses one of its members to serve as president pro tempore when the Vice President is absent.

**Clause 6**   The Senate acts as a jury if the House impeaches a federal official. The Chief Justice of the Supreme Court presides if the President is on trial. Two thirds of all senators present must vote for *conviction,* or finding the accused guilty. No President has ever been convicted. The House impeached President Andrew Johnson in 1868, but the Senate acquitted him of the charges (page 424). In 1974, President Richard Nixon resigned before he could be impeached.

**Clause 7**   If an official is found guilty by the Senate, he or she can be removed from office and barred from holding federal office in the future. These are the only punishments the Senate can impose. However, the convicted official can still be tried in criminal court.

**Clause 1** Each state legislature can decide when and how congressional elections take place, but Congress can overrule these decisions. In 1842, Congress required each state to set up congressional districts with one representative elected from each district. In 1872, Congress decided that congressional elections must be held in every state on the same date in even-numbered years.

**Clause 2** Congress must meet at least once a year. The Twentieth Amendment moved the opening date of Congress to January 3.

**Clause 1** Each house decides if a member has the qualifications for office set by the Constitution. A *quorum* is the smallest number of members who must be present for business to be conducted. Each house can set its own rules about absent members.

**Clause 2** Each house can make rules for the conduct of members. It can only expel a member by a two-thirds vote.

**Clause 3** Each house keeps a record of its meetings. The *Congressional Record* is published every day with excerpts from speeches made in each house. It also records the votes of each member.

**Clause 4** Neither house can *adjourn,* or stop meeting, for more than three days unless the other house approves. Both houses of Congress must meet in the same city.

**Clause 1** *Compensation* means salary. Congress decides the salary for its members. While Congress is in session, a member is free from arrest in civil cases and cannot be sued for anything he or she says on the floor of Congress. This allows for freedom of debate. However, a member can be arrested for a criminal offense.

**Clause 2** *Emolument* also means salary. A member of Congress cannot hold another federal office during his or her term. A former member of Congress cannot hold an office created while he or she was in Congress. An official in another branch of government cannot serve at the same time in Congress. This strengthens the separation of powers.

profit under the United States; but the party convicted shall nevertheless be liable and subject to indictment, trial, judgment, and punishment, according to law.

## Section 4.   Elections and Meetings

**1. Election of Congress**   The times, places, and manner of holding elections for Senators and Representatives shall be prescribed in each state by the legislature thereof; but the Congress may at any time by law make or alter such regulations, except as to the places of choosing Senators.

**2. Annual Sessions**   The Congress shall assemble at least once in every year, and such meeting shall be on the first Monday in December, unless they shall by law appoint a different day.

## Section 5.   Rules for the Conduct of Business

**1. Organization**   Each house shall be the judge of the elections, returns, and qualifications of its own members, and a majority of each shall constitute a quorum to do business; but a smaller number may adjourn from day to day, and may be authorized to compel the attendance of absent members, in such manner, and under such penalties, as each house may provide.

**2. Procedures**   Each house may determine the rules of its proceedings, punish its members for disorderly behavior, and with the concurrence of two-thirds, expel a member.

**3. A Written Record**   Each house shall keep a journal of its proceedings, and from time to time publish the same, excepting such parts as may in their judgment require secrecy; and the yeas and nays of the members of either house on any question shall, at the desire of one-fifth of those present, be entered on the journal.

**4. Rules for Adjournment**   Neither house, during the session of Congress, shall, without the consent of the other, adjourn for more than three days, nor to any other place than that in which the two houses shall be sitting.

## Section 6.   Privileges and Restrictions

**1. Salaries and Immunities**   The Senators and Representatives shall receive a compensation for their services, to be ascertained by law and paid out of the Treasury of the United States. They shall in all cases, except treason, felony, and breach of the peace, be privileged from arrest during their attendance at the session of their respective houses, and in going to and returning from the same; and for any speech or debate in either house, they shall not be questioned in any other place.

**2. Restrictions on Other Employment**   No Senator or Representative shall, during the time for which he was elected, be appointed to any civil office under the authority of the United States, which shall have been created, or the emoluments whereof shall have been increased, during such time; and no person holding any office under the United States shall be a member of either house during his continuance in office.

The Constitution

## Section 7.  Law-Making Process

**1. Tax Bills**   All bills for raising revenue shall originate in the House of Representatives; but the Senate may propose or concur with amendments as on other bills.

**2. How a Bill Becomes a Law**   Every bill which shall have passed the House of Representatives and the Senate shall, before it become a law, be presented to the President of the United States; if he approve, he shall sign it, but if not, he shall return it, with his objections, to that house in which it shall have originated, who shall enter the objections at large on their journal, and proceed to reconsider it. If after such reconsideration two-thirds of that house shall agree to pass the bill, it shall be sent, together with the objections, to the other house, by which it shall likewise be reconsidered, and, if approved by two-thirds of that house, it shall become a law. But in all such cases the votes of both houses shall be determined by yeas and nays, and the names of the persons voting for and against the bill shall be entered on the journal of each house respectively. If any bill shall not be returned by the President within ten days (Sundays excepted) after it shall have been presented to him, the same bill shall be a law, in like manner as if he had signed it, unless the Congress by their adjournment prevent its return, in which case it shall not be a law.

**3. Resolutions Passed by Congress**   Every order, resolution, or vote to which the concurrence of the Senate and House of Representatives may be necessary (except on a question of adjournment) shall be presented to the President of the United States; and before the same shall take effect, shall be approved by him, or being disapproved by him, shall be repassed by two-thirds of the Senate and House of Representatives, according to the rules and limitations prescribed in the case of a bill.

## Section 8.  Powers Delegated to Congress

The Congress shall have power

**1. Taxes**   To lay and collect taxes, duties, imposts, and excises, to pay the debts and provide for the common defense and general welfare of the United States; but all duties, imposts, and excises shall be uniform throughout the United States;

**2. Borrowing**   To borrow money on the credit of the United States;

**3. Commerce**   To regulate commerce with foreign nations, and among the several states, and with the Indian tribes;

**Clause 1**  *Revenue* is money raised by the government through taxes. Tax bills must be introduced in the House. The Senate, however, can make changes in tax bills. This clause protects the principle that people can be taxed only with their consent.

**Clause 2**  A *bill,* or proposed law, that is passed by a majority of the House and Senate is sent to the President. If the President signs the bill, it becomes law.

A bill can also become law without the President's signature. The President can refuse to act on a bill. If Congress is in session at the time, the bill becomes law ten days after the President receives it.

The President can *veto,* or reject, a bill by sending it back to the house where it was introduced. Or if the President refuses to act on a bill and Congress adjourns within ten days, then the bill dies. This way of killing a bill without taking action is called the *pocket veto.*

Congress can override the President's veto if each house of Congress passes the bill again by a two-thirds vote. This clause is an important part of the system of checks and balances (pages 208–210).

**Clause 3**  Congress can pass resolutions or orders that have the same force as laws. Any such resolution or order must be signed by the President (except on questions of adjournment). Thus, this clause prevents Congress from bypassing the President simply by calling a bill by another name.

**Clause 1**  *Duties* are tariffs. *Imposts* are taxes in general. *Excises* are taxes on the production or sale of certain goods. Congress has the power to tax and spend tax money. Taxes must be the same in all parts of the country.

**Clause 2**  Congress can borrow money for the United States. The government often borrows money by selling *bonds,* or certificates that promise to pay the holder a certain sum of money on a certain date (page 223).

**Clause 3**  Only Congress has the power to regulate foreign and *interstate trade,* or trade between states. Disagreements over interstate trade was a major problem with the Articles of Confederation (pages 199–200).

**Clause 4** *Naturalization* is the process whereby a foreigner becomes a citizen. *Bankruptcy* is the condition in which a person or business cannot pay its debts. Congress has the power to pass laws on these two issues. The laws must be the same in all parts of the country.

**Clause 5** Congress has the power to coin money and set its value. Congress has set up the National Bureau of Standards to regulate weights and measures.

**Clause 6** *Counterfeiting* is the making of imitation money. *Securities* are bonds. Congress can make laws to punish counterfeiters.

**Clause 7** Congress has the power to set up and control the delivery of mail.

**Clause 8** Congress may pass copyright and patent laws. A *copyright* protects an author. A *patent* makes an inventor the sole owner of his or her work for a limited time.

**Clause 9** Congress has the power to set up *inferior,* or lower, federal courts under the Supreme Court.

**Clause 10** Congress can punish *piracy,* or the robbing of ships at sea.

**Clause 11** Only Congress can declare war. Declarations of war are granted at the request of the President. *Letters of marque and reprisal* were documents issued by a government allowing merchant ships to arm themselves and attack ships of an enemy nation. They are no longer issued.

**Clauses 12, 13, 14** These clauses place the army and navy under the control of Congress. Congress decides on the size of the armed forces and the amount of money to spend on the army and navy. It also has the power to write rules governing the armed forces.

**Clauses 15, 16** The *militia* is a body of citizen soldiers. Congress can call up the militia to put down rebellions or fight foreign invaders. Each state has its own militia, today called the National Guard. Normally, the militia is under the command of a state's governor. However, it can be placed under the command of the President.

**Clause 17** Congress controls the district around the national capital. In 1790, Congress made Washington, D.C., the nation's capital (page 234). In 1973, it gave residents of the district the right to elect local officials.

---

**4. Naturalization; Bankruptcy** To establish a uniform rule of naturalization, and uniform laws on the subject of bankruptcies throughout the United States;

**5. Coins; Weights; Measures** To coin money, regulate the value thereof, and of foreign coin, and fix the standard of weights and measures;

**6. Counterfeiting** To provide for the punishment of counterfeiting the securities and current coin of the United States;

**7. Post Offices** To establish post offices and post roads;

**8. Copyrights; Patents** To promote the progress of science and useful arts by securing for limited times to authors and inventors the exclusive right to their respective writings and discoveries;

**9. Federal Courts** To constitute tribunals inferior to the Supreme Court;

**10. Piracy** To define and punish piracies and felonies committed on the high seas and offenses against the law of nations;

**11. Declarations of War** To declare war, ~~grant letters of marque and reprisal~~, and make rules concerning captures on land and water;

**12. Army** To raise and support armies, but no appropriation of money to that use shall be for a longer term than two years;

**13. Navy** To provide and maintain a navy;

**14. Rules for the Military** To make rules for the government and regulation of the land and naval forces;

**15. Militia** To provide for calling forth the militia to execute the laws of the Union, suppress insurrections, and repel invasions;

**16. Rules for the Militia** To provide for organizing, arming, and disciplining the militia, and for governing such part of them as may be employed in the service of the United States, reserving to the states, respectively, the appointment of the officers, and the authority of training the militia according to the discipline prescribed by Congress;

**17. National Capital** To exercise exclusive legislation in all cases whatsoever, over such district (not exceeding ten miles square) as may, by cession of particular states, and the acceptance of Congress, become the seat of government of the United States, and to exercise like authority over all places purchased by the consent of the legislature of the state in which the same shall be, for the erection of forts, magazines, arsenals, dock-yards, and other needful buildings;—and

**18. Necessary Laws**   To make all laws which shall be necessary and proper for carrying into execution the foregoing powers, and all other powers vested by this Constitution in the government of the United States, or in any department or officer thereof.

## Section 9.   Powers Denied to the Federal Government

**1. The Slave Trade**   ~~The migration or importation of such persons as any of the states now existing shall think proper to admit shall not be prohibited by the Congress prior to the year 1808; but a tax or duty may be imposed on such importation, not exceeding $10 for each person.~~

**2. Writ of Habeas Corpus**   The privilege of the writ of *habeas corpus* shall not be suspended, unless when in cases of rebellion or invasion the public safety may require it.

**3. Bills of Attainder and Ex Post Facto Laws**   No bill of attainder or *ex post facto* law shall be passed.

**4. Apportionment of Direct Taxes**   ~~No capitation or other direct tax shall be laid, unless in proportion to the census or enumeration herein before directed to be taken.~~

**5. Taxes on Exports**   No tax or duty shall be laid on articles exported from any state.

**6. Special Preference for Trade**   No preference shall be given any regulation of commerce or revenue to the ports of one state over those of another; nor shall vessels bound to, or from, one state, be obliged to enter, clear, or pay duties in another.

**7. Spending**   No money shall be drawn from the Treasury, but in consequence of appropriations made by law; and a regular statement and account of the receipts and expenditures of all public money shall be published from time to time.

**Clause 18**   Clauses 1–17 list the powers delegated to Congress. The writers of the Constitution added Clause 18 so that Congress could deal with the changing needs of the nation. It gives Congress the power to make laws as needed to carry out the first 17 clauses. Clause 18 is sometimes called the elastic clause because it lets Congress stretch the meaning of its power.

**Clause 1**   *Such persons* means slaves. This clause resulted from a compromise between the supporters and the opponents of the slave trade (pages 204–205). In 1808, as soon as Congress was permitted to abolish the slave trade, it did so. The $10 import tax was never imposed.

**Clause 2**   A *writ of habeas corpus* is a court order requiring government officials to bring a prisoner to court and explain why he or she is being held. A writ of habeas corpus protects people from unlawful imprisonment. The government cannot suspend this right except in times of rebellion or invasion.

**Clause 3**   A *bill of attainder* is a law declaring that a person is guilty of a particular crime. An *ex post facto law* punishes an act which was not illegal when it was committed. Congress cannot pass a bill of attainder and ex post facto laws.

**Clause 4**   A *capitation tax* is a tax placed directly on each person. *Direct taxes* are taxes on people or on land. They can only be passed if they are divided among the states according to population. The Sixteenth Amendment allowed Congress to tax income without regard to the population of the states.

**Clause 5**   This clause forbids Congress to tax exports. In 1787, Southerners insisted on this clause because their economy depended on exports.

**Clause 6**   Congress cannot make laws that favor one state over another in trade and commerce. Also, states cannot place tariffs on interstate trade.

**Clause 7**   The federal government cannot spend money unless Congress *appropriates* it, or passes a law allowing it. This clause gives Congress an important check on the President by controlling the money he or she can spend. The government must publish a statement showing how it spends public funds.

**Clause 8**  The government cannot award titles of nobility such as Duke or Duchess. American citizens cannot accept titles of nobility from foreign governments without the consent of Congress.

**Clause 1**  The writers of the Constitution did not want the states to act like separate nations. So they prohibited states from making treaties or coining money. Some powers denied to the federal government are also denied to the states. For example, states cannot pass ex post facto laws.

**Clauses 2, 3**  Powers listed here are forbidden to the states, but Congress can lift these prohibitions by passing laws that give these powers to the states.

Clause 2 forbids states from taxing imports and exports without the consent of Congress. States may charge inspection fees on goods entering the states. Any profit from these fees must be turned over to the United States Treasury.

Clause 3 forbids states from keeping an army or navy without the consent of Congress. States cannot make treaties or make war unless an enemy invades or is about to invade.

**Clause 1**  The President is responsible for **executing,** or carrying out, laws passed by Congress.

**Clauses 2, 3**  Some of the writers of the Constitution feared allowing the people to elect the President directly (pages 207–208). Therefore, the Constitutional Convention set up the electoral college. Clause 2 directs each state to choose electors, or delegates to the electoral college, to vote for President. A state's electoral vote is equal to the combined number of senators and representatives. Each state may decide how to choose its electors. Members of Congress and federal officeholders may not serve as electors. This much of the original electoral college system is still in effect.

Clause 3 called upon each elector to vote for two candidates. The candidate who received a majority of the electoral votes would become President. The runner-up would become Vice President. If no candidate won a majority, the House would choose the President. The Senate would choose the Vice President.

The election of 1800 showed a problem with the original electoral college system (page

---

**8. Creation of Titles of Nobility**  No title of nobility shall be granted by the United States; and no person holding any office of profit or trust under them, shall, without the consent of the Congress, accept of any present, emolument, office, or title, of any kind whatever, from any king, prince, or foreign state.

## Section 10.  Powers Denied to the States

**1. Unconditional Prohibitions**  No state shall enter into any treaty, alliance, or confederation; grant letters of marque and reprisals; coin money; emit bills of credit; make anything but gold and silver coin a tender in payment of debts; pass any bill of attainder, *ex post facto* law, or law impairing the obligation of contracts, or grant any title of nobility.

**2. Powers Conditionally Denied**  No state shall, without the consent of the Congress, lay any imposts or duties on imports or exports, except what may be absolutely necessary for executing its inspection laws; and the net produce of all duties and imposts, laid by any state on imports or exports, shall be for the use of the Treasury of the United States; and all such laws shall be subject to the revision and control of the Congress.

**3. Other Denied Powers**  No state shall, without the consent of Congress, lay any duty of tonnage, keep troops, or ships of war in time of peace, enter into any agreement or compact with another state, or with a foreign power, or engage in war, unless actually invaded, or in such imminent danger as will not admit of delay.

# Article 2.  The Executive Branch

## Section 1.  President and Vice-President

**1. Chief Executive**  The executive power shall be vested in a President of the United States of America. He shall hold his office during the term of four years, and together with the Vice-President, chosen for the same term, be elected as follows:

**2. Selection of Electors**  Each state shall appoint, in such manner as the legislature thereof may direct, a number of electors, equal to the whole number of Senators and Representatives to which the state may be entitled in the Congress; but no Senator or Representative, or person holding an office or trust or profit under the United States, shall be appointed an elector.

**3. Electoral College Procedures**  The electors shall meet in their respective states, and vote by ballot for two persons, of whom one at least shall not be an inhabitant of the same state with themselves. And they shall make a list of all the persons voted for, and of the number of votes for each; which list they shall sign and certify, and transmit sealed to the seat of the government of the United States, directed to the president of the Senate. The president of the Senate shall, in the presence of the Senate and House of Representatives, open all the certificates, and the votes shall then be counted. The person having the greatest number of votes shall be the President, if such number be a majority of the whole number of electors appointed; and if there be more than one who have such majority, and have an equal number of votes, then the House of Representatives shall immediately choose by ballot one of them for President; and if no person have a majority, then from the five highest on the list the said House shall in like manner choose the President. But in choosing the President the votes shall be taken by states, the representation from each state having one vote. A quorum for this purpose shall consist of a member or members from two-thirds of the states, and a majority of all the states shall be necessary to a choice. In every case, after the choice of the President, the person having the greatest number of votes of the electors shall be the Vice-President. But if there should remain two or more who have equal votes, the Senate shall choose from them by ballot the Vice-President.

**4. Time of Elections** The Congress may determine the time of choosing the electors, and the day on which they shall give their votes; which day shall be the same throughout the United States.

**5. Qualifications for President** No person except a natural-born citizen or a citizen of the United States, at the time of the adoption of this Constitution, shall be eligible to the office of the President; neither shall any person be eligible to that office who shall not have attained to the age of thirty-five years, and been fourteen years a resident within the United States.

**6. Presidential Succession** In case of the removal of the President from office, or of his death, resignation, or inability to discharge the powers and duties of the said office, the same shall devolve on the Vice-President, and the Congress may by law provide for the case of removal, death, resignation, or inability, both of the President and Vice-President, declaring what officer shall then act as President, and such officer shall act accordingly, until the disability be removed, or a President shall be elected.

**7. Salary** The President shall, at stated times, receive for his services, a compensation, which shall neither be increased nor diminished during the period for which he shall have been elected, and he shall not receive within that period any other emolument from the United States, or any of them.

**8. Oath of Office** Before he enter on the execution of his office, he shall take the following oath or affirmation:—"I do solemnly swear (or affirm) that I will faithfully execute the office of President of the United States, and will to the best of my ability, preserve, protect, and defend the Constitution of the United States."

237). Thomas Jefferson was the Republican candidate for President, and Aaron Burr was the Republican candidate for Vice President. In the electoral college, the vote ended in a tie. The election was finally decided in the House, where Jefferson was chosen President. The Twelfth Amendment changed the electoral college system so that this could not happen again.

**Clause 4** Under a law passed in 1792, electors are chosen on the Tuesday following the first Monday of November every four years. Electors from each state meet to vote in December.

Today, voters in each state choose *slates,* or groups, of electors who are pledged to a candidate for President. The candidate for President who wins the popular vote in each state wins that state's electoral vote.

**Clause 5** The President must be a citizen of the United States from birth, at least 35 years old, and a resident of the country for 14 years. The first seven Presidents of the United States were born under British rule, but they were allowed to hold office because they were citizens at the time the Constitution was adopted.

**Clause 6** The powers of the President pass to the Vice President if the President leaves office or cannot discharge his or her duties. The wording of this clause caused confusion the first time a President died in office. When President William Henry Harrison died, it was uncertain whether Vice President John Tyler should remain Vice President and act as President. Or should he be sworn in as President? Tyler persuaded a federal judge to swear him in. So he set the precedent that the Vice President assumes the office of President when it becomes vacant. The Twenty-fifth Amendment replaced this clause.

**Clause 7** The President is paid a salary. It cannot be raised or lowered during his or her term of office. The President is not allowed to hold any other federal or state position while in office. Today, the President's salary is $200,000 a year.

**Clause 8** Before taking office, the President must promise to protect and defend the Constitution. Usually, the Chief Justice of the Supreme Court administers the oath of office to the President.

**Clause 1** The President is head of the armed forces and the state militias when they are called into national service. So the military is under *civilian,* or nonmilitary, control.

The President can get advice from the heads of executive departments. In most cases, the President has the power to grant a reprieve or pardon. A *reprieve* suspends punishment ordered by law. A *pardon* prevents prosecution for a crime or overrides the judgment of the court.

**Clause 2** The President has the power to make treaties with other nations. Under the system of checks and balances, all treaties must be approved by two thirds of the Senate. Today, the President also makes agreements with foreign governments. These executive agreements do not need Senate approval.

The President has the power to appoint ambassadors to foreign countries and other high officials. The Senate must *confirm*, or approve, these appointments.

**Clause 3** If the Senate is in *recess,* or not meeting, the President may fill vacant government posts by making temporary appointments.

The President must give Congress a report on the condition of the nation every year. This report is now called the State of the Union Address. Since 1913, the President has given this speech in person each January.

The President can call a special session of Congress and can adjourn Congress if necessary. The President has the power to receive, or recognize, foreign ambassadors.

The President must carry out the laws. Today, many government agencies oversee the execution of laws.

*Civil officers* include federal judges and members of the cabinet. *High crimes* are major crimes. *Misdemeanors* are lesser crimes. The President, Vice President, and others can be forced out of office if impeached and found guilty of certain crimes. Andrew Johnson is the only President to have been impeached.

*Judicial power* means the right of the courts to decide legal cases. The Constitution creates the Supreme Court but lets Congress decide on the size of the Supreme Court. Congress

## Section 2.  Powers of the President

**1. Commander in Chief of the Armed Forces**  The President shall be Commander in Chief of the Army and Navy of the United States, and of the militia of the several states, when called into the actual service of the United States; he may require the option, in writing, of the principal officer in each of the executive departments, upon any subject relating to the duties of their respective offices, and he shall have power to grant reprieves and pardons for offenses against the United States, except in cases of impeachment.

**2. Making Treaties and Nominations**  He shall have power, by and with the advice and consent of the Senate, to make treaties, provided two-thirds of the Senators present concur; and he shall nominate, and by and with the advice and consent of the Senate, shall appoint ambassadors, other public ministers and consuls, judges of the Supreme Court, and all other officers of the United States, whose appointments are not herein otherwise provided for, and which shall be established by law; but the Congress may by law vest the appointment of such inferior officers, as they think proper, in the President alone, in the courts of law, or in the heads of departments.

**3. Temporary Appointments**  The President shall have power to fill up all vacancies that may happen during the recess of the Senate, by granting commissions which shall expire at the end of their next session.

## Section 3.  Duties

He shall from time to time give to the Congress information of the state of the Union, and recommend to their consideration such measures as he shall judge necessary and expedient; he may, on extraordinary occasions, convene both houses, or either of them, and in case of disagreement between them, with respect to the time of adjournment, he may adjourn them to such time as he shall think proper; he shall receive ambassadors and other public ministers; he shall take care that the laws be faithfully executed, and shall commission all the officers of the United States.

## Section 4.  Impeachment and Removal From Office

The President, Vice-President, and all civil officers of the United States, shall be removed from office on impeachment for, and conviction of, treason, bribery, or other high crimes and misdemeanors.

# Article 3.  The Judicial Branch

## Section 1.  Federal Courts

The judicial power of the United States shall be vested in one Supreme Court, and in such inferior courts as the Congress may from time to time ordain and establish. The judges, both of the Supreme and inferior courts, shall hold their offices during good behavior, and shall, at stated times, receive for their services a compensation, which shall not be diminished during their continuance in office.

## Section 2.  Jurisdiction of Federal Courts

**1. Scope of Judicial Power**  The judicial power shall extend to all cases, in law and equity, arising under this Constitution, the laws of the United States, and treaties made or which shall be made, under their authority; to all cases affecting ambassadors, other public ministers and consuls; to all cases of admiralty and maritime jurisdiction; to controversies to which the United States shall be a party; to controversies between two or more states; ~~between a state and citizens of another state~~; between citizens of the same state claiming lands under grants of different states, and between a state or the citizens thereof, and foreign states, citizens, or subjects.

**2. The Supreme Court**  In all cases affecting ambassadors, other public ministers and consuls, and those in which a state shall be a party, the Supreme Court shall have original jurisdiction. In all the other cases before mentioned, the Supreme Court shall have appellate jurisdiction, both as to law and fact, with such exceptions, and under such regulations as the Congress shall make.

**3. Trial by Jury**  The trial of all crimes, except in cases of impeachment, shall be by jury; and such trial shall be held in the state where the said crimes shall have been committed; but when not committed within any state, the trial shall be at such place or places as the Congress may by law have directed.

## Section 3.  Treason

**1. Definition**  Treason against the United States shall consist only in levying war against them, or in adhering to their enemies, giving them aid and comfort. No person shall be convicted of treason unless on the testimony of two witnesses to the same overt act, or on confession in open court.

**2. Punishment**  The Congress shall have power to declare the punishment of treason, but no attainder of treason shall work corruption of blood or forfeiture except during the life of the person attainted.

## Article 4.  Relations Among the States

## Section 1.  Official Records and Acts

Full faith and credit shall be given in each state to the public acts, records, and judicial proceedings of every other state. And the Congress may by general laws prescribe the manner in which such acts, records, and proceedings shall be proved, and the effect thereof.

has the power to set up inferior, or lower, courts. The Judiciary Act of 1789 (pages 222–223) set up a system of district and circuit courts, or courts of appeal. Today, there are 95 district courts and 11 courts of appeals. All federal judges serve for life.

**Clause 1  *Jurisdiction*** refers to the right of a court to hear a case. Federal courts have jurisdiction over cases that involve the Constitution, federal laws, treaties, foreign ambassadors and diplomats, naval and maritime laws, disagreements between states or between citizens from different states, and disputes between a state or citizen and a foreign state or citizen.

In *Marbury* v. *Madison* (pages 243–244), the Supreme Court established the right to judge whether a law is constitutional.

**Clause 2  *Original jurisdiction*** means the power of a court to hear a case where it first arises. The Supreme Court has original jurisdiction over only a few cases, such as those involving foreign diplomats. More often, the Supreme Court acts as an appellate court. An **appellate court** does not decide guilt. It decides whether the lower court trial was properly conducted and reviews the lower court's decision.

**Clause 3**  This clause guarantees the right to a jury trial for anyone accused of a federal crime. The only exceptions are impeachment cases. The trial must be held in the state where the crime was committed.

**Clause 1**  Treason is clearly defined. An **overt act** is an actual action. A person cannot be convicted of treason for what he or she thinks. A person can only be convicted of treason if he or she confesses or two witnesses testify to it.

**Clause 2**  Congress has the power to set the punishment for traitors. Congress may not punish the children of convicted traitors by taking away their civil rights or property.

Each state must recognize the official acts and records of any other state. For example, each state must recognize marriage certificates issued by another state. Congress can pass laws to ensure this.

**Clause 1**  All states must treat citizens of another state in the same way it treats its own citizens. However, the courts have allowed states to give residents certain privileges, such as lower tuition rates.

**Clause 2**  *Extradition* means the act of returning a suspected criminal or escaped prisoner to a state where he or she is wanted. State governors must return a suspect to another state. However, the Supreme Court has ruled that a governor cannot be forced to do so if he or she feels that justice will not be done.

**Clause 3**  *Persons held to service or labor* refers to slaves or indentured servants. This clause required states to return runaway slaves to their owners. The Thirteenth Amendment replaces this clause.

**Clause 1**  Congress has the power to admit new states to the Union. Existing states cannot be split up or joined together to form new states unless both Congress and the state legislatures approve. New states are equal to all other states.

**Clause 2**  Congress can make rules for managing and governing land owned by the United States. This includes territories not organized into states, such as Puerto Rico and Guam, and federal lands within a state.

In a *republic,* voters choose representatives to govern them. The federal government must protect the states from foreign invasion and from *domestic,* or internal, disorder, if asked to do so by a state.

The Constitution can be *amended,* or changed, if necessary. An amendment can be proposed by (1) a two-thirds vote of both houses of Congress or (2) a national convention called by Congress at the request of two thirds of the state legislatures. (This second method has never been used.) An amendment must be *ratified,* or approved, by (1) three fourths of the state legislatures or (2) special conventions in three fourths of the states. Congress decides which method will be used.

## Section 2.  Privileges of Citizens

**1. Privileges**  The citizens of each state shall be entitled to all privileges and immunities of citizens in the several states.

**2. Extradition**  A person charged in any state with treason, felony, or other crime, who shall flee from justice, and be found in another state, shall on demand of the executive authority of the state from which he fled, be delivered up, to be removed to the state having jurisdiction of the crime.

**3. Return of Fugitive Slaves**  No person held to service or labor in one state, under the laws thereof, escaping into another, shall in consequence of any law or regulation therein, be discharged from such service or labor, but shall be delivered up on claim of the party to whom such service or labor may be due.

## Section 3.  New States and Territories

**1. New States**  New states may be admitted by the Congress into this Union; but no new state shall be formed or erected within the jurisdiction of any other state; nor any state be formed by the junction of two or more states, or parts of states, without the consent of the legislatures of the states concerned as well as of the Congress.

**2. Federal Lands**  The Congress shall have power to dispose of and make all needful rules and regulations respecting the territory or other property belonging to the United States; and nothing in this Constitution shall be so construed as to prejudice any claims of the United States, or of any particular state.

## Section 4.  Guarantees to the States

The United States shall guarantee to every state in this Union a republican form of government, and shall protect each of them against invasion; and on application of the legislature, or of the executive (when the legislature cannot be convened) against domestic violence.

# Article 5.  Amending the Constitution

The Congress, whenever two-thirds of both houses shall deem it necessary, shall propose amendments to this Constitution, or, on the application of the legislatures of two-thirds of the several states, shall call a convention for proposing amendments, which, in either case, shall be valid to all intents and purposes, as part of this Constitution, when ratified by the legislatures of three-fourths of the several states, or by conventions in three-fourths thereof, as the one or the other mode of ratification may be proposed by the Congress; provided that no amendments which may be made prior to the year 1808 shall in any manner affect the first and fourth clauses in the Ninth Section of the First Article; and that no state, without its consent, shall be deprived of its equal suffrage in the Senate.

# Article 6. National Supremacy

## Section 1. Prior Public Debts

All debts contracted and engagements entered into, before the adoption of this Constitution, shall be as valid against the United States under this Constitution, as under the Confederation.

The United States government promised to pay all debts and honor all agreements made under the Articles of Confederation.

## Section 2. Supreme Law of the Land

This Constitution, and the laws of the United States which shall be made in pursuance thereof, and all treaties made, or which shall be made, under the authority of the United States, shall be the supreme law of the land; and the judges in every state shall be bound thereby, anything in the constitution or laws of any state to the contrary notwithstanding.

The Constitution, federal laws, and treaties that the Senate has ratified are the supreme, or highest, law of the land. Thus, they outweigh state laws. A state judge must overturn a state law that conflicts with the Constitution or with a federal law.

## Section 3. Oaths of Office

The Senators and Representatives before mentioned, and the members of the several state legislatures, and all executive and judicial officers, both of the United States and of the several states, shall be bound by oath or affirmation, to support this Constitution; but no religious test shall ever be required as a qualification to any office or public trust under the United States.

State and federal officeholders take an oath, or solemn promise, to support the Constitution. However, this clause forbids the use of religious tests for officeholders. During the colonial period, every colony except Rhode Island required a religious test for officeholders.

# Article 7. Ratification

The ratification of the convention of nine states shall be sufficient for the establishment of the Constitution between the states so ratifying the same.

During 1787 and 1788, states held special conventions. By October 1788, the required nine states had ratified the Constitution.

---

Done in Convention, by the unanimous consent of the states present, the seventeenth day of September, in the year of our Lord one thousand seven hundred and eighty-seven, and of the independence of the United States of America the twelfth. *In Witness* whereof, we have hereunto subscribed our names.

**Attest:** **William Jackson**
Secretary

**George Washington**
President and Deputy from Virginia

**New Hampshire**
John Langdon
Nicholas Gilman

**Massachusetts**
Nathaniel Gorham
Rufus King

**Connecticut**
William Samuel Johnson
Roger Sherman

**New York**
Alexander Hamilton

**New Jersey**
William Livingston
David Brearley
William Paterson
Jonathan Dayton

**Pennsylvania**
Benjamin Franklin
Thomas Mifflin
Robert Morris
George Clymer
Thomas Fitzsimons
Jared Ingersoll
James Wilson
Gouverneur Morris

**Delaware**
George Read
Gunning Bedford, Jr.
John Dickinson
Richard Bassett
Jacob Broom

**Maryland**
James McHenry
Dan of St. Thomas Jennifer
Daniel Carroll

**Virginia**
John Blair
James Madison, Jr.

**North Carolina**
William Blount
Richard Dobbs Spaight
Hugh Williamson

**South Carolina**
John Rutledge
Charles Cotesworth Pinckney
Charles Pinckney
Pierce Butler

**Georgia**
William Few
Abraham Baldwin

# Amendments to the Constitution

The first ten amendments, which were added to the Constitution in 1791, are called the Bill of Rights. Originally, the Bill of Rights applied only to actions of the federal government. However, the Supreme Court has used the due process clause of the Fourteenth Amendment to extend many of the rights to protect individuals against action by the states.

## Amendment 1
## Freedoms of Religion, Speech, Press, Assembly, and Petition

The First Amendment protects five basic rights: freedom of religion, speech, the press, assembly, and petition. Congress cannot set up an established, or official, church or religion for the nation. During the colonial period, most colonies had established churches. However, the authors of the First Amendment wanted to keep government and religion separate.

Congress may not **abridge,** or limit, the freedom to speak and write freely. The government may not censor, or review, books and newspapers before they are printed. This amendment also protects the right to assemble, or hold public meetings. **Petition** means ask. **Redress** means to correct. **Grievances** are wrongs. The people have the right to ask the government for wrongs to be corrected.

Congress shall make no law respecting an establishment of religion, or prohibiting the free exercise thereof; or abridging the freedom of speech, or of the press; or the right of the people peaceably to assemble, and to petition the government for a redress of grievances.

## Amendment 2
## Right to Bear Arms

State militia, such as the National Guard, have the right to bear arms, or keep weapons. Courts have generally ruled that the government can regulate the ownership of guns by private citizens.

A well-regulated militia, being necessary to the security of a free state, the right of the people to keep and bear arms shall not be infringed.

## Amendment 3
## Lodging Troops in Private Homes

During the colonial period, the British quartered, or housed, soldiers in private homes without the permission of the owners (page 166). This amendment limits the government's right to use private homes to house soldiers.

No soldier shall, in time of peace, be quartered in any house, without the consent of the owner; nor in time of war, but in a manner to be prescribed by law.

## Amendment 4
## Search and Seizure

This amendment protects Americans from unreasonable searches and seizures. Search and seizure are permitted only if a judge has issued a **warrant,** or written court order. A warrant is issued only if there is probable cause. This means an officer must show that it is prob-

The right of the people to be secure in their persons, houses, papers, and effects, against unreasonable searches and seizures, shall not be violated; and no warrants shall issue but upon probable cause, supported by oath or affirmation, and particularly describing the place to be searched, and the persons or things to be seized.

able, or likely, that the search will produce evidence of a crime. A search warrant must name the exact place to be searched and the things to be seized.

In some cases, courts have ruled that searches can take place without a warrant. For example, police may search a person who is under arrest. However, evidence found during an unlawful search cannot be used in a trial.

## Amendment 5
### Rights of the Accused

No person shall be held to answer for a capital, or otherwise infamous, crime, unless on a presentment or indictment of a grand jury, except in cases arising in the land or naval forces, or in the militia, when in actual service in time of war or public danger; nor shall any person be subject for the same offense to be twice put in jeopardy of life and limb; nor shall be compelled, in any criminal case, to be a witness against himself; nor be deprived of life, liberty, or property, without due process of law; nor shall private property be taken for public use, without just compensation.

This amendment protects the rights of the accused. **Capital crimes** are those which can be punished with death. **Infamous crimes** are those which can be punished with prison or loss of rights. The federal government must obtain an **indictment**, or formal accusation, from a grand jury to prosecute anyone for such crimes. A **grand jury** is a panel of between 12 to 23 citizens who decide if the government has enough evidence to justify a trial. This procedure prevents the government from prosecuting people with little or no evidence of guilt. (Soldiers and members of the militia in wartime are not covered by this rule.)

**Double jeopardy** is forbidden by this amendment. This means that a person cannot be tried twice for the same crime. However, if a court sets aside a conviction because of a legal error, the accused can be tried again. A person on trial cannot be forced to testify, or give evidence, against himself or herself. A person accused of a crime is entitled to **due process of law**, or a fair hearing or trial.

Finally, the government cannot seize private property for public use without paying the owner a fair price for it.

## Amendment 6
### Right to Speedy Trial by Jury

In all criminal prosecutions, the accused shall enjoy the right to a speedy and public trial, by an impartial jury of the state and district wherein the crime shall have been committed, which district shall have been previously ascertained by law, and to be informed of the nature and cause of the accusation; to be confronted with the witnesses against him; to have compulsory process for obtaining witnesses in his favor, and to have the assistance of counsel for his defense.

In criminal cases, the jury must be **impartial**, or not favor either side. The accused is guaranteed the right to a trial by jury. The trial must be speedy. If the government purposely postpones the trial so that it becomes hard for the person to get a fair hearing, the charge may be dismissed. The accused must be told the charges against him or her and is allowed to question prosecution witnesses. Witnesses who can help the accused can be ordered to appear in court.

The accused must be allowed a lawyer. Since 1942, the federal government has been required to provide a lawyer if the accused cannot afford one. In 1963, the Supreme Court decided that states must also provide lawyers for a defendant too poor to pay for one.

## Amendment 7
### Jury Trial in Civil Cases

In suits at common law, where the value in controversy shall exceed $20, the right of trial by jury shall be preserved, and no fact tried by a jury shall be otherwise re-examined in any court of the United States than according to the rules of the common law.

**Common law** refers to rules of law established by judges in past cases. This amendment guarantees the right to a jury trial in lawsuits where the sum of money at stake is more than $20. An appeals court cannot change a verdict because it disagrees with the decision of the jury. It can only set aside a verdict if legal errors made the trial unfair.

The Constitution

# Amendment 8
## Bail and Punishment

Excessive bail shall not be required, nor excessive fines imposed, nor cruel and unusual punishments inflicted.

**Bail** is money the accused leaves with the court as a pledge that he or she will appear for trial. If the accused does not appear for trial, the court keeps the money. **Excessive** means too high. This amendment forbids courts to set unreasonably high bail. The amount of bail usually depends on the seriousness of the charge and whether the accused is likely to appear for the trial. The amendment also forbids cruel and unusual punishments such as mental and physical abuse.

# Amendment 9
## Powers Reserved to the People

The enumeration in the Constitution, of certain rights, shall not be construed to deny or disparage others retained by the people.

The people have rights that are not listed in the Constitution. This amendment was added because some people feared that the Bill of Rights would be used to limit rights to those actually listed.

# Amendment 10
## Powers Reserved to the States

The powers not delegated to the United States by the Constitution, nor prohibited by it to the states, are reserved to the states respectively, or to the people.

This amendment limits the power of the federal government. Powers not given to the federal government belong to the states. The powers reserved to the states are not listed in the Constitution.

# Amendment 11
## Suits Against States

Passed by Congress on March 4, 1794. Ratified on January 23, 1795.

The judicial power of the United States shall not be construed to extend to any suit in law or equity, commenced or prosecuted against one of the United States, by citizens of another state, or by citizens or subjects of any foreign state.

This amendment changed part of Article 3, Section 2, Clause 1. As a result, a private citizen from one state cannot sue the government of another state in federal court. However, a citizen can sue a state government in a state court.

# Amendment 12
## Election of President and Vice-President

Passed by Congress on December 9, 1803. Ratified on June 15, 1804.

The electors shall meet in their respective states, and vote by ballot for President and Vice-President, one of whom, at least, shall not be an inhabitant of the same state with themselves; they shall name in their ballots the person voted for as President, and in distinct ballots the person voted for as Vice-President, and they shall make distinct lists of all persons voted for as President, and of all persons voted for as Vice-President, and of the number of votes for each, which lists they shall sign and certify, and transmit, sealed, to the seat of government of the United States, directed to the President of the Senate; the President of the Senate shall, in the presence of the Senate and House of Representatives, open all the certificates and the votes shall then be counted; the person having the greatest number of votes for President shall be

This amendment changed the way the electoral college voted. Before the amendment was adopted, each elector simply voted for two people. The candidate with the most votes became President. The runner-up became Vice President. In the election of 1800, however, a tie vote resulted between Thomas Jefferson and Aaron Burr (page 237).

In such a case, the Constitution required the House of Representatives to elect the President. Federalists had a majority in the House. They tried to keep Jefferson out of office by voting for Burr. It took 35 ballots in the House before Jefferson was elected President.

the President, if such number be a majority of the whole number of electors appointed; and if no person have such majority, then from the persons having the highest numbers not exceeding three on the list of those voted for as President, the House of Representatives shall choose immediately, by ballot, the President. But in choosing the President, the votes shall be taken by states, the representation from each state having one vote; a quorum for this purpose shall consist of a member or members from two-thirds of the states, and a majority of all the states shall be necessary to a choice. And if the House of Representatives shall not choose a President whenever the right of choice shall devolve upon them, before the fourth day of March next following, then the Vice-President shall act as President, as in the case of the death or other constitutional disability of the President. The person having the greatest number of votes as Vice-President, shall be the Vice-President, if such number be a majority of the whole number of electors appointed, and if no person have a majority, then, from the two highest numbers on the list, the Senate shall choose the Vice-President; a quorum for the purpose shall consist of two-thirds of the whole number of Senators, and a majority of the whole number shall be necessary to a choice. But no person constitutionally ineligible to the office of President shall be eligible to that of Vice-President of the United States.

To keep this from happening again, the Twelfth Amendment was passed and ratified in time for the election of 1804.

This amendment provides that each elector choose one candidate for President and one candidate for Vice President. If no candidate for President receives a majority of electoral votes, the House of Representatives chooses the President. If no candidate for Vice President receives a majority, the Senate elects the Vice President. The Vice President must be a person who is eligible to be President.

This system is still in use today. However, it is possible for a candidate to win the popular vote and lose in the electoral college. This happened in 1876 (pages 430–431).

## Amendment 13
## Abolition of Slavery

Passed by Congress on January 31, 1865. Ratified on December 6, 1865.

**Section 1.**   Neither slavery nor involuntary servitude, except as a punishment for crime whereof the party shall have been duly convicted, shall exist within the United States, or any place subject to their jurisdiction.

**Section 2.**   Congress shall have power to enforce this article by appropriate legislation.

The Emancipation Proclamation (1863) only freed slaves in areas controlled by the Confederacy (pages 401–402). This amendment freed all slaves. It also forbids **involuntary servitude,** or labor done against one's will. However, it does not prevent prison wardens from making prisoners work.

Congress can pass laws to carry out this amendment.

## Amendment 14
## Rights of Citizens

Passed by Congress on June 13, 1866. Ratified on July 9, 1868.

**Section 1. Citizenship**   All persons born or naturalized in the United States and subject to the jurisdiction thereof, are citizens of the United States and of the state wherein they reside. No state shall make or enforce any law which shall abridge the privileges or immunities of citizens of the United States; nor shall any state deprive any person of life, liberty, or property, without due process of law; nor deny to any person within its jurisdiction the equal protection of the laws.

This section defines citizenship for the first time in the Constitution, and it extends citizenship to blacks. It also prohibits states from denying the rights and privileges of citizenship to any citizen. This section also forbids states to deny due process of law.

Section 1 guarantees all citizens "equal protection under the law." For a long time, however, the Fourteenth Amendment did not protect blacks from discrimination. After Reconstruction, separate facilities for blacks and whites sprang up (page 431). In 1954, the Supreme Court ruled that separate facilities for blacks and whites were by their nature unequal. This ruling, in the case of *Brown* v. *Board of Education,* made school segregation illegal.

This section replaced the three fifths clause. It provides that representation in the House of Representatives is decided on the basis of the number of people in the state. It also provides that states which deny the vote to male citizens over age 21 will be punished by losing part of their representation in the House. This provision has never been enforced.

Despite this clause, black citizens were often prevented from voting. In the 1960s, federal laws were passed to end voting discrimination.

This section prohibited people who had been federal or state officials before the Civil War and who had joined the Confederate cause from serving again as government officials. In 1872, Congress restored the rights of former Confederate officials.

This section recognized that the United States must repay its debts from the Civil War. However, it forbade the repayment of debts of the Confederacy. This meant that people who had loaned money to the Confederacy would not be repaid. Also, states were not allowed to pay former slave owners for the loss of slaves.

Congress can pass laws to carry out this amendment.

*Previous condition of servitude* refers to slavery. This amendment gave blacks, both former slaves and free blacks, the right to vote. In the late 1800s, southern states used grandfather clauses, literacy tests, and poll taxes to keep blacks from voting (page 431).

Congress can pass laws to carry out this amendment. The Twenty-fourth Amendment barred the use of poll taxes in national elections. The Voting Rights Act of 1965 gave federal officials the power to register voters in places where voting discrimination was found.

**Section 2. Apportionment of Representatives** Representatives shall be apportioned among the several states according to their respective numbers, counting the whole number of persons in each state, excluding Indians not taxed. But when the right to vote at any election for the choice of electors for President and Vice-President of the United States, Representatives in Congress, the executive and judicial officers of a state, or the members of the legislature thereof, is denied to any of the male inhabitants of such state, being twenty-one years of age and citizens of the United States, or in any way abridged, except for participation in rebellion, or other crime, the basis of representation therein shall be reduced in the proportion which the number of such male citizens shall bear to the whole number of male citizens twenty-one years of age in such state.

**Section 3. Former Confederate Officials** No person shall be a Senator or Representative in Congress or elector of President and Vice-President, or hold any office, civil or military, under the United States, or under any state, who, having previously taken an oath, as a member of Congress, or as an officer of the United States, or as a member of any state legislature, or as an executive or judicial officer of any state, to support the Constitution of the United States, shall have engaged in insurrection or rebellion against the same, or given aid or comfort to the enemies thereof. But Congress may, by vote of two-thirds of each house, remove such disability.

**Section 4. Government Debt** The validity of the public debt of the United States, authorized by law, including debts incurred for payment of pensions and bounties for services in suppressing insurrection or rebellion, shall not be questioned. But neither the United States nor any state shall assume or pay any debt or obligation incurred in aid of insurrection or rebellion against the United States or any claim for the loss or emancipation of any slave; but all such debts, obligations, and claims shall be held illegal and void.

**Section 5. Enforcement** The Congress shall have power to enforce, by appropriate legislation, the provisions of this article.

## Amendment 15
## Voting Rights

Passed by Congress on February 26, 1869. Ratified on February 2, 1870.

**Section 1. Extending the Right to Vote** The right of citizens of the United States to vote shall not be denied or abridged by the United States or any state on account of race, color, or previous condition of servitude.

**Section 2. Enforcement** The Congress shall have power to enforce this article by appropriate legislation.

## Amendment 16
## The Income Tax

Passed by Congress on July 12, 1909. Ratified on February 3, 1913.

The Congress shall have power to lay and collect taxes on incomes, from whatever source derived, without apportionment among the several states, and without regard to any census or enumeration.

Congress has the power to collect taxes on people's income. An income tax can be collected without regard to a state's population. This amendment changed Article 1, Section 9, Clause 4.

## Amendment 17
## Direct Election of Senators

Passed by Congress on May 13, 1912. Ratified on April 8, 1913.

**Section 1. Method of Election** The Senate of the United States shall be composed of two Senators from each state, elected by the people thereof, for six years; and each Senator shall have one vote. The electors in each state shall have the qualifications requisite for electors of the most numerous branch of the state legislatures.

This amendment replaced Article 1, Section 2, Clause 1. Before it was adopted, state legislatures chose senators. This amendment provides that senators are directly elected by the people of each state.

**Section 2. Vacancies** When vacancies happen in the representation of any state in the Senate, the executive authority of such state shall issue writs of election to fill such vacancies: *Provided* that the legislature of any state may empower the executive thereof to make temporary appointments until the people fill the vacancies by election as the legislature may direct.

When a Senate seat becomes vacant, the governor of the state must order an election to fill the seat. The state legislature can give the governor power to fill the seat until an election is held.

**Section 3. Exception** ~~This amendment shall not be so construed as to affect the election or term of any Senator chosen before it becomes valid as part of the Constitution.~~

Senators who had already been elected by the state legislatures were not affected by this amendment.

## Amendment 18
## Prohibition of Alcoholic Beverages

Passed by Congress on December 18, 1917. Ratified on January 16, 1919.

**Section 1. Ban on Alcohol** ~~After one year from the ratification of this article the manufacture, sale, or transportation of intoxicating liquors within, the importation thereof into, or the exportation thereof from, the United States and all territory subject to the jurisdiction thereof for beverage purposes is hereby prohibited.~~

This amendment, known as **Prohibition,** banned the making, selling, or transporting of alcoholic beverages in the United States. Later, the Twenty-first Amendment **repealed,** or canceled, this amendment.

**Section 2. Enforcement** ~~The Congress and the several states shall have concurrent power to enforce this article by appropriate legislation.~~

Both the states and the federal government had the power to pass laws to enforce the amendment.

**Section 3. Method of Ratification** ~~This article shall be inoperative unless it shall have been ratified as an amendment to the Constitution by the legislatures of the several states, as provided in the Constitution, within seven years from the date of the submission hereof to the states by the Congress.~~

The amendment had to be approved within seven years. The Eighteenth Amendment was the first amendment to include a time limit for ratification.

# Amendment 19
## Women's Suffrage

Passed by Congress on June 4, 1919, Ratified on August 18, 1920.

Neither the federal government nor state governments can deny the right to vote on account of sex. Thus, women won **suffrage,** or the right to vote. Before 1920, some states had allowed women to vote in state elections.

**Section 1. The Right to Vote**   The right of citizens of the United States to vote shall not be denied or abridged by the United States or by any state on account of sex.

Congress can pass laws to carry out the amendment.

**Section 2. Enforcement**   Congress shall have power to enforce this article by appropriate legislation.

# Amendment 20
## Presidential Terms; Sessions of Congress

Passed by Congress on March 2, 1932. Ratified on Janurary 23, 1933.

The date for the President and Vice President to take office is January 20. Members of Congress begin their terms of office on January 3. Before this amendment was adopted, these terms of office began on March 4.

**Section 1. Beginning of Term**   The terms of the President and Vice-President shall end at noon on the 20th day of January, and the terms of Senators and Representatives at noon on the 3rd day of January, of the years in which such terms would have ended if this article had not been ratified; and the terms of their successor shall then begin.

Congress must meet at least once a year. The new session of Congress begins on January 3. Before this amendment, members of Congress who had been defeated in November continued to hold office until the following March. Such members were known as **lame ducks.**

**Section 2. Congressional Sessions**   The Congress shall assemble at least once in every year, and such meeting shall begin at noon on the 3rd day of January, unless they shall by law appoint a different day.

If the President-elect dies before taking office, the Vice President-elect becomes President. If no President has been chosen by January 20 or if the elected candidate fails to qualify for office, the Vice President-elect acts as President, but only until a qualified President is chosen.
   Finally, Congress has the power to choose a person to act as President if neither the President-elect or Vice President-elect has qualified to take office.

**Section 3. Presidential Succession**   If at the time fixed for the beginning of the term of the President, the President-elect shall have died, the Vice-President-elect shall become President. If a President shall not have been chosen before the time fixed for the beginning of his term, or if the President-elect shall have failed to qualify, then the Vice-President-elect shall act as President until a President shall have qualified; and the Congress may by law provide for the case wherein neither a President-elect nor a Vice-President-elect shall have qualified, declaring who shall then act as President, or the manner in which one who is to act shall be selected, and such person shall act accordingly until a President or Vice-President shall have qualified.

Congress can pass laws in cases where a Presidential candidate dies while an election is being decided in the House. Congress has similar power in cases where a candidate for Vice President dies while an election is being decided in the Senate.

**Section 4. Elections Decided by Congress**   The Congress may by law provide for the case of the death of any of the persons from whom the House of Representatives may choose a President whenever the right of choice shall have devolved upon them, and for the case of the death of any of the persons from whom the Senate may choose a Vice-President whenever the right of choice shall have devolved upon them.

The Constitution

**Section 5. Date of Implementation** ~~Sections 1 and 2 shall take effect on the 15th day of October following the ratification of this article.~~

Section 5 sets the date for the amendment to become effective.

**Section 6. Ratification Period** ~~This article shall be inoperative unless it shall have been ratified as an amendment to the Constitution by the legislatures of three-fourths of the several states within seven years from the date of its submission.~~

Section 6 sets a time limit for ratification.

# Amendment 21
# Repeal of Prohibition

Passed by Congress on February 20, 1933. Ratified on December 5, 1933.

**Section 1. Repeal of National Prohibition** The eighteenth article of amendment to the Constitution of the United States is hereby repealed.

The Eighteenth Amendment is repealed, making it legal to make and sell alcoholic beverages. Prohibition ended December 5, 1933.

**Section 2. State Laws** The transportation or importation into any state, territory, or possession of the United States for delivery or use therein of intoxicating liquors, in violation of the laws thereof, is hereby prohibited.

Each state was free to ban the making and selling of alcoholic drink within its borders. This section makes bringing liquor into a "dry" state a federal offense.

**Section 3. Ratification Period** ~~This article shall be inoperative unless it shall have been ratified as an amendment to the Constitution by conventions in the several states, as provided in the Constitution, within seven years from the date of the submission hereof to the states by the Congress.~~

Special state conventions were called to ratify this amendment. This is the only time an amendment was ratified by state conventions rather than state legislatures.

# Amendment 22
# Limit on Number of President's Terms

Passed by Congress on March 12, 1947. Ratified on March 1, 1951.

**Section 1. Two-Term Limit** No person shall be elected to the office of the President more than twice, and no person who has held the office of President, or acted as President, for more than two years of a term to which some other person was elected President shall be elected to the office of the President more than once. ~~But this Article shall not apply to any person holding the office of President when this Article was proposed by the Congress, and shall not prevent any person who may be holding the office of President, or acting as President, during the term within which this Article becomes operative from holding the office of President or acting as President during the remainder of such term.~~

Before Franklin Roosevelt became President, no President served more than two terms in office. Roosevelt broke with this custom and was elected to four terms. This amendment provides that no President may serve more than two terms. A President who has already served more than half of someone else's term can only serve one more full term. However, the amendment did not apply to Harry Truman, who had become President after Franklin Roosevelt's death in 1944.

A seven-year time limit is set for ratification.

**Section 2. Ratification Period** ~~This Article shall be inoperative unless it shall have been ratified as an amendment to the Constitution by the legislatures of three-fourths of the several states within seven years from the date of its submission to the states by the Congress.~~

## Amendment 23
## Presidential Electors for District of Columbia

Passed by Congress on June 16, 1960. Ratified on April 3, 1961.

This amendment gives residents of Washington, D.C., the right to vote in Presidential elections. Until this amendment was adopted, people living in Washington, D.C., could not vote for President because the Constitution had made no provision for choosing electors from the nation's capital. Washington, D.C., has three electoral votes.

**Section 1. Determining the Number of Electors** The District constituting the seat of Government of the United States shall appoint in such manner as the Congress may direct:

A number of electors of President and Vice-President equal to the whole number of Senators and Representatives in Congress to which the District would be entitled if it were a State, but in no event more than the least populous State; they shall be in addition to those appointed by the States, but they shall be considered, for the purposes of the election of President and Vice-President, to be electors appointed by a State; and they shall meet in the District and perform such duties as provided by the twelfth article of amendment.

Congress can pass laws to carry out the amendment.

**Section 2. Enforcement** The Congress shall have the power to enforce this article by appropriate legislation.

## Amendment 24
## Abolition of Poll Tax in National Elections

Passed by Congress on August 27, 1962. Ratified on January 23, 1964.

A *poll tax* is a tax on voters. This amendment bans poll taxes in national elections. Some states used poll taxes to keep blacks from voting. In 1966, the Supreme Court struck down poll taxes in state elections, also.

**Section 1. Poll Tax Banned** The right of citizens of the United States to vote in any primary or other election for President or Vice-President, for electors for President or Vice-President, or for Senator or Representative in Congress, shall not be denied or abridged by the United States or any state by reason of failure to pay any poll tax or other tax.

Congress can pass laws to carry out the amendment.

**Section 2. Enforcement** The Congress shall have power to enforce this article by appropriate legislation.

## Amendment 25
## Presidential Succession and Disability

Passed by Congress on July 6, 1965. Ratified on February 11, 1967.

If the President dies or resigns, the Vice President becomes President. This section clarifies Article 2, Section 1, Clause 6.

**Section 1. President's Death or Resignation** In case of the removal of the President from office or his death or resignation, the Vice-President shall become President.

**Section 2. Vacancies in Vice-Presidency**  Whenever there is a vacancy in the office of the Vice-President, the President shall nominate a Vice-President who shall take the office upon confirmation by a majority vote of both houses of Congress.

When a Vice President takes over the office of President, he or she appoints a Vice President who must be approved by a majority vote of both houses of Congress. This section was applied after Vice President Spiro Agnew resigned in 1973. President Richard Nixon appointed Gerald Ford as Vice President. After President Nixon resigned in 1974, President Gerald Ford appointed Nelson Rockefeller as Vice President.

**Section 3. Disability of the President**  Whenever the President transmits to the President pro tempore of the Senate and the Speaker of the House of Representatives his written declaration that he is unable to discharge the powers and duties of his office, and until he transmits to them a written declaration to the contrary, such powers and duties shall be discharged by the Vice-President as Acting President.

If the President declares in writing that he or she is unable to perform the duties of office, the Vice President serves as Acting President until the President recovers.

**Section 4.**  Whenever the Vice-President and a majority of either the principal officers of the executive departments or of such other body as Congress may by law provide, transmit to the President pro tempore of the Senate and the Speaker of the House of Representatives their written declaration that the President is unable to discharge the powers and duties of his office, the Vice-President shall immediately assume the powers and duties of the office as Acting President.

Thereafter, when the President transmits to the President pro tempore of the Senate and the Speaker of the House of Representatives his written declaration that no inability exists, he shall resume the powers and duties of his office unless the Vice-President and a majority of either the principal officers of the executive department or of such other body as Congress may by law provide, transmit within four days to the President pro tempore of the Senate and the Speaker of the House of Representatives their written declaration that the President is unable to discharge the powers and duties of his office. Thereupon Congress shall decide the issue, assembling within 48 hours for that purpose if not in session. If the Congress, within 21 days after receipt of the latter written declaration, or, if Congress is not in session, within 21 days after Congress is required to assemble, determines by two-thirds vote of both houses that the President is unable to discharge the powers and duties of his office, the Vice-President shall continue to discharge the same as Acting President; otherwise, the President shall assume the powers and duties of his office.

Two Presidents, Woodrow Wilson and Dwight Eisenhower, have fallen gravely ill while in office. The Constitution contained no provision for this kind of emergency.

Section 3 provided that the President can inform Congress that he or she is too sick to perform the duties of office. However, if the President is unconscious or refuses to admit to a disabling illness, Section 4 provides that the Vice President and cabinet may declare the President disabled. The Vice President becomes Acting President until the President can return to the duties of office. In case of a disagreement between the President and the Vice President and cabinet over the President's ability to perform the duties of office, Congress must decide the issue. A two-thirds vote of both houses is needed to find the President is disabled or unable to fulfill the duties of office.

# Amendment 26
## Voting Age

Passed by Congress on March 23, 1971. Ratified on July 1, 1971.

**Section 1. Lowering of Voting Age**  The right of citizens of the United States, who are 18 years of age or older, to vote shall not be denied or abridged by the United States or any state on account of age.

In 1970, Congress passed a law allowing 18-year-olds to vote in state and federal elections. However, the Supreme Court decided that Congress could not set a minimum age for state elections. So this amendment was passed and ratified, giving the right to vote to citizens age 18 or older.

**Section 2. Enforcement**  The Congress shall have the power to enforce this article by appropriate legislation.

Congress can pass laws to carry out the amendment.

The Constitution

# An Overview of Citizenship

This overview of citizenship gives a general outline of the skills, attitudes, and knowledge that go into American citizenship. As you review the outline, you will gain insight into the rights and responsibilities of being an American citizen in today's world. The page numbers in parentheses refer to examples of the various aspects of citizenship. By studying these examples, you will learn how the rights and responsibilities of citizenship have developed throughout American history.

I. **Rights and Responsibilities.** What are the rights and responsibilities of citizenship?

    A. **Definition of citizenship.** What is a citizen?

        1. **Allegiance.** A citizen pledges allegiance to the government—national, state, and local. (p. 177)

        2. **Privilege and protection.** A citizen is entitled to the privileges and protections of these governments. (p. 431)

    B. **Becoming a citizen.** How does a person become a citizen?

        1. **Citizen by birth.** A citizen by birth is either born in the United States or born in another country but with at least one parent who is a citizen and who has lived in the country at some time. (p. 423)

        2. **Citizen by naturalization.** A foreign-born person becomes a naturalized citizen by taking an oath of allegiance to the United States after meeting other qualifications. (p. 236)

    C. **Rights of citizenship.** What are the rights of citizens?

        1. **Legal basis of rights.** Legal rights of citizenship, such as the right to vote, are protected by the laws and courts of the country. (pp. 91–92, 251, 355)

        a. **Laws protect rights.** The laws of the land that protect these rights are the Constitution—including the first ten amendments, known as the Bill of Rights, and other constitutional amendments—and federal, state, and local laws and ordinances. (pp. 211–12, 427)

        b. **Courts defend rights.** The courts that protect these rights include the Supreme Court, other federal courts, and state and local courts. (p. 382)

        2. **Citizens protect rights.** Citizens help to protect the rights of citizenship by exercising these rights and respecting the rights and responsibilities of others. (pp. 423–24)

        3. **Leaders protect rights.** Citizens' rights are also exercised and protected by chosen leaders who represent the citizens in a republican form of government. (p. 212)

    D. **Responsibilities of citizenship.** What are the responsibilities of citizens?

        1. **Becoming informed.** Citizens are informed, analyzing issues and candidates and making thoughtful judgments. (pp. 231–32, 384)

        2. **Serving on juries and in the armed forces.** Citizens serve the community and nation on juries and in the armed forces. (pp. 181–82, 187, 228–29, 404)

        3. **Paying taxes.** Citizens pay taxes to support government programs, employees, and public services. (pp. 158, 406)

        4. **Obeying laws.** Citizens obey federal, state, and local laws and ordinances. (p. 78)

        5. **Participating, volunteering, and holding office.** Citizens participate responsibly and serve as volunteers and elected officials. (pp. 51, 344)

II. **A Government of Laws.** What is a government of laws, and why is this kind of government needed?

    A. **Government serves needs.** Laws state what the government can and cannot do to serve the needs of the people. (pp. 94, 106, 198)

        1. **Protection of life, liberty, and the pursuit of happiness.** People need the government for protection and to

maintain law and order. (pp. 149–50, 173, 310)

2. **Services.** People need the government to provide services. (pp. 44, 426)

3. **Efficient law-abiding government.** People need the government to be organized, efficient, and law-abiding to serve their needs well. (pp. 34, 153, 200)

B. **Democratic foundations of government.** The government of the United States is founded on democratic beliefs and values that are guaranteed by the laws of the land. (pp. 92, 101–3, 106–7, 109, 113–17, 124, 165, 198–99)

  1. **Declaration of Independence.** The Declaration of Independence states the basic beliefs of freedom and the rights of citizens to take part in the government. (pp. 178–79, 351, 598–601)

  2. **Constitution.** The Constitution is the "Supreme Law of the Land," which identifies the principles and the powers of the government and describes how the government operates democratically. It also states how the Constitution can be changed. (pp. 202–10, 374, 413, 602–23)

III. **Organization and Function of Government.** How does the federal government function?

A. **Three Branches.** Who makes up the three branches of government—executive, legislative, and judicial—and what are their duties and responsibilities? (p. 222)

  1. **Executive.** Article 2 of the Constitution created the executive branch headed by the President, who leads the country, recommends new laws, and can veto bills passed by the legislative branch. As the chief of state, the President is responsible for carrying out the laws of the country and the treaties and declarations of war passed by the legislative branch. The President also appoints federal judges and is the commander in chief of the military when it is called into service. Other members of the executive branch include the Vice President and members of the cabinet, ambassadors, presidential advisers, members of the armed forces, and other appointed and civil servants of government agencies, departments, and bureaus. (pp. 608–10)

    Citizens influence, as well as are influenced by, the leadership of the President and members of the executive branch. The executive branch listens to public opinion when deciding issues. Also, the President is elected to office and therefore needs to know what the majority of the voters want and believe is right. (pp. 207, 242–43, 245, 283, 318, 393, 401)

  2. **Legislative.** Article 1 of the Constitution established the legislative, or law-making, branch called Congress. It is made up of two bodies: the Senate and the House of Representatives. Voters in all states elect representatives to serve in each body of Congress. The legislative branch is responsible for making laws, raising and printing money, regulating trade, establishing the postal service and federal courts, approving many of the President's appointments, declaring war, and supporting the armed forces. Congress also has the power to change the Constitution and impeach the President. (pp. 602–8)

    Citizens have an important responsibility to voice their needs and opinions on public issues so that their elected legislators can fairly represent the will of the people. (pp. 207, 256, 323, 423–24)

  3. **Judicial.** Article 3 of the Constitution established the judicial branch headed by the Supreme Court. The Supreme Court can rule that a law passed by Congress or an act of the executive branch is illegal if the Court decides it is in conflict with the Constitution. Citizens, businesses, and government officials can also ask the Supreme Court to review a decision made in a lower court if someone believes that the ruling by a judge is unconstitutional. (pp. 610–11)

    The judicial branch includes lower federal courts known as federal district courts that have been established by Congress. These courts try law breakers and review cases referred from other courts. (pp. 207, 222–23, 382)

B. **System of checks and balances.** How is the government based on a system of checks and balances? (p. 101)

1. **Restraint.** Each branch—executive, legislative, and judicial—has the power to limit, or check, the action of the other branches. (pp. 208, 244)

2. **Separation of powers.** The Constitution clearly defines the separation of powers of the branches of government so that no one branch can become too powerful. (p. 207)

C. **Agencies, departments, and bureaus.** What are the agencies, departments, and bureaus of the government, and what do they do? (p. 222)

1. **What they are.** The administrative arm of the executive branch of government is made up of many agencies, departments, and bureaus, such as the Departments of State, Defense, Treasury, and Education, the Environmental Protection Agency, the National Aeronautics and Space Administration, and the National Security Council.

2. **What they do.** These groups carry out government programs and advise the President and Congress.

IV. **Selecting Leaders.** How do citizens select leaders for the government?

A. **Elections.** Citizens take active parts in the election process by working for candidates and voting for the candidates of their choice. (pp. 322, 375)

B. **Becoming a voter.** Citizens become voters by meeting certain requirements, registering to vote, and participating in elections. (pp. 101, 198)

C. **Qualities of leadership.** Some qualities of good leaders include honesty, outspokenness, dependability, good judgment, good communication skills, sensitivity to others, and intelligence. (pp. 39, 221, 257, 295–96, 326)

D. **Political parties.** Political parties raise issues, take positions, stand for political values and beliefs, and support candidates for office. They also try to influence government decisions and public opinion. (pp. 229–33, 383, 386)

E. **News media.** The news media help to shape public opinion as well as report the news. (p. 231)

F. **Interest groups.** Like political parties, interest groups support certain political values and beliefs and try to influence government decisions and public opinion. (pp. 210–11)

V. **Local and State Governments.** What makes up state and local government?

A. **State governments.** What do state governments do?

1. **Organization.** State governments also have three branches. The executive branch is led by the governor. The law-making branch is made up of a one- or two-house state legislature. The judicial branch has a state supreme court and lower courts. (pp. 197–98)

2. **Powers.** State governments share some functions with the federal government, such as the power to tax citizens, make and enforce laws, and borrow and spend money. Other functions are reserved for states only, such as the power to regulate trade within a state, set up local governments, and hold elections. (pp. 207, 300, 359, 419)

B. **Local governments.** What are local governments, and what do they do? (pp. 134, 270–76)

1. **County, city, and township.** Local governing bodies at the county, city, and township levels are usually run by elected officials. They provide public services and carry out other business.

2. **Other elected or appointed bodies.** Boards and commissions such as school boards are elected or appointed to oversee the work of specific local groups.

3. **Family and juvenile law.** Local laws and courts protect the health and safety of citizens and juvenile concerns. Possible issues include rights of students, rights of parents and schools, and child labor laws.

VI. **Citizen Involvement.** How do citizens take an active part in influencing government decisions and actions?

A. **Taking positions.** How do citizens help change laws, create new laws, and elect officials? (pp. 133–34, 160)

1. **Voting.** Citizens vote on issues, candidates, and constitutional amend-

ments in free elections. (pp. 205–6, 293)

2. **Writing.** Citizens express individual beliefs and try to win support for candidates or issues by writing letters to newspapers and public officials. (pp. 163, 353, 378)

3. **Petitioning.** Citizens work with groups to petition, or formally request, that issues or candidates for office be placed on the ballot to be voted on by the public in free elections. (p. 159)

4. **Speaking.** Citizens speak before legislative bodies or interested groups to gain support for issues or candidates. (pp.131, 210–11, 356)

B. **Responsive governments.** How does the government respond to the needs of the people? (pp. 44–45, 82, 356–57, 426)

1. **Provides services.** The government builds roads, hospitals, schools, and zoos and provides police and fire protection as well as other assistance and services to the public.

2. **Advises where to seek help.** The government helps citizens find information and sources of assistance to meet their needs and solve problems.

3. **Listens to citizens.** Government officials and formal procedures protect the rights of citizens to be heard on public issues. Elected representatives listen to and reflect the interests of the people who elect them to office.

VII. **Government and the Economy.** How do the government and the public control and influence the economy to protect the rights of consumers and producers?

A. **Regulation.** What is the role of the government in regulating the economy? (p. 164)

1. **Free market.** The government oversees the supply of money and financial policy to support free enterprise and a strong economy. (pp. 199, 278, 297)

2. **Costs and benefits.** Economic regulation by the government works toward encouraging competition, preventing monopolies, and supporting public and private projects that will serve the public good but need gov-

ernment assistance to succeed. (pp. 53, 113, 304)

B. **Protection.** How does the government protect the consumer and the producers of goods and services? (p. 164)

1. **The consumer.** Citizens and other consumers have rights to safety, honesty, and free choice in the goods and services they decide to use and own. Laws, regulations, and government agencies protect these consumer rights. Consumers influence the quality, quantity, and price of goods and services through what they buy and say they want. (p. 299)

2. **The producer.** Citizens and businesses have rights as producers to protection under the laws and courts. Protections include the right to employ workers, own property, and trade in a free market. (pp. 225, 277–79, 334, 337–38)

C. **Encouragement.** How does the government encourage the free market system?

1. **Incentives.** The government works to support the benefits to both consumers and producers so that they will want to do business in a free market. (p. 278)

2. **Government spending.** The government supports the free market system by spending money to purchase goods and services, promote research, develop public services, and help citizens as workers, employers, producers, and consumers. (pp. 223, 266, 276, 292)

3. **Private ownership.** The government protects the rights of citizens and businesses to own and use private property as they legally choose. (pp. 127, 382)

D. **Response: Citizen roles.** How do citizens influence economic decisions by the government?

1. **Right to petition.** Citizens petition, or formally ask, the government for assistance, change, or relief. (p. 352)

2. **Voter influence.** Citizens vote for candidates who agree with their economic views. (pp. 297–99)

3. **Active involvement.** Citizens work with government officials to make and change economic programs. (p. 225)

# Index

Page numbers that are *italicized* refer to illustrations. An *m, c,* or *p* before a page number refers to a map (*m*), chart (*c*), or picture (*p*) on that page. An *n* after a page number refers to a footnote. Black dots are next to names of people.

## A

**Abolition movement,** 352–54, 374, 384, 420; blacks in, 352; John Brown and, 381, 384–85; Kansas and, 380, 381; political parties and, 375, 383; responses of North and South, 354; underground railroad, 353, *p354. See also* Antislavery movement; Slavery.
**Act of Toleration,** 110
• **Adams,** Abigail, 180, *p233,* 234, 291
• **Adams,** John, 161, 166, 174, 180, 192, 227, 242, 291, 500, *p588,* Boston Massacre, 163; Declaration of Independence, 178, *p179;* election in 1796, 231, *p233;* in election of 1800, 237; as President, 233–36, 243, 244; as Vice President, 213, 220
• **Adams,** John Quincy, 260, 294, *p588;* election in 1824, 291–92; in election of 1828, 293; as President, 292, *p292;* as Secretary of State, 282–83
• **Adams,** Samuel, 161, 163, 165, 174
**Adams–Onís Treaty,** 282
**Adobe,** 34
**Africa,** *m51, m61;* European trade and exploration, 53, 54–55, *m57;* return of blacks to, 352
**African slaves,** 80, 130–31. *See also* Slavery.
**Agriculture.** *See* Farming.
**Alabama,** 271, *m272, m572–73,* 578
**Alamo,** 316–17, *m317, p318*
**Alaska,** 20, 23, *m24, m572–73,* 578; climate, 27, *m28*
**Albany,** N.Y., 67, 86, *m127,* 153, *m154,* 271, *m272;* in American Revolution, *m182, 183*
**Algonquins,** *m38, p74,* 87, 150; in American Revolution, 186
**Alien,** 236
**Alien Act,** 236, 237, 242, 243
**Allegheny River,** 152, *m154*
• **Allen,** Ethan, 173–74, *m175*
**Almanacs,** 136
**Amendments,** constitutional, 213. *See also* specific amendments.
**American Colonization Society,** 352
**American Indians,** *See* Native Americans.
**American Revolution,** 172–81, 192, 280, 295, 327; blacks in, 187–88, 193, *p205;* in Boston area, 174–77; in Canada, 177; events leading to,

156–69; France and, 184; independence declared, 177–79; Lexington and Concord, 168–69, 173; in Middle Colonies, 181–85; money borrowed during, 223, 224; money printed in, 199–200, 211; Native Americans and, 186–187; peace treaty, 191–92; at sea, 187; in South, 189–91; in West, 186–87; women in, 184, 188–89, 193; Yorktown victory, 191
**American System,** 279
• **Amherst,** Jeffrey, 154, 157
**Anasazis,** 34–35, 38
• **Anderson,** Robert, 389
**Andes Mountains,** 26, 29, *p32,* 44, *m45,* 281, 282
**Anglos,** 325
• **Anthony,** Susan B., 356
**Antietam,** Battle of, 399, *m399,* 402, *p405,* 408, 562
**Antifederalists,** 211, 212, 232, 511
**Antislavery movement,** 350, 351–54, 362; women in, 355. *See also* Abolition movement; Slavery.
**Apaches,** *m38,* 315, 319
**Appalachian Mountains,** 23–25, 84, 128, *m136,* 157, *m186;* crossing, 270, 271, *m272*
**Appomattox Courthouse,** *m311;* surrender at, 413
**Apprentice,** 135
**Arapaho,** *m38,* 456
**Arawaks,** 57
**Archaeologists,** 33–34
**Arctic climate,** 28, *m28*
**Arctic Ocean,** 22
**Argentina,** 29; independence, 281, *m282, m570–51*
**Arizona,** 27, 35, 149, 319, 324, *m572–73, 578*
**Arkansas,** *m572–73,* 578; Civil War, 397; secession, 394; statehood, 375
**Arkansas River,** 25, 49
• **Arkwright,** Richard, 266
• **Arnold,** Benedict, *m175,* 177, *m182,* 183, 184, 190
**Arsenal,** 385
**Art:** African, *p55;* American, 361, 363, 365; Aztec, *p63;* Civil War photography, 405; colonial, 82; Native American, *p39, p43. See also* Culture.
• **Arthur,** Chester A., *c440, p590*
**Articles of Confederation,** 196, 198–202, 203, 204; text, 507
**Artists,** American, 1820–1860, 361, 363, 365. *See also* specific artists.
**Asia:** European trade with, *m51,* 53, 55, 60; land bridge between North America and, 20, *m21;* sea route to, 53–59, 60–61, 65–68
**Assemblies,** colonial, 101, 107, 110, 115, 117
• **Astor,** John Jacob, 310
**Astoria,** Ore., 310, *m310*
**Astrolabe,** 54
**Astronomy,** 42, 44, 54

**Atahualpa,** 63
**Atlanta,** Ga., in Civil War, 411, *m411,* 412, 417
**Atlantic Ocean,** *m21,* 22, 25, *m58, m61, m66;* Columbus and, 55–57
**Atlantic Plain,** *m24,* 25
**Attorney General,** 222
• **Attucks,** Crispus, 162–63
• **Austin,** Moses, 315
• **Austin,** Stephen, 315, *p316*
**Austria,** 227, 282, *m570–71*
**Aztecs,** *m38,* 42, 44, *p44, m45,* 82; fall of, 62, 63

## B

**Backcountry:** in Middle Colonies, 128, 129; southern, 130, 133–34
• **Bacon,** Nathaniel, 110
**Bacon's Rebellion,** 110, 481
**Badlands,** 24, 25
• **Balboa,** Vasco Núñez de, 60, *m61,* 63
**Baltimore,** *p99, m112, m127, m130,* 133, *m136,* 141, 335; in Civil War, 394; in War of 1812, *m258,* 259, 261
• **Baltimore,** Lord, 109, 110, *p110*
**Bank of the United States,** *p223,* 224, 230, 243, 305; Andrew Jackson and, 297, 299; second, 278
**Banks:** Panic of 1837 and, 304; pet, 299
• **Banneker,** Benjamin, 234, 237, *p237*
**Barbary States,** 250, *m250*
• **Barnum,** P.T., 378
• **Barton,** Clara, 407
**Baton Rouge,** 86
**Battles.** *See* names of battles.
• **Baumfree,** Isabella, *p355*
**Bear Flag Republic,** 323
• **Becknell,** William, 319
• **Beckwourth,** James, 311, *p311*
• **Bell,** John, 386, *m387*
**Bennington,** Battle of, *m182,* 183
**Bering Sea,** 20, *m21*
• **Berkeley,** Lord, 107
• **Bickerdyke,** Mary Ann, 407, *p407*
• **Biddle,** Nicholas, 297
**Bill,** steps to become law, 208–10, *c209*
**Bills of rights:** English, 114; state, 198; American, 213. *See also* Constitution, U.S.
**Billy Yanks,** 403
• **Bingham,** George Caleb, 291, 365
**Birmingham,** Ala., 427
**Black Americans,** *p139, p311;* in abolition movement, 352, *p353,* 353, 354; in American Revolution, 187–88, *p189,* 193, *p205;* in California, 329; Civil Rights Act of 1866 and, 423; after Civil War, 418, 421, 423–28, *p429,* 431; in colonies, 117; in Confederacy, 402–03; education, 360, 418, 420; in 1820s, 303; Fugitive Slave Law and, 377–80; Ku Klux Klan and, 427; in North, 340; novelist, 362; in Reconstruction

governments, 425, *p426;* segregation in South, 431; southern, 344, 346–47; in Texas, 319; in Union, 402, *p429;* voting and, 198, 294, 344, 420, 423, 424, 427, 431; women's rights and, 355–56. *See also* Free blacks; Slavery.
**Black codes,** 421, 423, 567
**Blackfeet,** *m38*
•**Blackwell,** Elizabeth, 358
**Bleeding Kansas,** 381
**Blind,** education for, 360
**Blockade,** 177; in Civil War, 397–400, 407, *m411;* in War of 1812, 257, *m258,* 260, 267
**Blue Jacket,** 228
**Bolivar,** Simón, 281, *p281*
•**Bonaparte,** Napoleon, 236, 245
**Bonds,** 22; in American Revolution, 223, 224; in Civil War, 406
*Bonhomme Richard,* 187, *p187*
•**Boone,** Daniel, 271, *p271*
**Boonesboro,** Ky., 271, *m272*
•**Booth,** John Wilkes, 418, 419
**Border Ruffians,** 381
**Border states,** 394, *m394*
**Boston,** Mass.: in American Revolution, 174–88; blacks, 360, 380; colonial, 100, *m102,* 122, *m136,* 138, 139, 485; resistance to British policies, 158, 160, 161, 162–63, 165–66, *m169*
**Boston Associates,** 267
**Boston Massacre,** 162–63, 497
**Boston Tea Party,** 165–66
**Bounties,** 404
•**Bowie,** Jim, 318
**Boycott,** 159, 163, 164, 168
•**Braddock,** Edward, 153
•**Bradford,** William, 93–94, 121
•**Brady,** Mathew, 405, *p405*
**Brandywine,** Battle of, *m182,* 183, 184, 193
•**Brant,** Molly, 151
**Brazil,** 29, *m61, m78, m570–71;* discovery, 60; independence, 282
**Breadbasket Colonies,** 126. *See also* Middle Colonies.
•**Breckenridge,** John, 386, *c387*
**Breed's Hill,** 174, 175, *m175,* 176
•**Brent,** Margaret, 109–10, 117
**Bridges:** in 1800s, 272; Incas, 44
**British East India Company,** 163–64
•**Brock,** Isaac, 257
•**Brooks,** Preston, 382
•**Brown,** John, 381, 384–85, *p385,* 557
•**Brown,** Joseph, 406
•**Brown,** Moses, 266
•**Brown,** William Wells, 362
•**Bruce,** Blanche, 425
•**Buchanan,** James, 383, *p589*
**Buena Vista,** Battle of, 323, *m324*
**Buffalo,** 25, 28, 39
**Bull Run,** Battle of, 398, *m398*
**Bunker Hill,** Battle of, 174–76, *p173, m175,* 188, 193, 499

**Burgesses,** *p74,* 92
•**Burgoyne,** John, *m182,* 183, 184
•**Burr,** Aaron, 230–31, 237
•**Butler,** Andrew, 381–82

# C

**Cabinet,** 222
•**Cabot,** John, 65–66
•**Cabral,** Pedro Álvares, 60, *m61*
•**Cadillac,** Antoine, 84
**Cahokia,** *m186,* 187
**Calendar:** Aztec, 44; Maya, 42
•**Calhoun,** John C., 277, 278, 279, 299–300; slavery and, *p300,* 376, *p376,* 377, 530, 553
**California,** 149, 308, 319–23, *m572–73,* 578; Bear Flag Republic, 323; cession to U.S., 324; Gold Rush, 327–29, *p329;* land and climate, 27, 320; mix of peoples, 328–29; Native Americans, *m38,* 320–21; slavery question, 375–77; Spanish missions, 320–21; statehood, 328; war with Mexico and, 323
**California Trail,** *m320, m328*
•**Calvert,** Sir George, 109
**Canada:** in American Revolution, 173, *m175,* 177, *m192;* border agreement, 261; French and Indian War, 155–156; exploration, 67; French, 150; geography, 20, 23, *m24,* 25, 26; independence, 280; Quebec Act, 166; War of 1812 and, 254, 255, 257, *m258,* 260
**Canadian Shield,** *m24,* 25
**Canals:** in 1800s, 275–76
**Canoes,** 36–37, 84
**Cape Cod,** 93, *m94, m102*
**Cape of Good Hope,** 55, *m57, m61*
**Cape Horn,** 60, *m61*
**Capital,** 90
**Capitalists,** 266
**Caravels,** 54
**Caribbean Sea,** 22, 57, *m58, m570–71*
•**Carillo,** Jose, 329
**Carolinas,** 110–11, *c115,* 117, 133. *See also* North Carolina; South Carolina.
**Carpetbaggers,** 425, 427
•**Carter,** Jimmy, *c440, p591*
•**Carteret,** Sir George, 106
•**Cartier,** Jacques, 66–67, 467
•**Cartwright,** Edward, 266
**Cascade** Mountains, 23, *m24,* 27
**Cash crops,** 126
**Catholics,** 51, 68, 78, 100, 280, 340; in colonies, 103, 108, 109, 110; in Texas, 315
**Cattle,** *m122, m127, m130,* 315; in California, 321
**Caucus,** 295
**Cavalry,** 184
**Cayugas,** 40, 311, 312, 313

**Central America,** 29, 42, 77; independence, 281, *m282*
**Central Plains,** 24; climate, 28
**Century,** 167
•**Champlain,** Samuel de, 83, *m85*
**Chancellorsville,** Battle of, 409–10, *m411*
**Chapultepec,** Battle of, 323–24
•**Charles I,** King of England, 100, 109
•**Charles II,** King of England, 98, 106, 110
•**Charles V,** King of Spain, 77
**Charles River,** 168, *m169*
**Charles Town.** *See* Charleston.
**Charleston,** S.C., 110, *m112, m130, m136,* 141; in American Revolution, *m169,* 174, 175, 190, *m191;* in Civil War, 389, 417; resistance to British policies, 158, 160–61; as trade center, 129, 133
**Charter,** 89–90
**Checks and balances,** 208, 210
**Cherokees,** *m38, m255,* 258, 301, 303; in American Revolution, 186; Trail of Tears, 303, *p303*
**Chesapeake Bay,** 90, *m94,* 109, 182, 258
•**Chesnut,** Mary Boykin, 388, *p388*
**Cheyennes,** *m38*
**Chickasaws,** *m255,* 301, *m302*
**Chief Justice,** 222; John Marshall as, 243–44, *p243*
**Children,** in factories, 268
**China:** European trade with, 53, 60; Marco Polo's visit, 48, *m51,* 52; Yankee trade with, 249–50, 336
**Chinese Americans,** in California, 329
**Choctaws,** 301, *m302*
**Christians:** Crusades, 51–52; Native Americans and, 78, 84, 88
**Chronological order,** 167
**Church of England,** 68, 93, 94, 98, 100, 107, 134
**Church of Jesus Christ of Latter Day Saints,** 325–27
**Circuit courts,** 223
**Cities,** in early 1800s, 269–70, 438
**Civil Rights Act** (1866), 423
**Civil rights movement,** 431
**Civil war,** 376
**Civil War,** 392–413, 421, 424, 429; advantages and disadvantages of each side, 395, *m396;* blacks in, 402–03; draft laws, 404, 406; in East, 398; economy, 406–07; Emancipation Proclamation, 401–02; events leading to, 372–89, goals of each side, 397–98; leadership, 395, 397; public opinion, 393–94, 401, 404, 406, 412; at sea, 398–99; surrender of South, 412–13; wartime life, 403–04; weapons, 403–04; in West, 399–401, *m411;* women in, 407–08. *See also* specific battles.
**Civilians,** 407

- **Clark,** George Rogers, *m186*, 187
- **Clark,** William, 246–49, *m247*, *p248*, 250, 310
- **Clay,** Henry, 254, 277, 278, 279, 291–93, 300, 322, 522; Bank of the U.S. and, 297; slavery compromises, 373–77, *p376*
  *Clermont,* 275
- **Cleveland,** Grover, *c440*, *p590*
  **Cliff Dwellers,** 35, *p35*
  **Climate,** 26–29; changes in, 20, 26; North America, 27–29
- **Clinton,** DeWitt, 276
- **Clinton,** George, 230, 231
  **Clipper ships,** 335–36, 541
  **Clothing,** colonial, 125, 135–36
  **Coastal Plains,** *m24*, 25
  **Coinage Act** (1792), 211
  **Cold Harbor,** Battle of, 412, *m412*
- **Cole,** Thomas, 365
  **Colleges:** blacks and, 360; first, 134; women and, 357, 358
  **Colombia,** 281, *m282*
  **Colony,** 58; proprietary, 106–07; royal, 107. *See also* names of colonies.
  **Colorado,** *p35*, 83, 249, 319, *m572–73*, 578
  **Columbia River,** *m247*, 248, 250, 310
- **Columbus,** Christopher, 36, 55–58, 59, *p59*, 464
  **Comanches,** *m38*, 315
  **Committees of correspondence,** 163, 166
  *Common Sense* (Paine), 178, 182
  **Compass,** 54
  **Compromise,** 204
  **Compromise of 1850,** *p376*, 377, 379
  **Concord,** Battle of, 168, *m169*, 173, *m175*, 188, 193
  **Conestoga wagons,** 129–29
  **Confederacy.** *See* Confederate States of America.
  **Confederate Army,** 393, *p393*, 394, 395, 397, 398; combat life, 403–04; *p404*, draft law, 406; surrender, 413
  **Confederate States of America,** 392, 393, 401, 418; advantages and disadvantages, 395; blacks in, 402–03; border states, 394; draft law, 406; economy, 406–07; formation, 388; goals, 397; navy, 398–99; seizure of federal property, 388; states' rights in, 406. *See also* Civil War; Confederate Army; South.
  **Congress,** U.S., 261, 327; annexation of Texas, 322; under Articles of Confederation, 198, 199, 200, 204, 206; Bank of the U.S. and, 278, 297, 305; in Civil War, 402; declaration of war, 1812, 256; development, at Constitutional Convention, 203–04; election of 1800 and, 237; election of 1876 and, 431; first, 213, 222, 224, 225; Andrew Johnson and, 419, 420, 423, 424; Ku Klux Klan and, 427; Mexican War, 323; organiza-

  tion and powers, 207, *c208*, 209–11; during Reconstruction, 418, 419, 420, 421, 423, 424, *p430;* slavery issue, 204, 205, 373–77, 379, 382; tariffs, 279, 299, 300. *See also* House of Representatives; Senate.
  **Connecticut,** *m122*, *m127*, *m136*, 166, 197, *m199*, *m572–53*, 578; in American Revolution, *m175*, 176; colonial, 101–02, 105, *m107*, *c115*
  **Conquistadors,** 62–64, 65, 77
  **Conservatives,** 426–27, 429, 431
  *Constitution,* **U.S.S.,** 235, *p241*, 257
  **Constitution,** U.S., 196, *p197,* 197–213; amending, 213; Bill of Rights, 211–13; checks and balances, 208–10; electoral college, 207–08; federalism, 206–07; habeas corpus, 406; impeachment, 424; interpretations of, 230, 509, 510; ratification, 210–13; text of, 602–23. *See also* specific amendments.
  **Constitutional Convention,** 196, *p197*, 202–05, 273
  **Constitutional Union Party,** 386
  **Constitutions,** 197; Confederate, 406; state, 197–98. *See also* Constitution, U.S.
  **Continental Army,** 174, 176–77; blacks in, *p185*, 188
  **Continental Congress:** in American Revolution, 188, 193; Declaration of Independence, 178, *p179;* First, 166, 168; money printed, 199, 211; Second, 174, 177, 178, 179, 182, 184
  **Continental divide,** 248
  **Convention of 1800,** 236
- **Coolidge,** Calvin, *c440*, *p590*
- **Cooper,** James Fenimore, 362
  **Copperheads,** 404
  **Corduroy roads,** 272, *p273*
- **Cornwallis,** Charles, 182, 191
- **Coronado,** Francisco, *p17*, 63, *m64*
  **Corruption,** during Reconstruction, 426, 430
- **Cortés,** Hernando, 61–62, 63
  **Cotton,** 332, 335, 341–42, *p343;* Civil War and, 398, 407; cotton gin, 266, 341, *p343;* during Reconstruction, 427; slavery and, *p341,* 342, 344, *c345,* 354; in Texas, 315; trade with England, 113
  **Cotton gin,** 266, 341, *p343*, 540
  **Cotton Kingdom,** 341–42, *m342*
  **Coureurs de bois,** 83–84, 85
  **Courts:** federal, 207, *c208,* 222–23. *See also* Judicial branch of government; Supreme Court.
  **Cowpens,** Battle of, 191, *m191*
- **Crawford,** William, 291, 292
  **Creek Indians,** *m38*, 112, *m255*, 258, 282, 296, 301, *m302*
  **Creoles,** 79
- **Crittenden,** John, 386
  **Croatoan Island,** 89
- **Crockett,** Davy, 318
  **Crusades,** *m51,* 51–52, *p52*

  **Cuba,** 57, *m58, m64,* 280
- **Cuffe,** Paul, 139, *p139,* 508
  **Culture,** 33; American, 361–65, 378, 439–40; colonial, 134–37
  **Cumberland Gap,** 271, *m272*
  **Currency.** *See* Money.
  **Cuzco,** 44, *m45,* 63

# D

- **Da Gama,** Vasco, *p16,* 55, *m57*
  **Dakota Indians,** 25, *m38*
  **Dallas,** Tex., 24, *m317*
- **Dare,** Ellinor, 89
- **Dare,** Virginia, 89
  **Dartmouth College,** 360
  **Daughters of Liberty,** 160, 161, 165
- **Davis,** Jefferson, 388, 395, 406, 407, 412
- **De la Cruz,** Juana Inés, 82
- **De Las Casas,** Bartolomé, 79, 80
- **De Soto,** Hernando, 63–64
  **Deaf,** education for, 360
  **Decade,** 167
- **Decatur,** Stephen, 250, *p251*
  **Declaration of Indepedence,** 178–80, 197, 202, *p203,* 240, 269, 305, 351, 500; blacks and, 188; text of, 598–601; signing, 179
  **Declaration of Sentiments,** 356
  **Declaratory Act,** 159
- **Deere,** John, 334
  **Delaware,** *m199,* 212, *c115,* 127, *m130,* *m572–73,* 578; in Civil War, 394; colonial, 108–09, *m112*
  **Delaware Indians,** *m38,* *m94,* 108, 154, 157, *m255*
  **Delaware River,** 87, *m94,* 106, 107, 108, 126, 181, 182, 273
  **Democracy,** 296, 351; growth in 1820s, 293–95, 303
  **Democratic government,** 102
  **Democratic Republican Party,** 231, *c231. See also* Republican Party.
  **Democratic Party,** 297, 305, 322, 379, 383; in election of 1864, 412; election of 1876 and, 430, 431; formation, 294–95; during Reconstruction, 421, 426–27, 429, 430; slavery and, 375; split in 1860, 386, *m389*
  **Depression.** *See* Economic depression.
  **Desert:** early peoples, 34–36; climate, in U.S., 27–28
  **Detroit,** Mich., in War of 1812, 257, 258
- **Dias,** Bartolomeu, 55, *m57*
  **Discrimination,** 303, 329, 340, 438
  **Disease:** in cities in early 1800s, 270; Native Americans and, 63, 79, *c81,* 87, 311–12; wagon trains and, 314
  **District of Columbia,** 224. *See also* Washington, D.C.
  **District courts,** 223
- **Dix,** Dorothea, 358–59, *p359, 361, 407*
  **Dominican Republic,** 57n, *m570–71*

**Dominion of Canada,** 280
**Dominion of New England,** 114
**Dorchester Heights,** Mass., *m175,* *p176,* 177
•**Douglas,** Stephen, 377, *p384,* 393–94; in election of 1860, 386, *m387;* and Kansas–Nebraska Act, 379; Abraham Lincoln and, 383, 384
•**Douglass,** Frederick, 352, 353, *p353,* 428, 539, 555
**Draft laws,** in Civil War, 404, 406
•**Drake,** Sir Francis, 68, *p69,* 310
**Dred Scott decision,** 382, 423, 555
**Drought,** 35
**Due process of law,** 213
**Dumping,** 278–79
•**Duquesne,** Marquis, 150
•**Durand,** Asher, 365
**Durham Report,** 280
**Dutch colonies,** 86–88; housing, 127; New Netherland, 105–06
**Dutch West India Company,** 106

# E

**East Indies,** *m51,* 53, 60
**Eastern Woodlands Indians,** *m38,* 40–41
**Economic depression:** after American Revolution, 200–01; defined, 201; Panic of 1837, 304–05
**Ecuador,** 82, 281, *m570–71*
**Education:** for blacks, 360, 400, 418; colonial, 134–35, 488, 489; for disabled, 360; public, 134, 359–60; women and, 357–58
•**Edwards,** Jonathan, 137
•**Eisenhower,** Dwight D., *c440, p591*
**El Paso,** Tex., 83, *m317*
**El Salvador,** 281
**Elections,** Presidential: (1789) 213; (1796) 231, 233; (1800) 237; (1808) 253; (1816) 277, 529; (1824) 291–92, 293; (1828) 293; (1832) 297, 299; (1836) 304, 534; (1840) 305; (1844) 322; (1848) 375; (1852) 379; (1856) 340, 383; (1860) 386, *m387;* (1864) 412; (1868) 424; (1872) 430; (1876) 430–31
**Electoral college,** 207–08; in election of 1800, 237
**Electricity,** 265; Franklin's experiments, 136, *p137*
**Elevation,** 22
•**Elizabeth I,** Queen of England, *p17,* 68, *p69,* 76, 93
**Emancipation Proclamation,** 401–02, *p563*
**Embargo,** 253, 254
**Embargo Act,** 253, 278
•**Emerson,** Ralph Waldo, 168, 362
**Emigration,** 100
**Encomiendas,** 79
**England,** 53, *m66,* 87, 99; disputes with American colonies, 148–69; Glorious Revolution, 114; representative government in, 92; rivals for North America, 149–56; search for northwest passage, 65–68; trade with American colonies, 113–14, *c140;* war with Netherlands, 106; war with Spain, 68–69. *See also* English colonies; Great Britain (for years after 1707).
**English Bill of Rights,** 114
**English colonies,** *p75, m85,* 88, 98–117; cities, 139, 141; conflicts with French, 149–151; daily life, 120–41; education, 134–35; founding of, *c115;* French and Indian War, 151–56; governing, 113–15, 117; growth of, *m136;* Middle Colonies, 105–09, 126–29; Native Americans, 150–51, 157; New England Colonies, 99–105, 121–25; resistance to British policies, 148, 157, 158–69; social classes, 135–36; Southern Colonies, 109–34, 129–34; trade 113–14; 138–40; war for independence, 172–81. *See also* Middle Colonies; New England; South; specific colonies.
**Enumerated articles,** 113
•**Ericson,** Leif, *p16,* 49–50, 462
**Erie Canal,** 275–76, *m275*
**Eskimos,** 36, 37, *m38, p67*
•**Estevanico,** 65, *p65*
**Europe,** *m51, m57, m58, m61, m64, m66, m570–71;* Civil War and, 395, 397, 398, 402, 407; early claims to North America, 59–69; factory workers, 338; Monroe Doctrine and, 283; search for new routes to Asia, 53–59; trade with, 249
**Executive branch,** 203, 207, *c208. See also* Presidency.
**Explorers,** 48–49, 53–68, *p75. See also* names of explorers.
**Exports,** 113
**Extended family,** 346

# F

**Factories,** 278; closing in 1837, 304; in North, 332, 333–34, 336, 337–39, 343, 523, 542; in South, 332, 403
**Factory system,** 266 – 69
**Fallen Timbers,** Battle of, 228–29, 254
**Famine,** 339–40
**Far North,** 36, *m38*
**Farming,** 23; California, 321; in Civil War, 406; desert, 34–35; early peoples of America, 20; English colonists, 92, 150; Industrial Revolution and, 265, 267, 268; in Middle Colonies, 126, 127; Mormons, 326; Native Americans, 39–42, 45, 319; in New England Colonies, 121–22; in New France, 84–85; new inventions for, 334; in North, 333, 337; during Reconstruction, 428–29; Shays' Rebellion, 200–01; in South, 110–12,
129–30, 132, 332, *p333,* 342–44; in Spanish colonies, 78, 79
**Federal City,** 224, 234, *p237. See also* Washington, D.C.
**Federal government,** powers of, 206–10. *See also* Congress; Constitution, U.S.; Government.
**Federalism,** 206–07
**Federalist Papers,** 211
**Federalist Party,** 210–11, 212, 231, 233, 236, 240, 242, 243, 260; decline, 237, 277; split in, 235
•**Ferdinand,** King of Spain, 53, 55
•**Fern,** Fanny, 363
**Feudalism,** 50
**Fifteenth Amendment,** 424
•**Fillmore,** Millard, 377, *p589*
**First Amendment,** 213, 236
**First Continental Congress,** 166, 168. *See also* Continental Congress.
**Fishing,** 122, *m130,* 138, 139, *m141*
**Fisk University,** 420
•**Fitch,** John, 273
**Five Forks,** Battle of, 412
**Florida,** 25, 63, 156, 430, 431, *m572–73,* 578; acquisition by U.S., 282, *m326;* under Spanish rule, *m85,* 110, 112, *m130,* 149, *m150,* 184, 192, *m199,* 245, *m258,* 259; statehood, 375
**Flow chart,** 209
•**Ford,** Gerald, *c440, p591*
**Foreign policy:** of John Adams, 234–36; of Jefferson, 245–46; of Monroe, 282–83; of Washington, 226–27, 229
**Fort Detroit,** 84, *m136,* 157
**Fort Donelson,** 400, *m411*
**Fort Duquesne,** 152, 153, 154
**Fort Henry,** 399, *m411*
**Fort McHenry,** 261
**Fort Necessity,** 152–53
**Fort Niagara,** *m136,* 154
**Fort Orange,** 86, *m87*
**Fort Oswego,** 153, *m182*
**Fort Pitt,** 154, *m186*
**Fort Sumter,** 388–89, 393, *m411*
**Fort Ticonderoga,** *m154, p176, m182,* 183; Battle of, 173–74, *m175,* 177, 188
**Fort William Henry,** 153
•**Forten,** James, 205, *p205,* 340, 352
**Forts,** French, 150, 152, 154. *See also* names of specific forts.
**Forty-niners,** 327, 328, *p329*
**Fourteenth Amendment,** 423
**Frame of Government,** 107
**France,** 53, 230, 232, 282, *m570–71;* John Adams and, 234–36; in American Revolution, 189, *m191;* Canada and, 280; French and Indian War, 151–56; Louisiana Purchase, 245–46; Revolution, 226–27, 245; search for northwest passage, 65, 66–67; seizure of American ships, 251, 253, 254; treaty with U.S. (1778), 184; wars with Great Britain, 227,

251–53; XYZ Affair, 234–35. *See also* French colonies; New France.
• **Francisco,** Peter, 193, *p193*
• **Franklin,** Benjamin, 136–37, *p137,* 138, 141, 153, 178, 179, 187, 490; at Constitutional Convention, 202, 509; in France, 184, 192
**Fredericksburg,** Battle of, 408–09, *m411*
**Free blacks:** in American Revolution, 187–88; antislavery movement, 353; in California, 329; in Civil War, 402, 406; education and, 360; Emancipation Proclamation and, 402; Fugitive Slave Law and, 377; Liberia and, 352; in North, 340; in South, 344. *See also* Freedmen; Slavery.
**Free Soil Party,** 375, 381, 383
**Free states,** 352, 373–75, 377, 379, *m380,* 382
**Freedmen,** 418, 423, 427, 428, 431; black codes and, 421
**Freedmen's Bureau,** 418, 420
• **Frémont,** John, 323, *m324, 383*
**French colonies,** 83–86, 88, 149, *m150;* French and Indian War, 151–56, *m154;* Native Americans and, 150, 151. *See also* New France.
**French and Indian War,** 151–56, 184
**Frigates,** 235, *p235*
• **Frobisher,** Martin, *m66, 67*
**Fugitive slave laws,** 376, 377–80
• **Fuller,** Margaret, 363
• **Fulton,** Robert, 273, 275
**Fundamental Orders of Connecticut,** 101–02
**Fur trade,** *p75,* 83–84, 250, 335, *p365;* decline, 311; Dutch, 87; French, 83–84, 85, 150; in Oregon Country, 310, 311

# G

**Gadsden Purchase,** 324, *m326*
• **Gage,** Thomas, 168, 174, *m175*
• **Gallatin,** Albert, 242, 243
• **Gallaudet,** Thomas, 360
• **Galvez,** Bernardo de, 184
• **Garfield,** James A., *c440, p589*
• **Garrison,** William Lloyd, 353, 354, 362, *p374*
*Gaspee,* 164, *p164*
• **Gates,** Horatio, *m175, m182,* 183–84
**General Court,** 101, 103
**Geneva College,** 358
**Gentry,** 135, 136
**Geography,** 19
• **George II,** King of Britain, 111, 112
• **George III,** King of Britain, 159, 166, 173, 174, 177, *178n,* 179, 182, 232, *p253, 363*
**Georgia,** *c115,* 129, *m130, m136,* 149, 166, *m199,* 342, *m572–73;* American Revolution, 190; Civil War, 406; colonial, 111–12; removal of Native Americans, 301, 302

**German settlers,** 108, 319, 340; houses, 127
**Germantown,** Battle of, 183, *p183*
**Gettysburg,** Battle of, 410, *m411*
**Gettysburg Address,** 410
**Ghana,** Africa, *m57, m570–71*
**Ghent,** Belgium, 260
• **Gilbert,** Sir Humphrey, 68
**Glaciers,** 19–20, *m21*
• **Goddard,** Mary Katherine, 179
**Gold,** *p16,* 63–64, *p74,* 79, 83; in California, 327–29, 540
**Gold Rush,** 327–29, *p329*
*Golden Hind,* 68, *p69*
**Goliad,** Battle of, *m317*
**Gonzales,** Tex., 316, *m317*
**Government:** under Articles of Confederation, 198–201; democratic, 102; developed at Constitutional Convention, 203–05; English colonies, 101–02, 106–10, 113–15, 117, 124; Jamestown, 90–92; Native American, 39, 40–41, 44; New France, 85; Plymouth, 93; representative, 91–92; in South during Reconstruction, 425–26; Spanish colonial, 77–78; state, 197–98; U.S., 205–10, 443–44. *See also* Congress; Constitution, U.S.
**Governors,** 198; colonial, 115
**Grand Canyon,** 23, *p23*
**Grandfather clauses,** 431
• **Grant,** Ulysses S., *p589;* in Civil War, 399, 400, *p407, p409,* 410–13, 565; election in 1868, 424; reelection in 1872, 430
**Great Awakening,** 137
**Great Britain,** *151n,* 199, 226, 228, 230, 232, 340, *m570–71;* American Revolution, 172–81; Canada and, 280; Civil War and, 398, 402, 407; claim to Oregon Country, 310, 314, 322, 323; dumping of goods in 1814, 278–79; French and Indian War, 151–56; Industrial Revolution, 265–66, 267; Jay's Treaty with, 227; Monroe Doctrine and, 283; North American claims in 1783, *m192;* Pontiac's War, 157; Proclamation of 1763, 157; seizure of American ships, 251–54, 256; steamships, 336; taxation of American colonies, 148, 158–69; War of 1812, 256–61, 278; war with France, 227, 251–53. *See also* England (for years before 1707); English colonies.
**Great Compromise,** 204
**Great Lakes,** *m24,* 26, 84, 150, *m154;* control of, 260–61
**Great Migration,** 100, 101
**Great Plains,** 24; climate, 28; Native Americans, *m38,* 39; settlement, 309
**Great Salt Lake,** 23, *m572–73*
**Great Serpent Mound,** 34, *p35*
**Great Wagon Road,** 128, *m130,* 133, 271

• **Greeley,** Horace, 308
**Green Mountain Boys,** 174, *m175, p176,* 183
**Greenbacks,** 404
• **Greene,** Nathanael, *m175,* 191
• **Grenville,** George, 158, 159
• **Griffith,** John, 335
• **Grimké,** Angelina, 353, 355
• **Grimké,** Sarah, 355
**Guatemala,** 32, 281, *m570–71*
**Guam,** 578, *m570–71*
**Gulf of Mexico,** *m24,* 25, *m64,* 65, 84, *m85,* 248
**Gulf Plain,** *m24,* 25

# H

**Habeas corpus,** 405
**Haiti,** *57n,* 245
• **Hakluyt,** Richard, 76, 468
• **Hale,** Nathan, 181
*Half Moon,* 67
• **Hamilton,** Alexander, 202, 211, *p223,* 227, 243, 516; conflict with John Adams, 235–36; as Secretary of Treasury, 222, 223–25, 230, 231, 232
**Hampton Institute,** 420
**Hampton Roads,** Va., 399, *m399*
• **Hancock,** John, 179
• **Harding,** Warren G., *c440, p590*
**Harpers Ferry,** Va., 385, *m399*
• **Hargreaves,** James, 266
• **Harrison,** Benjamin, *c440, p590*
• **Harrison,** William Henry, 254, 255, 258, *p588;* election in 1840, 305
**Hartford Convention,** 260
• **Harvard,** John, 134
**Harvard College,** 138, 360
**Hawaii,** *m24, m28,* 448, *m572–73,* 578
• **Hawthorne,** Nathaniel, 362, 363
• **Hayes,** Rutherford B., 430–31, *c440, p589*
• **Hays,** Mary Ludwig, 189
• **Henry,** Patrick, 161, *p161,* 172, 212
• **Henry,** Prince of Portugal (the Navigator), 53, 54
• **Henry VII,** King of England, 65
**Hessian troops,** 177
• **Hidalgo,** Miguel, 281
**High Federalists,** 235, 236
**Highlands climate,** *c27, m28*
**Hills,** 22
**Hispaniola,** 57. 58, *m64*
**Hogans,** 39
**Hohokams,** 34–35
• **Homer,** Winslow, 351
**Honduras,** 281, *m282, m570–71*
• **Hooker,** Thomas, 101, 102
• **Hoover,** Herbert C., *c440, p591*
**Horses,** 62, *p63;* American, *45n*
**Horseshoe Bend,** Battle of, 258, 296
**House of Burgesses,** *p74,* 92, 161
**House of Representatives,** 295; blacks in, *p426;* election of 1800 and, 237; election of 1824 and, 292;

formed at Constitutional Convention, 204; Andrew Johnson and, 424; organization and powers, 207, 209, 210; during Reconstruction, 421; slavery issue, 374, *c377*
**Houses:** in cities, early 1800s, 269; Middle Colonies, 127–28; Native American, 34–36, 38–40, 42; in New England Colonies, 124–25; in Southern Colonies, 132
**Houston,** Tex., 25, *m317*
• **Houston,** Sam, 316–18, 322
**Howard University,** 420
• **Howe,** Elias, 333
• **Howe,** Samuel Gridley, 360
• **Howe,** William, 175, 181, *m182*, 183
• **Hudson,** Henry, *m66*, 67–68, 86
**Hudson Bay,** *m66, 68*
**Hudson River,** 67, 86, *m87, m94*, 126, 127; in American Revolution, 181, *m182;* steamboats on, 275
**Hudson River School,** 365
• **Hull,** Isaac, 257
• **Hull,** William, 257
**Humid continental climate,** *c27*, 28
**Humid subtropical climate,** *c27, m28*, 29
**Hunting:** early peoples, 20; Native Americans, 36, 39, 40, *p41*, 319
**Hurons,** *m38*, 150, 157
• **Hutchinson,** Anne, 103
• **Hutchinson,** Thomas, 148, 165

# I

**Ice age,** 19–20
**Idaho,** 309, 323, *m572–73*, 578
**Igloos,** 36
**Illinois,** 200, *m201*, 271, 273, *m572–73*, 578; Mormons in, 326
**Immigration,** 236; 1820–1860, 332, 339–40; later, 437–38
**Impeachment,** 210; Andrew Johnson, 424
**Imports,** 113, 279, *c279*
**Impressment,** 251; of American sailors, 251–52, *p252*, 256, 260, 520
**Incas,** *p33*, 44–45, 82, 461; Pizarro and, 63
**Income tax laws,** 406
**Indentured servants,** 117, 130, 484
**Independence,** Mo., 312, *m320*
**Independence Day,** 178, *p212;* symbols for, 269
**India,** *m51, m61*, 407; European trade with, 55, *m57*
**Indian Ocean,** 55, *m57, m61*
**Indian Removal Act,** 301–02, 303
**Indiana,** 200, *m201*, 271, 273, *m572–73*, 578
**Indiana Territory,** 254
**Indians.** *See* Native Americans.
**Indigo,** 129, *m130*, 133, 138–39, *m141*
**Industrial Revolution,** 264, 265–70, 333, 341
**Industry:** Bank of the U.S. and, 278; Civil War and, 395, *c396*, 406; for-

eign competition, 278–99; in North, 1820–1860, 222–37, 223; in South, 341–43, 427–28
**Inflation,** 406
**Interchangeable parts,** 268
**Interior Plains,** 23–26, *m24*
**Intermountain region,** 23, *m24*, 309, 310; Native Americans, 38
**Intolerable Acts,** 166, 168, 174
**Inventions,** 333–35, 441, 446. *See also* Industrial Revolution.
**Iowa,** *m572–73*, 578; statehood, 375
**Ireland,** *m570–71;* immigrants from, 339–40
**Iron,** *m122, m127, m141;* in Middle Colonies, 126–27
**Iroquois,** *m38*, 40–41, 66, 87, 151, 459; alliance with English, 150, 153, 154; in American Revolution, 186
**Irrigation,** 27, 35, 319, 325, 326
• **Irving,** Washington, 361–62
• **Isabella,** Queen of Spain, 54, 55–57
**Isthmus,** 22
**Isthmus of Panama,** 22, 60, *m61*

# J

• **Jackson,** Andrew, 295–96, 530, *p588;* Bank of the U.S. and, 297, 299; cabinet, 296–97; election of 1824 and, 291, 292; election of 1828, 290, 293; election of 1832, 297, 299; growth of democracy under, 303; Native Americans and, 258, 301–03, 533; as President, 290, 294, 295–304, *p296, p297, p298*, 318; spoils system and, 296; tariffs and, 299–301; in War of 1812, 259–61, 295
**Jackson,** Miss., 400, *m411*
• **Jackson,** Thomas (Stonewall), 398, 409
• **James I,** King of England, 89, 90, 93, 94, 100
• **James II,** King of England, 114
**Jamestown,** 89–93, 110, *m112*, 129
• **Jay,** John, 192, 211, 223, 227
**Jay's Treaty,** 227, 234
• **Jefferson,** Thomas, 240–53, *p242*, 299, *p588;* cabinet, 242; Civil War and, 372; conflicts with Alexander Hamilton, 227, 230–31, 235, 514; Declaration of Independence, 178, 179, 232, 351, 352; democratic beliefs, 241–42; in election of 1796, 231, 233; election in 1800, 237; foreign trade under 249–53; national expansion under, 244–49; as President, 240–52, 259, 518; as Secretary of State, 222, 223, 227; Supreme Court and, 243–44; in Virginia, 161, 166, 199; as Vice President, 233, 236
**Jews,** in colonies, 103, 108, 110
• **John,** King of Portugal, 55, 60, 92
**Johnny Rebs,** 403
• **Johnson,** Andrew, *p589;* becomes President in 1865, 419; conflicts

with Congress, 419–21, 423–24; impeachment, 424
• **Johnson,** Lyndon B., *c440, p591*
• **Johnson,** William, 150–51
**Joint stock company,** 90
• **Joliet,** Louis, 84, *m85, p86*, 472
• **Jones,** John Paul, 187
• **Juana,** Sor, 82, *p82*
**Judicial branch of government,** 203, 207, *c208*, 210, 222–23
**Judicial review,** 244
**Judiciary Act,** 222, 244
**July Fourth.** *See* Independence Day.

# K

**Kansas,** *m572–73*, 578; slavery question in, 378–81
**Kansas–Nebraska Act,** 379–80, 384
**Kaskaskia,** *m186*, 187
• **Kearny,** Stephen, 323, *m324*
• **Kennedy,** John F., *c440, p591*
**Kentucky,** 20, 186, 271, *m272, m572–73*, 578; in Civil War, 394
**Kentucky Resolutions,** 236, 299
• **Key,** Francis Scott, 261
• **King,** Rufus, 277
**King Philip's War,** 105
**Kitchen cabinet,** 297
**Know–Nothing Party,** 340
• **Knox,** Henry, *m175*, 222
• **Kosciusko,** Thaddeus, 184
**Ku Klux Klan,** 427, *p427*

# L

• **La Salle,** Robert, 84, *m85*
• **Lafayette,** Marquis de, 184, *m191, p192*, 226, 227, 503
**Laissez faire,** 243
**Lake Champlain,** 173, *m175*
**Lake Erie,** *m24*, 26, 271, *m272*, 276; in War of 1812, 257, *m258*
**Lake George,** 153, *m153*
**Lake Huron,** *m24*, 26, *m85*
**Lake Michigan,** *m24*, 26, 84, *m85*
**Lake Ontario,** *m24*, 26, *m85*, 153
**Lake Superior,** *m24*, 26, *m85*
**Lancaster Turnpike,** 271–72, *m272*
**Land Ordinance of 1785,** 200
**Latin America,** 83, *m282*, 448; Monroe Doctrine and, 283; revolutions in, 280–82
**Latitude,** lines of, 56, *m57*
**Law,** steps for bill to become, 208–10, *c208. See also* Due process; Judicial review.
**Lawrence,** Kan., *m380*, 381
**Laws of the Indies,** 77, 78
**League of the Iroquois,** 41
• **Lee,** Richard Henry, 178
• **Lee,** Robert E., 385, 393, 398, *p409;* in Confederate Army, 397, 399, 408, 409–10, 412, 413, 418, 561
*Legend of Sleepy Hollow,* (Irving), 361–62

**Legislative branch,** 203, 207–10. *See also* Congress; House of Representatives; Senate.

**Legislatures:** colonial, 115, 117; state, 198

• **Legree,** Simon, 378

• **L'Enfant,** Pierre Charles, 234

• **Lewis,** Meriwether, 246–49, *m247, p248,* 250, 310

**Lewis and Clark expedition,** 246–49, *m247, p248,* 250, 310, 519

**Lexington,** Battle of, 168, *m169, p169,* 173, *m175,* 188, 193

**Lexington,** Ky., 186

*Liberator, The,* 353, 354

**Liberia,** 352, *m570–71*

**Liberty Bell,** 269

**"Liberty tea,"** 165

**Liberty Trees,** 161, 225

• **Lincoln,** Abraham, 383–84, *p384, p410, p589;* assassination, 418–19, *p419;* Civil War, 393–95, 397, 398, 401, 404, *p405,* 406, 412; debates with Stephen Douglas, 384; election in 1860, 386, *m387;* Emancipation Proclamation, 401–02; Gettysburg Address, 410; as President, 388–419; Reconstruction, 418; reelection in 1864, 412

• **Lincoln,** Mary Todd, 393

**Line of Demarcation,** 60, *m61, m78*

**Literacy tests,** 431

**Literature,** American, 361–63

• **Little Turtle,** 228

• **Livingston,** Robert, 178, 245, 246

**Log cabins,** 127, 129, *p305*

**Lone Star Republic,** 317–19, *m317*

**Long houses,** 40

**Long Island,** N.Y., 20, *m87, m102;* Battle of, 181

• **Longfellow,** Henry Wadsworth, 363

**Longitude,** lines of, 56

**Lords,** feudal, 50

**Los Angeles,** Calif., 23, 83

• **Louis XIV,** King of France, 84

• **Louis XVI,** King of France, 184, 186, 227

**Louisbourg,** Nova Scotia, 154, *m154*

**Louisiana,** 84, *m85, m150, m156,* 184, *m192, m199,* 244, *p333,* 342, 397, 430, 431, *m572–73,* 578; statehood, 249, 271, 373

**Louisiana Purchase,** 245–46, *m326;* Lewis and Clark expedition, 246–49, *m247;* slavery in, 372–74

**Louisville,** Ky., 186, *m272*

• **L'Ouverture,** Toussaint, 245, *p245*

• **Lowell,** Francis Cabot, 267

**Lowell,** Mass., 267

**Lowell mill,** 339, 343, 523

**Lower Canada,** 280

**Loyalists,** 179, 181, 190–92, 280, 502

• **Lucas,** Eliza, 133

• **Ludington,** Sybil, 193, *p193*

**Lumber,** *m130,* 138, 139, *m141,* 335

• **Luther,** Martin, 68

• **Lyon,** Mary, 357

# M

• **Madison,** Dolley, 259, *p259*

• **Madison,** James, 196, 202, 205, 211–13, 224, 230, 240, *p588;* as President, 253–61, 277, 282; as Secretary of State, 242; War of 1812 and, 254, 256–58, 260

• **Magellan,** Ferdinand, 60–61

**Magna Carta,** 92, 158

**Magnetic compass,** 54

**Maine,** 83, *m122, m136, m199,* 361, *m572–73,* 578; admission as free state, 373; in American Revolution, *m175,* 177; colonial, *m102, m107*

**Malaria,** 45

**Mali,** 54, *m57*

**Mammoths,** woolly, 20, *p20*

**Mandans,** *m138,* 246

**Manhattan Island,** 86, *p88*

**Manifest Destiny,** 321–24, 538

• **Mann,** Horace, 359, 360

**Manor,** 50, 127

*Marbury v. Madison* (1803), 244

• **Marina,** Doña, 62, *p62*

**Marine climate,** in U.S., 27, *m28*

• **Marion,** Francis, *p190,* 191–92

• **Marquette,** Jacques, 84, *m85, p86,* 472

• **Marshall,** John, 243–44, *p243,* 301, 327

**Martial law,** 394

**Maryland,** 113, *c115, m127,* 128, 129, *m130,* 133, *m136, m572–73,* 578; Articles of Confederation and, 199; in Civil War, 394, 399; colonial, 109–10, *m112,* 117

**Mason–Dixon Line,** *188n*

**Massachusetts,** 199, *m572–73,* 578; abolition of slavery, 188; in American Revolution, *m175,* 176, 186; black regiments in Union army, 402; British laws against, 166, 168; colonial, *m107, c115, m122, m127;* education, 134, 359; government, 197; Shays' Rebellion, 201

**Massachusetts Bay Colony,** 100–01, 102, *m102,* 103–04, *c115*

**Mayas,** 32, *m38,* 42, *p43, m45*

*Mayflower,* 93, *p95*

**Mayflower Compact,** 93

• **McClellan,** George, 398, 399, *p405;* in election of 1864, 412

• **McCormick,** Cyrus, 334

• **McKay,** Donald, 336

• **McKinley,** William, *c440, p590*

• **Meade,** George, 410

**Medicine:** Native American, 44; women in, 358

**Mediterranean climate,** in U.S., 27, *m28*

**Mediterranean Sea:** attack of American trading ships in, 250; trade route, 53, *m57*

• **Melville,** Herman, 362, 363

**Memphis,** Tenn., 400, *m411*

**Mental illness,** reform in treatment, 358–59

**Mercantilism,** 113

*Merrimac,* 398–99

**Mestizos,** 79

• **Metacom,** 105

**Mexican Americans,** *p321,* 324–25, 329. *See also* Spanish colonies; New Spain.

**Mexican Cession,** 324, *m326;* slavery question in, 372, 374, 375, 377

**Mexico,** 23, 29, 42, 63, *m78,* 82, 83, 319, 320, *m570–71;* Cortes and, 61–62, 63; Gadsden Purchase, 324; independence, 281, 315; Mexican Cession, 324, *m326;* Native Americans, 321; Texas and, 315–18; war with U.S., 322–24, 374, 395, 539

**Mexico City,** *m78,* 82, 323, 471

**Miami Indians,** *m38,* 157, 187, 228, 255

**Michigan,** 200, *m201, m572–73,* 578; statehood, 375

**Middle Ages,** 50–52, 53

**Middle Colonies,** 99, 105–09, *m107,* 126–29; in American Revolution, 181–85; founding of, *c115;* houses, 127–28; land and climate, 126; manufacturing and crafts, 126–27; *m127;* schools, 134; trade, 138; westward expansion, 128–29. *See also* English colonies; specific colonies.

**Middle East,** *m570–71;* Crusades, 51–52, *m52*

**Middle Passage,** 131, *p131,* 487

**Militia,** 168

**Mills,** 266–68, 278, 337, *p338,* 339, 341, 343, 427, 542

**Mining,** 325

**Minnesota,** *m572–73,* 578

• **Minuit,** Peter, 86

**Minutemen,** 168, 174, 188

**Missionaries,** 88; French, 84; in Oregon, 311; Spanish, 78, 79, 82, 83, 315

**Mississippi,** 271, 342, *m342, m572–73,* 578; in Civil War, 400, 558; Native Americans, 39; statehood, 271

**Mississippi River,** *m24,* 25, 26, 84, *m85,* 149, *m150,* 248, 249; in Civil War, 397, 399, 400–01, *m411;* currents, 273; steamboats, 275; use by farmers, 244, 245

**Missouri,** 379, *m380,* 381, *m572–73,* 578; in Civil War, 394; slavery question in, 372, 373

**Missouri Compromise,** 374, 376, 379, *m380,* 382, 386

**Missouri River,** 20, *m24,* 25, *m85,* 311; Lewis and Clark and, 246, *p248;* steamboats, 275

*Moby Dick* (Melville), 362

**Mohawks,** 40, 150, 151, *p493*

**Molasses,** 139, *m141;* British tax on, 158

**Money:** in American Revolution, 199–200, 211, *p211;* American system of, 206, 211; in Civil War, 406

*Monitor,* 399
**Monmouth,** Battle of, 189
**Monongahela River,** 151, *m154*
•**Monroe,** James, 240, 245, 246, *p588;* election in 1816 and 1820, 277; foreign policy, 282–83; as President, 291, 352
**Monroe Doctrine,** 283, 527
**Montana,** 83, 309, *m572–73,* 578
•**Montcalm,** Marquis de, 155, 495
•**Montezuma,** 62
•**Montgomery,** Richard, *m175,* 177
**Montreal,** *m154,* 155; in American Revolution, *m175, 177*
**Moore's Creek Bridge,** Battle of, 189
**Morehouse University,** 420
•**Morelos,** José, 281
•**Morgan,** Daniel, *m175,* 191
**Mormon Trail,** *m320*
**Mormons,** 325–27, *p327*
**Morristown,** Battle of, 182, *m182*
•**Morse,** Samuel F. B., 334
**Morse code,** 334
•**Mott,** Lucretia, 356
**Mound Builders,** 34, 39
**Mount Holyoke,** 357
**Mount Vernon,** 193
**Mountain Men,** 310–11, *p311*
**Mountains,** 22; climate and, 27
•**Musgrove,** Mary, 112
**Muslims,** 51, 53

# N

•**Napoleon,** 251, *p253,* 254, 257, 258
•**Narváez, Pánfilo,** *m64,* 65
**Natchez Indians,** *m38,* 39–40, *m255*
**National debt,** 23, 223–24
**National Republican Party,** 294, 297. *See also* Whigs.
**National Road,** *m272,* 273
**Nationalism,** 254
**Native Americans,** 23, 32–45, *p44,* 58, *p62, p67, p73, p80, p108;* alliances with French and English, 150–51, 153, 154; in American Revolution, 186–87; in California, 328; culture regions, 36–41, *m38;* disease and, 63, *p73,* 79, *c81,* 87, 311–12; Dutch and, 86, 87, 88; Eastern Woodlands, 40–41; effects of European settlement on, *c81,* 87–88; English colonists and, 88, 95, 104–05, 108, 129, 150–51, 157; European explorers and, 57–58, 62–64, 66–67; in Far North, 36, 37; French and, 83, 84, 87, 88, 150, 153; Indian Removal Act, 301–03, *p303;* Jamestown and, 90–93; land lost before 1810, *m255;* Lewis and Clark expedition and, 246, 248, 249; Mormons and, 327; in Northwest, 36–38, 228–29; in Oregon Country, 311, 314; Pontiac's War, 157, *p157;* readings, 456, 457, 466, 483; in Southeast, 39–40; Southern colonists and, 110, 112, 130; in Southwest, 34–

35, 38–39, 319, 325; Spanish and, 58, 61–64, 78–82, 88, 320–21; in Texas, 315; trade with, 76, 250; voting and, 293–94; in War of 1812, 257, 258; westward expansion and, 254–56. *See also* names of specific people and nations.
**Nativists,** 340, 543
**Nauvoo,** Ill., 326
**Navajos,** *m38,* 39
**Navigation,** 53
**Navigation Acts,** 113–14, 139
**Nebraska,** *m572–73,* 578
**Nebraska Territory,** 378, *m380*
**Netherlands,** 65, *m66,* 67; Pilgrims in, 94; war with England, 106; war with France, 227. *See also* New Netherland.
**Neutrality,** 186, 260; American, in British–French wars, 227, 251
**Neutrality Proclamation,** 227
**Nevada,** 27, 83, 319, *m572–73,* 578
**New Amsterdam,** 86, 87, *m87, p88,* 105
**New England:** in American Revolution, 173–77, *m175,* 183, 184; colonial, 99–105, *m102, c115,* 121–25, 137; Dominion of, 114; economic activities, 113, 122–23, *m122;* education, 134, 135; family life, 124–25; industry, 337, *p338;* land and climate, 121–22; Native Americans and, 104–05; opposition to War of 1812, 256–57, 260, *p277;* towns, 123–24; trade, 138, 139, 249, 250, 253, 254, 256–57, 260; voting laws, 294; women, 125.
**New England Anti-Slavery Society,** 353
**New France,** 84-86, *m85,* 149, 150, *m150,* 153, *m153,* 154, 155. *See also* French colonies.
**New Hampshire,** 122, *m127, m136,* 199, *202n,* 212, *m572–73,* 578; abolition of slavery, 188; colonial, *m102,* 104, *m107, c115*
**New Haven,** Conn., *m102, c115, m122*
**New Jersey,** *c115,* 127, *m136, m199, m572–73,* 578; in American revolution, 181, *m182;* colonial, 106–07, *m112;* voting, 198
**New Jersey Plan,** 204
**New Mexico,** 35, 63, 149, 249, 308, 319, 322–24, 379, *m572–73, 578*
**New Mexico Territory,** 319, *m320,* 324; slavery in, 377
**New Netherland,** 86–87, *m87, p88,* 103, 105–06, 127, 480
**New Orleans,** La., 25, 84, *m85,* 199, 423; Battle of, 292, 295, *p296;* in Civil War, 400, 401, *m411;* as port, 244–45
**New Spain,** 77, *m78,* 82, 87, *m150, m192. See also* Spanish colonies.
**New Sweden,** 87, *m87*
**New World:** exploring, 58–65; naming, 59

**New York,** 66, *c115, m127, m136,* 199, 212, 361, *m572–73,* 578; in American Revolution, 181, *m181;* colonial, *m102,* 106, *m107;* manor system, 127; public education, 359, 360
**New York City,** N.Y., *m102, m127, m136,* 139, 141, *p419;* early 1800s, 269, 270; Erie Canal and, 275–76; first capital, 213, 220; resists British policies, 158, 159, 161–62; riot of 1863, 404, 406
**Newfoundland,** Can., *50n,* 66, *m66,* 83, 150
**Newspapers:** colonial, 138, 141, 158, 160, 161, 165; growth of political parties and, 231
**Nez Percés,** *m38,* 248
**Nicaragua,** 281, *m570–71*
•**Nixon,** Richard M., *c440, p591*
**Nominating conventions,** 295
**Nonimportation agreements,** 160, 161, 163
**Nonintercourse Act,** 253
**North,** 332–40, 347; in Civil War and after, 393–98, *c396,* 403–06, 417; conflicts with South, 202–04, 224, 225, 299–301; discrimination in, 303; economy, 333–39, *m334;* education, 359, 360; election of 1860 and, 386; free blacks in, 340; immigration, 339–40; railroads, 335, 337; slavery issue, 204–05, 318, 323, 352, 354, 372–78, 380, 382–85; tariffs and, 299; voting laws, 294
•**North,** Lord, 191
**North Africa,** 250, *m250, m570–71*
**North America:** geography, 22–29, *m58, m61;* early claims to, 65–69; early peoples, 34–41; first exploration, 49–50; land bridge between Asia and, 20, *m21;* readings, 454; rivers and lakes, 25–26; in 1753, *m150;* in 1763, *m156;* in 1783, *m192*
**North Carolina,** *c115,* 129, *m130, m136,* 212, *p429, m572–73,* 578; in American Revolution, 189, *m191;* colonial, 111, *m112;* secession, 394
**North Dakota,** *m572–73,* 578
**Northwest Coast,** peoples of, 36–38
**Northwest Ordinance,** 200
**Northwest passage,** 65–68
**Northwest Territory:** Native Americans in, 228–29; settlement, 200, *m201,* 271
**Nueces River,** 322, 323, *m324*
**Nullification,** 236, 299–301
**Nullification Act,** 300

# O

**Oberlin College,** 360
•**Oglethorpe,** James, 111–12, p111
**Ohio,** 200, *m201,* 273, *m572–73,* 578; statehood, 254, 271
**Ohio River,** 20, *m24,* 25, *m85,* 150, *m154,* 271; in American Revolution, *m186,* 187; steamboats, 275

**Ohio Valley,** 150, 151, 156–57, 199, 227, 228

**Oklahoma,** *m572–73,* 578

• **Old Hickory,** 296. *See also* Jackson, Andrew.

**Old North Church,** 168, *m169*

**Olive Branch Petition,** 174, 177

• **Oñate,** Juan de, 319

**Oneidas,** 40–41

**Onondagas,** 40–41

**Ontario,** Can., 280

**Oregon,** 308, 309, 322, *m572–73,* 578; statehood, 323

**Oregon Country,** *m247,* 308–14, *m326;* conflicting claims, 310; division in 1846, 323; early settlers, 311–12; land and climate, 309–10

**Oregon Trail,** *m310,* 312–14

• **Osceola,** Chief, 303

• **Otis,** James, 188

**Ottowas,** 157

**Overriding,** of Presidential veto, *c208,* 210

# P

**Pacific Coast,** 23, *m24,* 309–10

**Pacific Northwest,** 27, 250, 309; Lewis and Clark in, 248–49

**Pacific Ocean,** *m21,* 22, 60, 61, 68, 310; Lewis and Clark and, 248–49

• **Paine,** Thomas, 178, 182

**Panama,** 60, 63, 281, *m570–71*

**Panic of 1837,** 304–05, 318

**Parliament,** 92, 100, 266; taxation of American colonies, 158–61, 163, 164, 166, 168

• **Paterson,** William, 204, 243

**Patriots,** 179, 181, 186, 188

**Patroons,** 105, 127

• **Peale,** Charles Wilson, 365

**Pemaquids,** 95

**Peninsulares,** 78, 79

• **Penn,** William, 98, 107–08, *p108,* 126

**Pennsylvania,** 113, *c115,* 127, *m130, m136,* 166, *m119,* 271, *m272, m572–73,* 578; in American Revolution, 181, *m182;* colonial, 107–08, *m112,* 116, 126–28; government, 198

**Pennsylvania Dutch,** 108

**Pensacola,** Fla., *m258,* 259

**Pequots,** war with colonists, 104–05

• **Perry,** Oliver Hazard, 257, 261

**Peru,** 29, *p32,* 44, 63, 77, *m78,* 82, 83, 281, *m282, m570–71*

**Pet banks,** 299

**Petersburg,** Va., 133; siege of, *m412*

**Philadelphia,** Pa., *m107, m112, m127, m130, m136,* 137, 166, 174, 486; in American Revolution, *m182,* 183, 184; and Constitution, 201, 202, 212–13; colonial, 108, 498; growth of, 141; as nation's capital, 224

*Philadelphia* (ship), *p235,* 250

• **Philip II,** King of Spain, 68, 105

**Philippine Islands,** 61, *m570–71*

**Pickett's Charge,** 410

**Pictographs,** 42

• **Pierce,** Franklin, 379, 395, *p589*

• **Pike,** Zebulon, *m247,* 249

**Pike's Peak,** *m247,* 249

**Pilgrims,** *p77,* 93–95, *p95,* 100, 475

• **Pinckney,** Charles, 133, 237

• **Pinckney,** Eliza Lucas, 133

• **Pinckney,** Thomas, 231, 245

**Pinckney Treaty,** 245

• **Pitcher,** Molly, 189

• **Pitt,** William, 153–54

**Pittsburgh,** Pa., *m136,* 154, 271

• **Pizarro,** Francisco, 62–63

**Plains,** 22

**Plains of Abraham,** 153

**Plan of Union,** 153

**Plantations,** 111, 112, *p121,* 129–30, *p333, p341,* 343–47, 428; in Civil War, 403, 417, 418; life on, 132–33, *p132;* slaves on, 130-31, 344, 346; in Spanish colonies, 79, 80; in Texas, 315; in West Indies, 79, 88

**Plateaus,** 22

*Plessy* v. *Ferguson* (1896), 431

**Plow,** steel, 334

**Plymouth,** Mass., *m102,* 104, *c115, m122,* 161; Pilgrims, 94–95, 99

• **Pocahontas,** 90, 91, *p91*

**Poets,** American, 362–63

**Political parties,** 229–33, *c231;* Democratic Party in 1860, 386, *m387;* in 1820, 294–95; Free Soilers, 375, 381, 383; during Reconstruction, 418–21, 423–26, 429, 430; Republican Party formed, 383. *See also* names of specific parties.

• **Polk,** James, 322, 323, *p589*

**Poll taxes,** 431

• **Polo,** Marco, 48, *p49, m51,* 52, 463

• **Ponce de León,** Juan, 63, *m64*

• **Pontiac,** 157, *p157,* 301

• **Poor,** Salem, 193, *p193*

*Poor Richard's Almanac* (Franklin), 136, 187

**Popular sovereignty,** 374, 375, 377, 379, 380, 384

**Population,** *c81, c145,* 153; in West, *c274;* growth, 1790–1830, *c278*

**Port Royal,** 83, *m85*

**Portsmouth,** N.H., 122, *m122*

**Portugal,** 56, *m57,* 282; lands in New World, 60, *m78;* rise of, 53; trade and exploration, 53–55, *m570–71*

• **Portolá,** Gaspar de, 320

**Postal service,** colonial, 38

**Potlatch,** 37–38

**Potomac River,** *m94,* 224, 234; in Civil War, 398

**Pottawatomie Creek,** Kan., 381

• **Powell,** John Wesley, 22, *p22*

• **Powhatan,** 90, 91, *m94, m255*

**Prejudice,** 340. *See also* Discrimination.

• **Prescott,** William, 174–75, 176, 193

**Presidency:** and Constitution, 207–10, *c208;* candidates for, 295; Twelfth Amendment and, 237

**Presidios,** 78

**Primary sources,** 43

**Prime Meridian,** 56, *m57*

**Princeton,** Battle of, 182, *m182*

**Printing press,** 52; colonial, 138

**Prison reform,** 358–59

**Proclamation of 1763,** *m156,* 157

**Profiteers,** in Civil War, 406

• **Prophet,** The, 254, 255, *p256*

**Proprietary colony,** 106–07

**Protective tariff.** *See* Tariffs.

**Protestant Reformation,** 68

**Protestants,** 68, 340; in Canada, 280; in colonies, 108, 110, 117; Quakers, 107; in Texas, 315

**Prussia,** 184, 185, 227, 282

**Public schools,** 134, 359–60

**Pueblo Bonito,** N.M., 35

**Pueblo Indians,** 38–39, 319

**Pueblos,** 35; in Spanish colonies, 78

**Puerto Rico,** 58, 63, 282, 448, *m570–71,* 578

• **Pulaski,** Casimir, 184

**Puritans,** 100–04, *p103,* 106, 107, 114, 121, 123–24, 134, 137, 362

# Q

**Quakers,** 98, 107, 128, 131, 352

**Quartering Act,** 161–62, 166

**Quebec,** 83, 154–55, *m156,* 280; in American Revolution, *m175,* 177

**Quebec Act,** 166

# R

**Racism,** 130, 322. *See also* Prejudice.

**Radical Reconstruction,** 423–24

**Radical Republicans,** 421, 423, 428, 429

**Railroads,** 337, 379; in Civil War, 395, *c396,* 407, 411, 417; growth of, 335, *c335,* 445, *p445;* during Reconstruction, 426, 427

• **Raleigh,** Sir Walter, 89

**Ranches,** 319, 321

• **Randolph,** Edmund, 203, 222

**Ratify,** 192

• **Reagan,** Ronald, *c440, p591*

**Reaper,** 334, 406

**Reconstruction,** 416–31, 568; Johnson's plan, 419–20; Lincoln's plan, 418; Radical, 423–24; southern resistance to, 426–27

**Reconstruction Act,** 423

**Red Stick faction,** 258

**Reform,** 1820–1860, 350–60, 365; alcohol, 360–61; education, 359–60; slavery, 351–54; social, 358–59; women's rights, 355–58, 363

**Relief,** in maps, 21

**Religion:** European wars over, 68; freedom of, 102, 103, 107, 108, 110; Native American, 34, 36, 38–40, 40, 42, 44; in New England Colonies, 123–24; as reason for immigrating to America, 99–100

Religious Society of Friends, 107
Renaissance, 52–53
Rendezvous, 311
Representative government, 101; in Virginia, 90–91. *See also* Constitution, U.S.; Government, U.S.
Republic, 205–06
Republic of Texas, 316, *m317*, 317–19. *See also* Texas.
Republican Party, 231, *231n*, 233, 236, 240, 277, 291, 294, 297; election of 1800, 237; election of 1860, 386, *m387;* election of 1876, 430, 431; form in 1850s, 383; during Reconstruction, 418–24, 427, 429, 430
•Revels, Hiram, 425
•Revere, Paul, *p162*, 163, 168, *m169*, 363, 497
Rhode Island, 102–03, *n102*, *c115*, *m122*, *m136*, 164, *m199*, 202, 212, *m572–73*, 578; in American Revolution, *m175*, 176; government, 197
Rice, 129, *m130*, 131, 138, *m141*, 341, 342
Richmond, Va., *m136*, *m191;* in Civil War, 397, 398, 408, 411, 412, 417
•Rillieux, Norbert, 344
Rio Grande, *m24*, 26, 322, 323, *m324*
*Rip Van Winkle* (Irving), 361, 362
Roads: early 1800s, 271–73, *m272;* federal and state, 207; Inca, 44
Roanoke Island, 89, *m94*
•Robbins, Parker, 429, *p429*
•Rochambeau, Comte de, 191, *m191*
Rocky Mountains, 23, *m24*, 27, 86, 309–11; Lewis and Clark and, 246–48
Roman Catholics. *See* Catholics
•Roosevelt, Franklin D., *c440*, *p591*
•Roosevelt, Theodore, *c440*, 448, *p590*
•Ross, Betsy, 188–89
Royal colony, 107
Rush–Bagot Agreement, 261
Russia, 282, 283; claims in North America, 156, 310

# S

•Sacajawea, 246, 248, *p248*
Sagres, Portugal, 54, *m57*
Saguenay, 66–67
St. Augustine, Fla., *m78*, 83, *m112*
St. Lawrence River, 26, 66–67, 83, 84, *m85*, 150, *m154*, 155
•St. Leger, Barry, *m182*, 183
St. Louis, Mo., 24, 319, *m320*
Salem, Mass., 100, *m102*, *m122;* witchcraft, 104
•Salomon, Haym, 193, *p193*
Salt Lake City, Utah, *m320*, 326, 327
•Samoset, 95
San Antonio, Tex., 83; Battle of, 316, *m317*
San Diego, Calif., 320, *m320*, 321, 323
San Francisco, Calif., 23, *m320*, 321; Gold Rush and, 327, 328

San Jacinto, Battle of, 317, *m317*
•San Martín, José de, 281
•Santa Anna, Antonio López de, 316, *m317*, 318, 323, *m324*
Santa Fe Trail, 319, *m320*, 323
Saratoga, Battle of, *m182*, 184, 191
Savanna climate, 29
Savannah, Ga., 112, *m132*, *m136;* in American Revolution, 190, *m191;* in Civil War, 417
Scalawags, 425, 427
Scale, in maps, 21
Schools: for blacks after Civil War, 418, 420; public, 134, 359–60; during Reconstruction, 426, *p426*
•Scott, Dred, 382, 423, 557
•Scott, Winfield, 323, *m324*
Secession, 300, 375, 376
Second Continental Congress, 174, 175, 177, 178
Sectionalism, 374
•Sedgwick, Catharine, 363
Sedition, 236
Sedition Act, 236, 237, 242, 243
Segregation, 431
Seminole War (1835–1842), 303
Seminoles, *m38*, *m255*, 282, 301, *m302*, 303
Senate, 204, 207–10, *c209;* blacks in, 425, *p426;* Andrew Johnson and, 424; during Reconstruction, 421; slavery controversy, 374, 376, *c377*, 381–82
Seneca Falls Convention, 356–57
Senecas, 40–41, 157
Separation of church and state, 102, 103
Separation of powers, 207
Separatists, 93
•Sequoyah, 301, *p301*
Serfs, 50
•Serra, Father Junípero, 320
Seven Cities of Gold, 63, *m64*, 65
Sewing machine, 333–34
Sharecroppers, 428–29
Shawnees, *m38*, 157, *m255*, *m302*
Shay's Rebellion, 200–01
Shenandoah Valley, 133; in Civil War, 410–12
•Sheridan, Philip, 411, 412
•Sherman, Roger, 178, 204
•Sherman, William Tecumseh, *p407*, 411, 412
Shiloh, Battle of, 399–400, *m411*
Shipbuilding, 113, 122, *m122*
Ships: clipper, 335–36; flatboats, 271; frigates, 235; steamships, 273, 275, 336
Shoshones, 38, 246, 248, 519
Sierra Nevada, 23, *m24*, 27, *p311*
Silver, 63, 79, 83, 325
•Singer, Isaac, 333
Skilled workers, 338
•Slater, Samuel, 266, 268
Slave codes, 130, 420
Slave states, 372–75, 377, 379, *m380*, 388; in Union, 394, 401, 404

Slave trade, 54, 55, 80, *111n*, 131, *p131*, 139, *m141;* banning in Washington, D.C., 377
Slavery, 80, 105, 130–32, *p131*, 372–86, 418, 487, 545, 548; antislavery movement, 350–54; California and, 328, 375, 376, 377; in Civil War, 401–03, 404, 406, 408; Compromise of 1850, 377; cotton and, *p341*, 342, 344, *c345;* daily life, 346, *p347;* Declaration of Independence and, *178n;* decline in North, 188; Dred Scott decision, 382; election of 1848 and, 375; election of 1860 and, 386; Emancipation Proclamation, 401–02; Free Soil Party and, 375; Fugitive Slave Law, 377–78, 380; in Southern Colonies, 130–31; as issue at Constitutional Convention, 204–05; Kansas–Nebraska Act, 379–80; Lincoln–Douglas Debates, 384; Mexican Cession and, 374, 375; 552; Missouri Compromise, 373–74; Native Americans and, 58, 63, 64, 79–80, 88, 105; Northwest Ordinance and, 200; popular sovereignty, 374, 379, 380, *m380;* resisting, 346–47; slave codes, 347; in South, 111, 112, 132, 343, 344; in Texas, 316, 318, 319; Thirteenth Amendment, 419, 421; *Uncle Tom's Cabin*, 378–79; work of, 344, 346
•Smith, John, 90, 91, 122
•Smith, Joseph, 325, 326, *p327*
Social class, in colonies, 78–79, 135–36
Songhai, 54, *m57*
Sons of Liberty, 160, 161, 163, 165, 168, 193
South, 332, 341–47; American Revolution, 181, 189–91; backcountry, 133–34; blacks, after Civil War, 416–21, 423–26, 428, *p429*, 431; colonial, 109–12, *c115*, 129–34, 141; conflicts with North, 204–05, 224, 225, 299–301; cotton, 341–42, *p343;* education, 134, 359–60; free blacks, 344; growth of slavery, 130–31; industries, 342–43; land and climate, 129–30; products, *m130*, *m342;* railroads, *c335;* Reconstruction, 416–31; secession, 386, 388; tariffs and, 279, 299–301; trade, 138–39; War of 1812 and, 256–60. *See also* Confederate States of America and names of specific states.
South America, *m21*, *m61;* climate, 29; Europeans claims to, 59–60; Native American empires, 44, *m45;* landscapes, 22, 26; Spanish colonies, 77, *m570–71*
South Carolina, *m112*, *c115*, 129, *m130*, 133, *m136*, 166, 342, 343, 425, 430, 431, *m572–73*, 578; American Revolution, 190, 191; Civil War, 388, 389, 402; secession, 300, 386
South Dakota, *m572–73*, 578

**South Pass,** 311, *m320*
**South Pole,** 27, 56
**Southeast Indians,** *m38,* 39–40, 301–03, *p303*
**Southwest,** *m320;* land and climate, 319; Native Americans, 34–35, 38–39; settlement, 315, 325; Spanish influence, 83
**Spain,** 53; Asian trade and exploration, 55–58, 60; California and, 320–21; Louisiana and, 244–45; New World exploration and empire, 59–64, *m66,* 156; relations with U.S., 199, 226, 448; rivalry with England in North America, 149; war with England, 68–69, 112. *See also* New Spain; Spanish colonies.
**Spanish Armada,** 69
**Spanish colonies,** 57–60, *m58,* 77–83, *m78,* 88, 149, *m150;* culture, 80, 82–83; government, 77–78; Native Americans and, 79–80; revolutions in, 280–82; social classes, 78–79. *See also* New Spain.
**Spanish Florida,** *m85,* 110, 112, *m130,* 149, *m150,* 184, 192, *m199,* 245; cession to U.S., 282, *m326;* in War of 1812, *m258,* 259
**Speculator,** 224
**Spice Islands,** *53n*
**Spice trade,** 52, 53, 55
**Spinning,** 265–66, 267
**Spoils system,** 296
• **Squanto,** 95
**Stamp Act,** 148, 158–59, *p158,* 161
**Stamp Act Congress,** 159
• **Stanton,** Edwin, 397, 402
• **Stanton,** Elizabeth Cady, 356, 549
***Star-Spangled Banner, The,*** 261
**States:** governments formed, 197–98; powers, under Constitution, 206, 207. *See also* States' rights.
**States' rights,** 236; in Confederacy, 406; nullification and, 299–300
**Statistics,** 81
**Steam,** 265
**Steamships,** 336, 525
• **Stephens,** Alexander, 420
**Steppe climate,** *c27, 28*
• **Steuben,** Friedrich von, 184–85
• **Stevens,** Thaddeus, 421, 424, 429
**Stockade,** 92
**Stocks,** 123, *p123*
• **Stowe,** Harriet Beecher, 378, 379, 555
**Strait of Magellan,** 22, 60, *m61*
**Strikes,** 338, 339
• **Stuart,** Gilbert, 365
• **Stuyvesant,** Peter, 106, *p106*
**Subarctic climate,** *c27, 28*
**Subsistence farming,** 121
**Suffrage,** 293. *See also* Voting.
**Sugar,** 79, 139, *m141,* 341, 343
**Sugar Act,** 158, 159
• **Sumner,** Charles, 381–82, 421, 424, 429
**Supreme Court,** 207, *c208,* 210, 222–23; Bank of the U.S. and, 297; Dred

Scott decision, 382, 423; under John Marshall, 243–44; Native Americans and, 301; *Plessy* v. *Ferguson* (1896), 431
**Surplus,** 121
**Sutter's Mill,** *m320,* 327, *m328*
**Sweden:** settlers from, 87, 127

**T**

**Tainos,** 58, 63, 82
• **Taft,** William Howard, *c440, p590*
• **Talleyrand,** Maurice de, 234, 235, 245
• **Taney,** Roger, 299
**Tariffs,** 225, 279, *c279,* 299, 300–01, 305, 421, 423, 526
**Taxation:** of American colonies by British, 148, 158–69; under Articles of Confederation, 198–200; Congress and, 207, 225; on income, 406; during Reconstruction, 426; tax-in-kind, 406
• **Taylor,** Zachary, 323, 375, 377, *p589*
**Tea,** 160, 163–66, 250
**Tea Act,** 164
• **Tecumseh,** 254–58, *p256,* 301, 521
**Telegraph,** 334–35
**Temperance movement,** 360–61
**Ten Percent Plan,** 418
**Tenant farmers,** 127
**Tennessee,** 271, *m272,* 423, *m572–73,* 578; in American Revolution, 186; in Civil War, 399–400, 417–18; secession, 394, 419; statehood, 271
**Tenochtitlan,** 42, 44, *m45,* 62, 82
**Terre Haute,** Ind., 86
**Texas,** 308, 315–19, *p316, m317, p318,* 342, *m572–73,* 578; American settlement, 315; annexation, 322, 323, *m326;* Civil War, 397; conflicts with Mexico, 315–16, 536; Republic of, 316, 317–19; statehood, 375; war of independence from Mexico, 316–17
**Textile industry,** 265–66; mills, 266–68, 337, *p338,* 341, 343, 427
**Thames,** Battle of, 258, *m258*
**Thanksgiving,** origin, 95
**Third Amendment,** 213
**Thirteenth Amendment,** 419, 421
• **Thoreau,** Henry David, 362–63, 383, 551
**Three Fifths Compromise,** 204–05
**Tidewater,** 30, 133
**Tikal,** 42, *m45*
• **Tilden,** Samuel, 430–31
**Timbuktu,** 54, *m57*
**Tippecanoe,** Battle of, 255, 305
**Tobacco,** 91, 92, 110, 113, 129, *m130,* 139, *m141,* 335, 341–43
**Toleration,** 102, 103, 107–08, 110
***Tom Thumb,*** 335
**Totem poles,** 37, *p37*
**Town meetings,** 124, 166
**Townshend Acts,** 159–63
**Township,** 200, *m201*
**Trade:** American ships and, 335–36;

Barbary States and, 250; colonial, 113–14, 138–40, *m141;* 1800–1812, 251–54, *c252;* European–Asian, 48, 51, 52, 53–59; after American Revolution, 249–50; regulation of, 207; tariffs and, 279, 299; triangular, 139, *m141,* 158; War of 1812 and, 257
**Trade unions,** 338
**Trail of Tears,** 301–02, *p303*
**Traitor,** 178
**Transportation:** colonial, 138; railroads, 335; ships, 335–36; westward expansion and, 270–76; later, 444–46. *See also* Canals; Railroads; Roads; Ships.
• **Travis,** William B., 318
**Treaty of Ghent,** 260
**Treaty of Greenville,** 229, 254
**Treaty of Guadalupe Hidalgo,** 324
**Treaty of Paris,** 155–57, 192
**Treaty of Tordesillas,** 60
**Trenton,** N.J. *p221;* Battle of, 182
**Triangular trade,** 139, *m141,* 158
**Tributaries,** 25
**Tripoli,** war with, 250, *m250, p251*
**Tropical climate,** 27, *c27, m28*
**Tropical rain forests,** 29, 42
• **Truman,** Harry S., *c440, p591*
• **Truth,** Sojourner, 355–56, 407–08
• **Tubman,** Harriet, 353
• **Turner,** Nat, 354
**Turnpikes,** 271–72
**Twelfth Amendment,** 233, 237
• **Tyler,** John, 305, *p588*

**U**

***Uncle Tom's Cabin,*** (Stowe), 378–79, 555
**Underground railroad,** 353, *p354*
**Union** (in Civil War), 392–413, *m411;* advantages and disadvantages, 395, *c396;* blacks, 402; draft law, 404, 406; economy, 406; goals, 397, 401; public opinion, 393–94, 401, 404, 412. *See also* Civil War; North; Union forces.
**Union forces,** 393–95, 397, 398, 560; blacks in, 402, 408; combat life, 403–04; draft law, 404, 406; nicknames, 403; in West, 399–401
**Unions,** trade, 338, 446–47
**United Provinces of Central America,** 281, *m282*
**Unskilled workers,** 338–39
**Upper Canada,** 280
**Utah,** 319, 379, *m380;* Mormons in, 326–27; *m572–73,* 578; slavery in, 377; statehood, 327

**V**

**Valley Forge,** *m182,* 183–85, *p187*
• **Van Buren,** Martin, 296–97, 304–05, 338, 375, *p588*

Venezuela, 281
Veracruz, 323, *m324*
Vermont, 86, *m122*, 127, 188, *m199*, *m572–73*, 578
• Verrazano, Giovanni da, 66
• Vespucci, Amerigo, 59
Veto, *c208*, 210
Vice President, 207, 208, 237
Viceroy, 77
Vicksburg, Miss., in Civil War, 400, *m411*
Vigilantes, 328
Vikings, 49–50, *m51*
Vincennes, *m186*, 187
Vinland, 50
Virginia, 90–94, *c115*, *m127*, 128, 129, *m130*, 133, *m136*, 161, 166, 212, *m572–73*, 578; American Revolution in, 191; Civil War in, *p405*, 408–10, 412–13; claims to western lands, 199; colonial, 109, 110, *m112*, 474; government, 198; secession, 394; slavery, 188
Virginia Company, 89–92
Virginia Plan, 203–04
Virginia Resolution, 236, 299
Voting: in American colonies, 117; blacks, 198, 294, 344, 420, 423, 424, 427, 431; in 1820s, 293–94; free blacks, 344; of Southerners after Civil War, 420; women, 355, 356–57; later changes, 441–42, 443

# W

Wade–Davis Bill, 418, 421
Wagon trains, 312–14, 326
• Walker, David, 350, 354
Wampanoags, *m94*, 95, 105
War of 1812, *p241*, 256–61, 269, 273, 278, 291, 295; Rush–Bagot Agreement, 261; at sea, 257; Treaty of Ghent, 260; in West, 257–58
War Hawks, 254, 256, 257, 278
War for Southern Independence, 393. *See also* Civil War.
• Warren, Mercy Otis, 161
Washington, 309, *m572–73*, 578; statehood, 323
• Washington, George, 494, *p588*; in American Revolution, 156, 161, 174–

78, 180–85, *p185*, 189–93, *p192*; cabinet, 222; at Constitutional Convention, *p197*, 202, 203, 205, 212; election,213; Farewell Address, 229, 513; foreign policy, 226–227, 229, 244–45; French and Indian War, 152–53, *p152*; Native Americans and, 228–29, 504; as President, 220, *p221*, *p222*, 221–29, 233–34, 512
• Washington, Martha, 189, *p222*
Washington-on-the-Brazos, 316, *m317*
Washington, D.C., 224, 377; building of, 234, *p234*; burning, in War of 1812, 258–59; in Civil War, 412
• Wayne, Anthony, *m175*, 228–29
Weather, 26, *c27*
• Webster, Daniel, *p277*, 277–78, 297, 300, 305, 531, 554; slavery and, 376–77
West, *m199*, 264, *p265*, 270–76, 308–29; in American Revolution, *m186*, 186–87; California, 320–21; canals, 275–76, *m277*; in Civil War, 397, 399–401, *m411*; Lewis and Clark and, 246–49; Manifest Destiny, 321–22; Mexican War, 322–24; mix of peoples, 328–29; Native Americans, 36–38, 254; roads and railroads, 271–73, *m272*, *m320*, 337; slavery and, 373–76, *m380*; Spanish culture in, 320, 324–25; steamboats, 273, 275; War of 1812 and, 256, 257, 260. *See also* Pacific Northwest; Southwest.
• West, Benjamin, 363, 365
West Africa: European exploration, 53, 54; gold kingdoms, 54, *m57*
West Indies, 57–58, 77, *m78*, 79, 82, 88, 105, 133, 149, *m150*, 156, 249; colonial trade with, 139, *m141*
West Point, 190, 395, *395n*
West Virginia, *394n*, *m572–73*, 578
Western Hemisphere, 22
Whaling, 123, *p336*
• Wheatley, Phillis, *p189*, 504
Whigs, 294, *p297*, 305, 322, 383; slavery and, 375
• Whipper, William, *p374*
Whiskey Rebellion, 225, *p225*
• White, John, *p74*, 89

• Whitman, Marcus, 311–12
• Whitman, Narcissa, 311–12
• Whitman, Walt, 362
• Whitney, Eli, 266, 268, 341, 343, *p343*, 540
• Whittier, John Greenleaf, 362
Wilderness, Battle of, 412
Wilderness Road, 271, *m272*
Willamette River, 310, *m310*
• Willard, Emma, 357
• Williams, Roger, 102–03
• Wilmot, David, 374, 552
Wilmot Proviso, 374
• Wilson, Woodow, *c440*, *p590*
• Winthrop, John, 101, *p101*, 102, 103
Wisconsin, 200, *m201*, *m572–73*, 578; statehood, 375
Witchcraft, 104, *p104*, 478
• Wolcott, Laura, 188, *p188*
• Wolf Clan, John, *p151*
• Wolfe, James, 154, *p155*, 495
Women: in American Revolution, 180, 184, 188–89, 193; in Civil War, 407–08; education and, 135, 357–58; in factories, 267, *p268*, 339; limited rights in 1820s, 303; in Native American cultures, 37, 39–41; in New England Colonies, 117, 125; in New France, 84; in Reconstruction, 425, 426; in Southern Colonies, 133; in Virginia, 92; voting and, 198, 293; women's rights movement, 355–57, 363; writers, 363
Writers, American, 1820–1860, 361–63
Writs of assistance, 160
Wyoming, 311, *m572–73*, 578

# X Y Z

XYZ Affair, 234–35

Yale College, 134
Yankees, 139
Yellowstone River, *p19*
• York, *p248*
Yorktown, Battle of, 191, *m191*, *p192*, 505
• Young, Brigham, 326, 327
Zuñis, 63, *m64*, 65, 319

Index

Historical Pictures Service, Chicago; **158** NYPL; **160** John Carter Brown Library, Brown University; **161** Patrick Henry Memorial Foundation; **162** LC; **164** Rhode Island Historical Society; **165** LC; **169** NYPL, Stokes Collection; **173** Yale; **176** Joseph Dixon Crucible Collection; **179** Yale; **183, 185** Valley Forge Historical Society; **187** American Antiquarian Society; **188** Yale, Bequest of Mrs. Katherine Rankin Wolcott Verplanck (detail); **189** LC; **190** The Granger Collection; **192** Abby Aldrich Rockefeller Folk Art Collection, Williamsburg, VA; **193** US Postal Service; **197** Independence National Historical Park; **198** The Granger Collection; **200** Abby Aldrich Rockefeller Folk Art Collection; **203** The Granger Collection; **205** Historical Society of Pennsylvania; **211** MMA, Gift of Mrs. A. Wordsworth Thompson, 1899; **212** Courtesy of Kennedy Galleries, Inc., NY.

**UNIT 4  Pages 218–219** *l to r* NYSHA; Washington University Gallery of Art, St. Louis, MO; The Granger Collection; Irving S. Olds Collection; MMA, Rogers fund, 1942; **221** Mr. and Mrs. John Harney; **222** Brooklyn Museum; **223** *t* NYPL, *b* City Art Commission of New York; **225** MMA, Gift of Edgar William and Bernice Chrysler Garbisch; **226** Bibliothèque Nationale; **228** Courtesy, Henry Francis duPont Winterthur Museum; **229** NA; **233** *l and r* Massachusetts Historical Society; **234** LC; **235** The Granger Collection; **237** NYHS; **241** Courtesy United States Naval Academy Museum; **242** *l* Edwin S. Roseberry, Thomas Jefferson Memorial Foundation; *r* Independence National Historical Park; **243** Library of Boston Athenaeum; **245** The Granger Collection; **248** Thomas Gilcrease Institute of American History and Art, Tulsa, OK; **251** Courtesy of the Mariners Museum, Newport News, VA; **252** The Granger Collection; **253** *l* Field Museum of Natural History; *r* NMAA, SI, Gift of Mrs. Joseph Harrison, Jr. (detail); **259** NYHS, **260** New Orleans Museum of Art; **261** NYPL, I.N. Phelps Stokes Collection of Historical Prints; **264** Maryland Historical Society, Baltimore; **267** SI; **268** Yale, Mabel Brady Garvan Collection; **269** NYSHA; **271** Filson Club; **273** MFA; **276** NYSHA; **277** Dartmouth College Museum and Galleries; **281** Caribbean Tourism Association; **283** Courtesy of the Essex Institute, Salem, MA.

**UNIT 5  Pages 288–289** *l to r* SI, Lee Boltin for American Heritage; Memphis Brooks Museum of Art; Texas Memorial Museum; The Rockwell Museum; National Portrait Gallery, SI; **291** St. Louis Art Museum; **292** MMA, Gift of I.N. Phelps Stokes, Edward S. Hawes, Alice Mary Hawes, Marion Augusta Hawes, 1937 (37.14.34); **294** LC; **296** Chicago Historical Society; **297** Boston Public Library; **298** The Granger Collection; **300** National Portrait Gallery, SI; **301** The Granger Collection; **303** Michal Heron; **305** NYHS; **309** Corcoran Gallery of Art; **311** State Historical Society of Colorado; **312** Culver Pictures; **314** Thomas Gilcrease Institute of American History and Art, Tulsa, OK; **316** Texas State Capitol, Austin, TX; **318** State of Texas, Governor's Mansion; **321** Thomas Gilcrease Institute of American History and Art, Tulsa, OK; **327** Church of Jesus Christ of the Latter Day Saints; **329** California State Library; **333** Louisiana State Museum; **336** The Whaling Museum, New Bedford, MA.; **338** Yale; **339** The Granger Collection; **341** State of North Carolina, Department of Cultural Resources, Division of Archives and History, Raleigh; **343** Yale, Gift of George Hoadley, B.A. 1801; **347** *l* Missouri Historical Society, *r* LC; **351** MMA, Gift of Christian A. Zabriskie, 1950; **353** LC; **354** Cincinnati Art Museum, purchased from the Webber Estate by a popular subscription fund (detail); **355** NYHS; **356** Bettmann Archive; **357** The Granger Collection; **358** Bettmann Archive; **359** By permission of the Houghton Library, Harvard University; **360** Yale, Mabel Brady Garvan Collection; **361** NYPL, Astor, Lenox, Tilden Foundation; **365** MMA, Morris K. Jesup Fund, 1933.

**UNIT 6  Pages 370–371** *l to r* Musée de Pau; NYPL; Missouri Historical Society; N.S. Meyer, Inc.; NYHS; The Granger Collection; **373** Brooklyn Museum, Gift of Miss Gwendolyn

O.L. Conkling; **374** Bancroft Library; **376** The Granger Collection; **378** NYHS; **381** The Granger Collection; **382** The Granger Collection; **384** Illinois State Historical Library, Old State Capitol; **385** Pennsylvania Academy of Fine Arts; **388** National Portrait Gallery, SI; **389** Harry T. Peters Collection, MCNY; **393** The Granger Collection; **400** Corcoran Gallery of Art; **402, 404, 405** *t and b* LC; **407** Kean Archives; **408** The Granger Collection; **409** *l* NA, *r* LC; **410** LC; **413** West Point Museum; **417** LC; **419** Anne S.K. Brown Military Collection, Brown University Library; **420** The Granger Collection; **424** LC; **426** Chicago Historical Society; **427** Alabama Department of Archives and History; **428** LC; **429** State of North Carolina, Division of Archives and History; **435** NYPL.

**A LOOK AHEAD  Page 437** Indianapolis Museum, Gift of a Couple of Old Hoosiers; **438** Greenwood/Gamma Liaison; **439** *t* Wally McNamee, Woodfin Camp and Assoc.; *b* Kings's Highway Elementary School, Westport, CT; **441** NASA; **442** Michal Heron; **443** Collection of the Whitney Museum of American Art; **445** Thomas Gilcrease Institute of American History and Art, Tulsa, OK; **447** Arnold Zann, Black Star; **449** LC; **450** © Rick Friedman/Black Star.

## Illustrations for Readings and Other Sources

**UNIT 1  Page 453** Bettmann Archive; **455** Fred J. Maroon/Louis Mercier; **457** AMNH; **458** AMNH; **461** AMNH; **463** Bibliothèque Nationale; **465** Bibliothèque Nationale; **467** National Gallery of Canada; **469** LC.

**UNIT 2  Page 470** Courtesy of Glenbow Museum, Calgary, Alberta; **473** National Gallery of Canada/Gift of the estate of the Hon. W.C. Edwards, Ottawa, 1928; **475** LC; **477** Dan McCoy/Rainbow; **479** NYPL; **480** NYPL/Stokes Collection; **482** North Carolina Archives; **485** Colonial Williamsburg; **487** Bettmann Archive; **488** NYPL; **491** Insurance Company of North America.

**UNIT 3  Page 493** *t* NYSHA, *b* Albany Institute of History and Art; **495** National Gallery of Canada; **497** LC; **499** LC; **501** Historical Society of Pennsylvania; **505** Wide World; **506** NYPL; **507** NYHS; **509** Mary Anne Stets Photo/Mystic Seaport; **510** NYHS.

**UNIT 4  Page 512** Washington University Gallery of Art, St. Louis, MO; **514** NYHS; **516** Historical Society of Pennsylvania; **519** NYPL; **521** NYHS; **524** Courtesy of the Museum of Fine Arts, Boston (M. and M. Karolik Collection); **526** LC.

**UNIT 5  Page 529** The Rockwell Museum; **530** Smithsonian National Collection of Fine Arts; **533** National Portrait Gallery, SI, Washington, DC/Lent by National Museum of American Art; **535** Oregon Historical Society; **536** Institute of Texan Cultures, San Antonio; **539** NYPL; **541** Peabody Museum of Salem; **543** LC; **545** LC; **547** Gemini–Smith; **549** LC; **550** St. Louis Art Museum.

**UNIT 6  Page 552** Musée de Pau; **553** *l* NA, *r* MMA, Gift of I.N. Phelps Stokes, Edward S. Hawes, Alice Mary Hawes, Marion Augusta Hawes; **556** NYPL; **559** The Granger Collection; **561** The Granger Collection; **563** NG, Gift of Edgar Wm. & Bernice Chrysler Garbisch; **567** LC; **569** *l* LC, *r* American Heritage Picture Collection.

## Illustrations for Reference Section

**Page 570** *t* Minneapolis Institute of Arts, Julia B. Bigelow, Fund by John Bigelow; *b* MMA, Gift of Christian A. Zabriskie; **571** *l* National Portrait Gallery, SI; *r* National Portrait Gallery, SI; **572** *t* Laurie Platt Winfrey, Inc.; *b* Laurie Platt Winfrey, Inc.; **573** *tl* Thomas Gilcrease Institute, Tulsa, OK; *bl* American Museum of Natural History; *r* The Granger Collection; **574** *t* BBC Hulton/Bettmann Archive; *b* Prints Collection/NYPL, Miriam & Ira D. Wallach Division of Art, Prints & I. Noual MEZL + Photographs, Astor, Lenox & Tilden Foundations; **575** *t* Museum of Fine Arts, Boston, M. & M. Karolik Collection; *bl* NYHS; *br* Rare Book Div./NYPL, Astor, Lenox & Tilden Foundations; **576** *t* Museum of Fine Arts,

Gift by Subscription & Francis Bartlett Fund; *b* Dept. of Ethnology, Royal Ontario Museum, Toronto, Canada; **577** *l* Minneapolis Institute of Arts, Julia B. Bigelow, Fund by John Bigelow; *tr* Daniel J. Terra Collection, Terra Museum of American Art; *br* Oakland Museum, Gift of Kahn Foundation; **578** *t* Nelson-Atkins Museum of Art (Nelson Fund); *b* Oakland Museum, Gift of Mrs. Leon Bocqueraz; **579** *t* Gift of William Wilson Corcoran, Corcoran Gallery of Art; *bl* Laurie Platt Winfrey, Inc.; *br* Laurie Platt Winfrey, Inc.; **594** *l* Independence National Historical Park; *r* Thomas Gilcrease Institute of American History and Art, Tulsa, OK; **595** *l* The Granger Collection; *r* MMA, Gift of Christian A. Zabriskie; **596** *l* Wally McNamee, Woodfin Camp and Assoc.; *r* NASA; **597** *l* Curtis Publishing Company, *r* John and Kimiko Powers; **600–604** portrait nos. 1,2,4,5–7,9,10,12–18,20,21,25–27 National Portrait Gallery, SI; portrait nos. 3,8,11,19,22–24,28–40, White House Historical Association, Photos by National Geographic Society; portrait no. 41, © Larry Downing, Woodfin Camp and Assoc.